HoD

Please renew/return items by last date
shown. Please call the number below:

Renewals and enquiries: 0300 1234049

Textphone for hearing or
speech impaired users: 01992 555506

www.hertfordshire.gov.uk/libraries   **Hertfordshire**
L32

SHAKESPEARE AT STRATFORD

Published by The Arden Shakespeare in association with
The Shakespeare Birthplace Trust

General Editor: Robert Smallwood, The Shakespeare Centre

Associate Editors: Susan Brock, The Shakespeare Centre Library
Russell Jackson, The Shakespeare Institute

KING RICHARD III   *Gillian Day*
THE MERCHANT OF VENICE   *Miriam Gilbert*
THE WINTER'S TALE   *Patricia E. Tatspaugh*

Forthcoming titles:
ROMEO AND JULIET   *Russell Jackson*
THE TEMPEST   *David Lindley*
AS YOU LIKE IT   *Robert Smallwood*

SHAKESPEARE AT STRATFORD

THE WINTER'S TALE

PATRICIA E. TATSPAUGH

The Arden website is at
http://www.ardenshakespeare.com

Shakespeare at Stratford: *The Winter's Tale*
first published 2002 by The Arden Shakespeare
in association with the Shakespeare Birthplace Trust

© 2002 Patricia E. Tatspaugh

Arden Shakespeare is an imprint of Thomson Learning

Thomson Learning
Berkshire House
168-173 High Holborn
London WC1V 7AA

Typeset by LaserScript, Mitcham, Surrey

Printed by Zrinski in Croatia

British Library Cataloguing in Publication Data
A catalogue record for this book is available from the British Library

Library of Congress Cataloguing in Publication Data
A catalogue record has been applied for

ISBN 1-903436-16-8 (pbk)
NPN 9 8 7 6 5 4 3 2 1

THE AUTHOR

Patricia E. Tatspaugh, who has held academic and administrative posts in the USA and the UK, writes about the theatre and about filmed versions of Shakespeare's plays. Her essays include the performance history of *The Winter's Tale*, in the New Variorium edition of the play edited by Robert K. Turner and Virginia Haas (forthcoming), and 'The Tragedies of Love' for *The Cambridge Companion to Shakespeare on Film*, edited by Russell Jackson (Cambridge, 2000). Her theatre reviews have appeared in *Shakespeare Bulletin*.

For

LOUISE DEMARR TATSPAUGH

AND IN MEMORY OF

WALTER LUDLOW TATSPAUGH

CONTENTS

LIST OF ILLUSTRATIONS

Cover Photograph
Richard McCabe as Autolycus, 1992
Photograph: Donald Cooper

SOURCES

Joe Cocks Studio: The Joe Cocks Studio Collection, The Shakespeare Centre Library, Stratford-upon-Avon

Malcolm Davies: The Shakespeare Centre Library, Stratford-upon-Avon

Ernest Daniels, Angus McBean and Reg Wilson: The Royal Shakespeare Company Collection, The Shakespeare Centre Library, Stratford-upon-Avon

Donald Cooper

Richard Mildenhall

Every effort has been made to contact copyright holders and the publishers will be happy to include further acknowledgements.

GENERAL EDITOR'S PREFACE

The theatre archive housed in the Shakespeare Centre Library here in Stratford-upon-Avon is among the most important in the world; for the study of the performance history of Shakespeare's plays in the twentieth century it is unsurpassed. It covers the entire period from the opening of Stratford's first Shakespeare Memorial Theatre in 1879, through its replacement, following the fire of 1926, by the present 1932 building (renamed the Royal Shakespeare Theatre in 1961) and the addition of the studio theatre (The Other Place) in 1974 and of the Swan Theatre in 1986, and it becomes fuller as the years go by. The archive's collection of promptbooks, press reviews, photographs in their hundreds of thousands, and, over the last couple of decades, archival video recordings, as well as theatre programmes, costume designs, stage managers' performance reports, and a whole range of related material, provides the Shakespeare theatre historian with a remarkably rich and concentrated body of material. The wealth and accessibility of this collection have sometimes tended to give general performance histories of Shakespeare's plays an unintentional Stratford bias; the aim of the Shakespeare at Stratford series is to exploit, and indeed revel in, the archive's riches.

Each volume in the series covers the Stratford performance history of a Shakespeare play since World War II. The record of performances at Stratford's various theatres through this period unquestionably offers a wider, fuller and more various range of productions than is provided by any other single theatre company. It may fairly be said, therefore, that a study of the Stratford productions since 1945 of any Shakespeare play provides a representative cross-section of the main trends in its theatrical interpretation in the second half of the twentieth century. Each volume in the Shakespeare at Stratford series will, however, begin with an introduction that sets this Stratford half-century in the wider context of the main trends of its play's performance history before this period and of significant productions elsewhere during it.

The organization of individual volumes is, of course, the responsibility of their authors, though within the general aim of the series to avoid mere chronicling. No volume in the series will therefore offer a chronological account of the Stratford productions of its play: some will group together for consideration and analysis productions of similar or comparable style or approach; others will examine individual aspects or sections of their plays across the whole range of the half-century of Stratford productions' treatment of them. Illustrations are chosen for what they demonstrate about a particular production choice, a decision that, on some occasions, may be more important than photographic quality. Given the frequency with which individual plays return, in entirely new productions, to the Stratford repertoire, most volumes in the series will have some ten or even a dozen productions' approaches and choices to consider and contrast, a range that will provide a vivid sense of the extraordinary theatrical diversity and adaptability of Shakespeare's plays.

The conception and planning of this series would not have been possible without the support and enthusiasm of Sylvia Morris and Marian Pringle of the Shakespeare Centre Library, Kathy Elgin, Head of Publications at the Royal Shakespeare Company, Jessica Hodge and her colleagues at the Arden Shakespeare, and above all, my two Associate Editors, Susan Brock of the Shakespeare Centre Library and Russell Jackson of the Shakespeare Institute. To all of them I am deeply grateful.

ROBERT SMALLWOOD
The Shakespeare Centre, Stratford-upon-Avon

ACKNOWLEDGEMENTS

I am grateful to Roger Pringle, Director of the Shakespeare Birthplace Trust, for a grant from the Jubilee Education Fund that made possible extended visits to the Shakespeare Centre Library. It is a pleasure to record here my indebtedness to the unfailingly courteous and helpful staff of the library and, especially, to Susan Brock, Head Librarian, Sylvia Morris, Deputy Librarian, and Joanna Lockhart, who assisted with the selection and identification of illustrations and coordinated the preparation of the photographs. Stephen Cleary of the National Sound Archives kindly answered queries about its collection.

It is with pleasure that I record also my thanks to those who generously gave time to answer queries, to revisit productions they were associated with, to read drafts of the manuscript, to offer words of advice and encouragement. Following the style in which the RSC announces its company, I list them in alphabetical order: Katy and Gordon Clark, Janet Dale, Paul Greenwood, Roger and Nichola Gregory, Miriam Gilbert, Erica Groat, Judith Hill, Roger Howells, Russell Jackson, Gemma Jones, Linda Merians, Giuseppe Scavizzi, Bruce Smith.

My close association with *The Winter's Tale* on the stage began with the invitation to prepare its performance history for the New Variorum edition of the play. I am happy to acknowledge Barbara Mowat, Director of the Folger Institute, and the general editors of the New Variorum: Richard Knowles, Robert K. Turner, Paul Werstine.

I have enjoyed working with Hannah Hyam, who edited the manuscript with a keen eye and a great deal of patience. I am grateful to Jessica Hodge and Andrew McAleer of Thomson Learning for involving me in various decisions about the style and design of the series.

Finally, I am grateful to Robert Smallwood for many many conversations about the theatre at Stratford, for inviting me to contribute to this series, and for his perceptive and encouraging reading of the manuscript.

PATRICIA E. TATSPAUGH

London, May 2001

INTRODUCTION

For many years it was commonplace to dismiss *The Winter's Tale* as too complex or too crudely constructed to be staged successfully. Theatre reviews and scholarly articles decried its 'problems': Leontes' sudden and apparently inexplicable jealousy; the abandonment of his infant daughter 'Where chance may nurse or end it' (2.3.182); his public humiliation of Hermione; his responsibility for the death of his son; the apparent death of Hermione; the abrupt leap forward sixteen years; the introduction in the penultimate scene of three gentlemen to describe the long-anticipated ending in the reunion of Leontes and his daughter; Hermione's restoration and reunion with Leontes and their daughter; finding for Shakespeare's Sicilia and Bohemia countries and periods that can accommodate disparities such as the oracle of Apollo, a bear, Time, a sheep-shearing festival, the roguish Autolycus, Christian imagery; the density of some speeches; the mixture of genres.[1] Performances, however, testify to its stage worthiness and its potent effect on audiences, especially when the statue of Hermione comes to life. Reviewers' assessments of the last scene reveal something of the power of the play in performance:

> To see them and their children touching hands in a silent circle of reunion is a spectacle that really touches the heart.   (*Times*, 1969)[2]

> When we return to the court and the reconciliation of father, wife and daughter the stage fills with a sense of mystery and strangeness

1

that passes rational explanation or the power of language to
describe.   (*Guardian*, 1976)

The beauty and gravity of those final scenes, with the statue coming
to life amid flickering candles, will long stay with me.

(*FT*, Oct 1984)

Only the hardest-hearted will be able to sit through its magnificently
moving conclusion without blinking back the tears.

(*D. Telegraph*, 1992)

Each reviewer was responding to the closing moments of a
production at Stratford-upon-Avon since the war, the subject of
this study.

This book explores how directors, designers and actors have
explored the richness of Shakespeare's late romance and how their
explorations have realized the compelling nature of the play
in performances at Stratford since the first post-war production in
1948. This study of nine productions reveals a representative
cross-section of the main trends in the theatrical presentation of
The Winter's Tale since 1945. It discusses a range of directorial
approaches to staging issues, such as the presentation of the
statue. This book treats the issues as integral parts of the
production, not as isolated moments in performance, and places
each director's staging in the larger context of the approaches of
his post-war Stratford colleagues. To return to the example of the
statue scene. The discussion in chapter 5 of Adrian Noble's staging
(1992), which Charles Spencer calls 'magnificently moving', looks
back to chapter 1, which describes the opening visual image and
illustrates it with a photograph (Figure 8). The blocking of the
statue scene, where Hermione stands downstage centre looking
toward the court gathered within a large gauze box centre stage
(Figure 41), parallels the blocking of the opening of the
production, where her young son, Mamillius, sits downstage
centre and looks toward the court crowded within the gauze box.
Chapter 5 places Noble's staging of the statue scene in the context
of other presentations at Stratford. The discussion, illustrated by

eight photographs (Figures 35–42), records the cross-section of solutions by Stratford directors to one of the so-called staging problems of *The Winter's Tale*. These photographs, together with thirty-five others, shed light on the ways Stratford directors have used design and stage picture to convey their readings of the play.

A brief survey of *The Winter's Tale* in performance provides an historical framework for post-war Stratford productions. An introduction to post-war solutions of selected staging issues, which are representative of the types of decisions directors, actors and designers must make, draws on the historical overview and offers a contemporary context for assessing the solutions taken by the artistic teams at Stratford.

THE WINTER'S TALE IN PERFORMANCE

HISTORICAL OVERVIEW

The first reference to a performance of *The Winter's Tale* occurs in the diary of Simon Forman, who records his visit to the Globe on 16 May 1611 and draws a warning from Autolycus: 'Beware of trustinge feined beggars or fawninge fellouss'.[3] Court records list five performances, at Whitehall, one of them in a season of fourteen plays in the winter of 1612/13 to celebrate the marriage of Princess Elizabeth. No performances in London during the Restoration have been recorded and only sixteen took place in the eighteenth century. Of the three adaptations performed as afterpieces in the second half of the eighteenth century, David Garrick's *Florizel and Perdita*, based on the Bohemian scenes and relocating the statue scene to Bohemia, was the most popular. In the early nineteenth century John Philip Kemble began the gradual restoration of Shakespeare's script, explored the characters of Leontes and Hermione and made the first attempts to 'place' Sicilia and Bohemia.

In the second half of the nineteenth century, the focus shifted from the text to spectacle: lavish designs, thrilling effects and a heavily cut text were characteristic. Charles Kean (Princess's Theatre, London, 1856), who led the way, set the Sicilian scenes in ancient Greece. Crowded onto a set representing the theatre at Syracuse, more than 170 extras witnessed Hermione's trial. The set for Bohemia was 'A Pastoral Scene in Bithynia. With a Distant View of the City of Nicaea, on the Lake Ascaria; together with the Chain of Lofty Mountains, known as the Mysian Olympus'.[4]

Harley Granville-Barker's production at the Savoy in 1912 and his *preface* to the acting edition initiated the re-examination of the play in the twentieth century. Unlike those who found a problem-filled script that needed cutting and the support of scenic effects, Granville-Barker celebrated the challenges of Shakespeare's late play. In his *Preface* to the acting edition, he writes: 'The technique of it is mature, that of a man who knows he can do what he will, lets himself in for difficulties with apparent carelessness, and overcomes them at his ease' (Granville-Barker, 91). Granville-Barker played a full or nearly full text; his ensemble company presented realistic characters; his stage pictures were representational, not pictorially realistic; his adjustments to the Savoy's stage broke down the artificial barrier between actor and audience.

Granville-Barker's ideas lay almost dormant until mid-century, a slumber partially induced by two world wars and a worldwide economic depression. During these years *The Winter's Tale* was revived regularly – if not especially memorably – in summer seasons at Stratford, at the Old Vic, London, and in the United States. Its history at Stratford stretches back to 1895 and in the fourteen productions prior to 1945 one finds not only traces of nineteenth-century production values but also themes that post-war Stratford directors would explore, such as an emphasis on the private, not the regal and public, life of Hermione and Leontes, and the introduction of domestic chores for the women attending Hermione in 2.1. Throughout this period reviewers identify Bohemia with the Cotswolds and disapprove of Hermione's giving Leontes even the slightest cause for jealousy.

Peter Brook's production at the Phoenix Theatre, London, in

1951, staged as part of the Festival of Britain, is one of the most significant post-war productions outside Stratford. J.C. Trewin praises John Gielgud's Leontes: 'no other actor in my recollection has turned this gnarled verse to music, and Gielgud manages to touch us deeply as the tyrant in repentance'.[5] It would no longer be possible, he thought, to label the part 'unplayable'.[6] Trewin, whose reviews of five post-war Stratford productions will figure in later chapters, also points out that Brook read the statue scene as 'the truth of the play', a reading central to post-war productions and in contrast with Granville-Barker's treatment of it as a stage effect.[7] Unlike all of the post-war Stratford directors, Brook experimented with the placing of the interval. Playing all of the Bohemian scenes as an act, he introduced for transition from 3.3 to 4.2 a 'blizzard through which Time appears to lead us to the pastorals of Bohemia'.[8] Stage design based on Elizabethan principles allowed Brook to experiment with fluid movement between scenes, such as that from 3.3 to 4.2.

During the second half of the century *The Winter's Tale* gradually increased in popularity, an observation attested to by the listings of productions in the annual bibliography of *Shakespeare Quarterly*. This brief chronology presents a framework for the discussion of staging issues which follows, and of the post-war Stratford productions. At Stratford, Ontario, in 1978, director Robin Phillips introduced a candle-banked statue and gave prominence to the reunion of Hermione and Perdita, not Hermione and Leontes. In 1986, also at Stratford, Ontario, David William explored both the private and public roles of Leontes and Hermione, in a production staged as part of a series of the late plays. At the National Theatre, London, in 1988, Peter Hall directed a season of three late plays performed by the same company of actors, opened them at the Cottesloe and, after a tour including the Tokyo Globe Theatre, transferred them to the Olivier's large open stage. Some critics reminded their readers that Shakespeare's company, the King's Men, also performed the play in two contrasting spaces: indoor hall theatres and the open-air

Globe.[9] In Paris in 1988, Luc Bondy's production introduced middle-aged and somewhat unattractive kings and cast Hermione as distinctly younger than either of the kings.[10] Bondy's production in Berlin in 1991 featured an Autolycus 'instantly recognisable as one of the new breed of East European wide-boys, who have made Berlin their headquarters since the opening up of the Wall ... , selling smuggled knick-knacks, changing currency and playing games of chance'.[11] Ingmar Bergman's production for the Royal Dramatic Theatre of Sweden in 1994 was staged as a play within a play, with an onstage audience of actors, and provided a Christian frame of reference by, for example, setting 5.1 'in a monastery with several rows of nuns and monks singing religious music' and setting 5.3 in a chapel, with the statue presented on a catafalque (Ranald, 15). At Shakespeare's Globe in 1997, David Freeman set Sicilia in a barren African community and introduced elements of black magic. In Declan Donnellan's production for the Maly Theatre, St Petersburg (1999), we were 'invited to see events through a child's eyes' and 'domestic violence was never far away' (Phillips, 31).

One important characteristic of the 1990s was the number of productions designed for small spaces, small touring companies and even small members of the audience. At the Young Vic, London, in 1991, David Thacker directed a cast of fourteen and stressed the private, not the public, lives of Leontes and Hermione. Théâtre de Complicité toured the UK in 1992 with a cast of nine actors directed by Annabel Arden. As in Brook's production, a stunning image effected a transition, this time from Bohemia to Sicilia:

> Holding model galleons aloft, the people making the trip start a progress round the stage. Then, snow starts to fall and, as this is a production where the actors play more than one role, the group of travellers slowly transforms itself, before your very eyes, into the funereal procession that trudges after Leontes in his daily circuits of repentance. It's a haunting, unforgettable sequence.[12]

Stéphane Braunschweig, whose production for the Centre Drama-
tique National Orléans-Loiret played at the Edinburgh Festival in
1994, cast ten actors and in the final scene introduced Mamillius'
tunic, a potent funerary symbol of loss. For the touring company
Method and Madness in 1997, Mike Alfreds relied on eight actors
and highlighted storytelling techniques, taking as his key phrase
'A sad tale's best for winter'. In Richmond, Surrey, in 1996, the
Orange Tree Theatre Primary Shakespeare Project, directed by
James Brining, toured local primary schools and played briefly at
its intimate, black-box theatre. The effect of Leontes' jealousy on
his wife, son and daughter silenced and stilled its audience, which
burst into helpful shouts to save Perdita and Antigonus from the
pantomimic bear and readily participated in the sheep-shearing.
This young audience made Hermione's return to life and the
reunion of mother and daughter poignant in a way unmatchable
by audiences chiefly adult.

STAGING ISSUES IN THE TWENTIETH CENTURY

Four principal types of staging issues emerge from an overview of
the performance history of *The Winter's Tale*: the eruption of
Leontes' jealousy; the period and place of Sicilia and Bohemia; the
presentation of the choric figure, Time; and the blocking of the
final scene.

After Hermione convinces Polixenes to extend his visit,
Leontes first states his suspicions:

> Too hot, too hot!
> To mingle friendship far, is mingling bloods.
> I have *tremor cordis* on me:
>
> (1.2.108–10)

Writing about Leontes, a role he played at Stratford in 1981,
Patrick Stewart explains that it is possible to play Leontes' jealousy
as predating the action of the play or as something that erupts
suddenly. He reminds us that 'something profound is happening

to all those three characters which will scar them and lead them to waste sixteen years of their lives' (Stewart, 258–9). At the National Theatre in 1988, Tim Pigott-Smith conveyed 'the *tremor cordis* ... and the twinges of his jealousy as a physical symptom, recurring later in the action at moments of especial stress' (Wells, 144). In Berlin in 1991 Hans Christian Rudolph adopted a similar approach: his Leontes' jealousy was 'a physical pain burning in his heart' (*Times*, 3 Jan). Other actors ascribe to Leontes a psychological weakness. At Stratford, Ontario, in 1978 Brian Bedford's Leontes was a 'superbly repressed autocrat.... [The lines] became not outpourings of paranoia, but the marks of a festering passion' (Berry, 168). At the Young Vic (1991) Leontes, played by Trevor Eve, displayed 'a kind of derangement, a fevered paranoia fed by insecurity' (*Guardian*, 16 Sep). The 1986 production at Stratford, Ontario, presented Leontes (Colm Feore) as weaker than Polixenes, Hermione and Paulina, a decision that suggested a reason for 'Leontes's sudden explosive insecurity' (Weil, 234). In some productions Hermione, as she did at Stratford in 1942 and 1943, provokes Leontes' jealousy.[13] In Paris in 1988, Bulle Ogier's Hermione seemed at moments to be drawn to the Polixenes of Bernard Ballet (Campos, 43). In Bergman's production, Pernilla August's Hermione 'had a seductive friendliness that made Leontes' [Börje Ahlstedt] unwarranted suspicion almost palpable' (Ranald, 15). Some directors introduce technical effects to chart the development of Leontes' character. Bergman used changes in lighting to mark Leontes' 'inner development':

> When his jealousy was kindled, the windows were lit deep red. Later, when his love for Hermione had died, or rather lay dormant, a cold winter night with a starry sky and a frosty moon above snow-clad trees could be glimpsed outside the windows.   (Törnqvist, 85)

In Braunschweig's production 'the movements of the stage', marked 'the shifts in Leontes's mind' (*Times*, 25 Aug 1994).

A second issue is the determination of a period that will support the actor's interpretation of Leontes and accommodate the disparate characteristics Shakespeare assigns to his Sicilia and Bohemia. Since World War II many directors have sought to make the play accessible to their audiences by setting it within a period readily recognizable. In his essay about the production at Stratford, Ontario, in 1978, Richard P. Knowles records that Phillips and his designer sought an autocratic period within the 'historical memory' of their audiences. For Leontes' Sicilia they chose Czarist Russia in 1880, and for Bohemia, the Ukraine in 1896 (Knowles, 26–7). Although David William and his designer did not make 'period authenticity' a priority in their 1986 production at Stratford, Ontario, they too chose settings within the audience's historical memory: a European court of the 1830s for Sicilia and 'a Hardyesque rural community' for Bohemia (Warren, 166). William's production demonstrates another post-war trend: he focused on the private relationships of Leontes and Hermione. In productions such as William's, the characters may be stripped of sceptre, orb and crown, but more often than not they retain an aristocratic manner. At the Young Vic in 1991 even that aristocratic status was sacrificed. Eve's Leontes had 'no court, no system of power, no trappings of authority' (*Plays & P.*, Nov). It was 'a very private affair – played inside a tight family circle' (*S. Telegraph*, 22 Sep).

A third issue is the presentation of Time. To bridge the gap between the Old Shepherd's discovery of the infant Perdita, 'A very pretty barne!' (3.3.70) and sixteen years later when she presides over the sheep-shearing festival, Shakespeare presents Time, who introduces himself as 'I that please some, try all' (4.1.1). Expanding the scene, Kean presented Time as a classical figure in a three-part allegory. Many contemporary directors also expand the role, but they do so by introducing Time as a silent witness to other scenes or by assigning him (and, occasionally, her) lines scripted for other characters. At Stratford, Ontario, in 1958, for example, his unscripted appearances before the play began, and his speaking several minor parts, helped to convey that time is crucial for 'the repentance of the sinner and the return of the lost' (*Christian Cent.*, 29 Oct). In a production in

Birmingham (1986) his role was expanded; Time spoke not only his own lines but also those of Archidamus, the Gaoler and the Mariner and appeared as the bear (Cochrane, 90). When he directed the play for the Maly Theatre, Donnellan expanded the role by introducing Time as a silent character. 'Time ... first appear[ed] as a bowed peasant woman sweeping the stage at the beginning and end of the first half only to throw off her shawl to deliver her long speech in 4.1 as a robust young wench' (Phillips, 30). At the close, Mamillius entered with Time. Even when Time appears only in 4.1, his central role may be reinforced by significant doubling. Mamillius (New York, 1985; Paris, 1988) and Hermione (Edinburgh, 1994) have spoken the lines, which include references to 'Th' effects' of Leontes' jealousy and to 'Perdita, now grown in grace / Equal with wond'ring' (4.1.18, 24–5). Presenting Time as a gardener, Théâtre de Complicité presaged the interpolated business of Polixenes and Camillo 'tending their flowers' (*Indep. Sun.*, 5 Apr 1992) and Perdita's speeches on art and nature. More cynically, Time has been doubled with an Autolycus presented as a cider-swilling beggar who emerged from the yard at Shakespeare's Globe.

The statue presents a different set of staging issues. It has, traditionally, been placed centre stage, facing the court and the audience. The obvious advantage is that the audience can watch the gradual awakening of Hermione and, depending on the blocking (and the location of one's seat), may also observe the response of other characters. In his production for the National Theatre, Hall reversed the picture, placing Hermione downstage centre, her back to the audience, and allowing the spectators to see the faces of Leontes and the court. Hall's staging not only reversed the usual stage picture for the statue scene, it was also a mirror image of his staging of the trial scene, where Hermione defended herself from centre stage and Leontes sat in judgement downstage centre, his back to the audience. Evoking a parallel with the trial scene, Hall suggested that Leontes was now the defendant. Hall's staging delayed the audience's view of Hermione.

Christopher Edwards describes the effect: 'when Hermione does come alive, the sight of Sally Dexter's gracious, mature beauty – lined with hurt as well as age – is very moving. We have a powerful sense of the cost of Leontes's psychotic jealousy' (*Spectator*, 28 May 1988). Stanley Wells characterizes the reunion as 'no easy happy ending.... There was a world of unspoken emotion between husband and wife as, left alone together, they tentatively, sombrely, joined hands again' (Wells, 144). Hall's staging of a hesitant reunion of Hermione and Leontes looked back to Granville-Barker's, where Lillah McCarthy's Hermione 'exhibited a comparative coldness' in the statue scene (*Westm. Gaz.*, 23 Sep 1912). A number of other late twentieth-century directors have closed their productions with a cold reunion or a dysfunctional couple. They include Phillips (Stratford, Ontario, 1978), Bondy (Berlin, 1991) and Braunschweig (1994). A review in the *Scotsman* describes the reunion in Braunschweig's production: 'the resurrected queen and her reunited king intone their ostensibly joyous lines in halting monotone: no happy ending, but an intimation that life goes on, at bitter cost' (25 Aug). Stephen Phillips characterizes Donnellan's production for the Maly Theatre as 'the bleakest production of *The Winter's Tale* I have ever seen'. His description of the closing moments reveals the contribution of cuts and interpolated characters:

> The resurrection of Hermione evoked fear and sadness rather than harmony. Natalia Akimova had visibly aged. Her face expressed anguish, and she moved as if emerging from a coma. Leontes knelt beside her; Perdita fell and kissed her foot. She spoke only three lines of her final speech – 'You gods, look down, / And from your sacred vials pour your graces / Upon my daughter's head!' [5.3.121–3] – and the rest of the play was cut. The actors froze. Mamillius entered to inspect the tableau and finally placed his hand on his father's head in blessing before Time drew the boy away.   (Phillips, 31)

This selection of productions concentrates on the bleaker resolutions; the work of Stratford directors has so far presented more hopeful reconciliations.

THE WINTER'S TALE AT
STRATFORD-UPON-AVON SINCE THE WAR

Since World War II productions at Stratford have made substantial contributions to the performance history of *The Winter's Tale*. Directors, actors and production staff have explored the text and attended to verse-speaking; responded artistically to contemporary trends and events; mounted productions in which design supports the text; introduced interpretations and designs that would be adapted by other directors and designers. The work at Stratford looks back, sometimes intentionally, sometimes unintentionally, to earlier productions. Transfers to London (1969, 1981, 1986, 1992, 1999) and UK and international touring have given the work an audience far larger than that which can be accommodated in the theatres at Stratford.

THE PRODUCTIONS

Three years after the close of the war, Anthony Quayle's production of *The Winter's Tale* showed some lingering influences of Charles Kean. Quayle staged – but in a considerably more modest fashion, appropriate to post-war rationing – a banquet in honour of Polixenes and closed the statue scene with a procession. A more immediate influence was Quayle's wartime experience in eastern Europe. Setting Sicilia in eastern Europe, Russia, perhaps, and presenting Leontes as a tyrant, unsettled some reviewers. Bohemia, they reported with some relief, was very firmly located in the familiar Cotswolds.

The next two productions were presented as part of a 'season' of plays. The programme for Peter Wood's production, 1960, announces 'A Season of Shakespearean Comedy'. A programme note explains how *The Winter's Tale* fits into the scheme:

> In the late romances the dark side is as strong as in the comedy of Shakespeare's great tragic period. ... The dark opening gives way to a

world of pastoral, and Leontes' contrition leads to a happy ending,
in some sort religious as well as romantic.

Costumes and sets identified Sicilia with the world of Renaissance
humanism. Wood's production compared favourably with Peter
Brook's important production; Eric Porter, who took on Leontes at
short notice, was, critics argued, as compelling as John Gielgud
had been in 1951.

In 1969 *The Winter's Tale* was linked with *Henry VIII* and *Pericles*
in a season of 'rarely performed' late plays. In a lengthy
programme note, Trevor Nunn, the RSC's artistic director and
director of *The Winter's Tale*, argues the importance of the plays
and their 'speak[ing] to a time in need of moral certainty'.
Opposite Nunn's statement, the programme prints the strongly
worded disagreement of Milton Shulman, who reviewed the
season for the *Evening Standard*. By far the most successful of the
three productions and the only one to transfer to London, Nunn's
Winter's Tale proved seminal to the staging of Shakespeare in the
late twentieth century and, as we shall see, to the performance
history of *The Winter's Tale*. In brief, Nunn worked within the
tradition begun by Granville-Barker; he set Sicilia and Bohemia on
the same basic set – a white box; he introduced minimal, symbolic
stage properties; he stressed the private lives of Leontes and
Hermione, not their position as monarchs; he was the first
modern director to double Hermione and Perdita; he set Bohemia
in the 1960s English countryside. In post-war productions at
Stratford, Nunn was the first director to alternate child actors
as Mamillius. For this reason two names appear in the cast list in
Appendix 1.

John Barton, with Trevor Nunn, directed the play during the
1976 season. Although it was played on the season's permanent
set, which incorporated features of an Elizabethan stage, Barton
did not explore Elizabethan stage conventions and instead
identified Sicilia with a Scandinavian community within the
Arctic Circle. Barton reassigned lines and introduced silent

characters and stage business to call attention to the ethos of the relocated Sicilian community. Barton's production was also the first to include in the souvenir programme several pages of information explaining the design. It was, some would argue, essential to read the programme before the performance.

In appearance, Ronald Eyre's production (1981) was quite different from Barton's. The set itself, of highly polished wood, gave no hint of time and place. In the early Sicilian scenes the only stage furniture was a simple stool carried on when it was required. Scenes changed quickly. The predominantly white Sicilian costumes evoked the Regency, as they had in 1969. Whereas Barton had interpolated characters to build the theme of community, Eyre limited scenes to the minimum required by the dialogue. Patrick Stewart – then, in his pre-*Star Trek* days, best known for solid company work with the RSC – was Leontes.

Technically speaking, the next production (1984), which did not include Stratford on its tour dates, is outside the scope of this study. But there are compelling reasons for including it: its director was Adrian Noble, who would in 1992 direct the play on the main stage at Stratford; its company drew upon regular RSC actors; and it is the only one of these nine productions that was not designed for proscenium-arch theatres. Paired with *The Crucible*, Arthur Miller's dramatization of witchcraft in seventeenth-century Salem, Massachusetts, it toured fourteen venues in England and Northern Ireland, ranging from sports centres and a cattle shed at an agricultural showground to the medieval splendour of Lincoln Cathedral, which had been Noble's inspiration for the tour (Noble, xiii). After the tour of small towns and communities, it played a brief season in London at Christ Church, Spitalfields, Nicholas Hawksmoor's baroque masterpiece. Under the sponsorship of the British Council, it travelled in early January 1985 to Poland, for performances and workshops in Warsaw and Wroclaw. Reviews attest to the high degree of audience involvement. Writing about the tour, Noble describes *The Winter's Tale* as 'a great healing play' and notes that it seemed somehow symbolic that so often in 1984–5 we were visiting communities that were divided against themselves: in Poland certainly, but also in a number of mining districts in the hateful months of the long [coal miners'] strike. We hoped that somehow Shakespeare's play sowed seeds of harmony.   (xiv)

Noble set the play in mid-century Italy and presented Leontes as a Mafia godfather.

Terry Hands's production (1986) looks back, in some ways, to Nunn's white-box version. Hands doubled Hermione and Perdita, used changes in lighting to signify the development of Leontes' jealousy, costumed his characters in white Regency clothing, and introduced nursery toys. But Hands's production did not emulate the simplicity of Christopher Morley's design for the 1969 production. Stage design, costumes, props, lighting, music and sound – all contributed to a rich (too rich, said some) overlay of symbolism. Sicilia was a nursery kingdom ruled ineffectively by Jeremy Irons's Leontes. Reproducing E.H. Shepherd's illustration for A.A. Milne's poem 'If I were king', the programme suggests a link between a child's fantasy and Leontes' immaturity.

When he returned to the play in 1992, Noble placed Sicilia in an early twentieth-century aristocratic society, improving Leontes' social class but still not giving him the accoutrements of a monarch. The dominant feature of the design was a large gauze box that functioned, as we shall see, practically as well as symbolically. Bohemia recalled small towns in England between the wars, such as Cookham, the Berkshire town made famous in Stanley Spencer's paintings. Singing 'When daffodils begin to peer', Richard McCabe's Autolycus descended slowly into Bohemia on a parachute made of balloons (cover photograph).

In 1999 Gregory Doran restored Leontes' crown and gave him an eastern European country to rule. Doran placed the play at the turn of the century and, by presenting a sickly Mamillius, seemed to suggest pre-Revolutionary Russia. There was also a practical reason for Mamillius' wheelchair. It helped disguise the fact that

Mamillius was played by an adult, who doubled the part with Perdita.

PROCEDURES AND SOURCES OF INFORMATION

This study treats each act of *The Winter's Tale* in a separate chapter and presents 'Time' (4.1) as a brief transitional section to mark, as it does on the stage, the passage of sixteen years. Three chapters – those for Acts 2, 3 and 5 – break the act into its scenes; the other two do not. Each chapter, and each scene of chapters 2, 3 and 5, opens with a series of questions, which, it is hoped, will encourage the reader to consider various performance and staging options. Although many of the questions can be answered 'yes' or 'no', I urge the reader to hear another monosyllable: 'why?' and to consider also the impact of one decision on other decisions that must be made about a particular act or scene. The chapters do not attempt to answer all the questions, but present, rather, many of the answers provided by post-war productions at Stratford.

The questions thus function also to introduce the nine productions, which are discussed in chronological order. The first chapter, for example, raises a series of questions about the opening moments of performance. The chapter then describes how the directors, from Anthony Quayle in 1948 to Gregory Doran in 1999, chose to open their shows. Subsequent chapters trace how – if at all – the staging of the opening moments impacted on the rest of the production.

Even if the archives made it possible to recreate in detail each of the nine productions, such descriptive analysis would be beyond the scope of this series. I have, therefore, sought a compromise. Each chapter draws on as wide a selection of resources as possible and thus gives a comprehensive overview of the practice of performance criticism and the writing of performance history. But the treatment of each production within the chapters is necessarily selective. For productions since 1969 the archives offer more information than is available for 1948 and 1960. I have, therefore, drawn more fully on the promptbooks for 1948 and 1960 and suggested how decisions about text affected presentation of character. Similarly, for some scenes in each production there is very little evidence other than promptbook markings. Paulina's visit to the prison (2.2), the return of Cleomenes and Dion from Delphi (3.1) and the three gentlemen's account of offstage reunions (5.2) are seldom photographed or reviewed. Discussing the productions, I have attempted to corroborate evidence and examine what was attempted, not what should or could have been attempted.

Any effort to describe performance must come to terms with the mutability of performances, especially in productions with a long stage life, and acknowledge that reviewers 'see' performances from different perspectives. Promptbooks for productions such as 1969, which toured Japan and Australia before transferring to the Aldwych Theatre, London, record some changes but do not record all or attempt to (indeed, cannot) 'fix' the performance text as it progresses from theatre to theatre. The promptbook for 1981 records an order of entrances for the opening masque and an order for the final exit that differ from the one filmed at the Barbican, London, in 1983. Sometimes blocking is left open. The 1992 promptbook records that the blocking when Paulina enters to announce the death of Hermione is not set because 'Gemma Jones wants to try something different each time'. Sometimes an unusual, and potentially interesting, innovation cannot be corroborated. In the promptbook for the touring production (1984), this cue appears: '"spirit" Paulina picks up the baby' and exits, but there is also a cue for Antigonus to exit with the baby.

Inevitably, a collection of reviews of a production, many of them written about the same press-night performance, will include contradictory observations. It is, of course, sometimes difficult to pin down the period of the costumes, the exact location of the setting, the influences on the music. Reviewers may have blind spots, favour some actors or styles of acting or sounds of voices over others, write for a readership of a particular interest or set of values, and may come to the production with preconceived notions of how the play should – or should not – be presented (or even, in some cases, if it should be presented at all). For productions since the late 1960s, there is a wider selection of reviews to choose from, some of them quite detailed.

Photographs supplement the text. From the wealth available, I have selected photographs to illustrate different ways of staging key scenes, such as the statue; two presentations of Time; sets and costumes for each production; and dominant traits of actors' performances. These illustrations serve also to give an overview of fifty years of designs for Shakespeare. Today, for example, the proscenium arch (Figure 2) and its curtain, especially, the drop cloth, would be unusual; in 1948, they were a convention of theatre architecture and design. The designs for the Sicilian scenes in both 1960 (Figures 3 and 16) and 1999 (Figure 9) were based on a series of arches that could be adjusted to vary the stage picture.

Programmes have changed dramatically since the one announcing Anthony Quayle's 1948 cast. In 1960 the first programme notes appeared: an unsigned overview of the season of comedies of love and Ivor Brown's succinct introduction to the play. By 1969 the programme had swollen to twenty pages, an innovation introduced in 1964 by John Goodwin, Head of Publicity and Publications (Addenbrooke, 71). Twelve pages announce the cast and their credits, provide historical and critical commentary on the play, introduce other relevant pieces (including Louis MacNeice's 'Autolycus' and an excerpt from T.S. Eliot's 'Burnt Norton'), and reproduce rehearsal photographs, photographs from past productions, and engravings selected to add a visual dimension to the critical commentary. The white cover with an embossed title was appropriate to a production in which the Sicilian scenes were played on a white set by actors in white costumes. To provide a context for Nunn's presentation of Bohemia, Stuart Hall, then acting director of the Centre for Contemporary Cultural Studies, University of Birmingham, contributed a piece defining hippie love. The programme enhanced one's understanding of the performance, but it was not essential to read it before the lights dimmed.

Subsequent programmes, which vary in length, follow the same basic format: a cover linked in some way to the design or dominant mood of the production, information and photographs introducing the company and their roles, performance history with photographs, literary criticism, and several pages of information relevant – or sometimes, even essential – to understanding the thesis of the production. In 1976, for example, the front cover features twelve signs 'of middle European origin', which were also part of the design for the show. A note explains that they represent

> man; woman; man and woman united; pregnant woman; woman bears child; man, woman and children; friendship of two men; men fighting; death of child; mourning mother with remaining child; death of mother; one surviving child bearing within him the seed of a new family.

Within the programme three double-page spreads explore themes central to the production: 'the winter world', 'the summer world' and 'the bear facts'.

The programme for 1981 challenged the audience to draw links between *The Winter's Tale* and illustrations of six spirals, including an airline flight path, an aerial view of a copper mine and a roller coaster. The illustrations are juxtaposed with three pages of literary criticism and MacNeice's poem. The programme for the touring production (1984), designed for audiences who were, perhaps, seeing live theatre for the first time, is a production pack titled 'Making It Happen'. It offered, as its subtitle states, 'The Inside Story of The RSC/NatWest Tour'. The 'story' covers the writers (Shakespeare and Miller), directors, actors and staging.

The final three programmes follow the pattern of those for the other main-house shows. In words and pictures the programme for 1986 examines three topics: 'fathers and tyrants', 'time', 'endings and beginnings'. In 1992, excerpts are presented under two headings: 'To Be a Boy Eternal' and 'Dressing up as Shepherds'. Seven years later, excerpts in poetry and prose offer definitions of jealousy and introduce seasonal affective disorder, a psychological condition that one might find in the grey world that opened Gregory Doran's production.

ARCHIVES

This study relies almost exclusively on the collection of the Shakespeare Centre Library (SCL). Of primary importance are the deposits from the Shakespeare Memorial Theatre (Royal Shakespeare Theatre from 1961), an ever-growing collection that includes promptbooks, stage managers' scripts, properties and wardrobe lists, lighting cues, music cues and manuscripts, gramophone records, production photographs, souvenir programmes, postcards and posters, publicity materials, and numerous miscellaneous documents relating to each production. In addition to the theatre's collection of photographs, the library has its own extensive collection, as the generous selection in this volume testifies. It holds black and white photographs and contact prints for each production; colour photographs and contact prints and/or slides from 1960. It has also fixed-focus video recordings (with the limitations implicit in 'fixed focus') of performances for 1981 (filmed at the Barbican in 1983), 1986, 1992 and 1999. Theatre Records, a series of large volumes of news cuttings, contain theatre reviews, interviews and items related to the company and the artistic and administrative departments of the theatre. The volumes also include items about the personal lives of the company. In 1948, for example, Anthony Quayle and his family lived at Hall's Croft, in the last private rental of the property. In 1960 Elizabeth Sellars (Hermione) was in a car crash and later – the two items are not related – married a Harley Street doctor. A comprehensive collection of secondary materials, including scholarly periodicals such as *Shakespeare Survey*, supplements the primary documents in the collection. A final resource, one not listed in the SCL's card or computer catalogues, is the very knowledgeable and helpful staff. The National Sound Archives (NSA) at the British Library holds audio recordings made during the London runs of four productions: 1969, 1986, 1992, 1999. Appendix 1 lists the recording dates.

DOCUMENTATION

Appendix 1 presents the production credits and complete cast list for each production, identifying each actor announced for the press night. Reading through the lists of the earliest productions, one finds the names of established actors who, early in their careers, played small or anonymous roles: in 1960, Diana Rigg was cast as a lady-in-waiting; Philip Voss, the Second Lord; and Ian Richardson, one of the three gentlemen. As young men, a number of actors, now better known for major Shakespearean roles, played the Clown. The list includes Paul Scofield (1948), Ian Holm (1960) and Simon Russell Beale (1986). So too in 1948 Claire Bloom, then seventeen, played Perdita; and in 1960 twelve-year-old Dennis Waterman, as Mamillius, made his first appearance on the stage. Five actors have played in more than one Stratford production: Paul Hardwick (1948, 1960), Geoffrey Hutchings (1969, 1981), Gemma Jones (1981, 1992), Roger Rees (1969, 1976) and Graham Turner (1981, 1984, 1992).

The cast lists are followed by miscellaneous information, including size of companies, which numbered between twenty-one (1984) and thirty-four (1960) actors, date of press night, details of transfers and tours, and dates of video and audio recordings.

Appendix 2 lists all the reviews cited in the text, in alphabetical order by journal (the abbreviations used in the text are listed in Appendix 3). The selection represents a cross-section of the available reviews: national broadsheets and tabloids; local and regional papers; theatre-centred journals, such as the *Stage* and *Plays and Players*; scholarly journals, such as *Shakespeare*

Survey; and periodicals directed toward a specific audience, such as the *Tablet* and *New Statesman*.

The sources for descriptions not otherwise attributed are the promptbooks and videotapes at the SCL and, for 1992 and 1999, my notes from performances. All references to the text of *The Winter's Tale* are to the Arden edition, edited by J.H.P. Pafford, reprinted 1991.

NOTES

1 In defence of *The Winter's Tale*, see Coghill.
2 See Appendix 2 for full dates and reviewers' names.
3 The sources for this performance history are Bartholomeusz and Tatspaugh, and my viewings of productions.
4 Playbill, Folger Shakespeare Library.
5 'Raising a storm', *Illustrated London News*, 21 July 1951, 110, reprinted in Williamson.
6 'Town and country', *Illustrated London News*, 15 September 1951, 418.
7 Trewin, 1971, 60. On Brook's production, see also Rylands and Venezky.
8 *Illustrated London News*, 21 July 1951, 110.
9 For discussions of the two seasons of late plays, see Warren, 1990.
10 For a comparison of Hall's and Bondy's productions, see Campos. Campos places the productions in the context of English and French approaches to Shakespeare and to acting styles.
11 Denis Staunton, *Times*, 3 January 1991.
12 Paul Taylor, *Independent*, 4 April 1992.
13 *Stratford-upon-Avon Herald*, 1 May 1942, 7 May 1943.

1

SICILIA

hakespeare identifies Leontes as King of Sicilia, but productions seldom set *The Winter's Tale* in Sicilia – or any other Mediterranean location. In 1948 Anthony Quayle and his designers placed Sicilia in eastern Europe (Figure 1). Nearly three decades later John Barton, with Trevor Nunn, located Leontes' kingdom in a Scandinavian tribal community (Figure 11). Christopher Morley's costumes for Nunn's production (1969) suggested the Regency; but the set (a white box) and the props (nursery toys) were symbolic rather than realistic (Figure 4). As the illustrations confirm, design sheds light on the character of Leontes. Enthroned before a display of spears, Esmond Knight's Leontes in 1948 conveys a forceful authority. He is not the sort of man who would comfortably ride – as did Barrie Ingham in 1969 – a white hobbyhorse with his son.

The focus of this chapter is 'Sicilia': Sicilia the kingdom and Sicilia the monarch. Looking in some detail at how a number of productions treat Act 1, it provides essential background for subsequent chapters and a context for viewing other productions of *The Winter's Tale*. Three interrelated topics are central. First, the opening moments. How does the production begin? The Folio stage directions read simply '*Enter Camillo and Archidamus*', and their forty-four lines of courtly dialogue follow. Does the production open with an evocative visual image? Is there distinctive music or a sound effect? Is there interpolated action, such as the 'entertainment' Archidamus refers to? Does the director introduce characters other than the two lords who speak? The second topic is design. What does the stage look like? Has the permanent stage been altered? What do the sets and costumes indicate about Sicilia, the Sicilians and the two Bohemians? Is there an historical or social significance to the design? Are there props, such as the hobbyhorse, that may offer clues to character or theme? Third, Leontes. What clues help establish his relationship with Hermione, Polixenes, Mamillius? How does Leontes convey his jealousy? Do we observe the onset of that jealousy or merely its first manifestation? Do Hermione and Polixenes give him provocation? How much of the conversation between Hermione and Polixenes does he observe? How old are Leontes, Hermione and Polixenes? Do costumes, props, stage business establish similarities between Leontes and Mamillius? How does Mamillius respond to Leontes? Hermione? Polixenes? Is he a pawn between his parents? Is Leontes jealous of Polixenes' relationship with Mamillius? Is Mamillius puzzled by Leontes' outburst? Does he intuit what's happening? Take sides? Does the setting help to explain why Leontes might be of a jealous nature? Do lighting, music or sound effects feature in the presentation of the jealousy? Does the interpretation seem to stress Leontes as king or Leontes as man?

In 1948 the National Anthem opened the evening. Then the curtains parted and, as the orchestra played the overture, a puzzling drop cloth gave audiences their first impression of Motley's designs for Quayle's directorial debut at Stratford-upon-Avon. Two figures dominate. On the right an angel floats, wielding a trumpet as a weapon. Cowering from the threat is another supernatural figure, its face obscured by wings attached to its chest, its scaly flesh and cloven feet identifying it as a devil. In the background starfish and clouds float in the same element, and three columns – not in familiar classical orders – are the only evidence of the natural and human worlds. The supernatural beings and allusion to elements of earth, air and water contrast sharply with the art deco proscenium arch and doors of the Shakespeare Memorial Theatre and the platform jutting toward the auditorium. After the overture, this striking drop cloth rose to reveal a scene that the promptbook describes as

> Leontes' palace. It is evening and a sumptuous entertainment is drawing to an end. Last 8 bars of girl's song. Applause. While the musicians have their glasses filled and stand to toast the two kings, their viziers exchange a word.

The 'viziers' exchanged more than a word, but only approximately one-third of Shakespeare's dialogue. The promptbook calls for twenty-four performers, including six orchestra, a singer and a dancer.

'Sumptuous' may have been the intended effect, but reviewers more often characterized the entertainment as 'barbaric'. It was 'a Bacchanalia, a scenic overture preparing our minds by its barbaric intensity' (*Times*). Sicilia was a 'savage sort of place with a wild monarch [and] savage warriors' (*SA Herald*). The promptbook calls for a dancer to throw his knife and a girl to scream; for guests to cry out 'zanskali' and 'skali'. In Figure 1 Diana Wynyard's Hermione, Timothy Harley's Mamillius and Michael Godfrey's Antigonus may smile; but the stern expression of the two kings (Polixenes: Manfred Priestley) and Leontes' pose, with his back to his chief guest, belie the sincerity of Sicilia's invitation to extend the visit 'One seve'night longer' (1.2.17).

Quayle placed Leontes' kingdom behind the Iron Curtain, the term Winston Churchill had coined in 1946 for eastern Europe and the Soviet Union and terrain Quayle knew first hand from his wartime experiences in Albania. Some reviewers identified the set as 'Byzantine', 'Asian', 'Scythian'; but a majority favoured Russian, finding authority in Hermione's 'The Emperor of Russia was my father' (3.2.119). The *Manchester Guardian*'s reviewer finds it 'startling that she should have altered not only the costumes of her new court but also the local architecture'. It was, notices the *Birmingham Gazette*, 'a lurid household coloured in red, black and

FIGURE 1 Esmond Knight's stern Leontes (1948), enthroned with Hermione (Diana Wynyard) before a display of spears, listens to Polixenes (Manfred Priestley) explain why he must return to Bohemia. Mamillius (Timothy Harley) sits at his mother's side; Antigonus (Michael Godfrey) stands behind her. The tip of a guard's spear in the upper-right corner indicates that weapons in this Iron Curtain Sicilia were practical, not just ornamental. (1.2)

gold'. Motley's set for the opening scene (Figure 2) further explored the three motifs that the drop cloth had introduced: the human, natural and supernatural worlds. A geometrical display of spears symbolizes a military monarch, whose throne is the low, irregular-shaped object covered in animal skins and placed before a barren tree with gnarled trunk and eerie branches, representative of a sterile natural world. A celestial globe, the only other prop, introduces a civilizing note to the human world and

FIGURE 2 In 1948 Motley's design for Leontes' palace, which draws upon motifs from the human, natural and supernatural worlds, creates an appropriate backdrop for Esmond Knight's 'barbaric' Leontes.

links it with the natural world. Astronomical figures and geometrical signs and symbols decorate the walls and curtains. Motley's costumes (Figure 1) are formal, heavy, with bulky ornamentation and jewellery; crowns clearly identify Leontes, Polixenes and Hermione.

To one group of critics, Esmond Knight's Leontes was 'as barbaric in his jealousy as in his garments' (*D. Telegraph*). His Leontes was 'a snorting, snarling and violent man' (*Birm. Gaz.*), a 'raving maniac' (*Leam. Spa Cour.*), 'an advanced case of homicidal mania' (*D. Telegraph*). A number of reviewers observed the way Knight used his vocal power to sustain the intensity of Leontes' jealousy. The source of his jealousy, suggests the *Stage*, was 'an infection from the outside world rather than an emotion from within himself'. The production, argues the *Stratford-upon-Avon Herald*, 'solved the problem of Leontes' jealousy by making Sicilia a savage sort of place with a wild monarch capable of anything'. How, wonders the *Leamington Spa Courier*, did 'Hermione put up with him so long'. Two reviewers, responding unfavourably to Knight's interpretation, faulted him for omitting traits, traits that would have been inappropriate to his interpretation. Leontes' 'misery and anger would have been more convincing had they been less forcefully presented, and had they been allowed a subtle growth rather than release in a torrent of often incomprehensible wrath' (*Warwick Adv.*). Because Knight did not establish a bond with the audience, his Leontes did not invite sympathy (*Leam. Spa Cour.*), even when his lines and the blocking would seem to call for it: when he spoke about Mamillius – 'Who I do think is mine, and love as mine' (1.2.331) – Knight was on his knees, in tears and on the apron of the stage. As we shall see, other actors chose to give a less forceful presentation and to establish a bond with the audience. Alterations to the Stratford stage aided several of Knight's successors to work more closely with the audience.

Leontes' interaction with Hermione, Polixenes, Mamillius and Camillo gives a fuller picture of his jealousy and the responses to it. A foil to both Leontes and the setting, Diana Wynyard's Hermione 'touched the early scenes with gaiety' (Kemp and Trewin, 229), was 'gay and golden' (*Man. Guardian*), 'warmly human' (*SA Herald*). In Quayle's production, unlike the wartime productions in 1942 and 1943,[1] Hermione and Polixenes did not give Leontes cause for jealousy. Moreover, as the promptbook records, Leontes was offstage (1.2.48–86) and could not have observed how Hermione convinced Polixenes to remain.

The production, which cut Camillo's and Archidamus' description of Mamillius (1.1.34–45), introduced the young prince sitting at his mother's side. But his prop – a bow and arrow – and stage business marked him as Leontes' son. Leontes and Mamillius delighted in rough play. When Leontes looked into Mamillius' face and saw 'myself unbreech'd, / In my green velvet coat'

(1.2.155–6), he threw Mamillius to the ground, put his foot on Mamillius' chest, fought, drew Mamillius up to a sitting position, and 'chuckled'. Ordered to 'play, boy, play' (187) Mamillius stalked behind pillars, aimed an arrow at his father and laughed. Reviewers praised Harley for his 'spirited performance' (*Stage*) and for bringing the character to 'bounding life' (*Birm. Mail*). With Camillo, played by Julian Amyes, Leontes' fury was not a game: accusing Camillo of lying, Leontes beat him (300).

Observing that Knight was 'not for the moment on terms with his surroundings', the *Times* found in the setting a context for the interpretation:

> The Asiatic setting is not only strange and beautiful in itself but the strangeness suits a tale which asserts at every turn the right of romance to laugh at psychology. Leontes striding amid violent contrasts of colour to the barbaric clash of cymbals has no obvious need for evidence to sustain his tantrums of jealousy. He is the tyrant of a fairy-tale.

The dark moods of Knight's Leontes were complemented by the sombre tones of the sets and costumes designed by Sophia Harris, Margaret F. Harris and Elizabeth Montgomery, the trio of young designers known as Motley and providing the third of their sixteen designs for productions at Stratford.

A more civilized celebration, one in keeping with its Renaissance setting and Eric Porter's urbane Leontes, opened Peter Wood's production in 1960. 'One thunderous stroke across a gong' (*Nott. Guard. J.*) signalled servants to rush across the stage with food for the offstage banquet in honour of Polixenes. Guests feasted, according to a properties list, from a large tray of fruit, a bowl of fruit (so weighty that it required two servants to carry it), trays with peacock feathers, pheasant feathers, a boar's head, and then drank from goblets filled from a large jug of wine. Instead of cutting lines from 1.1, like Quayle and many other directors, Wood kept all of the dialogue and illustrated it with stage pictures. Leontes' bounty having been displayed, the stage picture reinforced Archidamus' anxiety that 'we cannot with such magnificence' (1.1.12) entertain the Sicilians. A second interpolated entrance is more significant. The entrance of Dennis Waterman, playing Mamillius, with three grey-bearded Renaissance scholars provided a stage picture for the dialogue. The 'gallant' Mamillius (38) bowed to Camillo. The old gentlemen nodded to confirm the importance elderly Sicilians attached to Leontes' having an heir. Pictured between two of his tutors in an archival photograph, Mamillius, his sword at his side, is in miniature – to borrow Ophelia's description of a more famous prince – a courtier, soldier, scholar. More importantly, Mamillius' tutors will reappear as silent witnesses in four other scenes (1.2, 2.1, 2.3, 3.2). When at last they speak (5.2), it will be to announce that the king has found his heir.

Jaques Noel's sets, formal and functional, drew upon Renaissance architecture and perspective views by Sebastiano Serlio and Andrea Palladio. A series of black arches formed by plain sliding pillars and triangular pediments receded to an upstage focal point. In 1.1 a candelabrum caught the eye; in 1.2 an ornate archway. Red drapery extended from the pillars into the wings. As Figures 3, 10, 16 and 26 reveal, the size and shape of the arches could be changed to create space appropriate to the action and the number of characters. The simplicity suitable for a conversation between two lords in 1.1 was transformed to a grander, more spacious setting for the entrance in 1.2 of Leontes, Hermione, Polixenes and seventeen courtiers and candelabrum-bearing attendants (Figure 3). Note that Hermione stands behind Polixenes, not beside her husband. Just before Leontes delivered the speech beginning 'Too hot' (1.2.108), the stage emptied, leaving Leontes, Hermione and Polixenes in the space dominated by lofty arches and twin medallions of lions' heads. The set functioned as an architectural backdrop for stage pictures created by actors in Renaissance costumes. Leontes wore 'elaborate ceremonial costumes ... with red cloak', which picked up the hue of the draperies and which announced 'his passionate nature before he

FIGURE 3 Surrounded by his court on Jaques Noel's wide, deep stage, Eric Porter's Renaissance king (1960) encourages Polixenes (Patrick Allen) to extend his visit. Hermione (Elizabeth Sellars) stands behind Polixenes; Paulina (Peggy Ashcroft) observes from the extreme right. (1.2)

utters a word' (*Plays & P.*). For Polixenes the costume list mandates 'contrast with Leontes – must seem Bohemian for first scene but magnificent nevertheless'. Figure 3 illustrates how such things as the shape of their collars, the cut of their robes and the style of their shoes distinguished between the kings of Sicilia and Bohemia. Reviewers praised Noel for the uncluttered design and the symbolic use of colour to mark the phases of the comedy: 'the red of passion, the purple of repentance, and the gold of celebration' (*SQ*, 452). One final point – the stage itself – is crucial, especially as it may have contributed to the audience's perception of Porter's Leontes. Peter Hall, in his first season as director of the Shakespeare Memorial Theatre, and assistant director John Barton, with consultant Henry Bardon, 'substantially redesigned' the Stratford stage for the 1960 season. They gave it 'a rake, a new false proscenium arch, and an apron stage that jutted fourteen feet into the auditorium'.[2] Quayle's production had been designed for a picture-frame stage; the alterations, and especially the enlarged apron, offered Porter the option of a closer relationship with the audience than Knight had enjoyed.

Porter's acclaimed Leontes was a man for whom the audience could feel some sympathy. He had a 'natural kindness' (*Theatre W.*). Leontes' 'sudden' suspicion (*Theatre W.*) seems to have been provoked by Hermione, played by Elizabeth Sellars, and Patrick Allen's Polixenes, who did 'indeed behave in a manner likely to raise the eyebrow of the most indulgent husband – "paddling palms and pinching fingers" [1.2.115] is no overstatement' (*S. Times*). A sequence of cues in the promptbook sheds light. Urging Polixenes to remain a week longer (46–56), Hermione clasped his hand; Polixenes kissed her hand ('Your guest then, madam', 56), returned a chain to her ('To be your prisoner should import offending', 57) and kissed her after she said 'Not your gaoler then, / But your kind hostess' (59–60). Hermione drew Polixenes down centre. The gestures may be read as innocent signs of friendship. However, the court turned away, Leontes watched them suspiciously and the chain may have made tangible Leontes' complaint 'he that wears her like a medal, hanging / About his neck' (307–8). Cues supplied for one of Leontes' speeches suggest Hermione's hands have a private significance to her husband:

> Why, that was when
> Three crabbed months had sour'd themselves to death,
> Ere I could make thee open thy white hand,
> And clap thyself my love; then didst thou utter
> 'I am yours for ever.'

(101–5)

As he spoke, Leontes took Hermione's hand, opened it, clasped his hand into hers. She embraced Leontes, but immediately afterwards she embraced Polixenes and drew him downstage of Leontes, where they clasped hands. As Hermione and Polixenes circled to upstage centre, where they talked, the court, which had turned aside from them when Polixenes kissed Hermione (60), exited. Leontes, downstage and off the rostrum, watched them. The *Times* praises Porter's portrayal of the 'onset' of Leontes' jealousy, which he 'conveyed most neatly by an infatuated fondling of his queen's shoulders and an infantile search for sympathy in the scene with his son'.

One way directors such as Wood have created sympathy for Leontes is by casting suspicion on Hermione and Polixenes. Another way is by establishing an affectionate bond between Leontes and Mamillius. The photographs and the promptbook reveal how Porter and Waterman presented that bond. Costumed as a miniature of his father, Mamillius did not enter the second scene until the close of Leontes' anguished 'Too hot' (108–19). Mamillius startled Leontes by grabbing him about his waist. Leontes welcomed him, and, records the promptbook, 'bends like a matador and plays with Mamillius'. 'His sinister doubts concerning Hermione's fidelity are', observes one reviewer, 'indicated with particular subtlety during his vigorous games with his little son, Mamillius. He tries to concentrate upon them, but with increasing frequency he turns away to watch the Queen's conversation with his distinguished guest beneath a distant archway' (*Morn. Adv.*). Questioning Mamillius' paternity, Leontes 'falls forward on knees, Mamillius puts his arm around him'. Mamillius exited with the three tutors, bowing gallantly to Camillo, as he had done in 1.1. In this act Mamillius was associated with his three tutors and his father, and briefly with Camillo and Polixenes. There are no stage directions for Mamillius and Hermione.

Trevor Nunn's innovative production (1969) was startlingly different from those of his predecessors. Nunn was concerned 'with the human personalities of a king or queen rather than with their public roles' (*Plays & P.*). His creative use of music, sound, lights and design, together with Christopher Morley's redesign of the Stratford stage, bridged the gap between the world of the play and the restlessness of the 1960s. It became the benchmark against which Nunn's immediate RSC successors would be measured and influenced directors around the world (Warren, 1990, 10–13). Before the house lights dimmed, a sitar, an instrument made popular by the Beatles' fascination with India, 'provide[d] an atmosphere of calm, repose, and spiritual meditation'.[3] Dispensing with the traditional, interpolated 'entertainment' for Polixenes (and with the National Anthem, no longer played at performances at the Royal Shakespeare Theatre), Nunn opened the performance with the voice of Time, whose speech

> comes to us disembodied, amplified through the theatre (and most beautifully and compellingly spoken by Alton Kumalo ...), while the eye is invited to look upon the foundations of humanism in a representation of Leonardo's drawing of a man, encased in a great transparent cube, upon which a stroboscopic light plays.
>
> (SA Herald)

The three-dimensional 'representation' in the perspex box was, in fact, Barrie Ingham, who played Leontes. Roger Gregory, who stage-managed the production, recalls that Ingham stood

> on a mini revolve like they use for shop window dummies – going slowly round. Meanwhile the box was on a track moving from upstage to downstage centre on the stage rake. So poor Barrie had quite a balancing act to perform, what with the jerky box movements, the rake and the revolve – and he had his arms outstretched like the Leonardo drawing. Then there was a black out, and we had to wind him quickly upstage so we could release him for the first scene.

When the stage darkened, a spot lighted upon 'another glass box, a tiny one this time, with a tiny mannikin revolving in it'. When the lights came up, it was revealed to be a toy Mamillius would play with (FT). The complexity of the visual image resonated throughout the production: the image alluded to Renaissance humanism, and the words recalled the traditional figure of Time; however, the presentation was contemporary. Sitar cascades and sound effects backed Kumalo's speaking of Time's disembodied words; strobe lighting distorted Time's image. Time, argues Ronald Bryden, was the protagonist and 'the stroboscope is its perfect symbol: light and dark, either in itself offering a coherent view of the world, alternating in scrambled, bewildering energy' (*Observer*). In a programme note to the season of late plays (*Pericles* and *Henry VIII* played in repertoire with *The Winter's Tale*), Nunn observes that they speak 'to a time in need of moral certainty, but the direction they suggest is not easy'. In the *Sunday Times* J.W. Lambert describes the late 1960s as a time 'when a whole culture seems to be disintegrating, when destruction is ... the staple diet of the mass media' and defines the theme of the late plays as presenting 'the possibility of redemption through courage, endurance and patient love'.

The cube enclosing Leontes foreshadowed the shape of his kingdom and his being trapped by his predicament. For the season Morley transformed the Stratford stage to create 'a "chamber setting" ... an enclosed setting in which the private rather than the public lives of characters could be explored' (Addenbrooke, 170). There was 'a conscious stripping away of everything extraneous, creating a stage that was like a great empty box' (Beauman, 301). The Sicilian scenes were played in a white box – its sides 'slatted ... like tall sunblinds' (*D. Telegraph*, 1970) and its minimal, stark white props clearly marking it as Mamillius' nursery. In Figure 4, Leontes and Mamillius, played by Jeremy Richardson, sit astride a white hobbyhorse, and Judi Dench's Hermione rests her hand on its head. Polixenes (Richard Pasco), outside the frame, watches approvingly seated on one of several white cubes that doubled as seats and toy boxes. Toys abounded: a top, yo-yo, kaleidoscope, a 'one-eyed broken doll' (*D. Telegraph*, 1969). The whiteness of the set and properties (and programme), and the pseudo-Regency costumes suggested innocence, purity and winter. Hilary Spurling places the setting in the context of the RSC's work: 'The setting evokes no place or time, unless perhaps the present – in the sense that, where this company's designers

FIGURE 4 Setting 1.2 in Mamillius' nursery, Trevor Nunn (1969) stressed the private, not the public, lives of Sicilia's royal family. Hermione (Judi Dench) stands before the hobbyhorse ridden by Mamillius (Jeremy Richardson) and Leontes (Barrie Ingham). Richard Pasco's Polixenes (not shown), seated on a toy box downstage of his host, watches affectionately.

once drew on Rembrandt or the Tuscan painters of the Renaissance, Christopher Morley's plain, white set now explores the formal severity and the luxurious delight in colour of contemporary painting' (*Spectator*).

Nunn stripped the monarchs of their crowns, other symbols of state and their courtiers. Other Stratford directors would present Leontes, Polixenes and Hermione without crowns, but only Nunn denied them attendants in this scene. Backed by a music box playing 'Jack and Jill', Hermione, Leontes and Polixenes entered playing tag, with Mamillius being 'it'. Instead of presenting Mamillius as a miniature adult, the production introduced adults, and monarchs at that, playing nursery games with the heir to the throne. The stage picture conveyed a young family and their cherished friend. British audiences may well have been reminded of a 1960s television documentary that gave a similar glimpse behind the scenes of its own queen, her husband and their young children. Spurling notes:

> Everything, from the costumes – ruffled shirts, flared jackets and high-waisted trousers ... suggests the youth, wealth and arrogance of the Sicilian court. And nothing could be more fetching than the mutual satisfaction of Leontes and Polixenes – with themselves, each other and the two young princes of whom their fathers are so inordinately fond. The whole scene is suffused with a sense of almost voluptuous well-being. (*Spectator*)

In this context Leontes' jealousy was sudden and inexplicable.

Ingham did not convey an earlier suspicion of Hermione or an unstable personality. Dench's gracious Hermione and Pasco's urbane Polixenes gave no hint of impropriety. Nunn's innovation was to introduce technical effects that allowed the audience to see through Leontes' eyes. Sudden changes in lighting from a warm golden to cold, steely blue froze Hermione and Polixenes in compromising gestures. In the *New Statesman*, Benedict Nightingale writes that 'Hermione's voice becomes salacious, inviting, and Polixenes wolfishly strokes her pregnant stomach'. Their voices were distorted; Dench's warm laugh turned sinister. At line 108, for example, the promptbook cues Hermione to whisper in Polixenes' ear, and at lines 181–5 for Hermione and Polixenes to 'mime kissing etc' and for the freeze to break when Hermione laughs. Several reviewers pointed out that Nunn borrowed cinematic techniques 'to contrast', as Sheridan Morley puts it in the *Tatler*, 'what is real with what exists only in Leontes' fevered imagination'. Other reviewers commented on the darkness Leontes' jealousy introduced. In the *Observer* Bryden likens the effect to one of the defining moments in the 1960s: 'The air darkens, gestures are frozen as in those photographs of the Dallas crowd . . . when the first bullet flung Kennedy's hand in the air. In that pause, the world looks different'. The NSA recording adds an aural dimension to the promptbook. Heartbeats underscore the speech in which Leontes refers to '*tremor cordis*' (110); in some speeches his voice is miked. Ingham speaks 'Inch-thick' (186) in isolated anger, seeking no allies in the audience. In Leontes' speeches, and most markedly in the speeches to Nicholas Selby's Camillo, the sound of the words echoes the sense. Leontes' anger was irrational; on 'hobby-horse' (276) he pushed the nursery toy. He was quite terrifying with Camillo, especially when he accused him of lying. Polixenes entered before his cue; then froze; again Leontes pushed the hobbyhorse. Throughout the scene, taunting sound effects heightened Leontes' misery: humming tops, heartbeats, a music box distorting the nursery rhyme 'Jack and Jill'. Reviewers welcomed Nunn's innovative presentation of Leontes' jealousy. Bryden explains the decision in terms of the stroboscope that had lit the opening image of the production. 'Leontes's jealousy', he argues, 'requires no motivation: it is simply the dark view of life crowding out the bright one' (*Observer*). Writing in the *Times* in 1969, Irving Wardle points out that 'Mr Nunn simply makes [Leontes' unmotivated jealousy] a condition of the story'. Wardle finds Nunn's staging of Leontes' jealousy 'the first of several marvellous transitions between dream and reality'. Robert Speaight sees in the 'sudden change of lighting a reminder that in what is described to us as an "old tale" we must take its arbitrariness on the chin' (*SQ*, 437). On the other hand, in his review for the *New Statesman*, Benedict Nightingale complains that the production did not 'prepare for the first outburst of jealousy. Leontes usually broods; his wife's fond treatment of his friend is open to misinterpretation; Polixenes may even be quietly in love with her'.

By the close of the scene, the set and the apparently innocent toys had begun to take on a darker significance. The white box trapped Leontes, and the nursery toys suggested he had not developed beyond the stage when children find it difficult to share their friends with others. Speaight sees the hobbyhorse, which has a textual basis (1.2.276), as symbolic of innocence and sin (*Tablet*). The top, which also has a textual basis (2.1.103), had a similar significance. Polixenes spun the 'school-boy's top' when he recalled his childhood days with Leontes; distorted, the hum commented ironically on Leontes' jealousy. Mamillius and Leontes took turns looking at the ever-changing designs in the kaleidoscope. The second time his father ordered him to 'Go, play, boy, play' (1.2.190), Mamillius selected a yo-yo. In the final movement of the scene, Polixenes played with the yo-yo; Camillo put away toys. The aural and visual images would resonate through the production. The chamber setting privileged the actor – 'his words, thoughts, fantasies and language' (*Plays & P.*); the visual imagery appealed to an audience educated in the film technique of visual 'telling'. Nunn's successors would adopt such things as lighting effects, symbolic toys, colour symbolism and the concentration on the private rather than the public lives of Hermione and Leontes.

For the 1976 season John Napier and Chris Dyer transformed the Stratford stage to recall an Elizabethan one. Figure 5 illustrates its features. A platform jutted into the auditorium with the audience seated on its three sides. Scaffolding with two galleries enclosed the acting space and extended into the auditorium. Given this transformation, one would expect the season to experiment with Elizabethan staging practices. However, as Figures 5 and 11 reveal, Di Seymour's design for the production, directed by John Barton with Trevor Nunn, relocated *The Winter's Tale* to an unspecified time somewhere within the Arctic Circle, well north of Sicilia. (In the same season Barton moved *Much Ado About Nothing* east from Messina to India.) In addition to relocating *The Winter's Tale*, the design introduced three key images: the seasons, a domestic setting, storytelling.

As the programme explains, the transplanted Sicilians celebrated the winter solstice festival of Jul. 'Garlands of holly and ivy' decorated the walls (*Cahiers Elis.*, 91). The props list calls for

FIGURE 5 Staged on the permanent, Elizabethan-style set for the 1976 season, John Barton's production introduced a symbolic, barren tree. Runic symbols on the curtains, explained in the programme notes, told a story similar to that of *The Winter's Tale*.

'5 skulls' to be hung from the posts of the galleries, and, ominously, the promptbook directs Polixenes to lift Mamillius up to put a garland on a skull as Leontes begins the speech 'Too hot' (1.2.108). Brown and beige hangings covered the Renaissance galleries and introduced through runic symbols a narrative similar to that of *The Winter's Tale*. For those wanting a key to unlock the meaning, the programme provided an explanation (see above, p. 19). Set against this backdrop picturing 'a sad tale', patterned carpets, three pouffes and two wooden chairs covered with bearskins defined a domestic space for the first act. The props list calls for games and toys for Mamillius: nine men's morris, a box of toys, rattles and flutes, a basket of wooden figures and a doll, a wooden top with whip. A barren tree served double duty as an indicator of the season and a symbol to be explored through performance. (It was, in fact, the trunk of a dead apple tree from

production manager Roger Howells's Warwickshire garden.)
Seymour designed costumes 'in Scandinavian furs and folk-woven
materials, hot reds and oranges predominating' (*SS*, 173). More
sober, Leontes wore an austere, dark brown priestlike cassock. Guy
Woolfenden's 'haunting' music enhanced 'the mood of remote
melancholy' (*D. Express*). Camillo played a cymbalum, or
dulcimer, associated with Hungarian bands. The design and
music, far removed from the Elizabethan platform on which the
play was performed, were also outside the traditional social and
historical settings for the play. More typically productions seek an
historical period that both accommodates the play and is, like the
Renaissance or Regency, within the audiences' frame of historical
reference. In the *Sunday Times*, Harold Hobson finds science
fiction in the set, which he read as looking forward to the 'new ice
age we are promised'. Richard David complains that 'the ultimate
effect of the outlandish setting was to remove the play altogether
into a two-dimensional world of make-believe' (David, 223).

Quayle's eastern European setting had helped explain Leontes'
jealousy, and it was reasonable to expect similar aid from this
setting remote in both time and place. But Barton used a change
in lighting. In 1969 strobe lights had caught Hermione and
Polixenes in the compromising gestures Leontes imagined. In
1976, 'the switch from normal stage lighting to weird coldness ...
emphasize[d] the sudden way in which fantasies seize[d] upon
Leontes's fevered brain' (*SS*, 173). One consequence of the
technique, Roger Warren explains, was that 'it greatly aids the
actor, since it uses an extreme, startling technical effect to parallel
Shakespeare's own extreme, daring psychological technique for
Leontes' (*SS*, 173). In 1969 Dench's Hermione and Pasco's
Polixenes had been beyond reproach. In 1976, however, the
behaviour of Marilyn Taylerson's Hermione and John Woodvine's
Polixenes was, according to some reviewers, suspicious. Hermione
was 'demonstrative' (*Tatler & Bys.*) and Polixenes was 'remarkably
familiar with Hermione, adjusting her dress over her ankles when
she sits, holding her hand as they talk together, and her husband's

jealousy really seems to have a solid ground' (*FT*). Hobson exonerates Hermione, who possessed 'not a scrap of flirtatiousness in her' (*S. Times*). David describes her as 'not the simple symbol of nobility and sincerity that is sometimes seen, but a conspicuously foreign princess. Her somewhat mannered courtesies made her opaque so that her innocence was never self-evident though she protested it with passionate grandeur' (223). Leontes' jealousy, he argues, was an 'innate quality', which 'springs imperiously out of Ian McKellen's masterly performance'. Similarly, Michael Billington describes Leontes as 'a man seething with "diseased opinion". Into an idyllic image of family life, he suddenly injects a racked sexual anguish spitting out words like "sluiced" and "bedswerver"' (*Guardian*).

In the 1976 Scandinavian *Tale*, runic symbols decorated the wall hangings in Sicilia and signalled the importance of folk tales, of narrative. The dominant visual motif of 1981, directed by Ronald Eyre, was that of the theatre, of performing a story. A low rostrum centre stage was the main acting space, entered primarily through three double doors in the upstage wall. The largest, central door was reserved for dramatic entrances. In early performances two pairs of tailors' dummies, costume rails and a props table on the upstage wall continued the theatrical motif; but these were gradually stripped away, as Gemma Jones recalled in a conversation with me, and attending to the dialogue took prominence. To direct the audience's attention to the speakers, four coldly clinical lamps shone down on the rostrum, where the main dialogue was spoken. On the proscenium and around the rostrum, actors appeared to be sometimes 'in the wings' awaiting their cue, and at other times commented ironically on the main action. The walls that enclosed the rostrum and the surrounding space created areas blocked from the view of the audience: spectators were not to be made privy to all the magic of the theatre; or, perhaps the court whispered and spied out of sight. Although the tones of the wood were warm, the highly polished floor, the starkness of the set and the institutional lamps made the space sterile and unwelcoming. Pure white costumes for Leontes (Patrick Stewart), Polixenes (Ray Jewers) and Mamillius and the white background of the dress worn by Gemma Jones's Hermione offered neither relief from the coldness nor clear statement of period. A number of reviewers described them as Regency or Regency-inspired; in the *Financial Times*, B.A. Young guesses they could be placed 'in some vague date between 1500 and 1900 but veering mostly towards the later time'.

The promptbook and videotape help to reconstruct the first act; some cues reveal what was intended when the set was dressed with the props table and tailors' dummies. After stagehands removed the cloth cover from the rostrum, which the company nicknamed 'the hotplate' (Jones, 158), Bernard Lloyd's Camillo and Brian Poyser's Archidamus opened the play in very formal tones. Before they finished their conversation, the tone shifted and the static stage picture gave way to one filled with action. Actors entered from the wings, chose props and costumes and assumed their places. Hermione picked up a sheaf of wheat; Leontes and Polixenes put on robes and crowns that had been displayed on the dummies. Voices off, a drum roll and a trumpet heralded a masque, directed by an energetic Leontes and performed on the central platform. Leontes darted anxiously about the stage, wearing a clown's red bulbous nose, blowing a toy trumpet and carrying a jester's bladder. Entering first, Autolycus, clad in black suit and top hat, led in an enormous black bear. A polonaise signalled the entrance of Hermione, partnered by Polixenes. The Bohemians danced on to folk music. As a clock began to strike, the huge upstage doors opened, Cleomenes and Dion entered, then a gigantic figure of Father Time, his arms outstretched to reveal symbolic figures on sleeves sweeping to the floor. (For a similar presentation, see Figure 24.) At the stroke of twelve – and to the delight of the court – Mamillius emerged from beneath Time's cloak and raced to his parents. Bells peeled; scene 2 began. Played on the platform, Leontes' masque announced the centrality of playing a role and anticipated the mauling of

Antigonus, the springtime of Bohemia and the mystical and healing powers of Time. In the programme, notes explore the meaning of Time and the sixteenth century's fascination with masques; early maps of constellations suggest a source for the figures on Time's cloak; illustrations from the sixteenth to twentieth centuries challenge the audience to attend to the significance of spirals.

Leontes may have controlled the masque, but his darting about the stage may be read as more than the first-night nerves of an amateur director. Writing about the role, Patrick Stewart discusses the formality of Leontes' relationship with Polixenes and explores the language of Leontes, Polixenes and Hermione. Stewart explains that

> it is possible to play Leontes as a man who becomes suddenly jealous, or as a man who is jealous all the way through. There is a tension underneath the scene; the actors have to respond to the complexity of what Shakespeare is trying to say.   (Stewart, 258–9)

In Stewart's performance, argues Irving Wardle in the *Times*, Leontes' jealousy emerged suddenly and had a devastating effect on him. 'It is', writes Wardle, 'as though he is having a heart attack. He gulps for air, loosens his clothes, his arms flail and when he regains equilibrium, his frank smile is replaced with a smilingly poisoned mask'. Roger Warren takes the opposite view: Stewart's Leontes was 'jealous from the start' (*SS*, 148). The jealousy of Stewart's Leontes seemed to predate the action of the play and suggested an ulterior motive to his pairing Hermione with Polixenes in the masque. Leontes was 'rash, fierce and choleric' (*Guardian*). The videotape provides examples: Stewart asks 'Is he won yet?' (1.2.86) in a harsh tone; he punches at Hermione; he slaps her hand as he says 'I am yours for ever' (105); he crosses over to Hermione and accuses her with 'and so prove, / As ornaments oft do, too dangerous' (157–8). When he describes their alleged misbehaviour, Leontes does not look at Hermione and Polixenes, whose actions belie Leontes' words. When he touches Hermione – and also Polixenes and Mamillius – Leontes is awkward, ill at ease. Jones's Hermione, who has given no cause for suspicion, has a natural warmth. In her essay about playing Hermione, Jones records that she, Stewart and Jewers

> exchange[d] experiences of pregnancy. I admit to a state of introverted self-satisfaction which allowed for no intrusion and blinded me to needs outside myself, while the men acknowledge certain feelings of impotent isolation and rejection. Might this account for Hermione's apparent unawareness of Leontes' condition and her innocently provocative behaviour. (Jones, 158)

In rehearsals they improvised playing 1.2 as though Hermione had been unfaithful: 'but observation on the exercise is that it is perverse and destructive to attempt to give Leontes a rational jealousy. Hermione must personify all that is pure and right in order to illuminate the irrationality of his jealousy and the extent of his loss' (159). In Figure 6 Leontes sits on the floor beside Hermione and childlike rests his head on her; she smiles at Polixenes, who kneels as if he is her suitor. In the *Times* Wardle, arguing for the sudden emergence of Leontes' jealousy, describes the significance of the moment: 'the first sight of what is to come appears when he is lying at Hermione's feet, his face staring out front and turning to stone in the midst of the surrounding gaiety'. On the other hand, the photograph also supports the actors' personal experiences of pregnancy. Hermione's 'introverted self-satisfaction' and the men's 'feelings ... of isolation and rejection'. The production did not portray a closeness between Leontes and Mamillius. Disrupting the bond between Polixenes and Mamillius, Leontes pulled his son away from Polixenes (171). Later, he stuttered his insecurity about Mamillius' paternity: 'Who I do think is mine' (331). Unlike Leontes, Hermione and Polixenes were able to give affection. A most telling example was their spontaneous compassion for Leontes when they realized he was troubled (146). Wracked with pain, Leontes put Polixenes and Hermione's hands together and dismissed them.

FIGURE 6 Leontes (Patrick Stewart) listens as Hermione (Gemma Jones) pleads with Polixenes (Ray Jewers) to stay longer. Hermione's crown, laced with flowers, and the pattern on her dress introduce a motif to be repeated by Perdita's costume and the curtain hiding the statue. (1.2, 1981)

Adrian Noble's 1984 small-scale tour introduced details that he would draw upon for his main-house production in 1992. Visual borrowings are easily identified. Balloons, to take just one obvious example, added festive colour to celebrations in Bohemia in 1984 and in Sicilia and Bohemia in 1992. What interests us here is Noble's reading of the play and the ways he translated his reading for two quite different theatrical events. In his introduction to an edition of the play, Noble describes *The Winter's Tale* as 'a great healing play, both through the extraordinary spiritual journey that is undergone by the protagonists and also through the sane, healthy influence that the humble Bohemians have on their mighty masters' (Noble, xiv). Of necessity Noble relied on different designs for that journey.

The basic features of Bob Crowley's design for the two promenade shows of 1984 were two large rostra, steps leading to each rostrum, and an abundance of oriental carpets. For the first three acts of *The Winter's Tale* the rostra were at opposite ends of a rectangular playing space covered by the richly patterned carpets. By the close of 2.1 the two rostra and the central space had clearly defined associations with characters. With seating limited to forty-eight places for the elderly and disabled, the audience promenaded along the sides of the playing space and, in some scenes, sat on a rostrum or its steps. Minimal props identified the location: for the beginning of Act 1, eight gold chairs were placed in a tight circle facing outwards; just above them hung a chandelier. Modern costumes, described as 'post-war Sicilian Mediterranean' (*FT*, Oct) and modern music, played by three musicians on keyboards, percussion and flute and saxophone, established time and place. The entertainment of Polixenes was formal, private, not ostentatious. Janet Dale, who played Paulina, likens it to an ambassadorial reception. Production photographs record a formal evening party, where Lynn Farleigh's Hermione wears a tiara and the men display medals on bright red sashes. The promptbook offers no evidence to counter the claim that 'there was only barely enough in her manner towards the rather serious Polixenes of Julian Curry to arouse the fanatical jealousy of Leontes' (*Cahiers Elis.*, 87).

Throughout the Sicilian scenes, visual images and stage business emphasized a division within the Sicilian society along lines of gender, not political status or class. One cluster of images centred on Christopher Lahr's Mamillius. Like his predecessors in the previous three Stratford productions, Mamillius played with a young child's toys, not with miniature bows and arrows, daggers or swords. The promptbook calls for him to have a toy cart with a bear, a panda, a lamb and cards in it, a drawing book and a glove puppet. In the opening scene Polixenes gave him another toy – a top – as a birthday gift, which, notes Robin Thornber, was 'a powerfully telling visual symbol of frail security' (*Guardian*). It was a symbol that Nunn had introduced in 1969 and that Noble would return to in 1992. Two of the numerous cues in the promptbook for

Mamillius to play coincide with Leontes' complaint: 'Most dear'st, my collop! Can thy dam? – may't be? – / Affection! thy intention stabs the centre' (1.2.137–8). The cues, which may be read as a symbolic representation of Leontes' abuse of Hermione, call for Mamillius to creep up with the glove puppet to frighten the lamb and to attack the lamb with the little bear. The business also anticipated 3.3, when the bear was attracted to Perdita before it pursued Antigonus. In the first act Noble also introduced the importance of Hermione's female attendants. Assuring Alun Armstrong's Leontes 'I am like you, they say' (208), Mamillius clearly identifies the women as 'they' by stressing the word. Toys and the business with Mamillius were realistic details that helped portray the world of women and children. The other world was the male world, dominated by Leontes and presented as one in which the key relationship was between a Mafia godfather and his subordinates. Dale recalls that Armstrong was encouraged to be an irrational, cruel autocrat, used to getting his own way and demanding allegiance from the lords who attended him. (Writing in the *Observer* in 1982 (1 Aug), Robert Cushman had predicted that it was 'only a matter of time before someone tries a Mafia setting'.)

In its stark white Regency-inspired costumes, predominantly white set, nursery toys, and lighting effects to mark the inception of Leontes' jealousy, Terry Hands's production (1986) looked back to Nunn's. But as Figure 7 reveals, Hands's production achieved a quite different effect. Its richness of detail – excessively rich in the eyes of some reviewers – created a series of stunning stage pictures. The opening moments, as recorded on the videotape, established a romantic atmosphere. Upstage of the scrim that divided the acting space, figures in graceful slow motion threw snowballs. Highly polished surfaces reflected the playful fight and the flame flaring from a fire bowl. Overhead and upstage of the scrim a large disc caught light. A celeste and a treble chorister, both of which would become aural motifs, introduced an ethereal effect to the winter festivities. As Richard Easton's Camillo and Stanley Dawson's Archidamus spoke, the scrim was raised and revealed

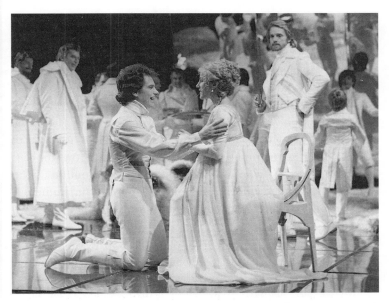

FIGURE 7 Polixenes (Paul Greenwood) and Hermione (Penny Downie) flirt, watched suspiciously by Camillo (Richard Easton), Leontes (Jeremy Irons) and courtiers. His back to the couple, Mamillius catches their reflection in the mirror. White was the dominant colour in the Sicilian scenes in 1986. (1.2)

the oversized polar bear skin – a visual motif – that dominated the stage floor and was reflected in the angled panel of mirrors upstage (partially visible in Figure 18). When the revellers moved downstage, servants passed among them with trays of drinks. Costumes, music, lighting and stage business introduced an attractive, early nineteenth-century world. But the set suggested also an imaginary realm, a darker atmosphere: reflections cast on the floor and on the upstage panel sounded a warning against reading too much romance into the fairy-tale prettiness.

It was a chilly marriage in which Penny Downie's Hermione dominated Leontes, played by Jeremy Irons, and seemed happier with Paul Greenwood's Polixenes, a point illustrated by the videotape and production photographs. Hermione's laughter mocked Leontes before he queries 'Tongue-tied our queen?' (1.2.27) and she chastised him for 'too coldly' (30) urging Polixenes to extend his visit. Hermione's voice conveyed the excitement of having a new admirer. She took Polixenes' hands and placed them on her belly. Polixenes knelt beside her and whispered affectionately in her ear. Figure 7 captures Hermione and Polixenes caught up in their own little world and oblivious to Leontes (centre, behind Hermione) and Camillo (to the left behind Polixenes), who watch them, and to Mamillius, who catches their reflection in the mirror, and to the numerous courtiers and servants. Nicholas Shrimpton notes that

> Hands ... seemed ... to be suggesting that Hermione and Polixenes were indeed lovers. Penny Downie offered an exceptionally flirtatious and ingratiating Hermione in a décollettée maternity dress. Paul Greenwood's Polixenes lavished cuddles, back-rubs, and love-lorn gazes upon her so ostentatiously that Camillo's 'Come, sir, away' (1.2.465) became a desperate attempt to avoid public scandal.   (SS, 178)

Greenwood recalls that Hands urged them to be flirtatious. As Hermione exited with Polixenes her laugh ironically answered Leontes' 'allowing husband!' (185). He and Mamillius turned to wave to the departing couple, but they were too late. Hermione and Polixenes justified Leontes' jealousy and even raised suspicions in her son. Mamillius took the earliest opportunity to escape from Polixenes, who embraced him as he recalled Leontes and himself 'as twinn'd lambs' (67), and to return to his father. He watched Polixenes kneeling beside his mother as Leontes observed 'women say so, / (That will say anything)' (130–5). Mid-speech Leontes picked Mamillius up. However, given the tortured mind uttering disjointed phrases, it was hardly a rescue to preserve what remained of the innocence of childhood. Hermione asked Mamillius, not Leontes, 'Are you mov'd, my lord?' and Leontes answered for his son, 'No, in good earnest' (150). Polixenes was very much at home in Sicilia.

As his rigid posture indicates (Figure 7), Leontes was considerably less comfortable. If Hermione gave Leontes cause for jealousy,
the production and the programme offered reasons why her
affections might have strayed. Irons's Leontes was emotionally
immature. Memories of childhood upset him. His voice had a
pathetic quality when he recalled the 'Three crabbed months' he
had courted Hermione (102). Sound effects, symbolic of youthful
innocence and evoking the apparently happy opening moments,
accompanied key speeches. Spoken against the faint treble of the
chorister, 'and so prove, / As ornaments oft do, too dangerous'
(157–8) was a remark that pointed to Leontes' lost childhood, and
his failure to come to terms with adulthood. The tinkling bells of
the celeste were an ironic counterpoint to the tortured speeches
'Too hot' (108) and 'Inch-thick' (186). Lighting – 'a sudden switch
[from blue] to white' – reinforced the point (*Cahiers Elis.*, 94). For
comfort and in fear of losing his son, Leontes clung to Mamillius,
who seemed to sense the tension and to side with his father.
Excerpts and illustrations in the programme trace the father–son
conflict, but more tellingly quote Peter Pan's assertion: 'I want
always to be a little boy and have fun'. Reminiscing, Polixenes
tells Hermione 'We were, fair queen, / Two lads that thought there
was no more behind, / But such a day to-morrow as to-day, / And
to be boy eternal' (62–5). Polixenes had made the leap of faith to
adulthood; Leontes had not. Mamillius, forced to witness his
mother's flirtations and to hear his father's suspicions, was
learning something of 'The doctrine of ill-doing' (70). To a greater
extent than had his Stratford predecessors, Irons sought a
complicity with his audience. Warren describes the effect:

Jeremy Irons played Leontes for laughs a great deal. 'I am angling
now,' [180] spoken confidentially to the audience, had a dangerous
whiff of Master Ford. His extended vision of universal cuckoldry
culminating in 'Many thousand on's / Have the disease and feel't
not' [206–7] was delivered directly to his fellow-cuckolds in the
audience as if to say 'we're all in the same boat, aren't we?' So the
audience laughed at phrases like 'sluiced,' 'his pond fished' and 'a

bawdy planet' [194, 195, 201]; the gross, obsessive sexuality of these expressions was sanitized by laughter. Instead of seeming a violent aberration totally at odds with the true facts of the situation, Leontes's speech came across as a knowing statement of an even more dangerous consequence: the whole play became a trivial domestic comedy in which adultery was a topic for smutty jokes.

(SQ, 86)

The three key features in Anthony Ward's design for Noble's 1992 main-house production were a giant gauze box; a cyclorama with the countryside low on the horizon and vast skies across which white fluffy clouds floated or storm clouds scudded; a raked floor of jagged boards (see Figures 8, 32, 41 and cover photograph).[4] The gauze box was at once eye-catching and puzzling. Lighting effects made it opaque or translucent, bright and warm or grey and dull. Varying the number of sides or raising it from the floor also changed its effect or meaning. On a practical level, it functioned as an attractive solution to the demands of the script and limitations of the Stratford stage. It helped to make the stage flexible, to accommodate large public scenes and smaller intimate ones, to bleed one scene into another and to conceal characters entering from upstage or on a trap. On a metaphorical level it offered a visual statement of Noble's reading of the play and a key to Leontes.

The production opened with the full company frozen within the gauze box and Mamillius, downstage centre, looking at them and holding a glass globe with a winter scene in it (Figure 8). As he raised the toy and caused the 'snow' to fall, the gauze box was flown out and the company 'spilled out'. Mamillius chased after Paul Jesson's Polixenes to capture the gift teasingly offered him, returned to his spot to unwrap the box, and spun his new top. As it hummed, the company froze. Samantha Bond's Hermione, Leontes, played by John Nettles, and Polixenes focused on Mamillius, who played where sixteen years later his mother would appear as a statue. At opposite edges of the platform

FIGURE 8 In the opening image of Adrian Noble's 1992 production, Mamillius (Marc Elliott) looks upstage toward the court, their party-going temporarily frozen within the gauze box. Hermione (Samantha Bond) glances at her son; Leontes (John Nettles) stands behind her; Polixenes (Paul Jesson) sits opposite her.

Benjamin Whitrow's Camillo and John Bott's Archidamus spoke their lines, closing with 'it is a gallant child' (1.1.37–8). The words were, records the promptbook, Mamillius' cue: he snatched up the top, went to his mother and hugged her.

Probably the most obvious feature of Noble's opening scene was the predominance of colour and the creation of a sense of inclusive society that welcomed attendants and a young child to an evening party. Bright red, yellow and blue balloons were tied incongruously to court chairs; ladies wore long gowns of velvet and satin in rich shades of greens, blues and mauves; Leontes and Polixenes wore jackets of forest green and burgundy, respectively. Lighting designer Chris Parry bathed the stage in warm tones, and Shaun Davey contributed festive music. Camillo, Archidamus, Antigonus and Paulina, as well as attendant lords and ladies, chatted amiably, danced, and 'canoodled' on cue. Mamillius entertained Hermione's ladies with magic tricks. The friendship of Polixenes and Leontes seemed on firm ground. Noble explains that they made 'the whole of the first act a party for Polixenes' departure, at which Mamillius was a beloved and treasured guest, allowed to stay up late as a treat' (Noble, xiv). In the opening sequences, however, Noble subtly foreshadowed Leontes' shattering of the attractive image: the spinning and humming of Mamillius' top; a melancholy motif and instrumentation slipped into Davey's music; the fissures in the floor; shadows cast by clouds; the court, frozen in arrested motion and contained within the gauze box.

Nettles conveyed Leontes' jealousy as striking suddenly and without warning. A series of freezes of the party-goers, which captured moments as would snapshots, changes in lighting from warm to blue, and Leontes' stage position intensified his misreading of Hermione and Polixenes. Robert Smallwood describes Leontes as

> hover[ing] round the fringes of the group, an isolated and furtive figure, peeping and spying and sharing his desperate imaginings with the audience in a dislocated, clipped, staccato delivery, with angry changes of rhythm surging through the lines, a delivery that seemed to me highly effective in suggesting a mind almost audibly cracking up. (SQ, 349)

The promptbook records that Leontes moved upstage at line 46, when Hermione says 'Verily! / You put me off with limber vows', and did not return until just before he asks 'Is he won yet?' (1.2.86). As Leontes watched from outside the circle of party-goers, Hermione and Polixenes waltzed, kissed, but gave no cause for alarm, as had Hermione and Polixenes in 1986. Morever, in the initial image of the production – the company frozen within the gauze box (Figure 8) – and in Polixenes' opening speech, the two men conveyed that they had maintained their childhood 'affection' (1.1.23). Nor did Nettles's Leontes suggest an emotional immaturity or a predilection to jealousy. At moments it even seemed as though he recognized, as did the audience, Hermione's affection for him. On the sound recording, Hermione speaks gently, not in the teasing or cool tone of other Hermiones in the speeches beginning 'What! have I twice said well?' (1.2.90) and 'Why lo you now; I have spoke to th' purpose twice' (106). In the intervening speech, Nettles's Leontes conveys his fondness for Hermione.

Nettles moved downstage centre to complain 'Too hot' (108). Behind him the revellers were frozen in a blue light; and a top hummed as he spoke. The lights went down for the passage beginning 'I am angling now' (180), throwing Leontes' shadow upstage of him. Nettles addressed 'Sir Smile' (196) to the audience but he did not seek to involve the audience by picking out as fellow sufferers men sitting in the stalls.

For the Sicilian scenes in Gregory Doran's production (1999) Robert Jones designed five pairs of sliding panels.[5] Set for Act 1, the panels narrowed in perspective to an upstage focal point – a ceremonial entrance – and provided four sets of parallel entrances from the wings. Jones's use of perspective, like that of Noel in 1960, looked back to the Italian Renaissance. Wood used Noel's set as an architectural background for painterly groupings. In Doran's production the sliding panels closed in on Antony Sher's Leontes and helped visualize his descent into instability. The billowing cloth ceiling hung ominously, cloudlike (Figure 9). As had, for example, Nunn and Hands, Doran suggested period – early twentieth century – and place – Russia or, perhaps, eastern Europe – and carefully planted clues that would chart Leontes' disintegration and Hermione's response. Sound, costume and stage picture were key elements in Doran's approach. First, the sound designer suggested Leontes' predisposition to suspicion. As the house lights dimmed, waves of whispers seemed to emanate from courtiers and servants hidden behind the tunnel of walls or entering for the first act. A few decipherable phrases – 'Is whispering nothing?' (1.2.284), 'Too hot, too hot!' (108) –

identified the source as Leontes' feverish brain. Inserted business shifted the focus to Leontes as monarch. A trumpet fanfare announced him; he entered alone through the central door, wearing a red velvet, ermine-edged gown, and a crown. (See Figure 20 for the costume, which he also wore in the trial scene.) Leontes collected Polixenes (Ken Bones), also in regalia, and Alexandra Gilbreath's Hermione, who entered from opposite wings, and led them downstage and then back up to the central doors to receive subdued applause from offstage crowds 'from what was clearly this kingdom's equivalent of the Buckingham Palace balcony' (SS, 263). As Polixenes made his last public appearance in Sicilia, Geoffrey Freshwater's Camillo and Peter Macqueen's Archidamus spoke the opening scene. Their public obligations having been met, Leontes and Polixenes cast aside the trappings of medieval monarchy to reveal the sombre suits of well-dressed early twentieth-century gentlemen. To sharpen the distinction between Bones's relaxed Polixenes and Sher's uptight Leontes, Doran divided the stage picture (Figure 9). To the audience's left Hermione assumed with grace her husband's charge to entertain Polixenes. They settled on a chaise to talk; Polixenes was solicitous; he helped her up to put a record on a gramophone; they danced. On the right, Leontes, having abdicated the uncomfortable role of host (whatever was Archidamus on about: 'we cannot with such magnificence' entertain, 1.1.12) did paperwork at his desk. The heartsick father shared his half of the stage with his physically ill son. Emily Bruni's Mamillius, wheelchair-bound and oblivious to others (hardly seeming to offer 'the greatest promise' or to be 'gallant', 36, 38), read a book.

Unlike his boyhood companion, Sher's Leontes was socially insecure. He spoke 'We are tougher, brother, / Than you can put us to 't' (1.2.15–16) with a false jollity. He delivered 'At my request' (87) with a boyish astonishment, pushed into Hermione to punish her success (89), refused to be drawn into a dance with Hermione and Polixenes, and spoke 'to your graver steps' (173) in a hurt voice. As Hermione and Polixenes waltzed upstage of Leontes, the

FIGURE 9 With the ceiling louring above him and the walls receding upstage of him, Leontes (Antony Sher) enjoins Hermione (Alexandra Gilbreath) to convince their guest (Polixenes: Ken Bones) to remain in Sicilia. Mamillius (Emily Bruni) pouts. Significant props are the chaise (behind Hermione and Polixenes), Leontes' desk and Mamillius' wheel-chair. (1.2, 1999)

stage darkened, shadows were cast, and Leontes slowly and painfully spoke 'Too hot' (108). He mistook Hermione's deep sigh, very clearly associated with her pregnancy. Polixenes asked 'What means Sicilia?' (146) because Leontes took the needle off the gramophone record, scarring the record in his haste. Leontes used his memories of their shared childhood (153–60) to regain his composure. Recapturing the old days for a moment, Leontes and Polixenes spoke 'As ornaments oft do' (158) in unison, turning the words into an admonitory saying from their youth. There was something almost incongruous in the way Sher's repressed little bureaucratic monarch found evocative language to describe Hermione's supposed adultery. Having risen from his desk to query 'Is he won yet?' (86) Sher held the stage until exhausted, then he returned to the relative safety of his desk (325). Surprised that Hermione and Polixenes had 'Gone already!' (185), Leontes sniffed Hermione's shawl for incriminating evidence. (When Polixenes returned, he folded it carefully and held it as he talked with Camillo.) Aware of the damning nature of his actions, Sher's Leontes justified himself by directing 'There have been' (190ff.) to the audience, moved to the apron, and pointed to members of the audience to demonstrate the prevalence of cuckoldom. A bold, some would argue cruel, decision, it evoked nervous laughter, not the sort Irons had received in 1986. A provocative gesture illustrated 'It will let in and out the enemy' (205). Broken and alone with Camillo, Leontes had trouble confessing his conviction. He took a long pause before 'slippery': 'My wife is slippery?' (273). Camillo's defence of Hermione provoked enraged shouting and screaming and storming up and down the stage. Greatly anxious, Leontes promised to 'seem friendly' (350) and left the stage to Camillo.

As he explained in an interview with Charles Spencer, Sher researched the role by visiting a number of psychiatrists, who offered various diagnoses of Leontes' condition: schizophrenia, manic depression, a sense of loss, psychotic jealousy. The condition most accurately describing Leontes, Sher decided, was 'psychotic jealousy'. Spencer summarizes its traits: it 'descends from a clear blue sky. The patient becomes irrationally convinced that his partner is betraying him and it causes wildly obsessive behaviour, morbid fantasies and paroxysms of rage and violence followed by periods of intense remorse' (*D. Telegraph*). Sher's performance was a detailed portrait of those symptoms.

The nineteen illustrations discussed or alluded to in this chapter are a useful tool for reviewing how Stratford directors have approached the three interrelated topics with which we began and how they have answered some of the questions raised about the three topics: opening moments, design, Leontes. Most of the productions began with either interpolated action, such as the masque initiated by Leontes in Eyre's production (1981), or with a strong visual image, such as that which opened Noble's 1992 production: sitting downstage centre, Mamillius turns to look at party-goers frozen in a gauze box centre stage (Figure 8). The evocative scene Mamillius observes leads directly to the second topic: design. Glancing through the illustrations, one is struck by the variety of designs, which could serve as an overview of a half century of theatre design. Several themes central to the performance history of *The Winter's Tale* also emerge. First, the introduction of symbolic objects and properties, such as the display of spears behind the crowned heads of Leontes and Hermione in 1948 (Figure 1), the barren trees in 1948 (Figure 2) and 1976 (Figure 5), the hobbyhorse ridden by Leontes and Mamillius in 1969 (Figure 4), the clown's red bulbous nose that Leontes wears and the fool's bladder he carries in 1981, the tilted panel of mirrors in 1986 (Figure 7) and the gauze box that encloses the court in 1992 (Figure 8). Fabrics, such as the curtains in 1948 (Figure 2) and 1976 (Figure 5) and Hermione's dress (Figure 6) and Time's garment in 1981 (Figure 24), introduce signs and symbols to be decoded. The illustrations also reveal ways in which the stage picture affects our perception of characters. In 1960 the use of perspective draws the eye upstage of the formal grouping of crowned monarchs and the Sicilian court (Figure 3). In 1999 walls enclose and a cloth ceiling droops threateningly over Polixenes, Hermione, Leontes and Mamillius (Figure 9). Looking back over the nine productions one finds symbolic properties that have a textual basis: a schoolboy's top, a hobbyhorse, bears, timepieces. Some of these, such as the top and clocks, introduce sound effects; heartbeats echo Leontes' '*tremor cordis*'. Two Stratford directors (and others as well) followed Nunn's lead in dressing the Sicilian characters in white costumes based on Regency designs.

The illustrations usefully place the eight main-house presentations of Leontes in a social or political context, give them costumes and properties and capture a visual image – one moment of their relationships with Hermione or Polixenes or

Mamillius. To convey the sudden onset of Leontes' jealousy four directors, beginning with Nunn in 1969 and followed by Barton in 1976, Hands in 1986 and Noble in 1992, used technical devices: changes in lighting, sound effects, freezes. In 1999 sound effects signalled that Leontes' suspicions predated the action; in 1981, Leontes' properties and frantic direction of the masque suggested a mind already disturbed. Performances presented various causes. In 1986 (Figure 7) and to a lesser extent in 1960, Hermione and Polixenes provoked Leontes' jealousy. In 1948 Esmond Knight's barbaric Sicilia helped reviewers explain his unprovoked jealousy. In 1999 Sher portrayed an insecure monarch suffering psychotic jealousy. Whatever the cause, Leontes' jealousy propels Hermione and Paulina, as well as himself, on long journeys. The next chapter examines how productions at Stratford have embarked upon those journeys.

NOTES

1 *Leamington Spa Courier*, 24 April 1942; *Stratford-upon-Avon Herald*, 7 May 1943.
2 Beauman, 239. See also Pringle.
3 Jacket notes, gramophone record.
4 The account here and in other chapters draws on my viewings of the production.
5 The account here and in other chapters draws on my viewings of the production.

2

SICILIA

CHAMBERS AND PRISONS

In Act 2 the scene shifts from a farewell appropriate to the departure of a royal guest and boyhood friend of the King of Sicilia to three more private scenes, dramatizing the immediate consequences of Leontes' jealousy (2.1 and 2.2) and its effects on him (2.1 and 2.3) over the more than three weeks since Polixenes and Camillo hastily set sail for Bohemia. In the title of this chapter 'prisons' alludes not only to the place where Leontes incarcerates Hermione but also to Leontes' constricted mental state, especially in 2.3. On stage, as in life, however, a private scene in the chambers of a royal family almost always includes some members of the royal household. One focus of this chapter is the reactions of Hermione, Mamillius and the royal household to Leontes' accusation of Hermione. Paulina, whom many productions include in 1.2, is, of course, of primary importance. But the anonymous lords, ladies and attendants, who may have helped fill in the stage picture in Act 1, also claim our attention. Has the director introduced guards or attendants or, as did Peter Wood (1960), minor characters from another scene? Have lines been reassigned to elevate less important characters, such as Paulina's Steward, or to make a point about the marriage of Paulina and Antigonus? Has the gender or status of a role been altered, by, for instance, assigning a lord's line to a lady or a servant's line to a doctor? In these three scenes, the minor characters begin to reveal something of their relationship with Hermione and Leontes and to comment – with words and actions and as silent witnesses – on the consequences of Leontes' jealousy.

This chapter continues the examination of the design of productions. Entrance cues and embedded stage directions help place each of the three scenes in a chamber (2.1 and 2.3) or a prison (2.2), but there are few embedded cues for props. How does the designer define each of the places and how, if at all, does the design link each scene with the previous one? How does the director handle scene changes? Is there continuous action, or does a blackout allow a set change, which is then revealed to the audience? What kind of music and sound effects are introduced? Is the production developing a musical motif or repeating a significant sound? What do costumes – and especially a character's change of costume – reveal?

2.1

HERMIONE'S CHAMBER

A sad tale's best for winter

The first scene, which may be broken into four phases, takes place in a room associated with women and children. Since Trevor Nunn's production (1969), it has, typically, been set in a domestic space and its furnishings and/or stage business often anticipate the imminent royal birth. As we shall see, design, props and music may also link this domestic scene with the preceding scene, in which Leontes reveals his 'diseas'd opinion' (1.2.297). Thus the designer's concept of the production may underscore the dramatic irony of the first phase of the scene (lines 1–32), the innocent banter of Hermione, Mamillius and the ladies. In the second phase (33–55), stage design and blocking usually present the visual irony through a split stage: Leontes and the lords converse (33–55) while Mamillius whispers to Hermione his 'sad tale'. The next phase (56–125), Leontes' accusation of Hermione, opens and closes with an important exit. Is Mamillius taken off on cue ('Bear the boy hence', 59), or does the child hear any of Leontes' accusation? Who takes him off? Is there any force? Does Mamillius resist? And for Hermione a similar set of questions, with particular attention to the possible use of force. Does Leontes physically abuse his pregnant wife? Who takes her off and is force employed? How does Hermione respond to Leontes? Does she reach out to him or touch him or attempt to touch him? Does she acknowledge Leontes before she leaves the stage? In the final phase (126–99), the focus shifts to Leontes and the lords, a passage that may be played as an ironic contrast with the female-dominated moments at the beginning of the scene. The playing script is of particular interest from the accusation to the close of the scene. In the accusation Leontes has approximately forty-one lines to Hermione's thirty-two, but some productions alter the relationship by cutting a higher percentage of Leontes' lines. (Of course throughout Shakespeare's plays it's not just the number of lines; the substance and delivery of a speech may increase its importance or the importance of an apparently slim role.) In the final phase Leontes and his lords share an equal number of lines, but cuts and reassignments of roles may alter the balance.

In 1948 simple adjustments transformed Motley's set for Act 1 (Figure 2), dominated by a military motif, to one more suitable for a domestic scene that Anthony Quayle opened with Diana Wynyard's Hermione, Timothy Harley's Mamillius, Paulina, played by Ena Burrill, Emilia and four ladies. The celestial globe was removed, the 'throne' became a couch, and curtains were drawn over the display of shields behind it. The military was still present, however: the sharp tips of spears, which in Figure 2 outline the entrance upstage centre, were reminders of the tyrannical nature of Esmond Knight's Leontes. As they had in Act 1, the monarchs wore crowns. Extant production materials leave some questions unanswered. How, for example, did Hermione, Mamillius and the ladies spend their leisure time?

Did the ladies engage in household tasks? What does the scene reveal about them, their relationship with Hermione, their relative importance in the royal household and the household itself? More crucially, what was Paulina's role in this scene? As he had in the first act, Quayle introduced Paulina as a silent witness. How did she respond to Leontes' treatment of Hermione? The only lines cut from the first phase of the scene are the Second Lady's reference to Hermione's pregnancy (19–20). They seem to have been cut because they were extraneous, not because the language was deemed unsuitable. Angus McBean's photograph in the SCL collection, which captures the moment when Mamillius responded to Hermione's 'come sit down' (29), suggests affection between mother and son but it also reveals a youth past the age and size for sitting on his mother's lap.

As Mamillius whispered his story, Leontes, Michael Godfrey's Antigonus and five lords entered downstage, swelling the number on stage to fifteen actors. Quayle shortened this phase of the scene (33–55) primarily by moving the first ten lines of Leontes' speech 'How blest am I' (36–45) to the third scene of the act. The alteration lessened the irony in the speech by stripping it from the visual context provided by Hermione and Mamillius. In the next phase (56–125) the promptbook, and especially the paring down of Leontes' speeches from thirty-seven to sixteen lines, suggests the swift and decisive behaviour of a tyrant. Leontes dragged Mamillius from Hermione's knees and dispatched him under the guardianship of one of the lords. Leontes did not charge Hermione with confederacy with Camillo. From the promptbook, one may infer that Leontes came across as a plain, blunt man, one who had made up his mind and did not waste words justifying his decision or revealing his anguish. Another effect of the cuts was to enhance Hermione's role. Hermione spoke twenty-six lines; Leontes, twenty-one. The promptbook also offers a revealing insight into Hermione. Instead of responding immediately to Leontes' charges, and completing his half lines, Hermione paused.

LEONTES   She's an adultress!

HERMIONE   [pause] Should a villain say so
    (The most replenish'd villain in the world)
    He were as much more villain: you, my lord,
    Do but mistake.

                                        (78–81)

LEONTES   Away with her, to prison!
    He who shall speak for her is afar off guilty
    But that he speaks.

HERMIONE   [pause] There's some ill planet reigns:

                                        (103–5)

These and other pauses suggest a reflective and astonished woman
and anticipate Hermione's delivery of her self-defence in the trial
scene. Two of her ladies were at her side throughout the
accusation.

    In the final phase of 2.1 (126–99), which lost half its lines,
Leontes sank onto the couch (126) and was approached by the
lords, at least one of whom knelt to him (129). Knight's Leontes
dealt as economically with Godfrey's Antigonus and the lords as
he had with Hermione. His speedy stanching of much of their
defence of Hermione added another dimension to his tyranny.

    As Figure 10 illustrates, Peter Wood (1960) and his designer,
Jaques Noel, shifted from the deep formal set for 1.2 to a more
intimate space downstage centre by simply drawing a curtain
from the stage left wings to mid-stage. But the stage picture and
business, as recorded in production materials, made 2.1 a formal
scene. Wearing her crown and costume from Act 1, Hermione,
played by Elizabeth Sellars, was carried on by two litter bearers
and placed before the curtains. Emilia, played by Mavis Edwards,
and three ladies, also wearing their costumes from the previous
scene, surrounded her. As in each of the previous scenes, Dennis
Waterman's Mamillius entered with the three pedants, the
promptbook's term for the three old gentlemen. The women
did not engage in hobbies or undertake chores; Mamillius was
not associated with games or toys. A stage direction calls for the

FIGURE 10 Crowns clearly identify Hermione (Elizabeth Sellars), who listens to Mamillius (Dennis Waterman), and Leontes (Eric Porter), who prepares to shatter the domestic calm. Hermione is attended by, from the left, Lady (Diana Rigg), Second Lady-in-Waiting (Maroussia Frank), Lady (Wendy Gifford), Emilia (Mavis Edwards). One prop – Hermione's chaise – and the curtains drawn behind the group clustered about the chaise transform the stage to a space suitable for Hermione's chamber. Leontes' attendants are Antigonus (Tony Church), Second Lord (Philip Voss), Third Lord (Donald Douglas), Cleomenes (James Kerry), First Lord (Donald Layne-Smith). (2.1, 1960)

pedants and the ladies to crowd around the chaise for Mamillius' story. When Eric Porter's Leontes, Tony Church's Antigonus, the First Lord, two other men and a soldier entered downstage to a point diagonal to the group clustered around Hermione's chaise, the scene was swollen to fifteen characters, nine of whom were on Hermione's part of the stage. A costume list calls for Leontes to dress in a 'military and severe' manner; he, too, wore a crown. The promptbook indicates that Mamillius was seized by Leontes and taken off upstage centre by a servant; the three tutors followed their pupil. As in the 1948 production, there was a pause between Leontes' charge and Hermione's response, but the cue calls for the pause after the accusation of adultery, for the court, which now numbers eleven, to respond and then for Hermione to answer. Pausing before 'thing', Porter seemed to have found a temporary lapse in Leontes' otherwise vivid vocabulary:

> O thou [pause] thing –
> Which I'll not call a creature of thy place,
> Lest barbarism, making me the precedent,
> Should a like language use to all degrees,
> And mannerly distinguishment leave out
> Betwixt the prince and beggar.
>
> (82–7)

As the lords and ladies watched, Hermione knelt to Leontes after 'and so / The king's will be perform'd' (114–15). The servant who had taken Mamillius off re-entered, accompanied by two men with pikes (103). The servant put manacles on Hermione; Emilia glanced at Leontes; Leontes turned away. Manacled and under armed guard, Hermione moved upstage and turned, but the promptbook does not record if she glanced at her accuser. Assessing Sellars's performance in the play, not just in 2.1, reviewers praised her for giving Hermione 'firm assurance and appealing purity' (*Yorks. Post*), 'dignity and courage' (*Evesham J.*), 'sincerity and nobility' (*SA Herald*, Sep).

In 1948 and 1960 directors relied on groupings of actors to create a stage picture. Wood's innovation, introducing three old gentlemen as silent witnesses, added choric figures to the scene. Beginning with Nunn's production in 1969, directors and designers introduced significant props and teased the audience to place the props not only within the context of the language of the play and the design for the production, but also within cultural and social history. During the blackout between scenes – and while the auditorium was filled with a burst of laughter from Judi Dench's Hermione and a music box playing the nursery rhyme 'Jack and Jill' – stagehands replaced the hobbyhorse with a spinning wheel. On the most basic level, the exchange of properties announced a move to an activity associated with women, and Hermione held a tangled lump of wool, which she dropped downstage centre when Barrie Ingham's Leontes accused her of adultery. The spinning wheel may also be read in conjunction with the sheep-shearing scene. Hermione's entrance with Mamillius recalled their closeness in 1.2 and Nunn's emphasis on the private, not the public, lives of Hermione and Leontes. Mamillius' toys continued to offer symbolic readings. He carried a teddy bear, which he dropped centre stage when he was seized, and a puppet, which by substituting 'puppet' for 'pinched thing' and 'toy' for 'trick' Leontes made self-referential:

> and I
> Remain a puppet; yea, a very toy
> For them to play at will.
>
> (50–2)

A 'sense of dislocation', which Hilary Spurling had found in 1.2, appeared 'most strongly' in 2.1:

> a scene in which the soft voices of her ladies, the pert child slithering between their satin laps, the queen's pallor and fatigue suggest a serenity already blurred and damaged, less by the impending childbirth than by something infinitely more barbaric.
>
> (*Spectator*)

In the text Leontes' 'How blest am I' (36–52) is preceded (33–6) and followed (52–5) by dialogue about the surreptitious departure of Polixenes and Camillo. Nunn highlighted Leontes' speech by placing 52–5 after 33–6 and by amplifying Leontes' voice. On the NSA recording Hermione's laughter at Mamillius' story coincides with the first words of Leontes' accusation, which Ingham shouts rapidly and with no misgivings. The stage picture sharpened Leontes' cruelty. In 1.2 only Leontes observed Hermione's and Polixenes' actions. In 2.1 Antigonus and four lords and five women witnessed Leontes' abuse of Hermione. On the recording, Dench's voice is calm, hurt. She says firmly:

> Good my lords,
> I am not prone to weeping, as our sex
> Commonly are.

(107–9)

One of several reviewers who praised Dench in this scene, Benedict Nightingale (*New States.*) observes that 'Judi Dench has clearly pondered Hermione's "I am not prone to weeping, as our sex commonly are", and achieves a dignified splendour in her defiance of her husband'. She paused after 'now / I' and whispered 'trust I shall' (123–4). Before exiting upstage, Hermione turned and looked downstage at Leontes, who stood by the spinning wheel. Heavy cuts in the last phase of the scene – approximately one-fifth of the lines – helped to shift the focus of 2.1 to the accusation. The words of Morgan Sheppard's Antigonus closed the scene, and a lord picked up the teddy bear Mamillius had dropped. Antigonus growled at it and hit it on the head, and the 'sinister music box' played 'Jack and Jill'.

Playing 2.1 on the permanent set for the 1976 production (Figure 5), John Barton and Nunn introduced stage business to mark the shift from a celebration of the winter festival of Jul back to ordinary domestic life. Marilyn Taylerson's Hermione entered with Emilia, gave her a set of keys and sent her on an errand. Cleomenes and Dion entered, two other lords entered, Cleomenes put a bear on the sofa, Hermione kissed them and they exited. Two young women sat on pouffes to the left of the chair where Hermione sat, their sewing baskets on their laps. A third sat downstage centre, her back to the audience. Meanwhile Mamillius, who had entered first in 1.1 and was again first on stage, was no

FIGURE 11 Leontes (Ian McKellen) seizes Mamillius from Hermione (Marilyn Taylerson). Antigonus (Griffith Jones, to Leontes' left), First Lord (Dennis Clinton) and Paulina's Steward (Richard Durden, at the right) attend Leontes. Hermione's attendants, Second Lady (Judith Harte) and First Lady (Susan Dury), perform domestic chores. (2.1, 1976)

longer on the good behaviour exhibited during the festivities of the first act. He charged at Hermione (presumably with the harpoon he carried), was carried away by one of the two lords, broke and ran to sit beside Emilia. As he began his story, Mamillius pointed to the drawing of a man with a spear on the screen downstage right of the chairs where he and Hermione sat. (See Figure 5, first panel on the left.) Unlike productions where Leontes entered with Antigonus, a number of lords and a show of force to restrain Hermione, Ian McKellen's Leontes entered with three other men (Figure 11): Antigonus (Griffith Jones), the First Lord (Dennis Clinton) and Paulina's Steward (Richard Durden). Leontes, who had revealed in 1.2 a fondness for Mamillius, was rougher with him than his predecessors had been: he shoved his son to the First Lord ('Bear the boy hence', 59) and ordered them off. The First Lord returned for Hermione, but she exited, followed first by her ladies and then by the First Lord.

In the final phase of the scene, Paulina's Steward spoke the lord's lines (126, 129–33, 139, 158–61, 188). The reassignment reinforced the production's emphasis on a closely knit, closed community and prepared the audience for the appearance of Paulina's Steward in 5.2 as one of the three gentlemen. But the gain was at some expense. The alteration diminished the anonymous chorus of voices urging Leontes to 'call the queen again' (126), risking the wrath of the monarch and willing, as was the anonymous lord

> For her, my lord,
> I dare my life lay down, ...
> ... that the queen is spotless
> I' th' eyes of heaven, and to you – I mean
> In this which you accuse her.
>
> (129–33)

In this phase of the scene, Barton cut fewer lines than had his Stratford predecessors.

In 1969 Nunn's cutting back on attendants in Act 1 and the first scene of Act 2 had called attention to the private, not the public, lives of Hermione and Leontes. Including a few more actors in each of the Sicilian scenes in 1976 Barton redefined 'public' as a Nordic community sharing an ethos and a mythology. By explaining its festivals and narratives, programme notes helped to make the community accessible to the audience. Stage business in 2.1 gave insight into the community and anticipated the next five scenes. The keys of housekeeping foreshadowed the keys of the Gaoler. Hermione bade farewell to Cleomenes and Dion, without knowing the purpose of the journey they embarked upon; Mamillius called attention to a runic narrative in a series of decorative wall hangings. The bear anticipated the destruction of Antigonus. The permanent set, with its runic symbols, continued to work on at least three levels: as had the chamber in 1969, it 'cabin'd, cribb'd, confin'd' Leontes; it established a sense of place, of community; it alluded to the community's rich, mythic heritage, its storytelling tradition.

The 1981 production, like the productions of 1969 and 1976, was played on a permanent set designed for the season. Unlike 1969, changes in properties did not define change of place – or introduce something new to look at; unlike 1976, the set did not feature a detail, such as the curtains with drawings, that could be examined or that added interest. Blackouts and music bridges linked most scenes in 1969; stage business created a Nordic society in 1976. In 1981, one scene bled into another; music and sound effects seldom announced a change of place or mood.

In 1969 and 1976 directors introduced symbolic props and actions, especially the spinning wheel (1969) and women sewing (1976). The only prop in 1981 was a low stool, which one of Hermione's attendants carried on for her. (In 2.3, a lord performed a similar service for Leontes.) The 1981 production relied simply on the fondness between mother and son. Mamillius and Gemma Jones's Hermione entered together, Mamillius teasing his mother by winding a scarf around her. Figure 12, in which Mamillius kneels at his mother's side and whispers his sad tale, conveys something of their closeness and the calm about to be shattered by the men.

Simultaneous with the entrance of Hermione, Mamillius, Emilia and two ladies onto the platform (the 'hotplate') two groups of lords entered and took their places upstage and downstage right of the platform. Ronald Eyre staged Leontes' entrance and Mamillius' story as parallel actions. As Mamillius announced his story 'Of sprites and goblins' (26), Patrick Stewart's Leontes entered eight lines earlier than usual; when Hermione answered her son, 'Let's have that, good sir' (26), the lord entered to meet Leontes. As Mamillius and Hermione talked (26–32), Leontes and the lord whispered at the side of the rostrum. Then the image was reversed: Mamillius whispered his story (Figure 12) and Leontes interrogated the lord about his story (33–6). Leontes

FIGURE 12 Mamillius (Timothy Sullivan) whispers his tale 'Of sprites and goblins' to Hermione (Gemma Jones). (2.1, 1981)

crossed onto the rostrum for 'How blest am I / In my just censure! in my true opinion!' (36ff.). His voice cold and deliberate, Leontes pulled Mamillius from Hermione and pushed him to the lord. With Mamillius struggling, they exited on cue (59) and before Leontes began to raise his voice. Shouting the accusation, Leontes pushed Hermione (78) and bumped into her as he said 'The centre is not big enough to bear / A school-boy's top' (102–3). In the video recording, Leontes rushes offstage when Hermione begins 'There's some ill planet reigns' (105) and does not return until she has finished speaking. The promptbook cues her to curtsy to him before he asks 'Shall I be heard?' (115). Hermione exited first; her attendants waited until Leontes dismissed them.

Adrian Noble's modern-dress touring production (1984) placed 2.1 in a nursery and further explored gender-based divisions in a society dominated by a Mafia godfather. For the first time in the productions under discussion, props and stage business not only placed the scene but also developed a close relationship between Lynn Farleigh's Hermione and the women. Played on the oriental carpets between the two rostra, the scene was established by props associated with Mamillius in the first act (a toy basket with three soft toys) and one that would feature again in 5.1 (a tricycle). Hermione's women folded linens, including baby clothes. Christopher Lahr's Mamillius, who entered with his teddy bear, burned off the last energy of the day by 'annoying Hermione's feet' and 'running thru a sheet – ghost like'. Hermione's call for a story was a mother's ploy to calm her child for bed. As Emilia and the women folded linens and looked after Mamillius, the Third Lady 'bathed' Hermione and rubbed her shoulders. In 1960 Wood had transformed the three gentlemen into Mamillius' tutors. Noble expanded the role of the Third Lady to identify her as Mamillius' nurse: she accompanied Mamillius when he was seized and returned in 2.3 to report that Mamillius 'took good rest to-night. / 'Tis hop'd his sickness is discharg'd' (10–11) and in 3.2 to announce Mamillius' death (142–5). When Noble returned to *The Winter's Tale* in 1992, he kept the business in 2.1 and the assignment of lines in 2.3 and 3.2.

Alun Armstrong's Leontes with the Antigonus of Paul Webster and four other men entered onto one of the rostra, a vantage point from which Leontes could look down on Mamillius whispering his story to Hermione. Reviewing the production during its London run, Michael Ratcliffe (*Observer*, 16 Dec) praised the 'power' with which Leontes spoke 'I have drunk, and seen the spider' (2.1.45). Ratcliffe, who judged the production one of the best in 1984 (*Observer*, 30 Dec), singled out Leontes entering the nursery as an example of the effectiveness of the promenade style:

> This apparently spontaneous tumble of players and punters
> produces confrontations and images which few who see them will
> quickly forget: Leontes in his anger ... scatters spectators to one side
> as he runs up the steps to poison the nursery calm.   (*Observer*, Oct)

Antigonus 'snatched' Mamillius. Hugging his teddy bear, Mamillius
was led off by one of the lords and followed by his attendant, the
Third Lady.

When he accused Hermione of mistaking Polixenes for
Leontes (81–2), Leontes attempted to strike her, but, directs the
promptbook, her ladies 'rushed to protect her'. He succeeded in
throwing her to the floor before ordering 'Away with her, to
prison!' (103). Antigonus, who with the other lords had watched
with concern when Leontes had attempted to strike Hermione,
tried to calm him. Leontes pushed him away. Having been helped
up by her women, Hermione began the speech 'There's some ill
planet reigns' (105–15). In this phase of the scene, Leontes lost
nearly half his lines; Hermione lost two.

The final phase of the scene was staged as an ironic comment
on the intimacy with which it had opened. Considerably
shortened (it played just over half the lines) and with Antigonus
assuming the brief speeches of the lord, it offered a glimpse into a
male world dominated by Armstrong's Leontes, 'fuming with
jealousy' (*D. Telegraph*).

In 1986 2.1 was also set in a nursery, but the effect was quite
different from that of the touring production. The toys showered
on Mamillius presented him as the most indulged Mamillius in
the history of the play at Stratford (and, perhaps, anywhere else).
For his pleasure, the prop list specifies: toy box, teddy bear,
spinning top with whip, toy drum and drumsticks, hoop and
stick, four large alphabet blocks. He entered, according to the prop
list, on a 'pony on wheels ... pulled on by ladies'. He wore a
plumed helmet with a visor and a white double-breasted suit with
long trousers and carried a rapier. The promptbook includes a cue
for him to ask one of the ladies to 'knight' him. Another group of
props, from the same list, is for the nursery and preparations for

the new baby: nursing rocker; a crib, dressed and ready for a baby, with a loose blanket on top; knitting; a christening gown, to be held up by a lady. Jean Fuzier and Jean-Marie Maguin (*Cahiers Elis.*, 94) observe

> all the stage furniture is endowed with singularly strong readability. Hermione's maternity chair whether in use or not has a haunting presence equal to that of the cradle for the expected infant, or Mamillius' toy boxes, large blue cubes whose sides are painted with letters and figures.

Joe Cocks's photograph in the SCL collection pictures the scene just before Mamillius begins his story: Penny Downie's Hermione, costumed as in Figure 7, sits in the nursing rocker with Mamillius seated on an alphabet block beside her. The composition of the photograph very closely resembles that of Figure 12, but the costumes and wigs express the difference between the two sets of mothers and sons.

Jeremy Irons's Leontes and nine men – treble the attendants for Hermione – entered from opposite sides upstage, Leontes coming downstage onto the bear's head, an entrance similar to Mamillius' in 1.2. Lights, which had come up on the entrance of the men, gave way to a spot on Leontes as he rejoiced 'How blest am I / In my just censure! in my true opinion!' (36–7). When Leontes orders 'Bear the boy hence' (59), the promptbook indicates that Mamillius tried to run back to his mother but was stopped and taken upstage. There is no exit cue for him in the promptbook. Terry Hands cut Hermione's first denial, 'But I'd say he had not' (62–4). Mamillius, who had watched the flirtations of his mother and Polixenes and who had then sought refuge in his father's arms, may have been within hearing distance when Leontes called the lords over to 'Look on her, mark her well' (65). Irons injected a chilling confidence into his denunciation of Hermione. He 'prowl[ed] up and down before pouncing with, "She's an adulteress" [78]' (*FT*). Complaining that 'The centre is not big enough to bear / A school-boy's top' (102–3), Leontes played with one. 'And', complained Nicholas Shrimpton, 'just in case we missed the point, he spoke his lines throughout with infantile exaggeration' (*SS*, 177). During Hermione's speech beginning 'There's some ill planet reigns' (105–15), Leontes circled the stage, then paced about. The final phase of the scene began with Leontes sitting in Hermione's nursing rocker, feet up, rocking. He returned to the bear's head to announce the messengers to Apollo's temple and asked 'Have I done well?' (187) in the tone of one requiring reassurance. As Antigonus (Raymond Bowers) spoke the final lines, the signature bells and boy's treble voice closed the scene as it had begun. The promptbook cues the large disc upstage of the scrim to turn and stop.

In 1992 Noble played the first phase of 2.1 before the gauze box, which created a space appropriate for a domestic scene. The promptbook calls for the 'top' box from the first act, a baby basket with baby things, sheets, cushions. A passage from *Peter and the Wolf* introduced the scene, and, as they had in Noble's touring production, the women folded linens. Mamillius teased Samantha Bond's Hermione, hitting her with a cushion, and played ghost with a sheet the women were folding. As Mamillius whispered his story, lights came up on Leontes (John Nettles) and six men, who had entered the box from a trap. The amplified voices of Leontes and the lord were backed by the humming top, identified in the promptbook as a 'single synchronized chord'. Leontes lost about seven lines detailing Camillo's alleged treachery, the first cuts in the scene. Moving forward when he began to identify himself as one who had seen the spider (42), Leontes put his hands on the downstage panel of the box. Rebecca Flynn describes the juxtaposition: 'Rendered invisible by the gauze, Leontes became a subliminal manifestation of Mamillius' ghost story. Leontes himself became the hidden spider, as he spread his fingers, spider-like, against the gauze' (*Cahiers Elis.*, 88). The downstage panel was raised and Leontes broke the calm of the domestic scene. Mamillius, his exit delayed until line 82, witnessed the accusation. As cued by the promptbook, he ran forward and shouted 'no' when Leontes called Hermione 'O thou thing', hit her, and she fell to the floor. Mamillius was pulled back by one of Hermione's ladies and they exited. Losing twenty of his thirty-seven lines, Leontes spoke eleven fewer lines than Hermione, who lost only four of her thirty-two. As he had in the first act, Nettles signalled an unwillingness to believe Hermione had been unfaithful. He paused between each word on the line 'She's an adultress!' (78), substituting two words for the contraction. The promptbook cues him to kiss the back of her neck (102). He took a long pause before banishing her to prison (103). In the final phase of the scene, which played forty-two of its seventy-four lines, pauses before 'familiarity' (175) and 'business' (197) suggested that Leontes sought synonyms for 'adultery'.

Gregory Doran (1999) introduced a number of innovations to this scene, recorded on the videotape. Unusually in these productions, both male and female servants set and removed properties for 2.1 and attended Hermione and Mamillius. Doran did not require them to perform domestic chores. Doran also broke with the long-established tradition which, following the text, juxtaposed Mamillius' whispering his story 'Of sprites and goblins' (26), with Leontes' more frightening imaginings. Leontes' voice was first heard from offstage, asking about the escape of Polixenes and Camillo. Hermione, Mamillius and their attendants as well as the lords accompanying Leontes heard his speech beginning 'How blest am I / In my just censure! in my true opinion!', in which he introduces the analogy of the spider (36–53). Hermione answered Leontes' rough actions with remarkable restraint. She beseeched him in the speech beginning 'Should a villain say so' (78–81), she moved slowly toward him and touched him (95–100), and knelt to him:

> Adieu, my lord:
> I never wish'd to see you sorry; now
> I trust I shall.

(122–4)

Hermione gestured for him to help her up and then got up, alone, with difficulty. The *Oxford Times* describes Hermione as 'almost in labour'; Robert Smallwood highlights the image of her husband's cruelty: Leontes 'ignored her and lit a cigarette' (*SS*, 264). In the *Daily Telegraph* Charles Spencer describes the setting as

> a claustrophobic court at the height of the Victorian age ... With battalions of officials and flunkeys, it is a place of stultifying protocol, which makes the sudden eruption of Leontes's jealousy all the more shattering.... The fact that she is being abused in front of so many of her devoted servants adds a cruel twist to the pain.

Leontes, who had sniffed her shawl for incriminating scents, searched her handbag for concrete evidence. In the *Sunday Times* John Peter explains that the 'greatest subtlety' of Sher's performance

> lies in portraying the side of Leontes that Leontes does not know. He knows that jealousy is terrible to feel but not that it is undignified to see. Sher shows its ridiculous aspect: the tetchy, irascible little man scavenging for clues in Hermione's handbag and convulsively stoking up his own rage, as if to justify it to himself.

2.2

THE PRISON

My poor prisoner,
I am as innocent as you

Scene 2 contains the stuff of tabloid journalism: accused woman – or, more likely, adulterous wife – gives birth in prison. It is one of those Shakespearean scenes where one wishes to see the place and events that the dialogue describes or alludes to and one puzzles over how such an offstage scene might be played (or, as would today be more likely, be interpolated into a film). Is Hermione, like some imprisoned women in these more enlightened times, manacled and guarded during childbirth? Or does she have any of the apparent comforts that visitors to the Tower of London see in Sir Walter Raleigh's quarters in the Bloody Tower? Has her infant daughter been swaddled and placed in a comfortable cot? A second omission is more frustrating. In lines cut by each of the nine productions, Emilia reveals that Hermione had thought about sending her infant daughter to Leontes:

> Who but to-day hammer'd of this design,
> But durst not tempt a minister of honour,
> Lest she should be denied.
>
> (49–51)

Had Emilia brought Hermione's infant daughter to Paulina, then we could 'read' the child for messages from Hermione to Leontes. Did Hermione, for example, wrap the baby in a garment Leontes would recognize? But 2.2 is crucial not just because the prison-childbed reinforces the extremity of Leontes' jealousy but also because it introduces Paulina, who will become the agent of his recovery. Although some productions, such as those of 1948, 1960 and 1992, include Paulina in the first act, and Quayle even introduced her as a witness to 2.1, Paulina's first lines come in this scene. She issues a command to the gentleman who enters with her: 'The keeper of the prison, call to him'.

Photographs of Motley's set for Quayle's production (1948) place the action before a curtain that blocks off the raised platform, visible behind the globe in Figure 2. The promptbook calls for a soldier to be discovered, and for Emilia to greet Paulina by 'crossing to Paulina's arms' and to cry and return to Paulina's arms after

> the queen receives
> Much comfort in 't; says, 'My poor prisoner,
> I am as innocent as you.'
>
> (27–9)

In 1960 2.2 was played before a prison wall, with bars, a large ring (associated with some method of torture?), and stairs leading from the first to the second level flown in behind. 'Through the special stage facilities now installed at Stratford', observes one reviewer, 'palaces change with exceptional smoothness to prisons' (*Morn. Adv.*). The props list calls for five hand manacles and one neck manacle. There is an entrance cue for three manacled prisoners and their attendants; the Gaoler also entered with two attendants. A photograph by Angus McBean in the SCL collection shows one of the half-naked prisoners behind the bars. The scene offered another example of Wood's method of illustrating scenes with mime; in this instance it not only gave a glimpse of Sicilia's less fortunate subjects but also suggested Hermione was under heavy guard in a mixed-sex prison. Had Emilia brought the infant out to Peggy Ashcroft's Paulina, the prison walls would have provided a sharp visual image. When the attendants protested Paulina's 'Withdraw yourselves' (16), she 'silence[d] them'.

In 1969 Nunn's production seems to have sought a lighter tone. Music cues call for the 'sinister music box', which had closed 2.1, to be followed by laughter, which Antigonus had predicted at the close of 2.1, and the nursery rhyme. On the sound recording, made after the production transferred to London's Aldwych Theatre, Elizabeth Spriggs, who took over the role of Paulina during the run, gets a laugh on 'Here's ado' (9). One can almost hear Spriggs drawing herself up to a full and commanding height when she imperiously addresses the Gaoler. Speaking to Emilia, she uses a conversational tone, and her description of the child as 'prisoner to the womb' (59) earns an approving laugh from a guard, and the audience. Spriggs found in the scene wit, warmth, and the imperiousness that drove Paulina. At Stratford, Brenda Bruce's performance, to be discussed more fully in 2.3 and 3.2, was praised as 'powerfully direct' (*SA Herald*).

The 1976 production offers a revealing contrast with the staging of 2.2 in 1960. Presenting the prison scene on the permanent set and making only slight adjustments to the script, Barton continued to signal close ties in the tribal community. Attended not by an anonymous gentleman and other attendants but by her steward, who with Antigonus had attempted to dissuade McKellen's Leontes in 2.1, Barbara Leigh-Hunt's Paulina asked for the keeper of 'her', not 'the', prison. Hermione's gaoler was not a commoner, but the First Lord, who had led Mamillius away and who returned to escort Hermione to prison. In the sentence opening his review of the production, J.C. Trewin speaks of the power of Paulina's entrance: 'As soon as Barbara Leigh-Hunt's Paulina takes the Stratford stage, the voice of honesty and reason, we wonder how the narrative of *The Winter's Tale* can stand against her impact' (*Birm. Post*).

For the first time in the production of 1981 there was a blackout and sound effects – the clangs of prison gates – between scenes. Roger Warren terms Sheila Hancock's Paulina one of the 'two masterly performances' in the production. (The other, he thought, was Patrick Stewart's Leontes (*SS*, 149).) 'Most Paulinas', he reminds us,

> are effective in a fearsomely humorous way; the immediately noticeable thing about this Paulina was that she was not fearsome at all, explaining patiently to the bureaucratic gaoler that the child is prisoner to the womb and now freed by nature. (148)

In the video recording made after the transfer to London, Hancock's Paulina is compassionate and gentle, but firm. She does not seek laughs from her auditors or the audience, and she is not imperious with those in a lower social class.

In 2.2, as in 2.1, Noble (1984) introduced stage business to mark the shift to a prison. A gaoler, carrying a lighted torch, paced from one side of the carpeted area to the other and two women ran on with a torch and 'birth implements . . . bowls, jugs of water, towel'. The *Guardian* (Aug) notes the 'economical' use of sound – an echo – to suggest place. Janet Dale, who played Paulina, recalls that she met Emilia on top of a table placed off-centre of the acting space. Paulina spoke 'Commend my best obedience to the queen' (36) as a farewell. In an innovative reading, the decision to appeal to Leontes through his daughter was played as an afterthought.

As a bridge between 2.1 and 2.2 Hands (1986) introduced extra-textual mime to reinforce the childishness of Jeremy Irons's Leontes. The Sicilian monarch sat on the bear's head, with the lords behind him; later he sat downstage right, around his shoulders a blanket from the cradle that had been prepared for the new baby. When he heard the newborn baby cry, he sat up but lay down again as the lights went down, wrapping himself in the blanket. The mime, recorded in the stage manager's notes, as well as in photographs and the videotape, attested to Hands's heavy symbolism. Leontes remained on the forestage throughout the scene, the stage was set with 'furniture as in nursery', and the prison scene was played on the bear. Upstage, snow fell throughout the scene. With its familiar bearskin rug, white costumes, reflecting panels, and fire bowl blazing upstage right, the scene lacked the power of Noel's set for 1960.

The gauze box having been flown out, 2.2 was played on a bare stage in Noble's main-house production (1992). A trap centre stage provided the entrance to the prison. The promptbook includes a sound cue for a 'woman in childbirth', an aural signal similar to the business Noble had introduced in 1984. In this scene with a gaoler and Emilia, Gemma Jones's tone made clear Paulina's social superiority. Jones's manner also announced that this Paulina would bear the angry truth:

> If I prove honey-mouth'd, let my tongue blister,
> And never to my red-look'd anger be
> The trumpet any more.

(33–5)

In 1999 Doran played 2.2 in subdued light, with shadows of prison bars cast across the stage. From the brief exchanges with the Gaoler and Emilia, one sensed that Estelle Kohler's Paulina, whom Paul Taylor describes as 'a sublime mix of the formidable and the humorously humane', was equal to the task that lay ahead (*Independent*).

2.3

LEONTES' CHAMBER

Nor night, nor day, no rest

The second act, which opens with Hermione and her attendants, closes with Leontes and his. In 2.1 Leontes disturbs a child's bedtime story; in 2.3 Paulina forces her way into the presence of the insomniac Leontes, assuring his attendants 'I come to bring him sleep' (33). The rest she offers comes in the form of what is, arguably, the most important prop to this point: Leontes' newborn daughter. In productions, the appearance and presentation of the infant varies considerably. Is she swaddled in her mother's shawl or some other piece of clothing easily identified as Hermione's? Has she been placed in a Moses basket or some similar object? Does Paulina shield the infant from Leontes' sight until she announces 'Here 'tis' (66)? Does she place the baby in his arms? put it on the floor before him? Does it cry or gurgle? How does Paulina address the lords who would block her entrance? her husband? her monarch? Does she find humour in the scene? How does Leontes respond to his subject's determination? How many attendants does he have? What show of force does he rely on for Paulina and for Antigonus? What do the set and his costume contribute to the dominant tone of the scene? If there are symbolic props, are they introduced for the first time in the production or are they familiar from an earlier scene? If the set features a significant object, such as the rostrum (1984) or the gauze box (1992), what role does it play in this scene? What is the closing image of Leontes and what does it reveal about his mental state?

When the scene drop rose in 1948 on Quayle's setting for 2.3, Leontes was discovered resting on a couch on the platform stage right (Figure 2). Upstage and with their backs to him, Michael Godfrey's Antigonus and three soldiers afforded security and the appearance of privacy. A bearskin covered the couch, the only piece of furniture. Curtains were drawn across the upstage openings. Leontes wore a loose gown. Quayle cut approximately one quarter of the scene, including, since he had cut the characters, the reference to Cleomenes and Dion's return from Delphos. Immediately after Leontes' opening exclamation 'Nor night, nor day, no rest' Quayle inserted Leontes' musing on the spider in the cup (2.1.36–45), and he replaced lines about Camillo and Polixenes (2.3.23–6), which are often cut, with lines 4–9 from the opening soliloquy. At Paulina's entrance, the promptbook calls for lines 26–32 to be spoken simultaneously, a babble provoking Leontes' query 'What noise there, ho?' (39). When Paulina put the baby before Leontes, he rose 'holding the bearskin'. Leontes signified his determination by holding a sword to Antigonus' neck.

In 2.1 and 2.2 Wood (1960) had called attention to Leontes' show of force. In manacles, Hermione was led away under armed guard to be incarcerated in a secure prison. His staging of 2.3 associated Leontes with military equipment and victories. The location was described as 'a golden armoury' (*SA Herald*, Sep) and 'a trophy room' (fly cue). A photograph of the set, with its displays of spears around Leontes' chair and of trophies, supports both descriptions.

Not surprisingly, when Leontes asked 'Who's there?' (9) the three gentlemen entered and one of them reported on the health of their pupil. The weapons and five attendants at Leontes' disposal did not deter Peggy Ashcroft's Paulina from entering the king's presence. Cues call for her to kneel before Leontes and then to take the Moses basket from an attendant and place it before Leontes. Paulina showed 'the cankered King his new-born daughter with exquisite pathos' (*S. Times*). Leontes glared at it and paused before commanding Paulina to leave (66). When Leontes demanded 'On your allegiance, / Out of the chamber with her!' five men with halberds surrounded Paulina and pointed their weapons toward the cradle (120–1). After Tony Church's Antigonus pledged to do anything 'To save the innocent: anything possible' (166), Leontes drew his sword; Antigonus knelt over the cradle, protecting it and ready to 'pawn the little blood which I have left' (165).

As with their assessments of Leontes and Hermione, critics' generalizations shed some light on Ashcroft's performance in this scene, which the promptbook labels 'Paulina'. Ashcroft's Paulina was 'superb in her indignation' (*News Chron.*), a 'practical, downright strong-willed woman with the honesty of the country-side about her' (*Yorks. Post*), 'pleading ... with the right power and passion, insistent but not strident or too ranting' (*Evesham J.*).

In 1969 the music between 2.2 and 2.3 repeated the sitar cascade from the opening moments and introduced again the music box distorting 'Jack and Jill'. Nunn continued his ploy of using provocative toys and games and of setting the stage with one dominant object. Leontes, Antigonus and four lords were discovered, Leontes downstage centre puzzling a move on an oversized chessboard set with red and white pieces in non-traditional shapes. In production photographs the doll, which the promptbook calls for, is a limp rag doll resting against one of the white cubes downstage.

In 2.3, as he did in 2.1, Nunn amplified voices to distinguish between silent characters (2.1, women and Mamillius; 2.3, Leontes) and speaking characters (2.1, Leontes and lords; 2.3, Paulina and lords). The promptbook calls for the heavily cut dialogue between Brenda Bruce's Paulina and Leontes' attendants (26–39) to be amplified in the auditorium. On the NSA recording, Spriggs conveys a variety of tones: lighthearted (relationship with Antigonus), quiet (presentation of baby to Leontes, 65–6), gentle (comparison of infant's features with its father's, 97–107), firm ('heretic that makes the fire', 114), loud ('Look to your babe', 125), quiet and prayerful ('Jove send her', 125–6), firm and very hurt ('we are gone', 129).

In 1.2 strobe lighting accompanied Leontes' sudden, inexplicable jealousy. In 2.3, as the sound recording testifies, Ingham's voice conveyed the depth of Leontes' despair. Speaking of Camillo and Polixenes, he wept before saying 'Laugh at me' (24). With Paulina he shouted and worked himself into a state. Contemplative, he quietly observed 'I am a feather' (153) and relented, 'be it: let it live' (156). But Leontes closed the scene in noisy desperation, shouting at Antigonus, who gently urged 'Sir, be prosperous / In more than this deed does require' (188–9), and at the departing servants. Gareth Lloyd Evans notes Leontes' 'descent (superbly counterpointed by the lighting) into the twilight world of mental illness' (*SS*, 134). B.A. Young, who found little in the production to praise, disagrees: 'lowering a great bank of light onto Leontes as he spits out the entirely neutral words, "think upon my bidding" [206] ... seem[ed] ... irrelevant and irritating' (*FT*). In the promptbook the last cue for the scene is for Leontes to be upstage beneath Apollo, which, explains Roger Gregory, the production's stage manager, 'was a huge cone of lights about five-foot square, which descended from the grid, lights blazing, to hover over Leontes and then blackout'.

Nunn was the first post-war Stratford director to introduce the business of Paulina's giving Leontes his infant daughter. The promptbook and a series of photographs taken by Joe Cocks shed some light on the playing of the scene. As Paulina approached, Leontes turned his back on her and covered his ears with his hands. Saying 'Here 'tis: [the queen] commends it to your blessing' (66), Paulina put the baby into Leontes' arms (Figure 13). Then she 'eased left centre'. With no success, Leontes offered the child to Paulina, to the lords, to Antigonus. He held his daughter until line 93: 'It is the issue of Polixenes', when he put the infant on the chessboard. Paulina picked it up and the lords drew around her to look at the 'copy of the father' (99). Directors who continued the practice varied the timing and the presentation, but in future Stratford productions the essential feature of handing over the infant daughter to her father can be traced to Nunn's production.

In 1976, 2.3 opened with Leontes alone and sitting on one of the large pouffes that were permanent props in the first three acts.

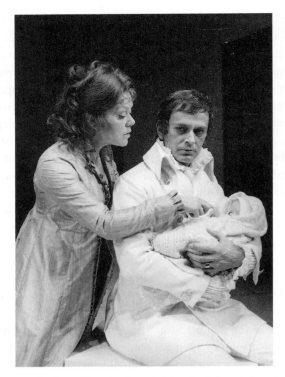

FIGURE 13 Paulina (Brenda Bruce) tries to interest Leontes (Barrie Ingham) in his newborn daughter, whom she has just thrust into his arms. (2.3, 1969)

As Leontes' soliloquy closed, the First Lord (by now familiar as the one who had removed Mamillius in 2.1, returned for Hermione and served as Hermione's gaoler) tiptoed upstage of Leontes. And this First Lord, not an anonymous servant, now answered Leontes' queries about his son. Paulina, with the infant hidden beneath her cape, 'quell[ed] the restraining courtiers with a dragon-like air' (*Tatler & Bys.*). In 2.3, writes B.A. Young (*FT*),

> we encounter the full vigour of Barbara Leigh-Hunt's Paulina, a performance of some subtlety. She can have an ordinary domestic

disagreement with her husband Antigonus.... But in conflict with Leontes, she is another woman, tough, determined, never discourteous beyond the bounds of necessity, and doing magical things with her lines.

Barton continued the business of Paulina's giving Leontes his infant daughter, but there was a slight variation from 1969. After reminding Leontes of the 'good queen' (64), Paulina put the baby in Leontes' lap (Figure 14). Michael Billington describes the effect on press night: 'when his new born daughter is deposited in his lap, he lifts his curled, white knuckled hands above his head as if fearing physical contamination' (*Guardian*). McKellen's 'staccato spitting venom', observes Rosemary Say (*S. Telegraph*), was 'most effect[ive] against his sharpest adversary, Paulina – "a callat of boundless tongue" as he calls her [90–1] – whose advocacy of the docile Hermione's cause makes the strongest scene in Barbara Leigh-Hunt's clear-cut authoritative interpretation'. At 'Commit them to the fire!' (95) Leontes left the baby on the pouffe. Because of cuts in the text, the baby was in Leontes' lap for fewer lines (22) than Ingham had held it in 1969 (27). Billington enjoyed the 'moment when Barbara Leigh-Hunt's excellently brisk and down-to-earth Paulina demonstrates that the baby, Perdita, has her father's smile and all heads turn to look at a dismayingly frowning Leontes' (*Guardian*). Before leaving, Paulina kissed the baby and Antigonus. Accusing Antigonus of treachery, Leontes cut down with his sword the wreaths that Hermione and Mamillius (with Polixenes' help) had hung during the interpolated celebration of Jul in the first act. The stillness of Paulina's Steward, sitting and holding the infant, counterpointed Leontes' wrath. 'I am a feather for each wind that blows' (153) was, claims Billington, the key to McKellen's interpretation.

> He suddenly switches from demonic tyranny, aided by Di Seymour's Boyar fur costumes, to the pathos of a man destroyed by his own sexual fantasies. And it is this feeling of a good man afflicted by sudden sickness that makes the final reconciliation scene so deeply moving.   (*Guardian*)

FIGURE 14 Leontes (Ian McKellen) recoils from the infant that Paulina (Barbara Leigh-Hunt) has placed on his lap. Antigonus (Griffith Jones), First Lord (Dennis Clinton) and Paulina's Steward (Richard Durden) attend their king. The barren tree foreshadows the loss of an heir. (2.3, 1976)

After Antigonus exited with the infant, Mamillius entered and went over to his father. The First Lord entered with news of the imminent arrival of Cleomenes and Dion. Leontes carried Mamillius off. 'Particularly revealing', writes Robert Cushman (*Observer*), 'is his clinging to his son counterbalancing his revulsion from his wife'. Richard David terms the decision a 'dubious and sentimental conclusion devised by the directors, who brought on Mamillius to be sung to sleep (naturally with the "theme-song") by his distracted father' (David, 224). The scene closed with a stanza from one of Autolycus' ballads:

> But shall I go mourn for that, my dear?
>   The pale moon shines by night:
> And when I wander here and there,
>   I then do most go right.

(4.3.15–18)

As in earlier scenes in the 1981 production, the stage picture was split in 2.3 between action on the platform (or 'hotplate') and the silent characters on the stage around them. Patrick Stewart's Leontes was alone for the soliloquy at the beginning of the scene, but two lords were close at hand. Cocooned in a boldly patterned blanket worn over his white nightgown, he cringed on the stool downstage centre. In two previous productions, Leontes had changed costumes for this scene: a loose gown (1948) and a robe de chambre (1960). But in 1981, the regal Leontes, gowned and crowned (but wearing a clown's nose) to direct the masque that opened the production, had declined into an insomniac, who had pulled a blanket off the bed to cover his long white gown (Figure 15). As it had in 2.1, the scene drew a sharp contrast between the frenetic motion and shouting of Leontes and his female adversary. Sheila Hancock's Paulina was the calm, still voice of reason. Paulina, who had hidden the infant beneath her shawl, placed it in its basket, on the floor downstage centre. Warren applauds the originality of Hancock's interpretation: Paulina

> point[ed] out the baby's dimples with a smiling tenderness which led easily to her invocation of 'good goddess Nature' [103] without any tiresome pushing for 'significance'. 'Let him that makes but trifles of his eyes / First hand me' [62–3] lost nothing by its softness; and 'I pray you, do not push me' [124], instead of being stridently aggressive, was spoken quietly as if to suggest that there was no need to imitate Leontes's brutal disregard of common humanity.   (*SS*, 148)

After Paulina exited, the infant cried. The lords were unable to quiet it, but Leontes' glance silenced it. The otherwise humourless Leontes sometimes got a laugh when he whispered and shushed Antigonus, whose loud voice might have awakened the child. His back to the lords and the departing Antigonus, Leontes did not acknowledge Antigonus' 'Sir, be prosperous / In more than this deed does deserve [*sic*]' (188–9). The scene closed as it had begun, with Leontes very much alone, his heart burdened.

FIGURE 15 His infant daughter in a Moses basket on the floor before him, Leontes (Patrick Stewart) makes clear to Antigonus (Robert Eddison) that the child is to be cast out. Leontes' servant (Brian Poyser) and an Old Lord (Bert Parnaby) attend. (2.3, 1981)

Noble (1984) set 2.3 on the rostrum now firmly established as Leontes' space. Props conveyed an atmosphere redolent of a Mafia godfather's office or study: a side drinks cupboard, a brown armchair, a grandfather clock, and objects such as a cigarette case, lighter, ashtray. Alun Armstrong's Leontes paced back and forth on the rostrum, Antigonus and a lord sat behind him, a third man paced from one side of the carpeted area to the other. The Third Lady brought Leontes news of his son. As Leontes asked her 'How does the boy?' (10) Antigonus poured Leontes 'another brandy'.

That a masculine world dominated by Leontes had already been established paid dividends in this scene. Leontes was still pacing when Paulina entered with her steward. The guard shone his torch on them and tried to stop them; Antigonus ran to the steps to quiet Paulina. The promptbook says 'her lines stop' those who would restrain her, and it is worth noting the cuts in, and reassignment of, speeches. Paulina lost her first speech (27–30); her husband, Antigonus, not a servant, explained that the insomniac Leontes had 'commanded / None should come at him' (31–2). Paulina's arresting response was simply 'Not so hot, good husband [*sic*]; / I come to bring him sleep' (32–3). That is, before the intervention of Leontes, Paulina spoke twelve syllables of the ten or so lines written for her. Paulina forced her way onto the rostrum, laid the infant at the centre edge, on a direct line with Leontes' armchair, and unwrapped it – it was covered with Hermione's mantle. Paulina, with Leontes' infant daughter, had successfully invaded Leontes' space. In a conversation with me about the scene, Dale explained that putting the baby on the floor increased the chances that Armstrong's Leontes would pick up his newborn daughter. But Leontes did not yield. The baby remained on the floor except when Paulina picked it up to compare it with its father (97–107). In 1969 Bruce had moved in close to Leontes and put her arm about him when he was holding the baby (Figure 13). Bruce appealed to a vulnerable streak in Ingham's Leontes. In 1984 the promptbook calls for Paulina to 'move closer onto Leontes', but Armstrong's Leontes did not hold the infant and the cue comes toward the close of Paulina's confrontation with him. To move towards Armstrong's autocratic Leontes was far bolder, a statement that Paulina, unlike the lords who surrounded him, was not afraid of him. One exchange, as Matt Wolf (*City L.*) points out, had a heightened resonance when *The Winter's Tale* was played in tandem with *The Crucible*, 'an analogous study of the effects of irrational hysteria':

LEONTES   I'll ha' thee burnt.
PAULINA   I care not:
   It is an heretic that makes the fire,
   Not she which burns in't.

(113–15)

The only production to lay all three scenes on a site-specific set – the nursery – Hands's (1986) began 2.3 with the mute image of white nursery furniture: a nursing rocker, a cradle, toys, oversized alphabet blocks. The promptbook, photographs and videotape contribute to the impression that this Leontes had not grown up, a thesis expounded in the programme notes and examined by many reviewers. Leontes, who had slept on the forestage throughout 2.2 and was trying to sleep longer, spoke his opening speech as though thinking aloud. Petulant and childlike, he crawled over to a block. Leontes was still on the floor when Paulina entered, as had Mamillius in 1.2 and Leontes on several occasions, along the length of the large bear rug. As she approached, he covered his head with the white baby blanket, which he had been wearing as a shawl since the close of 2.1. The effect, notes Irving Wardle, was 'one of comic absurdity' as Leontes tried 'to escape the sledgehammer accusations of Gillian Barge's Paulina' (Times). Paulina hid the baby until she surprised Leontes by putting it in his arms and he was 'left, gnashing his teeth, holding the baby' in another moment of 'comic absurdity' (Times). When Paulina left, the baby cried, and snow fell. Jeremy Irons 'assume[d] a rueful humour, as when he focus[sed] on us for a quizically camp "I am a feather for each wind that blows" [153]' (FT). Leontes, who had pushed Antigonus to the ground by pointing a sword at his chest, seemed determined: 'The bastard brains with these my proper hands / Shall I dash out' (139–40). As Leontes pronounced his daughter's sentence, the lights went down and music, a flute and the celeste, began to mark the transition to 3.1. The scene closed with Leontes kneeling and his eight lords coming down to him as Antigonus exited with the baby.

In 1992 the gauze box served as a backdrop against which 2.3 was played and as an antechamber where lords could guard Leontes' privacy. His 'courtiers', notes Robert Smallwood, 'watched him through the box, almost as if he were a psychiatric patient under observation, as he struggled with his insecurity and despair' (SQ, 349). John Nettles played the scene in a white shirt and the trousers of the suit he had worn in the previous scenes.

Assigning, as he had in 1984, the servant's lines to one of Hermione's ladies, Noble stressed that young Mamillius was still in the care of the nursery staff. The promptbook calls for Leontes' infant daughter to be wrapped in a shawl and Hermione's jacket, clothing that might soften Leontes' resolve. True to her word, Gemma Jones's Paulina was firm with Leontes and answered his shouts with shouts. Stage business shed light on the marriage of Paulina and Antigonus and anticipated Paulina's grief at the close of the play. On the videotape Antigonus seems to cower behind her, but he hugs her at the close of the speech in which she demonstrates that the baby is the 'copy of the father' (99). She slaps her husband playfully when Antigonus answers Leontes' threatening 'Hang all the husbands / That cannot do that feat, you'll leave yourself / Hardly one subject' (109–11). Shouting at Leontes, Antigonus echoes Paulina's courage. Ethereal music accompanies the announcement of the return of the emissaries and prepares for the shift to their scene.

In Act 1 of Doran's production (1999), the panels of the set receded, tunnel-like, to the upstage vantage point from which Leontes, Hermione and Polixenes, clad in royal regalia, accepted applause from an offstage crowd. By 2.3 changes in the set and Leontes' costume marked the sharp decline in his mental and physical state. The panels closed in on him, restricting him to considerably less playing space. Darkness and prison-like shadows cast a gloomy spell. Leontes' dishevelled state and dressing gown testified to the insomnia he confessed in the first line: 'Nor night, nor day, no rest.' The braided uniforms of his attendants, correct in every detail, and, later, Paulina's long, elegant coat, provided a sharp contrast with his appearance. On the audio recording one hears first Leontes' scream, as though he is awakening from a nightmare. A shriek precedes the entrance of a servant, played as a doctor with his medical report on Mamillius. Speaking of his son's illness, Antony Sher slows down, like an old gramophone running out of power. A telling characteristic of the opening moments of the production recurs: the voices Leontes had heard were presented now as Hermione's laughter and a cue for his 'Camillo and Polixenes / Laugh at me' (23–4). Unlike his Stratford predecessors, Doran did not juxtapose the entrance of Paulina, a voice of sanity and reason, with an image of the distraught Leontes. Disturbed by the laughter he had imagined, Leontes had exited; from offstage he queried 'What noise there, ho?' (39) and rushed on in response to Paulina's answer. In this royal household with many servants, Paulina did not carry the infant; rather she called for it to be brought on in its Moses basket just before she knelt and presented it to Leontes. He picked up the baby, but put it back when he proclaimed Paulina a 'witch' (67). Vivian Thomas describes Kohler as

> a Paulina of towering physical and moral presence. When dressed in magnificent fur-lined coat and Russian-type hat she dwarfed Sher – and everyone else.... Head thrown back, the strongest voice in the company, mobile face with flashing eyes, all served to give her an untouchable quality. *(Cahiers Elis.*, 77)

Leontes delivered the command to Antigonus in a jagged voice (172–82) and knelt during the last five lines. In excited voices, the servant and the lord announced the imminent return of Cleomenes and Dion. But Leontes' energy was long spent. With difficulty he rose, then fell backward. To those who would help him up, he said 'Leave me' (205). The scene closed with 'While she lives / My heart will be a burden to me' (204–5).

The second act, which opens with Hermione's playful 'Take the boy to you', closes with Leontes' banishment of his infant daughter to 'some place / Where chance may nurse or end it' (181–2) and his ordering preparations for 'A just and open trial' (204) for Hermione, 'Our most disloyal lady' (202). In 1999 the servant's excited announcement of the return of Cleomenes and Dion suggested that Leontes' household did not, as his fevered brain imagined, whisper about his being a cuckold. Doran juxtaposed this hope that the oracle's message would be restorative with an image of Leontes' psychotic jealousy: 'While she lives / My heart will be a burden to me' (204–5) and a dramatic faint. Eyre's production also focused on Leontes' despairing isolation. By closing with Leontes' cradling Mamillius, Barton offered an image of the family Leontes was destroying. Other directors introduced lighting or sound effects that anticipated Apollo's judgement. Nunn's five-foot square of blazing lights diminished Leontes and fitted into a pattern of lighting effects that had opened the play and marked the emergence of Leontes' jealousy. In Hands's production the signature flute and celeste bridged the scenes, and in Noble's 1992 production ethereal music presaged the brief scene in which Cleomenes and Dion recall the mystery of their journey to Delphos and anticipate the Oracle's message. The intention of them all was to provide a telling image, anticipatory and usually ominous, of a king's decision that will bring destruction on his family and plunge his kingdom into a leaderless abyss. The next act presents and explores the devastation wrought by Leontes' jealousy.

3

OPEN SPACES

A t the close of the second act, Leontes welcomes the news that Cleomenes and Dion have returned from Delphos and takes the 'good speed' of their journey as a sign that 'The great Apollo suddenly will have / The truth of this appear' (2.3.199–200). A central focus of Act 3 is journeys – journeys real and spiritual. Cleomenes and Dion return safely and in good time from Delphos (3.1). Less fortunate, Antigonus and the Mariner land on the shores of Bohemia, where they lose their lives: Antigonus, famously, to a ravenous bear, the Mariner and his mates to angry seas (3.3). Between these two voyages, the truth appears; but Leontes overrules the great Apollo and embarks on his long journey of atonement (3.2). His behaviour propels Paulina and Hermione on a spiritual journey.

In the third act, the scenes shift from interior spaces to open spaces. Cleomenes and Dion await fresh horses for the journey from the Sicilian coast to the court; Hermione is tried in a public court, apparently 'i' th' open air' (3.2.104); on the coast of Bohemia Antigonus abandons Perdita to 'A lullaby too rough' (3.3.55). One overarching focus of this chapter is an exploration of how directors and designers have staged these three apparently dissimilar scenes. Have they, for example, found or introduced links between or among them? Do they reintroduce significant props, costumes or music from the first two acts? A second major focus continues the examination of characters, especially the decisions taken by the actors playing Leontes, Hermione and Paulina.

3.1

Hasting to th' court

This, the shortest scene in *The Winter's Tale*, acts as a bridge or chorus between Leontes' night terrors in 2.3 and the trial. Cleomenes and Dion recall the climate, geography and architecture they encountered at Delphos, the awe-inspiring ceremony performed by Apollo's priests, and 'the ear-deaf'ning voice o' th' Oracle' (9). With compassion they hope the oracle will clear Hermione's name; with diplomacy they refer to 'These proclamations' (15) and 'The violent carriage of it' (17), not to Leontes and his instigation of the proceedings. Their costumes – casual, military, religious, court – may reveal not only something about the envoys but also something about Leontes and the forthcoming trial. Although brief, the scene, which introduces a number of motifs that resonate through the rest of the play, invites directors and designers to treat the conversation of Cleomenes and Dion as something more than a welcome break from events in Sicilia. Productions may, for example, stage a contrast between the reported religious ceremony and Leontes' judicial ceremony. When Leontes defies the oracle, 'ear-deaf'ning' thunder may express Apollo's anger. Another possibility is to call attention to the parallels between the supernatural event the travellers have witnessed and the shepherds' experience of meeting 'with things dying' and 'things new-born' (3.3.112–13) and their faith in fairies, in 3.3. Although it may be more apparent in the study than on the stage, there is a similarity of mood in the closing speeches:

DION   And gracious be the issue.

(3.1.22)

SHEPHERD   'Tis a lucky day, boy, and we'll do good deeds on 't.

(3.3.136–7)

Only Gregory Doran (1999) played the entire scene. Anthony Quayle (1948) omitted it, and seven other directors cut between four syllables (Peter Wood, 1960) and one third (Adrian Noble, 1984) of its twenty-two lines. Most of the cuts fall somewhere between lines 14 and 22. Following the textual cues, most directors place 3.1 on land, though Wood placed it on the sea and cut only the unnecessary command 'Go: fresh horses!' (21). Withdrawing the pillars and pediments of the first two acts (Figure 3), Wood opened up the stage to create a wide, deep space for Cleomenes and Dion. A single sail was flown in above a railed platform that suggested the prow of a ship and would become in the next scene the dock from which Hermione stood trial (Figure 16).

Returning the scene to land, Trevor Nunn (1969) played it on a bare stage. Horses' hooves echoed. Dressed for riding, Cleomenes and Dion wore short capes over their suits and high boots. On the NSA recording of the London transfer, the voices of Cleomenes and Dion convey the wonder of their experience. Sound effects indicate that in 1970 they journeyed by train.

In 1976 John Barton, with Nunn, moved the scene indoors, introduced six other characters and, continuing the stress on community, staged a tribal ceremony. Cleomenes and Dion entered with the oracle; the First Lord and Paulina's Steward entered at line 13 with the box it was to rest on, which they placed downstage centre. Paulina, Emilia and two other ladies joined them. After Cleomenes put the oracle on the box, the group clustered around it, hugged each other and then together touched the oracle. The First Lord spoke Dion's wish that 'gracious be the issue', and as Ian McKellen's Leontes entered, all drew back quickly.

In 1981 music, played for the first time since the masque that had opened Ronald Eyre's production, created a sense of wonder and anticipated the entrance at the trial of Cleomenes and Dion with the oracle. Identified in the music cues as 'oracle song preview', it was scored for wind instruments (horns, bassoons and clarinet) and voice (singer: Bernard Lloyd). On the video recording, it is the music, rather than the voices of Cleomenes and Dion, that conveys the spiritual aspect of the journey they have made. A silent figure upstage of the emissaries receives the command 'Go, fresh horses!'.

Adrian Noble's promenade production (1984) used to advantage the audience clustered on the rostrum from which Leontes' emissaries spoke. Reviewing a performance in Barrow-in-Furness, Michael Ratcliffe reports that Cleomenes and Dion stood 'in light at the top of a sprawl of people, like immigrant survivors on a raft, stunned and humbled by the momentous nature of what they have just seen' (*Observer*, Oct). In a production that associated alcohol with Leontes and his followers, it was, perhaps, not surprising that the promptbook calls for Cleomenes and Dion to share a hip flask.

Unscripted business in Terry Hands's production (1986) shed light on Leontes and foreshadowed the futility of Dion's desire that the journey would 'Prove ... successful to the queen' (12). While Cleomenes and Dion revisited the wonders they had seen and hoped Apollo's oracle would 'Turn all to th' best!' (15), Leontes himself (Jeremy Irons) was setting the stage for the trial and upstage seven lords draped themselves in scarlet cloaks in preparation for their roles in the next scene.

Noble (1992) bled 2.3 into 3.1. As Leontes commanded the lords to prepare for the trial, Cleomenes and Dion entered upstage of the gauze box, from which they spoke in amplified voices. Carrying suitcases like their predecessors in 1984, the envoys, observes Robert Smallwood, 'in their linen jackets and straw hats, looked like characters in a Forster novel and must surely have traveled with the help of a Baedeker guide' (*SQ*, 349).

As had Wood in 1960, Doran (1999) pushed back the walls that had seemed to close in on Leontes and introduced Cleomenes and Dion on a wide and deep stage. Wearing military-styled jackets and waist-length capes, they carried the chest to the apron, where they knelt and touched it from time to time, their reverential gestures anticipating the religious ceremony to be introduced when the oracle was brought into court.

3.2

A just and open trial

Shakespeare embedded many stage directions in the script of this crucial scene. Among the cues in the first ten lines are Leontes' acknowledgement of a 'great grief', the Officer's calling for 'Silence!', and Hermione's entrance. In planning and rehearsing a production, directors, designers and actors investigate these and many other cues in the script. They almost certainly explore many of the questions on the following far-from-comprehensive list. Where does the trial take place, and how do props and attendants define the place? How does Leontes enter, what does he wear and who attends him? How does Hermione enter, what does she wear, who attends her and is she restrained? How does Leontes open the proceedings? How does Hermione argue her case, how does she approach Leontes and to whom does she address 'the Emperor of Russia was my father' (119)? How does Leontes respond to her argument and gestures, if any, of reconciliation? What, if any, ceremony attends the entrance of Cleomenes and Dion and the opening of the oracle? Does someone other than an anonymous servant announce the death of Mamillius, and what point is made by the assignment of the line? Who witnesses Leontes' request for Apollo's pardon? How do Paulina and Leontes play the final phase of the scene? What is their relationship? Does Paulina use physical force? raise laughter? How do witnesses respond to the scene? What response does Leontes evoke from the audience? How does the scene close?

Motley's set (1948) continued the emphasis on supernatural and decaying natural worlds and Leontes' power, as illustrated in

Figures 1 and 2. Motley announced the change from Leontes' chamber to a public scene by replacing his couch with a large throne and by providing bench seating in recesses on both sides of his throne and opposite, behind the tree. A bold emblem – an eagle or a phoenix – was the backrest to Leontes' solid throne. The three large spears to the left of the tree took on a sinister aspect when Hermione entered, under the guard of three soldiers pointing spears at her.

Although he fell far short of the more than 170 extras Charles Kean had introduced in 1856, Anthony Quayle filled the Stratford stage with more actors than any of his successors used. In addition to the seven speaking parts and three soldiers, the call list for the trial includes two hornblowers, which the promptbook places at the left and right edges of the apron, and fifteen witnesses (eleven men and four women), who take their places on the benches. Ena Burrill's Paulina, who had made an unscripted appearance at the accusation, did not witness the trial; one of the lords spoke her line 'This news is mortal to the queen' (148).

The promptbook calls for Diana Wynyard's Hermione to enter, guarded, between the spears and the tree upstage left. As she moved to the witness stand centre stage, drums beat at four-second intervals and the spectators murmured. The Officer's call silenced the drums and spectators. Angus McBean's photograph of Hermione pictures her in a black dress appropriate to her status as queen; she wears a crown and veil. There was, apparently, no attempt to use costume as a device to remind the audience that she had recently delivered a child in prison or that she had been 'hurried / Here, to this place, i' th' open air, before / I have got strength of limit' (104–6).

The promptbook indicates that Hermione paused frequently, as she had in the accusation scene, especially during her first speech (22–54, seventeen times) and during the speech beginning 'Sir, spare your threats' (91–116; nine times). *Punch* admires 'her gentle delivery of the defence speech [which was] in sharp relief to the storms of the court'. Hermione, observe T.C. Kemp and

J.C. Trewin, 'stood trial with patient grace' (Kemp and Trewin, 229). Wynyard gave a 'lovely and gracious study, in which the quiet dignity of the injured Queen was revealed' (*Leam. Spa Cour.*) and 'stood with serene and tragic beauty' (*Birm. E. News*). Throughout the trial the spectators, who had been vocal guests at the entertainment in Act 1, murmured or growled or whispered. Quayle added two more words to the apparently invented language he had given them then: 'ska' and 'hakarni' presumably signalled support for Hermione. Certainly the spectators applauded the oracle: the promptbook cues five cries of 'Apollo', 'Great God Apollo', 'Blessed Apollo' during the Officer's reading of the verdict.

Quayle reversed the order of lines in Leontes' denial of the oracle and introduced business to stress the king's folly. Esmond Knight's Leontes left the rostrum and crossed down left centre to announce 'The sessions shall proceed: this is mere falsehood' (141). At this point everyone collapsed and one of the lords caught Hermione. Proclaiming 'There is no truth at all i' th' Oracle' (140), Leontes sank to his knees and 'a sensational moment of thunder and lightning ... play[ed on the] semi-scorched earth with the stage in darkened prelude' to Bohemia (*Evesham J.*). More immediately, the scene was set for what must have been a dramatic entrance to announce the death of Mamillius.

On his knees and with the rest of the court and spectators on the floor behind him, Leontes begged Apollo's pardon in a speech shortened to nine lines (153–61). To them Paulina entered crying 'Woe the while!' (172–4). Reviewers praised the 'power and passion ... the voice and presence' (*SA Herald*), the 'dignity and sympathy' (*Leam. Spa Cour.*) of Burrill's Paulina. She portrayed 'all righteous indignation springing from a large heart' (Kemp and Trewin, 229) and she conveyed 'a clear understanding of the full power of feminine force – insistent but not strident' (*Stage*). She found in Paulina the universal quality of 'such honest, fearless women, standing by their instincts to the limit of peril' (*SA Herald*). 'A prosecutor at whom any tyrant might tremble' (*Punch*), Burrill moved Knight's tyrant king to tears.

FIGURE 16 On a set that emphasizes the height and depth of the stage, Eric Porter's Leontes glares defiantly ahead while the Officer (Roger Bizley) reads the indictment of Hermione (Elizabeth Sellars), whose costume calls attention to neither her royal status nor the recent childbirth. Paulina (Peggy Ashcroft) is at the right behind the Officer. (3.2, 1960)

Although Wood (1960) seems to have set 3.2 indoors, the space, as McBean's photograph confirms, was far more open than it had been in Acts 1 and 2 (Figure 16). Slender pillars give the set height, and a plain drop cloth upstage gives the appearance of depth. The props are simple: a dock, which in 3.1 had functioned as the prow of the ship carrying Cleomenes and Dion homeward; a throne for Leontes; a bench for two of the five attendant lords. (Hermione, as well as her five attendants, stand.) A canopy, held by an attendant, helps establish Leontes' status, as do two gold banners topped by lions' heads and crowns. Two guards in crested helmets stand at attention. The wardrobe list calls for Leontes' costume to be 'jewelled but sombre'. Photographs of Hermione suggest that her costume revealed neither her regal status nor the recent childbirth. She wears a dark, full-length, hooded cape over a light-coloured dress.

The promptbook calls for two trumpeters to announce the scene, for the Officer to stamp his pike and for the Hermione of Elizabeth Sellars to kneel before Eric Porter's Leontes and then to enter the dock. When the women attempted to approach Hermione, an officer held them back with a pike. The court reacted to the oracle and joined with Hermione to say 'Praised!' (137). The trial over, the dock was struck. Leontes knocked the offending oracle from the Officer's hand. Mamillius' three tutors entered and the one charged with conveying the news of their pupil's death knelt down centre and moved on his knees towards Leontes. Three claps of thunder sounded Apollo's wrath: one after the tutor spoke 'Is dead' (145); one after Leontes' 'the heavens themselves / Do strike at my injustice' (146–7) and one after Leontes besought Paulina to administer to Hermione 'Some remedies for life' (153).

Reviewers were generally complimentary to Sellars and Porter. In the *Birmingham Post* Trewin records that 'two very real people confront each other' and that Leontes was 'alive with dangerous passion'. Sellars was 'at her best in the trial scene when her bewilderment, courage of heart, and love for Leontes are impressively revealed' (*Stage & TV*). The *Times* praises Sellars's Hermione for defending herself 'with fluent poetry and changes of tone'.

Toward the close of the scene in many productions, Leontes falls down or kneels after he pleads with Paulina to 'Go on, go on: / Thou canst not speak too much; I have deserv'd / All tongues to talk their bitt'rest' (214–16). His tears are the cue for a compassionate Paulina to observe 'he is touch'd / To th' noble heart' (221–2). In Wood's production, Paulina herself, played by Peggy Ashcroft, was moved by the power of the speech beginning 'I say she's dead' (203–14), which closes with an evocative picture:

> A thousand knees
> Ten thousand years together, naked, fasting,
> Upon a barren mountain, and still winter

> In storm perpetual, could not move the gods
> To look that way thou wert.
>
> (210–14)

Before approaching Leontes, Paulina sought comfort from one of the lords.

Ashcroft's Paulina was much praised. Paulina's 'cries at the injustice of a king [were] touchingly streaked with pity' (*Coventry Sta.*). Ashcroft had 'great authority and remarkable sensibility'; her 'pride and regal bearing' were 'very effective, particularly in her fiercest encounters with Leontes' (*Stage & TV*). McBean's photograph in the SCL collection illustrates the close of the scene: Paulina kneels down beside Leontes, who had reached out to her.

In keeping with the concept of a chamber production that examined the private lives of the characters, Nunn (1969) played 3.2 on a stage with a single prop – Leontes' throne, making its first and only appearance – and with fewer actors than had his predecessors in 1948 and 1960. The promptbook calls for Leontes, Hermione, Paulina, five other men and five other women. Leontes' throne was placed downstage right; the Officer stood opposite. Judi Dench's Hermione entered upstage left, paused at the top, and crossed to centre stage. For the first time in post-war productions at Stratford, Hermione evidenced the effects of childbirth and imprisonment. She stumbled as she entered; she wore a very plain white dress and neither jewellery nor make-up and looked washed out. J.W. Lambert praises her 'superb, lonely, Attic entrance' (*S. Times*). Trewin, whose collection of productions of *The Winter's Tale* stretched back at least to the 1930s, writes of Dench's Hermione:

> we have not had in our time a performance of more simply-expressed emotion, especially when she came forward, a slight, resolute figure, dwarfed by ... [the] permanent setting ... to defend herself before the King who will not look at her.   (*Birm. Post*)

The Officer's call for silence was, Benedict Nightingale notices, 'in an ironic whisper: the court is already standing in mum misery, watching the mad king as he sits hunched and scowling on his throne' (*New States.*).

The dominant characteristic of Dench's voice, as recorded in London by the NSA, is a quiet firmness. Pauses reinforce her argument, and her weariness. She takes a long pause, for example, before she begins her defence, and before 'You, my lord, best know' (32). Dench also heightens the effectiveness of her appeal by occasionally raising her voice or stressing a word. Several examples, in which the stressed words are italicized, illustrate:

> But thus, if powers divine
> Behold our human actions (*as they do*)
> (28–9)

> since he came,
> With what encounter *so uncurrent* I
> Have strain'd t' appear thus:
> (48–50)

> *all* I know of it,
> Is that Camillo was an honest man
> (73–4)

> Now, my liege,
> *Tell me what blessings* I have here alive,
> That I should fear to die?
> (106–8)

On the NSA recording the speech beginning 'The Emperor of Russia was my father' (119–23) sounds as if it is a private plea to the court for compassion.

Critics remarked the dignity of Dench's performance. In the *Times* (1969) Irving Wardle praises her 'superb dignity'; in the *Guardian* Philip Hope-Wallace, her 'simple dignity'. After the oracle was read, Hermione went over to Barry Ingham's Leontes and embraced him; he pushed her downstage. 'It is', writes Wardle, 'only at the climax, when the news from the oracle seems to reverse the judgement against her, that she breaks down and opens her arms to Leontes' (*Times*, 1970). At 'Hermione's great swoon at the news of her child's death, an eerie dusk descends, and the acting goes into slow motion'. The lighting, Hope-Wallace points out, was 'curiously effective'.

Hearing the news of Mamillius' death, Leontes suffered 'a kind of stroke'; Robert Speaight calls it 'a mistake to let this impede his speech just at the moment when the clearing of Leontes' mind and the cleansing of his soul are indicated by a new-found freedom in the verse' (*SQ*, 437). In the NSA recording Leontes sounds very broken, and Ingham's delivery of the final speech is slow. The stroke, which Nightingale characterizes as a 'psychosomatic symptom' of the illness that led him to suspect adultery, also caused 'the slight dragging of a foot' (*New States.*). Reviewing the London transfer, Wardle notes 'a twisted arm and a speech impediment' (*Times*, 1970). Ingham did 'the impossible with Leontes by making him sympathetic throughout. His crumpled figure as he hears of the death of his queen possesses the moving pathos of a broken doll' (*Morn. Star*), an image that may have been suggested by the limp rag doll in 2.3.

Paulina announced Hermione's death in the longest speech in the production (41 lines), created by cutting the two interruptions by lords (174, 202). To Ingham's physically and emotionally broken Leontes, Brenda Bruce's Paulina played spiritual healer. Bruce, observes Gareth Lloyd Evans, 'grips Paulina's sturdy honesty and intuition firmly and ... explained ... why the character is so important – she is Leontes's confessor, through her he talks out his own sickness' (*Guardian Week.*). Lambert characterizes her as 'radiat[ing] behind all the nagging a priestess-like embrace which makes it no surprise that ... it is to her, his principal scourge, that Leontes turns in his agony of heart and mind' (*S. Times*). Ronald Bryden describes the close of the scene: 'Barrie Ingham, speech slurred like a man's after a stroke, lets Brenda Bruce lead him off like an aged child, knees trembling, one foot dragging' (*Observer*). As they exited, the first two lines of 'Jack and Jill', the signature nursery rhyme, played slowly and distortedly.

In 1976, the sudden entrance of Ian McKellen's Leontes marked a shift from the interpolated ritual that eight members of the tribal community had performed in honour of the oracle. Leontes kissed the indictment and placed it on the ornamental block where the community had laid the oracle. For the public trial, Leontes wore a crown, the plain cassock of the first two acts and a modestly decorated coat; he carried a sword. He took his place stage right and with the block and the seven witnesses formed a circle. Her wrists bound with suede ties and wearing a light-coloured shift, Marilyn Taylerson's Hermione stood in the centre and faced the block that held the indictment and Apollo's judgement (Figure 17). Richard David records that Taylerson

> found it awkward and unnatural to address her protestation to the audience as if they were the public attending the trial; she felt it essential to have someone on stage to whom she could appeal directly and personally. Hence the stage audience, interposed between Hermione and the audience proper but seated on the ground so as not to mask her. (David, 12)

Trewin refers to Taylerson's 'eloquence at her trial' (*Birm. Post*). Roger Warren observes that 'Taylerson's frail, delicate Hermione rose splendidly to a powerful defence, though she pushed the climax into rant.' Behind her the barren tree 'provided a stark background ... , a suggestion of "this place i' th' open air" [105]. This suggestion was badly needed, since the permanent set robbed the trial of a sense of space, of sinister occasion' (*SS*, 173).

However, the set, blocking and reassignment of lines did continue the emphasis on a closed community, its myths woven into the decor and its faith enacted in the ritual reading of Apollo's oracle. The First Lord assumed the role of court officer and shared with Paulina's Steward the swearing in of Cleomenes and Dion. The reading of Apollo's oracle was staged as a communal ceremony. Hermione knelt and rested her bound hands on the oracle stand; the others knelt in a circle behind her. The oracle was passed around the circle, and seven speakers each read a segment.

FIGURE 17 Encircled by Leontes (Ian McKellen) and the domestic household, Marilyn Taylerson's Hermione – her hands bound – pleads her case in a tribal ceremony. The oracle has been placed on its stand; Leontes wears his crown for the first time in the production. The community includes Paulina's Steward (Richard Durden) to Leontes' left, Second Lady (Judith Harte), First Lady (Susan Dury), First Lord (Dennis Clinton), before the tree and, to his left, Paulina (Barbara Leigh-Hunt). (3.2, 1976)

As each person handed the oracle on, they joined hands with the preceding person. Paulina read the prophecy: 'and the king shall live without an heir, if that which is lost be not found' (134–6). Then all except Leontes held up their hands, stood and hugged Hermione. They all answered Leontes' 'Ay, my lord' and Paulina added 'even so / As it is here set down' (138–9). When Emilia announced Mamillius' death, the crowd collapsed on the floor. Before fainting on the block, Hermione reached out to Leontes. David did not like the staging: the trial scene was reduced

almost to a pow-wow before the chief's wigwam. The circle of attendants, including the Queen's ladies, who squatted on the

> ground to hear the case against Hermione, was far too tribal and
> nomadic a court for the solemn arraignment to which Leontes
> subjects the daughter of the Emperor of Russia.   (224)

Warren argues that 'it was Paulina rather than Hermione who
balanced Leontes ... her "thousand knees" speech ... was, like
Mr McKellen's speeches, charged with a powerful clarity totally
free from rant: a superb performance to match his' (*SS*, 173).
Paulina's Steward, not an anonymous lord, urged his mistress to

> Say no more:
> Howe'er the business goes, you have made fault
> I' th' boldness of your speech.
>
> (216–18)

Unlike its predecessor, Eyre's 1981 production did not establish
a community and staged the trial with the minimal necessary
props and actors. Stephen Wall describes the stage as 'generally
under-populated.... It's hard to believe in Leontes's tyrannical
power when there are so few to exercise it on. In the trial scene the
audience is half-heartedly drafted for jury service' (*TLS*). In
Hermione's chamber (2.1) and Leontes' chamber (2.3) and earlier
in the trial scene (3.2), the scarcity of courtiers and servants may
have suggested that Leontes lacked subjects to tyrannize and
contributed to a sometimes static stage picture. But especially
in 2.3 and 3.2, it may also be read as establishing an isolation in
sharp contrast to the exuberant Leontes who stage-managed the
opening masque and as providing a space that privileged
language. Leontes' and Hermione's costumes, and especially his
crown and the chains binding her wrists, made visible the king's
tyranny. Leontes' costume, a dark cassock with a patterned stole,
was sombre. Gemma Jones's Hermione, barefooted and with her
hair cropped short, wore a plain white shift.

Jones contrasts her first thoughts about 3.2 with the discoveries
made during rehearsal. I quote at length:

> I will beat my breast, tear my hair and emit real tears.... I fancy
> being dragged on by what is left of my hair, in chains from head to

foot. But ... we realize that Hermione's speech in the trial scene cannot be performed on an emotive wail.... The speech is too long; it becomes self-pitying, which Hermione is not.

Her speech has a fluidity and simplicity compared to the more complex intellectual agility of the first scene, where she played with words. She is articulate, objective and strong, because she is right. She is innocent and she knows it. She does not have to plead her cause or prove that she is true. She has faith.... To present the words as naked of imposition or comment as possible and yet to endow them with the full value of their worth is a challenge that I trust, if but partly achieved, will prove more moving, and a simple shift, bare feet and hand-cuffs will suggest all that needs to be said about her physical condition. (Jones, 161)

Trewin praises Jones for 'resist[ing] the grand manner; she is instead a dignified and heart-breaking innocent' (*Lady*); Michael Billington characterizes her as 'moving' and observes that 'even when manacled and arraigned, [she] casts looks of pitying wonder at her demented husband' (*Guardian*).

Cleomenes and Dion, robed in white-hooded cassocks and carrying the oracle in an ornate trunk, entered through the large upstage doors reserved for entrances such as the opening masque. The oracle music, now played more slowly, accompanied them. Trewin reports that Patrick Stewart's Leontes responded to the oracle's message by 'climbing to a pitch of fury' (*Lady*). Observing that lights underscored turning points, Wardle records the 'awesome blackout when Leontes rips up the oracle's message' (*Times*). To John Elsom it seems that Apollo 'is so angry with Leontes ... that he tries literally to strike him with lightning, instead of figuratively so, through the death of Mamillius' (*Listener*). On a lighter note, Jones records a disappointment, and a glimpse behind the scenes:

We rehearse my being carried from the stage at the end of the trial scene. My hopes of a pathetic exit in the arms of one strong man are dashed with the humiliating realization that I am too heavy and am therefore bundled into the wings by two. I bruise my knee falling to the floor and resort to wearing knee pads under my shift. I then

bruise my elbow, but draw the line at yet more padding, or I'll end
up with shoulder pads and a visor like an American football player.

(163)

In the last phase of the scene, as Warren explains, Sheila
Hancock's Paulina became Leontes' 'healer'. Hancock

delivered the long speech which culminates in the announcement
of Hermione's 'death', and which parodies Leontes's own extravagant hyperboles, without a trace of rant but with maximum
impact; and her disclaimers about reminding him of his crimes ('lo,
fool again!' [228]) were genuine rather than rhetorical. The stress on
compassionate friend rather than tart scold established the start of a
close relationship between her and Leontes, which enabled her to
educate him back to human feeling, to be the healer rather than the
scourge of his mind; and so the extraordinarily moving and
suggestive final scenes gained more conviction than usual by being
prepared for in this way. (SS, 148)

Bob Crowley's set for the 1984 touring production provided a
dramatic setting for the trials in this play and its travelling
companion, *The Crucible*. On the rostrum already established as
his space, Alun Armstrong's Leontes sat in an oversized armchair
of red and gold. On the rostrum opposite him, Lynn Farleigh's
Hermione, in a two-piece suit, hat and gloves, began her defence.
Both speakers used microphones. Reviewing a performance at
Lincoln Cathedral, Anthony Masters notes that

the central acting area was based halfway down the nave but
stretched virtually from the crossing to the west door for major
confrontations like the trial scenes ... Hermione's was breath-
takingly staged, with innocent queen and jealous king facing each
other across half a mile of carpet cordoned off by officious ushers like
a royal procession. (*Times*)

The cast – wearing coats and hats to signal the cold weather – and
audience crowded together behind the ropes. Anthea Robbins
comments on the involvement of the audience: 'we were all the
people of Sicilia watching in horror as Leontes unjustly accused

his wife of adultery and treachery' (*Scun. E. Tel.*). Hermione left the rostrum and approached Leontes, but he remained seated and in the dominant position. In this, the production most evocative of Italy (albeit of the Sicilian underworld), bells tolled from the entrance of Cleomenes and Dion with the oracle through to its reading.

Throughout the production minor details, as well as the visual image of the set, helped to create a conflict between the worlds of men and of women and to stress distinguishing traits of each world. One such detail was to assign the responsibility for announcing Mamillius' death to the lady who would be familiar from stage business in 2.1, not to an anonymous lord, as is usual. (The speech prefix is simply '*Servant*'.) When he returned to the play in 1992, Noble retained the line assignment.

Convinced that Hermione's faint was fatal, Leontes fell to the floor. Billington describes him as 'gradually dwindling into a carpet-gnawing wretch at the queen's expiry' (*Guardian*). One motif of the reviews of Armstrong's Leontes is that an actor 'born to play Bardolph' so convincingly portrayed a jealous tyrant (*D. Telegraph*). Ratcliffe, who reviewed performances in Barrow and London and listed the production as one of the best of the year (*Observer*, 30 Dec), writes that 'it is terrible to watch Mr Armstrong weep, because he does not look the weeping kind' (*Observer*, 16 Dec).

Some credit for Leontes' tears must go to Janet Dale's Paulina, who entered through the audience shrieking 'O cut my lace' (173), flung her coat onto the floor, and climbed onto Hermione's rostrum to berate Leontes. The lords, who had attempted to block her entry in 2.3, were stunned into submission. Paulina, as had Hermione during the trial, appealed to the audience. Her 'power', writes Eric Shorter, was 'enough to stop the most sceptical adolescents chewing their gum' (*D. Telegraph*). As the scene drew to a close, Paulina knelt to console Leontes and took his hand as the lords led him off.

In 1986, the stage, which Leontes himself had set during the previous scene, was an extraordinarily strong visual statement of

Sicilia as a nursery kingdom. Leontes' 'throne' was Hermione's nursing rocker placed on a dais formed by pushing together the four oversized alphabet blocks. The crib and blanket were downstage centre. A small sword, spinning top, teddy and cloth ball were mute reminders of Mamillius. Upstage, snow fell throughout the scene, now connoting the sombre symbolism of winter, not, as at the beginning of the production, inviting a playful snowball fight. Two fires, a large one next to Leontes' throne and a smaller one on what would become Hermione's side, glowed. The angled wall of mirrors upstage reflected the set, the proceedings and the somewhat distorted faces of the audience in the front stalls.

The visual richness of Hands's production, which divided critics, elicited more discussion than did the acting in this and other scenes. It is, however, possible to draw some conclusions from the production materials, photographs and the fixed-focus video recording of the performance. First, with Hermione, Leontes exhibited marks of emotional immaturity. He snapped his fingers to command Hermione to move forward; when she approached him ('You knew', 77), he got up and moved away from the crib, where he had been kneeling; he drove her away when she tried to touch him ('Your actions', 82); he kicked the crib ('I but dream'd it!', 84). As the references to Hermione suggest, she attempted through gestures to reinforce the truthfulness of her self-defence. She knelt at the crib during Leontes' speech about the outcast brat (87); she fell to her knees for the apostrophe to Apollo (116); she spoke the 'Emperor of Russia' (119) as an aside to her five attendants. Hermione's costume and wig did not convey the deprivations of her having given birth in prison.

Most productions introduce some ceremony attendant upon the oracle, but in 1986 the ceremony centred on Leontes. Hermione's 'Therefore proceed' (108) was Leontes' cue to prepare himself for the revealing of the oracle's judgement. As she spoke, Leontes was helped into a very full gold robe with ermine trim and a crown too large for his head. Two of his lords helped him onto

FIGURE 18 Hermione (Penny Downie) pleads her case with Leontes (Jeremy Irons), who has donned full regalia and stands on a dais made of large alphabet blocks. Note the cradle before her and the bear's head just visible at the right edge of the photograph. (3.2, 1986)

the throne. Three others held the sceptre, orb and state sword. When Hermione said "'Tis rigour and not law' (114), Leontes turned, in full and ill-fitting regalia, his appearance (Figure 18) ironically illustrating the truth of her argument and alluding to E.H. Shepherd's drawing for 'If I were king' (see p. 15). Here, as in 3.1 when Leontes set the stage during the conversation of Cleomenes and Dion, the blocking makes an ironic comment and reveals Leontes' nervous compulsion to 'do something'. But the blocking may also have been introduced to reveal Leontes' immature need to be the centre of attention: in 3.1, he upstaged actors reporting on a place unlike Sicilia and in 3.2, Hermione's closing argument.

Penny Downie's Hermione may not have convinced Leontes, but she did engage the court, whose members moved forward to support her. The Officer read the oracle's words in an excited voice and the court rushed to Hermione's side of the stage. Opposite them the nursery tyrant stood on the dais, defied Apollo and plunged the stage into darkness.

In the final phase of the scene, the empty crib continued to be an important symbol. Paulina pushed Leontes toward it; later he crawled toward it; photographs record that he put his crown in it, a visual symbol of the end of his dynasty. The chorister's voice and the celeste, which had signified innocence and hope at the beginning of the production, sounded hollow in the context of Mamillius' death, the apparent death of Hermione and the casting out of the infant daughter. Helped up by a lord, Leontes reached down to help Paulina up, a gesture that may be read as his looking for the first time outside himself, an important initial step in his recovery. Broken and speaking in a faltering delivery, Leontes was helped off by Paulina and the lords. For the first time in Hands's production, Leontes left the stage. The signature tune, played on the celeste, and the revolving of the crystal, closed the scene.

Noble (1992), the only Stratford director to take Hermione's 'i' th' open air' (105) as a literal statement for the location of the trial, introduced a storm of *Lear*-like intensity. The scene opened with sombre ceremonial music, rain, and storm clouds skudding across the cyclorama. His voice grief-stricken, Leontes spoke against steady rainfall. The court, in long black coats and hats, sheltered under large black umbrellas. The crowd parted to allow Hermione and her gaoler to enter from upstage and make a long slow passage to the apron. Hermione limped; her clothes were in disarray; an umbrella held by the Gaoler shielded her from the rain. Samantha Bond defended herself with 'an impressive dignity and a calm, steely pride' (*SQ*, 349). Production materials record that she reached out to Leontes: she put her hands on his chest ('My life stands in the level of your dreams', 81); she rested her head on his shoulder ('Your actions are my dreams', 82); she put her hands over his mouth to try to prevent his saying 'You had a bastard by Polixenes' (83). Bond spoke with 'the fire and pride of a young Judi Dench' (*S. Times*). Before 'Therefore proceed' (108) she took a long pause and shifted to a quiet tone for the last part of the speech. To the Gaoler, who had supported her when she seemed to falter, she uttered 'The Emperor of Russia was my father' (119), a decision Smallwood finds 'inspired: instead of a superfluous boast of what members of the court all knew perfectly well, it became a touching invocation of the last trusting relationship left to her' (*SQ*, 349).

The kettledrums that accompanied Hermione's entrance foreshadowed a greater storm when Leontes defied the oracle (Figure 19). Perhaps taking a cue from Paulina's 'still winter / In storm perpetual' (212–13), Noble introduced, as the promptbook records, 'lightning flashes, smoke on stage, thunder and rain, drums, wind machine'. The gauze box dropped from twenty to eight feet above the stage. From Leontes' 'the heavens themselves / Do strike at my injustice' (146–7) to the entrance of Paulina (172), 'the wind machines are on and the company fall on the ground as the oracle strikes and then they and their umbrellas get blown around'.

The storm was theatrically effective and fitted in with several themes explored by the production. The autumnal colours of the first act gave way to darkness and storms of winter. Apollo's fury, expressed by the storm and the loss of Mamillius and Hermione, set Leontes on the road to spiritual regeneration and opened the way for a re-examination of Paulina's role. The storm also linked Sicilia and Bohemia. From as early as 1869 (Charles and Adelaide Calvert, Manchester), directors have used 'the heavens themselves / Do strike at my injustice' as an embedded cue for a storm employing advances in lighting and sound technology. In these productions storms linked the action in Sicilia and on the seacoast of Bohemia, where the Mariner warns Antigonus:

> the skies look grimly,
> And threaten present blusters. In my conscience,
> The heavens with that we have in hand are angry,
> And frown upon's.

> (3.3.3–6)

FIGURE 19 After Leontes (John Nettles) defies the oracle, a violent storm throws the king and courtiers (Lord, John Hodgkinson; Dion, James Walker) to the ground and scatters their umbrellas. Note the jagged cracks on the stage floor. (3.2, 1992)

In 1992 the storm proved to be one of several parallels between Sicilia and Bohemia, where sixteen years later a sudden summer storm broke up the sheep-shearing festival.

Impressive though the storm was, the language, as Peter Holland points out, was 'lost in the theatrical tempest' (*SS*, 174). The storm may also be read as evidence of Leontes' deranged mental state: staging a trial out of doors on a cold, stormy winter day is not the action of one sound in mind. Paul Taylor expresses a similar point about the intensity of the storm: 'when Gemma Jones's excellent Paulina cries "This news is mortal to the Queen" you simply feel that she's not the only one who will be a goner if they stick around in these spectacularly inclement conditions' (*Independent*).

The blocking for Paulina's speech beginning 'What studied torments' (175) was not set, records the promptbook, because

Jones wanted to try something different each time. There is, however, a cue for Leontes to let out an anguished cry and to fall forward at the close of the catalogue of his transgressions and before she announces Hermione's death. Smallwood records that 'Gemma Jones's powerful, bossy grande dame of a Paulina punctuated her indictment of Leontes with fists thudding on his shoulders as he crouched on the floor seeking shelter from the storms, meteorological and verbal' (*SQ*, 349–50). In 3.2 the dominant traits of Jones's Paulina were her class ('distinctly upper-crust', *D. Telegraph*; a 'county lady', *SS*, 175; 'a tad too elegant and refined', *FT*, 1993); her fierceness ('formidable lady', *Times*; 'terrier-like tenacity', *Guardian*, 1993); and her 'loyalty towards her queen ... both slightly comic and intensely moving' (*Guardian*, 1993). Usually Jones raised laughter, of relief or at the character's expense, when, for example, Paulina tried to repent and unwittingly reminded Leontes of the very things – his wife, his children, the banishment of Antigonus – she would have him forget. But she was also compassionate. She knelt and cradled Leontes in her arms. As the box was flown in for the next scene, Paulina helped Leontes off.

Of Doran's production (1999), Maeve Walsh writes 'at the trial, accused and accuser are physically wrecked' (*Indep. Sun.*). Antony Sher's Leontes entered as he had done at the beginning of the production, in full regalia from the upstage centre entrance. Smallwood describes Leontes, wrought by jealousy:

> Exhausted still [from 2.3], and demented, he limped down the length of the stage for the trial scene, a terrible parody of his opening energetic entrance, stumbled up the steps of a huge throne, and made a pitiful mess of speaking the indictment against Hermione, fumbling with notes and spectacles, getting to the end with the utmost difficulty and to the excruciating embarrassment of his court. (*SS*, 264)

As he explained 'Your actions are my dreams' (82), Sher came dangerously close to losing control. His eyes started, and when

Alexandra Gilbreath's Hermione addressed the audience, which he had taken into his confidence in the first act, he stared at it.

Hermione entered from the wings (in this Sicilian court, the massive upstage opening was reserved for the monarch) 'in a filthy prison shift, bloody from child-birth, her hair matted, her face ashen, her eyes staring, the entire court gasping in shock at her appearance' (*SS*, 264). Manacled and leaning on the rails for support, she took her place in a small dock opposite Leontes, dwarfed by his throne (Figure 20). She spoke 'with simple humility and utterly unaffected dignity' (*Times*) and looked on Leontes 'with eyes of pity, not revenge' (*Guardian*). Throughout her defence, Gilbreath directed some lines to the audience. She opened her arms out in appeal ('Your honours all, / I do refer me to the Oracle: Apollo be my judge!', 114–16) and 'in a trance she insist[ed to the audience] that "the Emperor of Russia was my father" [119]' (*Indep. Sun.*).

The oracle, which Cleomenes and Dion had treated with reverence (3.1), was brought on in a religious ceremony. An Eastern orthodox priest, richly robed and mitred in gold and red, was attended by acolytes bearing incense, a candle and a crozier. He intoned the Officer's speeches. Leontes' defiance of Apollo could, thus, also be read in Christian terms. He left his throne, took the oracle from the priest, and paused before proclaiming 'There is no truth at all i' th' Oracle' (140). The priest and his acolytes, silent witnesses to the rest of the scene, were the last to leave the stage.

The cluster of religious men and symbols counterpointed Estelle Kohler's Paulina, who, notes Christopher Cannon, 'assume[d] the authority necessary to rebuke, punish and finally redeem a king' (*TLS*). Kohler provided 'the emotional heart of the evening with her beautifully moving performance as Paulina, who stands up to Leontes and forces him to confront his folly' (*D. Telegraph*). She 'engage[d] Leontes in eyeball-to-eyeball contact' (*Guardian*). Paulina pushed and punched Leontes, threw him across the stage, and he fell. She picked up the oracle as she began the catalogue of

FIGURE 20 All but destroyed by psychotic jealousy, Antony Sher's Leontes interrogates Hermione (Alexandra Gilbreath), whose bloodstained shift contrasts sharply with Hermione's costume in Figure 16. The First Lord (Christopher Wells) observes. (3.2, 1999)

his offences and threw it down before announcing Hermione's death. At the close of the scene, Leontes, reduced to tears and 'retch[ing] with grief' was 'led off like an infant' (*New States.*). In a production that displayed the trappings of kingship and its official church, it was significant that Paulina spoke with 'vehement moral urgency' (*FT*).

3.3

Some remote and desert place

The third scene contains Shakespeare's most famous stage direction: '*Exit, pursued by a bear*' (58). Scholars have explored its significance and sought to prove – or disprove – that Shakespeare's company borrowed (or hired) a bear from the Bear Gardens, near the Globe (Williams). In the playhouse, directors and designers have grappled with the challenge of representing a bear on stage. Over the years bears, looking like bears, have been frightening, ludicrous, vaudevillian, pantomimic and cuddly.[1] Other directors introduced lighting and sound effects, not a predatory bear.[2] Bears have also been represented by symbolic figures, by Hermione, and by actors in running shorts and track shoes and in a dancer's practice clothes.[3] Preferring dinner, not a midnight snack, most bears ignore the infant Perdita. On occasion, Antigonus and Hermione have diverted the bear from Perdita.[4]

But the scene contains far more than a man-eating bear, a ravenous special effect or a comic turn. In several centuries of theatre reviews, a common theme is the similarity between Bohemia and Shakespeare's Warwickshire. (No one mentions that neither has a sea-coast.) In English reviews, one can almost hear a collective sigh of relief when the shepherd enters – for it is, after all, the people, not the place, that evoke the warm response. The main discussion of staging Bohemia and the Bohemians belongs in chapter 4. In this chapter, the topic is a more practical one: how to shift from the trial in Sicilia to the sea-coast of Bohemia. The scene – and recent productions – raise a number of other questions. Does Hermione speak the lines in Antigonus' dream? Does she appear at any point in the scene? Does Antigonus attempt to provide adequate cover for the infant? How does Antigonus convey his belief that Hermione has died and that Apollo's ruling names Polixenes as the father of Perdita? Has a garment associated with Hermione been left with the infant? What do lighting and sound effects contribute to the shift in tone from the bear to the shepherds? Does the director introduce extras, such as the hunters the shepherd refers to? Is the director establishing a pattern in the placing and reception of the infant by Leontes, Antigonus, the Old Shepherd? And, of course, what does the bear look like?

In Motley's Sicilia (1948), a barren tree with sinister branches represented the natural world. Bohemia, and especially the

Bohemians, on the other hand, reminded viewers of Warwickshire. A photograph of the set, labelled 'sea coast', shows several large rocks, trees with leaves, a path leading to distant hills. An owl in a tree seems to signify that, in contrast with Sicilia's fantastic birds and beasts, homely wisdom and familiar bird and animal life inhabit Bohemia. According to *Punch* the production 'drench[ed] the sea-coast of Bohemia with the theme-song of the B.B.C. seagull'.

Having cut the visit of Cleomenes and Dion to Apollo (3.1), Quayle sacrificed the opportunity to contrast its supernatural elements with the beliefs of the Old Shepherd and his son.[5] *Punch* reports that the production was 'unusual in giving us a glimpse of the bear', but it does not describe the brief appearance. Cutting the last eleven lines of the scene denied Paul Scofield's much-praised Clown the generous gesture of burying what, if anything, was left of Antigonus. The scene – and the first half of the production – closed with the Old Shepherd's 'come, good boy, the next way home' (124–5; Figure 21), not the warmly humane ''Tis a lucky day, boy, and we'll do good deeds on 't' (136–7). Nevertheless, John Kidd's Old Shepherd and the Clown possessed a

> rich humanity and humour [which] help[ed] to make Bohemia a land where it is natural to expect the lost to be found and kindness to heal the wounds of cruelty. From their first entrance we are assured that the 'blossom' baby cast at their feet will be treated with tender devotion.   (*SA Herald*)

It is difficult to draw many conclusions about Wood's production of the scene (1960), which cut only two lines. Perdita was in a cradle, which gave her a little more protection from the storm than most Perditas are granted. The usual sound cues for thunder, horns and seagulls signalled the storm, the hunters and the calming of the storm. The promptbook has a stage direction for the bear to enter upstage, cross upstage, and then to exit at the proscenium, but Trewin refers disapprovingly to a 'shadow-bear' (*Illus. Lon. News*). The huntsmen, about whom the Old Shepherd

FIGURE 21 'come, good boy, the next way home'. John Kidd's Old Shepherd and Paul Scofield's Clown carry the infant Perdita and the 'fairy gold' to their cottage. (3.3, 1948)

complains, crossed the stage, one of them with a crossbow. Writing in the *Financial Times*, Richard Findlater praises James Bree as the Old Shepherd and Ian Holm as his son for playing the scene 'with just the right – and oh so elusive – simplicity, humour and innocence'.

In Nunn's production (1969) the nursery rhyme that accompanied Leontes' exit from the previous scene bled into seagulls. Nunn was the first post-war Stratford director to introduce the voice of Hermione for her words in Antigonus' dream (27–36).

The bear was horrific and, records the *Birmingham Post*, 'nobody laughed'. Hilary Spurling describes it as

> rearing up some twelve feet tall as his victim bolts across the floor, so that Antigonus becomes a squirming dwarf, grappled and finally enveloped, the pair of them dwarfed in turn by the set's wall rearing at least forty feet above. The whole calamity has a nice turn of speed, and an even nicer blend of visual elegance and nonchalant absurdity. *(Spectator)*

'A frenzy of strobe lighting', which intensified the 'chilling horror', suggested a link between the bear and the emergence of Leontes' sudden destructive jealousy in 1.2 (*E. Standard*). Sydney Bromley's Old Shepherd gave the Bohemian scenes a 'lovely start' (*Guardian*, 1970).

By doubling the bear and Time, Barton (1976) explored a different link. Roger Warren reads the bear as 'another primitive folk emblem, an actor in a huge mask *guiding* Antigonus off to slaughter' (*SS*, 174). In the runic narrative on the curtains, the bear appears as an oversized figure in the panel upstage of the tree (Figure 5). Laroque applauds the decision to link the bear with Time: 'By transforming the bear into an allegory of Death and making Antigonus a victim of Time, we have a tempting and intelligent solution to a major difficulty of the play' (*Cahiers Elis.*, 91). The bear evoked several different responses from reviewers. It was 'grimly stylised' and not played for laughs (*Birm. Post*). It was likened to 'a wizard' (*FT*), 'a walking totem-pole' (*Observer*), 'a witch doctor' (*New States.*). Benedict Nightingale describes him as a 'voodoo-man. At any rate, a grim gentleman wearing an animal mask and brandishing human skulls looms over the frozen Antigonus, who mutters "this is the chase" and allows himself to be ushered offstage' (*New States.*). Antigonus left Perdita in a cradle with a cover; the coat Hermione wore in the first two acts was bundled and placed with the box of gold and the fardel. The shepherds wore warm clothes, hats and snowshoes, and carried harpoons. Robert Cushman praises David Waller's Old Shepherd for his 'warming first moments', but argues that the 'totem-pole, which escorts [Antigonus] offstage', rendered the Young Shepherd's 'speech describing his dismemberment by the bear neither credible nor funny' (*Observer*).

In Eyre's production (1981), the baby, who had cried when Paulina left it with Leontes (2.3), cried again in 3.3. Stephen Wall finds the sound effect less moving than the 'nobly compassionate tone' of Robert Eddison's Antigonus (*TLS*). In a production that was often stark or static, Eyre introduced a series of stunning entrances or effects and suggested links among them. The 'most massive and malignant of bears' (*Birm. Post*) made a dramatic entrance through the large upstage centre doors, as had Cleomenes and Dion with Apollo's oracle. Nunn's lighting effects had drawn a parallel between Leontes' destructive jealousy (1.2) and the bear; Eyre intensified the horror by repeating the effect that signalled Apollo's ire with Leontes: after an 'awesome blackout ... Antigonus ... meets the giant bear in a flash of lightning' (*Times*; Figure 22). The 'double-decker' bear 'engulf[ed] rather than pursue[d] Antigonus' (*TLS*).

As the scene shifted to the shores of Bohemia, the promenade audience for the 1984 touring production assumed a more active role. Actors invited members of the audience to help create the sea by raising and lowering a cloth. In Scunthorpe, *Guardian* critic Robin Thornber 'watched one little girl's jaw drop and eyes light up as she helped to billow the cloth that blows up a storm'. Noble explains that 'we drew attention to the dramatic nature of this event by placing the baby on a huge sheet of cloth and giving dozens of people a corner each, with the responsibility of saving the child' (Noble, xv). The bear looked at the infant before striking Antigonus, a more satisfying meal. The shepherds entered to find not only Perdita and the fardel but also Antigonus' hat, shoe, torch and bloody handkerchief.

In 3.3, as in 3.2, the technical effects in Hands's production (1986) garnered more words from the reviewers than did the actors. Subject to the same weather as Sicilia, Bohemia received a

FIGURE 22 Antigonus (Robert Eddison) faces a stunning – and most terrifying – bear. Antigonus stands between Perdita and the bear. (3.3, 1981)

fresh snowfall and Antigonus, thoughtfully, covered Perdita with his own coat. In 1969 Nunn, as mentioned above, was the first post-war director at Stratford to use Hermione's voice for her lines in Antigonus' dream. Hands was the first to fly Hermione in to speak her lines. The gigantic bear rug from Leontes' Sicilian palace was raised to its full height, its eyes flashing red; Antigonus turned as though to save Perdita, then turned upstage to sacrifice himself. The crystal disc turned again as the shepherds, clad in heavy coats and woolly boots, left the stage. The celeste marked the close of the first half of the production.

In 1992 Antigonus confronted a large shaggy black bear, which entered on all fours and reared up menacingly on its hind legs. Lightning flashed when it roared and when it reared up. The bear dropped down to sniff the baby, which cried. To distract it, Hermione appeared, an apparition flown inside the gauze box. The bear and Antigonus looked at Hermione. The bear hit Antigonus, who reeled offstage and was duly pursued by the bear. Hermione's unscripted appearance to preserve Perdita from the bear was what is usually referred to as a bold decision. Nightingale pronounces 'the hovering mum ... a bit preposterous', but applauds Noble for being 'prepared to take imaginative risks' (*Times*). Peter Holland observes 'it only muddles things – it is one of those moments when I want to sound very pedantic and to say that if Shakespeare had intended Hermione's ghost to appear he would have written the scene that way' (*SS*, 175).

Shakespeare, one suspects, would have approved of the warmth and wit of Jeffery Dench's Old Shepherd and Graham Turner's Clown. The first thing Dench's Old Shepherd did was to cover the infant, a spontaneous and reassuring gesture. Smallwood observes 'the splendidly unsentimental geniality' of the Old Shepherd and 'the Stan Laurel-esque innocence' of the Clown (*SQ*, 350). Rebecca Flynn places the scene in the context of Noble's exploration of fathers and children: 'It is characteristic of Noble's imaginative response to the patternings of the play that as the Old Shepherd peered curiously and charitably down at the abandoned baby, his own child's voice was heard offstage calling "Father, Father!"' (*Cahiers Elis.*, 89).

For the transition from the trial to Bohemia, the walls in Doran's production (1999) were withdrawn and the drapery that had functioned as the ceiling of Leontes' palace (Figure 9) was adjusted and became 'splendidly evocative of clouds heavy with snow' (*Mail Sun.*). Hermione spoke her dream message but did not appear. The cloth, which had been transformed from ceiling to cloud, changed again to represent the bear 'looming growlingly over the front stalls as it shaped itself into two huge clawed paws to fall and envelope the fleeing Antigonus' (*SS*, 265). The bear, 'twice as big as a man, and shrouded in mist [was] quite scary' (*TLS*). As had Leontes when he sought fellow-cuckolds in the audience, and Hermione when she appealed for witnesses to her innocence, so the Old Shepherd (James Hayes) addressed the audience. Noble had called attention to the shepherd as a caring father. By having a bleeting lamb echo the baby's cry, Doran called attention to the Old Shepherd's vocation and – in a production that introduced ritual and Eastern orthodox clerical garb and symbols – hinted at the Christian symbolism of the shepherd. Christopher Brand's Clown, a lanky, doltish lad, told his story in a matter-of-fact manner, not with the compassion with which other young shepherds recount the mauling of Antigonus. Perdita was wrapped in Hermione's elegant shawl, which Leontes had sniffed for incriminating evidence.

Two series of photographs resonate with the closing image of Act 3. In one, Leontes seizes, or stands ready to seize, Mamillius (Figures 10 and 11); in the second, he refuses to acknowledge his infant daughter (Figures 13–15). Against these may be juxtaposed a photograph from Quayle's production (Figure 21), which pictures the Old Shepherd and Clown carrying the infant and which captures the optimistic note on which nearly all productions break for the interval. The visual image of the two rustics and, unknown to them, the infant princess and the Old Shepherd's words (which only Quayle cuts) offer promise: ''Tis a lucky day, boy, and we'll do good deeds on 't' (136–7).

NOTES

1 At, respectively, Stratford, 1969; Chicago, 1994; New York, 1985; Young Vic, London, 1981; Alabama Shakespeare Festival, Montgomery, 1976.
2 Young Vic, 1991.
3 At, respectively, Stratford, 1986; Shakespeare's Globe, 1997; Venice Beach, California 1979; Washington, DC, 1987.
4 Ashland, Oregon, 1984; Stratford, 1992.
5 Two programmes (1948 and 1981), following the Folio, identify the Old Shepherd's son as 'Clown'. The others identify him as 'Young Shepherd'.

TIME

I that please some, try all

Directors of other Shakespearean plays have to decide where to place the interval, and other volumes in this series may discuss the advantages and disadvantages and significances of various choices. *The Winter's Tale* has a natural break before the leap forward of sixteen years. The challenge to its directors is how best to introduce the figure of Time as Chorus. In his – for at least in the Stratford productions a man has personified Time – speech of thirty-two lines, Time tells us that he uses his wings and turns his glass. But Time, as the Introduction points out, does not always have wings or carry an hourglass.

Anthony Quayle's production (1948) presented Time (William Squire) as the traditional figure of Father Time (Figure 23). He wore a floor-length, hooded gown; his long white beard reached nearly to his waist; his wings, with designs resembling art nouveau patterns, were longer than he was tall and more than equal to the task of winging him around the world. In his left hand he held an oversized scythe, the handle a knotted branch from a tree. In his right hand he carried his glass. The act curtain rose on this figure, standing before Polixenes' palace, its façade decorated with a telescope, stars and zodiacal signs. Time moved slowly to the forestage for his speech, from which Quayle cut nine lines. Squire gave 'humour and dotage (and, incidentally, the incoherence of old age), to Time's tottering lines' (*Birm. E. News*).

FIGURE 23 In this traditional presentation, Father Time (William Squire) has wings and carries a scythe. He stands before the curtain representing the façade of Polixenes' palace. (4.1, 1948)

Derek Godfrey's 'serenely aristocratic' Time (1960) created a quite different effect (*Nott. Guard. J.*). He carried a bow and an object described by the props list as an 'hour glass device' and by a reviewer as 'a remote-controlled hourglass' (*SA Herald*, Sep). A common theme in the reviews is that Godfrey spoke beautifully. Godfrey's Time possessed a 'dazzling French elegance, fantastic but memorable' (*Liv. Post*). Another reviewer likened him to a French aristocrat (*Birm. Post*). Godfrey's Time had 'a twinkling eye and a merry heart' (*Evesham J.*). He was, notes the *Morning*

Advertiser, 'an elegant genial fellow with a black silk cloak and a beige waistcoat, and his commentary [was] accompanied by reminders of past sorrows and hints of joys to come'. As he had in earlier scenes, Wood introduced mime to illustrate the speaker's words. On Time's cue, Leontes paced across the stage, motioning away Dion and Cleomenes. Florizel entered with a falcon; Perdita entered from the opposite side, met him, they passed around each other, gazed at each other, and exited. No lines were cut.

In 1969 Trevor Nunn reintroduced the Apollo light cube that had blazed over Leontes at the close of 2.3. Before this lighting effect and against the background of the hum of a spinning top and whistling wind, Time spoke his lines. The sound and lighting effects fitted into the pattern Nunn was weaving, the first details of which appeared in the opening image of the production.

John Barton and Nunn (1976) assigned the lines to John Nettles, who had represented the bear. Benedict Nightingale records that 'the same figure reappears, removes his bear's head to reveal the yellowish jowls and droopy whiskers of what seems to be a Chinese magician', and delivers Time's speech (*New States.*). When Time introduced Florizel and Perdita, they entered upstage, looked at each other, and were waved off by Time. Closing with 'th' argument of Time' (29), he picked up the bear's head and exited. Nightingale reads the innovation as a reminder that 'Time can be a destroyer and can be a creator' and as an aspect of the directors' 'emphasis on cyclical change, decay and renewal'.

Ronald Eyre's staging of 4.1 (1981) looked back to the masque that had opened the production, as these details from the promptbook and videotape reveal. An oversized figure of Time, led on by Cleomenes and Dion, 'gave birth' to Mamillius, who emerged from beneath his gown. In 4.1 Time (Robert Eddison) – now a human-sized figure – entered from upstage centre; Cleomenes and Dion carried his gigantic scythe and lantern (Figure 24). Time's appearance in the opening masque made his second appearance 'less artificial', argue Jean Fuzier and François Laroque (*Cahiers Elis.*,116). The effect Eyre achieved did more than

FIGURE 24 Time's gown, based on the winter constellations illustrated in the programme, links the figure, portrayed by Robert Eddison, with death. Attendants Dion (Peter Land) and Cleomenes (Hugh Quarshie) carry the scythe and lantern so that Time can reveal the figures on his gown. (4.1, 1981)

decrease the artificiality of an allegorical figure. Staging, costume and casting – Eddison doubled Antigonus and Time – were part of Eyre's solution to the problem of joining the two halves of the play. In both the masque and 4.1, Time entered from upstage centre accompanied by Cleomenes and Dion; the cut of both of his costumes was the same, and the designs were similar. In 4.1 the design was based on the winter constellations, illustrated in the programme.

As had Eyre, Adrian Noble (1984) doubled Antigonus and Time and drew, through sound effects, links with earlier scenes. The second half began with Camillo and Polixenes playing boules. The hum of a spinning top, familiar from the opening scene, interrupted their game; they froze, as had the company in the opening scene. As Time, Paul Webster entered and took in the whole audience with his speech, shortened by approximately one third. Amplified ticks of a grandfather clock recalled the prop prominent in scenes set on the rostrum associated with Leontes.

Implicit in Terry Hands's staging of Time (1986) was an association with the bear. Having devoured Antigonus, the gigantic bear dropped into a stage trap. Emerging from the same trap, Henry Goodman's Time, presented as a large white bird with a wing span twice its length, flew up and toward the audience, and then landed on the stage. The mirrors upstage reflected his emergence, his flight and his landing. Fuzier and Jean-Marie Maguin admit 'the comic twist is hard to justify but the whole scene is a visual delight' (*Cahiers Elis.*, 95).

In 1986 Time flew; in 1992, it floated. As he had in 1984, Noble opened the second half with Polixenes and Camillo. Seated downstage in wicker chairs, Paul Jesson's Polixenes dozed under a Bohemian newspaper and Benjamin Whitrow's Camillo worked the crossword in his Sicilian newspaper. Camillo not only spoke of letters from Leontes but also received from Time a message, which drifted down on the string attached to a red balloon. Camillo read Time's speech and awakened Polixenes by puncturing the balloon, a device that alerted the audience to watch for parallels between Sicilia and Bohemia and made Time, if not ordinary, at least not of mythic stature. Robert Smallwood points out a disadvantage of making Camillo privy to Time's message:

> When, however, Whitrow's Camillo seemed to understand the import of what he read (for example, his noting the name of Perdita), then one was forced to believe that his Act 4 intervention on Florizel's behalf derived from his 'acting upon information received' (as police press-releases always say) and thus removed from the solution of the lovers' problem that element of fortune integral to romance.   (*SQ*, 350).

Gregory Doran (1999) devised a simple but effective way to join Sicilia and Bohemia, Antigonus and Time. Devoured by a bear shaped from the billowing cloth that had been the ceiling in

Leontes' palace and stormy skies in Bohemia, Jeffry Wickham's Antigonus returned, draped in the same cloth to impersonate Time and to introduce Florizel and Perdita on cue. As the *New Statesman* notes, 'Antigonus ... emerges from the silk that engulfed him'.

Without exception the presentation of Time at Stratford has derived from the concept of the production. He has been linked with recurring stage business, as in 1960, when interpolated mime illustrated his lines. He has been linked with the design, as in 1948, when Polixenes' palace provided an appropriate backdrop, and in 1986, when he flew from the stage trap into which the bear had disappeared, and in 1992, when his words arrived on a balloon. Doubling the bear and Time (1976) made the link concrete, not metaphorical as in 1986. The three productions that doubled Antigonus and Time (1981, 1984, 1999) reminded the audience of Antigonus' role in preserving Perdita. Two productions made Time a motif: in 1969 Time's words opened the play; in 1981 his entrance was the optimistic climax of the masque. The presentation has varied, but the intent has usually been to treat the allegorical figure with respect.

4

BOHEMIA

I n spite of Time's efforts to ease the transition from Leontes' court to Polixenes' Bohemia sixteen years later, many productions seem to struggle to make Act 4 work. Directors must find a way to encourage the audience to suspend its curiosity about Leontes and to engage instead with the sheep-shearing and characters chiefly rural. Michael Billington refers to the difficulty of finding 'the right metaphor for communal joy' (*Guardian*, 1976), and Harold Hobson, to the difficulty of conveying 'simple happiness' (*S. Times*, 1976). Robert Speaight sounds a warning to directors:

> you cannot produce the pastoral fourth act of *The Winter's Tale* with any hope of success unless you are prepared to take peasants as naturally and seriously, as realistically, and also as unromantically, as Shakespeare took them. His 'sea coast of Bohemia' is geographically improbable but sociologically exact. (*SQ*, 20, 1969, 437)

Implicit in these references to 'communal joy', 'simple happiness' and natural, realistic peasants are challenges to the composer and the choreographer, who must decide the most appropriate style and period for the music and dances. Directors must decide how, if at all, to link the two halves of the play. Are they distinct and irreconcilable? Are the Bohemian scenes chiefly entertainment, a chance for party pieces, such as the trio sung by Dorcas, Mopsa and Autolycus, and interpolated business? Or is there a thematic unity between Sicilia and Bohemia? If there is a unity between Sicilia and Bohemia, does it reveal, as did Peter Hall's production (National Theatre, London, 1988), a negative view of human nature? Or does the unity, as in Adrian Noble's productions (1984, 1992), focus on a positive view?

This chapter explores where and when post-war Stratford directors have located Bohemia, a choice influenced, of course, by the placing of Sicilia; how they have addressed the challenges stated by Billington, Hobson and Speaight; how they have staged script-based thematic links; and how they have introduced devices such as interpolated characters, doubling, and aural and visual parallels. Four characters are of particular interest, their presentation helping to determine whether the Bohemian scenes are integral or entertainment: Autolycus, Polixenes, Perdita and Florizel. What is Autolycus' function? Is he mean-spirited? happy-go-lucky? shy? sardonic? cynical? What disguises does he adopt? Can he sing? Has Polixenes aged over the sixteen years? Have events in Sicilia scarred him? Does he seem to recognize Hermione in her daughter? Is his outburst motivated by concern for the future of the crown? jealousy? snobbery? To what extent does his outburst recall Leontes' sixteen years earlier? How does Perdita greet Polixenes? Does Perdita bear any physical resemblance to Hermione? Do they share character traits? If the parts are doubled, how does the actor distinguish between mother and daughter? Does Perdita reign as a reluctant or confident queen of the sheep-shearing? What leads Polixenes to say of her 'nothing she does or seems / But smacks of something greater than herself, / Too noble for this place' (4.4.157–9)? Does either staging or costume link Perdita in 4.4 with Hermione in the trial or the statue scene? What is her relationship with the Old Shepherd and the Clown (and have they aged sixteen years)? Is the actor comfortable with Perdita's poetry, especially the exchange with Polixenes? Are the passages between Perdita and Florizel played convincingly? Are Florizel and Perdita conveyed as engaging young people or as less attractive, one-dimensional characters whose social position is solely dependent on a father's wealth? How does Florizel respond to Polixenes' argument that 'a father / Is at the nuptial of his son a guest / That best becomes the table' (395–7)? How does he respond to 'Mark your divorce, young sir' (418)? How does Perdita deliver the speech beginning 'Even here, undone' (442–51) and are there echoes of Hermione's manner?

A final set of topics includes the text (what's cut, what's added or reassigned or transposed, in this, the longest scene in the play and a scene longer than any of the Sicilian acts and the second longest in Shakespeare, after the final scene in *Love's Labour's Lost*); the relationship between stage and audience, music and dance, and the length – real and apparent – of the Bohemian scenes. This final topic brings us full circle to the three critics cited above. Productions that find 'the right metaphor for communal joy'; that convey 'simple happiness'; that are 'sociologically exact' tend to set sail for Sicilia before the audience tires of Bohemia.

In Anthony Quayle's production (1948), the decor of Leontes' palace featured weapons, an unnaturally distorted tree and the supernatural (Figure 2). The drop cloth before which Manfred Priestley's Polixenes and Julian Amyes's Camillo played 4.2, a representation of Polixenes' palace, suggested the Bohemian king's fascination with the stars. On one side of the off-centre entrance a telescope, mounted on a swan-shaped cart, pointed toward the stars; the signs of the zodiac decorated the other side. (Part of the zodiac may be seen in Figure 23.)

As Figure 25 reveals, Motley's set for 4.4 draws upon realistic features from the Stratford countryside: seats hewn from Cotswold stone, on either side of the false proscenium; the Old Shepherd's rustic cottage, with a pole supporting a vine-covered shelter; distant hills. Framing the main acting space, a stylized drop cloth pictures English vegetation: forming the sylvan arch are oak, chestnut and other native leaves. Although the set bears Motley's distinctive characteristics, its shepherd's cottage and other pastoral details look back to traditional designs for Bohemia. The Bohemian costumes, like the set, contrast with those worn in Leontes' court

FIGURE 25 Motley's design for Bohemia (1948) introduces traditional costumes and the Old Shepherd's cottage. Characters, from the left, include the Old Shepherd (John Kidd), Clown (Paul Scofield), Mopsa (Jean Fox), Dorcas (Elizabeth Melville), Perdita (Claire Bloom), Florizel (John Justin), Camillo (Julian Amyes) and Polixenes (Manfred Priestley). (4.4)

(Figures 1 and 25). The design is simple; the fabrics plain. Some of the men wear smocks. The young women's dresses are unadorned except for decorative garlands and belts, and their hairstyles are simple. Some characters wear sandals and others are barefooted. Having stated some reservations about Quayle's Slavonic Sicilia, reviewers welcomed a familiar Warwickshire or Cotswold setting for Bohemia. One critic contrasts the 'deep hues and dim lights' of Sicilia with the 'pastoral gaiety' of Bohemia (*Birm. E. News*); Kemp and Trewin, 'the disruption of the turbulent court' with 'the healing breezes' in Bohemia (229). The country dancing, such as that illustrated in Figure 25, is quite different from the frenzied, barbaric dance in the first act. Quayle cut the satyrs' dance.

The acting was also well received. Claire Bloom's Perdita was praised for her 'tenderness and warmth' (*Birm. E. Desp.*), her 'wit and gaiety of spirit' (*Leam. Spa Cour.*) and her 'pliant, childlike beauty' (*Coventry Sta.*). Looking back on her debut at Stratford, Bloom, who was then seventeen, paints a different picture. She assesses her performance as 'a failure. I could discover little about her character and fell instead into reciting and posing. Everything was studied and "poetic", and I came to dread the evenings when that play was to be performed' (Bloom, 73). John Justin's Florizel conveyed a 'real charm in the naturalness and spontaneity of Florizel' (*Leam. Spa Cour.*) and a 'handsome heroic dash' (*Birm. E. News*). As had long been the tradition, modesty governed Florizel's exchange of garments with Autolycus, which took place behind one of the rocks. Alfie Bass's Autolycus was 'a gay rascal, cunning but without cynicism' (*Evesham J.*). Kemp and Trewin think he made 'the rascal obvious instead of artful' (229). He was 'rather too zealously grotesque', complains the *Manchester Guardian*.

John Kidd's Old Shepherd and Paul Scofield's Clown, 'whose rich humanity and humour' (*SA Herald*) had closed the first half of the production, were welcomed back. Most praised of all the Bohemians was Scofield's Clown, 'a deeply amusing moonstruck country lad' (*News Chron.*), who was 'vastly and rustically endearing' (*Observer*) and who possessed a 'slow-witted, good-natured rusticity' (*Coventry Sta.*). Speaking in a 'broad dialect [he was] not merely conventionally amusing but genuinely funny' (*Punch*). In his biography of the actor, Trewin recounts Scofield's playing of the Clown in 4.3, a role he had played for the Birmingham Rep:

> Scofield came – as he did at Birmingham – straight from the wattle-cotes of Arden to the Bohemian pastoral: a slow, moony, furry-vowelled boy, going to buy sugar and currants and rice and saffron for the revel, or listening, a frozen shudder, great eyes staring, hair wild, to those torments thought up by the relishing Autolycus.
>
> (Trewin, 1956, 51–2)

Dame Laura Knight's painting of Scofield as the Clown is displayed in the RSC's collection at the Swan Theatre.

Quayle's promptbook raises questions for which other production materials and reviews yield no answers. Polixenes, not Camillo, speaks the line 'I should leave grazing, were I of your flock, / And only live by gazing' (4.4.109–10). Was it spoken as a compliment with no subtext? Or did Priestley's Polixenes convey jealousy of his son's youth and his attractiveness to Perdita? Did he, as do some actors, suggest that Polixenes recognized Hermione in her daughter?

In Peter Wood's production (1960), costumes and sets also suggested Warwickshire. As Figures 25 and 26 illustrate, the costumes and wigs are similar to those Motley had designed for Quayle's production: simple, unadorned dresses, long hair worn loose or in plaits for the shepherdesses; tunics and trousers for the shepherds; some wear sandals; others go barefooted. In two ways, however, the designs were significantly different. Wood's Renaissance Sicilia, like his Cotswolds Bohemia, was familiar, not foreign, territory (see Figures 1 and 3). Jaques Noel's stylized set suggested rather than pictured the countryside (Figures 25 and 26). In 4.3 Autolycus (Jack MacGowran) entered a wide, deep stage, decorated with only a line of seven scarecrows receding to the horizon. Set on the rostrum, a horizontal grouping of seven trees, lanterns nestling in the branches, was the backdrop for 4.4. The sheep-shearing took place at twilight and in the early evening. The property list calls for a barrel, baskets of wool, a bale of hay, a small basket of loose wool and baskets of food and flowers. Autolycus carried a 'travelling shop', a frame on which he displayed his wares. The masks that he peddled to the shepherds had grotesque features ('ugly', says Speaight, *SQ*, 453) and were 'made out of leaves and other sylvan materials' (*Morn. Adv.*). One rests on the knee of a shepherd in Figure 26.

In Bohemia, as in Sicilia, the set complemented rather than competed with the actors. Although it is a posed photograph lit by the photographer, not stage lighting, Angus McBean's photograph (Figure 26) suggests how Wood employed stage pictures. The promptbook records more instances of Wood's interpolation of

FIGURE 26 In 1960 the costumes were traditional but the trees, festooned with lights, were representational. Characters include Mopsa (Gloria Dolskie, seated), Florizel (Dinsdale Landen, foot on table), Perdita (Susan Maryott), Shepherd (Clive Swift, strap across chest), Clown (Ian Holm), Dorcas (Mandy Miller), Polixenes (Patrick Allen) and Camillo (Paul Hardwick, standing right). (4.4)

action based on the script. Arrows shot from the wings prepared for the entrance of Polixenes, played by Patrick Allen, with Paul Hardwick's Camillo and three huntsmen. To offstage cries of 'stop, thief', Autolycus, whose 'traffic is sheets' (4.3.23), entered 'running with linen' and stood downstage posing as a scarecrow. Chasing him with pitchforks, Mopsa and Dorcas (Gloria Dolskie and Mandy Miller) ran on and off, upstage of him.

Wood staged the dancing as 'a full-blooded fertility rite. In place of the genteel trippings we are too often given, these barefoot peasants stamp their dances to finger-click and pipe and tambourine' (*S. Times*). Richard Findlater describes the scene as 'a decorated night-piece, with suggestions of carnival sophistication, [through which] Mr. Wood achieve[d] a certain *visual* unity'.

Although Wood avoided 'the peril of suggesting a Cecil Sharp House party', Findlater points out another problem: 'the rustic Bohemians – except for Mr. Bree and Mr. Holm – seem[ed] self-conscious among the rather confused revels' (*FT*). Later in the season, the *Stratford-upon-Avon Herald* critic, who pronounced the production the best of the season, faults the dance for falling into another trap. 'On the first night', he recalls, 'we were fascinated by the finger-snapping, the stamping, the hot-blooded dance which seemed to have its origin in Spain'. But it went on too long, and in November was 'over the edge'. The production, argues Findlater, 'recover[ed] its grip ... as soon as it plunge[d] back into semi-realistic action, when Polixenes 'turn[ed] savagely upon his son, echoing the crazed despotism of Leontes'.

Critics divided over the degree of success achieved by Wood's Bohemian scenes. There was general agreement that Bree's Old Shepherd and Holm's Clown were successful. MacGowran gave his 'immensely sly' Autolycus (*Punch*) an Irish accent and was 'rather a lonely figure ... [who] suggested an underlying melancholy unusual in this part' (*Theatre W.*). It was also unusual, noted a number of reviewers, to cast an actor without a good singing voice. In Figure 26 Susan Maryott's sour expression belies the critics who describe her Perdita as 'sunny, sensitive' (*Evesham J.*) and 'passionate' (*S. Times*). Perhaps the photograph captures the 'one statuesque pose' noticed by Jeremy Brooks (*New States. & Nat.*). Dolskie (Figure 26, seated with hat) earned praise for her Mopsa's 'tiny vignette of bashful talent' (*New States. & Nat.*).

Choosing a familiar, contemporary – and somewhat controversial – setting, Trevor Nunn (1969) presented the sheep-shearing scenes 'as a free-ranging, *Hair*-type musical'. As Nunn explains,

> without vulgarising the Perdita theme, we tried to make an entertainment within the centre of the play which would actually have the value of an awakening, to make everyone in the audience come suddenly alive. This is the allegorical meaning of the end of the play, a slow miraculous awakening inside Leontes ....
>
> (*Plays & P.*)

(It may not have been a coincidence that the cover of the programme – white with embossed lettering – bore a resemblance to the Beatles' 'White Album', released in November 1968.) Under the caption 'I with things new born', the programme carried four items and an engraving that throw light on Nunn's reading of Bohemia. E.M.W. Tillyard's praise of the scenes, the engraving and Sir Thomas Overbury's character of a milkmaid place the scene in the English countryside. Juxtaposed with these traditional views of Bohemia was Stuart Hall's definition of hippie love (1968): 'In the Hippie alphabet, Love stands for something wider and more inclusive than sex. It is a complex affirmation. It has a widening circle of resonances.' One of those resonances identifies hippie love as offering 'a sacred respect for personal relationships (in a world where personal relationships are fragile and contingent)'. The final selection, Louis MacNeice's 'Autolycus', describes the rogue as 'Hot from Eastcheap'. Nunn would seem, then, to identify Autolycus as an urban hippie (or as an urbanite disguised as a hippie) intent on conning the rural, Bohemian hippies.

The costumes – bell-bottomed trousers, skimpy skirts and short shorts, bare chests and midriffs and feet, long hair worn by men and women – contrast with those worn by the Warwickshire peasants in 1948 and 1960. The exuberance of Derek Smith's Autolycus extended to his sartorial sense: a richly coloured medley of ill-fitting and ill-matched garments such as one might select on a blitz shopping spree at Oxfam and well befitting a 'snapper-up of unconsidered trifles' (4.3.26). A fright wig completes his outfit (Figure 27). Sheepskin waistcoats hinted at the occupations of the Old Shepherd and Clown. To one critic Judi Dench's Perdita was 'a delightful, rural hippie' (*Morn. Star*); in one dance she looked 'exquisitely Botticelli-like', an image captured by Figure 28 (*SS*, 134).

Played in the three-sided white box and with 'new buds sprouting out of rotten old trunks' (*Times*, 1969) and bright sunlight to mark a shift from gloomy Sicilia to Bohemia, the Bohemian scenes appealed directly to Stratford and London

FIGURE 27 In Nunn's hippie Bohemia (1969), Autolycus (Derek Smith) dances with Mopsa (Susan Sheers) and Dorcas (Lisa Harrow). (4.4)

audiences. Reviewing the production for the *Guardian*, Gareth Lloyd Evans records that Derek Smith's Autolycus 'performs to the audience and is near the point of making us all sing with him'. Guy Woolfenden's music, available on record, had a lively, contemporary (some said 'shocking!') beat, and was 'designed to build up the pastoral scenes into something more robust' (*Times*, 1970). The Clown 'twangle[d] that fashionable fancy the jew's harp', and Autolycus gave 'a few toots on a kazoo' (*S. Times*). Autolycus' first song 'sen[t] up the more lunatic sort of pop singer' (*S. Times*). Costumed as a Green Man and wearing huge Wellington boots, Alton Kumalo, whose distinctive voice spoke Time's lines at the beginning of the production and again in 4.1, contributed a show-stopping African boot dance. The 'men of hair' (4.4.327), commented, or complained, reviewers, alluded to *Hair*, the American musical drawing crowds in London and celebrating 'flower power' and 'the age of Aquarius'. (The music

FIGURE 28 Perdita (Judi Dench) is admired by Camillo (Nicholas Selby) and Polixenes (Richard Pasco). Mopsa (Susan Sheers) and the Clown (Geoffrey Hutchings) are at the right. (4.4, 1969)

of both *Hair* and the Bohemian scenes sounds dated, even to ageing hippies.)

In many reviews of Nunn's Act 4, the focus is hippie Bohemia rather than the acting or the thematic relevance of Bohemia to Sicilia. Some critics approved of Nunn's staging: his Bohemia did all it should do (*Birm. Post*); it presented a 'vigorous and virile interpretation of pastoral innocence and fecundity' (*SA Herald*); its 'music and the dancing ... have a primitive, thumping base with chanting and body movements giving the shepherds' life a wonderfully earthy flavour' (*Birm. Sun. Mer.*). Many echoed the *Daily Telegraph*'s assessment that Bohemia was 'fun' (1969). Others found the staging disappointing, too long or inappropriate. J.W. Lambert reminds his readers that 'Morris dancing, so long mocked, was a highly sophisticated form compared with the rough and ready stomping which is all we can offer today' (*S. Times*). Those who identified hippies with urban, not rural, lifestyles, did not approve of Nunn's Bohemia. Benedict Nightingale, for example, objects on the grounds that 'hippies are essentially urban dropouts, and this is a triumphant pastoral, celebrating the integration of man (labouring man) with nature' (*New States.*); Speaight argues that 'a crowd of haggard Hippies are no substitute for the healthy sensuality of the scene' (*Tablet*). Be they rural or urban, hippies represented freedom from the restraints of society and provided, argues Nunn, an 'image of what has to be rediscovered by Leontes. He has to recover a sense of positives – a zest and belief in life' (*Plays & P.*).

Nunn's production introduced several links between Sicilia and Bohemia. The permanent set, which enclosed the free spirits, may be read as an ironic comment on, as well a visual reminder of, Sicilia. The doubling of Hermione and Perdita, for the first time since Mary Anderson's production in 1887, introduced another link. Lambert called Dench's doubling 'the thread' that held the play together (*S. Times*). Listening to the NSA recording, one is struck by an attractive similarity between mother and daughter. Hermione has a characteristic laugh; Perdita, a giggle. The chief echo of Sicilian events and the rigid restraints of convention against which the Bohemians rebelled was, however, Richard Pasco's Polixenes, who had 'shrivel[ed] sadly into brittle middle-age' (*Times*, 1969).

John Barton (1976), as had Nunn, staged the Sicilian and Bohemian scenes on a set with only minimal props to indicate a change of time and place. In 1976, tapestries and the spindly, barren tree remained; carpets covered the main playing space downstage left, behind which was the tree; bales of wool replaced the pouffes (Figure 5). 'In Bohemia', argues Roger Warren, 'the designs became schematic and constricting, instead of liberating as in the abandoned *joie-de-vivre* of the earlier [1969] version' (*SS*, 173–4). Speaight is not convinced by the setting:

> the shearing of sheep was implausible in a landscape where no sheep could have pastured, and the flowers 'from the waggon'

FIGURE 29 Cherie Lunghi's Perdita welcomes Camillo (Bob Peck, kneeling) and Polixenes (John Woodvine). The Old Shepherd (David Waller, standing centre) and Clown (Roger Rees, kneeling, to his left), Florizel (Nickolas Grace, downstage of Perdita), shepherds and shepherdesses, watch. (4.4, 1976)

would hardly have bloomed, at any season of the year, where no vestige of a leaf was seen to burgeon on a single tree.   (*SQ*, 188)

François Laroque, on the other hand, finds that the setting 'laid stress on the play's symbolism and deliberately laid aside all realistic approaches.... The last part of the play [from 4.4 was] synonymous with a general thawing of the ice and the return of spring' (*Cahiers Elis.*, 91).

The change of season allowed characters to shed outer layers of costumes, essential in Leontes' cold court, but the costumes retained basic features of the Sicilian ones: warm colours, Scandinavian designs and fabrics (Figure 29). Unlike her post-war Stratford predecessors, Cherie Lunghi's Perdita was 'Most goddess-like pranked up'. Warren likens her to a 'Byzantine icon' (*SS*, 174).

Photographed greeting John Woodvine's Polixenes and Bob Peck's Camillo, Perdita wears what the property list describes as a gold and white silk gown, a gold diadem, a gold collar. Barely visible in the photograph, the collar seems to have been created from layers and layers of gold coins. Was it formed from the gold left with the infant Perdita, or was it a collar belonging to Hermione? The promptbook calls for Polixenes, after removing his disguise, to rip off the necklace and throw it down.

The shepherds' dance took place around the barren tree and the dancers may have carried bells on sticks and worn bells on their wrists and ankles. The property list also calls for two drums and two pieces of wood for percussion. The 'men of hair' wore furry headdresses and fur on their lower legs. Laroque describes the dance as 'a sort of sword-dance accompanied by a mock fight between two "wild-men"' (*Cahiers Elis.*, 92). A cue in the promptbook directs the group to 'pounce' at the close of the dance on the actor representing a bear. A photograph records that the Clown harpooned the bear. The ram's head, worn by another dancer, may be a visual allusion to the ivory tusk that held Apollo's oracle.

As seems so often to be the case with Autolycus, reviewers were either charmed or unamused by his wit, songs and disguises. Warren, for example, thought that Michael Williams 'worked so hard that the effort showed' (*SS*, 174). Hobson, however, enjoyed his 'overflowing mischievousness' and concluded that Williams 'must be the best Autolycus we have ever seen. Gaiety bubbles out of him, it is not imposed from the outside' (*S. Times*). Autolycus introduced his wares 'like glove puppets through a curtain before emerging as a trinket-laden Father Christmas' (*SS*, 174).

Michael Billington points out three ways in which Barton 'stress[ed] the play's underlying unity': the 'hieroglyphics and symbols' in both societies; 'the parallel tyranny of Leontes and the intemperate Polixenes'; 'a dreamlike element about both the accusations of adultery against Hermione and her daughter's love for a king's son'. He continues, 'but in forging a link between the two halves of the play, Barton underestimates the change of tone and mood imposed by the 16-year time-gap' (*Guardian*). The two halves were also linked by props, such as Camillo's cymbalum, which fascinated Mamillius in 1.2 and Perdita in 4.4, and the two celebrations – Jul and the sheep-shearing – and the roles Hermione and Perdita played in the celebrations. Placing the statue on the same side of the stage where Perdita had welcomed Polixenes and Camillo and where Autolycus had played puppeteer suggested a link between 4.4 and 5.3.

To bring the Bohemian scenes alive in what Billington describes as a 'gigantic cabinet' – a set less flexible than the white box in 1969 or the mock Elizabethan/Scandinavian design in 1976 – was the challenge Ronald Eyre and his company faced in 1981. For Billington (*Guardian*) and Stephen Wall (*TLS*) the set did not work. Warren, however, disagrees and finds a similarity between the sheep-shearing and

> the harvest supper in *Far from the Madding Crowd*. Surprisingly, this actually worked better than the customary outdoor setting, the forestage defining and holding together a scene which tends to sprawl, especially the very tricky final sequence where Camillo supervises the flight to Sicilia. (*SS*, 147–8)

Reviews and production archives suggest that Eyre sought to convey a village atmosphere. The promptbook refers to 'villagers', not shepherds and shepherdesses, and the *Oxford Mail* places it as an 'Edwardian country village'. In business reminiscent of Wood's production (1960), a gunshot preceded the entrance of Autolycus (Geoffrey Hutchings), chased by villagers; he escaped by posing as a scarecrow. Villagers decorating the hall announced the transition to 4.4. They formed an arch with poles, strung pennants from the arch, placed bales as seats, and, their chores completed, posed for a group photograph. Instead of mute lords sitting on the benches or standing along the edges of the 'hotplate', as had been the case in Sicilia, musicians and villagers not directly involved in the main action participated in the celebration. Gemma Jones records her disappointment that the orange-seller she had looked forward to impersonating was cut from 4.4 (Jones, 155, 162).

Hutchings's Autolycus and Stephen Oliver's music contributed significantly to the festive atmosphere of the scene. Autolycus was, observes John Elsom, 'a wide-boy', 'a cockney con-man', 'a conjurer' (*Listener*). Oliver's music was pastiche Gilbert and Sullivan ('Get you hence') and music hall, anachronistically reminiscent of Flanagan and Allen ('Sweet of the year'). Autolycus, with Dorcas and Mopsa (Clare Travers-Deacon and Diana Hardcastle), sang from a Victorian music sheet entitled 'White Slave'. The promptbook cues a waltz. A trouserless villager joined the four satyrs in their dance. After Polixenes unmasked himself, the villagers took down the decorations and the arch became 'a symbolic gibbet' (*FT*). This Hardyesque symbol linked the darker side of Sicilia and Bohemia, of Hermione's fate and Polixenes' threatening Perdita with 'a death as cruel for thee / As thou art tender to 't' (4.4.441–2). Spirited like her mother, Perdita said, not only 'plainly', but also firmly, 'The selfsame sun that shines upon his court / Hides not his visage from our cottage, but / Looks on alike' (445–7). A more fruitful set of images linked Hermione and Perdita and anticipated the final scene. In the masque preceding 1.1, Hermione carried a sheaf of wheat and wore a crown laced with flowers and a white gown patterned with red flowers and leaves (Figures 6 and 12). Perdita's costume for the sheep-shearing was so similar that it seemed at first glance to be a copy. She wore a similar crown and carried a sheaf of wheat. In 5.3 the curtain shielding the statue would be another variation of the pattern on Hermione's costume.

In contrast with the eight Stratford productions, Noble's 1984 promenade production was played on a set and in spaces conducive to successfully involving the audience in the Bohemian scenes and, especially, the sheep-shearing. Having placed the Sicilian scenes in 1950s Italy, Noble staged the sheep-shearing as a village fête. Photographs record that John Dougall's Prince Florizel affected the casual dress favoured by undergraduates in the late

1950s and early 1960s: a checked shirt, a jumper tied loosely about his shoulders, and khaki trousers. Perdita, played by Jenifer Landor, wore a peasant blouse and a lacy apron over a gathered skirt. The carefully defined villagers anticipated Noble's 1992 production. Margery Mason, a sorrowing, anxious Emilia, appeared as a lewd, cackling village woman. Putting aside Paulina's costume – and character traits – Janet Dale disguised herself as a pig woman in a pink sweater grubby with pig muck, a skirt and headscarf. The props list, which calls for balloons, party poppers, blow-outs, bubble blowers, garlands and lights to string on poles, hints at the festive mood. Actors moved freely among the audience and distributed bread and wine (alas, it was Ribena) to the audience, some of whom sat at tables placed along parallel sides of the rectangular space. When he needed a bolt hole, Ron Cook's Autolycus hid among the spectators. Entering on stilts, Ian Talbot's 'sympathetic, rosy-cheeked Young Shepherd ... threatened at any moment to tip over on to Autolycus and audience alike' (*Cahiers Elis.*, 86). In Sicilia the rostra at either end of the rectangular playing space had been used to separate or contrast groups of characters. In Bohemia, with the band at one end and some of the entertainment at the other, they tended to extend the festivities the length of the playing space. Autolycus lured Dorcas and Mopsa (Caroline Milmoe and Julia Dearden) on stage to sing 'Whither, oh whither'; surrounded by villagers and the audience, Florizel and Perdita watched from a bench placed in the centre of the carpeted rectangle (Figure 30). In addition to Autolycus' songs, set to lively music, his magic tricks, his wares displayed in numerous pockets inside a capacious overcoat, and the satyrs' spectacularly rude country dance (Alun Armstrong, briefly interrupting Leontes' penitence, joined the dance), the entertainment included a congo line of girls led by the Clown, inserted to provide time for four actors to do a quick change from shepherds to furry satyrs.

By drawing the audience into the fête, Noble heightened the effect of Polixenes' rage at Florizel and Perdita, which, points out Martin Hoyle in the *Financial Times*, revealed 'an emotional

FIGURE 30 At the village fête, Perdita (Jenifer Landor), Florizel (John Dougal) and members of the audience enjoy a trio sung by Autolycus, Mopsa and Dorcas. (4.4, 1984)

weakness that counters Leontes' ... and adds to what too often seems mere unlikeable snobbery'. Describing a performance at Barrow-in-Furness Michael Ratcliffe praises the Bohemian scenes for

> sustaining a bucolic energy, spirit and charm that do not falter until Polixenes breaks them, punching his son to the floor, kissing Perdita ... on the mouth and hurling the shepherds' table to the ground. There were gasps of horror from members of the audience to my right .... Perdita's cry of pain, 'even here, undone!' [4.4.442], carries an unwontedly woeful force. (*Observer*, Oct)

The upturned table, according to the promptbook, rested on its side until toward the close of the scene, some eighty-nine lines later in Noble's promptbook. Camillo and Perdita turned it upright while Florizel and Autolycus exchanged garments (*c.* 644), an exchange, one may infer from the photographs and promptbook, which was played for humour: Florizel put Autolycus' trousers on after they did the 'taking off the undies' gag.

Adverse criticism of the Bohemian scenes, as of the Sicilian scenes, focused primarily on the discomforts of promenading. Robert Hewison, who saw the show at the Poole Arts Centre, writes:

> There has to be some compensation for sometimes not being able to see, not being able to hear, and being uncomfortable for most of the time. There has to be a different kind of magic .... Ideally, the audience should become part of the action.   (*S. Times*)

In the Bohemian scenes the magic worked for him: 'The playing area became a village square, and like tourists seated at café tables we watched stout peasant dancing, with food and wine served by the cast' (*S. Times*). Robin Thornber, who charted the stages of the actor–audience relationship at the Doncaster Road Baths in Scunthorpe, notes that

> the blurred boundary between performance and spectators did enhance the impact of the playing and after the interval, when the action explodes into the rustic jollity of the Bohemian sheep shearing festivities, the party spirit pulled us in, involving the audience more intimately.... This is just the sort of show – where you share bread and wine with the shepherds – to tour to places starved of live theatre, turning on an audience by bringing Shakespeare home and bringing him alive in every sense. (*Guardian*)

Promenading 'probably also recalled theatre-going in Shakespeare's day, which cannot have been comfortable either' (*Cahiers Elis.*, 87). Michael Ratcliffe, who saw the production on tour and during its London fortnight, observes wryly that 'the bucolic scenes work a little less well with the shy London folk than they did in Furness' (*Observer*, 16 Dec).

In 1984 critics did not ponder over the geographical location of Noble's village fête. Two years later, the design and music of Terry Hands's production suggested an eclectic mixture of locations, none of which was Bohemia or a familiar Warwickshire. Richard

Edmonds placed the costumes in the nineteenth century and the dance in the twentieth, where 'the actors jig about to a rock band and occasionally break into a tango wearing Hawaiian leis' (*Birm. E. Mail*). Nicholas Shrimpton identified the costumes as 'hover[ing] indecisively between Jacobean sheep-shearing and a Hawaiian beach party' (*SS*, 178). Still a third, Ann FitzGerald, observed 'Turkish bloomers and turbans' (*Stage & TV*). Nicholas de Jongh found the costumes 'far from the Regency' and saw in them 'shades of Tahiti'; he heard a 'heavily mythical Mummerset accent' from Penny Downie's Perdita (*Guardian*). Others were reminded of a 'South Seas disco' (*Bristol E. Post*), 'Club-Mediterranean' (*Cahiers Elis.*, 94) and 'Asia Minor' (*FT*). The exact location could not be pinned down, and the eclecticism did not seem to be making a point. But there was agreement that the colourful costumes – russets, reds, golds – gave to the Bohemian scenes a festive warmth missing from the formal white Regency dress in Leontes' snowy Sicilia.

More easily placed, the music was 'thoroughly modern' (*Guardian*) and, argues John Pitcher, bore a resemblance to contemporary musicals:

> the rustic songs and games . . . are delivered by athletic young people as if they were in an episode from *Fame*, or in an inert bit from a Lloyd Webber musical. Even the normally splendid Joe Melia is drawn into an underpowered version of Autolycus, which begins a shade too close to Joel Grey's Emcee in *Cabaret*.   (*TLS*)

The scores call for 'When daffodils' and 'Jog on' to have a 'steady ragtime' beat, for the alto sax in 'Come buy' to be 'dirty and cheeky', and for 'Whither' to be a 'dramatic tango'. The video and photograph collection record a Hawaiian look for 'Whither'; Melia presented 'When daffodils' as a music-hall entertainer and closed 4.4 with a patter version of 'Jog on'.

The set retained several of the dominant features of Sicilia: the mirrors, the revolving disc, and in 4.2 and 4.3, snowfall upstage. Visually 4.2 looked back to Sicilia: although Polixenes and

Camillo had aged, they wore the same white Regency costumes of sixteen years earlier; they played the scene before mirrors reflecting themselves as well as sheet-shrouded objects and the first rows of the stalls. Snow fell upstage of them and of Autolycus, who entered wearing a long white bearskin coat and a bear's head. Having frightened some shepherds with his disguise, he placed the bear's head downstage centre, where it remained, a potent symbol. The shift from winter to spring was accomplished when Autolycus stole the sheets from the shrouded objects, which were revealed to be three sloping green mounds; the snow ceased; silvery green tree trunks were flown in. It may have been a sheep-shearing festival, but a bearskin rug, not a sheepskin, was provided for Perdita and Florizel.

Nathaniel Parker's Florizel was 'very sensitive' (*Birm. E. Mail*), 'gentle' (*Glasgow Her.*), 'positive and stylish' (*FT*), and, adds the *Stage and Television Today*, with Autolycus 'one of the few really secure performances'. Downie's Perdita had a 'wise innocence' (contrasted with her Hermione's 'innocent maturity') (*S. Times*), was 'sweet but unsickly, spirited and fresh' (*FT*). She was not, laments the *Yorkshire Post*, 'an image of nature's bounty', nor did she 'touch the heart', as either Perdita or Hermione (*D. Telegraph*). She was 'as skittish as her mother but, surprisingly, deeply admired for it by a handsome, serious and sincere Florizel' (*Stage & TV*). Photographs suggest that she also had her mother's stylish dress sense. Other photographs hint at a forwardness shared with Hermione. When Autolycus and Florizel exchanged costumes, she helped the prince by pulling his trousers down.

Photographs and the videotape record Polixenes' warm greeting of Perdita. He 'fancie[d]' Perdita (*Wantage Gro. Her.*) and gave 'a look of cold fury when he sees himself supplanted by his son' (*Time Out*). Or perhaps he recognized Hermione in her daughter. In conversation with me, Paul Greenwood recalled thinking 'it's her'. Some critics read the denunciation not as jealousy but as snobbery directed at 'Perdita, the humble shepherdess, for aspiring to marry a prince' (*SA Herald*).

Playing his first season with the RSC, Simon Russell Beale, a 'splendid' young shepherd, seemed 'to have cornered the market in grinning simpletons' (*S. Today*). Melia's Autolycus garnered praise for introducing 'much needed vibrancy to the production' (*SA Herald*) and for his 'lovable roguishness' (*S. Today*). His skills included dancing and singing 'with all the cheery exuberance of an Edwardian Music Hall comedian' (*S. Telegraph*), performing a puppet show of the prodigal son (4.3.93–4), and playing a Turkish peddlar, who entered 'astride a stuffed white angora goat on wheels' (*FT*; Figure 31). Melia's Autolycus was 'one great clown played by another' (*Times*).

The thematic unity of Hands's production was firmly centred on technical devices: colour (such as the whiteness of 4.2); props (the bear, snow); design (the mirrors, the revolving disc); music (the treble voice and celeste). As Pitcher points out, the treble voice, established 'as the signature for loss in Sicily', recurred at significant moments in the sheep-shearing (*TLS*). On the video recording, one hears the treble voice when Polixenes first sees Perdita and when Florizel and Perdita dance; the celeste is played when Polixenes denounces Perdita and does not cease until she says 'Even here, undone' (4.4.442). The treble voice accompanies Camillo's plan for the voyage to Sicilia and his anticipation of Leontes' reception of Florizel and Perdita. In both Sicilia and Bohemia lights and reflection, as well as music, underscored the emotional content. In Bohemia, lights came up for a lively dance, went down for a slow one, and came back up for another lively one. They went down again when Polixenes asks 'Pray, good shepherd, what fair swain is this / Which dances with your daughter?' (168–9). The dancing couple, like the flirtatious couple in the first act, was reflected in the mirror. 'While technically flawless', write Jean Fuzier and Jean-Marie Maguin, 'the style of the event remains irreconcilable with the issues of the play' (*Cahiers Elis.*, 94). Pitcher laments the lack of 'any poetic continuity with [Hands's] version of Sicily' (*TLS*).

In 1984 residents of towns and villages visited by Noble's touring production had helped the cast to establish a sense of

FIGURE 31 Wearing a Turkish costume, Joe Melia's Autolycus makes a show-stopping entrance on a white angora goat. (4.4, 1986)

community for the sheep-shearing. Sitting at tables alongside the acting space, they sipped wine, nibbled bread and applauded the songs and dances. The staging was such that the members of the audience seemed a natural extension of the actors who watched, for example, Dorcas, Mopsa and Autolycus sing 'Get you hence' (4.4.298). For his 1992 main-house production, actively involving the audience was not an option. 'I knew', writes Noble, 'I had to create a real, recognizable community, and drew inspiration from the work of Stanley Spencer, who painted sacred subjects in the context of a small English village between the wars' (Noble, xv). A photograph of Noble's creation (Figure 32) captures the villagers and illustrates many of the details recorded by reviewers. 'There was', writes Peter Holland, 'in this very English, Edwardian village fete something comfortably and nostalgically recognizable, a myth of England past, jellies and trifles, small boys in short-trousered suits and the town band' (*SS*, 173). In a densely

FIGURE 32 Bohemia (1992) evoked a village fête between the wars. Here a villager (John Hodgkinson) blows a bubble while his neighbours dance and chat. Mopsa (Stephanie Jacob) and the Clown (Graham Turner) dance (at the left side); next to them a villager (Roger Frost) dances with Dorcas (Jenna Russell); Perdita (Phyllida Hancock), wearing a crown of flowers, is in the centre at the back; the Old Shepherd (Jeffery Dench) sits upstage; other villagers (Ian Taylor and Angela Vale) dance, at the right. (4.4)

packed piece of descriptive writing, Robert Smallwood introduces the set, music, dance, costume and several characters:

> There was a touch of Stanley Spencer's Cookham about it, with painted kitchen chairs in ill-assorted colors, trestle tables, bunting, balloons ... and a chirpily self-confident oompah-pah band (the vicar on drums) playing foxtrots and quick-steps for the villagers, who wore Fair Isle pullovers, linen dresses (Perdita's with a pattern of ripe cherries), and tweed jackets, and the disguised Polixenes and Camillo, wandering in as if from an Alpine holiday, looked faintly like an illustration from *Heidi*. (SQ, 350)

'The vicar on drums' points to a major strength of Noble's Bohemia: the recognizable yet individualized characters and actions. A very uptight man and his son danced awkwardly; a plain woman hit Autolycus with her handbag when he approached her daughter; a villager photographed Perdita and Florizel dancing. The Old Shepherd sat with a child on his lap, his feet tapping time to the music. 'There was the same Spencerian pleasure in the diversity and eccentricity of human shapes and faces', observes Rebecca Flynn (*Cahiers Elis.*, 89). Holland, who had 'never seen it done better', credits its success to 'the familiarity and fine detail of the characters at the feast' and to Richard McCabe's Autolycus (*SS*, 173).

Legendary moments in theatrical annals tend to be serious ones, such as Garrick's Richard III on the eve of battle, Macready's Leontes when the statue moves and Olivier's Coriolanus falling to his death. A list of lighter moments must include the entrance of Richard McCabe's Autolycus, captured mid-air in Donald Cooper's photograph on the cover of this book. Smallwood describes it as

> something of a coup de théâtre. Against a glorious blue-sky cyclorama, dangling from the end of a huge parachute made of enormous green balloons – like some gigantic bunch of grapes – Richard McCabe's astonishing Autolycus floated down in a battered straw hat and huge-pocketed overcoat, singing with massive enthusiasm and only moderate tunefulness.   (*SQ*, 350)

Writing about his role, McCabe makes the point that Noble wanted Sicilia and Bohemia to 'be as different as possible, as if moving from darkness into light'. Autolycus' entrance was

> a bold gesture that told the audience we were now entering a different world.... I remember that when the screen lifted to reveal a sky-blue cyclorama and brightly coloured balloon tree, the feeling of release in the audience was almost palpable.   (McCabe, 63)

In his essay McCabe explains the sources for some of the decisions he took and explores Autolycus' function. A television programme on overreachers in the City inspired the explanation for his being 'out of service' (4.3.14): the banner headline in the *Bohemian Gazette*, which he produced on cue, read 'Servant

Guilty', the implication being that there had been financial irregularities. 'An ugly purple bruise' on his neck made painfully clear why he feared 'beating and hanging' (29). McCabe discusses also how he and Graham Turner, who played the Young Shepherd, devised the gulling of this character, and how entering the sheep-shearing, when 'the party [was] in full swing', he approached and manipulated the villagers. McCabe defines Autolycus' function:

> By excusing his sins we are more able to pardon the repentant Leontes, and accept the enchantment of the final scene. He acts as a bridge. Without Autolycus there could be no 'happy' ending. He allows us to forgive and move on and, as such, is central to the heart of the play. (70)

McCabe's Autolycus earned high praise: he was the best Peter Porter had seen (*TLS*), a 'dynamic, razor-sharp con-man' (*Tribune*) and the 'star turn of the liveliest Bohemian party I can remember' (*Indep. Sun.*).

The 'star turn' attracted more press than others in Bohemia, but there were brief notices for the 'lovely performances ... from Jeffery Dench as the kind old shepherd and Graham Turner as his delightfully dim son' (*D. Telegraph*) and for 'particularly fine performances' from Jenna Russell as Dorcas and Stephanie Jacob as Mopsa (*Tribune*). Benjamin Whitrow's Camillo 'movingly captures the passage of time' (*D. Telegraph*). 'Alan Cox's eager, touchingly ardent Florizel ... spoke his love to Phyllida Hancock's warmly sensual Perdita for all the village to hear – which they did, with affection and applause' (*SQ*, 350–1). Hancock's Perdita had an 'unaffected charm' (*Plays & P.*). Perdita exuded a 'warm sexuality' (*D. Telegraph*) but turned modestly aside when Florizel and Autolycus exchanged costumes.

Unlike some of his predecessors, Noble wanted to avoid 'a stylistic connection between Sicilia and Bohemia to make the play a unified whole' (McCabe, 63). There were, however, echoes of Sicilia in Bohemia. Michael Coveney notices Perdita's 'uncomplicated instinct for hospitality', a trait, he might have added, she shared with her mother (*Observer*). Listeners to the audiotape may be struck by two occurrences of a waltz: in 1.2 when Hermione urges Polixenes to stay, and in 4.4 when Perdita and Florizel dance. Just as Perdita echoed her mother's warmth so Polixenes' pushing Florizel to the ground recalled Leontes' shoving Hermione. Leontes' jealousy had broken up the party his son enjoyed; Polixenes' anger broke up Perdita's reign as queen of the sheep-shearing. A fierce storm, like the one at the close of the trial, sent the Bohemians scurrying to clear up before too much damage was inflicted on musical instruments, food and furniture.

In 1992 'the play's shift from emotional winter to spiritual spring [was] moving as well as fun' (*Times*) and introduced 'fresh comic pleasure. It is never a lumpen, mirthless comedy of rural folk. Noble avoids the usual emphasis on the glories of rural spring and sap rising in young lovers' (*E. Standard*). He achieved his goal of distinguishing sharply between the darkness of Sicilia and the light of Bohemia. But he also, without being heavy-handed, introduced visual and aural details that gave a unity.

In Act 1 of Gregory Doran's production (1999) Antony Sher's Leontes had attended to the business of state: taking a bow with the royal guest and Hermione and diligently perusing documents at his desk while his queen entertained his childhood friend. Sixteen years later, another monarch tended to recreational pursuits: Polixenes, played by Ken Bones, carefully examined a row of plants before asking Geoffrey Freshwater's Camillo about the royal offspring.

Instead of celebrating in a communal space or before the Old Shepherd's cottage, as have so many other shepherds and shepherdesses, Doran's Bohemians gathered in 'a wool warehouse' (*SS*, 265) or 'a sort of fleece-baling factory, complete with pulleys and iron wheels' (*Times*). The acting space was wider and deeper than it had been in Leontes' constricting Sicilia, but the stacked bales of wool, the machinery and the interior setting hinted at the product and its market, not at shepherds and shepherdesses tending their flocks under sunny skies. 'Robust as it is', observes the *Stage*, 'this is also very much a workaday, slightly charmless sheep-shearing, all Victorian sideburns and lashed with libidinous rustic simplicity'. From time to time reviewers have credited the Old Shepherd with funding the feast from Perdita's inheritance, but the set suggested to some critics that her wealth had underwritten her foster father's business ventures and the sheep-shearing was 'a celebration financed by a *nouveau-riche* shepherd' (*Times*).

The billowing cloth, which had served as a ceiling in Leontes' palace, Bohemian mountains, storm clouds and the bear, played a lighter role in Bohemia. Draped across the floor midstage, it hid Autolycus (Ian Hughes) the sheet-stealer, who emerged singing. As he sang, from beneath it appeared, one by one, several of his doxies. Disguised as a Church of England vicar, Autolycus met Christopher Brand's Young Shepherd, a 'charming dunderhead' (*New States.*), for

> a scene of pure physical theatre. In a series of deftly executed moves
> – between actors who seemed to have a height differential of at least
> two feet – the Young Shepherd is unwittingly divested of not just his
> wallet but his entire outfit.   (*Indep. Sun.*)

'An admirably versatile Autolycus', Hughes appeared next as a 'Jewish pedlar with his ballads as old 78 gramophone records' and then as a 'Lytton Strachey look-alike for the scene with the departing Shepherd and his son' (*SS*, 265). Hughes was 'a nimble, slightly saturnine Autolycus' (*S. Times*). He sang 'Jog on' in falsetto and 'Will you buy' and the scene-closing reprise of 'Jog on' in a plaintive tone.

Emily Bruni doubled the wheelchair-bound Mamillius with a hoydenish Perdita, who, some reviewers remarked, belied the compliments given her by the revellers and their guests. At a preview, 'her voice and all her gestures, especially her habit of wiping her nose on the back of her hand, suggest a peasant girl like all of the others' (*S. Times*). She was 'too awkward (proclaiming her lines with bawdy knowingness) and exuberant' (*TLS*). Ryan McCluskey's 'beautifully played' (*Birm. Post*) Florizel was 'fittingly passionate and sensitive' (*Stage*).

Polixenes' interest in horticulture having been established, Bones's king was better equipped than most Bohemian royalty to appreciate Perdita's knowledge of flowers. He 'engage[d] in discussion with Emily Bruni's hoydenish Perdita with all the enthusiasm of an anorak' (*Time Out*). Continuing the theme, the *Spectator* notes that he may have been an 'expert in the cross-pollination of orchids but erupt[ed] as dangerously as Leontes at the prospect of this human coupling' (Figure 33). Polixenes' 'splendid fit of temper ... produc[ed] respondent violence from Florizel in protection of Perdita' (*SS*, 265). Despite the doubling of Mamillius and Perdita, the parallel drawn between the outbursts of Leontes' jealousy and Polixenes' anger and the redefinition of the billowing cloth, Doran did not relate Bohemia thematically to Sicilia. The Bohemian scenes, 'performed like an old-fashioned opera, with young men in big boots and jerkins and semi-circles of giggling peasant girls' (*Observer*), contrasted with Leontes' grey Sicilia but did not shed light on it.

The Bohemia that best achieved the three traits – 'the right metaphor for communal joy', 'simple happiness' and natural, realistic peasants – with which this chapter began was Adrian Noble's in 1992. The 1950s village fête in the touring production in 1984, upon which Noble's main-house version drew, and Nunn's contemporary Bohemia in 1969 both very successfully involved their audiences. Nunn's hippie Bohemia, illustrated in Figures 27 and 28, may not have pleased all the critics, but by freeing Stratford productions from a traditional Cotswold countryside (Figures 25 and 26), it encouraged directors to seek new settings, such as those in Figures 29 and 32. In most of these new locations, directors introduced some link with the Sicilia Polixenes had visited sixteen years earlier. The text itself makes one link explicit: Polixenes' temper – captured in Figure 33 – like Leontes' jealousy, impels others, as well as himself, on journeys. Camillo, who had enabled Polixenes to escape Leontes' wrath, arranges now for Florizel to flee his father's anger and sets in motion events

FIGURE 33 Polixenes (Ken Bones) reminds Florizel (Ryan McCluskey) of the duties a son owes his father. (4.4, 1999)

that will lead to the fulfilment of the oracle's prophecy. In the next act, Leontes, who had branded his baby daughter 'bastard' (seven times) and 'brat' (twice) and demanded of his lords 'Shall I live on to see this bastard kneel / And call me father?' (2.3.154–5) will welcome Florizel's 'Libyan' wife as 'fair princess, – goddess!' (5.1.130).

5

'SUCH A DEAL
OF WONDER'

When we last saw Leontes, at the close of the trial scene (3.2), he vowed a daily visit to the chapel where Hermione and Mamillius lay dead and enjoined Paulina to 'lead me / To these sorrows'. Sixteen years later, at the beginning of Act 5, a courtier urges the penitent king, who has 'done enough' and has 'perform'd / A saint-like sorrow' (1–2), to turn his thoughts to the future by remarrying and fathering an heir to secure the kingdom. Throughout Act 5, and most especially in the first scene, past sorrows intrude upon the present: the deaths of Hermione, 'the sweet'st companion' (11); of Mamillius, the 'Jewel of children' (116); of Perdita, the 'lost child' (40); and of Paulina's Antigonus. Once again opposing the courtiers, Paulina places faith in another past event: the oracle's prophecy that the lost child will be found. Because Shakespeare has already let the audience in on the fulfilment of this prophecy, those who are seeing or reading the play for the first time will endorse her faith in Apollo. But Paulina has reserved the greatest wonder, withholding it until fifty-two lines before the play ends.

This chapter, like its predecessors, first considers some of the overarching topics addressed by directors, actors and the production team; second, it introduces questions pertinent to each of the three scenes; lastly it examines some of the decisions taken by the nine post-war productions at Stratford.

At the beginning of Act 4, Time eased our passage forward sixteen years to Bohemia, seen only briefly before as a storm-ridden sea-coast where two compassionate shepherds had found the abandoned Perdita. In the first scene of Act 5, the many references to the past may be read as embedded cues to directors and designers charged with staging the return to Sicilia. As in Act 1, the presentations of Sicilia the kingdom and Sicilia the monarch are central. How does design, for example, signal the changes in the kingdom? If the production has introduced symbolic objects, such as Mamillius' toys or the bear's head, are they still present? Does interpolated stage business link Sicilia then and now? What does a comparison of one's first impression of Sicilia with the impression at the beginning of Act 5 reveal? How do the dominant characteristics of Sicilia compare or contrast with the earlier Sicilian scenes? How, if at all, do costume, make-up and props age the characters? Do set, costume, music, or sound effects introduce a real or implied connection with Bohemia? What physical signs reveal the effect of sixteen years' penance on Leontes? Do these physical signs alter during the act? How important are the symbols of monarchy or protocol? What other props are associated with Leontes? How do earlier impressions of Leontes – as host, jealous husband, prosecuting monarch – contrast with the penitent Leontes?

The fifth act offers the opportunity to review not only Leontes but also Paulina. What are the dominant traits of her personality and her relationship with Leontes? How does the Paulina of 5.1 and 5.3 compare or contrast with the woman who visited the prison, implored Leontes to accept his infant daughter and announced Hermione's death? How has she aged? What are the stages in the triangular relationship of Leontes, lords, and Paulina?

Another general topic focuses on the familiar subject of the larger stage picture. Are the scenes played as private or public scenes? That is, how many characters other than those required by the speech prefixes does the director introduce and what is their function? Does the director seem to be drawing parallels between any of these three scenes and earlier ones? Are, for example, both the trial and statue scenes played with extras in attendance or with similar blocking for the prisoner's dock and the statue? What is the dominant tone of each scene and how is it achieved? What do music, sound effects and lighting contribute? A final general topic returns to the playing script. Has the script been reshaped? Have characters been added, deleted, combined? Has the timing of entrances been altered? What kinds of cuts does the director introduce and what are the effects on character, pace of production, resolution, nature of the reconciliations?

5.1

Welcome hither,
As is the spring to th' earth

Questions pertinent to 5.1 centre on Leontes. What does the blocking reveal about the relationship between Leontes and Paulina, Leontes and the lords, Paulina and the lords? Is the entrance of Florizel and Perdita staged to delay the moment when Leontes sees Perdita? What effect does the arrival of Perdita have on Leontes? Does either Leontes or Paulina see a resemblance between Perdita and Hermione? Has Perdita been costumed to resemble a Libyan princess ('She came from Libya', 156) or Hermione? Are there any similarities between Leontes' reception of Perdita and Polixenes' meeting her in 4.4? How does Leontes say 'Would he do so, I'd beg your precious mistress, / Which he counts but a trifle' (222–3)? Does anything other than Leontes' words prompt Paulina's 'Sir, my liege, / Your eye hath too much youth in 't' (223–4)?

When the curtain rose on the final act of Anthony Quayle's production (1948), Esmond Knight's Leontes was kneeling downstage centre, attended by five lords and Paulina, played by Ena Burrill. He remained kneeling until Paulina and a lord helped him up, just before the entrance of Florizel and Perdita (122). His penitent posture introduced a religious tone, which was a motif of Quayle's Act 5. The *Observer* contrasts Sicilia with sixteen years earlier:

> When we return to a Sicilia lapped now in charity and the quiet airs of reconciliation, the Leontes of Esmond Knight finds in autumnal repentance a command missed in the toils of jealousy's yellow fever; and Ena Burrill's Paulina retains the clear constancy that has marked it from the first.

The *Warwick Advertiser* describes Knight's Leontes as more 'convincing', more 'moving'; in the fifth act 'the gentle hand of time and grief had done their soothing work'.

Quayle's playing script, especially in 5.1, moved quickly toward the statue scene. Quayle cut approximately two thirds of 5.1, reducing it to the minimum essential to convey the plot. His cuts and a reordering of lines altered the characters, especially of Leontes and Paulina. A brief conversation between a character identified in the promptbook as Lord A, who spoke Cleomenes' and Dion's lines, and Paulina about Leontes' remarriage (1–6, 24–6, 35) opened the scene. Although the disagreement reveals Paulina's power and makes Leontes a silent witness to a conversation about himself, the cuts, as they had in 3.2, softened Paulina. Burrill's Paulina did not remind Leontes that he had 'kill'd' Hermione (15), a reminder that in Shakespeare's script looks back to her long speeches in 3.2 (175–202, 203–14, 218–32) and provokes remorse from Leontes:

> I think so. Kill'd!
> She I kill'd! I did so:
>
> (16–17)

and also Leontes' rebuke of Paulina:

> but thou strik'st me
> Sorely, to say I did: it is as bitter
> Upon thy tongue as in my thought. Now, good now,
> Say so but seldom.
>
> (17–20)

Silent for the first sixteen lines of the scene, Leontes enters the dialogue with a stunning metaphor of eight monosyllables. He describes Hermione: 'Stars, stars, / And all eyes else, dead coals!' (67–8). In this second section of the scene (67–75, 81–4), he promises not to remarry without Paulina's consent. Then Paulina reminds Leontes and the lords about Apollo's prophecy (35–40). In addition to reinforcing Paulina's power over Leontes – he accedes to her wish before she reminds him of Apollo – this reordering of lines set the stage for the announcement of the arrival of Florizel 'with his princess' (86), who will fulfil the prophecy. Heavy cuts in the next section – only nine of thirty-three lines remain – include Paulina's apostrophe to Hermione (95–103) and a reminder, not welcomed by Leontes, that 'Had our prince / (Jewel of children) seen this hour, he had pair'd / Well with this lord' (115–17). The final phase of the scene cut directly from Leontes' greeting of Florizel and Perdita (123–37) to the announcement that Polixenes has arrived (180). The scene moved swiftly to its close, sacrificing the references to the Old Shepherd and the Clown (189–92; 197–201), Perdita's lament 'O my poor father!' (201) and the exchange between Paulina and Leontes about Perdita:

PAULINA   Sir, my liege,
   Your eye hath too much youth in 't; not a month
   'Fore your queen died, she was more worth such gazes
   Than what you look on now.
LEONTES   I thought of her,
   Even as these looks I made.

                                        (223–7)

Peter Wood (1960) retained considerably more of the script than Quayle had played. In 5.1 his three-quarters to Quayle's one-third made it possible for Eric Porter's Leontes to convey his penitence through language as well as the symbolic gesture of kneeling. Wearing what the wardrobe list describes as a 'penitent costume' in 'the purple of repentance' (SQ, 452) and with 'the droop of penitent shoulders' (*SA Herald*, Sep), Porter was a 'benign penitent' (*FT*).

Wood was the only Stratford director to stage separate entrances for Florizel and Perdita. Dinsdale Landen's Florizel – in a 'brilliant rich costume' – entered first. Pausing before he spoke, Leontes seemed to recall his charging Hermione with adultery:

> [pause] Your mother was most true to wedlock, prince;
> For she did [pause] print your royal father off,
> Conceiving you.
>
> (123–5)

The entrance of Perdita, played by Susan Maryott, was staged for dramatic effect. Costumed as a 'princess (from Libya) exotic, mysterious, veiled', she entered from upstage centre and went downstage along an aisle formed by rows of servants holding candelabra. As he welcomed her, Leontes lifted her veil, turned to look at Florizel, and took her hand.

When the lord announced the arrival of Polixenes, Leontes dismissed Dion and Cleomenes and the six servants; the rest of the scene was played as a private moment, with just the four principals. Crossing to Florizel, who had fallen to his knees on 'Beseech you, sir' (217), Leontes put his hands on the supplicant's shoulders: 'But your petition / Is yet unanswer'd' (227–8). A cue for Paulina to go over to Perdita and look at her suggests that she might intuit the identity of the Libyan princess. Leontes and Florizel exited together. Peggy Ashcroft's Paulina held her hands out to Perdita and they followed the men. Wood cut three of Leontes' references to Polixenes: his repentance of wrongs against the Bohemian king (146–50); his description of Polixenes (169–75); his regret that Florizel has offended his father (210–12).

In Trevor Nunn's production (1969) a sitar cascade, last heard at the close of the prison scene, marked the transition from Bohemia to Sicilia. Barrie Ingham's Leontes still suffered the side-effects of the stroke that had crippled him when he defied the oracle. His 'right arm [lay] dead at his side' (*S. Wales E. Arg.*); he limped; he had a speech impediment (*Times*, 1969). He was 'shrunk and grey with pain ... , like a man emerging shakily from a long illness' (*Spectator*). On the NSA recording, Paulina (Elizabeth Spriggs) is gentle with him, and their voices have an antiphonal tone. Although it may be only a side-effect of the stroke, Ingham's slow delivery makes it seem that Leontes relives his loss when he says:

> I lost a couple, that 'twixt heaven and earth
> Might thus have stood, begetting wonder, as
> You, gracious couple, do: and then I lost –
> All mine own folly – the society,
> Amity too, of your brave father,

(131–5)

In a production that doubled Hermione and Perdita, one expects to find a reviewer who comments on Leontes' reception of Perdita. But the journals listed in Appendix 2 and other news cuttings at the SCL do not refer to this moment. At the close of the scene, a musical motif underscored Leontes' loss: several bars of 'Jack and Jill', last heard as a bridge between the trial scene (3.2) and the arrival of Antigonus and Leontes' infant daughter on Bohemia's stormy shores (3.3).

A dominant characteristic of John Barton's production (1976) was the introduction of interpolated characters and business to remind the audience of the importance of community and ritual to the Sicilians, whom Barton had relocated to a spot on the northern edges of Europe. The promptbook provides details. Cleomenes and Dion entered with the box that had held the oracle and placed it downstage centre. Following them, Ian McKellen's Leontes, with long blond hair and wearing a priestly cassock – 'seraphically saintly', says Harold Hobson (*S. Times*) – carried the oracle's scrolls, kissed them, knelt before the oracle stand, placed them on it, then stood. Leontes' participation in the ritual was significant: in 3.1 his entrance had interrupted the ceremony attending the return of Cleomenes and Dion with the oracle; his restoration to the community was a sign of his repentance. After his speech beginning 'I think so. Kill'd!' (16) he knelt again where he remained until he swore – with Barbara Leigh-Hunt's Paulina kneeling beside him – not to remarry without her consent (71, some 44 lines in Barton's playing script).

McKellen's 'ageing effortlessly across three acts makes the king of Sicilia a genuinely believable and sympathetic figure' (*Oxf. Mail*). McKellen, argues the *Daily Telegraph*, 'discovers a winning simplicity in the old king, sane and bitterly repentant of his cruelty'. Roger Warren records that his 'delivery was very moving in its simplicity' (*SS*, 174). François Laroque observes that 'something has definitely been broken in him ... and when his long winter is interrupted by the arrival of Florizel and Perdita there is nothing left for him but to bless his successor to the throne, who we feel will not have to wait long' (*Cahiers Elis.*, 91).

As he had in the earlier scenes, Barton reassigned lines scripted for lords and gentlemen to stress the centrality of a close community. In 5.1, Dion and Cleomenes, Paulina's Steward and the First Lord, familiar from the earlier Sicilian scenes, shared the lines. Barton cut approximately two-fifths of 5.1. Paulina lost lines about Antigonus; Paulina and Leontes lost lines including the reference to the 'sainted spirit' of Hermione (54–67); Paulina lost her insistence that she choose Leontes' new queen, if there were to be one (76–84); Leontes lost 'What might I have been, / Might I a son and daughter now have look'd on, / Such goodly things as you!' (175–7).

In the masque that had opened Ronald Eyre's production in 1981, Patrick Stewart's exuberant Leontes had darted about the stage directing the participants. In 5.1 stillness characterized the entrance of the 'stricken and aged' king (*SS*, 148), a 'penitential Christ-like figure' (*Cahiers Elis.*, 116) carried in on a litter. Leontes was, writes Irving Wardle, 'almost unrecognizably altered into a feeble unshaven recluse with the delayed responses and cracked delivery of senility' (*Times*). In conversation with me Robert

Smallwood remembered thinking 'how dusty he looked, like some old statue in an ill-kept church'. Sheila Hancock's Paulina, her voice having aged, was gentle with him; the promptbook calls for her to put a blanket over his knees and on the videotape she places a shawl about his shoulders. In Eyre's spare, uncluttered production, character – and especially Hancock's Paulina – rather than design and significant properties linked the Sicilia of sixteen years earlier with Act 5. Hancock's Paulina, observes Warren, was 'the healer rather than the scourge of his mind; and so the extraordinarily moving and suggestive final scenes gained more conviction than usual by being prepared for in this way' (SS, 148). Warren records that, when Florizel and Perdita entered, Leontes 'rose at "Welcome hither, / As is the spring to th'earth"' (150–1). On the videotape recorded later in the run, Leontes seems to collapse and to be helped up by Peter Chelsom's Florizel. Warren notes the 'vigour returning to him with the arrival of Perdita, whom he treated with a mixture of enthusiasm and the hesitancy of a man caught between the happy present and the painful past' (SS,148–9). Leontes' standing close to Leonie Mellinger's Perdita and holding her hand evoked Paulina's warning: 'Your eye hath too much youth in 't' (224). Restored by the arrival of the young couple, Leontes was able to walk off.

Adrian Noble's touring production (1984) returned to a Sicilia, as the promptbook and photographs record, shrouded in dust covers. Alun Armstrong's Leontes walked with the aid of a stick, Cleomenes and Dion lighted the way with torches. 'Sobrely overcoated [they presented a] stoically mournful picture of a Sicilian aristocracy in emotional exile from itself' (FT, Oct). Janet Dale's Paulina, who had 'softened both in manner and make-up to mellow convincingly' (Cahiers Elis., 87), shone her torch on a toy lamb in the centre of the acting space and lifted a dust cover to reveal Mamillius' top and, under another, the grandfather clock, which had apparently lain beneath dust covers for sixteen years. These objects, as well as a toy basket and a tricycle also called for by the promptbook, symbolized the loss occasioned by Leontes' defiance of the oracle. During her apostrophe to Hermione (95–8), Paulina started the clock, a gesture that foreshadowed the final scene. But for the moment, Leontes, slumped in an armchair, measured his 'leisured remorse with the solid tick of a clock' (*Guardian*, Aug). More forcefully, as Anthony Masters records, at Lincoln Cathedral 'one of England's loudest cathedral chimes toll[ed] the advancing hours in Sicilia' (*Times*). For their appearance before Leontes, Perdita wore a two-piece suit and Florizel, 'the uniform of a full navy captain, ... [but with] the now inappropriate tousled appearance of his initial courtship of Perdita' (*Cahiers Elis.*, 86).

In Terry Hands's production (1986) Sicilia itself had not changed significantly in the intervening sixteen years, but props marked the passage of time and called attention to the family Leontes had destroyed. Courtiers still wore white Regency costumes, but their walking sticks were practical, not solely ornamental. The angled mirrors reflected actors and the front rows of the stalls as well as 'Hermione's chair, Mamillius' toy box, and the baby's cradle spinning slowly, emptily as we return to Leontes' waste land' (*Cahiers Elis.*, 95). Behind the wall of mirrors the crystal disc still revolved, stopping at significant moments. The bear's head, placed downstage centre by Autolycus after he had frightened shepherdesses with it in Bohemia, looked back to the bearskin rug in Sicilia and to Antigonus' '*Exit, pursued by a bear*'.

As had his post-war Stratford predecessors, Jeremy Irons portrayed both the 'saint-like' penitent (2) and the king crippled by guilt. His hair, now shoulder length, and his beard, had whitened with age; his face was hollow; he wore a long white hospital nightgown; he was confined to a white wheelchair pushed by Paulina, played by Gillian Barge. He expressed an 'inconsolable grief' (*S. Wales Arg.*) and was 'noble in his sadness' (*Glasgow Her.*).

The entrance of Nathaniel Parker's Florizel and Penny Downie's Perdita, wearing rich turquoise and glittering costumes, introduced not only youthfulness but also a welcome splash of colour. The colour looked back to the first act, where shifts from blue to white lighting marked the eruption of Leontes' jealousy and anticipated the dominant colour in the next two scenes. In a 'moving moment' Leontes lifted Perdita's veil and 'recognize[d] the features of the wife he killed' (*Cahiers Elis.*, 95). It was, of course, a literal recognition because Penny Downie doubled the roles. Meeting Perdita in Bohemia, Paul Greenwood's Polixenes had experienced a similar shock. The sight of Perdita, as it had in 1981, restored Leontes – 'the years visibly fall from him' (*Glasgow Her.*) – and he was able to walk off with the aid of a cane supplied by the ever-helpful Paulina.

In Noble's main-house production (1992), the return to Sicilia was announced by the reappearance of the gauze box that was central to earlier Sicilian scenes. As the lights went up, Leontes, played by John Nettles, was discovered wearing a heavy overcoat and sitting in the centre of the box in a high-backed chair, which the promptbook labels 'throne'. Gemma Jones's Paulina, in the same costume she had worn sixteen years earlier but now with a matronly shawl around her shoulders, stood to his left, a comforting hand on his shoulder. Wardle describes the transition from 'the liveliest Bohemian party I can remember: icily followed by a return to the grey light of Sicily and the desolate Leontes against a blank horizon' (*Indep. Sun.*). On the NSA recording Nettles draws out Leontes' first speech, and Paulina quickly agrees with him in a matter-of-fact tone. One of the lords speaks to him in the tone reserved for speaking to children. Leontes was a 'stumbling, broken old man' (*S. Telegraph*) who walked with a stick.

In 1960 Wood staged the welcome of Florizel and Perdita to delay as long as possible Leontes's first view of Perdita. First Florizel entered, then Perdita. Noble sought a similar effect by different means. Entering with Florizel, Perdita wore a costume and a long single braid that called attention to her close resemblance to her mother. When they knelt before Leontes, Perdita bowed her head, until Leontes referred to her as 'your fair

FIGURE 34 In a stage picture similar to the one that closed 3.2, Paulina (Estelle Kohler) comforts Antony Sher's distraught Leontes. (5.1, 1999)

princess' (130). In productions such as 1969 and 1986, when Hermione and Perdita are doubled, one expects Leontes to be startled by Perdita's looking just like her mother. Noble's staging surprised the audience as well as Leontes, who paused in wonder before he spoke. Perdita's resemblance to her mother further developed a motif introduced in the Bohemian scenes: similarities between the mother and daughter's graceful hosting of parties and spirited response to false accusations. Stage position – downstage centre – also recalled Mamillius at the beginning of the production and presaged the statue scene.

The opening image in Gregory Doran's Act 5 (1999), as had that of Noble's production in 1984, gave the impression that time had stood still for sixteen years. At the close of the trial scene, Antony Sher's Leontes was 'sobbing, hunched on the floor, where we were to find him, still in much the same position, still attended by Paulina [Estelle Kohler], . . . a little bespectacled old lady who was still watching over him when the play returned to Sicilia for its conclusion' (*SS*, 264, 265; Figure 34). Two attendants sat upstage of them, smoking and playing cards. David Jays likens Sher's Leontes to 'a Tolstoyan penitent, squatting over his Bible. He has given away all the furniture – dust and paper crumple across bare floors. Sher's ice-splintered voice is warmer, furred with regret and wonder' (*New States.*). Receiving Florizel and his princess, Leontes was 'rocked backward by the filial image of Perdita' (*Guardian*). When Perdita is doubled with Hermione, as in Nunn's and Hands's productions, or costumed like her, as in Noble's 1992 production, Perdita reminds Leontes of his dead queen. Doubling Mamillius and Perdita, Emily Bruni's Perdita reminded Leontes of his dead son.

5.2

The Oracle is fulfilled

In 5.2 Shakespeare not only denies the audience a scene it would enjoy, he uses language that, J.H.P. Pafford reminds us, is 'ornate and artificial', the 'courtly language of the time' (Pafford, lxxxviii), to describe the offstage reunions. Appropriate to the three gentlemen who speak it, the language demands close attention from the audience and is one of the reasons the scene was not played for many years. Granville-Barker restored it, but modern directors tend to make more cuts here than they do in the lines spoken later in the scene. Although each gentleman speaks the language of his station, Shakespeare distinguishes between the three of them, not only in how much they know but also in how they speak. Do productions make a similar distinction? Whatever the decision about the three gentlemen, productions make clear the distinction between their costume and language and the appearance and expression of the Old Shepherd and his son, each now a 'gentleman born'. The script invites other questions about the scene. Are the three gentlemen presented as three new characters, or has the director combined a number of roles and introduced one or more of these three speakers in earlier scenes? How do the three gentlemen play the scene? How do they respond to Autolycus? How do they play the death of Antigonus, 'He was torn to pieces with a bear' (64)? Does the Third Gentleman, the one who heard the news first hand, have an air of superiority over his less fortunate colleagues? (When he enters he is referred to as 'the Lady Paulina's steward', 26.) What do the new clothes of the Old Shepherd and the Clown reveal about their sartorial tastes? How do they adjust to their new positions? How do they treat their lessers? How does Autolycus play the scene?

Quayle (1948), who had played approximately one-third of 5.1, retained just over half of 5.2. He cut the first nineteen lines, in which the First Gentleman tells Autolycus what little he knows about the Old Shepherd's revelations, and opened the scene with Autolycus' lament 'Now, had I not the dash of my former life in me, would preferment drop on my head' (113–23). The text that remained was a straightforward eyewitness account, not entirely stripped of wonder. John Kidd's Old Shepherd and the Clown of Paul Scofield played three-quarters of their lines, losing the exchange about false swearing (161–72). 'Even when they become "gentlemen born", we do not fear', comments the *Stratford-upon-Avon Herald*, 'any corruption of their courtesy or kindness or any diminution in laughter'.

In 5.2, as in 5.1, Wood's (1960) promptbook retains about three-quarters of Shakespeare's script. It calls for 5.2 to open with the 'same movement of servants' that had opened the first scene of the production, and the property list again supplies them with foods prepared for a feast: a large tray of fruit and large trays displaying peacock and pheasant feathers, two dishes of sweet-meats, a tray of goblets and a large jug of wine. Having appeared in three scenes as Mamillius' tutors, the two old gentlemen and Paulina's Steward (Roy Dotrice, Ian Richardson, Peter Jeffrey) were no strangers to the audience. J.C. Trewin enjoyed the 'three ancients ... who turn Shakespeare's information service into a quite bewitching exercise in comic garrulity. The sudden senile cackle at "He was torn to pieces with a bear" [64] should now become accepted practice' (*Illus. Lon. News*).

Cutting Autolycus' soliloquy, with which Quayle had opened the scene, Wood moved directly to another comic vignette. The promptbook calls for the Old Shepherd, played by James Bree, and Ian Holm's Clown to enter flanked by servants, one of whom fanned them. The Clown wore a broad-brimmed hat with a single feather, a tunic decorated with a few stars, and cross-gartered trousers, sandals, a cloak. Wearing basically the same costume as his son, the rank-conscious Old Shepherd added decorative details to his costume to denote his new status as 'brother' to two kings (141). After the Old Shepherd said 'Come, boy; I am past moe children, but thy sons and daughters will be all gentlemen born' (127–8), he clapped his hands to dismiss the servants, who were, no doubt, amused by his ill-fitting authority. In business similar to that of his first encounter with the Clown, Autolycus, who 'glances at the audience', fell on his face and tricked the Young Shepherd into helping him up and embracing him. Autolycus stole the Young Shepherd's purse, but put it back. Trumpets and noises off announced the final scene.

During its journey from Stratford to Australia to London, Nunn's (1969) script for 5.2 underwent several changes. The promptbook records cuts, then reinstates them; the NSA recording does not follow the prompt script. Trewin, who enjoyed Wood's staging of the three gentlemen as a comic set piece, 'rather regretted' Nunn's playing them seriously. Autolycus lost his soliloquy (113–23). On the recording, the announcement of Antigonus' demise was played for laughs, as was the Clown's 'and so we wept' (144). Closing the brief scene, the evocative sitar prepared for the statue scene.

Like Quayle, Barton (1976) opened 5.2 with Autolycus' soliloquy (113–23). The three lords, represented by Cleomenes, Dion and Paulina's Steward, entered backwards, 'as if they were just quitting the royal presence' (*SQ*, 189). Repeating the stage picture of 3.1 and 3.2 (Figure 17), Barton stressed the importance of the oracle and the community's faith in it. On command from Paulina's Steward, Autolycus, Cleomenes, Dion, Emilia and three lords sat in a circle and joined hands. From the privileged place in the centre, Paulina's Steward revealed how 'one joy crown[ed] another' (45). Before David Waller's Old Shepherd and the Clown of Roger Rees entered, Cleomenes and Dion removed the block on which the oracle had rested. Barton cut just over one-fifth of the scene.

In Eyre's (1981) Sicilia, which had seldom heard music and sound effects, the peal of bells that had opened 5.1 continued softly as the gentlemen and Autolycus, played by Geoffrey Hutchings, entered. Autolycus, who had been chased on stage in 4.3, was again pursued – perhaps having been expelled from the meeting of the two kings. The three gentlemen wore white cassocks, similar to those worn by Cleomenes and Dion when they presented the oracle at the trial and similar to those to be worn in the statue scene. The court clothes worn by John Rogan's Old Shepherd and Gerard Murphy's Clown were also white, and of a design similar to those worn by the court in earlier acts. Like Barton, Eyre cut about a fifth of the scene.

In Noble's touring production (1984), the bursting of balloons, pealing bells, a chiming clock and rain signalled the transition from a shrouded to a celebratory Sicilia. Paulina's Steward and two gentlemen rushed on with umbrellas (one of Noble's favourite props) to discuss the amazing news. Running on, Autolycus tried to stop the men bursting balloons and to query them about the cause of the festivities. Noble, as had Quayle, cut more than two-fifths of the scene.

Hands (1986) played 5.2 before the opaque white curtain, last used as a scrim behind which courtiers had engaged in a snowball fight. Entering with the news from court, Paulina's Steward, played by Henry Goodman, jumped for joy over the bear's head, to the amusement of the other two gentlemen. The Third Gentleman used 'Did you see' (40–1) to arrest the exit of the other two, who assumed his story was finished. On 'I would fain say, bleed tears' (87–8), the Third Gentleman put his handkerchief to his eyes; the other two followed suit. Joe Melia's Autolycus mocked him and began a gag of stealing handkerchiefs, undercutting the wonder of the Third Gentleman's report. The Old Shepherd of Bernard Horsfall and Simon Russell Beale's Clown took pride in their sartorial splendour, but production photographs reveal that their new blue satin suits did not sit as gracefully on their shoulders as did the similar costumes of courtiers. The Old Shepherd's gait pointed toward too many celebratory drinks, and they both spoke more loudly than they had in Bohemia. The props list calls for the Clown to have rings, bracelets, a hip flask, a money purse, removable buckles, a lace hankie, rich pickings for Autolycus, who wore the clothes he had got in the exchange with Florizel. To close the scene, Hands reversed the pattern that had introduced Autolycus (4.3). To the sound of trumpets, Autolycus picked up the bear's head, put it on and exited. Nicholas Shrimpton's

> best guess as to the point [of the bear motif] was that it was an attempt to make much of the Clown's observation, at 4.4.791 [803–4], that 'authority be a stubborn bear', thus putting the ursine bad temper of Leontes (and subsequently Polixenes) in symbolic perspective. If so, I can only say that the simple game was not worth the expensive candle. (SS, 178)

The 1992 promptbook calls for the front gauze to be flown in, and against this backdrop Noble staged 5.2, playing approximately three-fifths of the lines. The practical effects of the box were to provide an appropriate playing space for a scene with few characters and to suggest the offstage space where the reunions took place. Richard McCabe's Autolycus entered first. Ignoring Autolycus' attempts to get attention, three city gentlemen rushed on and off, carrying folded umbrellas and wearing bowler hats and long black coats. Added business alluded to Autolycus' notoriety and the banner headline – 'Servant Guilty' – he had shared with the audience. Autolycus took the earliest opportunity to steal the First Gentleman's umbrella. But the First Gentleman had the last word. Retrieving his umbrella just before his exit, he made clear that Autolycus was not welcome to follow him to court: 'Who would be thence that has the benefit of access?' (109–10). Jeffery Dench's Old Shepherd and Graham Turner's Clown had celebrated their rise to respectability 'with a shepherds' spending spree, staggering on stage under the weight of carrier bags from Fortnum and Mason' (*S. Telegraph*). The promptbook cues business for Autolycus and the Clown. When Autolycus sees the Old Shepherd and the Clown entering, he 'jumps into the audience, uproots a member of [the] audience and takes their seat'. Walking along the apron taking pictures with his new camera, the Clown spotted Autolycus and pulled him from the audience. On the audiotape the Clown warns 'madam, check your handbag'. Peter Holland commends McCabe's performance: 'I could not quite believe in an Autolycus who reformed at the end of 5.2, stealing the Young Shepherd's watch again and then, overcome with remorse, dropping it back into the Young Shepherd's carrier-bag, but McCabe made it coherent' (*SS*, 173).

Whereas flying in the gauze box had restricted stage space in Noble's production, opening out the set provided space for the extra characters Doran introduced in 1999. Approximately nine servants, including women, footmen and the doctor who had attended Mamillius and Leontes, participated. Some spoke lines; others shared lines, such as when two women queried in unison 'Has the king found his heir?' (29–30). Doran's staging looked back to earlier scenes: the opening scene, where it appeared that gossiping servants might be the source of the whispers Leontes imagined; the accusation, witnessed, unusually, by both male and female servants; the close of 2.3 and the excitement in the voice of the servant who announced the return of Cleomenes and Dion. In Leontes' household in 5.2, servants, hitherto silent witnesses, found their voices. In their formal finery, with satin scarves and waistcoats, the Old Shepherd of James Hayes and Christopher

Brand's Clown 'begin to restore colour and ornament to the grief-stricken kingdom' (*TLS*).

5.3

It is requir'd
You do awake your faith

The penultimate scene closes with the Clown's invitation to Autolycus: 'Hark! the kings and the princes, our kindred, are going to see the queen's picture. Come, follow us: we'll be thy good masters' (172–5). But on the stage, Autolycus and even the 'kindred' may not join the principals who see 'the queen's picture'. Where does the production place 5.3, the statue scene, and what props, other than the statue, are present? How does the setting contrast with the other Sicilian scenes? If the production has relied on a dominant image or device such as the gauze box, how does the final scene treat that image or device? Has the meaning assigned to it been made clear? Has the image or device enhanced or detracted from the production? Has it revealed or intruded upon the script? Does the production evoke the memory of Mamillius? Where is the statue placed and what effect does the blocking have on Hermione's awakening? Is the audience to see Hermione's face, Leontes' face, or the profiles of each of them? Does the blocking of this scene resemble that of the trial? What does the statue look like? Does either costume or hair style resemble an earlier appearance of Hermione? How is the statue lighted? If an actor doubled Hermione and Perdita, how does the production solve the problem presented by the characters appearing together in this scene? Does the blocking enable Paulina to include the audience when she exhorts 'resolve you / For more amazement' (86–7), 'It is requir'd / You do awake your faith' (94–5) and 'those that think it is unlawful business / I am about, let them depart' (96–7)? What music awakens the statue? Does it repeat motifs presented earlier? How does the production

FIGURE 35 In 1948 ornate costumes and the set gave the statue scene an Eastern aura. Leontes (Esmond Knight) stands next to the statue of Hermione (Diana Wynyard). Perdita (Claire Bloom) kneels before it; Florizel (Dinsdale Landen) kneels behind her. Camillo (Julian Amyes) stands behind him. The Old Shepherd (John Kidd), with his distinctive white hair, is at the extreme right. (5.3)

handle the reunions of Hermione and Leontes, Hermione and Perdita, Hermione and Polixenes, the betrothal of Paulina and Camillo? Do Hermione and Leontes follow the embedded cues or do they play against the text? What is the closing image of the production?

Quayle staged the statue scene as a public event, calling the full company of thirty-five actors. Angus McBean's photograph (Figure 35) places the statue centre stage, facing the audience and with the witnesses grouped on either side. Perdita kneels before the statue; Florizel kneels behind Perdita; Camillo (Julian Amyes, with a cross on his chest) stands behind Florizel. In the formal photograph, neither Paulina nor Polixenes has a prominent place. At the right edge of the photograph is the distinctive white hair of the Old Shepherd, in ermine-collared cape, and the Clown. Dotted amongst the crowd, several pikes and spears may look back to the military ethos of Act 1 (Figures 1 and 2) and the force that attended Diana Wynyard's Hermione at the trial, but they do not dominate. The costumes and the backcloth with its stylized angels and stars, onion domes and spires, convey the Eastern influence. Leontes' heavy crown and embroidered stole are at once regal and ecclesiastical. Hermione wears a similar stole. Four laurel wreaths, which hang from the lintel of the canopy shielding Hermione, anticipate the reconciliation.

After Hermione embraced Leontes (111), the promptbook calls for a procession to begin (135) and for the production to conclude with a 'Hymn to Apollo' (146). The lyrics, like those in nineteenth-century productions, praise 'Apollo, Great God of the Sun / ... Who through Thy Oracle, / Had shown to us where duty is'. At its conclusion as in the opening entertainment, Quayle's production showed the lingering influence of Charles Kean (see p. 12) and elaborate mid-nineteenth-century stagings of *The Winter's Tale*.

But World War II and its aftermath were the more immediate influence on Quayle's production. In his review for the *Birmingham Post*, T.C. Kemp alludes to the post-war world: *The Winter's Tale* was welcome 'surely, never more than now when reconciliation and forgiveness are far to seek in a grey and withered world'. Kemp's words echo Ben Iden Payne's in 1942, as reported by the *Stratford-upon-Avon Herald* (1 May). Iden Payne finds *The Winter's Tale* relevant 'since it breathes the spirit of forgiveness and reconciliation which is essential to the peace of the world'. The Sicilia of Act 5, with, in Kemp's words, its 'fairy-tale statue scene and the happy ending', was more in keeping with reviewers' expectations than had been Quayle's Iron Curtain setting of Acts 1 to 3, and Knight's tyrannical Leontes. Kemp may have called the statue scene 'fairy-tale', but the *Stage* finds a religious tone, 'the full glory of triumphant faith', in Hermione's playing. Wynyard was 'particularly entrancing ... when Hermione changes from a thing of marble to a living creature of beauty and life. It was not only a scene beautifully staged but deeply moving' (*Warwick Adv.*). The *Stratford-upon-Avon Herald* pronounces Leontes as 'fundamentally a well-meaning and lovable person, capable of a saint-like sorrow for deeds against his own real character'. (It did not mention the effect of his deeds on Hermione, his son and daughter.)

In contrast with Quayle, who had staged 5.3 with a full company and added a procession and a 'Hymn to Apollo', Wood played the statue scene as a private, family one, calling only the seven speakers (Figure 36) and relying on their words and Jaques Noel's stage design. Alone among the Stratford designers, Noel provided Paulina's gallery, which gave Leontes and his companions 'much content / In many singularities' (11–12). A photograph of the set pictures three statues in Grecian drapery upstage of Hermione. Writing in the *Tablet*, a Roman Catholic journal, Robert Speaight sets the stage:

> The scene is generally produced in a dim religious light; the effect is incense-laden and cloistral. But Mr. Wood has seen the resurrection of Hermione as a mystery *en pleine lumière*. He uses the whole space of an uncluttered stage, with towers and steeples in perspective against a cloudless sky. We are on the roof, so to speak, not in the chancel or the crypt – and Heaven is not far away. Moreover, everyone, except the grave and good Paulina, is dressed in festive gold. I do not know whether this Paschal effect was intentional, but it was extremely felicitous. For we had already seen Leontes in the penitential weeds of his perfect contrition, and it was right, not only that he should be seen to be reconciled with Hermione, but that all their world – all Shakespeare's world – should be visibly transfigured. ... When Mr. Eric Porter, as Leontes, takes Hermione into his arms and exclaims, 'Oh, she is warm,' poetry and emotion are transmuted into purest gold.

Details in the promptbook shed additional light on the playing of the scene. Unusually, Paulina entered her gallery first, alone, and as Speaight points out, not dressed in gold. Wearing what the wardrobe list describes as a 'costume of Peace' and what Speaight

FIGURE 36 Wearing what one critic calls the 'gold of celebration' Eric Porter's Leontes gazes at Hermione (Elizabeth Sellars), sculpted in Grecian drapery. With only Paulina (Peggy Ashcroft, leaning on stick), Polixenes (Patrick Allen), Florizel (John Justin), Camillo (Paul Hardwick) and Perdita (Susan Maryott) in attendance in 1960, the statue scene is more private than it had been in 1948. (5.3)

calls 'the gold of celebration' (*SQ*, 452), Leontes entered arm in arm with Perdita. The monarchs and their children wore crowns. When Hermione awakened, she stretched out her hand to Leontes. Speaight describes the moment when Leontes' fingers reached out to touch Hermione's hand as being 'on the hither side of eternity' (*SQ*, 453). After they kissed, Leontes' words '"If this be magic, let it be an art lawful as eating" (110–11), trembled with wonder and hope, and saw the end of torment' (*Coventry Sta.*). As the script requires, Leontes matched Camillo with Paulina, who accepted with 'humor' (*SQ*, 453), called upon Hermione to 'look upon my brother' (147) and introduced Hermione to Florizel (149–51). The closing moments celebrated the forthcoming marriages and the reconciliations. Camillo and Paulina, Florizel and Perdita, then Polixenes exited; after kissing downstage centre, Hermione and Leontes followed.

In 1969 Nunn, for whom Judi Dench doubled Hermione and Perdita, faced the same problem in presenting the reunion of mother and daughter that Mary Anderson had faced in 1887. Playing just under one-half of Shakespeare's lines, Anderson cut both of Perdita's speeches and introduced a double to receive Hermione's blessing. The *Times* objects that 'the beauty of the scene ... is seriously impaired by the presence among the spectators of the strange, veiled, speechless figure, who keeps her back to the audience and is addressed as Perdita' (12 Sep 1887). Nunn relied on a technical effect to allow Dench to appear first as Perdita and then as Hermione. He reintroduced the perspex box, a device first used in the opening moments of the production. Then it had enclosed Leontes and reminded the audience of Leonardo's drawing; Time's speech linked the three-dimensional representation of Leonardo's drawing with *The Winter's Tale*. It was replicated by the white box of the set; by a child's toy at the edge of the stage; by the white cubes, which doubled as toy boxes and seats; and by the cube of lights lowered to represent Apollo's oracle in 2.3 and before which Time spoke (4.1). Placing the statue – an actress standing in for Judi Dench – within the cube made visual the thematic importance of time: it looked back to the initial image and presaged the last piece of Time's news (4.1.26). Robert Speaight describes how Dench left the stage as Perdita and returned as the statue:

> It was solved by placing Hermione's statue – not, at first, Hermione herself, for Perdita still has some words to speak – on a revolving

pedestal. When Leontes is overcome by the likeness and Paulina closes the curtain, Perdita discreetly disappears in the shadows; and when the curtain is opened again, the real Hermione is there on the pedestal, and the substitute Perdita, who has nothing more to say and is exactly of Miss Dench's height and coloring, slips on from the other side of the stage, keeping her face averted from the audience. Technically, this worked to perfection; but we were so busy admiring the sleight of hand that the emotional impact of the scene was blunted.   (*SQ,* 437)

Judi Dench acknowledges that the switch

did not work for me. Even when it did work well, it left the audience wondering how on earth it had happened, instead of feeling the emotion of what was happening between the characters. I didn't feel so much moved as breathless, by the time I had swapped with the double who played Perdita and rushed round to take the statue's place in the perspex box at the back of the stage, but I did feel as though I was another actress, which is a very strange sensation.

(Dench, 206)

Despite the drawbacks Speaight and Dench point out, Nunn's solution, unlike Anderson's, reordered some lines but did not do serious damage to the text. Doubling the roles linked Sicilia and Bohemia and stressed similarities of mother and daughter in appearance, character and fate. But as other productions reveal, doubling is not the only way to achieve these goals. No matter how smoothly and cleverly the double is handled, there remains an overwhelming drawback. Hermione directs her only words to Perdita:

> You gods, look down,
> And from your sacred vials pour your graces
> Upon my daughter's head! Tell me, mine own,
> Where hast thou been preserv'd? where liv'd? how found
> Thy father's court? for thou shalt hear that I,
> Knowing by Paulina that the Oracle
> Gave hope thou wast in being, have preserv'd
> Myself to see the issue.

(121–8)

One wants Perdita herself, not a double introduced in the last scene, to hear her mother's words.

The music that awakened the statue was the by now very familiar sitar, played 'soft, distant rising' according to the music cue. The sustained note, then the crescendo, as heard on the NSA recording, create an ethereal effect. On the recording Paulina takes a long pause after 'You perceive she stirs' (103). John Barber records that Hermione 'holds the audience breathless when she stirs and moves down from her dais' (*D. Telegraph*). Another long pause followed Hermione's reunion with Perdita (NSA). Nunn had, apparently, considered closing the production with a song or chorus. In the production copy of the Arden edition, marked with music cues, appears the annotation 'final beautiful song', as Leontes says 'hastily lead away' (155). But the cue list does not mention the song, the scores do not include a song, and the NSA recording does not close with vocal music. The production closed instead with a visual image praised by several reviewers. In the *Times*, Irving Wardle writes 'To see them and their children touching hands in a silent circle of reunion is a spectacle that really reaches the heart' (1969). Neville Miller observes that 'Leontes becomes whole again and able to join hands with the five principals of his story in a circle of love' (*S. Wales E. Arg.*). Speaight complains that Leontes still limped: 'let him limp no longer when Hermione has been restored to him' (*SQ*, 437).

The doubling of Hermione and Perdita necessitated two cuts. Leaving the stage as Perdita and reappearing seconds later as Hermione, Dench could not appear 'wrinkled' (28) and 'aged' (29). Cutting Paulina's request to Perdita 'Please you to interpose, fair madam, kneel / And pray your mother's blessing' (119–20), kept the focus on Hermione – 'Turn, good lady, / Our Perdita is found' (120–1) – rather than on the stand-in Perdita. Other cuts in the promptbook include the reference to the paint not being dry (47–8), and Leontes' 'If this be magic, let it be an art / Lawful as eating' (110–11).

FIGURE 37 Having drawn the curtain to reveal the statue of Hermione (Marilyn Taylerson), Paulina (Barbara Leigh-Hunt) studies the responses of Florizel (Nickolas Grace), Leontes (Ian McKellen) and Perdita (Cherie Lunghi). Placing the statue at the side of the stage made it possible for the audience to see the faces of all the principals. (5.3, 1976)

Among post-war Stratford directors, Barton was the first to stage the scene so that the audience could see the faces of all the principal characters and the statue (Figure 37). He placed the statue on a dais downstage left, close to where Perdita had welcomed Polixenes and Camillo (Figure 29); on a diagonal, Leontes, Perdita and Florizel faced the statue; Paulina, her steward, Polixenes, Camillo, Cleomenes, Dion and the First Lord took their places alongside or behind Leontes and the couple. For the unveiling, Paulina moved to the spot before the barren tree from which Marilyn Taylerson's Hermione had defended herself in the trial scene. Speaight, whose reviews of 1948 and 1960 have been cited, ranks the staging as better than any other he had seen; it was 'brilliantly lit, the amazed spectators were not obliged to turn their backs on her. . . . she held her pose beautifully' (*SQ*, 189).

Roger Warren describes the effect of the scene as 'very moving in its simplicity'. Hermione's

> brief utterance skilfully suggest[ed] how strange it seemed to be among people again after that long seclusion. As in 1969, the moving quality of the scene was intensified by having Leontes and his family touching hands in a silent circle of reunion, filling the stage, as one critic [Michael Billington] finely put it 'with a sense of mystery and strangeness that passes rational explanation or the power of language to describe'. (*SS*, 174)

In his review, Billington characterizes the scene as 'pure magic because it restores an authentic husband–wife relationship' (*Guardian*). The scene 'brought tears' to the eyes of John Barber: 'the ethereal Marilyn Taylerson kept incredibly still, and when she spoke seemed to have returned from the grave' (*D. Telegraph*). Barton's promptbook, which cuts approximately one-third of the script, more than his three immediate Stratford predecessors had cut, calls for the rest of the company to enter when Perdita kneels to receive her mother's blessing (120). In a production stressing the centrality of community and its rituals and narratives, the statue scene celebrated, in the words of Billington, 'the ultimate restoration of harmony'.

In 1981 the oversized doorway upstage centre was reserved for significant entrances: the interpolated masque; the bear; Time; and the torchlight procession at the beginning of the statue scene. In addition to contributing to the atmosphere, the procession, recorded on videotape, hid the stage hands who pushed on the prop that would enclose the statue and also gave Hermione time to take her place. The statue in place centre stage, the eleven actors who had formed the procession exited, and the principals entered from three separate entrances: Leontes with Polixenes and Camillo; Perdita and Florizel; Paulina. Visual details linked the statue scene with earlier scenes. In the masque actors had covered their white costumes with colourful royal robes; in the statue scene they assumed a uniform appearance by wearing white robes

FIGURE 38 Leontes (Patrick Stewart), Hermione (Gemma Jones) and Perdita (Leonie Mellinger) join hands in a circle, watched by Paulina (Sheila Hancock). The statue stood on the tournament-tent shaped object and was hidden by a curtain with a design similar to the one on costumes worn earlier by Hermione (Figures 6 and 12) and Perdita. (5.3, 1981)

over their costumes (Figure 38); in the previous scene the three gentlemen wore white robes. Another set of visual details linked Hermione with earlier scenes. The design of flowers and vines on the curtain shielding the statue (Figure 38) was very similar to the designs of Hermione's costume in Acts 1 and 2 (Figures 6 and 12) and Perdita's in the sheep-shearing. The Christian imagery introduced by Leontes' Christ-like appearance in 5.1 was made more explicit. Photographs, including Figure 38, record that Leontes, Polixenes and Hermione wore identical crowns, the dominant feature of which was a cross, and there was a cross on top of the austerely modern version of a medieval tournament tent that encloses the statue. (The enclosure also resembled, in the words of Gemma Jones, 'a shower cabinet'. Her task, 'to keep very still', was not helped 'when it is suggested to me, just before I go on, that I should be revealed wearing a bath hat and singing "I'm going to wash that man right out of my hair"' (Jones, 163).)

When Paulina drew the curtain to reveal the 'still dignity' of Jones's Hermione, Leontes and Perdita were downstage right and left, respectively. The promptbook identifies the music as 'Cantas Firmus', to be played by three recorders. The scene 'paced with much humanity by Sheila Hancock's Paulina, makes its usual and infallibly heart-stopping effect' (*TLS*). Jones's 'excellent and moving Hermione' (*Cahiers Elis.*, 116) took a long pause before she spoke. Leontes nearly fainted and just as Florizel aided him in 5.1 so now, the videotape reveals, Ray Jewers's Polixenes comforted him. In Eyre's staging, Leontes and Polixenes were fully reconciled before their entrance together for the final scene. Hermione reached out to draw Perdita over to her; Leontes joined them; Hermione, Leontes and Perdita linked hands (Figure 38). Warren describes the scene and Paulina's role in it:

> In the statue scene the sight of Hermione, and then her revival, were almost too much for him; Sheila Hancock controlled this scene with consummate skill, coaxing Hermione into life and Leontes into accepting her, Paulina's culminating act as the rebuilder of their marriage. Leontes seemed to acknowledge her crucial role as confessor, teacher and friend as he gently matched her with Camillo who had previously performed the same 'priest-like' function; and the little bow and smile with which she acknowledged the appropriateness of the match were simply perfect: I have never seen the part better, more subtly played.   (*SS*, 149)

According to the promptbook, Eyre followed the usual pattern of having Paulina and Camillo, then Polixenes, exit first. But then followed Hermione and Leontes and finally, Florizel and Perdita. Perhaps this reversal of the usual order was meant to remind the audience of the lost Mamillius or to celebrate the fulfilment of the prophecy. The 1982 production at the Barbican, London, that has been recorded on the videotape reverts to the usual order.

In 1981, the torchlit procession entered from upstage centre and made the same exit after it had served the practical purpose of providing cover for the statue. In Noble's touring production (1984), the cast formed a candlelit procession, entering through the promenading audience and taking their places around the edges of the rectangular playing space. Singing 'Lucis Creator', a hymn written for the production, the procession announced a religious tone for the final scene. Veiled and in classical drapery, the statue was placed on the platform previously associated with Leontes and his mafioso cronies. The two rostra, which had anchored the extremities of the acting space and symbolized the split in Sicilia, were pushed together. As production photographs reveal, candles along the edges of the carpeted acting space gave the statue a religious aura. Gradually the principals joined Paulina on the rostrum with the statue. First Leontes went onto the rostrum, then Perdita, who carried a bunch of flowers to place at the base of the statue of her mother (Figure 39). Her offering of flowers, a poignant, simple gesture, is unique in these productions and is one I have neither seen nor read about in other productions. To comfort Leontes – 'Dear my brother' (53) – Polixenes went to the rostrum; later Florizel joined the group. Encouraging the reunited family to 'Go together, / You precious winners all' (130–1), Paulina, directs the promptbook, 'makes all join hands'. Paulina was 'almost as emotional as Leontes at the reunion of the family' (*Cahiers Elis.*, 87). At the close of her speech, the promptbook cues her to leave the group 'grief stricken'. Leontes summoned Camillo and joined their hands. The promptbook closes with the cue 'Exit all onto floor level and move in clockwise direction around rostra. Hermione leading off'. Of a performance at Lincoln Cathedral, Michael Coveney writes:

> The beauty and gravity of those final scenes, with the statue coming to life amid flickering candles, will long stay with me; all the more effective at Thursday's matinee, when the dappled natural lighting effect of sunshine refracted through the cathedral's stained glass windows gave way to the bleak and wintry greyness of a dying afternoon. Alun Armstrong's Leontes and Lynn Farleigh's

FIGURE 39 Carrying a bouquet of flowers to honour the memory of her mother, Perdita (Jenifer Landor) approaches the statue of Hermione (Lynn Farleigh). In the background, Paulina (Janet Dale) holds one of the many candles that contributed to the religious aura of the scene. (5.3, 1984)

> Hermione were tumultuously reunited in a scene as poignantly moving as the same actors' prison cell farewell in *The Crucible*.
>
> (*FT*)

It was, of course, a visit to Lincoln Cathedral that had inspired Noble to direct *The Winter's Tale* for a tour of non-traditional playing spaces.

In 1986 Hands, as had Nunn, doubled Hermione and Perdita and had to solve the problem of presenting them on stage together. His solution – the introduction of a veiled figure – owes more to Anderson than to Nunn. Leontes and Perdita, veiled to disguise the actor standing in for Downie, led the procession that opened the statue scene. As white had once dominated Sicilia, so now blue, reintroduced to Sicilia by Florizel and Perdita, was omnipresent. All were costumed in rich shades of blues and bluish greens. Hermione's statue, which rose from a trap centre stage, was sculpted in deep blue with gold accents; it stood on a blue cube placed on the blue-tiled floor. A white curtain fluttered before it. In Act 1 blue lighting was associated with the period before the inception of Leontes' jealousy, signified by a switch to white lights. In the statue scene, blue may also be read in religious terms, as an allusion to paintings in which the Madonna wears blue. However, Hermione's costume and coiffure do not conjure very strong associations with traditional representations of Mary. Behind the statue the mirrors reflected actors and audience (Figure 40). In 1.2 they had reflected the worried face of Mamillius when Hermione and Polixenes flirted downstage (Figure 7); in 5.3 they reflected the face of the stand-in Perdita, who did not resemble Downie and who did not speak. The crystal turned.

Hands directed the scene 'with a slow grace' (*Glasgow Her.*). Once more, the treble voice, now a choir of them – and here the religious effect was clear – was called upon to mark a significant moment, the awakening of the statue. The video and a series of contact prints record the reconciliation of Leontes and Hermione, the mute Perdita seeking her mother's blessing, the reunion of Hermione and Polixenes, the betrothal of Paulina and Camillo, who put his arm around her waist. Gold-dust sequins, not the snow of earlier scenes, fell upstage; the sun rose behind the scene.

In Noble's touring production, the full company had entered in candlelit procession singing a hymn, and the two rostra, symbols of division, had been pushed together. In 1992 Noble again introduced the full company and a 'symbol of isolation and division', the gauze box. The company swirled on from stage right, a mass of richly coloured satins and velvets moving downstage and then circling upstage to enter the gauze box. As if by magic, Hermione emerged downstage centre on the spot where Mamillius had spun his top and, like Mamillius, with her back to the audience and facing the court frozen within the gauze box (Figure 41). Noble's staging shifted the centre of attention from Hermione to the court, which looked downstage 'through the gauze box as if through a barrier to belief' (*SQ*, 351). The

FIGURE 40 Paulina (Gillian Barge) comforts the stand-in Perdita, who kneels before Hermione (Penny Downie). Leontes (Jeremy Irons), his back to the audience, Florizel (Nathanial Parker) and Camillo (Richard Easton, reflected in the mirror) ponder the miracle. The mirror reflects not only the characters but also the tiled floor on which the statue rests. (5.3, 1986)

audience 'watches the amazed faces of the court rather than wonder[ing] if Hermione will betray herself by twitching the odd muscle before time' (*FT*). Noble's staging placed Hermione at the centre of a circle, with the audience completing the circle begun by the court. Another effect of Noble's staging was that Paulina seemed to include the audience when she said, for example, 'Either forbear, / Quit presently the chapel, or resolve you / For more amazement' (85–7) and 'those that think it is unlawful business / I am about, let them depart' (96–7). Paulina, 'tears streaming down her cheeks, voice cool with irony and hot with rage, memorably brings this rich feast of a production to its finale'

FIGURE 41 Her back to the audience and in the same stage position Mamillius had assumed at the beginning of the performance (Figure 8), Hermione (Samantha Bond) faces the court. Perdita (Phyllida Hancock) kneels; Paulina (Gemma Jones) stands behind her. Polixenes (Paul Jesson) comforts Leontes (John Nettles). (5.3, 1992)

(*E. Standard*). Gemma Jones recalled in conversation with me that they tried several ways of staging the scene, right up to the opening, and that placing the statue down centre was 'lovely' for the cast, which could see Hermione awaken and move. Jones admits to being 'always moved ... to a fault' by the scene. Reviewers describe their response to Noble's reversal of the usual stage picture. Rebecca Flynn notes that 'we had to study Leontes' face for the first sign of warmth' (*Cahiers Elis.*, 89). Peter Porter records that 'as the screen lifts, she comes alive, still with her back turned, and we glean how the transformation develops from the courtiers' faces, not hers' (*TLS*). When Hermione turned, 'we could see the tears on her cheeks' (*SQ*, 351).

As Smallwood points out, 'those who want to watch Hermione's face as she first sees her husband after sixteen years of separation would never approve' of Hermione's turning her back to the audience (*SQ*, 351). Noble's decision to reverse the usual stage picture fitted, however, smoothly into the dominant visual motif. It was appropriate that Leontes and the court, not Hermione, be placed within the gauze box. The placing of Hermione where her son was first discovered suggested to Michael Billington that the scene was 'haunted by the spirit of the dead Mamillius whose wishes finally seem fulfilled in the linked, loving hands of father, mother, and Bohemian king' (*Guardian*). At the National Theatre in London four years earlier, Peter Hall had also placed Hermione's back to the audience, focused on the responses of Leontes (Tim Pigott-Smith) and the court, and joined court and audience in a symbolic circle with Sally Dexter's Hermione at the centre. But Hall's production explored a darker theme. When Hermione turned, she 'moved forward unsmiling. ... There was a world of unspoken emotion between husband and wife as, left alone together, they tentatively, sombrely, joined hands again' (Wells, 144).

In 1992, as he had in 1984, Noble directed the final scene to convey his conviction that *The Winter's Tale* 'is a great healing play, both through the extraordinary spiritual journey that is undergone by the protagonists and also through the sane, healthy influence that the humble Bohemians have on their mighty masters' (Noble, xiv). Smallwood describes the closing image:

> Then, after the embrace of husband and wife, came the hesitant handshake with Paul Jesson's gentle and still rather perplexed Polixenes, ... who now joined hands with his friend and his friend's wife in a gesture of love and forgiveness, relief, and faint uncertainty, that provided the last splendid image of hard-won joy in this impressive production. (*SQ*, 351)

The promptbook calls for Paulina and Camillo to lead the full company around 'in a swirl'.

Doran's 1999 staging of 5.3 drew upon the stage pictures in his earlier Sicilian scenes. The most obvious parallel was with the trial scene. As the statue, Hermione stood 'in the same trellised dock in which the queen had been so viciously humiliated, now transformed into a sacred shrine aglow with candles' (*Spectator*). The statue was 'a silvery candle-lit madonna' (*Observer*) and, in keeping with the Eastern setting, 'a hauntingly beautiful icon of the loss she both represents and redeems' (*TLS*). Figure 42 captures Hermione when Paulina says 'You perceive she stirs' (103). In the trial scene, Alexandra Gilbreath's Hermione had reached out to Sher's Leontes, a gesture she repeated when the statue awakened (*SS*, 265). Other visual parallels were more subtle. Emily Bruni's Perdita, for example, wore her mother's shawl, the shawl Leontes had sniffed for evidence of his wife's infidelity and which Polixenes had so gently and skilfully folded a few moments later. Bruni's doubling of Perdita and the wheelchair-bound Mamillius also cast a glance back to the opening scenes and to the consequences of Leontes' defiance of the oracle.

In the *Financial Times*, Alastair Macaulay characterizes the 'journeys of the spirit' enforced upon Paulina and Hermione. Estelle Kohler's was 'a journey of sympathy and of time's depredations'; Gilbreath's 'a journey of suffering innocence and of endurance'. Smallwood captures the effect achieved by the final moments of the production:

> But there was something about the choice of stillness and awed bewilderment that made one aware of the fragility of the scene's beauty and wonder and which rang true with the play's final lines. '*Hastily* lead away', he said, as if the overwhelming joy of this moment might be jeopardized if it were over-indulged; and the jeopardy derived from his preceding admission that he, like everyone else, must '*answer* to his part', in his case a part responsible for the '*wide gap*' of time' through which they had all been 'dissevered'. There is guilt, and waste, within the joy and fulfilment of the end of *The Winter's Tale*, and this production found them all.
>
> (*SS*, 265–6)

One theme dominates reviewers' reception of the final scene of these productions: its power to move. The productions themselves

FIGURE 42 The music commanded by Paulina (Estelle Kohler) having awakened Hermione (Alexandra Gilbreath), she startles Leontes (Antony Sher) when she begins to stir. The candle-banked platform had served as the dock in 3.2. (5.3, 1999)

reveal a cross-section of directorial decisions about staging the scene – and the nine stagings fit gracefully into the dominant motifs of each production. Stratford's directors have staged the statue scene as a public gathering of as many as thirty-four persons witnessing Hermione's reawakening and as a private one limited to the seven persons most immediately affected by the consequences of Leontes' jealousy. Crowned monarchs and their entourage have admired the statue of a queen; laying aside the accoutrements of power, the monarchs have stressed the common humanity of Leontes, Hermione and Polixenes. They have entered Paulina's gallery in procession, sometimes in candlelit procession, sometimes singing a hymn or accompanied by religious music. And they have entered silently in groups of two or three. The statue crafted by Julio Romano has worn Grecian drapery and costumes of the period of the production. Colour has linked

Hermione with the Madonna, as has her pose and the bank of candles enclosing her. The statue has most often been placed centre stage facing the audience; twice it was at stage left, placed so the audience could watch Hermione 'be stone no more' (99) and the faces of the court; once it was downstage centre, its back to the audience, which attended to the responses of Leontes and those gathered around him. The two productions that doubled Hermione and Perdita chose different solutions to presenting both of them in the final scene. Two productions introduced visual reminders of the dead Mamillius, but the reminders were subtle ones, unlike productions where Mamillius himself appears or his clothing hangs as a trophy near his mother's statue. The reintroduction of familiar and provocative visual devices, such as the perspex cube that displays the statue or the gauze box that encloses the court, helps directors to convey their readings of the play. The singing of an especially written hymn or the resurgence of theme music offers an aural reinforcement of the reconciliations. Whatever the location of Sicilia – eastern or northern Europe, Renaissance Europe, post-war Italy, Regency, Edwardian or contemporary England – *The Winter's Tale* has spoken to post-war audiences. Playing it in the context of a season of Shakespeare's plays about love or with other of his late plays and pairing it with *The Crucible* have highlighted its various facets. Stratford's directors and actors have explored the text and with the help of designers of the set and costumes, lighting effects and music conveyed their readings. The one reading they have not staged, to which a number of other late twentieth-century directors have been drawn, is the dark theme that reunites a dysfunctional couple. In the post-war world, Stratford's productions of *The Winter's Tale* have so far chosen to carry its theme of reconciliation to audiences in Stratford and around the globe.

PRODUCTION CREDITS
AND CAST LISTS

Programmes supply production credits and cast lists; in every case the listing is the announced one for the first performance. The card catalogue of the Shakespeare Centre Library and its production archives provide the incidental details, such as press night.

1948

Director	Anthony Quayle
Designer	Motley
Music	Leslie Bridgewater
LEONTES	Esmond Knight
MAMILLIUS	Timothy Harley
CAMILLO	Julian Amyes
ANTIGONUS	Michael Godfrey
POLIXENES	Manfred Priestley
FLORIZEL	John Justin
ARCHIDAMUS	William Squire
OLD SHEPHERD	John Kidd
CLOWN	Paul Scofield
AUTOLYCUS	Alfie Bass
MARINER	David Wroe
GAOLER	Norman Mitchell
LORDS OF SICILIA	Douglas Wilmer (A)
	Paul Hardwick (B)
SERVANT TO LEONTES	Arnold Diamond
MESSENGER	Robert Urquhart
CITIZENS	Michael Gwynn, Harold Kasket,
	Tom Kneale
SHEPHERD BOY	Michael Bates
DANCER	Edmund Purdom

HERMIONE	Diana Wynyard
PERDITA	Claire Bloom
PAULINA	Ena Burrill
EMILIA	Ailsa Grahame
MOPSA	Jean Fox
DORCAS	Elizabeth Melville
LADY	Jean Fox
TIME	William Squire

LORDS, LADIES, MUSICIANS, SHEPHERDS, GUARDS:
Michael Bates, Alexander Davion, Alan Dipper, Jean Fox, Keith Herrington, Norman Mitchell, Mairhi Russell, Robert Urquhart, John Van Eyssen, Clifford Williams, David Wroe

Number in company	33
Press night	4 June 1948

1960

Director	Peter Wood
Designer	Jaques Noel
Music	Lennox Berkeley
Lighting	Maurice Daniels
Choreography	Pauline Grant

LEONTES	Eric Porter
MAMILLIUS	Dennis Waterman
CAMILLO	Paul Hardwick
ANTIGONUS	Tony Church
CLEOMENES	James Kerry
DION	Julian Battersby
POLIXENES	Patrick Allen
FLORIZEL	Dinsdale Landen
ARCHIDAMUS	William Wallis
OLD SHEPHERD	James Bree
CLOWN	Ian Holm
AUTOLYCUS	Jack MacGowran
MARINER	Walter Brown
GAOLER	Clive Swift
PAULINA'S STEWARD	Peter Jeffrey
FIRST OLD GENTLEMAN	Roy Dotrice
SECOND OLD GENTLEMAN	Ian Richardson
FIRST LORD	Donald Layne-Smith
SECOND LORD	Philip Voss
THIRD LORD	Donald Douglas
OFFICER OF THE COURT	Roger Bizley
FIRST SHEPHERD	Dave Thomas

HERMIONE	Elizabeth Sellars
PERDITA	Susan Maryott
PAULINA	Peggy Ashcroft
EMILIA	Mavis Edwards
MOPSA	Gloria Dolskie
DORCAS	Mandy Miller
SECOND LADY-IN-WAITING	Maroussia Frank

TIME   Derek Godfrey

LADIES, SERVANTS, SOLDIERS, SHEPHERDS AND
SHEPHERDESSES:
Roger Bizley, Walter Brown, Maroussia Frank, Wendy Gifford, Diana
Rigg, David Sumner, Clive Swift, Dave Thomas, William Wallis, Don
Webster

Number in company	34
Press night	30 August 1960
Audio recording	Trial scene (3.2) with Leontes (Eric Porter), Hermione (Elizabeth Sellars) and Officer (Paul Hardwick) (Argo RG 289)

1969

Director	Trevor Nunn
Designer	Christopher Morley
Music	Guy Woolfenden
Lighting	John Bradley, Christopher Morley

LEONTES	Barrie Ingham
MAMILLIUS	Sam Rich/Jeremy Richardson
CAMILLO	Nicholas Selby
ANTIGONUS	Morgan Sheppard
CLEOMENES	Anthony Pedley
DION	Philip Taylor
POLIXENES	Richard Pasco
FLORIZEL	David Bailie
ARCHIDAMUS	John Berwyn
OLD SHEPHERD	Sydney Bromley
CLOWN	Geoffrey Hutchings
AUTOLYCUS	Derek Smith
MARINER	James Vallon
GAOLER	Boyd Mackenzie
FIRST LORD	John Hallam
SECOND LORD	Michael Shannon
THIRD LORD	Basil Clarke
FOURTH LORD	Myles Hoyle
FIFTH LORD	Roger Rees
OFFICER	Denis Holmes
FIRST SERVANT	Roger Rees
SECOND SERVANT	Myles Hoyle
HERMIONE	Judi Dench
PERDITA	Judi Dench
PAULINA	Brenda Bruce
EMILIA	Janet Henfrey
MOPSA	Susan Sheers
DORCAS	Lisa Harrow
LADIES	Juliet Ackroyd, Lisa Harrow, Susan Sheers, Janet Whiteside

TIME   Alton Kumalo

OTHER LORDS AND GENTLEMEN, LADIES, OFFICERS,
AND SERVANTS, SHEPHERDS, AND SHEPHERDESSES:
Juliet Ackroyd, John Berwyn, Basil Clarke, John Hallam, Lisa Harrow,
Janet Henfrey, Denis Holmes, Alton Kumalo, Boyd Mackenzie,
Anthony Pedley, Michael Shannon, Susan Sheers, Morgan Sheppard,
Philip Taylor, James Vallon, Janet Whiteside

Number in company	28
Press night	15 May 1969
Tour	Japan, 12–30 January 1970; Australia, 5 February to 18 April 1970
Transfer	London, Aldwych Theatre, 2 July 1970
Audio recordings	London, Aldwych Theatre, 27 January 1971
	Music by Guy Woolfenden (Grosvenor Records, 1970, GR1 000)

1976

Directors	John Barton with Trevor Nunn
Designer	Di Seymour
Music	Guy Woolfenden
Lighting	Clive Morris

LEONTES	Ian McKellen
MAMILLIUS	Richard Porter/Dorian Wathen
CAMILLO	Bob Peck
ANTIGONUS	Griffith Jones
CLEOMENES	Clyde Pollitt
DION	David Howey
POLIXENES	John Woodvine
FLORIZEL	Nickolas Grace
ARCHIDAMUS	David Lyon
OLD SHEPHERD	David Waller
CLOWN	Roger Rees
AUTOLYCUS	Michael Williams
MARINER	Peter Woodward
PAULINA'S STEWARD	Richard Durden
FIRST LORD*	Dennis Clinton
SHEPHERD'S SERVANT	Leonard Preston
SHEPHERDS	Dennis Clinton, David Lyon, Peter Woodward
HERMIONE	Marilyn Taylerson
PERDITA	Cherie Lunghi
PAULINA	Barbara Leigh-Hunt
EMILIA	Lea Dregorn
MOPSA	Pippa Guard
DORCAS	Frances Viner
FIRST LADY	Susan Dury
SECOND LADY	Judith Harte
SHEPHERDESSES	Lea Dregorn, Susan Dury, Judith Harte
TIME	John Nettles

*Identified in promptbook as Fourth Lord

Number in company	25
Press night	3 June 1976

1981

Director	Ronald Eyre
Designer	Chris Dyer
Music	Stephen Oliver
Lighting	Chris Ellis
Choreography	Sheila Falconer

LEONTES	Patrick Stewart
MAMILLIUS	Christopher Davies/Jeremy Sullivan/ Timothy Sullivan
CAMILLO	Bernard Lloyd
ANTIGONUS	Robert Eddison
CLEOMENES	Hugh Quarshie
DION	Peter Land
POLIXENES	Ray Jewers
FLORIZEL	Peter Chelsom
ARCHIDAMUS	Brian Poyser
OLD SHEPHERD	John Rogan
CLOWN	Gerard Murphy
AUTOLYCUS	Geoffrey Hutchings
MARINER	Brian Poyser
GAOLER	Colin Tarrant
PAULINA'S STEWARD	Colin Tarrant
OLD LORD	Bert Parnaby
FIRST GENTLEMAN	Christopher Hurst
SECOND GENTLEMAN	John McAndrew
OFFICER	Nigel Le Vaillant
SERVANT TO THE OLD SHEPHERD	Graham Turner
HERMIONE	Gemma Jones
PERDITA	Leonie Mellinger
PAULINA	Sheila Hancock
EMILIA	Diana Berriman
MOPSA	Diana Hardcastle
DORCAS	Clare Travers-Deacon
FIRST LADY	Clare Travers-Deacon

SECOND LADY	Julia Hills
BOLD SHEPHERDESS	Juliette Mole
TIME	Robert Eddison
Number in company	26
Press night	30 June 1981
Transfer	Newcastle, Theatre Royal, 2 March 1982
	London, Barbican, 28 July 1982
Video recording	7 February 1983

1984

Director	Adrian Noble
Designer	Bob Crowley
Costumes	David Short
Music	Guy Woolfenden
Lighting	Michael Calf
Choreography	Ian Spink
Sound	John A. Leonard

LEONTES	Alun Armstrong
MAMILLIUS	Christopher Lahr/Daniel Steele
CAMILLO	David Bradley
ANTIGONUS	Paul Webster
CLEOMENES	William Haden
DION	Graham Turner
POLIXENES	Julian Curry
FLORIZEL	John Dougall
ARCHIDAMUS	Ian Talbot
OLD SHEPHERD	Trevor Martin
CLOWN	Ian Talbot
AUTOLYCUS	Ron Cook
MARINER	Ron Cook
GAOLER	Trevor Martin
PAULINA'S STEWARD	Albie Woodington
FIRST LORD	Brian Horstead
FIRST GENTLEMAN	Paul Webster
SECOND GENTLEMAN	Graham Turner

HERMIONE	Lynn Farleigh
PERDITA	Jenifer Landor
PAULINA	Janet Dale
EMILIA	Margery Mason
MOPSA	Julia Dearden
DORCAS	Caroline Milmoe
SECOND LADY	Harriet Bagnall
THIRD LADY	Alibe Parsons

TIME	Paul Webster

SHEPHERDS, SHEPHERDESSES, LORDS, GUARDS, LADIES IN
WAITING:
Members of the company

Number in company	21
Tour	England (outside London) and Northern Ireland, 28 August to 8 December 1984; Christ Church, Spitalfields, London, 10–22 December 1984; Poland, 16–25 January 1985

1986

Director	Terry Hands
Designer	Gerard Howland
Costumes	Alexander Reid
Music	Nigel Hess
Lighting	Terry Hands with Clive Morris
Choreography	Chrissy Wickham
Sound	John A. Leonard

LEONTES	Jeremy Irons
MAMILLIUS	Martin Hicks/Richard Parry
CAMILLO	Richard Easton
ANTIGONUS	Raymond Bowers
CLEOMENES	Stanley Dawson
DION	Sean O'Callaghan
POLIXENES	Paul Greenwood
FLORIZEL	Nathaniel Parker
ARCHIDAMUS	Stanley Dawson
OLD SHEPHERD	Bernard Horsfall
CLOWN	Simon Russell Beale
AUTOLYCUS	Joe Melia
MARINER	Roger Watkins
PAULINA'S STEWARD	Henry Goodman
OFFICER	Mark Lindley
GENTLEMEN	David Glover, Brian Lawson
PASTORAL SERVANTS	Trevor Gordon, Gary Love, Roger Moss, Patrick Robinson

HERMIONE	Penny Downie
PERDITA	Penny Downie
PAULINA	Gillian Barge
EMILIA	Eileen Page
MOPSA	Cornelia Hayes
DORCAS	Caroline Johnson
LADIES	Susie Fairfax, Cornelia Hayes, Caroline Johnson

TIME	Henry Goodman

Number in company	27
Press night	30 April 1986
Transfer	Newcastle, Tyne Theatre, 10 March 1987
	London, Barbican, 14 October 1987
Video recording	10 December 1986
Audio recording	13 January 1988

1992

Director	Adrian Noble
Designer	Anthony Ward
Music	Shaun Davey
Lighting	Chris Parry
Movement	Sue Lefton
Sound	Paul Slocombe

LEONTES	John Nettles
MAMILLIUS	Marc Elliott/Stefan Weclawek
CAMILLO	Benjamin Whitrow
ANTIGONUS	Andrew Jarvis
CLEOMENES	Pearce Quigley
DION	James Walker
POLIXENES	Paul Jesson
FLORIZEL	Alan Cox
ARCHIDAMUS	John Bott
OLD SHEPHERD	Jeffery Dench
CLOWN	Graham Turner
AUTOLYCUS	Richard McCabe
MARINER	Ian Taylor
GAOLER	Roger Frost
PAULINA'S STEWARD	John Bott
LORDS	John Hodgkinson, Ian Taylor, Guy Williams
SHEPHERD'S SERVANT	Barnaby Kay
HERMIONE	Samantha Bond
PERDITA	Phyllida Hancock
PAULINA	Gemma Jones
EMILIA	Angela Vale
MOPSA	Stephanie Jacob
DORCAS	Jenna Russell
LADY	Catherine Mears
[TIME	Benjamin Whitrow]

CHILDREN: Fiona Bocock, Michael Hales, Robert Hales, Edmund Kingsley/Kate Kruszynskyj, Poppy Lawton, Kate Misson, Antony Woolf

Other parts played by members of the company

Number in company	24 adults, 7 children
Press night	1 July 1992
Transfer	Newcastle, Theatre Royal, 23 March 1993
	London, Barbican, 23 June 1993
Tour	7 September to 23 October 1993: Plymouth, Bath, Geneva, Paris, Dublin, Budapest
	1 March to 22 May 1994: Wellington, New Zealand; Tokyo; Brooklyn, NY; Washington, DC
Video recording	19 January 1993
Audio recording	6 July 1993

1999

Director	Gregory Doran
Designer	Robert Jones
Music	Ilona Sekacz
Lighting	Tim Mitchell
Movement	Sian Williams
Sound	Andrea J. Cox

LEONTES	Antony Sher
MAMILLIUS	Emily Bruni
CAMILLO	Geoffrey Freshwater
ANTIGONUS	Jeffry Wickham
CLEOMENES	William Mannering
DION	Steven Atholl
POLIXENES	Ken Bones
FLORIZEL	Ryan McCluskey
ARCHIDAMUS	Peter Macqueen
OLD SHEPHERD	James Hayes
CLOWN	Christopher Brand
AUTOLYCUS	Ian Hughes
MARINER	Nicholas Khan
GAOLER	Peter Macqueen
FIRST LORD	Christopher Wells
SECOND LORD	Nicholas Khan
DOCTOR	Sévan Stephan
GUARDS	Michael Moylan, Gil Cohen-Alloro
FOOTMEN	Jim Fish, Miltos Yerolemou
SHEPHERD'S SERVANT	Miltos Yerolemou

HERMIONE	Alexandra Gilbreath
PERDITA	Emily Bruni
PAULINA	Estelle Kohler
EMILIA	Myra McFadyen
MOPSA	Gail Ghislaine Sixsmith
DORCAS	Myra McFadyen
LADIES-IN-WAITING	Nancy Carroll, Emily Pithon, Paula Stephens

MAIDS   Vanessa Earl, Karen Bryson, Florence
                         Sparham, Gail Ghislaine Sixsmith

TIME   Jeffry Wickham

Other parts played by members of the company

Number in company	29
Press night	6 January 1999
Transfer	London, Barbican, 25 March 1999
Video recording	21 and 22 December 1998
Audio recording	5 May 1999

REVIEWS CITED

Useful collections of reviews may be found in the volumes of Theatre Records, SCL, and in *London Theatre Record*, 1981– (published as *Theatre Record*, 1991–), edited by Ian Herbert. With few exceptions, the dates given below are those supplied by either the Shakespeare Centre Library or *Theatre Record*. A selection of reviews of productions at Stratford (1960, 1969, 1976, 1981), as well as other significant productions, is reprinted in *Shakespearean Criticism*, 15 (1991), 396–500.

1948

Birmingham Evening Despatch, 5 June 1948, Brian Harvey
Birmingham Evening News, 12 June 1948, R.R.
Birmingham Gazette, 5 June 1948, J.M.C.
Birmingham Mail, 5 June 1948, C.I.W.
Birmingham Post, 5 June 1948, T.C. K[emp]
Coventry Standard, 12 June 1948
Daily Telegraph, 5 June 1948, W.A. Darlington
Evesham Journal, 12 June 1948, J.H.B.
Leamington Spa Courier, 11 June 1948, P.D.H.
Manchester Guardian, 7 June 1948, G.P.
News Chronicle, 11 June 1948, Alan Dent
Observer, 6 June 1948
Punch, 16 June 1948
Stage, 10 June 1948
Stratford-upon-Avon Herald, 11 June 1948, R.E.
Times, 7 June 1948
Warwick Advertiser, 11 June 1948

1960

Birmingham Post, 31 August 1960, J.C. Trewin

Coventry Standard, 2 September 1960, S.S.M.
Evesham Journal, 2 September 1960, John H. Bird
Financial Times, 31 August 1960, Richard Findlater
Illustrated London News, 17 September 1960, J.C. Trewin
Liverpool Post, 31 August 1960
Morning Advertiser, 12 September 1960, Geoffrey Tarran
New Statesman and Nation, 10 September 1960, Jeremy Brooks
News Chronicle, 31 August 1960, Elizabeth Frank
Nottingham Guardian Journal, 31 August 1960
Plays and Players, October 1960, Peter Roberts
Punch, 7 September 1960, Eric Keown
Shakespeare Quarterly, 11 (1960), 452–3, Robert Speaight
Stage and Television Today, 1 September 1960, R.B.M.
Stratford-upon-Avon Herald, 2 September 1960, Edmund Gardner
Stratford-upon-Avon Herald, 11 November 1960, Edmund Gardner
Sunday Times, 4 September 1960
Tablet, 24 September 1960, Robert Speaight
Theatre World, October 1960, Harold Matthews
Times, 31 August 1960
Yorkshire Post, 31 August 1960, Desmond Pratt

1969

Birmingham Post, 17 May 1969, J.C. Trewin
Birmingham Sunday Mercury, 19 May 1969
Daily Telegraph, 16 May 1969, John Barber
Daily Telegraph, 3 July 1970, Eric Shorter
Evening Standard, 16 May 1969, Milton Shulman
Financial Times, 16 May 1969, B.A. Young
Guardian, 16 May 1969, Gareth Lloyd Evans
Guardian, 3 July 1970, Philip Hope-Wallace
Guardian Weekly (Manchester), 22 May 1969, Gareth Lloyd Evans
Morning Star, 17 May 1969, Gordon Parsons
New Statesman, 23 May 1969, Benedict Nightingale
Observer, 18 May 1969, Ronald Bryden
Plays and Players, September 1970, Peter Ansorge (interview with
    Trevor Nunn)
Shakespeare Quarterly, 20 (1969), 435–7, Robert Speaight

Shakespeare Survey 23 (1970), 133–4, Gareth Lloyd Evans
South Wales Evening Argus, 19 May 1969, Neville Miller
Spectator, 23 May 1969, Hilary Spurling
Stratford-upon-Avon Herald, 23 May 1969, Sheila Bannock
Sunday Times, 18 May 1969, J.W. Lambert
Tablet, 7 June 1969, Robert Speaight
Tatler, June 1969, Sheridan Morley
Times, 16 May 1969, Irving Wardle
Times, 3 July 1970, Irving Wardle

1976

Birmingham Post, 7 June 1976, J.C. Trewin
Cahiers Elisabéthains, 10 (1976), 90–2, François Laroque
Daily Express, 1 June 1976, Herbert Kretzmer
Daily Telegraph, 5 June 1976, John Barber
Financial Times, 7 June 1976, B.A. Young
Guardian, 5 June 1976, Michael Billington
New Statesman, 11 June 1976, Benedict Nightingale
Observer, 13 June 1976, Robert Cushman
Oxford Mail, 4 June 1976, Don Chapman
Shakespeare Quarterly, 28 (1977), 188–9, Robert Speaight
Shakespeare Survey 30 (1977), 173–4, Roger Warren
Sunday Telegraph, 6 June 1976, Rosemary Say
Sunday Times, 6 June 1976, Harold Hobson
Tatler and Bystander, July 1976, Clare Colvin

1981

Birmingham Post, 1 July 1981, J.C. Trewin
Cahiers Elisabéthains, 20 (1981), 115–16, Jean Fuzier and François
    Laroque
Financial Times, 29 July 1982, B.A. Young
Guardian, 1 July 1981, Michael Billington
Lady, July 1981, J.C. Trewin
Listener, 9 July 1981, John Elsom
Observer, 1 August 1982, Robert Cushman
Oxford Mail, 1 July 1981, Don Chapman

Shakespeare Survey 35 (1982), 147–9, Roger Warren
Times, 2 July 1981, Irving Wardle
Times Literary Supplement, 10 July 1981, Stephen Wall

1984

Cahiers Elisabéthains, 28 (1985), 86–7, G.M. Pearce
City Limits, 21 December 1984, Matt Wolf
Daily Telegraph, 22 October 1984, Eric Shorter
Financial Times, 22 October 1984, Michael Coveney
Financial Times, 13 December 1984, Martin Hoyle
Guardian, 31 August 1984, Robin Thornber
Guardian, 12 December 1984, Michael Billington
Observer, 7 October 1984, Michael Ratcliffe
Observer, 16 December 1984, Michael Ratcliffe
Observer, 30 December 1984, Michael Ratcliffe
Scunthorpe Evening Telegraph, undated [August/September] 1984,
　A[nthea] R[obbins]
Sunday Times, 28 October 1984, Robert Hewison
Times, 27 October 1984, Anthony Masters

1986

Birmingham Evening Mail, 1 May 1986, Richard Edmonds
Bristol Evening Post, 3 May 1986, Brian Jones
Cahiers Elisabéthains, 30 (1986), 93–5, Jean Fuzier and Jean-Marie
　Maguin
Daily Telegraph, 2 May 1986, John Barber
Financial Times, 1 May 1986, Martin Hoyle
Glasgow Herald, 3 May 1986, Anne Donaldson
Guardian, 2 May 1986, Nicholas de Jongh
Shakespeare Quarterly, 38 (1987), 84, 85–6, Roger Warren
Shakespeare Survey 40 (1987), 177–8, Nicholas Shrimpton
South Wales Argus, 1 May 1986, Helen Birtwhistle
Stage and Television Today, 15 May 1986, Ann FitzGerald
Stratford-upon-Avon Herald, 9 May 1986, Viv Thomas
Sunday Telegraph, 4 May 1986, Francis King
Sunday Times, 4 May 1986, John Peter

Sunday Today, 11 May 1986, F[rancis] W[heen]
Time Out, 7–13 May 1986, Jane Edwardes
Times, 1 May 1986, Irving Wardle
Times Literary Supplement, 23 May 1986, John Pitcher
Wantage Grove Herald, 8 May 1986
Yorkshire Post, 2 May 1986, J.P.

1992

Cahiers Elisabéthains, 44 (1993), 88–9, Rebecca Flynn
Daily Telegraph, 3 July 1992, Charles Spencer
Evening Standard, 2 July 1992, Nicholas de Jongh
Financial Times, 3 July 1992, Malcolm Rutherford
Financial Times, 25 June 1993, Alastair Macaulay
Guardian, 3 July 1992, Michael Billington
Guardian, 25 June 1993, Lyn Gardner
Independent, 3 July 1992, Paul Taylor
Independent on Sunday, 5 July 1992, Irving Wardle
Observer, 5 July 1992, Michael Coveney
Plays and Players, August 1992, Garry O'Connor
Shakespeare Quarterly, 44 (1993), 349–51, Robert Smallwood
Shakespeare Survey 46 (1993), 173–5, Peter Holland
Sunday Telegraph, 5 July 1992, Kirsty Milne
Sunday Times, 5 July 1992, Robert Hewison
Times, 3 July 1992, Benedict Nightingale
Times Literary Supplement, 10 July 1992, Peter Porter
Tribune, 17 July 1992, Rod Dungate

1999

Birmingham Post, 8 January 1999, Richard Edmonds
Cahiers Elisabéthains, 56 (1999), 76–8, Vivian Thomas
Daily Telegraph, 8 January 1999, Charles Spencer
Daily Telegraph, 26 March 1999, Charles Spencer (interview with
    Antony Sher)
Financial Times, 8 January 1999, Alastair Macaulay
Guardian, 9 January 1999, Michael Billington
Independent, 8 January 1999, Paul Taylor

Independent on Sunday, 10 January 1999, Maeve Walsh
Mail on Sunday, 17 January 1999, Georgina Brown
New Statesman, 15 January 1999, David Jays
Observer, 10 January 1999, Susannah Clapp
Oxford Times, 15 January 1999, Jeannine Alton
Shakespeare Survey 53 (2000), 263–6, Robert Smallwood
Spectator, 16 January 1999, Patrick Carnegie
Stage, 14 January 1999, Ben Dowell
Sunday Times, 10 January 1999, John Peter
Time Out, 13 January 1999, Jane Edwardes
Times, 8 January 1999, Benedict Nightingale
Times Literary Supplement, 22 January 1999, Christopher Cannon

ABBREVIATIONS

NEWSPAPERS AND PERIODICALS

Birm. E. Desp.	*Birmingham Evening Despatch*
Birm. E. Mail	*Birmingham Evening Mail*
Birm. E. News	*Birmingham Evening News*
Birm. Gaz.	*Birmingham Gazette*
Birm. Mail	*Birmingham Mail*
Birm. Post	*Birmingham Post*
Birm. Sun. Mer.	*Birmingham Sunday Mercury*
Bristol E. Post	*Bristol Evening Post*
Cahiers Elis.	*Cahiers Elisabéthains*
Christian Cent.	*Christian Century*
City L.	*City Limits*
Coventry Sta.	*Coventry Standard*
D. Express	*Daily Express*
D. Telegraph	*Daily Telegraph*
E. Standard	*Evening Standard*
Evesham J.	*Evesham Journal*
FT	*Financial Times*
Glasgow Her.	*Glasgow Herald*
Guardian Week.	*Guardian Weekly (Manchester)*
Illus. Lon. News	*Illustrated London News*
Indep. Sun.	*Independent on Sunday*
Kidd. Times	*Kidderminster Times*
Leam. Spa Cour.	*Leamington Spa Courier*
Liv. Post	*Liverpool Post*
Mail Sun.	*Mail on Sunday*
Man. Guardian	*Manchester Guardian*
Morn. Adv.	*Morning Advertiser*
Morn. Star	*Morning Star*

New States.	*New Statesman*
New States & Nat.	*New Statesman and Nation*
News Chron.	*News Chronicle*
Nott. Guard. J.	*Nottingham Guardian Journal*
Oxf. Mail	*Oxford Mail*
Plays & P.	*Plays and Players*
Scun. E. Tel.	*Scunthorpe Evening Telegraph*
SQ	*Shakespeare Quarterly*
SS	*Shakespeare Survey*
S. Wales Arg.	*South Wales Argus*
S. Wales E. Arg.	*South Wales Evening Argus*
Stage & TV	*Stage and Television Today*
SA Herald	*Stratford-upon-Avon Herald*
S. Telegraph	*Sunday Telegraph*
S. Times	*Sunday Times*
S. Today	*Sunday Today*
Tatler & Bys.	*Tatler and Bystander*
Theatre W.	*Theatre World*
TLS	*Times Literary Supplement*
Wantage Gro. Her.	*Wantage Grove Herald*
Warwick Adv.	*Warwick Advertiser*
Westm. Gaz.	*Westminster Gazette*
Yorks. Post	*Yorkshire Post*

OTHER ABBREVIATIONS

NSA	National Sound Archives
SCL	Shakespeare Centre Library

BIBLIOGRAPHY

PRODUCTION ARCHIVES

The primary source for productions at Stratford-upon-Avon is the collection of the Shakespeare Centre Library. Its holdings include promptbooks for each post-war production of *The Winter's Tale*; other production-related manuscripts, such as music scores and cues; photographs (all productions) and colour slides since 1960; fixed-focus video recordings (1986, 1992, 1999, and London transfer of 1981); volumes of theatre records.

The National Sound Archives, British Library, holds audio recordings of the London transfers of 1969, 1986, 1992 and 1999.

BOOKS AND ARTICLES

Addenbrooke, David, *The Royal Shakespeare Company: The Peter Hall Years* (London, 1974)

Bartholomeusz, Dennis, *'The Winter's Tale' in Performance in England and America 1611–1976 (Cambridge, 1982)*

Beauman, Sally, *The Royal Shakespeare Company: A History of Ten Decades* (Oxford, 1982)

Berry, Ralph, 'Stratford Festival Canada', *Shakespeare Quarterly*, 30 (1979), 167–75

Bloom, Claire, *Limelight and After* (Harmondsworth, England, 1983)

Brown, Ivor and Anthony Quayle (eds), *Shakespeare Memorial Theatre 1948–1950* (London, 1951)

Campos, Christophe, 'Tales of two winters: Shakespeare in London and Paris', *Franco-British Studies*, 10 (1990), 35–53

Cochrane, Claire, *'The Winter's Tale'*, *Cahiers Elisabéthains*, 32 (1987), 90–1

Coghill, Nevill, 'Six points of stage-craft in *The Winter's Tale*', *Shakespeare Survey 11* (1958), 31–41

David, Richard, *Shakespeare in the Theatre* (Cambridge, 1978)

Dench, Judi, 'A career in Shakespeare', in Jonathan Bate and Russell Jackson (eds), *Shakespeare: An Illustrated Stage History* (Oxford, 1996), 197–210

Dessen, Alan C., 'Reviewing Shakespeare for the record', *Shakespeare Quarterly*, 36 (1985), 602–8

Ewbank, Inga-Stina, 'From narrative to dramatic language: *The Winter's Tale* and its source', in Sandra L. Williamson (ed.), *Shakespearean Criticism Yearbook 1989*, vol. 13 (London, 1991), 409–16

Granville-Barker, Harley, *Prefaces to Shakespeare: 'Cymbeline' and 'The Winter's Tale'* (London, 1984)

Holland, Peter, *English Shakespeares* (Cambridge, 1997)

Holland, Peter, 'Shakespeare performances in England', *Shakespeare Survey* 46 (1993), 169–71

Jones, Gemma, 'Hermione in *The Winter's Tale*', in Philip Brockbank (ed.), *Players of Shakespeare* (Cambridge, 1985), 153–65

Kemp, T.C. and J.C. Trewin, *The Stratford Festival* (Birmingham, 1953)

Knowles, Richard Paul, 'History as metaphor: Daphne Dare's late 19th- and early 20th-century settings for Shakespeare at Stratford, Ontario, 1975–1980', *Theatre History Studies*, 5 (1985), 20–40

McCabe, Richard, 'Autolycus in *The Winter's Tale*', in Robert Smallwood (ed.), *Players of Shakespeare 4* (Cambridge, 1998), 60–70

Mullin, Michael (ed.), *Theatre at Stratford-upon-Avon: A Catalog-Index to the Productions of the Shakespeare Memorial/Royal Shakespeare Theatre, 1879–1978*, 2 vols (Westport, Conn., 1980)

Noble, Adrian, Foreword to John F. Andrews (ed.), *The Winter's Tale* (London, 1995)

Pafford, J.H.P. (ed.), *The Winter's Tale*, The Arden Shakespeare (London, 1963, reprinted 1991)

Phillips, Stephen J., 'The Winter's Tale', *Shakespeare Bulletin*, 18 (2000), 30–1

Pringle, Marian J., *The Theatres of Stratford-upon-Avon 1875–1992: An Architectural History* (Stratford-upon-Avon, 1994)

Quayle, Anthony, *A Time to Speak* (London, 1990)

Ranald, Margaret Loftus, 'The Winter's Tale', *Shakespeare Bulletin*, 13 (1995), 14–15

Rylands, George, 'Festival Shakespeare in the West End', *Shakespeare Survey* 6 (1953), 142–6

Stewart, Patrick, 'Acting Leontes', in *Du texte à la scène: langages du théâtre*, ed. M.T. Jones-Davies (Paris, 1983), 251–9

Tatspaugh, Patricia, '*The Winter's Tale* on the Stage', in the New Variorum edition, eds Robert K. Turner and Virginia Haas (forthcoming)

Törnqvist, Egil, *Between Stage and Screen: Ingmar Bergman Directs* (Amsterdam, 1995)

Trewin, J.C., *Paul Scofield* (London, 1956)

Trewin, J.C., *Peter Brook* (London, 1971)

Venezky, Alice, 'Current Shakespearian productions in England and France', *Shakespeare Quarterly*, 2 (1951), 335–8

Warren, Roger, 'Shakespeare's late plays at Stratford, Ontario', *Shakespeare Survey 40* (1988), 155–68

Warren, Roger, *Staging Shakespeare's Late Plays* (Oxford, 1990)

Weil, Herbert S., Jr, 'Shakespeare Festival, Canada 1986', *Shakespeare Quarterly*, 38 (1987), 227–42

Wells, Stanley, 'Shakespeare performances in England, 1987–8', *Shakespeare Survey 42* (1990), 129–48

Williams, George Walton, 'Exit pursued by a quaint device: the bear in *The Winter's Tale*', *The Upstart Crow*, 14, 105–9

Williamson, Sandra L. (ed.), *Shakespearean Criticism*, vol. 15 (London, 1991), 393–540

Wilson, M. Glen, 'Charles Kean's production of *The Winter's Tale*', *Theatre History Studies*, 5 (1985), 1–15

INDEX

This index includes actors, directors, critics and other individuals mentioned in the main text who are connected with a production of *The Winter's Tale*. Productions referred to in the text by date are indexed by director. It also includes references to other Shakespeare plays. Page numbers in bold refer to illustrations.

Here is a vivid and stirring saga of a great American family, the deWitts, set against the changing panorama of a tumultuous century in American history. It is the story of The Interstate, a railway founded before the middle of the nineteenth century, which developed through a stormy hundred years into a vast enterprise.

In 1866, old Aaron deWitt watched his two sons struggling for control of the railroad he founded. There was Stephen, retiring, idealistic, quietly capable, and his younger brother Rufus, arrogant and flamboyant, certain that he would be his father's choice. The fatal splitting of the deWitt dynasty had begun . . . and within a few months it was intensified by the birth of two children— Laura, taken from the dying body of Stephen's young wife, and Cornelia, as red-headed and determined as her father. Then Aaron died, leaving control of his empire not to Rufus, but to the grief-stricken, broken Stephen. And so began the struggle of four generations for the control of the sprawling Interstate.

TAYLOR CALDWELL

Never VICTORIOUS Never DEFEATED

Man is never victorious, never defeated,
The cheater yields up his loot to the cheated,
Wisdom and folly can never be parted,
The waters return to the hills where they started.

TAYLOR CALDWELL

COLLINS
8 Grafton Street, London W1
1989

William Collins Sons & Co Ltd
London · Glasgow · Sydney · Auckland
Toronto · Johannesburg

ISBN 0 00 221379 6

First published 1954
This edition 1989

© Janet Reback 1954

Printed and bound in Great Britain by
Billings Book Plan, Worcester

Contents

PROLOGUE

IT WAS generally agreed, and with indignation by a few, that it had been a great scandal. Cornelia deWitt Marshall had not only insulted herself, but all her friends, and the company which her grandfather had founded.

The banquet honouring her and the one hundredth anniversary of the mighty Interstate Railroad Company was given in the main dining-room of Philadelphia's oldest and most aristocratic private club. Scores of the largest stockholders, including the younger Jay Regan of New York and one or two of the Vanderbilts, not to mention all the directors and officers of the company, were present. At the head of the table, with his mother at his right hand, sat DeWitt Marshall, president of the company, his son Rufus next to him. (Rufus was only twenty-one, but as he would one day be president himself, it was considered proper that he sit beside his father.) It was well known that Cornelia deWitt Marshall had been, and still was, "the guiding genius of the company." The gentlemen present (and there were only gentlemen in deference to Cornelia's aversion to women) regarded this seventy-year-old woman fondly as she sat there at the immense table in the glitter and glow of the crystal chandeliers.

Some of the expressions of fondness might be artificial, but the respect was real enough. She was called in private "the old red hellion." However, no one underestimated Cornelia. A masterful and powerful woman, a vindictive and humorous enemy—Cornelia.

There she sat in her thronelike gilt chair, and she was impressive. Even sitting, she towered over her neighbours. Some of the older men, Jay Regan among them, thought of an ancient phrase: "A fine figure of a woman." When she stood, she was five feet eight inches tall, and her figure might have been that of a woman forty years her junior. Her waist was slim, her breast full and white, though the neck above it was raddled. She could stride like a young woman, and her gestures were quick and dominant.

9

Never Victorious, Never Defeated

She could ride a horse like a young man, and she often drove her own car, and engaged, at intervals, in an excellent game of tennis and golf. When she sailed on her enormous yacht, *Rufus*, she would often take the wheel, to the awed admiration of the captain. She could swim like a vigorous child, swear like a New York policeman, outshout anyone at a football game, and dance like an adolescent. She also had an original and very large fund of ribald stories and could outdrink almost any man. She smoked constantly.

Seventy years old, and still full of immense vitality—Cornelia. It was amazing, thought her older male friends, some of whom tottered when they walked and had rheumy eyes. Cornelia never forgot anything, either. Her memory was a complete library of the whole railroad business.

The banquet was very good indeed. The chief and his assistants had outdone themselves on this occasion. Cornelia had eaten twice as much as anyone present. However, she did not appear satiated or sluggish, and she had drunk quantities of bourbon, her favourite beverage, not only before the banquet, but all through it.

So, there she sat, smiling, tall and stately in her chair, emanating energy and liveliness. She wore a silver gown, closely fashioned in order to show off her youthful figure and splendid white shoulders. A cascade of small white orchids flowed over her breast. A diamond necklace blazed about her throat; diamonds glittered in her ears, in her hair and on her fingers, and all up and down both long white arms. It was a crude display, and the more tasteful of the guests commented on this to themselves. But then, Cornelia had never pretended to have taste. She was vulgar and raucous and coarse, and gloried in it all. She displayed her vulgarity as she displayed her diamonds: proudly, and with wicked humour.

DeWitt, and his son Rufus, looked at Cornelia to-night with polite expressions, and murmured at her shouted remarks, which could be heard all through the banquet hall. They looked at her face; in contrast with the rest of her body it was showing her age to some extent. It was not the face of a seventy-year-old woman, but still it was a haggard face, over-rouged, the red lips tight and thin, the large curved nose very conspicuous, the hazel eyes shadowed too much with gleaming lavender, the eyelashes coated and stiff. She was at her best when she smiled or laughed, for her big white teeth were her own, and perfect, and shone like polished porcelain. Then her eyes would dance, the wrinkles almost disappear, and her humour and animal roughness and vitality would accomplish the miracle of making her seem at least thirty years younger.

Above this amazing face was an even more amazing pile of waved and shining red hair, interwoven with diamonds. It was not an auburn red, or a dandy red, or a golden red. It was frankly and simply, violently red. It was the colour of her youth. She had portraits to prove it. For the past thirty years, however, her hair had really been white. She did not care who knew that this redness she now displayed was only a dye. It was a work of art, and it was abundant and vigorous.

It was almost impossible to escape the sound of that booming voice; the waiters smiled discreetly, and chuckled to themselves when they caught some of her favourite and more indelicate jokes. There was a magnetism about Cornelia to which only her son DeWitt was immune. He would sometimes condescend to explain this thoughtfully: " I suppose it's because she's never cared about a living thing but herself. If you love yourself sufficiently everyone else will love you. They'll believe you must have some perfectly good reason for your opinion."

Father and son studied Cornelia to-night, seeing the rapt faces about her, watching her gay gestures, her swift and glittering smile, hearing her uproarious laughter and the laughter which joined hers. Rufus shifted uneasily in his seat and after a moment's hesitation whispered, " Have you noticed, Father? There's something diabolical about grandmother to-night. . . ."

"Nonsense," said DeWitt with disapproval. His son, whom he considered a rather hulking masculine edition of his mother—without Cornelia's brains of course—subsided, and a sulky expression settled on the big mouth so like his grandmother's. As if he felt his son's resentment, DeWitt shifted in his seat and played with his cane. Rufus annoyed him; everybody annoyed him, except Tony, and Tony was not here. For an instant, DeWitt, to his own disgust, felt the old familiar pang of desolation.

Old George Hill, one of the directors of the company, was lighting Cornelia's gold-tipped cigarette. His hand shook with age. He was cackling at her last joke. Then he became sober. He was to make the speech and the presentation of the medal.

Never Victorious, Never Defeated

He rose slowly to his feet and leaned on the table, a fat old man with glaucous eyes and a thick pink double chin. The waiters scurried from the room and closed the doors. A silence fell, and everyone waited. Cornelia blew a cloud of smoke before her face, and then another. The February night was unusually mild, and the air conditioning roared in the sudden quiet.

Mr. Hill glanced portentously about him. "Dear friends," he rumbled, "we're here on a very special occasion. Such an occasion might call for long speeches. But Cornelia—Mrs. Marshall—has asked for no speech at all! Isn't that so, my dear?" he asked, turning to Cornelia and gazing down at her affectionately.

Cornelia waved away the smoke, nodded, laughed exuberantly. "Even a railroad must be embarrassed to be one hundred years old," she said. Her eyes sparkled on each face, and there was something of reflection in them. Her stare came at last to her son and grandson, and her grin widened. DeWitt drew his black brows together and involuntarily stiffened. Rufus felt a curious thrill of alarm. He did not like his grandmother; he had always considered her intensely ugly, and sometimes hated his own appearance which was so like hers. His hand moved without volition, as if to touch his father's thin arm, then dropped on the table.

He thought: There is no denying that the old red devil has a mind, perhaps a better mind than all of us put together. But, there's also no denying she's a witch. He reached absently for a cigarette in a crystal box and began to puff amateurishly. There was something in the air, centred in "that old woman," which made him angrily apprehensive. For Cornelia's eyes had taken on a queer fixed brightness, a kind of glare, as she looked at her son, and her smile, to Rufus, was the ugliest smile in the world. The blinding light of the chandeliers shone on Mr. Hill's bald rosy head, and Cornelia's diamonds stunned the eye. She was one shimmer, like electricity. To Rufus she gave the impression of new balefulness, all of which was directed at DeWitt, his father.

Then, while old Mr. Hill rumbled on with his eulogies, her gaze shifted to her grandson Rufus. He watched her; she was laughing soundlessly, he could see. Yet there was an odd sort of triumph in her eyes now. Rufus was puzzled. He was no favourite of Cornelia's, but still there was that triumph, that assurance, in her eyes. What the hell is she up to, and how does it concern me? Rufus asked himself.

12

Never Victorious, Never Defeated

"We all know," said Mr. Hill, his voice trembling with emotion, "that it was Rufus deWitt, father of Mrs. Marshall, whose enterprise, vision, and determined courage—inherited from his own father, Mr. Aaron—set the Interstate Railroad Company on its path to huge success. But we also know that it was Mrs. Marshall's genius and ambition which caused our company to assume such gigantic proportions and importance. Always, she was her father's right-hand man. She was the light that never dimmed; her ideas, her enthusiasms, her plannings, are unique in the history of American railroading."

Rufus suddenly thought of his dead grandfather, Allan Marshall. He had known little of Allan. The family did not speak of him since his death; he was a man to be forgotten as quickly as possible. But no one can forget him, commented Rufus to himself. He is here, like a ghost, forceful and passionate and listening. Nobody can escape him.

"I wonder what my grandfather would have thought of all this?" Rufus asked his father. But DeWitt lifted a shoulder against his son, in contempt. Rufus lit another cigarette; his red brows drew together and he bent his head.

Mr. Hill had come to the conclusion of his rhapsodies. Everyone waited. Mr. Hill was holding a white satin box in his hand, worshipfully, as a priest would hold a chalice. Something shone in it: a big gold medal. Mr. Hill bowed, and laid the box before Cornelia, who glanced down at it with smiling tolerance. Then she looked up, and this time she did not direct her eyes to her son or grandson. She was looking at one of the sons of her cousin Laura, Miles Peale, executive vice-president of the company. Miles returned the look with the utmost gravity, and there was no expression on his face. Cornelia smiled, and chuckled. She removed the medal and examined it critically.

"Well, well," she said, holding up the medal. "Look at it, everybody! It's beautiful. On one side is our old wood-burning engine and on the other side is our latest locomotive. With cars, rounding a magnificent curve in the mountains. Wonderful. 1835 to 1935. One hundred years!"

The banquet hall thundered with applause and loving laughter. Cornelia passed the medal to her neighbour, who passed it on. It went from reverent hand to reverent hand, and Cornelia watched its passage. She was smoking rapidly, and through the smoke her sparkling eyes were full of evil mirth.

13

Never Victorious, Never Defeated

The medal reached young Rufus. The thing was cold and big and heavy in his hand. It represented incredible power. He passed it on to his father, who studied it closely and then seemed reluctant to pass it on. It reached Cornelia again, and her smile was very wide, as if she had noticed her son's desire to retain the medal.

It was then that the scandalous incident began. For Cornelia began to toss the medal in her hands, throwing it higher and higher each time. And as she did so she laughed, the laugh becoming more ribald, harsher, louder, with each burst. No one moved; no one spoke. All smiles had gone. Everyone watched the coin shining in the air, and they saw it fall, saw it rise again. They could not move even when Cornelia abruptly thrust back her chair and got to her feet, still tossing the coin, still shouting out her laughter, which now had a jeering note. A few started to rise, then froze in a half-sitting position, hypnotised by the extraordinary actions of that extraordinary woman.

Now the medal was whirling higher in the air so that it was a yellow blur of light under the chandeliers. Mr. Hill sat in his chair, paralysed, his mouth dropping open. Some of the men gripped the edge of the flowered table, leaning forward. DeWitt's hands, on the table, were like clenched and fleshless bones.

Nothing could have been more malefic or more appalling than Cornelia's hard and blatant face, the open mouth roaring with laughter. She rocked on her high silver heels, a silver-flaming and diamond-shining figure topped by a mound of vivid red hair.

Then, without a word, without a glance, she moved towards the door, still throwing the medal, and whooping at each rise and drop. She walked unsteadily, like one intoxicated. No one stood up, even now. No one followed her. She reached the door, flung it open as the medal spun in the air; she caught it, and passed out of the hall.

They could hear her laughter as she retreated.

PART ONE

CHAPTER ONE

FOR THREE days there had been the typical January thaw so that one might have thought spring had come.

Each day everybody prophesied snow for the morrow. But the snow did not come. Instead, the grass turned bright green, and the perennials in the gardens were brilliant with life against the wet black ground. The snow retreated like a white wave against walls and huddled in the hollows in the woods. A pale bright sun burnished the naked limbs of trees and struck the sides of houses with a glow. The river swelled darkly, and mists rolled down the mountains at sunset, and the sky became a soft and tender blue.

It might have been spring except that the earth gave out no scent and the balmy air and winds were sterile of all sweetness, and though the grass was green it had an artificial quality. No tree toads sang at twilight; no bird-song struck the ear. People looked uneasily at the sky or watched the rising river which threatened the valley.

On the fourth night rain began to fall, and there was an ashen look in the sky which slowly took on a pinkish colour. Black clouds began to drift rapidly against this eerie background, and suddenly vivid lightning slashed through them. A burst of thunder followed. The storm broke furiously over the countryside, and the bare trees lashed the roaring air, and mountain and valley quivered in the wild blazes of light and seemed to shake in the thunder. The river, illuminated with white flame one moment, then dark the next, tumbled in flight between the hills.

It was eleven o'clock, and in the midst of the storm, when Lydia deWitt rose slowly through the oblivion which had engulfed her for hours. Her dazed ears became aware of the battering against the windows, and then her eyes, feeble and still dim, caught the glare of the lightning between the folds of the red velvet curtains. She was very confused. She could not remember where she was. She heard the thunder and asked herself weakly: Is this summer? What has happened to me? The gutter streamed with water, and she could hear it, like a small cataract. Then she saw the lamplight in the room and tried to raise her head.

"Well!" exclaimed a hearty male voice. "She's awake at last! Our Liddie's awake!" The solid floor, heavily carpeted, shook slightly under someone's footsteps. The lamplight flickered before Lydia's vision, and she closed her eyes again. A woman was speaking now, in soft and servile tones: "She's all right now, Mr. deWitt. Our lady is all right. Aren't you, Mrs. deWitt?"

Lydia kept her eyes closed and swallowed against her nausea. She shivered when a violent peal of thunder exploded over the house. It was a great and sturdy house, but it trembled under that assault.

"A wonderful baby, Liddie!" said the male voice. "Won't you open your eyes again, and the nurse will bring her in."

Lydia sighed. Her lashes fluttered open. "A girl?" she whispered.

"A lovely girl," said the voice exuberantly. "Bright red hair. Cornelia! Yes, that's what we'll call her."

Cornelia. A hard and rocky name. Lydia lay flat in the huge bed and looked at her husband. She looked at him, and hated him, and turned aside her head. But he continued to stand near her, smiling, tall, wide, and strong, his red and waving hair afire in the lamplight. She could see him as he stood there, though her head was averted. She could see the massiveness of him, and his fine black broadcloth suit, and his black cravat with the pearl pin. She could see his large and ruddy face, his beaming hazel eyes, his thick lips parting widely over big white teeth. His hands were large and white and soft, and he wore a fine signet ring.

She could feel the magnetism that crackled about him, and his health and vitality. She knew he was still smiling broadly. She knew many more things about him, and her loathing mounted in her until she was afraid she would shriek. Her flesh turned hot and she clenched her hands. Her eyes fixed themselves intensely on the fire which spluttered and rose in golden sparks in the throat of the chimney. Then a stiff white skirt and apron intervened between her and the fire, and the voice of Mrs. Brunt, her nurse, spoke again: "I'll bring in the sweet baby for you to see, Mrs. deWitt. Such a beautiful baby girl!"

Never Victorious, Never Defeated

No, thought Lydia. I don't want it. I don't want to see it. A hand touched the long sweep of her dark hair which coiled on the pillows, and she winced.

"Such a hard time our girl had," said her husband murmurously, continuing to stroke her hair. "But everything's well now. Did you have a good sleep, darling?"

Lydia drew in an exhausted breath. She wondered if she could not throw herself back into that darkness forever. Someone kissed her cheek, and she shrank away. The presence of her husband overpowered her, and her flesh prickled. "Don't," she muttered. "Please don't, Rufus."

Rufus began to laugh. His hand touched her wet throat solicitously. "I don't mind that it's a girl, dearest," he said. "I wanted a boy, yes. But this baby is even better. She looks just like me, Dr. Worth said." His voice, always rich, became richer with pride. Lydia knew his chest was swelling. Red Rufus! she thought with bitter contempt.

She turned her head abruptly and looked at him, wanting him to see the hatred that boiled in her, and which had begun to boil in her less than three months after their marriage. She could not help herself now. Her large dark eyes brimmed with the fire of her hatred, and her pale mouth opened, involuntarily. She stared at her husband, her white face shining with the passion of detestation she had concealed for over two years. She did not care if he saw it; she willed him to see it.

Rufus stepped back. His reddish brows drew together as if he were bewildered. His face took on that anxious young look which was so appealing to women. Mrs. Brunt saw it, and clucked. "Sometimes ladies are disturbed at a time like this," she said consolingly. "Perhaps I'd better not bring in the baby yet. Mrs. deWitt ought to sleep some more."

But husband and wife regarded each other fixedly, and in silence. Then Lydia, looking only at Rufus, said slowly and clearly, "I don't want to see the baby."

"Of course not; not yet," said Mrs. Brunt soothingly. "We must sleep a little more. . . ."

Lydia said, "I want to see Alice and Stephen."

Rufus glanced away, and after a moment he said jovially, "Why, of course, my darling! They're still here. They never went away. And Mamma and Papa are waiting up."

He took a step towards the fire, and Lydia could see the strong

19

muscles of his back and shoulders. He began to stir up the coals; they shattered and filled the big warm room with yellow light. He stood there then and stared into the fire. He said softly, "What's the matter, Liddie?" He looked at the closed door through which Mrs. Brunt had vanished.

Lydia became aware for the first time of the huge pain in her body. She writhed with it, gripping the sheets. Sweat burst out over her face. The hatred in her mind and the pain in her flesh were too much to be borne. She cried out, suffocatingly. Rufus did not turn. He pushed a fallen coal back on to the hearth. His red hair was lighted up by the firelight, and it was like a nimbus over and around his large head.

"I'll never have another child!" exclaimed Lydia, and she writhed again in her agony. "Not ever by you, Rufus!"

He came to her now, apprehensive and genuinely concerned. He did not touch her. He began to frown, and he bit his underlip thoughtfully. He was uncertain and baffled. It could not be possible that Lydia hated him, he thought. It was just imagination, or the lamplight, or the suffering she had endured, which had given such a fierceness to her eyes.

"Why, Liddie," he said. " I don't understand. Of course, you've had a dreadful time, and women——"

Lydia lay on her pillows, panting, looking up at him, her hands tense and white as they pulled the sheet over her in a self-protective and instinctive gesture. She had no more words. The emotion that surged in her was too powerful for speech. It had been there, held down, kept in control, for over two years. Now it rose to her lips in a flood of cold rage and loathing. The habit of twenty-four years of gentle breeding could not be overcome, however, so she was silent.

Rufus spoke again, almost inaudibly, and as if to himself : "You look at me as if you hate me, Liddie. Why? What have I done? Have I hurt you in any way, my darling? You know how much I love you, don't you, Liddie? Was the pain too much for you? "

Lydia said through the hard muscles in her throat, "Yes."

He was satisfied, and relieved. Ladies like Lydia, who had always been protected and sheltered, sometimes became emotional after childbirth. Dr. Worth had warned him of this. There might even be a period of "depression" and "melancholy." It was quite usual. He looked down into Lydia's eyes, and saw the bright and staring fever of them, the furious concentration. He put his hands in his pockets and rocked on his heels, frowning again.

The firelight leaped and fell over the white walls, touched the crimson velvet curtains to a brighter colour, stretched in shadows over the white ceiling with its gold moulding. At Lydia's feet, the carved bedposts with their pineapple-shaped tops rose like the slender trunks of trees. Two blue velvet chairs were drawn near the fire, and there was a gold silk sofa near the window matching the soft gold of the carpet. A mirror over the fireplace reflected the room and its fine furnishings and the lamp which stood on a distant table.

"There's been a storm while you slept, dearest," said Rufus. "Thunder and lightning. Like summer." His voice was tentative and troubled.

Lydia turned away her head again and closed her eyes. Oh, God! she thought. If I never had to see him again! She did not think of the child at all.

The door opened and Mrs. Brunt appeared. She was a short stout woman with a coarse and friendly face, though her small eyes were fawning and obsequious. She smiled at Rufus archly, and lifted a fat finger in coy warning. "Mr. and Mrs. deWitt, sir. But only for a moment. Please. We must sleep, you know."

Lydia turned on her pillows eagerly. There was her sister, her dear sister Alice, and Stephen. They were coming towards her, walking gently. She held out her hand to Alice, and her fingers closed tightly about her sister's fingers.

"She's very tired. It's been hard," said Rufus. The handsome and ruddy face had turned cold, though it still smiled. It was impossible for Rufus not to smile. "She mustn't be disturbed too much."

Alice bent over Lydia and her pretty, light-blue eyes filled with tears and sympathy. One of her long pale curls touched Lydia's cheek. She whispered, "Dear Lydia, I'm so glad it's over. And such a beautiful baby. Hush, dear. Hush, hush." Lydia was trembling violently, and her fingers clutched Alice's hand in a kind of desperation.

"Don't leave me, Alice, don't leave me!"

Alice was alarmed. She stroked her sister's damp forehead and tried to understand the frantic expression in her eyes. This was not like Lydia, the quiet, the humorous, the steadfast and poised. She had never seen Lydia like this, not even when their parents had died after a long struggle against "lung fever." There was something frightfully wrong with Lydia. Was it so awful, then, to have a child? With apprehension, she thought of her own child, who would be born in three months.

Even in her suffering, Lydia at last saw the fear in her gentle sister's eyes. Alice was only twenty-one, three years younger than herself, and she had always protected her, for Alice was frail. She told herself sternly that she was frightening this young creature, and she despised herself for her emotionalism. She held her body stiff against her trembling, and tried to smile.

"Don't mind me," she said in a stifled voice. "I'm just tired, Alice." She pressed Alice's fingers lovingly against her cheek in an old gesture of affectionate protection. Nothing must hurt Alice, who had never known hatred and anger and who had never felt an overpowering detestation for anybody, and who had lived always in trust and under the shelter of the love of parents and sister. Nothing must disturb Alice's dream of life, in which all mankind was good and heroic, all things lovely and tender, with God in His heaven and war a nightmare which did not exist in reality. The dream had been so strong in this young woman, who in so many ways was only a child, that the war which had ended less than a year ago had not really touched her consciousness. She had been horrified at Mr. Lincoln's assassination, and had cried a little, and had been comforted by her husband, and everyone had conspired to drive the event from her mind. Within a few weeks she had forgotten. No one spoke of that death in her presence again.

"You are so white, Lydia," said Alice, and her voice shook.

Lydia called on her strength, and patted her sister's cheek. "It was nothing, dear. Nothing. I'll be well very shortly. You'll see."

There was no comfort anywhere for her, no consolation, no courage, no friend. All her life she had had to be the strong one in a family which never faced reality. She thought of her parents, so like Alice, so small and fragile and touching. As a sturdy child, she had known all about them, and had defended them against all ugliness and truth. She could not remember when she had first appointed herself as their protector; to her, it seemed that it had been forever.

She thought now of that gracious and charming home in which she had been born, and in which her parents had died.

Never Victorious, Never Defeated

She saw the timeless gardens with the fountainlike willows and the white beeches and the tall elm trees which massed their branches together in dark enchantment. She saw the lilacs and the rose gardens, the dial and the moss-covered flagstones; she heard the cheeping and the songs of birds in the misty sunlight. The very mountains which rose far beyond had a purple unreality about them, and even the storms and the winters were dreams.

The rooms of the house never echoed; the windows always seemed to shine softly. The fires never roared. Even the winds were quiet here, never once drowning out the sound of tinkling teacups, sweet low laughter, and gliding footsteps. Life had muted itself around that house. Nothing had ever caused a book to be dropped abruptly, nor had a voice ever been raised in annoyance or anger. When death came, it came noiselessly, without pain and without distress. Lydia remembered now, and the strange suffocating sensation which she had known for so many years in her parents' home returned to her overwhelmingly.

Recalling all this, and seeing her sister's lovely young face, Lydia demanded more and more of her strength. She kissed Alice's hand, and weakly tried to laugh.

"I'm almost well, now, dear Alice," she said. The sickness in her heart, the pain in her body, the wild hatred in her mind, must not be revealed to her sister again. She murmured lovingly when Alice bent over her even farther and pressed her soft cheek against her own. The pale curls lay across Lydia's lips, and she kissed them remorsefully. Alice's scent, as tenuous and as light as herself, filled Lydia's nostrils. She put her arms about the girl's shoulders, for Alice had begun to cry.

Someone was lifting Alice away from her. It was Stephen, brother of Rufus. Lydia looked up at him gratefully. He held Alice to him, while she wept gently, and smiled down at Lydia. She lifted a hand to him and he caught it and held it kindly and warmly. She did not see Rufus standing at a little distance with that cold smirk on his face.

Stephen deWitt was a tall, thin, and unprepossessing man of thirty-two, his brother's elder by two years. Nothing glowed or brightened about him. He gave an impression of muted brownness, of faded insignificance. His body was narrow, his face was narrow and without virility, and his eyes were small and light brown. He had a long and crooked nose, a quiet mouth under a large brown moustache, big ears and scanty brownish hair. He was like a shadow beside his brother's blazing colour; when Rufus was present he appeared to retreat, to become entirely inconspicuous, even absent. People always forgot him immediately. If they spoke of him at all they invariably remarked that he was repellent, uninteresting, without conversation or wit or charm, and that he had not much intelligence. It was "well known" that without Rufus's quick intellect and strength and tireless vitality Stephen would be "nothing."

Lydia had often overheard these remarks, and she had burned with anger. What did these fools know about Stephen? If he did not speak, she knew why he did not. If he drifted away from others, his head bent as if in apology, she understood. She was well aware of the contempt in which he was held; she knew of the sneers at his expense. His parents had not discouraged popular depreciation of their older son; in fact, they had encouraged it. Rufus, who might have turned more favour in his brother's direction, was careful only to hold him up to ridicule, to joke affectionately at his expense, to slap him too solidly on his thin shoulders, to laugh heartily as he rallied him. And this, too, Lydia understood. It was partly because of Stephen, and all that she had learned about the two brothers, that she had come to hate her husband.

"How are you, Lydia?" Stephen was asking, as he fondled his young wife's curls and pretty shoulders. His hand tightened on Lydia's, and his little eyes were shy and sympathetic. He had a hesitating, almost stammering, way of speaking, as if he were doubtful that his words would be comprehended by others. "Was it—very bad?"

"No," Lydia said. The bitterness and hatred subsided in her. Involuntarily she moved a little closer to Stephen and her sister. The tears still shone on Alice's face, but the girl was smiling like a young child and dabbing at her eyes. Her dark blue velvet dress was moulded over her lovely figure, swelling out in deep folds at her hips. She wore a white lace collar about her throat, and white lace cuffs on her sleeves. She looked defenceless and fragile as she stood, one arm about her husband's shoulder.

"She mustn't be tired," said Rufus, and now he came closer to the bed. Immediately all of them lost colour in the fire of his own colour. Alice was a puppet, Stephen a vagueness, and Lydia herself a figure in black and white.

"Why, why, of course," muttered Stephen. "Mustn't tire Lydia, must we?" He paused. "A nice baby, Lydia. She looks just like Rufus."

Lydia lost control of herself for the last time. "Don't leave me, please," she said, her voice breaking.

Rufus laughed richly and clapped his brother on the shoulder. "They're staying overnight, dearest. It's too far for them to go home now. Mamma and Papa have insisted that they stay."

"Oh, we wouldn't leave Lydia to-night," said Alice in her child's tone, so high and clear. She did not look at Rufus directly, for she was instinctively afraid of him.

"No, no, not at all," said Stephen hurriedly.

"And now," said Rufus in his loud and jubilant voice, "suppose we leave poor Liddie alone, to sleep and rest?" He bent over Lydia. She did not stir or glance at him. She suffered his warm kiss, the pressure of his lips on hers. She did not even wince now, when he stroked her hair and murmured fondly. She held to her self-control, for Alice was watching them and smiling with innocent tenderness.

Then she was alone, except for Mrs. Brunt, who officiously straightened the sheets and the quilts and talked inconsequentially with enthusiasm about the baby. Lydia heard her, but cared nothing for what she said. The nightmare was on her again, and the hatred and rage and pain. She closed her eyes and pretended to sleep, and Mrs. Brunt retreated to the fire.

The thunder and the lightning had gone, but a savage wind rushed against the windows. The fire leaped in answer. The yellow shadows jumped on the walls and ceilings. Mrs. Brunt snored in her chair.

CHAPTER TWO

THEY WENT down the white and gracefully curving stairway, with its deep crimson carpeting, Rufus gallantly assisting Alice, who shrank timidly and unconsciously from his strong grip, and Stephen following.

Stephen, as usual, was bemused by the charm and beauty of his father's house. As he walked slowly behind Rufus and Alice, he

25

looked at the gracious panelling of the wall to his left. Gold-coloured panels were set into creamy moulded wood, and where the staircase curved, there was an arched and leaded window looking out on to the dark and wintry garden. From the high white ceiling fell a magnificent chandelier blazing with candles, throwing its prismed light down on to the wide hall with its polished floor, its scattered Aubusson carpets, its cream-coloured sofa and delicate gold, blue, and rose damask chairs and fragile tables. Here, too, were panelled walls and gold wall brackets flickering with candles, and flowers from Aaron deWitt's conservatory, and a small white fireplace dancing with burning apple-wood logs. Warmth, the scent of the flowers, the odour of wax and fire, filled the quiet midnight air.

"Careful, my dear," said Rufus affectionately to Alice, as they neared the end of the stairway. His gestures were exaggeratedly solicitous. He knew that Alice was afraid of him and disliked him in her dreamlike way, and it amused him. Once he had seriously considered marrying Alice, having become fascinated by her pale gold and blue beauty, but Alice, always so gentle, always so considerate, had shown her guileless horror of him unmistakably. This had not angered or insulted him. He had immediately dismissed her from his mind as a woman without intelligence or discrimination, and had turned his attention to the dark and smiling Lydia who apparently appreciated him.

At the foot of the stairs Alice shook off his hand, and looked up pleadingly at her absorbed husband, who was trailing behind them. Stephen stopped on the fourth stair and surveyed the hall below as if he had never seen it before, and was enchanted. Alice uncertainly smoothed the flaring folds of her blue gown, and waited for him. He became aware of her then, and the anxious expression in her large eyes, and he hurried down the remaining stairs and took her hand. She smiled as if rescued, and moved closer to him.

He knew that she was afraid of Rufus and his parents, but he thought this was because she was still only a child in many ways. He, who was so perceptive, was often not very perceptive with regard to Alice, possibly for the reason that she never spoke of his family except with kindness and never criticised any of them, or possibly because his love for her was composed of deep protectiveness and paternal tenderness.

He held her hand tightly as the three of them moved towards

26

the great drawing-room where his parents were waiting to hear the news that Lydia had recovered consciousness. Inwardly, he began to shrink, and the old familiar coldness and aversion returned to him. He knew so much about his parents, as he knew so much about Rufus, but though he had such objective knowledge and clarity of understanding, he could not prevent the vague sense of tiredness and sickness which came to him when about to encounter his father and mother. They despised him, as nearly everyone despised him, and in spite of his intelligence it would come to him that perhaps, in many ways, he deserved it.

"Don't be so humble; don't have such a low opinion of yourself, Stephen!" Lydia had once exclaimed to him with unusual sharpness.

He was baffled and surprised, and had answered her uncertainly: "But I'm not in the least humble, nor do I have a low opinion of myself." He had reflected a moment, then had added, "However, is it possible to know anything about yourself without humiliation? Complete self-knowledge, I think, would lead to suicide."

They entered the drawing-room, and now the energetic Rufus was crying out buoyantly, "Lydia is quite well! She awoke, and now she is sleeping again! Mrs. Brunt is very capable, and the baby is asleep, too. What a night this has been! And listen to that wind. Like a tiger at the windows."

His parents were sitting near the fire, and he went to them in his exuberant way and kissed them heartily. His mother smiled at him with deep devotion, but his father, curiously, and for the first time in Rufus's memory, looked beyond him at Stephen.

Stephen was hesitating on the threshold as he always did, as if he were an intruder in the house where he had spent the greater portion of his life. The room was of majestic proportions, and had been exquisitely furnished, not by Aaron deWitt, but by a famous artist who had died on the very day he had entered the completed house. The walls of the room were panelled in white, with occasional panels of deep blue silk on which hung a few of the artist's smaller but finer paintings of mountain and river and forest. A dim heliotrope rug covered the floor, and upon this were scattered Aubusson carpets like oblongs of faded flowers. An enormous white fireplace, beautifully carved and fluted, dominated almost one entire wall, and the fire on its white hearth

27

fluttered and flamed in gold. Silver, bronze, and gilt lamps lighted up the room, and a curved sofa covered with a delicate rose and blue tapestry stood on one side of the fireplace. A large blue satin chair was drawn up opposite. Gilt cabinets occupied two distant corners, and on their crystal shelves were arranged wonderful statuettes of ivory and Dresden, little gold snuffboxes, tiny dolls' mirrors, and other *objets d'art* at which no one except Lydia and Alice and Stephen so much as glanced.

Aaron deWitt sat, slight and stiff, and in his red velvet dressing-gown, on the soft-hued sofa, and his wife, Sophia, sat opposite him in the blue satin chair. He had a short, pointed white beard, as stiff as his body, and a sunken, sallow face in which his small black eyes looked at the world with cold derision and ruthlessness. His bony nose jutted far out from his face like a sharp-edged stone, and under his thick white hair his forehead was rutted like old granite. He was much slighter than his son and his little feet, encased in warm carpet slippers, barely touched the floor. He gave the impression of complete and indomitable hardness, and there was an inexorable quality about him which intimidated everyone except his wife.

Sophia, his wife, was his own age, sixty-five. They had been married a long time before Sophia had borne her two sons. Unlike Aaron, she was tall. Where he was inflexible, she was arrogant, and this revealed itself in the haughty way she held her head, and the manner in which she preened. Her father had been the proprietor of an ill-paying general store in the village in the valley, and since her husband had become wealthy she had felt the necessity to assume a grandeur and pretentiousness not hers by birth. Her figure was still good, in spite of her age, and she wore, to-night, a rather old-fashioned if very rich black gown with immense hoops.

It was from Sophia that Rufus had inherited his flaming red hair, and though Sophia's hair, dressed very severely, was now almost entirely grey, threads of fire still ran through it. He had also inherited her eyes, her formerly ruddy complexion. She had once been a high-spirited woman, as he was now high-spirited, but as her earlier heartiness and joviality, her exuberance and gregariousness, her gaiety and boldness, had later taken on an aspect of "vulgarity" in her mind, she had repressed them.

"Well, come in, come in!" she shouted at Stephen and Alice as they still wavered on the threshold, uneasily. Then she lowered her voice and said, "Alice, sit by Papa, and Stephen . . ." She did not care where Stephen sat, so long as it was not near her; so Stephen wandered vaguely to a chair at some distance, sat down, and fumbled for his pipe. His chair was not near a lamp; he began to blend with the shadows, as he always did.

Rufus stood behind the sofa on which sat Alice and his father. He was too restless and too vital for much sitting. He put one hand on his father's shoulder, and his other hand was spread wide near Alice's young back. He beamed at his mother and said, "Everything is splendid now. Dear Liddie is resting. Isn't the baby beautiful? She looks like us, Ma."

Sophia smiled at him, and when she smiled the former spectacular colour which she had possessed seemed to envelop her in spite of her grey hair and lost complexion. Her small hazel eyes glowed with pride. She had kept her big white teeth, and they shone between her pale lips. She said, "Well, but it's a pity she isn't a boy."

Aaron deWitt spoke for the first time, and he had a singularly neutral and uninterested voice: "I'm glad it's a girl. No danger to Rufus, then."

Rufus laughed boisterously and patted his father on the shoulder. "Now, what do you mean by that, Pa?"

Aaron shrugged, coughed, and drew the folds of his dressing-gown close over his sunken chest.

"Your Pa doesn't mean anything, dear," said Sophia, frowning briefly at her husband. "He's teasing you. But we'll have a boy next time, eh?"

Rufus began to smile and nod, then stopped. He thought of Lydia's outburst against him, and his red brows drew together in a puzzled frown. "Liddie was a little hysterical," he commented. He straightened up, began to walk up and down behind the sofa.

"Was she?" asked Aaron, with the first interest he had shown. "Now I wonder why? What did she say?"

"Lydia is never hysterical, under normal circumstances," reproved Sophia. "Ladies after childbirth are often unstrung. One doesn't give any weight to what they say."

"What did she say?" repeated Aaron. He smiled coldly, and his yellow teeth glimmered in the firelight. "And stop walking up and down behind me, Rufe."

Rufus obeyed at once. "Frankly," he said, "I don't quite

remember. She seemed overwrought. But then, she's had so much pain to-day, and it was difficult. . . ."

His mother regarded him shrewdly. She did not like Lydia, but she remembered that it was Lydia's and Alice's money which had extricated her husband from a particularly perilous situation. She could command almost everybody, but she could not command Lydia, with her cool smile, her hidden amusements, her lack of illusion. She would have liked to question Rufus, also, but she knew, as he knew, that it was much more convenient, and safer, never to discuss or notice anything which might threaten one's personal comfort. If Lydia had been elliptical, and inscrutable, in her tiresome way, then it was best to ignore it. So Sophia said, with a twitch of her hoops, "It can't be important. Having a child makes a woman very nervous." She turned her head and looked at Stephen, and said with offended irritation, "Stephen! Are you smoking that abominable pipe? You know I don't like smoking in the house, and it is very bad for your father's lungs. Please stop it immediately."

Starting apologetically, Stephen began to knock the ashes from his pipe. It was then that Aaron said, "Let him smoke. Smoke, Steve, if you want to. Who cares?"

This was so extraordinary, and so without precedent, that both Rufus and Sophia stared blankly at Aaron, who was grinning wryly. They knew that Aaron had as low an opinion of Stephen as they had, and that it delighted him to discomfit his son, and to ridicule his diffidence, and to harass him.

"But Pa, your lungs," said Rufus.

"The devil with my lungs," replied Aaron. His wizened face sharpened, and he shrugged again. Stephen, as much surprised as his mother and brother, held his pipe in his hand as if he did not know what to do with it. Then, as he caught his father's derisive eye, he put the pipe back in his mouth. "This is an unusual occasion, isn't it?" added Aaron. Something seemed to be pleasing him, for he gave a low and bitter chuckle. "I think we should celebrate. Are the servants still up?" He tugged at a brocaded bellpull near him. "Whisky, Steve? Rufe? And what will you have, my dears?" he demanded of Sophia and Alice.

"A little hot milk," replied Sophia. Her withered cheeks were flushed; she tossed her head with suppressed anger and gave Stephen a glance of intense dislike.

"A little hot milk," said Aaron contemptuously. "For you, then, Sophie, if you will. But what of you, Alice?"

Alice had been sitting silently beside him all this time, shrinking, and looking only at the fire. She jumped nervously at this direct address, and blinked, and tried to smile. "Why, a little hot milk——" she almost whispered.

"Nonsense!" said Aaron. "You won't have whisky, of course, but sherry or port. Aren't you going to drink to your niece?" He watched her keenly. He thought her a pretty young thing, but without importance, and not very bright.

Alice was so afraid of him that she stammered incoherently, "I'm thinking of Lydia. She was so strange. It—it isn't like Lydia to be strange, or to cry."

"You'll discover it quite natural to be 'strange' when your own time arrives," interrupted Sophia, annoyed. This little mewling thing, this little white kitten! Only her money had made her tolerable to the strong Sophia. She dismissed Alice, and said righteously, "A cup of hot milk, Aaron, if you please."

"Whisky, of course, for me," said Rufus. He was leaning on the back of the sofa directly behind his father. He radiated pleasure and affection at everybody, including Stephen.

"Well," said Aaron impatiently to his older son. "Can't you speak up, Steve?"

As Stephen never "spoke up," this highly amused Rufus and Sophia, who laughed heartily. Alice looked slowly at them both, and something began to kindle in her sweet and gentle face, something like the shine of steel. She said clearly, "I think Stephen distinctly said 'whisky,' Papa deWitt!"

Sophia and Rufus gaped at her with unaffected astonishment. Alice, who was quiet, so shrinking, so like a small and timid mouse, had actually "spoken up," herself, for the first time to anyone's knowledge. There was a valiant look about her, and a breathlessness.

"Why, so Steve did," said Aaron, and chuckled again. Something had happened to make this child courageous, to reveal emotions no one had known she possessed.

A sleepy butler answered the summons, and Aaron gave his orders. There was a prolonged silence in the room. A plane had shifted; there was a different aspect to everything, queer and out of focus. Everyone was aware of it, especially the observant Aaron.

Never Victorious, Never Defeated

"Well!" exploded the confounded Sophia at last.

"Well, what?" asked her husband, as if interested.

Rufus and Sophia exchanged a glance. Rufus smiled easily, and Sophia stretched her neck high. "It seems we're all a little —high-strung to-night," she said. "It's so very late." She added, to Stephen, without turning to him, "The south bedroom is ready for you both, and I'm sure we'll all be glad to be in bed very soon."

Alice spoke again quickly. "I hope there'll be a fire for us. There wasn't the last time, and I took a chill, and so did Stephen."

"It doesn't matter," began Stephen, smiling tenderly at his wife. She turned rapidly on the sofa and exclaimed, "Indeed it does, Stephen! You have weak lungs, too, you know, and you shall not, you shall not enter a room where there is no fire!"

So the whimpering kitten had claws, had she? thought Sophia. This thought did not give her more respect for Alice; rather, it increased her contempt. These weak and vapid creatures sometimes flared up incontinently, and in desperation, but it was easy to subdue them. Sophia stared at Alice haughtily, and said in a most repressive voice, "It was an oversight. Besides, you don't intend to sit up all night in your room, do you, Alice? Or do you like a warm and uncomfortable room?"

But Alice was not subdued. "I like a warm room," she said, and her voice, though light and childish, had become inflexible. "I want a fire."

Aaron laughed his thin and acidulous laugh. He was more and more delighted. "A fire it will be, then," he said.

The butler returned to the drawing-room with the whisky, the hot milk, and the sherry. He was a short, stout man of forty, with hard and bulbous blue eyes, a milk-white bald head with a thin tuft of yellow hair curling over each extended ear. He placed the tray on the table before Aaron and smothered a sulky yawn. He looked up, and Rufus, still standing behind his father, winked at him. Immediately, he smirked.

"Seth," said Aaron abruptly, "is there a fire in the south bedroom?"

"No, sir," answered the man, his smirk disappearing. "It wasn't ordered."

"No?" Aaron raised his thick white brows. "Well, it is now. Make one immediately, for Mr. and Mrs. Stephen."

32

"At this hour, sir?" asked the butler incredulously. "It's almost one in the morning!"

Aaron played with the tassels of his robe and contemplated his servant. "Did I ask you the time, Seth?" He fixed his cold and implacable eyes on the other, and Seth stepped back. "Yes, sir," he muttered, and left the room hastily, his fat buttocks rocking under his long coat.

"You ought not to have bothered, Pa," Stephen began in his halting voice.

"Why not? Isn't this my house? Isn't he my servant?" Aaron began to pour the whisky from the crystal bottle. "Aren't you my guest, as well as my son?"

No one answered him. The queer silence returned to the room, and Rufus lifted himself from the protective pose he had assumed over his father, and this time, when his eyes met his mother's, there was consternation in them. Aaron extended a glass in Stephen's direction, and Stephen rose in long sections and went to take it. He stood there, like a stranger, between his father and mother, and could only look down at the whisky. He could not remember when his father had ever shown him any consideration; he could not remember when he had last said, "my son." But Alice's eyes gleamed at him with gallant love, and her chin tilted. Sophia sat upright in affront, and with an expression that resembled fear about her mouth. "Have you forgotten me, Aaron?" she demanded loudly. "I was under the impression that ladies were to be served first." Her voice shook with her anger and bafflement.

"The hot milk is as near to you, my dear Sophia, as it is to me," Aaron remarked indifferently. And then he lifted the glass of sherry and put it into Alice's hand. Again Rufus and his mother exchanged glances, and Sophia's face turned grim.

Rufus began to laugh easily, came from behind the sofa, and took his own glass of whisky. He said, "I can't last recall when we were all up to such an hour. Strange to say I am not in the least tired."

Alice rarely, if ever, spoke to anyone but Stephen and Lydia without being addressed first, but now she turned impetuously to Rufus and cried, "It was not you who had the baby! It was not you who suffered! Why should you be tired?" The sherry splashed over her agitated fingers. Her eyes were too brilliant, as though she were feverish. She went on: "I must know what has hurt Lydia. I must know!"

Stephen looked down at her compassionately, tried to smile his usual painful smile, then said nothing. Sophia clattered her teaspoon on her saucer and said, "Good heavens! What is wrong with you, Alice? You're quite a spitfire to-night, aren't you?"

"Shall we drink to the baby?" asked Aaron in a very mild voice. His evil smile made his eyes dance.

Stephen abstractedly put the glass to his lips, and the three men drank. Rufus's ruddy complexion became even ruddier. But Alice put down her sherry and sat again in rigid silence, looking beyond Aaron at the fire.

"Our heiress," said Aaron contemplatively, as he licked the last drops of whisky from the glass. He held up the glass and examined it with regret. Sophia had begun to smile and to nod her head with satisfaction. Rufus laughed aloud with pleasure, seated himself on the arm of the sofa, and flung his arm about his father's bony shoulders. Now the swift glance between mother and son was triumphant. It was always understood that though Stephen was vice-president of the State Railroad Company, and Rufus only superintendent, Rufus, the younger son, would inherit the presidency after his father's death. It was only right, Rufus and his mother had told each other. It was, he, Rufus, who was the farsighted member of the company, the intelligent one, the daring and the ambitious one. "Grey Stephen" was only the plodder, the conservative moderator, the dusty handler of papers, the silent guardian of files and books. Was it not Stephen who had said it would be almost impossible to secure that 999-year lease, and was it not Rufus, assisting his father, who had actually secured it? Had not Aaron, himself, declared that without Rufus this could not have been done?

Rufus and his mother had forgotten, though the event was very recent, that for months before, Stephen had prosaically, quietly, and with that colourless obstinacy of his, presented all the facts and the solid dull figures and the duller but insistent arguments to the men of power who had the authority to grant such a lease. Each time Stephen would go to Philadelphia, with his old-fashioned carpetbag, Rufus and his mother would laugh happily at "our bookkeeper," and amused themselves endlessly with speculations as to how Stephen would conduct himself in grand houses and great offices among sophisticated men. It never occurred to Sophia to question Aaron why he had sent Stephen to Philadelphia; she had assumed that there was not much importance in dry papers, and Stephen, "the paper man," was good only to marshal the routine facts before the real force of the family, Rufus, descended on Philadelphia with imaginative intelligence and eloquent persuasion.

No one ever knew what Aaron was thinking, but Rufus and his mother did not care, and Sophia did not even frown when Aaron, after his toast, poured himself another glass of whisky and tossed it down his shrivelled throat. It was only Stephen who said in his toneless voice, "Pa, do you think, after your illness, that you ought to be drinking whisky? Your stomach, you know. . . ." and the voice trailed off, as it always did, into uncertainty.

"It isn't every night we have an heiress born to us," said Aaron. He gave Alice a long and speculative glance. Then he yawned, suddenly and abruptly, and announced, "I'm going to bed. Sophie, are my pills on my dresser?"

"You're in pain, Aaron?" she asked, but only abstractedly, for she was still richly contemplating what Aaron had said about Rufus's child. Aaron stood up and studied them all, his eyes darting from face to face. He did not answer his wife, but as he smiled his yellowish smile, a spasm drew together the papery greyness of his facial muscles. He nodded, but as if to himself.

Without another word he walked out of the room. He had always walked quickly and lightly, as he was a small man. But lately he had been walking with feebleness, and slowly. Only Stephen remarked this, following his father with a long, concerned look.

Sophia rose with the fluid motions of a young woman, extended her hand to Rufus and said grandly, "My darling, I must have one last look at my first grandchild. Come, let us go." Rufus took her hand, but as he led his mother from the room, he turned his head to wink in a brotherly and conspiratorial fashion at his brother. It meant nothing; it was part of his good-humoured attitude towards everyone, and was almost automatic. Stephen did not see it, nor did Alice. They were standing close together on the hearth, and Alice's head was on Stephen's shoulder.

Sophia's hoops swayed lightly up the stairway, and the diamonds in her ears sparkled in the light of the chandelier. When she and Rufus had reached the head of the stairs she kissed

Rufus warmly, and suddenly, from behind the masquerade of her grey hair and faded cheeks and slightly purplish lips, blazed again the colour which she had once possessed, and which she had given to her second son. "You heard what Papa said!" she whispered exultantly. "You heard what he said!"

CHAPTER THREE

SLOWLY, Alice and Stephen followed the others, but not for some little time.

The south bedroom was the smallest of all the bedrooms in the house, and was reserved for the least important guests, or their servants. However, it was pleasant with bright chintzes, and had three windows facing south, and white woodwork and a little black marble fireplace. None of the luxury of the other rooms was here, but yet it was friendly and charming.

It had been taken for granted that when Rufus married Lydia they would live with Aaron and Sophia. And it had been taken equally for granted that when Stephen married Alice they would not live in this house. Instead, Aaron, with a mocking gesture of magnanimity, had given Stephen the old home in which both sons had been born, a dark, small-roomed, uncomfortable, and old-fashioned place with a brick-walled kitchen, tiny entries, a stark narrow parlour, a lightless dining-room, miniature bedrooms, and a dolorous and very dank garden. Alice, with her delicacy, had lightened the house with pale colours, had given warmth where there had been only chill, had set out a garden with burning flowers and bushes which mitigated the looming darkness of many trees. She had thrown away much of the heavy and ponderous furniture and had brought to the rooms considerable of the elegant and airy and discriminating pieces which had been saved from her parents' home. What had once been ugly and repellent was now lovely and attractive.

A fire had been grudgingly lit in the south bedroom at Aaron's direction, but had not burned long enough to dispel the fierce cold. The lamps had been lighted and the rose-chintz curtains drawn. Alice shivered when she and Stephen entered, and clasped her arms with her hands. Stephen noticed this and said, "Let us go to bed at once. It is so cheerful to watch the fire when one is in bed."

But Alice, always the complaisant and softly agreeable, went to the big poster bed, threw back the covers, and exclaimed, "There are no warming pans!" She turned to Stephen, her face unusually excited. He put his long thin arms about her. "What does it matter, dearest? I'll warm you. I'll hold you close."

He was astounded when she pulled away from him, ran to the bell rope, and jerked it violently. She was breathing fast; her eyes were vivid. Stephen could not understand, and when he attempted to take her in his arms again she thrust him from her. "Stephen!" she cried. "They shall not do this to you any longer!" She stamped her foot and burst into tears.

Stephen was greatly alarmed. "Don't disturb yourself so, darling," he said with anxiety. "What does it matter?"

A robe-clad and yawning maid, resentful and sullen-eyed, answered the bell. "Where are the warming pans?" demanded Alice, her little white fists clenched at her sides. "Mr. Stephen has not been well, and he shall not get into the cold damp bed. Bring the warming pans at once, without any delay!"

The maid, who knew Alice very well, saw the tears of anger and mistook them for signs of helpless frustration. She said, with grumbling contempt. "There aren't any coals for the pans, Mrs. deWitt."

"Alice," began Stephen, but Alice, to his increasing astonishment, gestured at him fiercely.

"Be quiet, Stephen. Edith, there are coals in the drawing-room. Fill the pans there. Two of them."

The maid, now wide awake and as astonished as Stephen, retreated as if in flight. Alice, full of an unprecedented energy, tore the yellow quilt from the bed, flung it about Stephen's shoulders, and pushed him into a chair near the fire. Then she sat on his knees, put her arms about his neck, and held him with unexpected and ferocious strength, her tears running down his neck. Stephen, petrified, could only sit in confounded silence while she wept.

"They shall not do this to you any longer!" she cried over and over. "All the insults, while you do the work! All the laughter and the jeers and the scorn, when they'd be nothing without you! Always ' grey Stephen,' while Rufus gets the credit! I can't stand it any longer, Stephen. Sometimes I hate you when you let them use you so disdainfully." She beat on his shoulders with her fists. "Let us go away, a long way, far off, where you'll be appreciated!"

Now Stephen was greatly frightened. He kissed her wet cheeks and tried to calm her awful trembling. "I don't know what's wrong with you, Alice. What does it matter what they think? I know what I am. It's good enough for me." He was quiet a moment, while sharp scenes from his whole sombre life ran before his eyes. "Life is so short," he commented, half inaudibly. "One does one's work to the best of one's ability. It's of no consequence if no one else appreciates it."

"It is, to a man's wife, to her sense of her husband's importance!" Alice was still trembling. Her soft hair was disordered, and stood about her wet and passionate face in a mass of gilt ringlets.

Stephen was silent. He smoothed Alice's hair, and he sighed, over and over. Then he tried to smile, that painfully uncertain smile of his. "It's been too much for you to-day, my Alice." But he was heavy with his memories. He was not angered by them, but only bewildered. It was true that Rufus was the one who had the brilliant appearance, strong imagination, and boldness. What was it in him, Stephen, that made others despise him, and hold him in low esteem? This thought had dogged all his unobtrusive and conscientious life.

Stephen had not yet reached the point in his thoughts when he could come to believe that mankind is entranced by pyrotechnic superficialities, by gay lies and a handsome exterior, by hypocritical grace and false good-fellowship, by a magnetism that was utterly selfish and so superbly self-centred that it excited adoration in others. It was necessary to believe in something. He believed in mankind with a kind of desperation, and if mankind despised him, it was because in some way *he* was wrong. He also believed in God.

The maid returned, full of umbrage, and dumped the filled pans on the bed. She was about to stamp out of the room when Alice called, "Put them between the sheets, Edith." Alice rose from her husband's knee and confronted the maid. Edith glared at her. For a hard moment or two Alice and the maid confronted each other in a test of will. Then Edith, muttering under her breath, wrenched apart the bedclothes and thrust the pans between them. It was as though she were handling weapons which she ached to employ. Then she went from the room, slamming the door noisily behind her. Alice began to laugh shakily. "I never knew," she said in wonder. "I never knew. And it's so very easy. I always hated to put people ' in their places,' as they say. But now I know. You must do it, pleasantly when you can, or in a callous way, if necessary, but you must do it when it has to be done."

Stephen said, speaking despondently, "I suppose I have no character."

Alice was quite intoxicated with her new discoveries. "You have a lot of character, Stephen! But you put on no airs, make no pretentions, demand nothing of anyone, treat everyone with consideration and gentleness. That is not wrong—at times. But those times come so very seldom. Self-abnegation and service inspire contempt. . . . Why, how awful!" Appalled, she clapped her cold little hands to her cheeks and looked at Stephen in horror. "What a frightful world!"

Stephen, very disturbed, got to his feet, the quilt hanging from his shoulders. He took the girl in his arms, pressed her face to his breast as if to hide from her the terrible thing she had seen in a moment of woeful revelation. He murmured over and over, as he smoothed her hair, "No, dear, you're wrong. It's all right. Edith was just tired and sleepy, and that's why she was so uncivil. How agitated you are. Let me help you to bed. My dearest, my dearest."

Alice cried silently as she undressed. When they were in bed he held her closely, her head on his shoulder, and he looked sadly into the darkness of the room. Between the slightly-parted draperies he could see the icy glimmer of the moon. The wind had fallen, and there was no sound at all but the slow dropping of the coals in the fireplace.

Alice curled closer to him, and her soft hand found his cheek. She made herself laugh a little. "It's so late, and we ought to be asleep," she said murmurously, clinging to him.

"Yes, yes," he said.

"I found out something else," said Alice, again with that note of wonder in her voice. "He hates everybody—but you."

"Who?" asked Stephen, confused.

"Your father." And then, incredibly, and after this incredible statement, she fell asleep.

Stephen lay beside her, staring dry-eyed at the slit of moon

39

showing between the draperies. He had immediately forgotten Alice's words. They were words of a beloved child, who knew nothing. He would often lie like this, lately, unable to sleep, and without warning, without his will, scenes from his past life would come to him, overwhelming in their clarity, crushing in their half-revealed significance.

Twenty years ago he had had but one desire. He was a young boy, lonely, forgotten, not considered by his parents, who were so engrossed by the lively and lovable Rufus. He had no friends, for even boys of his own age avoided him at his school. He had nothing to say to them, and what he overheard them saying to each other seemed so empty and so trivial, so without content or meaning, that it seemed impossible to him that they were interested in their own conversation. His teachers overlooked him completely, and were never conscious that he was there. He moved like a shadow through his childhood.

When he was ten years old he had wanted a dog to mitigate his loneliness. The dogs of his schoolmates raced after him, fawning, looking at him with strange and fathomless eyes. There was something in their brief presence which comforted him; they licked his hands, even when their masters called them impatiently, and they pressed against his knees. They filled him with warmth, made him feel at one with the world in which he lived, and in which he usually felt such a grief-stricken stranger. For just that little time when they leaped upon him, and tried to speak to him, he was no longer an alien, but was accepted into the universal brotherhood.

So Stephen had wanted a dog of his own. He never asked his parents for anything. It took him months to ask his father for a dog. Aaron had looked at him speechlessly. "It won't eat much," Stephen had pleaded. "I'll take care of it."

Aaron, at that time, was just beginning to acquire some wealth. He was crafty and noncommunicative about his new money. He considered Stephen, whom he was always forgetting, then said coldly, "A dog? What for? We can't have pets around here. I don't like them."

A few months later he bought Rufus a pony.

Stephen, lying beside his wife, was suddenly convulsed with the agony he had felt when his father had brought the pony home for Rufus, a pony jingling with bells, and with a saddle and harness of red leather and silver. Again, he heard Rufus's joyful cries,

40

the loud and loving laughter of Sophia, the pleased chuckling of Aaron. He stood apart from them all and watched, as he watched now, with the anguish in his heart fresh and keen. He had not been envious or angered. There had been no resentment in him, no indignation. Only pain.

He had crept away, unseen, unnoticed. He had not hated his father for this betrayal ; even then, he had believed it inevitable that his own desires should be disregarded. He had walked for a long time, up a hill, and then had sat on a stone, not grieving, only very still, and very cold. He had watched the round crimson sun go down beyond the distant mountains, and he was conscious only of his suffering.

He had never bought himself a dog when he had married and had gone away from his parents. He no longer wanted a dog. The dog he had desired was dead.

The maple clock on the mantelpiece chimed half-past two. Alice was breathing deeply beside Stephen. He touched her hair. He thought: why do I remember these things? What does it matter now? Why should they torment me, when they were so long ago?

CHAPTER FOUR

PORTERSVILLE STOOD on both sides of a narrow river that was spanned by a slender bridge, one side reserved for foot passengers and the other for vehicles.

It was a small and quiet town of some fifteen thousand people, and unusually sophisticated. It was not uncommon for the more affluent to go frequently to Philadelphia, which the State Railroad Company had made only forty-five minutes away. There they would attend the opera, the theatre, and social gatherings, for many had close friends and relatives in the big city to the east. They regretted .that Philadelphia probably would never engulf them in its prophesied growth, for here the mountains rose abruptly and the hills were too steep. However, they happily believed that some day they would regard themselves as a suburb of the beloved city. Some of them had homes high in the hills, similar to that of the DeWitts, and it was a local amusement to turn spyglasses in the direction of Philadelphia and declare that the smoke was quite visible.

Portersville had always, in a way, considered itself a suburb of Philadelphia, and there was little local industy. Before the advent of the State Railroad Company there had been much water traffic on the river between the various communities. This traffic had practically disappeared. The labour which supported the State Railroad Company lived in either Pittsburgh or Philadelphia, the two connecting cities, though the largest office force was in Portersville. The State Railroad Company had recently set up a small office in Philadelphia, which was being used more and more by Rufus deWitt, but most of the executive work was accomplished in Portersville.

It was a pleasant town, if rather quiet in colouring. The streets were as broad as possible, considering the shouldering hills and mountains. Many of the wealthier people owned hilly farms in the vicinity, and culled their farm labour from the East Town, as it was called, which was a section of three-storied, narrow houses of field-stone or brick, with winding streets suggestive of European hamlets. The white steeples of churches pierced the prevailing grey and brown and dark red of the section. There was a small sawmill here, cutting lumber for almost exclusively local use, and a few granaries and a flour mill. Three streets of shops, occupying three sides of the public square, serviced the modest needs of the working and lower middle-class people. Here lived the little merchants, the butchers, the harness and saddle makers, the labourers, and the domestic servants who worked in the fine, great houses of West Town. Portersville was proud that it had few, if any, slums, and it prided itself on the fact that its "stock" was German and English and Scotch. Here, as yet, there was no struggle between race and race, no antagonisms except that vaguely and good-humouredly felt for the very small Catholic population.

West Town was completely occupied by families of means, who drew most of their wealth from enterprises near Scranton, Pittsburgh, or Philadelphia. The majority of them had been born in Portersville, and nothing could induce them to leave for larger cities and more excitement. Their homes lay near the river, and for some distance beyond it, homes of the same field-stone and brick which housed their employees. Some few, like the DeWitts, had built their homes in the style of Southern

42

residences, with white pillars and pediments, and arched first stories, but in the main the houses, though large, suggested conservative quietness and solidity. A number of the people in this section had migrated, after acquiring considerable money, from East Town, but never did they refer to their former section with contempt or aversion. In fact, many wistfully remembered the more active community life, the bustle about the square on Saturday nights, the rumours and the laughter, and the naïve neighbourly friendships.

Very few despised their origin in East Town. The DeWitts, with the exception of Stephen, did. It had been quite "a feather in their caps" when the two sons had married the Fielding daughters, whose father and grandfathers had never engaged in "trade," but had drawn their money from England and from immense farms in the centre of the state. Again, with the exception of Stephen, the DeWitts had nothing to do with their old neighbours in East Town, who were not angered at this snobbery but found it immensely amusing.

Portersville's one bank was the Portersville National, on the east side of the river. It occupied a third of one of the streets of the little public square, and was its most imposing building, built of grey stone with wide polished windows and smooth granite steps. It was the centre of much activity, for the bank occupied only two stories, the other two being rented as offices for local lawyers, prosperous businessmen, two or three doctors, town administrators who could not be accommodated in the little town hall, and the State Railroad Company. If one could afford to rent "front" offices, one had definitely arrived. The rear offices, though not as large as the front ones, were as well lighted and as clean and busy. Sometimes, when fortunes changed decidedly, the gentlemen in the rear would take over the front offices, and the "front gentlemen" would move "temporarily" to the rear. It became quite an occasion for gossip and excitement when these changes took place, and so it was somewhat of a game, good-natured and happily competitive.

The State Railroad Company occupied three of the large front offices. One of the rooms was Stephen's, with gold lettering on the door: "Aaron deWitt, President," and contained two desks, Stephen's and his father's. Rufus, the superintendent, had a smaller room to himself. The other room was occupied by four bookkeepers, five clerks, and an office boy.

Never Victorious, Never Defeated

The DeWitts had another large and grimy office at the local railroad station, and Rufus was more often in this than in the one at the Portersville Bank building. His was the more active part in the running of the railroad, which had suited him splendidly until lately. His father had been ill for nearly a year, and had visited the offices only four times in eight months.

The offices looked down, from the third story, on the busy little square with its statue of Benjamin Franklin (very green and vague) in the centre. One had an excellent view of the square, its trees and winding paths, the opposite streets, the adjacent river, and the dark and imminent mountains rising beyond the town.

As the DeWitts were disliked, with the exception of the colourful Rufus (who had conveyed the impression that he still loved East Town and was apologetic over his family's snobbery), there was little traffic between the private offices above the bank and the offices of the State Railroad Company. What traffic there was occurred when Rufus was present, and then there would be much back-slapping, much laughter, much smoke, and many stories, with Rufus perched in all his informal splendour on the edge of his desk and his laughter louder than that of the others. They assured Rufus privately, and over and over, that he was being unjustly treated by his father, and that he, not Stephen, should be vice-president in spite of his age. To which Rufus would reply in smiling mock horror. "I? All that damned paper work? God save the thought! I'd rather be out where people live, and in here, where my friends are welcome."

The war had been able to create little bitterness in Portersville. There were a few who had dared to assert that the Southern states were within their rights to secede, and produced copies of the Constitution to prove it. These arguments had not been pushed aside, angrily and with patriotic vehemence; they had been soberly considered and even opponents had agreed with much of the contentions. No lasting enmities had resulted from the arguments; it was granted that one had a right to his opinions, and even those most passionately devoted to Mr. Lincoln had expressed their doubts of some of his unconstitutional actions and had declared that they regarded his inclination towards centralised government with considerable apprehension. Slavery was morally wrong, but everyone knew that slavery was not the issue. Had not Mr. Lincoln reiterated that over and over in his speeches? The issue was secession, which was constitutionally legal, but dangerous with Europe so watchful and so lustful across the Atlantic.

Even when some placards had appeared at night on the streets, with a caricature of Mr. Lincoln on them, and bearing the words: "Down with the Dictator!" no fierce rage or resentment had been engendered in the townsfolk. No windows had been broken; friends had not become enemies. But all this, too, would come later, much later.

When Gettysburg became the scene of a most terrible battle, Portersville was filled with the wildest excitement. Thousands gathered at the railroad station to mourn over the wounded, whether friend or "enemy." Women entered the coaches to minister to the soldiers, regardless of the uniforms, and came out bloodstained and weeping, in bombasine and woollen skirts, in velvet bonnets or with shawls over their heads, empty baskets, which had contained food and drink and bandages, in their hands. The doctors of Portersville had rushed to the assistance of their exhausted colleagues on the trains, and had not noticed whether these colleagues wore grey or blue. They had talked with their brothers, had shaken their heads over the war, had sighed, had even let the unashamed tears roll down their bearded cheeks. When the coaches went on, to the hospitals, they went accompanied by prayers.

When Mr. Lincoln was assassinated, he was mourned conservatively, and none of his former enemies in Portersville were looked at bitterly or condemningly. It was bad, very bad. But there was a Vice-President, and one must look to the future and help the South with her terrible problems, and her awful wounds. No people were more aghast, more indignant, more enraged against the "carpetbaggers" than the people of Portersville; and if any of the men of the town were involved in this shameless plunder of the defeated states, they kept it a dark and fearful secret.

Portersville had its own wounded, its own dead. The people of both sections mourned them, side by side, in the cemeteries. There were no social distinctions in the graveyards. This, too, would come later.

It was a good place to live, Portersville, in the sixties, in the noble Commonwealth of Pennsylvania.

Never Victorious, Never Defeated

Pigeons caught the lead-coloured light of the March morning on their wings, as they flew from window to window.

March was the hiatus between seasons, unsoftened by snow, a bare greyness, a dun neutrality, a sombre hollowness. The square below was mud, with patches of brown and sodden grass; the black trees tangled their branches together like the bare scaffolding of a ruined cathedral. Sometimes gales convulsed them under a livid sky in which the misty sun was only a blur of paler lividity. The dank coldness of the air penetrated clothing, and carriages moving along the streets of the square seemed to have become smaller, the horses languid with misery. The people walked as fast as they could, huddling themselves in their capes and shawls and greatcoats, their faces bent, the wind catching at skirts and whirling hats off unprotected heads. The grey light was reflected back from the polished windows of shops.

Beyond Portersville, from this view from the offices of the State Railroad Company, rose the sharp outlines of Knife Mountain. However, it resembled an enormous razor rather than a knife, a razor held horizontally and its handle dropping a little lower than the blade. Purple and clearly defined, it contrasted acutely against the cold and colourless sky, and added gloom to the general scene.

Stephen, since his father's illness, had occupied Aaron's desk near the window, a large square desk with a leather top. His own desk was bare, and smaller than Aaron's, and stood near a wall at right angles. The office was large and light; a crimson carpet covered the parquetry floor, and there were vivid hunting prints on the white walls. Leather chairs, in red and green, and ornamented with brass nailheads, were scattered neatly throughout the room, and a comfortable fire roared and leaped in a black marble fireplace. On the mantel stood a mahogany clock with pleasant chimes, and against another wall personal and secret filing cabinets of mahogany, always locked, contained documents pertinent to the company. In one corner lurked a small iron safe, the only ugly note in the office.

Stephen's brief case lay on his desk before him. He had withdrawn a few documents of considerable thickness, and he held them in his hand. But he was not looking at them now; his eyes were moving slowly and abstractedly over the square, and the gigantic razorlike mountain beyond the little city.

Alone, he could relax, and his natural melancholy lay like a dark shadow over his nondescript features and brown eyes and thin brown hair. His subdued clothing, not excellently tailored, bunched on his shoulders and arms.

Yet, in spite of the melancholy and the stillness of his attitude, and the arms bent awkwardly on the desk, his face revealed his sad intellectuality, his deep thoughtfulness and introspection. These traits, painfully hidden when he was in the company of others, gave him a look of quiet nobleness and dignified withdrawal.

He lifted his right hand and reflectively smoothed his moustache. When his hands moved at all, it was to be seen that they were thin and elegant, the hands of a philosopher and thinker. No one noticed this, of course, except Alice and Lydia, just as only they had ever seen him so contained and preoccupied with thought, and contemplative without fear or shrinking.

The scene outside the windows seemed part of him, part of his static despondency. He watched the pigeons flutter from window to window. For a few moments he fixed his unremarkable eyes on the mountain, and now they were no longer unremarkable. They were alive, not with vividness, but with resolution.

He did not hear the knock on his panelled door, and so he started quite noticeably when he heard Rufus's cheerful voice. "Plotting, Steve?" asked Rufus laughingly. It was a joke between him and his mother about Stephen's "plotting." It was understood between them that Stephen had too little intelligence for this.

Stephen, his back still to his brother, hastily caught up the documents before him and thrust them quickly into the brief case. Then he turned and gave Rufus his uncertain smile. His eyes were dull again, and lightless, and betrayed nothing of his thoughts. "Not exactly," he answered. The clock on the mantelpiece struck nine. Stephen was always the first at the offices, and since his father's illness he had taken to arriving as early as half-past seven. He lived closer to the town than did Rufus, who usually arrived later.

The grey light in the office was dissipated by the entrance of Rufus; it retreated to the corners of the room, as shadows retreat before the burst of the sun in the morning. Rufus seated himself on the edge of Stephen's desk, and his handsome face glowed with friendliness and goodwill. This expression was so natural for him, so automatic, that he could expend it as freely on his

47

brother as on his many friends, and so, in spite of his many long thoughts on the subject of Rufus, and his instinctive, sick knowledge, Stephen felt himself beguiled and confused, as usual.

A few weeks ago his best friend, Joseph Baynes, had said to him bitterly of Rufus, "' He hath a person and smooth dispose, to be suspected.'"

To which Stephen, faintly smiling, had murmured, "Yes, I know, Iago. But I think you wrong Rufus—in a way."

Mr. Baynes had thought this very naïve, and in spite of his affection for Stephen, he could not help thinking with a little contempt: ". . . Thinks men honest that but seem to be so."

Stephen studied Rufus's symmetrical and powerful body, his artless beaming face, his affectionate smile. The old aching bewilderment came to him. If Rufus was completely evil he would be universally avoided, unless—and for an instant the clue glimmered before Stephen's inner eye—there were some men who did not believe that what they did was evil, and were incapable of considering any of their actions evil. . . . The clue winked out, and Stephen shook his head slightly.

"What's the matter?" asked Rufus, interested. "Headache, Steve? By the way, nothing has happened as yet, has it?"

"No. But Dr. Worth thinks the child will be born any day now. Alice is very well, and we don't expect any trouble. I hope she won't have so hard a time as Lydia did."

For only a moment there was a tightening about Rufus's beaming eyes, and a little puckering about his smile. It was not a gentle expression, in spite of the bluff and engaging smile which remained fixed on his face. He lit a cigar, and the sulphur smell of the lucifer with which he had lighted it lingered acridly in the air.

"Yes, Liddie did have a hard time. Let's hope Alice has a better one. By the way, you and Alice haven't been up to the house for nearly a month, and Pa is asking for you."

Stephen, as usual, was quick to apologise, even when no apology was necessary. This fault came from his aversion for inflicting even unintentional slights or hurts on others. "But you bring me messages from him every day, Rufus, and instructions——"

"In a sealed envelope," interrupted Rufus, grinning wryly.

Stephen's thin cheeks took on colour. "Pa doesn't mean any offence to you. It's just his way; he always seals everything, even

48

of the most insignificant importance. The habit of a lifetime. You mustn't feel offended. After all, I show you the papers after I have opened them, Rufus."

"So you do." Rufus leaned towards his brother and put his hand affectionately on that meagre shoulder. "I'm not blaming you, not for a second."

Stephen was silent in his distress, and humbled. Rufus had not blamed him, but he felt a twinge of guilt. Perhaps he should write his father and ask him not to seal the envelopes. It was hardly fair to Rufus. Again, Stephen was betrayed by his abnormal compassion and consideration for others.

Rufus watched the wretched struggle in this "grey fish," and was pleased. His was a mind so acute that it could follow almost every thought in the minds of others, and this in itself was partly the secret of his popularity. He waited. However, Stephen, always sparing of words, was keeping silent too long, and Rufus's instincts stirred.

Now Stephen began to speak slowly: "Pa must understand that Alice can't ride any distance now, and I dislike leaving her even for a short time. Besides, for some reason, she has taken to crying at night, the poor child."

"Why, of course, of course," said Rufus in his rich voice of intimate understanding. "Liddie did that too."

"Did she?" Stephen was relieved. Then he stopped. Rufus had lied. Lydia was always serene; she had been especially serene, if a little too quiet, during the time she had been carrying Cornelia.

He looked up at Rufus, sitting there on his desk, smoking, all his glory of body and face artlessly and completely evident, all his friendliness and sympathy shining from his bright hazel eyes. Rufus said, "Any messages to our friends in Philadelphia? I'm going again to-morrow."

"To-morrow? You go very often now, don't you, Rufus?" The words were sincere and contained no undertone, but Rufus studied his brother with narrowed concentration. Sometimes he suspected that this shadowy and humble and gentle man had "depths" which were dangerous.

"Why, so I do," he said in that open and boyish way of his. He laughed. "More and more to do in our office in Philadelphia. And very convenient for our friends. No long letter-writing. Dispatch."

He stood up and stretched, and he was like a fine tawny lion in his colour and motions. He wandered to the window and looked at the square below. "Terrible day. Everyone hurrying. I don't like the idea, but I have to go down to the station." He began to hum musically to himself in a rich baritone. The smoke rose from his cigar. Finally he returned to Stephen, and again perched on the desk.

"Pa's very excited about our decision to run a line from Philadelphia to Washington, in competition with the Capital Railway." He spoke negligently, and implied that this was all Stephen's energetic idea. He admired Stephen with his eyes, and Stephen blushed. "Rufus, you know it was your thought, more than mine," he said.

"No, no, I won't hear that! You have so much self-depreciation, Steve. I only concurred in your suggestion." This had been quite true, but Rufus was so enthusiastic, so admiring, that Stephen was touched by a sense of guilt again, a guilt without reason.

Rufus exhaled blue smoke rings and watched them happily. "But I'm not without ideas of my own, Steve. Those small railroads running between Philadelphia and Washington: useless little affairs, just connecting odd communities, when they ought to be linked to the main railway—ours, and owned by us. . . ."

Stephen was alerted. He had heard these hints from Rufus before. He protested, saying, "But these ' useless little affairs ' are run by other families, and bring income to them. Why should we deprive others of income?"

Rufus laughed boisterously, and regarded his brother with a twinkle. "Why? Because we want to grow. Expand! That's the watchword since the war. Besides, these little railroads are practically bankrupt now. The banks in Philadelphia hold their bonds, and I hear the railroads can't even pay the interest, in many cases. If, for instance, we bought the bonds, we'd have these feeders to our line. We'd better think about it, before long. The Capital is thinking of it, I assure you!"

Stephen was now as cold as winter ice. He tapped his brief case with one lean finger. He murmured, "We talked this over and over——"

"I know, I know!" Rufus was all glowing and laughing sincerity. "But you've always opposed it, Steve, and Pa, for some strange reason, has upheld you. What's the matter with the two of you? You, I know, are conservative, but Pa was always an *entrepreneur.* Is he in his dotage or something? Where is his old imagination, his old plotting and boldness? Not that I'm belittling you, Steve. Not at all! Your work didn't include planning at any time. However, I do think that you, as Pa's deputy now, should pull yourself away from your everlasting papers and think about us, and the future."

Stephen was silent. He looked down at his brief case, and to him, it seemed to contain a high explosive. He put his hand on it, as if to protect if from Rufus. Rufus saw the gesture, and his ruddy brows lifted.

Then Stephen said, "Over half the feeders and little railroads running from community to community are owned by Joseph Baynes, who is a friend of ours."

Rufus laughed this off lightly. "Joseph Baynes, you know very well, Steve, is a stick-in-the-mud. He made money only during the war, carrying ammunition and soldiers and such to our main line. He never made a go of his business before the war, and hardly could pay his running expenses. The war saved him. But he isn't being saved now. Our good friend, Alex Peale, president of the Philadelphia Savings Bank, holds almost all of Joe's bonds. We could buy them up for a song."

Rufus had long hinted about this and had discussed Joseph Baynes's feeders and little local railroads with his father, and Stephen had listened. There had been hints, too, of the bonds. Stephen had paid all this little attention, until lately. His undistinguished face became closed and expressionless.

"We've talked of this before," added Rufus.

"I know." Stephen's voice was hardly audible.

"Well, why not think of it, fast! Alex's brother is Senator George Peale, and he's an even better friend of ours than Alex himself. We can spare the money for the bonds. And look what our income will be! We have ideas; we have imagination, a forward outlook."

Stephen's hands rested on the brief case. Of course, he had always known. But, in his belief that mankind was really inherently decent and honourable, he had not believed anything would come of discussions. Aaron often loved to speculate, just for the pleasure of speculation.

"What does Pa now say about your idea?" asked Stephen, keeping his head averted. He knew, even before Rufus answered with enthusiasm.

51

"Well, Pa's now come to my way of thinking, after all this time."

Stephen's bones were cold and felt stiff in his thin body. He said, "What will become of Joe? He owns the biggest block of stock in his feeders and railroads, and he is a director."

Rufus, though he knew Stephen, was taken aback by this puerility. "Joe? He'll be glad he doesn't have to wear himself out trying to borrow money to pay the interest on his bonds. It's too big a strain on a man his age."

"I happen to know he hasn't any reserves," said Stephen in his dull and abstracted voice. "What will he live on? How will he support his family?"

Rufus snapped his fingers. "Oh, Joe's an old friend. We can be generous." He was full of triumph. "Joe's a good railroader. We can even put him in charge of running the feeders, and connecting up the little railroads with our main line."

"You mean, he'd be working for us, as our employee?" Stephen showed no indignation, only a faint interest, and Rufus became excited.

"Why not? It would be a big relief for him. A good salary, no responsibilities. And, in a way, he'd be proud to see the expansion of what was once his own property. In himself, he has no progressive ideas."

Stephen leaned his elbows on his desk and cupped his narrow chin in his hands and stared out the window. "Joe," he said, "is a proud man. I don't think he'd survive what would practically be confiscation of his property. I don't think he'd work for us."

Rufus became affectionately impatient. "Steve! Joe's a practical man."

Stephen did not appear to have heard him. He went on: "If we buy up Joe's notes, his stock will become worthless. He'll have nothing to leave his family."

"Must we always consider others at our own expense?" Rufus was honestly outraged.

"Did we ever?" asked Stephen drearily.

This made Rufus laugh once more. He slapped Stephen on the shoulder again with rollicking amusement. "No, we didn't. How would we ever have made money if we had?"

"There's such a thing as principle," said Stephen hopelessly.

Rufus gaped. "In business? What are you talking about?" He was utterly sincere and utterly aghast at his brother's childishness. "Where would anyone get if one constantly thought about 'principles'? Why, nowhere, except to the poor farm. But, of course, you aren't serious."

Stephen said nothing.

"One must expand, or decline and go out of business," Rufus went on, encouraged by Stephen's silence. "One must be progressive. . . ."

Stephen stirred out of his apathy and lifted his small brown eyes to Rufus contemplatively. "Progressive? To where?"

Rufus stood up and began to walk up and down the room rapidly. "Steve, you surely know that we are on the brink of the age of expansion and progress! The whole damned country! The territories! Why, it's not a dream, linking the east coast to the west! Big railroaders are already talking about it, and it'll soon be a fact! There's no end to expansion. Progressive? Why not?"

Stephen said, "Can't there ever be progress without misery and despair and bankruptcy and exploitation—and betrayal?"

"No, there can't!" replied Rufus with annoyed vehemence. "And you know that, too."

"Yes," mused Stephen. "I know. Or at least I know that's what many men think. Look here, Rufus, this country's big enough for all of us, without cutting throats. It might take a little longer, but there would be national peace and confidence and co-operation, and more certainty in human lives. A man wouldn't need to be watching all the time, afraid of his competitors and his 'friends.'"

"Now you're really hidebound," said Rufus indulgently. "You know the idea is fantastic."

"Yes, of course I know," said Stephen. "I know it only too well."

Rufus was exultant. He stood behind Stephen and pressed his hands warmly on his brother's shoulders. "Competition is the life of all progress," he said. "You do believe that, don't you?"

"Certainly." Stephen's hands lay flexed on his brief case. "But can't it be honest competition?"

"No, it can't. It can only be dog eat dog. As for myself, I don't want to be a little dog. I want to be a big one," and he made an amusing sound as he clicked his teeth together.

"Even though Joe Baynes would be eaten up in the process?"

"Oh, Joe," Rufus removed his hands. "Joe's a businessman

53

himself. He wouldn't hold it against us. He'd do the same to us, you can be sure, if he had the opportunity."

"No, he wouldn't," said Stephen without emphasis. "I know him too well. He's twenty-two years older than you are, and twenty years older than I. I've been his closest friend for many years, and I've always admired him, and I know everything about him."

Rufus withdrew to the fire. He kicked at a coal thoughtfully. He said, "If we don't take over his bonds, the Capital will. That's certain. And the Capital won't give him a job, and so he'll have nothing. He's sensible. He'll accept half a loaf."

The Capital Railroad. Stephen wrinkled his dry brow. Rufus was right, of course. Stephen sighed, and the sigh was audible in the room. He snapped the lock of his brief case shut and straightened his shoulders.

"You think Alex Peale will sell the bonds to the Capital?"

"Why, unquestionably, Steve! In fact"—Rufus paused, then continued after his hesitation—"Alex as much as offered the bonds to us last week, when I saw him. He'd rather we'd have them, instead of Capital. But the bank can't go on, not collecting interest. Alex has to do something. Good God, he's a banker! Do you expect him to lose money?"

"No, I certainly don't."

"Well, then?"

"If Joe can continue paying the interest, if he can pay the interest now——"

"But he can't."

Stephen made no reply. His gaunt body was bent against the livid light that poured through the windows.

"Even if he could," said Rufus with sudden hard impatience, "as of to-day, he wouldn't be able to go on. He hasn't the imagination, the foresight, the daring. He'd be in trouble again, in a year, two years, three years. His properties don't pay their way, and you know it."

"We could help by putting links between his little railroads and our line," said Stephen.

Rufus was shocked. "You don't mean it!" he cried. "It'd cost us too much money, and the returns would not come in in any quantity for a long time. Why should we make him such a gift, friend or no friend? And what would our own stockholders say? They're all for rapid expansion. One has to consider one's stockholders." He waited: then, as Stephen did not speak, he went on in a louder and more incredulous voice: "But, of course, you aren't serious! Pa would never agree to it, and you know it."

"No, he wouldn't," assented Stephen sadly.

"There you are! And now Pa's all for buying up the bonds." Rufus added, "I wish you wouldn't talk so idly, Steve. It's time-wasting. You know that we don't have the time for mere fruitless conversation. What shall I tell Alex to-morrow? Of course, Pa and I have made up our minds, but we'd like your formal assent, as vice-president." He could not keep the edge of contempt out of his voice.

"Let me think about it for a few hours," replied Stephen. He stood up, and held his brief case in his hand. "In the meantime, I have to go out for a while."

"I'm going to the station," said Rufus, again the amiable brother. "Let me drive you." He had accomplished what he had come to accomplish, and was jubilant.

Stephen looked at him, his face greyer than ever in the grey light. "No, I have only to go to the bank downstairs, and then I must go on a little private business of my own."

CHAPTER FIVE

RUFUS LOOKED through the window, waiting for Stephen to emerge from the building. But some time passed. So, he had gone to the bank first, as he had said. Rufus had never had occasion to doubt Stephen's word, nor had he ever caught him in a lie; however, falsehood was so much a part of his own nature that he still could not believe that the truth lived in any man.

Stephen finally emerged from the general front door that led to the back and all the offices. His greatcoat was buttoned high on his neck; he wore that "damned old-fashioned tall hat" of his. It was like him never to know when a style passed and became ridiculous. The wind caught the "stovepipe" and Stephen, staggering a little under the assault of the gale, clutched wildly at his hat, his brief case abruptly swinging outward and catching the hat of a passer-by. Rufus could not hear what went on, but he saw that Stephen, very flustered and almost servile, was apologising, and the passer-by was glaring. The more Stephen explained and apologised, the more outraged was the other man, straightening himself up so that he towered over Stephen.

Rufus laughed boisterously, shook his head, and went back to Stephen's desk, which had been his father's. He sat down in Stephen's chair and methodically went through all the drawers and read all the papers. He was disappointed again. Then his eye lit on the files, and he went to them briskly. But they were locked. Aha! Rufus regarded the files with cunning satisfaction. So he was hiding something, was he, the grey fish? He was so pleased to discover that the files were locked that he never bothered to consider that perhaps Stephen, who locked the files at night, had as yet no occasion to unlock them this morning.

He sat on Stephen's desk for a few moments, gleefully reflecting on his triumph over Stephen this morning. It had been absurdly easy. He and his father would laugh at it to-night, and to-morrow he, Rufus, would have a fine dinner with his dear friend, Mr. Alex Peale, in Mr. Peale's splendid home, and all arrangements would be made to buy up old Joe Baynes's bonds. Perhaps the senator would be there, too. Certainly he would be there! He was in Portersville at this very moment, in his old home, mending his political fences and solicitously, and with tenderness, interviewing his constituents.

And then, after dinner, after cigars and port and conversation, he, Rufus, would go to a discreet "little place" with which he had become well acquainted the last month or two. His expression of anticipation and enjoyment slowly began to fade, and now a vicious look glinted in his eyes. Damn Lydia. It was all her fault. Sometimes he wanted to throw the obscene fact into her cold dark face, but after all there were some things a man did not say to his wife, even if she had taken another bedroom for herself and left her husband's bed. Rufus had never asked why. So far, he contented himself by looking wounded and sorrowful in Lydia's presence, and very stately, in his hurt. He would not answer his mother's pertinent questions; even with her he occasionally acted, for he was born theatrical and it gave him some satisfaction to exercise his natural histrionic gifts.

The strange thing was that he was truly hurt and wounded, and deeply puzzled. He loved his wife. There was a mystery about Lydia, an elusiveness, which had captivated him even when he had first been attracted to her sister. She was so complete,

56

so composed; she was a lady as his mother would never be a lady. There was such depthless enigma in her lovely dark eyes, such a perfect contour to her slim cheeks, such an exciting dark fire in her masses of hair. Her tall figure was excellent, and her taste could not be surpassed. She carried herself like a queen, serenely, without imperiousness, yet with soft and sure command. She did not sway languidly, as other women swayed, but walked smoothly and assuredly. Rufus, brooding over her and his baffling wrongs, thought of her long white throat, her long white arms and beautiful hands, her mouth that was strong and pink and firm. Lydia had "character." She was also amusing, as well as composed and equal to any contingency. She had loved him.

I love her, not just for her appearance, and her manners, and the fact that she is a lady, but because I can trust her. Rufus looked up, astonished. It was true. He trusted Lydia, he who had never trusted anyone else, not even his mother. Now his pain became a live and twisting thing in him. He remembered the earlier months of his marriage, and Lydia's passion for him, her joy in him, her infinite tenderness, her reciprocating love. Things had begun to go wrong only after her conception of Cornelia. Lydia had avoided him, averted her eyes from him, seldom spoke to him, answered him coolly when he insisted. He had attributed this to her pregnancy and had waited with eagerness for her to be delivered. But things had become untenable after the birth, rather than better.

Of course, he thought tentatively, he could demand his rights as a husband. But he, who shrank from nothing else, shrank from this. He knew that Lydia would submit if he insisted, but the submission would be loathsome to him who had known her responses. She must be won back from that strange and inimical world to which she had retreated, and from which she would not emerge even to nurse her child. This retreat had occasioned the immediate necessity and trouble of finding a wet nurse. Lydia, apparently, did not care. Sophia, outraged, reported that Lydia rarely went into the nursery.

Stephen walked some distance after leaving the bank, keeping his eyes down in his usual way and so avoiding the necessity for greeting any acquaintance. He knew in what derisive repute he was held by almost everyone, rich or poor or middle class, and it hurt him less to see no one than to catch the sliding eyes of mockery in otherwise friendly faces.

In his childhood and boyhood he had accepted all this, but now there was growing in him a bitter doubt and resentment. It was slowly becoming obvious to him—though he sternly tried to subdue the knowledge—that he knew too much about mankind, and had always known, that he saw mankind naked, not clothed in civilisation and restrained by Christianity, and what he saw was not good.

It was not awkwardness, shyness, and inadequacy, as most people believed, that made him drift away from groups and suffer agonies at social dinners, and so "make a spectacle of himself" in the opinion of others. It was fear. Fear of men filled him with an icy panic, a desperate if secret desire for immediate flight. It was complete understanding that made him apologetic in his manner towards those he encountered; he was so remorseful that he knew all about them!

Those small eyes, disconcerted, would move away from a direct look, so that he got the reputation of being furtive; but sometimes, when off guard, he would fix them on others with a curiously intent and penetrating expression, so that even passers-by, or those near at hand, became uneasy.

The wind tore at him as he raced on his long legs through the streets towards the river; several people smiled maliciously at the sight of him, at the ridiculous appearance he presented with his flapping coat-tails and flapping brief case. He did not see the smiles; he knew they were there, but in his compassion he refused to look. He reached the river street and found a hack. He directed that he be driven to 46 Elm Road.

The hack rumbled with hollow sound over the bridge; the grey light in the sky darkened before a coming storm. Then Stephen was being driven down the finest and most exclusive street in West Town, a street which faced the river across long sweeps of lawn. Even on this March day the houses seemed warm and imposing on their wide grounds, and the empty trees had a kind of stark grandeur about them. The cold grey and purplish river rushed rapidly along before these pleasant homes, and a livid light flowed over the wet roofs. Here the mountains were more emphatic in their nearness, roll and line and folds of them, a darker purple than the river, rising up in petrified chaos behind the city.

Never Victorious, Never Defeated

Rain suddenly lashed out of the sky and struck at the dirty windows of the hack. Almost immediately the windows clouded over from the slight warmth inside the vehicle, and Stephen rubbed one in order to peer out. Just then the hack came to a broad driveway of gravel, and turned in on its winding surface towards a house of grey stone with steeply-pitched roof, squat grey chimneys, and high leaded windows shrouded in silk. Even in this drear March weather the house stood in admirable proportions at the end of the drive.

The hack drew up under the porte-cochère, and Stephen, struggling with his long legs, alighted. The wind seized him and between his attempts to hold on to his hat, retain his brief case, which he clutched as though it held the secrets of a great empire, and keep his coat from being torn from his body while he fished for change in his pocket, he was a somewhat ludicrous figure. "Looks somethin' like old Abe Lincoln, with a moustache," thought the hack driver, watching Stephen calmly from his perch without offering any assistance at all, as he would have done with a more prepossessing man. It was his opinion that here was someone quite unimportant, a poor lawyer or something, or a half-starved constituent of the gentleman who lived in this house.

The gale had taken Stephen's breath, and there was a painful stabbing in his chest. Panting a little, he sounded the knocker, not in the bluff and confident manner of his brother, but tentatively, as if apologising for his intrusion. The door opened, and a portly butler faced him. The man frowned at this rather bedraggled man on the doorstep, with his old-fashioned hat and outmoded greatcoat, his red nose, wet shoes, and the big bushy moustache which was the only definite accent in his face.

"Well?" said the servant sharply, beginning to shut the door against one whom he suspected of being only a shabby opportunist or political beggar.

Stephen gathered himself together, pushed his hat at a less incongruous angle on his head, wiped his feet on the doormat. He said to himself, as he was beginning to do lately: Now. Just look him steady in the eye. Damn it, it hurts me to look at him like this: it hurts me to force myself to a pretentious dignity and make my voice cold. Why the hell can't people be decent? Why must a man act with his fellows as though they were at the best slightly contemptible and impertinent? He said, and his voice was a trifle stronger in tone than it had been some months earlier, " Please inform Senator Peale that Mr. Stephen deWitt is here."

The servant stepped back precipitously, his mouth falling open. He bowed so that his head was almost level with his knees. He began to stammer, " Why—why, sir, I didn't recognise you! I'm very sorry, indeed, sir, I'm very——"

Stephen, half envious, half condemning, had watched other men confronting a presumptuous servant and stopping their speech with a harsh glance, a gesture of lordly disdain. Stephen knew he should do this, he half desired to; and then, seeing the butler's frantic apprehension at his mistake, his heart melted in spite of all his efforts. No one should be so frightened by another man, he thought; no one should be forced to suffer so in his inner security, even if it is his own fault.

He said, " It doesn't matter. I've never been here before, so why should you know me? Thank you, thank you. I won't be long, I think. Just lay my coat and hat anywhere."

The servant, enormously relieved, was also taken aback. Stephen, with the old sinking feeling, saw the white face regain its colour and take on its original look of arrogance, though it was somewhat muted and secret. He knew exactly what the man was thinking: Is this Stephen deWitt, actually Stephen deWitt? What a miserable and inconsequential creature! If he were half a man he would knock me down.

The fact that Stephen neither physically nor by implication " knocked him down" lowered him in the servant's estimation. Stephen thought, as usual, that it was best not to notice too many things which wounded, and so he followed the man down a long, wide, and gloomy hall with polished floors, darkly panelled walls, heavy and gloomy furniture and big mirrors, and a pitched, beamed ceiling. He decided he did not like this great house, and he thought all that wood and all that unrelieved and crepuscular dimness was very depressing. Probably wants to chill constituents, he thought, and was pleased at his unkind thought.

He tasted it on his tongue, and its acrid sting was like an intoxicant. He needed this feeling, he remembered, and so it was a taller and straighter and less awkward Stephen who was ushered into a library immense as a meeting hall, full of brown and red and blue books, dim Oriental rugs and furniture made for a giant. A wall of grey, silk-covered windows faced what was probably a very desolate garden. But a good and roaring fire crackled on a hearth and shimmered on brass fenders, and two lamps were lit. Even at this distance the sound of the river could be heard plainly, like a thunderous counterpoint.

A man was reading before the fire, and comfortably smoking a pipe. He looked up alertly as Stephen was announced, and he rose at once, his short plump arms and hands extended, his smoking jacket falling open to show a flowered waistcoat which stretched over a big round belly. He was a completely bald man, and he had a good, kindly, and common face, full of open honesty and warmth, a broad coarse nose, and a happy smile. He exuded an odour of smoke and lemon-scented Cologne, and his handclasp was cordial and sincere. Seeing this lavish greeting of the " miserable creature," the butler was more disconcerted than before, and hastily retreated.

"My dear, dear Stephen!" cried Senator George Peale with paternal fondness. "How delighted I am that you finally visited me! I've asked you so often, you shrinking violet, but you never came until to-day. Well, is this a dragon's nest? Come, come, sit by the fire! Let us have a long visit. Wine? Whisky? Sherry? How damp you are; what a pity. So good to see you, you rascal! Whisky? Now then, now then; is that comfortable? How is your dear father, and our delightful Rufus, the scoundrel?"

Stephen was befuddled by all this cordiality and kindness and obvious pleasure. No one had received him like this before. He had to control his bemused enchantment and gratitude, and he clenched his hands on his brief case lest he forget.

He therefore sat stiffly on the edge of the comfortable chair, his legs spread ungracefully, the knees sticking uncompromisingly against the stuff of his pantaloons. He clutched the brief case. He said, "My father is still an invalid, and Rufus is well. Whisky, please, Senator. I hope I haven't taken another chill."

The senator standing over him, was concerned, and this made Stephen feel guilty. "It's nothing at all, nothing, Senator. I shouldn't have mentioned it." The senator was only forty-five, but Stephen treacherously thought of him as an affectionate uncle. He pulled his thoughts away from this beguiling picture and suddenly, unknown even to himself, his mouth tightened grimly under the moustache and his small eyes retreated in reserve. He must remember his errand, he said inwardly, with

61

cold anger directed only against himself, and nothing must shake him. Too much was at stake.

The senator pulled the bell rope near the fireplace, and directed all the tender solicitude he could summon at his "dear, dear Stephen." He sat down near Stephen, and nothing could have been more intimate and familiar than his smile. He cocked his head and regarded Stephen with humorous doting. "What a strange person you are, Steve. A strange, strange person. But I like you; I've always liked you better than our Rufus, and no words of mine can express how much I do like Rufus. He's like the sun, my dear wife says. But you, but you——" All at once the senator saw he had made a mistake, which could become offensive if tact were not immediately used. But who the devil was there with whom to compare Stephen deWitt? "Why, dammit!" he cried. "You look something like old Abe, of blessed memory."

That he had made an error he immediately saw, but why he did not know. For Stephen was saying with unfamiliar coldness, "I suppose you mean that as a compliment, Senator, and thank you. However, I don't think I resemble Mr. Lincoln in the slightest."

"Well, well," said the senator, nonplussed, wondering why anyone should resent being compared with Mr. Lincoln. Then he remembered Stephen's modesty and thought he had offered too extravagant a compliment. He smiled tenderly. "Of course, Mr. Lincoln had such a mop of hair, and there was a wart on his cheek, and he had a lantern chin. But, who cared? Such a spirit, such a nobility, such an inner glory!" He sighed. "You remind me of him in those ways."

Stephen was silent.

"When I received your note yesterday, I was too happy for speech," said Senator Peale, spreading his plump knees and resting a hand on each, and regarding Stephen with a benign expression. "I said to my dear wife, 'Anna, Stephen deWitt has finally consented to visit us!' She has always liked you extremely, you know, Stephen."

Stephen doubted this very much, but he remembered that Mrs. Peale was a very nice and gentle soul, and he winced. He wished this man were a villain, a big and thumping villain, or at least a hypocrite or possessed of narrow meannesses. It was so hard to feel bitter against this kind of man, who did not consider what he had ever done was villainous. He doubtless believed that he had lived a fine and Christian life, had done his duty as a representative of the people, had made a fortune as legitimately as possible, and was a good husband and father. And no doubt, reflected Stephen despondently, most people are heartily in agreement with him. He felt the damp leather of the brief case under his hands, and again his treacherous kindness almost overcame him.

He became conscious that Senator Peale had been talking on and on, with laughter and pleasure, and that he himself had been nodding without having heard a single word. The senator handed him a glass of whisky. The storm had darkened so steadily over the city that it might have been night instead of hardly noon. Stephen caught a word—". . . weather."

He assented, nodding his head again: "Yes, very bad, isn't it? I think we'll have snow."

Silence followed his remark, and he glanced up to see Senator Peale staring at him in perplexity. The senator looked down at his glass, a smile fixed on his kindly face, and Stephen knew, once more, that he had committed his too-familiar *faux pas*. He had, on the basis of a mere word, thought that he could come into a conversation that had left him far behind, and completely bereft of any idea about it.

"Your boy, Patrick, must be at least eleven years old now, mustn't he?". His voice wavered hopefully.

The senator looked up, smiled in a peculiar fashion, and said, "Yes. Yes, he is eleven now, Steve. More whisky?" asked the senator, rising with the agile air of a pleased host. Stephen held out his glass at the end of a stiff arm. Then the senator pulled the bell rope again and said, in too loud a voice, "He's right here at home, now! The climate in Washington doesn't suit the little fellow or his mother, and they've both had chills. They prefer Portersville, where we were all born, and they don't even care much for our home in Philadelphia. Nice little place, Portersville! Always delighted when I can come home."

The butler returned, carefully avoiding looking at Stephen, and the senator asked that Master Patrick be called to the library. Stephen was at once sickened with distress. To see the child, whom he remembered as a handsome, grave little boy, would make his work the harder. But there was no escape, and when Patrick entered the room, smiling at his father with his serious eyes, and then bowing to Stephen, it was almost more than the latter could endure. He addressed a few halting remarks to the child, which were politely answered. Then Patrick withdrew, and his father followed him with a long and moving look. When he turned to Stephen, his voice was more than a trifle shaken: "Our only child. But I feel that in Patrick heaven has blessed me. . . ."

A thousand small black faces rose up like an accusing chorus before Stephen's inner eye, and his shivering pity for the senator departed, leaving him cold and very still.

The senator, more disposed than ever to be kind to Stephen, whom he privately considered very queer, remarked, "But you'll be having one of your own very soon, my boy! Rufus has his girl; perhaps you'll have a son."

"Yes," said Stephen. He began to unfasten his brief case.

Oh, my God, thought the senator, sighing patiently. A petition or something! Well, that was one of the prices of being a senator. But it was odd that Stephen deWitt should be the one bringing a petition, signed, no doubt, by at least two thousand people. What did they want now, here in Portersville? Then he was electrified, for just as he was composing his features into the accepted fatherly expression and senatorial interest, he saw Stephen's eyes. Small and sunken behind his high cheekbones though they were, they were now the eyes of an enemy, not vindictive, but stern beyond the power of softening.

Stephen was holding a bound sheaf of papers in his hands, and he was extending the sheaf to the senator. "I have been gathering this information, and paying for the gathering, over a period of seven years, Senator," he was saying. "I thought you ought to see these copies. The other copies are in a safe place, in Philadelphia. You are running for the Senate again this year, are you not?"

Stunned, the senator took the papers, but he could not withdraw his attention from Stephen for several long moments. He began to shake his head, as though pestered by a strange sound. "Why, yes," he said at last, in a slow voice, "I am running again this year. I believe the people want me. . . ." Still gazing at Stephen, he asked, "Is this a petition, Steve?" He tried to smile, to change those inexorable eyes.

"Not a petition, Senator. Only a confidential résumé of your career while in the Senate."

The senator could not believe that he had heard what he had

heard. He held the sheaf of papers in his hands, and now they began to tremble slightly and make a fluttering sound.

"I want you to understand, Senator, that no personal animosity brings me here to-day," Stephen was saying. He wanted to avert his head, but he refused to permit himself to do this. It was almost the most untenable moment of his life, for he knew that he was about to strike at this man, perhaps mortally, this man who had been one of the closest friends of the DeWitt family for many years, and had given, and received, advantages during the relationship. So Stephen, not turning away his eyes, went on: "But I have thought, over all these years, that you ought not to be a senator of this Commonwealth, that you ought not to be elected."

"What are you saying, Steve?" whispered the senator disbelievingly. The papers fluttered louder in his hands. The rain beat wildly against the windows, and the red fire hissed and cracked. He must be mad, thought Senator Peale. He was always peculiar; yes, he must be mad. He cleared his throat, said weakly, "What do you mean? Your family has always supported me. Your father . . ." He had to swallow. "I'm sorry, Steve, if I have done anything in Washington that didn't meet with your approval, but——"

"You voted for a stronger and more centralised government, Senator, not only for the war period, but as a permanent thing." Stephen's voice rose clearly and incisively, for now he had his compassion under control, and could remember. "You voted for a measure that would have destroyed all that George Washington and Thomas Jefferson fought for, and prayed for, and lived for: the right of the states and the commonwealths to their own sovereignty. You did that, Senator, not for any evil reason, I am sure; you said, if I remember correctly, ' It's the trend of the times.'"

He shook his head. "No, Senator, it isn't the ' trend of the times,' it's the trend of tyranny. Washington knew that men would always rise up who would attempt to abrogate the rights of the states and the commonwealths and centralise government and make it all-powerful. The men who framed the Constitution knew it, too. That is why we have a system of checks and balances. But the men who want power hate those checks and balances, and I suppose, through all the generations of America, they will attempt to overthrow them." He paused, and then continued:

Never Victorious, Never Defeated

"I don't believe you want power more than does any other man. I know that the urge for power is strong in most people. I don't think you were plotting against America deliberately. But still, men like you are dangerous. Yes, I know all the arguments for centralised government: economy, more efficiency, quicker results by directives, more mobility during emergencies of any kind. Perhaps they're valid arguments in a way. However, they would lead to despotism, the kind of despotism that is crushing Europe to-day and has been crushing her for centuries."

It was the longest speech he had ever made in his life, and he poured it out on long breaths of powerful indignation. He could summon up this indignation when protecting a principle or a friend, or against injustice, where he could not do it for himself. His neutral-coloured face had flashed into life and strength. It was no longer a man of meekness and humility who sat opposite the stupefied senator, but a man who, in spite of his lean and lanky awkwardness, his clumsy gestures, his battered clothing, was a force. The senator was as much paralysed by this change in a man he had always considered a mere cipher as by his words.

Stephen was speaking again, more moderately, but still with anger: "You also voted in behalf of the bill to bring tens of thousands of hapless and starving Europeans to this country, Senator. On the surface, it is a charitable and Christian and worthy bill, and I would approve of it also, except for a very pertinent thing.

"We are expanding industrially. We need labour. So, again on the surface, all that you have voted for in that bill is excellent and praiseworthy. But let us think of our own native labour, and let us think of those Europeans, too. Let us, indeed, think of the Europeans first of all. Was there any strong provision made in that bill to protect European labour from the rapacity of our own people, our own employers? Was there any provision that these people be sheltered adequately, given the same rate of pay as our native labour receives? Were there any provisions for their health and safety? No, there were not. So now they are coming in by the shiploads, the endless thousands of them in the stinking holds of vessels, dirty, diseased, hungering. Where are they going? To the cities, to displace our native workers, to work for much less money, and to be bound for a whole year to the masters to whom they will be consigned, to be victimised by mills and factories and machines, virtual slaves who will never dare move

66

until their period of serfdom is over. And this thing was done to despairing creatures by wicked men who are taking advantage of their despair."

The senator put his hand to his cheek. His pleasant colour had faded. He was very pale. "Steve," he said, "please listen. Isn't it better for these men to be consigned to employers for a year, while they pay off their passage, than to starve to death in Europe or die in Europe's endless wars? They have their families with them. Within a generation they will be part of America. We need the labour, if we are to expand. . . ."

Stephen smiled sadly. "Yes, we are a rapidly growing country, a pioneering country, and we will now begin to push back frontiers in earnest. But it could have been done a little more slowly; the influx of Europeans could have been more carefully controlled, so that when they arrived there would be some respectable shelter for them, some provision. It could have been a slow process, with the help of our own native labour. I dislike prophecy, but now I shall predict the future: for many decades, because of this uncontrolled influx of people into a country not yet prepared to take care of them, there will be bloody riots, hatreds, and racial antagonisms which will last, perhaps, for decades.

"Those who voted for that bill, without any restrictions to amount to anything, without any normal and judicious control, are not good Americans. You were one who voted for it, Senator. And that is why I determined to help prevent you from returning to Washington this year."

The senator gazed at Stephen earnestly, and the shadow of his bewilderment was still in his eyes. He considered what Stephen had said, and when he spoke, his voice was no longer good and round, like a ripe plum. It was low and thoughtful.

"You are a fine and idealistic man, Steve. I honour you for it. But there are exigencies. . . ."

Stephen smiled mournfully. "Yes, there are always exigencies, Senator."

"However, Stephen, I don't think the people of Pennsylvania will refuse to re-elect me again to the Senate because of these two actions of mine, which were done with the utmost sincerity and in the firm belief they were best for America." He looked regretfully at the other man. "I hope this doesn't spoil our friendship, my boy."

Stephen pointed to the sheaf of papers in the senator's hands. "I brought those copies for you to read, sir."

The senator pulled his hypnotised eyes away from Stephen and began to read. The lamps in the room brightened as the day darkened outside; the fire was sinking into red embers; the rain hammered at the windows. Stephen lay back in his chair, utterly exhausted and dejected. Now his compassion returned to him, tearing at his unprotected heart. He could not look at the senator as he read. He might betray all his work if he did. He stared at the ceiling blindly, and his mouth was dry and there was a nauseous taste in it.

The senator, well accustomed to read rapidly, to skim, to gather all the information on a sheet of paper in one tight nut of facts almost at a glance, made no exclamation as he read the papers Stephen had given him. Stephen could hear the papers turning with monotonous swiftness. Ten, eleven, twelve. The senator had finished. Stephen turned his stare down from the ceiling. The senator was sitting in silence, his head bent, his eyes fixed on the floor between his knees. The papers were gripped in his hands. His face was grey and had fallen into folds which made him appear much older than he was.

Feeling that Stephen was looking at him, he raised his own eyes. There was a sick expression in them. "You did this—to me —Steve, to hurt me. . . ."

Stephen clenched his hands to hold back that hateful compassion. "No, not to hurt you, Senator. Believe me. Just to keep you from going to Washington again."

The senator spoke with difficulty: "You've had me spied upon for years. To destroy me. Steve, you know your father was in this—this—'blackbirding' too? You know that it was he who invited me to invest. . . . My brother Alex always had the money. I didn't. I wanted it. It's normal to want it, so I borrowed what I could, and I invested. . . ."

Stephen spoke gently but inflexibly. "You invested it in ships and in men to kidnap black men and women and children from Africa and to spirit them into the Southern states. You invested it in agony and suffering and slavery. You didn't think it was wrong; you never thought it was wrong; you don't, even now, think it was wrong. You were very patriotic during the war to free your victims, Senator, but then, you, like Mr. Lincoln, always said it was really a war to preserve the Union, and so it

68

was." He stopped for a moment. "I was informed, as you see, that you were one of only three senators whom Mr. Lincoln called to the White House to read the Emancipation Proclamation before it was issued. And I think you were the only one who told him it was 'ill-advised.' At least you had the honesty of your opinions, Senator, and I never condemn an honest opinion."

He pulled himself stiffly upright in his chair. "You made a lot of money, Senator, and according to your lights it was not an evil thing to acquire it as you did. It helped you to get elected the first time. It helped you to invest in a number of things which are paying you handsomely. But, Senator, you have forgotten one thing: there are, in this state, tens of thousands of fathers and brothers and sons and mothers who are grieving for their dead killed in the war. There is a battleground, Gettysburg, which the people will not forget just as they will not forget their dead. They remember that those soldiers died because of men like you. They won't re-elect you, Senator, when they know." Pain was in his face. "They will hate you until you die, yourself, Senator."

Senator Peale rubbed his damp forehead with the back of his hand. He spoke dully: "So you gathered all this blackmail so I wouldn't dare run for the Senate again. You are threatening to expose me because I believe in a strong, centralised government, and I approved of bringing Europeans to this country as fast as possible."

"Yes," said Stephen, and he could not help the note of pleading in his voice. "I believe you are dangerous in the Senate, sir. In a way you could call it blackmail. Perhaps others would think it patriotism."

The senator lifted his head and smiled drearily at Stephen. "I mentioned before that your father invited me to go into that —that thing. Steve, if you 'expose' me, I'll bring your father into it also. He won't like that, ill as he is, and he won't like the son who did it."

"He'll laugh," said Stephen contemplatively. "He has a great sense of humour. It'll amuse him inordinately. He'll laugh at you, Senator, and enjoy the laughing. He'll just remember that even if people are disgusted with him, and loathe him, they can't possibly refuse to ride in our trains. But they won't forget you, Senator. Senators are expendable."

The senator stood up, thrust his plump hands in his pockets, and looked at the embers of his fire. There was a slack and weary air about him, and Stephen had to remember so that he would not melt with sympathy.

"What you are trying to tell me, Stephen, is that I must not run for the Senate this year?"

Very gradually, Stephen got to his feet, "unfolding" himself, as Rufus often said. He put his elbow on the mantelpiece and covered his face with his long fingers. He spoke from behind them:

"That was my original intention, Senator. It isn't now."

The senator continued to look at the fire; then, with infinite slowness, he turned to Stephen, unable to speak.

Stephen's voice came muffled and mortally tired from its shelter behind his hand: "I'm here to make a bargain with you, Senator. This morning it was still the original bargain: your retirement, and my silence. But things changed in little more than an hour. I'll be brief: I want you to telegraph your brother Alex, in Philadelphia, not to sell Joseph Baynes's bonds to my brother Rufus to-morrow. I want you to telegraph him never to sell them without due notice to you, which you will pass on to me, secretly. I want you to get his promise not to sell those bonds under any circumstances to the Capital Railroad Company."

The senator was amazed, and with his amazement came a deep and confused respect. He tried to smile. "Oh. You want them yourself, is that it, Steve?"

Stephen dropped his hand and showed his haggard face. "No," he said. "I just want Joe Baynes to have them. You see, I'm going to lend—give—him the money to pay the outstanding interest."

The senator was amazed. He could not speak. He pulled at his fleshy face; he rubbed his chin. He reached out for a poker and stirred up the dying fire. He sucked in his lips, folded his arms on his knees, and regarded the embers in a long silence.

Then he spoke as if speaking aloud to himself: "I never considered myself a venal man."

"I know," said Stephen gently.

The senator put his hands over his face. "I never knew a good man before, Steve."

"I'm not"—and Stephen smiled involuntarily—"Joe Baynes is just my friend."

The senator dropped his hands and looked up at Stephen with deep penetration. Twice he started to speak, but stopped himself.

Then he laughed without real mirth. "And you would sacrifice even your principles for a friend—just one man?"

The great pain stood on Stephen's face, so great a pain that it was really anguish. "I'm afraid I would." He added, "You see, I'm not a good man at all, Senator."

Senator Peale took the copies and threw them into the fire. The two men watched the brief blaze. Senator Peale said, when the papers were ashes, "I'm getting much the better bargain. You're not getting anything, Steve, not anything at all. You confuse me."

"You find it very strange?"

The senator considered this. It was some time before he spoke again, and it was in a low tone. "Not for you, Steve. No, it's not strange for you."

When he looked up again, Stephen was gone.

CHAPTER SIX

THE WIND and the rain blended together in one vast and rumbling maelstrom as Stephen emerged from the senator's house. The butler looked out and said dubiously, eyeing Stephen the while with surly resentment that he had been so deceived, "Very bad, sir. Your hack has gone." He implied that a man who had no carriage, or who had not arranged for one of his own, was a man of very low degree. Stephen, vexed with himself for not having made some provision for the hack owner to wait for him, or at least call for him, contemplated the dark grey weather with consternation.

"I'll call a carriage for you, sir," said the butler, and by this offer he tendered forgiveness to Stephen and felt uplifted in consequence. "One of the senator's."

"Oh, please don't bother," Stephen began, with his customary dislike of inconveniencing anyone, but the butler had already disappeared. Within a few minutes a small carriage drew up with smartness before Stephen, who looked at it gratefully. Should he tip the butler? But the man was smiling at him in a very kindly, if superior, fashion, and in some way Stephen caught the diffused idea that the servant had conferred some mysterious favour upon him, Stephen, which would be nullified by a tip. So he merely smiled, crawled into the carriage, and was driven away.

He had succeeded. He had known that he would not fail. But such a depression fell on him now that his body collapsed against the smooth leather cushions of the carriage. For one man, one friend, he had betrayed his country. It was useless to tell himself that Senator Peale was no worse than any other politician and perhaps even better than any man who might replace him. The fact remained that he, Stephen, had lost a measure of his own integrity, had failed to do what he had set out to do originally. He remembered what the senator had said: "I'm not really a venal man." No, he was not. Unscrupulous slave dealers had demanded slaves, in spite of all the rigorous laws passed by the Southern States to prohibit the importation of the wretched black man.

"Blackbirding" was a crime in which Northerners had engaged to their own vast profit, and among the most vociferous of the Northerners demanding that the South be crushed had been men like Senator Peale. It was they, now, who were sending their hordes of hired "carpetbaggers" into the ruined South, and Senator Peale had his own agents among them. The weight on Stephen's concave chest became like iron.

Stephen had given the coachman his directions, and in an effort to forget his depression he looked out of the polished glass windows. The carriage was moving steadily through the streets of East Town, after having crossed the bridge, and now it was approaching the railroad tracks. Stephen had heard a dolorous howling in the distance. Old Sixty-three, he thought, glancing at his silver watch. Right on time, too. The carriage crossed the tracks hastily, and the howling filled the watery air, and a single glaring eye pierced through the ghostly gloom of wind and rain. You could always depend on old Sixty-three, for the engineer, Bill Laufer, was proud of his record, and was the State Railroad Company's oldest employee. He had lost three fingers of his right hand when he had been a "coupler," some fifteen years ago, and to him the loss was his prideful badge of service. Stephen understood the love of railroad men for the railroads, for he shared it himself.

The carriage was now rolling along a rather bleak street of warehouses and shabby offices. Stephen tapped on the glass and called out, "At the corner. Let me out, please." He fastened his coat, gripped his brief case again, settled his hat firmly, and unentangled his legs. He merged into the rain and ran into a doorway. No one moved along the street, except for a lumbering wagon or two, and the narrow brick walks glimmered wetly in the grey half light. The windows of all these offices ran with grimy water; the doors were old and splintered. Stephen entered a small and gritty hallway and approached a door on which was printed in faded letters, "Baynes Locals." He tapped, then entered.

The door opened on a small office furnished simply with a table, a roll-top desk, a black leather chair which was peeling, a bookkeeper's desk with a stool, and a small and frugal fire. The windows looked out on the dreary street, and had not been washed for a long time. The bare floor gritted under Stephen's boots, and he put on his usual gentle and diffident smile.

The man sitting at the desk was very small, even smaller than Aaron deWitt, and he turned eagerly at Stephen's entrance; his tired, thin face lit up. He was a man in his early fifties, but he was so drawn and worn, so weighted with chronic worry and anxiety, that he appeared much older. In spite of his carefully pressed old clothing, his patched boots, and neatly mended cravat, it was evident that he was a gentlemen, for his blue eyes were quick and intelligent, his features finely etched and clear. His thin hair had turned white during the past year, and was fastidiously combed and arranged to the best advantage.

"Steve!" he exclaimed, rising and holding out his hands, and looking up at Stephen with genuine pleasure and affection.

"You seem surprised to see me. Had you forgotten that I was coming?"

"No! Of course not. But Steve, it's always so good to see you. It's like a new gratification whenever you appear. How are you? Sit down in that damned chair. It's the best I have, as you know. Wait a minute; I'll stir up the fire and toss in some coals."

Stephen watched him. "I bought some more land near Scanton. Everybody laughs at me, but I think it'll be the best coalfield we've ever discovered."

"It was you who told them all that the iron was about played out and they'd better concentrate on coal," said Mr. Baynes, looking over his shoulder at his friend as he stirred up the fire. "Are you going to start digging soon?"

Stephen hesitated. He glanced at his brief case. "No, not yet. There's plenty of time."

The office might be small, dirty, and full of dreariness, the one kerosene lamp flickering on the brown walls, but Stephen felt peace and contentment. He laid his hat on the table, stretched out his legs to the fire, and pulled his pipe from his pocket. He filled it slowly, lit it carefully. Mr. Baynes perched himself on the chair of his desk and regarded Stephen with deep attachment.

"I've just remembered," said Stephen. "I'm hungry, and I've had no luncheon. Have you an extra sandwich, Joe?"

"I forgot to eat, and I'm glad now," replied the other man. He pulled open a drawer of his battered desk and brought out a small basket. He opened it, folded back the white napkin, and revealed buttered bread, some slices of ham, mustard, and two pieces of cake. He spread the napkin on the table and laid the food upon it. Stephen looked at it with satisfaction. He picked up two pieces of bread, laid a slice of ham upon it, and made a sandwich. "Joe," he said, "don't worry any more. I've brought some money for you, to pay the interest on your bonds."

Mr. Baynes turned in his chair and stared wretchedly at the windows. "I made a mistake, Steve, just as I always make mistakes. I thought the interest was due next week. It's to-day. I just went through my books. So you see, it's too late. I wrote Alex Peale to-day, begging for more time, because you had promised to help me. I sent the letter by special messenger on one of your trains. But to-night my bonds will be sold. There's somebody after them. Perhaps the Capital. . . ." His dry eyes did not turn towards Stephen, and he had spoken quietly, though his hands had been twisting together all the time in a gesture of despair.

Stephen bit a large piece from his sandwich and chewed it. He looked at his friend compassionately and swallowed. "You're wrong, Joe. Alex won't sell out your bonds, to anybody. I can promise you that on my word of honour." He laid down the sandwich and pulled his brief case to him. Slowly, unbelievingly, Mr. Baynes swung to face him. Stephen was piling bank notes on the table in precise heaps. "Five thousand dollars, Joe. That's your interest to date."

Dazed, Joseph touched one of the heaps with the tip of a finger, but he stared at Stephen. "I don't understand," he said, and his voice shook. "What do you mean? How could you, how did you stop him from selling me out? How do you know?"

"It's too complicated to tell you. You've just got to trust me, Joe."

"Trust you," repeated Joseph. And then he put his hands over his face and his shoulders heaved, and then he laid down his arms on the table and bent his head on them.

The dirty office was very still. Once or twice Stephen reached out to touch his friend, then drew back his hand, embarrassed. But his little eyes were bright with pity and sympathetic understanding. He picked up his sandwich and continued to eat it, and then he talked gently:

"It's all right, Joe. Did you think I wouldn't help you to the best of my ability? It wasn't important about the interest. Even if you didn't pay it, Alex Peale wouldn't sell you out. He never will now. You see, I talked with his brother, the senator, today."

Joseph lifted his head quickly from his arms. His face was strained with fatigue and emotion. "But I went to see the senator yesterday, Steve! I talked with him, asked him to intervene for me with his brother. And he said, very regretfully, that he could do nothing. And I've known George Peale since we were boys together, and we attended the same university and the same church!"

"You didn't use the right arguments, apparently," replied Stephen, hesitating over another piece of ham. "I can be very persuasive on occasion."

Joseph Baynes could not help his involuntary smile. Then he laughed a little, and Stephen joined him dryly. "Of course," Joseph said, blowing his nose, "he's always been such a good friend of your family's, though you haven't known him as long as I have. We lived next door to each other. Your father? Is it possible your father . . . ?"

Stephen stopped chewing. "My father? Good God, Joe! And that reminds me. You're not to tell anyone about all this, not even Elsa."

"You haven't even told me," suggested Joseph hopefully.

Stephen thought about his interview with the senator, and lost his appetite. He leaned back in his chair and regarded the fire sombrely. "There's nothing to tell," he said. "Nothing at all."

Never Victorious, Never Defeated

Now that the full awareness of his reprieve came to Joseph Baynes, tears gathered in the corners of his eyes.

"Steve, Steve! Do you know what I was thinking before you came? I had decided to kill myself. There was nothing else to do."

"That would be very helpful for Elsa and your children," replied Stephen calmly.

"It would. She would have gone home to her brothers and sisters in Philadelphia. I quarrelled with them all, years ago."

Stephen thought this over, then he said, "It's been my observation that no widow is welcome among brothers and sisters, especially if they have money, as I know Elsa's relatives have." Stephen was concerned, for the flush of joy had gone from Joseph Baynes's face; it was pale and exhausted again. His right hand, on the table, kept jumping as if pulled by strings.

"I suppose I'm a failure, Steve. I thought I had founded something completely sound and profitable. After all, as they say, we're expanding, and there's no limit to the expansion. And I do serve communities where your company, and the Capital's, don't go; I have my franchise, and no one can take it away from me unless I go bankrupt. And then I discover that I'm a miserable businessman. I'm not going to plead hard luck; that's the coward's way. Well, maybe I am a coward just the same.

"My lines aren't paying, Steve. And I don't know how to make them pay. I can't charge higher fares; the farmers, and the people in poor circumstances in the villages and in country employment——"

"You certainly can charge higher prices! Don't be a fool, Joe. The farmers? The people in the villages? Why, Joe, they've been coining money during the war! They always do. It's the so-called little people who make the cash during wars, in fistfuls. They know how: a dollar here, a dollar there, new money coming in all the time. Perhaps the towns and cities didn't do so well, except for the larger manufacturers who made things for the army. But the little fellows, in the out-of-the-way places—their expenses don't increase, they have nothing on which to spend money, and what comes to them they keep in iron fingers. They live on a patch of land or a farm, and they eat as usual, buy nothing, and hide it all away in local banks or in mattresses and teapots. And, of course, they whine if anyone raises necessary prices on them! Aren't they the unimportant folk, hidden away, living their 'modest' little lives? Who are the big men who would want to make them pay adequately for what is offered them? It's a sin; it's a crime! It's the same old human story, Joe, my friend."

Joseph listened with some surprise. "Steve, I never heard you talk this way before."

"I'm learning. I'm learning!" said Stephen grimly. "I learn every day. So, my friend, you are going to raise your fares immediately. You are going to balance your books properly. You are going to make a decent profit. I'm not suggesting you gouge, but you have as much a right to make a living as any farmer or villager on your lines. More so, in fact. You've supplied the brains and the equipment and the hardest work. They won't boycott you! How could they? They haven't any alternative means of transportation. Go over your books all the rest of to-day, Joe, and all to-night. Consider what would be just and fair profit to you. And then arrange your fares accordingly."

He waited. Joseph was frowning, and his eyes were glittering with excitement.

"As we expand, Joe, your lines will become more and more travelled, and important. There'll be travelling all the time. People move in an air of prosperity, even if they just move in the accustomed places. It's a kind of ferment."

Joseph picked up one of the piles of bills. "I'll pay you back, Steve. It may take some time, but I'll pay you back. And I'll get those bonds. Why, damn it, you've put fire into me! I'm a new man, Steve. God bless you."

Steve, disconcerted as always when thanked for anything, looked at his watch. "It's half-past two. I must get back to the office. Joe, give my love to Elsa and the children."

"You still haven't told me what you said to Senator Peale?"

Stephen bent his head. "Well, among other things, I told him that I did not believe he should be returned to Washington. As you know, you and I have discussed this innumerable times. . . ."

"You told him that?" cried Joseph incredulously.

"I did."

Joseph, staring at Stephen as at a madman, scratched his head. "And he promised to intervene for me with his brother, at your request?"

"He did. By telegraph."

77

Joseph's face became very thoughtful. "There's something you haven't told me, Steve. You're a secretive rascal. You never tell anyone anything, if you can help it. But it doesn't matter. There isn't a man in Portersville who has done as much good as you have, anonymously. The packets of money to war widows and orphans, the foodstuffs you bought for the sick and indigent in the towns and villages—which I moved on my own railroads—the nameless contributions to the soldiers' hospitals, the orphan asylum, the poor-house, the churches. Don't look so startled. You didn't even tell me about them, but I have ways of knowing. Gossip gets around, and sometimes, in spite of your unobtrusiveness, people remember. And"—Joseph's voice dropped—"you're the best friend a man ever had."

"Ridiculous," said Stephen. "You would do the same for me, wouldn't you?"

"Of course." Joseph could not look away from him, and his eyes were strange.

"Well, then?"

"I haven't asked you about Alice," said Joseph in a preoccupied voice.

"She's splendid. It will be any day now."

"If it is not to-morrow, will you come to our house for dinner? Elsa is much attached to you, Steve. And the children always enjoy your visits."

It was true about Elsa Baynes, thought Stephen. Such a pretty, gay little woman, with rumpled brown hair and vivid eyes. But the children did not like him, and this was odd, for he loved children, especially those who were very young. He frequently brought them gifts and tried to talk to them, for he was unique in his respect for youthful minds, but they would merely take his gifts, grin at him slyly, and let their eyes slide away to their corners. Well, well, thought Stephen, regretfully, it's not the children's fault if they do not like me. He said, "I never leave Alice alone at night, Joe. And after to-day, I'm not going to leave her alone for more than three hours in the morning, until the child is born."

He left his friend and went out into the cold storm. The rain had stopped, but the wind roared through the streets like a cataract. Bending his head, huddling himself together, Stephen began to walk back to his offices.

Joseph Baynes looked at the closed door for several minutes

after Stephen left, then he slowly walked back to the table. He counted the money. Five thousand dollars. More than enough for the present interest. He dropped one heap upon another, and his expression became very odd, dark and sick and full of self-hatred.

CHAPTER SEVEN

THAT LEAVES me very little in my personal account now, thought Stephen, but without regret, as he approached the bank building somewhat out of breath. He had hoped to be able to start digging in the coalfields near Scranton this spring. He had thought of the "Fielding money" which had been invested in the State Railroad Company, and which had enabled the company to extend its lines and to contemplate extending them again. Alice did not have much of her dower left at the present time; her husband had hoped to restore it. But there were so many desperate calls on his charity, which he answered anonymously. Rufus, he knew, was much more sensible than he. In fact, Rufus, who contributed meagrely to any request for aid, received enormous praise for what he did give, for he bestowed it with an air, an attitude of immense generosity and an implication of remorse that he could not do much more at the present time.

Stephen knew all this, but it meant nothing to him. Rufus's dazzling glory did not arouse his envy. It was enough for him that through his charity there was somewhat less suffering in Portersville. He had explained it all to young Alice, and she had agreed with him eagerly, not questioning him, but believing that whatever Stephen did was the wisest thing possible. Stephen, trudging into the bank building, thought: At any rate, we didn't take the money Alice will have when she is thirty-five. There is always that for her.

He started up the stairway, remembering Joseph Baynes's joy, and smiling in the remembrance. He was already building up a wall against the depression he felt when thinking of Senator Peale, and how, for the sake of his friend, he had betrayed his deepest principles. He reached his offices and was met by a circle of white-faced clerks and the bookkeeper.

"Mr. Stephen!" one exclaimed. "We've been trying to find you! Everybody has been trying to find you! Mr. Rufus said to go home immediately after you returned here! He is with Mrs. Stephen, and the whole family, he said."

Stephen stood and looked at them. "What?" he muttered. "What? What?"

"It's Mrs. Stephen," said the bookkeeper with a tragic look, and with obvious relish in the dramatic news he was imparting.

So, it had happened while he was away. There had been no way by which he could have been reached. He had not expected it, God forgive him, not this morning when he had left Alice smiling and serene in her bed, with her tray beside her. Would Alice forgive him for not being available in her extreme hour of suffering? He would tell her. . . . He stood there, his greyish face twitching—idiotically, in the opinion of his employees. "I think you'd better go home, sir," said the bookkeeper. It had been too much to expect that this absurd and stupid employer of theirs should show any emotion of alarm. "Shall I call you a hack at once?"

"Yes," said Stephen in a dull voice. He was suddenly very faint. He sat down on the bookkeeper's stool, and his hat toppled from his head. He looked at it emptily; wisps of his thin brown hair stood up all over his skull; his cravat was pulled to one side; his legs, like stilts, hardly seemed part of him but more like lathes of lumber. He had to clutch the side of the bookkeeper's high desk to keep from falling.

I've got to be calm and intelligent about this, he thought. I couldn't help being away. Alice isn't alone; the family is with her. Her sister, and Rufus, and probably my mother. Besides, babies aren't born that fast. I'll get to her in time. He said to the clerks, "How long ago was I called?"

"At ten o'clock, sir. It was very urgent. Your housekeeper sent the boy for Dr. Worth at once, and then he came here for you, in your carriage."

Ten o'clock. He was talking with Senator Peale at that very time. It was now half-past three. Stephen, with a strangled cry, got to his feet. "Has there been any more news?" he asked. Rufus had gone! Rufus had gone in his place! Why? Why? The child of Stephen and Alice would not seem important to Rufus, whose daughter had already been named "heiress" by her grandfather. Rufus would have waited until the evening, and then would have paid a casual brotherly visit. But Rufus had gone, Rufus who never cared for anyone.

Small pits of darker grey appeared in Stephen's gaunt face. Not bothering about his hat, and dropping his brief case where he had been sitting, he stumbled from the room. He flew down the stairway, passing acquaintances who looked after him with amazement. There was no end to the stairs; they went down eternally into nightmare. His heart was one hollow of agony and fear. Five and a half hours ago, Rufus had gone, precipitously, leaving everything! Rufus had gone—gone—gone—— It was clanging in Stephen's head, an uproar which rose to a tumultuous thunder as he burst into the street.

The bookkeeper was hastening towards him. "I can't find a hack, sir!" he cried desperately. "It's the weather. They're all being used. But wait——"

But Stephen, with a wild face and mad eyes, had charged past him, and was running, like a tall scarecrow, down the street. He flew across intersections, his coat sailing out behind him, his bare head streaming with water, for it had begun to rain again. He charged up hilly streets, his breath tearing in his throat. He collided with hurrying pedestrians and with umbrellas, rebounded from them, staggered, and then resumed his frantic speed.

Shadows of affronted faces flashed before him. As in a nightmare, he heard offended exclamations, saw angry glares. He slipped on muddy cobblestones, leaped across rushing gutters, was conscious of the clamouring river in the distance. His legs flailed and lifted his bounding body. His arms jerked back and forth, the elbows lifted high. The walls of buildings tilted toward him, tilted back; the sky flew up, flew down. Children coming home from school saw him and ran out of his way, or pursued him for a few feet, jeering and screaming. Once or twice he fell against passing carriages and hacks and even horses, and raucous shouts followed him, cursing. No one recognised him in that dimness and in that rain: he blew along like the wind. There was nothing in him but the dreadful necessity to get to Alice, and nothing but his terror. He was caught up in a spinning eternity, and though he did not utter a word he thought he could hear himself shrieking his wife's name.

Now he was on the steep rise of the road which led to his home. a trundling wagon with a farmer huddled on the seat was ahead of him. His strength was failing; his knees were swinging from side to side; the agony in his chest had become a boiling pool of blood which was strangling him. He yelled, and the sound seemed to come from the whole of his sweating body. The wagon rumbled to a halt, and the stout farmer turned as Stephen came alongside.

"Well, it warn't my fault," the farmer grumbled later to spellbound friends. "How'd I know it was Mr. Stephen? There it was, raining like the flood, and it was dark as seven o'clock, and the wind was somethin' to feel! And then this fellow lopes up, without a hat, and streamin' with water, and a face like I wouldn't want any of you to see. I tell you, it was a sight! His face a-pullin' like mad, like he had the fits or somethin', and the most God-awful noises you ever heerd comin' out of his mouth. What would a man think? That he'd got a loony on his hands, and there on the road without no house in sight, and everything mud, and the horses jumping up and down at the sight of him. And him holdin' on to the side of the wagon, makin' them sounds, and not even talkin' sensible, but just lookin' at me wall-eyed, and lookin' as if he'd been fished out of the river. What was I to do? Did he say, ' Look, my man, I'm Mr. Stephen deWitt. I must get home?' Well, then, wouldn't a fellow do anything for the DeWitts, seein' they're so important? But what does he say?" The farmer rubbed his beard in defiant bafflement. "He don't say nothin' for a moment, just jabbering and growling-like in his throat, and I got scared, I tell you. I lifted my whip and hit him across the shoulders, and then when that didn't do no good, I took the butt and hit it sharp across his hands. Brought him to his senses a little. He squeaked, ' My wife. I'll give you five dollars, now, but take me home. I can't run any longer.' And then, bejabbers, if he don't start to sob, just like a woman, and groan.

"Well, five dollars is five dollars, even for a loony, and then he fished out the gold-back, and I snapped it away from him, and he clambered up beside me and kept on makin' those damn sounds. I don't wonder now, but I did then, and am I to blame? I hit up the horses, wantin' to get rid of him fast; no telling what loonies will do in lonesome places. And there he sat, a-clutchin' his knees, and there was blood on his knuckles where I'd hit him, and it ran down with the rain, and he kept heavin' and lookin' ahead and a-moanin'. ' Can't you go faster, faster?' ' Look, mister,' I says, ' my horses are doin' the best they can, and it's better than walkin', though you can try it again if you want to.' And he don't answer, but looks at the back of the horses, and horses are nervous critters and they felt him lookin', and they begin to tear along like crazy, and I kept holdin' back on the reins. Frightened? I thought the devil had got in the wagon with me!

"Five dollars. That was a lot of money for a ride of less than two miles, and I got my suspicions it was stolen money, or maybe that Confederate money, and the fellow'd murder me up the road. And so I sneaked a look at it, and it was all right, and then I said, ' Shut up makin' those damned noises. What's the matter with you? Are you crazy, or somethin'? Somebody after you? It isn't my business, but——'

"And then he only says, and now he got a voice like a thread, like a baby's, kind of weak and broke off, 'I'm Stephen deWitt, and I'm afraid my wife is dying.'

"Well now," the farmer related, "you could've pushed me off the seat with one finger! I took a hard look at him in that damned funny light, and sure enough it was Mr. Stephen deWitt! Seen him hundreds of times on the street, but never rightly remembered him. Always skulkin' along, near the sides of buildings, and never noticin' anybody, and sidlin' away like a gun-shy dog. You had to see him a hundred times before you'd remember him, and me, my eyes ain't what they was. But it was Stephen deWitt all right, and I got to shiverin', and reached behind me for a blanket to cover him, him all wet the way he was. But he just kept on sayin', ' Hurry, hurry.' And I said, ' Mr. deWitt, sir, I didn't know you at all, and I'm sorry, damned sorry! and tried to give him back the gold note, but he pushed it away with his elbow, and said, like he was prayin', ' Faster, faster.'

" ' It was the damn storm, and the dark, sir,' I said, rememberin' that the bank holds my notes, and old Aaron deWitt's allus buyin' up notes and foreclosin' on the side—buying future right of way, he says. And my farm's right on his damn railway. So I whipped those damn horses to a gallop, and by and by we come to his house, all dark except for a couple of windows, and two carriages outside, and Mr. Stephen jumped from my wagon and was gone before you could draw your breath! Never saw legs go so fast—like a grasshopper's. Didn't seem to touch ground."

"Well, it sure was bad," said one of his listeners.

Never Victorious, Never Defeated

The farmer looked at him belligerently, even though he was ashamed. "It waren't my fault, I keep tellin' you. And he's got lots of money. They made lots during the war, on their railway." He added surlily: "Anyways, though I'm sorry, he don't have no use for the little folks around here. Don't even notice 'em. It's Mr. Rufus that's our friend, not him."

The chorus of assent reassured him, and the listeners' resentment vaguely began to extend itself to Stephen for no logical reason at all.

Stephen never remembered that awful running through the streets of Portersville, nor did he ever recall the farmer. He knew that in some way he must have got home, but the details were forever hidden from him, and he never tried to remember. After all, that had been nothing. The only thing that he could recollect was racing desperately up the walk towards the tall, narrow house which had been his father's, and straining his frantic eye at the two windows which were lighted, one his own and Alice's, and one the long living-room which Alice had transformed from bleakness into charm.

His hair plastered to his skull, his eyes distracted, his clothing sodden and muddy, his boots pouring water, he flung himself into the small hallway and began to cry out in a cracked voice, "Alice! Alice! Where is Alice?" He had to lean against the wall, for his breath was suddenly gone, and he had no more strength.

For he knew. He had known it all for what seemed like black and timeless hours. When Lydia and his mother and his brother ran out to him, and he saw their faces, he could make no outcry; he could just look at them dumbly, his breath harsh and fast and moaning. Even when they surrounded him, he could not speak or ask a single question; and when his mother, by the light of the small chandelier which hung from the high ceiling, saw his face, she burst into wails and covered her eyes with her hands. Lydia was weeping, her pale and slender cheeks raw with tears, and even Rufus was red and wet of eye.

It was Lydia who came to him and took his hand speechlessly. He could direct all the wild intensity of his regard only upon her. He did not know that his brother was supporting him; he did not hear his brother's voice. Something was happening to him internally; something was bleeding, pouring out all his life, something was twisting his heart in iron. He ought to have known! He ought to have known that he could never keep anything.

"Oh, Stephen, poor Stephen," Lydia was saying, and she reached up and kissed his collapsed face. "My poor Stephen. Rufus, he must sit down. He seems as if he is dying." A chair was forced behind Stephen's knees, and he sat down obediently, without removing his eyes from Lydia's face. She knelt beside him and put her arms about him, and her pretty mauve foulard dress was stained with his wetness and his mud. But his own arms hung slackly from his shoulders, and his breath was still a terrible thing to hear.

Sophia and Rufus stood near him, and Sophia sobbed loudly. Her crimson velvet dress had been put on hastily over her handsome figure, the lace collar awry, the pearl brooch at a sharp angle, and her grey hair was disordered. "My poor boy!" she moaned, and wrung her hands.

Rufus said, and his rich voice was queerly low and sustained, "Stephen, it couldn't be helped. She fell down the stairs about half-past nine, and at ten the boy went for you and the doctor. It was no one's fault; she tripped, poor Alice."

Poor Alice, poor Alice, poor Alice! There was a jangling in Stephen's ears, like a screaming of insane bells. Poor Alice, who had fallen, whose husband ought to have been with her, at home, helping her. But her husband was away, far away from her, helping a stranger, a friend. There was all that assistance for a friend, but none for Alice. The horrible refrain began once more: Alice! Poor Alice, poor Alice! Poor child, poor little one, poor bright blue eyes, poor happy voice, poor laughter, poor singing. Poor child who was all he had.

Now he could speak, and only one word, very rustily, "Alice?"

Lydia tried to pull his head to her breast, but he put her aside with a gesture which could be gentle even now. He spoke only to her: "Alice—the baby—they are dead?" His voice seemed to come back to him from a far place, hollow and echoing.

Lydia could not reply, and all at once he remembered, even in that agony which could not possibly be real, that Lydia was Alice's sister. He, with an effort so immense that it took his final strength, put his wet arm about her shoulders, and she fell against him, broken with anguish

There was nothing inside him now but an empty place howling

85

with exquisite torture. His blood and his organs had gone, and he was untenanted except for his suffering.

"I was away," he muttered. "I was far away, and I didn't know." He looked up at his brother, and his eyes were blank pits. "I shouldn't have been away. I didn't know."

Rufus put his hand on his brother's soaking head, and he was shaken. "You couldn't have helped. It happened too fast. Your idiot housekeeper was up the road buying eggs, and found Alice when she came back. She shouldn't have left her. Steve, don't look like that. It would have happened anyway. She was—she was—almost gone when she was found."

He could not tell Stephen that Alice's neck had been broken, and that she had lived only an hour after her fall, and had died even while her child was being delivered hastily on this very hall floor, by Dr. Worth. A rug had been thrown over the bloody pool which had stained the light carpet. There she had lain in her deathly ignominy, in her red-stained white morning-robe, while the doctor wrestled and struggled to bring forth the child before it, too, died. No, Rufus could not tell him this. He had seen it himself, for he had arrived with the doctor. He would never tell poor Steve of the tumbled mass of pale hair which had lain on the floor or the white still face, the glaring eyes upturned, the slack mouth open and emitting the gurgling sounds of death, and the pretty white arms and legs thrown wide in the last agonies. Rufus, who was rarely moved by anything, had been unbearably moved by this. The housekeeper had been useless, screaming in the background; but Rufus, in all his ruddy splendour, had knelt by the doctor and had assisted him. His own hands had been covered by gushing blood, and his own hands had touched the baby being wrested from the moribund body.

He could not tell Stephen, not so long as either of them lived, that at the final moment, before Alice died, her glazed eyes had taken on a gleam of consciousness, and that she had whimpered one lost and seeking question: "Stephen? Stephen?"

"She never recovered consciousness; she never knew," lied Rufus. "She never suffered. Even if you had been here, she would never have looked at you or known you."

Rufus rubbed his brother's head clumsily, and Lydia, unable even to weep now, pressed her body against Stephen's wet coat and could hear the slow thick beating of his heart under her ear.

Never Victorious, Never Defeated

"It's a girl; a very nice little girl," said Rufus, and his voice was changed and hushed. "Wouldn't you like to see—to—see——"

"I want to see Alice," said Stephen faintly. He put aside Lydia, and Rufus helped him to his feet. The brothers moved slowly to the stairs, and step by step, held strongly by Rufus, Stephen climbed them, sagging and reeling. Lydia followed; she saw Stephen's slipping and fumbling boots. The water and the mud ran over the light-blue carpeting, leaving footmarks that resembled dark blood. She did not know the truth, either, and Rufus had resolved that he would never tell her. She had accepted his lies, without question, and had arrived a considerable time after Alice had died and had been taken to her bedroom. Even she did not know what the small carpet covered in the hall below. But it was she, and not the shrieking Sophia, who had taken off that beautiful white velvet morning-gown, and who had washed and dressed the young and little sister who had always been in her care and under her protection. She had done this alone, in tearless and stony silence, for, until it was done she dared not let her grief overpower her. It had seemed, while she worked, that she was washing and dressing the small Alice of their childhood, and she had combed the bright pale hair neatly and had folded the colourless hands on that childish breast.

A dim light burned in the bedroom which Alice had made so attractive with the light and airy furniture of her parents' home. She lay in hers and Stephen's bed, her head turned slightly towards the door as if she waited for her husband, not in eagerness but with sleeping, smiling patience. Lydia had dressed her in her cherished bridal nightgown of white satin and lace. Her closed eyelids, veined and rounded, were like marble; her lips, too, were marble.

Stephen staggered to the bedside, held by his brother, and he looked down at his wife. He stood like that for a long time, then his knees bent and he laid his head beside Alice's on the same pillow, and he closed his eyes. The tears ran down Lydia's face, and Rufus made a move as if to put his arms about her, then did not. There was such a bitter coldness on Lydia's face, such a stiffness, such an anger.

Stephen's breath, inaudible now, flowed over Alice's serene and silent face. Rufus thought that he had fainted.

All that I had, all that had ever loved me, in all the world, Stephen was thinking. There is nothing now, just as there was nothing before I knew her. But it is worse than before; I have had her, and I've known what it is to have her, this dear thing, this loving thing, this sweetest of all things.

How could a man live when his darling was gone, when the voice that had coaxed, soothed, and comforted him, would never be heard again? What was there in life that could numb this desolation, take away this anguish, fill up the emptiness that had been full? She had been alone; he had not been with her; he had not been able to help her. She had died alone, and she had taken with her all the meaning of his existence and left him bereft. She had died while he was helping a friend, and with her had gone the sun and the warmth, the joy and the faith, the fire and the love.

He had not expected any reward for anything he had done, or for any suffering he had alleviated. It would never have occurred to him that he should have a reward. No, he had expected nothing.

But he had not expected to be punished because he had fed others and had consoled others. His punishment was too much, for what he had done.

CHAPTER EIGHT

THE GREAT wide window of what Sophia elegantly called "the large guest chamber" looked down precipitously upon a view which was conceded to be "one of the best in the state." The artist who had built this house had originally intended it for an upstairs study, but it had been later converted into a bedroom for the more honoured guests of the DeWitts. The high white walls, the carved white ceilings, the magnificent white fireplace, were backgrounds for the dimmest of blue and rose and gold Aubusson rugs, massive cherry furniture, gold-threaded rosy draperies, and gilt lamps.

For six months Stephen had occupied that big postered bed and this velvet chair by the window. For six months he had lived silently in the room, never reading, very rarely speaking, and looking down emptily at the magnificent scene far below him. For two of those six months his life had been in danger from "the lung fever" which he had hoped would kill him. For another two months he had fought his return to health, and had almost won. For the past two months his still-young body had begun to win the struggle against all his desires, all his anguished desires. He still had a passionate will to die, and sometimes, as now on this late October afternoon, the will gained temporary ascendency over the fighting flesh.

There he sat now, in the blue velvet chair, wrapped in shawls and blankets from which his narrow head and long grey face, so emaciated and so sunken, emerged like the head of a turtle from a large shell. His skeleton-like hands lay listlessly, palms upward, on the arms of the chair. The early twilight filled the room with a cold, wan light, like the reflection of snow, and the firelight raced over the white walls and ceiling in a dance of scarlet ghosts. Near the fire, as still as Stephen himself, sat Aaron deWitt in his dressing-gown, his pipe held reflectively in his hand, his eyes fixed on his son, who seemed totally unaware of his presence.

Stephen gazed down through the window, but he saw nothing. The panorama of grey and purple hills, tumbling in silent chaos in the distance, evoked no interest in him. The mountains circled towards the house and enclosed a narrow river, glinting in dull silver under a dull silver sky, which wound away mysteriously into mists towards the farther mountains. The wild autumnal colour, which had earlier fired the mountains into explosions of gold and crimson and unearthly greens, had subsided into the immense grandeur of cold lavenders and mauves and cobalt blues, retreating and unreal as a dream.

It was too early for sunset; the mountains beyond had not brightened as yet. The sky above them remained silvery. The fire crackled and spluttered: Aaron smoked thoughtfully; Stephen looked down vacantly at the ghostly river between the hills. The carved marble clock ticked on the mantelpiece, but this, and the snapping of the fire, were the only sounds in the wide room. They had been the only sounds for at least two hours. No other member of the family had entered the room, and no servant. Father and son sat alone, the father watchful, the son oblivious.

The will to die became stronger in Stephen, and as if he felt that desolate urging himself, Aaron stood up. He moved quietly and slowly to the small table near Stephen and carefully mixed some medicine into a glass of port wine. Then he touched Stephen's shoulder and Stephen started violently.

"Your tonic, Steve," said Aaron, and his yellow teeth gleamed between his bearded lips. Then an involuntary grimace ran over his face, and he bent a little in a kind of uncontrollable convulsion. He gave a sharp small cough, straightened, and again said, "Your tonic. Drink it down, my boy. It's time."

Stephen's lassitude was too enormous for ready responsiveness of movement. His left hand rose painfully inch by inch, and he took the glass. It was heavy for him, in his weakness, and so it shook in his fingers. He did not want the "tonic" and the wine; if he drank it he would feel returning strength. He let his hand droop towards the table. Aaron grinned, took the glass, and held it to Stephen's lips. "Come on, now; let's not be a baby," he said, with good humour. Stephen's mouth, cold and dry, resisted for a moment; then, without looking at his father, he drank the liquid. Aaron nodded, as if with satisfaction. He went back to his chair, refilled his pipe, and began to smoke again. Occasionally he grimaced, as he had done before, and once or twice he pressed his hand against his stomach. He had grown older and thinner and smaller these past months, to Sophia's dismay. She had attributed this to the grief Aaron had felt for the death of Alice and the collapse and suffering of his son.

Stephen's thoughts, as always, were vague and confused cloud-shapes in his mind. He could not follow a thought through; it ran from him like a dissolving dream. He could think only of Alice with any clarity, and then the thought was an exquisite agony. Over and over he would say to himself: I didn't know. I left her. I was helping. . . . There was the rain, and the river, and there wasn't a hack—just the wind. I couldn't run. But then, she was already dead. She was lying there, waiting for me. Alice.

He knew that he had been unconscious in that bed yonder when his wife had been buried. He had not as yet seen her grave. He had no desire to see it. Alice had gone; she was nowhere in the world. She would never enter through that door, nor stand beside him looking down at the river. She no longer existed. She had left him as if she had never known him. There was only an emptiness left, filled with unbearable pain. The pain did not lessen as the months went by; there was no dulling of the torture, no surcease. There was no consolation. His body might have grown stronger but his spirit lay in him bleeding and stricken to the death.

"He is making no real effort. I'm very disappointed," the doctor had confided to Aaron and Sophia. "If he goes on this way—and I had hopes for him a few weeks ago—he will die. That's what he wants. Medicine can only give him temporary strength, which he fights."

Sophia, whose sympathy and imagination were so small, had become impatient. After all, she would say to Aaron, Stephen was still a young man. There were other nice young women in the world. And there was work to do. It was really dreadful that poor Rufus should be so burdened, now that he had to do his own work *and* Stephen's. Had Aaron noticed how tired the boy seemed these days? It was a pity. Stephen should have some understanding of the hardship his brother was enduring. He should make an effort, especially since he knew very well that his father was still unable to return to his offices.

Lydia had given the baby her mother's name, Laura. Did Aaron remember the embarrassing day when friends had called upon Stephen, and had mentioned the child by name? He had looked at them vacantly, and had murmured, "Laura? Who is Laura?" Truly, Stephen was inflicting too much on his family.

Aaron had looked at her with his quick and evil smile. "Truly," he had repeated solemnly. Sophia had coloured angrily, then wondered if indeed Aaron was mocking her, and if so, why? He, who had always so derided Stephen and his tiresome grey ways, who had overlooked him in his childhood and his youth, and who had laughed at him so openly, could not possibly be mocking his wife when she had made a sensible complaint against their son.

Aaron had added no other comment to his single word, but had gone upstairs as usual to sit with Stephen. This baffled Sophia. It was so unlike Aaron. A few times she had crept to the door of the "guest chamber" and had listened. However, she never heard either man speak. Hours later, Aaron would emerge, go downstairs for a glass of whisky, or retire to his own room. Many times Sophia would desire to ask her husband why he stayed with Stephen for so long, but something prevented her from speaking. It was part of the tedious pattern of these months, and Sophia's impatience became mixed with sullen anger against her stricken son. A nebulous uneasiness began to pervade the days for her, a kind of foreboding of some danger.

Never Victorious, Never Defeated

To-day, Sophia, who was in her bed with a "chill," was again uneasy. Aaron had not come into her room to inquire as to her state of health. He was with Stephen again, in the fine chamber which he had insisted Stephen occupy, though the south bedroom was quite adequate. Were father and son speaking at last? She listened intently. Once she thought she had heard Aaron murmur something. She sat up in bed and listened intently. If Aaron had spoken, Stephen had not replied. Sighing with vexation, Sophia lay down again. Why wasn't it obvious to everyone as well as herself that Stephen was just indulging in self-pity?

The medicine and the tonic slowly relaxed Stephen's cramped and aching body. He saw the faint pink flush over the mountains deepen into a brighter rose, cold and without warmth. The mountains turned a darker purple, came into sharper focus. The river took on clearer tints of silver and scarlet. Mists began to rise on the narrow and hurrying waters, and they reflected the sunset in their passage through the close blue chasm.

The sleepless agony quickened in Stephen. He turned his head in a spasm of suffering. His eyes inadvertently fell on his father, sitting so quietly smoking by the fire. For the first time Stephen's absent gaze did not move away from Aaron. Reluctantly, he continued to observe his father, and now there was the dimmest stirring of anxious curiosity in him. Why was Aaron here? Why did he come, day after day, to remain hour after hour, rarely speaking, not reading, not moving.

Aaron suddenly turned his head and the two men looked at each other in a long silence. The room was darkening, though the sky outside was a flow of brilliant magenta over the mountains. The window flamed in it; red shadows struck the white ceiling, so that it seemed afire. Across the breadth of the room Aaron and Stephen gazed at each other through the dusk, and did not speak.

Then Aaron got to his feet and deliberately put down his pipe. He thrust his little hands in his pockets, teetered on his heels, and regarded the window reflectively. Stephen might not have been in the room at all. Aaron began to hum, hoarsely, a mannerism he had when he was alone. Then he pursed his lips and whistled softly a wandering tune such as a man makes when his mind is deeply occupied. He started to walk up and down the room, his head bent, his steps short and slow and feeble. His pointed beard caught the firelight as he passed to and fro before it. There were grey hollows in his face, but Stephen could see the alert gleam of his eyes as the firelight struck them.

Then he felt his father beside him. Aaron stood near his son's shoulder and looked at the sky also, rocking on his heels, his mouth pursed up soundlessly. Stephen wanted to ask about his health, with awkward uncertainty, but he was too tired. However, some discomfort came to him as his father continued to stand so near him in the thickening twilight.

There was a sound of carriage wheels outside, and Aaron shrugged. He said casually, "Well, Job, I see your three comforters have arrived again for their weekly visit." He laughed shortly, and then chuckled to himself. He went back to his chair, dipped a lucifer into the fire and relit his pipe. He had crossed his small legs, and he swayed one of them up and down. He appeared deeply amused. Stephen's hands moved restlessly on the arms of his chair. He wondered why his father often remained when Jim Purcell, Joseph Baynes, and Tom Orville visited him. He would not comment, or speak, unless appealed to directly, but he listened, and he would laugh soundlessly, to Stephen's embarrassed discomfiture.

Job. Aaron had called him Job. Was not Job the man of many afflictions, whom God and Satan had tested, and who had triumphed over his sufferings and his disasters? Why had Aaron spoken so jocularly of Job? What had Job to do with him, Stephen deWitt? Had there been cruelty, as usual, in Aaron's remark, or mockery? Stephen knew that his friends were not at ease in Aaron's company, or at least, Tom and Joseph were not. It was impossible to know what Jim Purcell thought, and it was even more impossible to know why he came to see Stephen at all. What few words he grunted added nothing to the general talk; he would sit, thought Stephen, startled into opening his eyes, as Aaron sat: listening, sometimes oblivious, and swinging one big leg as Aaron was swinging his small one now.

They were coming down the long wide corridor now, three dissimilar men. Tom Orville and Joseph Baynes were old friends and, with Stephen, they had formed a close companionship. Like Stephen, they had known Jim Purcell all their lives, and they did not like him. He had been a big lump of a boy, and he was a huge lump of a man now very rich, unmarried, coarse in his manners, grotesque in appearance, and in so far as his acquaintances knew, he had little wit and no subtlety. His life was restricted to the one urge of becoming the wealthiest man in the community. He had attached himself to Stephen when Stephen had been only nine years old, and he twelve. Even the very young Stephen had wondered why, and he still wondered.

There was a discreet knock on the door, and Aaron said jovially, " Come in, gentlemen, come in." The door opened, and the three men filed soberly into the room, glancing at Aaron with strained politeness, and, in the case of two of them, with constraint and fear. Aaron nodded at chairs; his yellow teeth glistened in the firelight.

"Welcome, good comforters," he said serenely. He settled himself deeper into his chair, with an expression of anticipatory enjoyment. He pulled the bell rope. "Whisky again, no doubt?" he remarked affably.

CHAPTER NINE

UNCOMFORTABLE UNDER the dancing eyes of Aaron, Joseph Baynes and Tom Orville seated themselves awkwardly, and glanced furtively at each other as if to say: Why does he have to be here? But Jim Purcell gave Aaron a long look and nodded slightly. His large and misshapen face resembled a mass of formless and colourless dough, all protuberances, swellings, and circular pits, in which his eyes were mere small lozenges of mud, so lightless were they, so without sparkle or expression. His lumpy nose was greasy, and seemed to have been stuck at a haphazard angle in the centre of his face, and his mouth was a mere crease in the general doughiness. Above a very low forehead rose a thin but tough layer of coarse brown hair, which apparently was never combed or brushed, and his large ears flew out from the sides of his big head like crudely fashioned wax. He gave an unperturbed impression of absolute and deliberate coarseness, and his rumpled clothing, his badly-tied black cravat, revealed his calm scorn for the niceties, as did his dark and enormous hands with their carelessly cleaned nails. His great boots were stained and coated with old mud, the colour of his eyes. There was a quality of brutality about him, a nonchalant contempt.

In contrast with him, the fastidious Joseph Baynes appeared a little too delicate, small and fragile. Tom Orville, a middle-sized man in his late thirties, shrank before this giant of a man, and his candid, fresh-coloured face and eager eyes became the face and eyes of a schoolboy. Jim Purcell drained maturity from the other two visitors. And though Baynes and Orville were men of presentable and pleasing appearance, it was paradoxical that this huge and ugly man could make them seem puerile and insignificant and without vitality in comparison.

Once Tom Orville, a good-natured and kind-hearted man usually, had remarked to Stephen that Jim Purcell was a "true prehistoric man," both in appearance and in his blunted nature. Stephen, always uneasy when a deprecating remark was made about anyone, had found himself involuntarily laughing. He was sorry for the laughter later, though he had admitted that there was some truth in Orville's flippant remark. But his perplexity over Purcell's silent attachment to him, the seeking out of him by this dull-eyed and expressionless giant from their earliest childhood, increased rather than decreased.

There was another bewildering circumstance which had occurred in 1863. Tom Orville possessed a modest but flourishing lumber business. In 1860, in anticipation of large war orders, Orville had taken widespread options on local timber tracts. Larger lumber companies in the vicinity, anxious to remove this small competitor, and enraged that he had outmatched them in his foresight, persuaded the bank in Portersville, and banks in other nearby towns, not to advance him any money when the options came due. Purcell, himself, was invested in two of the larger lumber companies, and his word was law among the bankers. He had given his orders: Orville, the presumptuous, was to be eliminated, forced into bankruptcy.

Orville had come to his friend, Stephen deWitt, as Joseph Baynes had come to him later, in despair and frantic helplessness, threatening suicide, weeping for his wife and children. Stephen had anxiously searched his own financial resources, but saw that they were inadequate. He had pleaded with the president of the Portersville bank; he had visited other bankers in other towns. He had even gone to Philadelphia, and had offered the bankers there his collateral in behalf of Orville. He had been received with warm, if sheepish, courtesy. It did not occur to him that his request would be refused, for was he not the son of Aaron deWitt, and was not Aaron the close friend and associate

95

of these men? But the request was refused, with inadequate excuses; and Stephen, sensing the acute embarrassment of the bankers, had had mercy on them, in spite of his own heart-sickness.

He had then gone to Purcell, as a last resort, Purcell who was his mysterious familiar. He had gone with the deepest shrinking and reluctance, practically assured in himself that he would, of course, fail. He had sat in Purcell's dusty, untidy, if luxurious, home, and he had advanced all the humanitarian and Christian arguments at his disposal, all the pleas for justice which could make his drab face so eloquent on occasion. And Purcell had listened patiently, but without expression. He had waited while Stephen made his promises to mortgage his future in behalf of his friend. He showed no quickening until this, and then he had fixed those lightless eyes upon Stephen with profound curiosity.

After all his pleas had been made, Stephen had sat exhausted, waiting for the inevitable refusal. And then Purcell had said in his hoarse voice, "You want him to get the money from the banks? All right."

They all sat about Stephen now. Purcell, after his first grunt of greeting, and his first muddy contemplation of Stephen, seated himself, swinging his great leg, and smoking an excessively foul pipe. He regarded space without expression, while Joseph and Tom asked Stephen about his health, and Aaron listened, silently chuckling.

Stephen tried to arouse himself from his lethargy. Not to speak, not to show some interest, would have seemed an unpardonable discourtesy to these kind and anxious friends of his. So he replied that he was improving; his voice was very weak and dwindled.

Joseph and Tom smiled at him with encouragement, but there was a crease of good-tempered impatience on Joseph's forehead.

"This has been a fine day," he remarked. "You ought to have aroused yourself and taken a drive, Steve."

He and Tom exchanged one of their mutually supporting glances, and Tom nodded. In their opinion "Steve" was making a fool of himself by his prolonged sorrow over his wife. True, Alice had been a "nice" young thing in her way, and it was all very tragic. But a man couldn't die because his wife had died, especially not a man Stephen's age.

"The doctor," Aaron placidly remarked from the fireplace,

"said to-day that Steve's not even well enough to sit out on that balcony yet." He waved in the direction of the western window where a small terrace, guarded by wrought iron, jutted out over the abyss.

Joseph moved uncomfortably on his chair. Like Orville, he was afraid of Aaron. He said, with almost too eager an attempt at placating, "Well, perhaps the doctor is right. But all these months. . . . Poor Steve. Never knew lung fever to last so long. Three months at the most. He should be getting his strength back now."

Jim Purcell said hoarsely, "Maybe he doesn't want it back. Maybe he's got reasons for not wanting it back."

This seemed utterly ridiculous to the other two men, who, however, dared not argue for fear of Purcell. Joseph leaned towards Stephen, trying to capture that sick and wandering eye, and he said with gentle earnestness, "Steve. What has happened is the will of God. Who are we to quarrel with Him? It's an affront to Him to question His decrees."

"Who says so?" Purcell asked. He turned in his chair and looked Joseph up and down with brutish dismissal.

"The Bible says so," Tom replied uncertainly. "Our churches teach so."

Joseph, who was superintendent of the First Methodist Church of Portersville, and who had long ago forgotten his own despair from which Stephen had saved him, said in a deepened and solemn voice, "Behold, happy is the man whom God correcteth: therefor despise not thou the chastening of the Almighty.'"

"Job," said Aaron, nodding in his glee. "It was one of Job's comforters who said that, didn't he? Eliphaz."

Joseph was astonished that one such as Aaron could know the Bible. He stammered, "You're quite correct, Mr. deWitt."

Jim Purcell nonchalantly emptied the contents of his odoriferous pipe in his hand, then tossed the brown mess into the fireplace. He very seldom remarked on anything, but now he quoted: "And Job replied, I kind of remember, "What is my strength, that I should hope? And what is mine end, that I should prolong my life?' And if I remember rightly, it wasn't Eliphaz who spoke in the name of God, who heard God. It was Job. Funny, isn't it?"

Stephen moved his head in pain. The voices came to him from a gathering of shadows, and he could not distinguish one from

G

the other. But an echo repeated itself over and over in the desolate and hollow places in his mind: "What is my strength, that I should hope? And what is mine end, that I should prolong my life?"

The others were too amazed at Purcell's rumbling quotation of the Bible to do anything but stare at him blankly, with the exception of Aaron. How dared this powerful rascal, this lumpish giant and brute, quote Holy Writ? It was blasphemy. Joseph ducked his head with apprehensive politeness towards Purcell, but had the courage to say, "Job said that when he was in the very pit of his lost faith in God. Later, he understood."

"You're wrong, Baynes. He never lost faith in God. It's just you mealymouths who never had faith in Him, and that's why you can quote Him so readily."

Purcell swung his huge body cumbrously towards Stephen, whose head was bent on his chest. "Steve," he called roughly. He waited. Stephen did not look up; he had not heard. Then Purcell lumbered to his feet, walked to the sick man, and pushed his shoulder none too gently. Stephen raised his head and tried to fix his glazed eyes on that doughlike face. "Steve," repeated Purcell, and his voice was almost a roar. "Listen to me. Grieve yourself out. If you find it's too hard goin', do somethin' about it. You hear? A man don't have to stand more than he can. It ain't expected of him. But don't linger on, tryin' to make up your mind. You got a kid here. Is she worth livin' for? Is she, Steve?"

That harsh and compelling voice caught Stephen's attention, and he heard every word. "My child?" he muttered. "Yes, my child."

"Well, then, is she worth livin' for, that young 'un? She's all you've got, from Alice. Who's goin' to take care of her? Want her out on the street, Steve? Want her left alone—Alice's kid? Goin' to desert her? Make up your mind, once and for all." He waited, then went on, more roughly than before, "You got an idea, way back in that soft skull of yourn, about what the world's really like, though you won't admit it to yourself. Want your kid to face the world alone, knowin' what it is? Like you faced it? Got no mercy on Alice, eh, or Alice's baby?"

Tears filled Stephen's eyes. The room was utterly silent. Aaron leaned forward in the dusk, intently watching, but Joseph and

98

Tom were looking at each other with carefully concealed and superior scorn.

"Make up your mind, Steve," said Purcell. "You're the one to decide. If livin's too much for you, do somethin' about it. If the kid's somethin' to you make up your mind about that. That's what you're tryin' to do, isn't it? Make up your mind?"

Joseph was moved to say, "Jim, are you trying to tell Stephen that he's deliberately——"

Purcell turned his mammoth head and surveyed Joseph with contempt. "Yes. And what about it? It takes a brave man to die, not a coward, like you church folk are always sayin'."

He came back to Stephen. "What about it, feller? Goin' to stay around and protect that kid from you-know-who, or goin' to shuffle off? I'd kind of like to know, so I can select the flowers."

"I think," said Aaron blandly, "that he's made his choice. He's moving away. Perhaps a good idea, considering everything. And Jim," he added, laughing, "you know the child won't be 'out in the street.' She's got a very loving family left, her grandpa and grandma, and her Uncle Rufus. And her cousin, too. We'll all take care of Laura. Steve, you can rely on that."

The world had come back to Stephen with awful clarity, for the first time since Alice died. Alice's child, and his, left to this world, this terrible and pain-filled world of loneliness and cruelty and hate! He had never thought of it before. He could not remember the face of his child; he could not remember if she had ever been brought to him. He stirred in his chair, and the movement was like a convulsion. He lifted up his wasted hands and cried out feebly. "The baby! I must see the baby!"

Purcell and Aaron exchanged a curious glance, then Aaron nodded and pulled the bell rope again. "Why do you torment him so, Jim?" asked Joseph, gaining courage in his concern for Stephen, so mercilessly attacked by this beast. "Let him rest."

"He's been too long tryin' to make up his silly mind," Purcell answered. "If he's got a mind at all, and not porridge in his skull."

Joseph hesitated. "Steve," he said, with kind urgency, "you must get well; we miss you, boy. It's been bad; but you still have your friends. . . ."

"Why, yes," grunted Purcell. "He still has his friends, don't he?" He left Stephen and went to the wide western window and looked out indifferently. His big fingers filled his pipe with remarkable precision and economy of movement. He struck a lucifer on the heel of his dirty boot, lit the pipe. He leaned against the side of the window. The stark mountains bulked in black and purple against the brilliant gold and scarlet sky, and the narrow river between the clefts of them ran in fire.

Tom joined Joseph. They stood on each side of Stephen, forgetting, in their distress for their friend, the two other inimical personalities in the room. They pleaded with Stephen; they exhorted, made small rallying jokes, laughed a little. They did not know that he did not really hear them at all. When they paused for a moment, he repeated in a thin, intense voice, "I want to see my child."

A servant entered the room, and Aaron said, "Ask Mrs. Rufus to bring in Mr. Steve's baby. She'll be in the nursery now." He carried a large glass of whisky to Stephen and pushed it into his hand. "Come on, drink. No more tonics. Throw this down like a man."

Joseph straightened, and said anxiously, "Do you think it's best, Mr. deWitt? I've heard that whisky is very bad for men who are recovering from lung fever."

Purcell, without turning, remarked to no one in particular, "When a man's got to make a decision, he'd better take the edge off himself. Hell. He never had lung fever anyway. Go on, Steve; drink it."

Stephen, finding a glass in his hand, automatically lifted it to his lips. Even in his anguish he was unable to offend anyone.

"That's right, throw it down," Aaron repeated. The fumes and the taste of the liquor revolted Stephen, and he made an instinctive gesture of repudiation. But when he looked up he saw not the faces of Joseph and Tom, silently protesting, but the grinning face of his father and the doughy mass which was the face of Jim Purcell.

Lydia deWitt entered the room carrying Stephen's child in a blue shawl. Her concerned eyes went to Stephen immediately, and she approached him at once. Joseph and Tom greeted her; Aaron ignored her, but Jim Purcell, leaning against the wall near the window, studied her with coarse openness. She saw this and smiled, and for a moment the protuberances and pits which formed the man's face moved into the formation of a smile also.

"I think," said Aaron, "that we'd better take our whisky

downstairs and finish it. Rufe's due home any minute now, and we can sit by the fire and have another drink with him."

The three men followed him, Joseph and Tom keeping well together, Jim Purcell following. The door closed behind them, and Stephen, darkly flushed and sweating with weakness, sank in the chair and closed his eyes. Lydia drew a small chair close to him and sat down, and then she waited. The child whimpered, and she began to sing to it softly, in her strong yet gentle voice, holding it close to her breast. The room filled with the sound of the fire, the crying of the wind, and Lydia's soothing lullaby. The dusk made everything shadowy in the room while the conflagration darkened beyond the window.

Finally Stephen said faintly, "Lydia." She raised her head and regarded him with grave attention. "Lydia," he repeated.

"Yes, Stephen?" The child lay on her knees, and she did not move. Stephen lifted his hand as though it was an enormous weight and indicated the baby with it. "I haven't seen—her, I don't believe," he whispered.

Lydia rose at once and went to him. She folded back the shawl, and he saw the face of his child for the first time. The baby lay in Lydia's protecting arms, a very small creature with thin little hands and a pale and pointed face in which the eyes were questioning grey circles. The last crimson light of the sunset illuminated the child, and Stephen, pulling himself away from the back of the chair with an effort that brought moisture visibly to his forehead, leaned forward, and father and daughter stared at each other mutely, each sombre and motionless.

Then Stephen's hand, moving like the hand of a blind man, fumblingly stretched itself out, hovered over the child. The hand sank, rose, hovered again. Finally it took the little hand of the baby, and held it. The fingers were as cold and as lifeless as his, and as still.

"It—she—is cold," said Stephen painfully.

"Yes," said Lydia, with softness and compassion. "She always is. Babies need love. And I'm afraid there isn't much love in this house for her. I do what I can. But children, even as young as this, seem to know."

There was no colour on the small cheeks or on the little mouth. There was a seeking and lost expression in the grey eyes which had fastened themselves unsmilingly on Stephen. He could not bear it; tears began to run down his cheeks, tears of grief and remorse and deathly illness. He said, his voice breaking, "Put her in my arms, Lydia."

He held his child to him, and kissed her, and she moved in his arms with a nestling movement, so that her small head was on his breast. Then Stephen cried out, "Look, Lydia! She is smiling!"

CHAPTER TEN

RUFUS WAS just entering the large and stately drawing-room and a maid was just lighting the lamps, when Aaron, Joseph, Tom and Jim Purcell entered through another door. A huge fire rioted in the great white fireplace and threw its amber shadows on the white and blue panels of the walls and on the carved ceiling. Now the lamps began to glow, silver and gilt, in the heavy dusk, and all the fine rugs and furniture took on identity.

Rufus was surprised that the weekly guests had not already departed, and for an instant his tired face changed. Then, very buoyantly, he greeted them. He could be unaffectedly friendly with Joseph and Tom, whom he good-temperedly despised as harmless failures and not likely to get into his way to any serious extent. Jim Purcell was another matter. Rufus was more effusively cordial with him, and was not concerned that Purcell merely grunted in reply to his greeting, and, without waiting for the others to be seated, sat down on the rose and blue tapestry sofa near the fire. "How is poor Steve?" Rufus asked of Aaron, who seated himself next to Purcell. "I see you've all got whisky. Mind if I order some for myself?" He pulled the bell rope, beamed down at his father genially.

"Poor Steve," said Aaron, "has had a jolt. He's coming out of things now. Thanks to Jim, here."

Rufus raised his ruddy eyebrows quizzically. He, like Aaron, knew quite well why Jim "haunted" Stephen. It was a standing joke between them, a comprehending but not ridiculous one. "What did you do, Jim?" he asked, seating himself in his mother's blue satin chair and giving himself over to be charming in spite of his fatigue. His intensely coloured face was overlaid with weariness, like dust, and his red hair did not flare up from his head as usual in its customary lion-like strength.

Jim did not answer his question, but Aaron chuckled thinly. "Oh, he recalled to Steve's mind what might happen to the baby in this den of wolves. That did it. Steve's got a lot of imagination, though you don't credit him with it, Rufe."

"Now what in hell do you mean by that, Pa?" asked Rufus, laughing. But he was not particularly amused.

The whisky, having been brought, was placed before Aaron, who poured a glass for his son, and refilled Purcell's glass and his own. Joseph and Tom refused, partly out of principle and partly because they wished to leave as soon as possible. However, like all good men, they were natural gossips, and they hoped to acquire a few scandalous little morsels to relate privately to their friends, morsels which would raise them in their friends' esteem as being intimate with the DeWitts in spite of their fear of the family.

"I hope Steve does come out of it," Rufus remarked, after a long and grateful drink. "Frankly, I'm no man for details and papers; and my clerk, and Steve's, too, are much too rabbity to make the smallest decisions for themselves. And though I can usually make friends with everybody, and can understand almost any man, I don't understand these Irish fellows we put on a few months ago. Wild. The farmers along our right of way are complaining. The boys have a habit of stealing apples and chickens, and romping, and raising hell generally."

"Steve, for some peculiar reason beyond my understanding, could always manage them," remarked Aaron, wiping his beard with the back of his sallow hand. You wouldn't have thought it. He could reason with them." He shook his head. "The most unlikely people take to Steve."

"You could, of course, give the Cork boys as much money for equal work as you do our native Americans," said Purcell in his rumbling voice. "But that wouldn't be good business."

There was no irony in his voice, and Rufus and Aaron understood this. "What they don't get from us they make up in what they get from the farmers," Rufus answered. "That doesn't bother me; it never did. But we're extending our line and we need some strips of land along the right of way. The farmers are rearing up; they were all for the extension, especially when they found out it would open new markets for them. They're willing to accept the benefits, but they're demanding ungodly prices for those worthless strips, and they want guarantees that we won't employ the Irish lads as gandy-dancers. We'll have to do what we've always done: promise them the earth with the moon thrown in, and let them try to do anything about it after the rails are laid."

Joseph Baynes, who had been listening intently, could not restrain his indignation: "It was all wrong, in the very beginning, to import those people. We have enough workmen of our own, but our workmen demand at least a semblance of livelihood." He paused; they were all looking at him, and he was vaguely frightened in spite of the apparently friendly interest. "These Irish fellows are always fighting, too. Remember those brawls last month? One of them was killed, and over a dozen others were badly injured. Similar riots, I've heard, are occurring wherever the Irish are employed on other railroads. Very odd and barbaric people."

"Steve understood them," said Aaron mildly. "He managed to keep apart what he called the ' Far-downers ' and the ' Corkonians.' Whatever they mean. And if, by any chance, these mysterious mobs got into fights Steve would go right down to them, even if it was in the middle of the night, and with a little abracadabra, which I never comprehended, would settle the whole matter."

"Why do they come here? Why don't they stay where they belong?" asked Tom in a tone of dissatisfaction. His round full face so jejune and so fresh, was profiled by the fire, and it fully revealed his pudgy, uptilted nose. It was an artless face, even a naïve one, and Rufus studied it smilingly, but with inner irritation.

Purcell was answering Tom: "For the same reason your ancestors came here, Orville. Why didn't they stay ' where they belonged? '" His dull voice, so without emphasis, was like a thud in the room.

Tom was affronted. "My ancestors, Jim, were English gentlemen. . . ."

"Funny," ruminated Purcell. "All ancestors were. Not a word about the bond servants, and the sweepin's of the gutters of London, and the deported criminals, and the fellers who couldn't get along with their neighbours and had to be kicked out. Oh, those poor fellers called it ' freedom of religion,' but they were just cantankerous Puritans who wanted lots of space where they could hang their religious opponents and burn those they called ' heretics ' and ' witches.'" He slumped deeper into his chair.

Aaron and Rufus burst out laughing, but Tom Orville was angered. "My grandfather often told me that his ancestors left England because of Bloody Mary. Their property was confiscated, their lives threatened, and they had to flee on the first clipper out of Liverpool."

"Wonderful how our ancestors always had manor houses," rumbled Purcell. "Mine lived in English slums, and when they got here they did good work."

"My ancestors went to Maryland, under a special grant from the king," said Joseph Baynes.

Purcell gave him one of his long and muddy and contemptuous stares. "Well, all I can say, Baynes, is that the Romans, who really got that grant, were mighty tolerant. Mighty tolerant. And it seems to me that I heard you once say that you didn't like Romans. That," he added, looking at Aaron, "sounds to me like ingratitude."

"More whisky, gentlemen!" cried Aaron with glee, and this time the angered Tom and Joseph forgot their principles in their agitation, and allowed their glasses to be refilled. The night had definitely settled down outside, and the lamps were reflected in the black windows.

Tom and Joseph exchanged one of their mutually comforting glances. Then Joseph said, "You employ Germans, too, Mr. deWitt. The Irishmen hate them worse than they hate each other. There's something about the Germans which maddens them, possibly because the Germans are so industrious and reliable, and will work for almost anything. You never hear a dependable German workman singing on the job or making jokes. Work is a serious matter to a German."

"Then why don't you employ some Dutch on your damned local wrecks?" asked Purcell. "Fallin' apart, every man jack of them. Need some new capital, and such, and new enterprise. Or, perhaps, new management. I've watched them stagger along, and expected every minute to see them collapse."

A sick sinking feeling came to Joseph, and now he vaguely understood why he had been pressed to stay longer to-night, an invitation never extended before. He was a subtle man, and Tom, his friend, sensed his fear.

Joseph tried to ward off what he felt was coming. "Mr. deWitt," he said, and his voice was tight with apprehension, "one of these days there's going to be grave trouble between the

Irish and the Germans most of the railroads hereabouts are now employing. I've already heard of massacres, elsewhere, and murders. . . ."

"Massacre and murder entered very largely into the building of America, and I seriously doubt if they won't enter again," interposed Rufus. He, too, knew what was coming, and a large part of his weariness went away and all his senses became alerted. He folded his fingers lovingly about his whisky glass and, leaning his elbows on his knees, bent forward, his handsome and massive legs spread, his boots glimmering richly in the firelight. "Despite what Steve is always pleading, it still happens, and happens regularly, that wherever the wilderness is hacked down, man hacks down his neighbours, too, in a general blood-letting of trees and men."

"Are you advocating murder, Rufe, as the price of advancing civilisation?" asked Joseph, aghast.

"I'm advocating nothing," said Rufus with good-natured impatience. "I'm just stating a fact. I suppose facts must sustain individual prejudices, to be accepted by a lot of people."

"I love whisky and I love facts," said Aaron happily. Now his shrunken face was no longer wizened and drawn; vitality temporarily replaced the brownish-grey of his complexion. He turned on the sofa, looked past Purcell, and addressed Joseph in the frankest manner and with the friendliest and most reasonable of smiles:

"How are your Locals doing, Joe? Getting enough business to make them profitable?"

Joseph was not deceived. He thought bitterly: As if you don't know all about it, you vicious little rascal! "I'm getting enough," he answered, with tightness and reserve. "I don't believe in gouging. I took Steve's advice, and raised the passenger and freight rates. . . ."

Aaron arched his pointed eyebrows diabolically. "Steve told you that? Well, well. Unlike him, isn't it? But good advice. You were undercutting us, in a way, and our customers were pointing you out to us as an excellent example of selfless business. What the hell do they want? Business run for the benefit of their own greed and interests? But, go on. You took Steve's advice and raised the rates. So you have a profit, and aren't worried any longer."

Joseph's delicate face sharpened. Who told you I was worried?

he asked inwardly. He said, "I'm not worried, sir. I treat my customers fairly." His eyes retreated, and darkened, and he bit his lip.

"Fair from your standpoint, or fair from theirs?" asked Rufus with his affectionate display of interest.

Joseph did not answer, but Purcell lifted himself from his Gargantuan slump. "I often wondered how you squeezed out from under the Capital, Joe. You didn't have no money, but you raised the interest, and you kept old Alex Peale from pullin' you in. Miracle, eh, Joe?"

Joseph, who had forgotten Stephen's part in his salvation, moved suddenly in his chair, pricked by the discomfort of his memory and a dim resentment of it, and by a sense of danger. "Miracle," he answered, looking into those lightless slits of eyes, and hating the man who possessed them. He glanced openly at his watch, looked at Tom, who nodded. Aaron lifted his hand. "Now, don't hurry, Joe. I wanted to talk business with you. Tell me, are you getting enough new ties at a reasonable price? Jim, here, said you weren't doing business with any of the lumber companies in which he is invested."

"I get my ties when I need them, from Tom, who gives me a reasonable quotation."

"I treat all my customers reasonably," said Tom with tense defiance. He drew a deep breath, and his fresh colour brightened almost to a blush. "And if anyone wants to know, I am doing well, myself."

"As Tom and I are ethical men, and believe there is a place in America for both large and small business, we are always at a loss to explain the unethical practices of expedient and avaricious men," Joe interposed, and his anger made him somewhat breathless. "They haven't hurt us so far, for which we thank God."

"It is never out of place to thank God," said Aaron seriously, but his eyes danced. "Now I'm going to tell you boys something we intend to do, ourselves, as part of the programme of an expanding America. We are looking over plans to run our road to Baltimore and Washington. Jim is interested in investing in this venture." He paused.

Rufus played his part well. "Do you think it wise to discuss these plans as yet, with those not directly involved, Pa?" he asked gravely.

107

Aaron waved him away, with smiling indulgence. "Shut up, Rufe. Why shouldn't Joe know, who is a railroader himself? Just a friendly discussion."

It it possible that he is suggesting that I invest in this big venture? Joseph asked himself incredulously, and with excitement. Visions rushed before him of such magnitude that he could hardly breathe comfortably. Where could he borrow the money? Old Steve, of course. He never failed a friend. Then the disquieting thought came to him that Stephen had already lent him five thousand dollars, none of which he had as yet repaid, for the simple reason that he could not repay it. His resentment quickened; it was unfair that such an astounding opportunity should be offered him when he had no money at all. Now Steve was a rich man, wasn't he, or how could he have given five thousand dollars in cash so casually?

Purcell, who always knew so much, was watching Joseph narrowly, and now he muttered "humph" and spat into the fire.

"I'm being candid with you, Joe, as a friend of Steve's," said Aaron, smiling at the younger man so that his feline teeth were widely displayed through his bearded lips. "Got any money you can invest with us? A wonderful opportunity. You'll never have such an opportunity again."

I must talk with Steve! thought Joseph desperately and with an obscure anger. He said, with eagerness, "Give me a little time, Mr. deWitt. I'll try to raise the money, somehow, very soon. . . ." The Fielding money! Old Steve was hoarding that. But surely he wouldn't desert a friend in this emergency!

Then Purcell said with loud and deliberate coarseness, "He's thinkin' of Steve, Aaron. He's thinkin' of borrowing from Steve again. Doesn't anybody ask me how I know, but he owes Steve nearly nine thousand dollars: four thousand borrowed four years ago, and five thousand borrowed—if you want to call it 'borrowed'—about six months ago. For interest on the bonds Alex Peale holds."

"What!" cried Aaron, with great and mendacious astonishment. "Well, well, I didn't know. But it's just like Steve, isn't it?"

Rufus suppressed a smile and turned to Joseph, who had become crimson. "Honestly, Joe? But good, if it is. You're paying interest to Steve on your notes, of course, and the principal, too, and that should impress the banks so that they'd lend you a reasonable sum of money to invest with us."

Joseph felt faint. He had no statements; he had no cheques. He had not even made a record of the loans from Stephen. But it's an honourable debt! he cried to himself. Why should he refuse to help me again; surely he isn't a stone, and will understand why I need money now? Involuntarily he began to rise; he must force Stephen to come out of that ridiculous lethargy and listen to him.

He did not know that Purcell, Aaron, and Rufus were watching him with devilish and hidden glee. Then Aaron said, "It's too bad it can't be arranged as a friendly matter, between you and Steve again, Joe. But Steve's in no condition to be harassed just now; I wouldn't permit it. Besides"—and he studied the paling Joseph blandly—"Steve hasn't any loose cash. But that doesn't matter, does it?" he added cheerily. "You've got a good credit rating with the banks, no doubt. Incidentally, Tom, how about you investing, too?"

Joseph fell back into his chair. It was Tom's turn to colour. He said without hesitation, however : "I haven't the money, Mr. deWitt. I couldn't raise it. I already owe the banks as much as I can carry. I don't believe in expanding beyond my reasonable capacity to repay promptly." He was genuinely astonished at hearing the news that Joseph had borrowed nine thousand dollars from Stephen deWitt, and he looked at his friend with mingled curiosity and interest.

Aaron shrugged regretfully. "Well, I'm sorry, Tom." Then he had an inspiration. "You've just bought up some new good tracts of lumber. Look here, Tom, we'll give you a first mortgage on those tracts, at six per cent, and you can invest the money with us! How about it? You'll never have such an opportunity again."

Tom was astute; he had some idea that all this was not being offered on the basis of a friendship which did not exist. But his eyes closed cunningly; did they think he wouldn't be able to repay the debt? He said, "Thank you. Suppose you let me think it over for a day or two, Mr. deWitt. But I think your offer is most generous, and I think I'll take it. I'll just have to look over my books." He glanced at Joseph speculatively. He said to himself: Why is old Joe so white? He looks as though he's been kicked in the stomach by a mule.

Aaron and Rufus were obviously pleased at Tom's implied promise to invest in the State Railroad Company. "That deserves another drink," said Rufus smoothly, and he refilled Tom's glass. Tom drank; his hands were shaking with his excitement.

"But Joe hasn't said whether or not he'll invest," said Aaron archly. "Don't you believe in us, Joe? How about it?"

Joe's extremity was so great that he blurted out, to his horror, "I can't. I haven't the money."

Aaron sighed, shook his head, planted his hands on his small and bony knees, and appeared to meditate. He sucked his lips in and out, blinked his eyes. Then he looked up and gazed at Joseph thoughtfully. "Joe," he said, "I've known you all your life. You've worked very hard. How old are you? Fifty-two? That's a hard age for anybody. You're running your locals practically single-handed, and you married late and your boys won't be able to take over for many years. It'll get harder and harder for you all the time. A one-man company is very hazardous, especially for a man your age who has no one to whom to delegate details and authority and responsibility. You are either at work, or you're not. Too big a load for you, Joe."

He waited a moment and surveyed Joseph with increasing sympathy. Joseph opened and shut his eyes and turned paler than ever.

"So," said Aaron kindly, "speaking as an old friend, and with no other motive in mind, don't you think it would be a good idea if you would relinquish your controlling interest in your locals to the State Railroad Company, so as to relieve you of responsibility, worry over financial matters, and constantly increasing labour troubles? Not to speak of the constant obsolescence of old equipment, such as yours. You'd be on a good salary, as manager of the locals—a permanent income without the anxiety—and you would have a much easier existence."

Joseph could not find his voice for a few moments; his heart was beating too painfully. When he could speak, it was almost inaudibly: "No. Thank you, Mr. DeWitt."

Aaron was all sympathy, but he became very serious. "Joe, I don't believe your locals are fully serving the community. A larger road, such as ours, can best serve it. We would expand your locals to our own lines. Think of what that would mean to the people you serve. No carrying and hauling of freight, no transfer of passengers by hack or carriage or wagon to make connections with our lines."

"Even by hauling, and the extra expense of transfer to the passengers, the cost is still cheaper than it would be if the locals were connected with State," said Joseph. His heart was slowing; he was breathing easier, though there was still a hunted look in his eyes, a dark shadow of fear. "The little people depend on me, sir."

Aaron shrugged, spread out his hands resignedly. "We all have our own opinions, Joe. I take it, then, that you aren't interested. Another drink?"

"No sir." Joseph edged forward in his chair, signalling to Tom Orville, who, however, was staring at Aaron with a fascinated frown. But Aaron, as if the whole matter was now off his mind, and of no further interest to him, remarked, "By the way, while we are now extending to Pittsburgh, the Chicago Railroad System is projecting lines from Chicago, Fort Wayne, and Columbus to Pittsburgh. That will give us the traffic from the west and the other companies will get it from the east." He smiled at Purcell. "Capital should be doing very well, then! And you're invested in it heavily, aren't you, Jim? The Chicago Railroad System is owned by scoundrels." He cackled affectionately. "But brilliant *entrepreneurs*. One of these days they'll be approaching us on a matter of business, and we're ready for them."

"Charming people, some of them," said Rufus, smiling.

The clock struck half-past six, and now Joseph, smothered in the presence of men who talked of large affairs, and remembering his small locals and their desperate state, got to his feet. Tom Orville rose with him, and the two men, as if they were escaping, left a hurried message for Stephen, and departed. Orville's carriage was brought around to the entrance, and a sudden cataract of rain fell as the two men seated themselves.

"I'm afraid of those scoundrels," said Joseph after a few minutes, as the carriage rolled down the long and winding road towards the valley. "They're up to something."

"They can't touch either of us so long as we're solvent," replied Tom sturdily. His words struck on Joseph's ear as the most puerile and threatening he had heard this evening. Solvent! It was all right for young Tom to talk of solvency.

Jim Purcell, leaving shortly after Tom Orville and Joseph

Baynes, could see their carriage lights winking far down on the narrow road to the city. He glanced back at the great house on the hill, wiping away the moisture of his own breath on the glass. There it stood, resembling a Southern house rather than a Northern one, with its enormous slender white pillars, its white walls and balcony, its white brick arches beneath the first floor. Every window glowed with soft gold; lavender mist drifted from its many chimneys and mingled with the rain. Jim Purcell sat back on his seat and sombrely pulled at his thick lower lip.

CHAPTER ELEVEN

SOPHIA DEWITT was guilty of what was almost her first lapse into maudlin sentimentality when, on January 2, 1867, she remarked to her sons, "It is just as if he had planned it, and perhaps he did. He left this world as a new year was being born, to begin a new life."

Stephen had been acutely embarrassed, and Lydia had averted her long dark eyes, but Rufus, after the first awkward moment when he had had difficulty in restraining a hysterical burst of laughter, gravely nodded his head at his mother. I can laugh later at the idea of Pa's beginning a "new life" anywhere, he thought, but it would certainly be out of place now. He thought of his father, lying in state in the enormous room which Sophia called the "drawing-room," and he reflected, with a sad amusement, that if Aaron was anywhere at all, it was in hell having a convivial drink with Satan himself. And probably plotting to take over the realm, too, he added.

Sophia, as "the Widow," moved about her dolorous duties with lofty stateliness, her head held high in the manner of a great lady, bearing her sorrow with dignity and importance. Her friends, including Senator Peale and his wife, and very distinguished people from Philadelphia, came in long carriage-streams up the mountain. The peak of her gratification and pride, however, was reached when Guy Gunther, the New York financier and broker of railroad stocks, arrived in Portersville for the funeral of Aaron deWitt. So overwhelmed was Sophia that she almost forgot her sincere grief for her husband, and she would remark to her friends in a broken voice, "Mr. Gunther is here; you know Mr. Gunther, the famous financier? He was such a dear friend of Aaron's. Ah, there he is now, speaking with Rufus; he has always been like a second father to Rufus."

"Ma is bearing up well," Stephen remarked hesitantly to his brother, the day of the funeral.

"But she always did," replied Rufus in surprise. "Ma needs only to be the focus of attention to be contented, even on such an occasion as this. She is what they used to call a ' lusty ' woman. Didn't you know?"

But Stephen, wandering about like a dazed grey shadow, did not know. He suffered no sorrow. He had known grief too great to be borne, and had endured too much; so even if he had loved his father he could not have been stricken too deeply. As usual, he was overlooked by the crowds who came to stare soberly at Aaron, to console Sophia, and peep at the gentlemen from Philadelphia and the fabulous man from New York. The rooms rustled with ladies' black dresses; the hall was full of canes and gloves and hats; the scent of flowers choked the warm air. A subdued murmur filled the house, and doors were constantly being opened and shut. Outside, the bitter white January day stormed against windows, and the hearths roared in answer.

Lydia, tall and thin in her black dress, attended to details which Sophia had delegated to her. Stephen thought, with dim admiration, that she was everywhere, tactful, kind, doing everything with grace and poise. Sometimes she would run upstairs to the nursery for a look at the children, and then she would be downstairs again, greeting new callers, leading them to Sophia, who sat in state near Aaron's casket. The servants, properly sniffling and overpowered, were almost inaudibly directed by her, receiving flowers still fresh and damp from hothouses, accepting cards, and divesting the ladies and gentlemen of their furs and coats. Lydia's face became dulled with fatigue, but her step did not slow. Her husband watched her with pride and love and desolation, and would sometimes wander towards her for the pleasure of meeting her eyes.

It seemed to the sons of Aaron deWitt and to Lydia that time had stopped entirely, and that for months they had not left these rooms, that Aaron had been dead for uncounted days, and that the hour of the funeral would never arrive. But eventually it was over, and then, to their exhausted amazement, it was the afternoon of the funeral and they were home again, numbed with cold; Aaron was in his grave, and the lawyers waited to read the will.

The short January day was ending, and every window was draped in snow. Sophia, Lydia, Rufus, and Stephen sat in the library, which was never used, and from whose wood and leathery walls there emanated a chill and musty smell. The fire on the black marble hearth had been lit for days, but still that pervasive odour persisted like a tangible presence. The crimson draperies were looped back from the tall and narrow windows, showing a view of black trees plastered with blobs of snow and shrouded gardens and distant white mountains. The furniture of red and black morocco leather loomed in the dusk, and the lamps could not lighten the gloom of the corners. Sophia, wrapped in a black shawl, shivered, and for the first time in these last days she seemed to shrink, to realise for the first time that her husband was dead. Rufus sat near her, his hand on her shoulder, and Lydia sat beside him gazing emptily through the nearest window. Stephen sat by the fire, unobtrusive as always, and wishing, with intense tiredness, that the portentous lawyers would speak and be gone.

But the lawyers, two old friends of Aaron's, were not going to be deprived of their own special hour and importance. They unfolded the long sheets of Aaron's will, coughed, delicately wiped their glasses, glanced with commiseration at the widow and the sons, consulted in murmurs with each other, verified each page, nodded severely. Then, one of them stood up and began to read, measuring each word. And as he read a stupefied incredulity fell on the bereaved family.

For Aaron had bequeathed to his son Stephen the controlling interest in the State Railroad Company. He had directed that Stephen assume the presidency of the company, and that Rufus be the executive vice-president. He had directed that Stephen pay "my beloved wife, Sophia," an annual income "to maintain her in her accustomed manner." "My house, upon my death, shall become the possession of my son, Stephen deWitt, and his heirs, and it is my desire that he and they reside therein."

There was much more, including provision for Rufus's salary, and minor bequests to charities and institutions. Lydia was not mentioned. And the child, Cornelia, Rufus's daughter, was omitted, also. But there was a codicil. "To my beloved granddaughter, Laura Fielding deWitt, I bequeath the sum of twenty-five thousand dollars, to be placed in trust for her until she is twenty-one years of age."

The lawyer's voice ended on an unctuous echo. He sat down beside his partner, and with impersonal malice and satisfaction they surveyed the four stunned and disbelieving faces before them. It was nothing to these men how Aaron deWitt had disposed of his holdings and his fortune, and whom he had made his heir. They personally disliked Stephen and derided him, and they admired Sophia and Lydia and were even fond of Rufus. But, as human beings engaged in an unusually dry and routine profession, they found a deep pleasure in the rare occasions when they could be part of an emotional disruption and violence, and when they could look, unconcerned, at the agitation and consternation of others. It gave a spirit to their methodical days, a winey glow to their desiccated lives.

Stephen's voice was a dry rustle: "But why, why? He hated me. He—he despised me. It isn't possible!"

The lawyer who had sat in silence cleared his throat: "My dear Stephen, I'm sure your father cared a great deal for you to entrust such an important post to you, and to make you his chief heir."

No one else stirred or spoke; no face changed from its rigid mask of repudiation and incredulity, but Stephen got to his feet and fumbled for the back of his chair. So lately delivered from death, himself, so lately rescued, he had to fight for breath, for the power to speak. "No," he whispered. "No, I can't take it."

It was then that Sophia gave a hoarse cry that was almost a scream. She threw her hands over her face and began to moan. "Aaron! My husband. To do this to me, to my son, to my Rufus, and his child! He must have been mad. Mad, mad!"

All Rufus's colour had gone completely. His large and handsome face fell into flabby folds, and turned bluish. "I don't understand," he stammered, and he looked ill. "I always thought—why, when my child was born he spoke of her as his ' heiress.'" He swallowed painfully. "It was always understood—I was his favourite."

One of the lawyers, delighting in all this drama, spoke soothingly: "I'm sure your father did what he thought was best. It was perhaps his opinion that his older son was best qualified. . . ."

"Rufus was, he is," said Stephen, still fighting for breath, still denying. He turned to his brother, and then stopped, for Rufus

115

was regarding him starkly, without his chronic amusement and tolerance, but only with the most desperate hatred and loathing. Stephen's hand, held out in pleading, dropped heavily to his side.

"I——" faltered Stephen, held in utter horror at what he was seeing on his brother's face, "am not capable. . . ."

Sophia was sobbing in complete abandonment, and Rufus sat beside her like a stone, still regarding Stephen with that undisguised, that complete and open hatred. "Undue influence," he muttered.

One of the lawyers cackled. "I hardly think so," he said, and sat back to enjoy to the fullest the debacle the will had created.

Stephen could not believe what he was seeing. Everyone vanished for him, except his brother. He tried again. "Rufus," he said, and his voice dwindled in his throat.

Rufus smiled then, an ugly and brutal smile. "It seems I'm at your mercy, old Steve," he said, in a slow and insulting voice loaded with his savage rage and disgust. This papier-mâché man, this drab, stringy creature, this imbecile rustler of files and foolscap, this inglorious clown with the sallow face and squeezed eyes and ink-stained fingers! The rage increased in Rufus to such a pitch that his head whirled and his ears rang. There must be a way to take revenge for his awful mortification, for the destruction of all his hopes. The bestial fury turned his face into a distortion, and suddenly he struck his knee with his clenched fist.

It was then that Stephen moved away from them all and left the room, and another part of him died, as it had died with Alice's death.

Slowly and wearily he climbed the stairs to the "guest chamber." The house was ominously silent about him, his father gone, the friends departed, the flowers vanished with only a ghost of their lost presence permeating the empty rooms. Not even a servant was about; no lamps had as yet been lighted. Stephen walked down the long hall, which fled with mysterious shadows. He entered the chamber where he had spent so many tortured months, and the low fire on the hearth threw coppery reflections of itself over the walls and ceiling. Here he could hear the wind that blew up from the low chasm below the room; it battered on the windows in a long curtain of snow. He did not light a lamp, but stood by the window which showed him the ranks of white mountains and the black slow river between them.

There was heat in his forehead, and he leaned it against the cold glass. He tried to think, to understand, but his mind was deeply confused and wretched. Part of him still denied what he had heard in the library, but now a bitter hardness like the stone in a withered fruit thrust itself into his thoughts. He could taste that bitterness, feel that jagged hardness; and it seemed to him that he had changed very much this past year and that something had become wizened in him, something which had been whole and sound. I did not know; I did not want it, he said to himself. Why did my father do this?

Now the fever in him became stronger, and he suddenly tore at the windows and opened them and stepped out upon the narrow iron balcony which leaned over the turbulent abyss falling down to the stones and river below. The wind assaulted him; the snow blinded him. He stood there, shivering but hot, feeling the hostility and rejection of the big house behind him, and unwilling to enter it again and see the inimical faces, the averted eyes, the scorn and detestation and suspiciousness. How was he going to live with his mother and his brother in this house, which had been given to him outright?

Then he knew that this was exactly what Aaron desired: that Stephen should find the presence of his mother and brother intolerable in this house, or that they would, if he offered them shelter here, contemptuously refuse.

He stepped out into the hall again, resolute. But for some reason obscure to him, the darkness and the flitting of pale shadows in the corridor made him hesitate, confused him again. He thought to himself vaguely; I must see the child. So, instead of turning towards the great staircase, he went to the nursery. He opened the door to firelit warmth and peace. The nurse was drowsing by the window, but she had not as yet lighted a lamp. Stephen crept soundlessly towards the two cribs where the babies lay, side by side, near the fire. Little Cornelia, a year old, was awake, and sitting up playing with her small rosy hands. She was a beautiful child, all amber and burnish and dimples, and she gave her uncle a gay smile and a chuckle. She was always ready to play, for she was full of health and vitality, like her father, and for some inexplicable reason she had taken an immense fancy to Stephen. Looking at that lovely baby now, her red hair a mass of bright curls over her head, Stephen was intensely struck by renewed anger and indignation against his father. Aaron had dispossessed this laughing little one; he had humiliated and almost destroyed her father; he had shamed her mother. She laughed aloud, pulled on his hand and tried to get to her plump feet. It was then that Lydia, unseen by Stephen in the shadows on the other side of the fireplace, stood up and approached him.

Of course, she can't bear to have me touch her child, thought Stephen humbly. He shrank away from the crib, and just stood there, his shoulders bent, his hands hanging at his side. Now mingled pity and scorn shone in Lydia's eyes, and she said quietly, "Did you come to see little Laura, Stephen? She is asleep." Lydia went to the other crib, bent over it, and regarded the child there with a strange and brooding expression. Stephen fumbled his way to the crib. There lay his daughter, small and slender and almost colourless in contrast with the flaming beauty of her cousin. For the first time Stephen thought with surprise: Why, she looks like Lydia! Tentatively, he touched his child's face with his forefinger, and a deep and intolerable yearning overwhelmed him again for Alice.

He muttered urgently to Lydia, "I'm sorry; I'm terribly sorry. . . ."

Still regarding little Laura, Lydia did not move. Her hands were clenched rigidly on the side of the crib. "For what?" she asked. He stammered: "For my father's will. I didn't know, believe me."

The nurse was rousing and getting to her feet sheepishly. Lydia turned her fine dark head and asked her to leave the room for a few moments. She waited until the woman had gone, then straightened up and stared contemplatively at Stephen. She said, "Of course you didn't know. Did I say that you did, Stephen?"

"But my mother, and Rufus——" Stephen began in his halting voice.

Lydia was silent. It was as if she were seeing him for the first time, and was not particularly pleased to what she saw. Finally she spoke, and there was an edge to her voice: "Stephen, I once thought I knew why Alice loved and married you. I'm not sure but what she was mistaken after all."

Stephen looked at her dumbly, and each of the cruel words

seemed to crash not only against his ears, but his heart. "What—what are you saying, Lydia? How can you speak so? Do you know what I am going to do? I am going to ask my mother and my brother to remain in this house, with me and my child. I am going to consult with Rufus about breaking our father's will. I am going to try to rectify this incredible wrong. What more can I do?"

Now the scorn in Lydia's eyes was an icy blaze. She tried to speak, then compressed her lips. She moved a few paces away from him and stood with her back to him, looking at the fire. He could see that her hands were gripped together as if she were fighting for control. Her tall thin figure was outlined by the fire, and the black silk glistened softly as it fell in folds from the tight bodice, and her black hair was outlined with an umber shadow. Never before had Lydia seemed formidable to the distressed Stephen, but now she was like a stranger. Then he heard her speaking: "I had hoped you were beginning to learn, to see a little. There is a difference between an utterly amoral man and a complete fool."

He could not understand her. He could only stand there, and she saw his gentle, haggard face, the suffering in his eyes, and the bewilderment. Her shoulders dropped as if in resignation, and her face softened as she sighed. She came to him and took his arm. "Stephen, try to see. Try not to be so enslaved to emotions. Come downstairs with me now, and talk with your mother and brother."

Grasping Stephen as if he were a prisoner who might try to escape, she led him from the room. In silence, they went down the stairs together. Lydia did not speak until they had reached the hall, and then she said in a low and peremptory voice, "Try to remember something, Stephen. Your father left you what he did; he had a reason. It is too much to expect that you might understand that reason, but at least you can put out of your mind that it was a malevolent one."

"What else?" he muttered, but she gave his arm a strong pull and he went with her into the drawing-room where his mother and brother were sitting in a bleak and violent silence, not looking at each other. When Lydia and Stephen entered they started, exchanged glances, then turned away. Lydia said in a slow and distinct tone, "Stephen has something to say to you, I believe." She dropped his arm, moved to the fireplace, and yet confronted him in upright challenge. Her eyes commanded him, gave him a warning he could not comprehend.

Sophia sat in her mound of rustling black silk, a commanding and dominant woman, her grey hair a little dishevelled, her large strong-featured face full of bitter hatred and aversion. She was ashen-pale; her hazel eyes blazed at Stephen as if all her long repudiation of him had come to a focus which would hurl him out of her sight. Rufus only sat there as if his brother were not present at all, one of his clenched fists ground into his ruddy cheek, his sleek legs coiled as though to spring and attack.

"What can he say?" cried Sophia harshly. "After what he has done?" She moved her body as if to start back from a repulsive presence, and she flung up one hand, glittering with diamonds, in a somewhat histrionic gesture.

Stephen, confronted by all this savage rage and disgust for him, could not speak. What have I done to deserve this? he thought. They have always hated me. . . .

"I have been thinking. This is your home, Ma, and it is your home, Rufus. Rufus, your child was born here, and you have lived here with your wife. I lived here but a short time, and then when Alice and I were married, Pa gave us our old house."

He paused, and a most shattering thought came to him: Why were Alice and I not invited to remain here? Why was it understood that we should understand that we'd not be welcome? Why did they despise Alice? Because she was good and innocent and gentle? Or because she was my wife?

Sophia and Rufus though manifesting complete contempt, and pretence that they had not heard Stephen, had become very stiff and still in their chairs. Lydia said sharply, "Stephen! Why have you stopped talking? They are waiting to hear what you have to say."

Alice, thought Stephen. She was exiled with disdain from this house. When she came, she came on sneering sufferance, and she was rallied and badgered. I used to see tears in her dear eyes. My little Alice. He straightened and involuntarily glanced at Lydia, and her pale face was very set and intent upon him. His voice was stronger when he went on: "It is my intention to ask you to remain in—in our—home. It is impossible that you, Ma, and you, Rufus, leave. In spite of the terms of Pa's will, this is your home. You can't leave."

Sophia exclaimed with loud loathing, "Indeed, sir! Do you

think for a moment that I intend to remain in a house, *my* house, from which I have been dispossessed? I don't know what you did to your father, or how you cajoled him all the months you were whining and sickening after Alice died, or how you persuaded him, when he was so ill and you lured him into the guest chamber so you could pervert his mind and turn his natural affections away from his wife and his son! But you did it! How could he know, ill as he was, and not in his right and legal mind, what you were doing to him, under your hypocritical pretending that you were grieving for your wife!"

Stephen listened to this with horror. He stepped back into the shadows. For almost the first time in his life his hands turned into fists. They believe this! he said inwardly. Revulsion so tremendous rushed into every part of his body that he began to tremble and his sallow face glimmered as if with lightning.

"'Not in his right and legal mind,'" repeated Rufus, as if struck. He sat up in his chair and his hazel eyes, so like his mother's, began to sparkle savagely. "Of course! He had been ill for long over a year, and had no control over his senses. Undue influence, as I said before."

Then Lydia spoke, and her voice was as clear and sharp as an icicle: "The will was made on February 15, 1865—two years ago. Have you forgotten?"

Sophia swung around in her chair and looked at Lydia with outraged violence. Her mouth opened to shout, and then the impact of what Lydia had said came to her, and her face collapsed into deep folds and wrinkles. Rufus fell back in his chair, and his features tightened.

"You have only one quarrel, if there is a quarrel, with the codicil, leaving little Laura that twenty-five thousand dollars," Lydia continued. "However, it can be proved that though Rufus and I have had returned to us my parents' money, none of Alice's share was so returned. And it was much more than twenty-five thousand dollars. It was nearly fifty."

She swung to Stephen, who stood in shadow, and she made an eloquent gesture with her hand to him as if saying: You see how it is.

"What have I done, Lydia, to turn you against me like this?" asked Rufus of his wife, and his voice was genuinely broken and husky. "Is it too much of a man to expect that his wife will be loyal to him, at least?"

"Oh, my God!" exclaimed Lydia with impatient vehemence. "Rufus, you aren't a fool. I was just stating a truth which you apparently were attempting to ignore."

Rufus considered this, and turned a deep red. "Yes, you are right, of course, Liddie. But somehow, the influence occurred. It was always understood——"

"By whom?" demanded Lydia. She came closer into the wide circle of firelight. "By you? By your mother?" Her face flamed with scorn.

"Pa spoke of Cornelia as his ' heiress,'" said Rufus, and it seemed from his tone that he was pleading with his wife. "It was in this very room, on the night our child was born."

Lydia laughed drearily. "Did it ever come to you that perhaps he was mocking you? You know how he was. He was an evil man——"

"How dare you, you wretch?" screamed Sophia, starting to her feet. "How dare you speak so of my husband?"

Now Rufus, angered, got up. "Ma! What are you calling Lydia, my wife?"

Lydia flashed him a wry, but gentle look. "Never mind, Rufus. One must remember the circumstances. But I haven't finished. I repeat that Aaron deWitt was an evil man, and he knew it, and enjoyed being evil. However, he wasn't stupid; he had a most excellent mind, astute and comprehending. And he made Stephen his heir for what seemed to him good and sufficient reasons. I don't intend to discuss those reasons, which are very obvious to unprejudiced people such as myself. Don't look at me so uncomprehendingly, Rufus; don't look so amazed. And your father didn't leave you penniless. We have a great deal of money, and you have a lot of stock in the company, and you are to be executive vice-president. It is your pride that has been attacked, and I sympathise though I don't agree."

All this time Stephen had not moved. He was lost in the shadows, his head bent. But he was thinking, and his bitterness was a deathly taste in his mouth. He said to himself: I've been a fool. I don't know just how, but I have. His sorrow for Alice was like a freshly-bleeding wound in him. He forgot what he had been about to offer his brother.

Sophia had fallen back into her chair, and she was sobbing desperately. "An evil man—my husband!" she cried. "My husband, my poor, betrayed husband, dying alone in his bed only three days ago! My husband, lied to, cajoled, tormented out of his wits by a thief and a rascal who used his wife's death to gain his ends!"

Stephen stirred from the shadow and came into the firelight. He looked only at his mother and his small brown eyes were like circles of phosphorescence. "Don't, Ma," he said in a very strange voice. "Don't lie any longer. And don't ever mention Alice's name again, ever. If you do, I shall ask you to leave this house and never put foot into it again."

Sophia dropped her hands from her wet face and stared at him with complete amazement. Rufus, standing beside his wife, was also astonished.

"What are you saying? Are you mad? You never talked like this before," said Rufus in a hushed tone.

"No, I never did," said Stephen. "Because you see, though it has always been there for anyone to observe, I was blind, and a fool."

Sophia was enormously shaken. She still could not believe that this unobtrusive and gentle son of hers, this hesitant and retreating son who was the object of the derision of a whole city, could speak as he had done. He had dared to put on the stature of a man, and this outraged her more than anything else.

She rose dramatically, and pointed her finger at him, but she looked at Rufus. "He dares to speak so to your mother, and you do not knock him down!"

Rufus smiled, and said dryly, "You are also his mother. And his objections are only just."

He bowed ironically at Stephen. "We accept your kind offer to remain in the house. Your house. And I must say, Steve, that had I been in your place, I wouldn't have made that offer."

CHAPTER TWELVE

Rufus SAT alone in his bedroom before the fire, wrapped in his dark blue dressing-gown and smoking a cheroot. He was lonely; it was midnight. The house lay about him in ponderous silence, an island cut off from the world by wind and snow and storm. He was thinking, and his thoughts were heavy and despondent and still black with rage. He no longer blamed Stephen for his father's will, but thinking of Aaron, consigned to his grave that day, his hatred became a violent thing in him. He glanced about his room, tenantless except for himself, and his hatred spread to everything and everybody. He ran his hands distractedly through his red hair, threw the cheroot into the fire, and cursed aloud. He had humour of an exceptional kind, but he could find nothing humorous in his present situation, the end of his hopes and plans. He got to his feet and began to pace the carpet, up and down, back and forth, rubbing his chin, clenching his hands, muttering under his breath.

He was by nature exuberant and immediate, and so, at first, his plans were all urgent and active. One by one, he discarded them regretfully. Intuitive and full of perception, he had known that when Stephen had accompanied Lydia down the stairs and into the drawing-room a few hours ago, Stephen had been prepared not only to offer his mother and brother a home for life in this house, but to offer to help break the will or rectify its provisions. If only Sophia had been more intelligent and less coarse and stupid! In less than ten minutes she had destroyed her favourite son's hopes and had set him here, plotting unnecessarily and almost futilely. But what, Rufus allowed himself to think in the midst of his searching, had come over old Steve, that he had not gone on with his offer? What had turned that undistinguished face into stone?

The time had gone, perhaps, when one could strike at Stephen through his absurd emotions, his reasonless and self-imposed guilts, his humility, his inability to wound others and to protect himself, his enormous lack of self-esteem, his conviction of his worthlessness. Some way, Stephen had mysteriously glimpsed a little of the truth which Rufus had always known: that he had intrinsic power and ability and keenness, and that without his really great mentality and planning and acumen the State Railroad Company might be less than it was. Aaron had known; it was unpardonable that, after his death, he had not let the comfortable deception persist.

Stephen had, in some way, caught a glimmering of the truth. Sophia had presented him with that glimmering. Yet, something else had also happened in that room in the space of a few moments, something which Rufus could not grasp. He did not waste time in attempting to grasp it; it was powerful, but it was intangible

124

too. He had to reckon with it, and so quell any immediacy.

Rufus's door opened; he heard it and started. Lydia was entering, closing the door behind her. She was dressed in a soft rose peignoir, and her long black hair fell to her waist. Rufus stared at her disbelievingly. He looked at her pale face and large dark eyes, and he saw that she was both sad and resolute. She had never entered this room since he had taken up occupancy, and she had never permitted him to enter her own bedroom from the time of Cornelia's birth. Rufus, his heart suddenly racing, his face flushing and his eyes brightening, got to his feet speechlessly.

She came up to him and looked into his eyes gravely. "I'm terribly sorry about the will, Rufus," she said in a low voice. "It must be dreadful for you."

She pitied him, he understood. He drew out a chair for her, and she sat down, clasping her hands on her knees. His breath was coming fast, and he knew that his features were thickening with desire for her, with love and passion for her. He sat near her and waited, and let his face become despondent and withdrawn.

"But nothing can be done, and it's best to go on in the most sensible way," Lydia continued. There was no uneasiness about her, no coldness, and Rufus's ears began to sing with joy and exultation. She was gazing at him so sympathetically, so kindly.

"Dear Lydia," he said softly. With genuine shyness, he reached out his hand and took one of her own. She did not resist, though she did not respond with any pressure. However, she leaned towards him, and her face softened almost to tenderness.

His first impulse was to speak with intimate contempt of Stephen, and to express bitterness against his father and his own "wrongs." But his perceptiveness held the impulse back. Lydia was not a woman of petty character, or feeble mind. So he said, very carefully and quietly, "Don't be too sorry, Lydia, my darling. Perhaps my father thought he was doing what was best."

He knew he had been right, for Lydia's face took on colour and more gentleness. Now she actually pressed his fingers. He became a little dejected, and somewhat angry. If he had hoped that her sympathy was tinged with indignation and scorn for Stephen, he was disillusioned. She was nodding her head. "You are perfectly right, Rufus." She smiled at him, and he was mortified that she so easily accepted the premise of the "value" of his brother as opposed to the lesser value of himself.

As if she understood what he was thinking, she said quickly, "I did not mean to appear disloyal to you to-day, Rufus. I was merely calling your attention to facts. Of course, I know that in your first shock you had forgotten that the will was made two years ago."

Rufus nodded. "But I still don't understand," he said. He held tighter to her hand, and she let it remain.

"It doesn't matter, after all," said Lydia. "We have a great deal, Rufus. I should like to leave this house with you and Cornelia, and have a home of our own. Your mother can remain with Stephen, of course."

He forgot all his distraction, momentarily, in his joy and relief. "You would honestly prefer that, Liddie? The three of us, alone?"

"I'd honestly prefer it."

Rufus considered. Apparently Lydia was offering her husband a normal family life again, and if this was so, then she loved him in spite of the coldly violent conversations they had had over the past months. This was enough to give him delight. He looked into her eyes and asked, "You do love me, don't you, darling?"

She was silent, and the colour left her face, and she gently withdrew her hand. But she did not look away from him. "I still love what I thought you were, up to six months after I married you, Rufus."

He stood up, his florid face darkening. "One of your serpentine remarks, Lydia. You've told me a dozen times this past year that what you thought I was, and what I really am, are two irreconcilable things. Therefore you have said, it was impossible to love the reality which is me. Are you still of that opinion?"

She waited a moment, then said with remorse, "Yes, I am."

He did not want to lose the joy and delight he had felt. He stood beside her and put his hand on her shoulder. "Lydia, let us be reasonable. Was it my fault that you had some impossible image of me in your mind? Was it my fault that you were deceiving yourself?"

"No."

"Then why should you punish me because I am not the man you thought I was? Did I ever deceive you about my character?"

She bent her head and began to cry silently. "What can I say,

126

Rufus? It isn't my intention to 'punish' you for my own ignorance and stupidity. I am punishing myself, and if you are hurt by it, I can only say I am sorry, and please forgive me. No, you never deceived me about your character. I was the one who was blind, and unable to see. But what you are, Rufus, completely and happily amoral, completely expedient and ruthless, is repulsive to me."

She lifted her wet face and gazed at him with real anguish. "Forgive me, Rufus, for my stupidity, and for the misery I must have caused you all this time."

He saw he had some strong advantage. He let his face express grim wretchedness and affront. "I find it hard to forgive you, Lydia. You've made my life almost impossible."

"I know." She thought of the poisonous little rumours she had overheard about Rufus's attachment to some easy lady in Portersville, the wealthy widow of a land speculator. She felt no humiliation or anger. It was her own doing, she told herself. She was too conscience-stricken to remark that it was a little absurd for Rufus to say that his "life had been made impossible."

She said falteringly, "Rufus, if you want me to, I'll stay here with you to-night, and any other night."

His first impulse was to take her in his arms with relief and happiness. He thought to himself: Perhaps I can overcome her distrust of me, and get her to abandon her foolish ideas. And, even if I can't, I'll at least have her, and perhaps that will be enough.

And then he knew it would not be enough. He loved her too much to take what she was offering in mortifying sympathy. He was sickened with his desolation, but he said, "I'm not quite so 'amoral' as you think, Liddie. For, you see, I don't want you in my room and in my bed if you don't love me. I could take advantage of this sympathy of yours, but I won't."

He sat down again, heavily, and stared at the fire. She watched him with grief for a while, then exclaimed, "Rufus, there must be some way to help you! It isn't fair for me to treat you like this, but I can't help it."

"Are you suggesting a divorce, Lydia?" he asked incredulously. "And on what grounds?"

Her whole face trembled, but she answered courageously, "I am sure you can get a divorce from me, Rufus. On the grounds of— desertion."

"And expose you, and me, to notoriety? And jeers? No, Lydia.

I, perhaps, as a man, would escape a lot of that. But not you."
He added, "And there is the child to be considered."

But he was also thinking of the laughter of his "friends" at his
desertion by Lydia. He was also thinking that he would have to
return the "Fielding money" to Lydia in the event of a divorce.

"I'm not afraid of any notoriety or jeers, Rufus. For, you see,
I don't like people, and I've come to know what they are, and
never in my life have I considered the opinions of others if those
opinions were trivial or impudent or none of their affair. Perhaps
that was selfish in a way, for loneliness breeds selfishness, but it
also made me indifferent to the passing views of strangers who
are nothing to me."

Rufus, who had always lived by and depended upon the good
and admiring judgments of his fellows, and who could not
endure life unless he was applauded, envied, and courted, felt that
he was listening to an esoteric philosophy expressed in an alien
language he only partly understood. He thought Lydia extremely
peculiar and unfathomable, and then he did not entirely believe
her.

"Divorce is out of the question," he said flatly. "I am surprised
you ever thought of such a disgusting thing." He stood up
again and began to walk up and down the room, frowning. He
was angry, and humiliated. He said, "No, I don't want you,
Lydia, except on my own terms, and you know what they are.
And we can't possibly leave this house."

"Why not, Rufus?" she asked pleadingly. "I never quarrel
with your mother, and we are on more or less amiable terms, but
still I'd like a home of my own. I never considered this my home,
and now, by the terms of your father's will, it isn't your home,
either."

He was so stung at this, and so enraged, that he shouted, "But
it will be, and perhaps not so long in the future, either!"

She stood up abruptly and her face whitened. "What are you
talking about, Rufus? You can't overthrow your father's will;
the lawyers said as much."

He stopped near her and they looked at each other, Lydia taut
and shaken. Rufus red and swollen of face, his hazel eyes on fire.
He told himself, in his fury, that he hated her, hated her shallow
and narrow principles, her smug judgment of him, her self-
assurance that dared her to judge him at all and believe that she
was right. What if he said to her that he had no intention of

letting Stephen keep what he had, that he would endlessly plot, day and night, to deprive that fool of what should be his, Rufus's, and that he would use every idi t weakness of character which his brother possessed to ruin him?

But it was his native caution, his mistrust of everybody, that held back what he wished to say. Lydia had become his enemy not only by her rejection of him but by her insistence that he abide by the terms of his father's evil will. She was no longer to be trusted; perhaps, he thought, he had never had any real reason to trust her.

He forced himself to relax. He made himself smile, as if with amusement. "Why are you so disturbed, Liddie?" he asked softly. "I was merely saying that I regard this house as my home, and that I have already accepted Steve's invitation to remain here. After all, I have lived in this house longer than he, and morally— you like that term, don't you?—it is my house as well as his."

There is something dangerous here, thought Lydia, with fearful anxiety. She regarded Rufus searchingly, but his smile was so open, so full of incipient laughter at her, that she began to feel foolish. Besides, what could Rufus do to Stephen? There was nothing he could do. She sighed. She began to move towards the door, her rosy gown trailing behind her. She hesitated on the threshold, then said gently, "Good night, Rufus," and closed the door behind her.

Then it seemed to Rufus incredible that he had let her go, and that he had not accepted her in her gesture of consoling sympathy, and that without her there was nothing of real substance in his existence. He ran to the door, opened it, and called her name. The hall was empty. He stood there deeply shaken, and said to himself: I would have had to give up all my life, if she had heard me, and if a man gives up his life, what else is there? He shut the door.

I

CHAPTER THIRTEEN

PORTERSVILLE WAS deeply shocked and incredulous when it was learned that grey Stephen had become Aaron deWitt's heir, and was now president of the State Railroad Company. No one could quite believe it, and for some time many persons were furiously sceptical. There had not been so much excitement in the city since the assassination of Mr. Lincoln, and vehement arguments went on in almost every house, particularly in the homes of those who personally knew the DeWitts. Rufus's friends, for a long time, made it a point of gathering together in groups and marching on the Portersville National Bank building, climbing the stairs with considerable racket to the offices of the State Railroad Company, passing the president's shut door with even more racket, and then entering Rufus's offices with outraged faces and loud expressions of indignation. For a few weeks Rufus permitted this, to assuage his own human bitterness, then his common sense intervened. These sympathising sorties, while consoling, would soon make him ridiculous, he saw, for he knew that eventually mankind comes to despise the man who has lost, or been victimised.

The board of directors of the State Railroad Company almost worked themselves up to a state of joint apoplexy, and had gloomy private talks in their lumber or steel or banking offices. The State Railroad Company, they darkly and gloomily hinted, would "come to an end" with such as Stephen as the head of it. What did the "gentlemen in Philadelphia" think of all this? they would ask themselves. The gentlemen in Philadelphia displayed a most reassuring lack of dismay, and the directors relaxed, still angered, but relieved. Jim Purcell, also a director of the company, said, in his uncouth manner, and after an obscene remark, "You're a lot of fools. The evidence was right there for you to see all the time, about Steve, but you've been bedazzled by the antics of Red Rufe. Forget his posturin's and his grinnin's. Look beyond them, at Steve, you fools."

When Portersville finally had to accept the fact that Stephen was president of the company, its resentment grew rather than lessened. Hundreds felt personally insulted, even those who had no direct connection with the State Railroad Company. Emotion ran high for Rufus as wrath increased against Stephen and the dead Aaron. It was impossible for Stephen, even in his deepest retreats, to be unaware of the feeling against him in the city. He condoned it for a long time, and in his compassion for Rufus, he blamed no one. Eventually, however, he could no longer avoid the recognition of the malice that is part of all human character, and he came to see that affection for Rufus was less the motivating power of the malevolence he encountered than aversion for himself.

But a strange thing happened to him. In the past he had accepted this aversion with humility, more than half believing that in some way he deserved it. Slowly, now, he began to question his humility, and something like the still anger he had experienced on the day of his father's funeral moved in him.

His face, diffident, shrinking, and gentle, began to take on an aspect of sternness and cold quiet. As time went on, his brown moustache became sprinkled with grey, as did his sparse brown hair. His mouth stiffened; his eyes forgot the habit of shyly sidling away and acquired remote directness which often disconcerted his enemies while it deepened their hatred for him.

Aaron's plan for the extension of the railroad to Baltimore and Washington was carried through, and after a meeting of the board of directors, at which Stephen presided in an almost total silence, and at which Rufus was at his most charming and enthusiastic, it was decided to rename the company the Interstate Railroad Company. One of the happy directors, not famous for tact, ended the discussion with a vibrant remark: "In a way, we should call it Rufus's Road!" Swamped by embarrassment, and after a slinking glance at Stephen's haggard and expressionless face, the directors began, very hastily, to speak of something else. They were still outraged, after four years, that Stephen should be their president; and they refused to admit, even to each other, that he was a most competent one. They declared that it was "all Rufus's doing, anyway," for where would Stephen acquire the intelligence, strength and imagination, which had resulted in the expansion of the road so successfully, especially in a time of increasing national insecurity?

Never Victorious, Never Defeated

The charitable organisations to which Stephen gave so generously were not permitted by him to make known his deep charity. This provision was not hard to enforce, for many of the directors of the charities were Rufus's friends; and they persuaded themselves that in some way Stephen "ought" to be contrite for what he had done to his brother, and that he was only just making "amends" to his conscience, if he had such a thing. So even his contributions were received with surliness and ingratitude. The fact that Rufus gave little or nothing was entirely overlooked, or explained away in terms that implied that he had been "robbed" and could temporarily give no more than he did. In the meantime, he had to conserve his resources for the coming "day."

There was no reason in all this Lydia would say to herself. But then, she would add, there is very little logic in mankind. Even when her bitterness against her husband had been at its strongest, she had felt nothing more inimical than dislike for him. Now she began to hate him for his smiles, and his silences, his pregnant implications, when, after so long a time, his friends tendered sympathy to him. But she never spoke of this. She merely avoided Rufus for days on end, and when forced to speak at all it was in monosyllables and of the most inconsequential social or household matters.

Sophia, too, added to the hatred directed against her older son. Though warned by Rufus not to employ such ludicrous terms as "undue influence" or "injustice done to my son Rufus," she nevertheless was able to convey to her eager friends that Stephen had "plotted" against his brother while his father was susceptible to such suggestions. It was argued among these friends that a mother would not be capable of falsehoods or acid bitternesses against one of her own children unless there was reason for it.

As if he were totally blind and deaf to all the local turmoil about him, Stephen worked endlessly, methodically, and tirelessly. He often drove down to the offices at dawn, and was there after Rufus left. But Rufus did not regularly leave his brother alone. His study of Stephen, and Stephen's methods, went on with the deepest of concentration. He knew, now, that he had been the colourful façade, the final verve, which had decorated the edifice already carefully and tediously built by Stephen. He himself had always had the knowledge, but the details, the hard driving work, the persistence, had bored him. He did not underestimate his own accomplishments, for he understood that even prosaic business must have its flare, its drama, and that businessmen, however dull-headed, appreciated a little life and excitement and the histrionic illusion that their affairs were not entirely a matter of cold figures. If he could achieve the potency of Stephen's management and clever planning, and combine it with his own characteristics, he believed, and rightly, that he would be irresistible. Hence, in his study of his brother, he never became bored since he had everything to gain.

He would say to himself: I am now thirty-two, thirty-three, thirty-four. I am moving along where I wish to go, and it is only a matter of time. I can wait.

He thought himself alone in his admiration for Stephen's real genius, for he almost always forgot Jim Purcell. He saw that Stephen was heavily, and constantly, investing in the coal mines around Scranton, to the extent of his financial ability. Only recently, in April 1871, Stephen had bought more undeveloped acreage, though Wall Street was uneasily aware of the growing depression throughout the country. On the Monday following Black Friday, on September 24, 1869 (when there had been a "corner" on gold), Stephen had quietly bought up huge tracts at an unbelievably low price. He had, two years later, been offered twice what he had paid for the land, though there was a feeling in the nation that a terrible panic was developing. Rufus, who had smiled contemptuously at Stephen's purchase, now, in November, 1871, cursed himself for his blindness. It takes time to understand everything about a man you intend to ruin, he would say to himself.

One of Rufus's plans was to eliminate any antagonism which existed between him and his brother, for he alone knew that Stephen had a latent tendency towards suspicion which was only recently becoming evident in small ways. This suspiciousness had formerly been sternly repressed by Stephen, who believed all men to be intrinsically good. Now he was exhibiting some disturbing discretion, if only spasmodically and at very infrequent intervals. Rufus went to the most delicate and strenuous extremes to destroy any possible distrust Stephen might have of him. He never made the smallest decision alone; he consulted Stephen at all times. He was open in his real admiration for his brother; he laughed at his own errors when he talked with Stephen and confessed to impulsiveness. When "troublemakers" on the road cried for an increase in wages, while wages were falling all over the country, and it was only sensible to deny the increases, Rufus upheld Stephen in his decision to accede to the demands in the face of the vehement protests of the board of directors. "Stephen knows what he is doing," said Rufus seriously. "Look at the trouble the other roads are having."

Slowly, by the most careful and subtle efforts, Rufus built up a solidarity between Stephen and himself.

There were only two people who dreaded, and suspected, this growing friendship and confidence between the two brothers, and these two were Lydia and Jim Purcell. Lydia dared say nothing to Stephen, for an inexplicable coldness had inserted itself in their formerly profound trust of each other. But Purcell shouldered his rough and massive way into Stephen's office one afternoon and said in his grating voice, "What is all this between you and Red Rufe? The whole town is talkin' about you two being so lovey-dovey, and cleavin' to each other. Are you a fool, eh, Steve? Don't guess for a minute what he's up to? Plain as the nose on your damn' silly face. He's out to ruin you, like the spider and fly business."

Stephen, who had always passively accepted Purcell's "haunting" as one of the mysteries of life, and as of no particular importance, had risen to a rare anger. "I don't know what you're talking about, Jim. Rufus ruin me? How? I am the president; I have fifty-one per cent of the stock. How could he take all this away from me? It's ridiculous. You never liked him; there has always been animosity between you two. . . ."

"Never asked yourself why, did you, Steve?"

"No. I never thought it was important." Stephen's pale face flushed.

Purcell pointed a big thick finger almost into his face. "It's because we're both scoundrels, Steve, and we both want the same thing: to be the most powerful and richest man in this city, and maybe in the state, sometime. We know all about each other. D'ye think for a minute Rufe's given up his idea, any more than I've given up mine? If you think so, you're an imbecile. And you're in danger."

"Rufus and I are friends," said Stephen stiffly.

Purcell nodded his huge and shapeless head, and the bulges and pits of his face expressed disgust at this childishness. "I know. He figured it this way. Smart feller, our Rufe. And you're fallin' right into the pit he's diggin' for you. I'm tryin' to warn you, that is all."

"Why? Why should it matter to you, Jim?"

Purcell was silent. He stood beside Stephen's desk and pulled at one of his loose and flabby lips. He stared at Stephen intently, then shook his head as if he had been arguing with himself over a hopeless matter. "You'll never know," he said at last.

Stephen did not see him again for six months.

Stephen tried to forget Purcell's warning, but it hovered uneasily in his mind as a kind of betrayal of Rufus. One time he tentatively tried to talk about the matter with his brother, and he said haltingly. "I haven't seen Jim Purcell lately. Is he out of town? No? He came in to see me one day, and . . ."

"And what?" Rufus asked the question smilingly.

But Stephen could not go on. It would be mortally humiliating to Rufus. So he stammered, "It was really nothing. Just a small matter; he's one of the directors, you know."

Rufus studied that distressed face, the shifting eyes, the expression of pain, and he knew at once. Rufus was amused, but also alarmed. He watched for any meeting between Stephen and Purcell, and as the months went by and there was no meeting, he was relieved.

One day Rufus and Purcell came face to face on the street. Rufus would have been content to smile and bow, and pass on, but right there, in the centre of Portersville, Purcell caught his arm and said loudly, "Look here, Rufe. I'm watchin' you. Any funny business, and I'll make you remember I'm one of the directors. Understand?"

Rufus laughed a little. "Why all this drama, Jim? No, I don't understand you. Why don't you visit us up on the hill and we'll all have a little talk about it—Steve, you and I? And now, please excuse me."

Purcell, of course, did not come. There were many things happening in the country this November of 1871. The prophesied panic was showing signs of materialising.

CHAPTER FOURTEEN

THE WAR Between the States had brought great industrial expansion to the North, even during the years of the war. Far behind British industrialisation, which was superb, complete, and universal, the Union discreetly headed by the new buccaneers, had a vision of the United States becoming the industrial empire of the world. Unperturbed, during the war, at the prospect of defeat at the hands of the Southern Confederacy, they were equally unperturbed at the collapse of government credit, for it brought debasement of the currency and a consequent inflation. The prices of all goods leaped upwards. Northern citizens, however, paid but vague attention to this, for they were engaged in the immense business of war, consuming and destroying, and over the North a bogus prosperity burgeoned which was enthusiastically proclaimed to be the beginning of "a new era of industrial expansion and limitless wealth and opportunity for all citizens."

Bankers and investors were able to raise a million dollars a day to pursue the conflict against the South. Meat had poured from Chicago in unbelievable quantities for the military and the people; the production of iron became mountainous; railroads expanded enormously; oil wells spouted in various sections; machines were rapidly invented for farm use in order that farm workers could be drawn off into the Union army. The factories making war goods bulged incredibly. The protective tariffs against foreign goods had operated to the advantage of native manufacturers in the throes of a delirious war prosperity. America, whose industrial growth had been sluggish, now found herself hurling madly into the industrial revolution. All this was regarded joyously by a heedless citizenry who never even dimly perceived that a prosperity created by a war must end in chaos at the end of a war.

Only the farmers were adversely affected. Believing, like their city brethren, that the golden tide of industrial expansion would pour over them also, they had incontinently expanded, and ran into debt. The western farmers particularly suffered. The hessian fly destroyed crops; the elevators offered but fifteen cents for corn; the farmers signed more notes at as much as fifteen or twenty per cent. Only the middleman of the cities prospered on the growing misery of the farmer, who had to pay excessive prices for necessary city-made goods during the war. The custom duties and the internal-revenue taxes were particularly oppressive to the farmer. While the buccaneers of the cities and other prosperous men engaging in the manufacture and sale of war goods to the government nimbly evaded taxes, the farmer could not escape the tax collector and his peering surveillance.

By 1871 the people of America became aware of a frightful breakdown in the morals of their government. Had the war prosperity continued, the citizens would not have cared that corruption extended from Washington into every city and hamlet. But the sudden decline of a war-fevered delirium in the cities, with desperate unemployment, gave the people leisure to observe what had happened and was still happening. There were countless instances of wholesale robbery, including the losses of the insurance companies. Business ethics were completely abandoned in the mad rush to acquire such properties as the railroads, oil wells, and mines, and speculation remained uncontrolled and unchecked. The wounded and exploited South continued to be victimised and made desperate by Northern robbers and swindlers, with the blessing of a supine and corrupt government whose members desired nothing but personal power and gain.

As the American people's faith declined in their government, their faith declined in themselves and the whole governmental and business structure. They did not hold themselves guilty of their misery and despair. They thronged the streets vainly looking for employment, while their families starved or became homeless. In the meantime, the banks uneasily remained on the alert, fearful of a run, which, however, was not to materialise for a few months.

The utter collapse of the American economy had been delayed for a short time after the War Between the States by the outbreak of the Franco-Prussian War. English and American industrialists, already disturbed over a threatened economic debacle in 1869, felt reprieved. They competed furiously with each other for the market supplying France and Germany with war materials, and bad feeling, already very intense between the British and

American Governments and people, grew to dangerous proportions. England believed the European continent to be her God-endowed source of industrial markets, but now, to her indignation, this new barbarian country, vastly growing and expanding in both cultivated territory and industry, was becoming a sinister threat to the British industrial empire. Britain had hoped that a divided America, still staggering bloodily after a terrible civil war, would be removed from competition in markets for a long time. But, on the contrary, the war had so expanded industry in the United States, and had revealed so many enormously rich natural resources, that for the first time in the nineteenth century Britain had occasion to pause and to fear.

Only a few men anywhere, among them Stephen deWitt, had begun to observe an ominous phenomenon in the world. In past centuries wars had occurred for territory, or by reason of private quarrels between royalty, or as a result of racial antagonisms. Never before had wars deliberately or inadvertently burst out for the control of industrial markets.

And now these few alarmed men began to suspect, without any other evidence but their intuition, that an industrial economy might have to be supported by future wars. As industry expanded, and more and more goods were available in a market bound to contract, or remain the same, or fail to keep up with production, wars would be necessary to produce national prosperity or to eliminate competitors. To these few men this was the utmost in human degradation and infamy.

A crisis had come upon the world, though few realised it. Stephen often thought to himself with consternation: No one has studied the possibility of creating new markets through aid to countries too poor to buy our immensely increasing goods. No one has lifted his voice to insist that progress does not necessarily mean steel mills and endless smoking factories where goods are produced which people cannot buy. There must be a healthy balance between agriculture and industry, or the warehouses of the nations will be heaped high with unsold goods while the cities starve for want of food. The rise of great cities will see the decline of agricultural acreage, and while we in America still have more than a safe margin between agriculture and industry, there may very well come a time when that margin is fatally narrowed.

In that event, we shall be forced to engage in wars to consume our goods and to compete for world markets. There is another alternative, and that is less emphasis on the mere possession of goods and more emphasis on spiritual values and the land. Food had always been the answer to men's problems, and it would remain the answer.

For the first time in the history of the world, men were confusing materialism with progress and civilisation. Out of that confusion catastrophe and war would leap from a million open hearts in hundreds of Pittsburghs. The roar of the catastrophe was already gathering sound in every corner of the Western world.

The industrial revolution might very well produce not only a revolution in man's physical existence but in his moral and spiritual life as well—to his desperate peril.

On November 11, 1871, Stephen deWitt received a letter from Mr. Guy Gunther, senior member of The Gunther Company of New York, financiers and brokers of railroad stocks and bonds. The firm consisted of four brothers, all astute, genial, and rapacious. Guy had been Aaron deWitt's friend, and between them had been a guarded respect for each other's *entrepreneur* qualities. Friendship, however, had not stood in the way of one or two attempts on Guy's part to secure the controlling stock of the Interstate Railroad Company on a certain occasion of crisis, some years ago, before the Fielding money had come to the rescue. Nor had Aaron held this against his friend. It was all business.

Rufus had understood this completely, and had never borne any resentment against the powerful New York financier. Only Stephen, the impractical and honourable, had been angered and disgusted. He had hardly acknowledged the presence of Mr. Gunther at his father's funeral, to the intense if hidden amusement of Rufus and the other man. "Stephen is—incomprehensible," Guy had murmured to Rufus on one occasion, keeping his face solemn. "He is an idiot," Rufus had replied, equally as solemnly. Mr. Gunther had smiled, just a little, and had moved away, and Rufus had wondered, with discomfiture, if he had said something ridiculous.

The letter to Stephen was a masterpiece of discreet flattery, admiration, and kindness, and Stephen, to whom hypocrisy was an esoteric language, felt some of the hard affront in him soften. Mr. Gunther was to be in Philadelphia for a few days, "visiting some old friends." He and Stephen and Rufus had not met for quite a few years, and Mr. Gunther "wondered" if the two brothers would be in "the city" during his, Gunther's, visit. "It would be refreshing to see you both again, and talk about my dear friend Aaron."

Stephen read and reread the letter several times. It was after the sixth reading that he became uneasy. He asked his clerk to get him "Mr. Guy Gunther's file."

Rufus had read some of the "dossiers" on businessmen and even on casual acquaintances. Nothing was too small for Stephen to note, whether it was to the effect that a local banker had recently bought a new and more elaborate home, or that a lumberman had married off his daughter to a member of a Philadelphia Main Line clan, or a notation that a certain coal-mine operator near Scranton was "drinking too much, according to reports." He has the instincts of a small-town gossip, Rufus would think, enjoying himself.

The Gunther secret file was one of the thickest and heaviest, and Stephen devoted over two silent hours to the study of it.

A few weeks ago Mr. Gunther had "visited" in Chicago, where his wife had some distant American relatives. This interesting fact had been mentioned proudly in the Portersville evening paper, for had not Mr. Gunther been Mr. Aaron deWitt's friend, and had he not attended Mr. deWitt's funeral? It was over this last item that Stephen spent at least twenty brooding minutes. Then he asked his clerk to bring him the dossier of the Chicago Railroad System.

The Chicago Railroad System, though not as old and established as the Interstate Railroad Company, was considered as "sound" as such a railroad could be. "Railroading" was still a precarious business, dependent upon crops and conditions in the nation generally. But precarious as it was, a decline in railroad stocks could bring the threatened "panic" closer, could aggravate it enormously. Stephen knew the officers of the company, and admired them as men of integrity. The Interstate Railroad Company had considerable stock in the System. Stephen's last notation was to the effect that the System, manned by ambitious men, was planning to build an independent line from the Pittsburgh terminal to Philadelphia, thus carrying all traffic direct from Chicago to Philadelphia and possibly New York. However, Stephen had jotted down with relief, "They are not in a financial condition to do this, thus competing with us, possibly to a disastrous extent. Must watch carefully. Gunther might finance them? In spite of a feud between the company and Gunther? Hardly think so; they despise him." Another notation: "Who would finance them?"

Stephen read on. The System had "passed" its last dividend. Was their report of their "plans" merely an attempt to bolster faith in themselves in the eyes of the public? Of course, other railroads had "passed" not one but several dividends over the past three years, because of national conditions. The Interstate Railroad Company and the Chicago Railroad System had been almost alone in paying dividends recently.

Stephen read on, his thin brown brows knotted together. Was there a connection between Gunther's visit to Chicago and the Chicago Railroad System, and another connection with his desire to see the sons of his "dear old friend," Aaron deWitt? Stephen had had Chicago papers sent to him, and had studied them for any hints that Gunther had met the men from the System. There had been nothing at all. But Stephen continued to frown. Something was moving, somewhere. The Gunthers produced nothing except over-extended markets for railroad stock, or panics. It was a horrible thing, to Stephen, that financial pirates were able to create panics at will, for their own profit. He believed there was something terribly wrong in the structure of an economy if the food and wages and shelter of a whole people were at the mercy of the Gunthers and their kind.

Stephen put aside the file and stared through the window at the ashy November sky. A few ruffled pigeons fluttered against it. The knifelike mountain lifted itself in a dark blur over the city. A few flakes of snow brushed the windows. Behind Stephen the fire blustered on the hearth. The afternoon began to darken rapidly.

Stephen's first impulse was to call his brother into consultation, and to speculate with him on the whole matter. He kept nothing from Rufus now, as he had done before Aaron's death. His hand kept creeping to his bell, which would summon his clerk, and inexplicably his hand kept withdrawing. Why should he not call Rufus? Why should he not tell Rufus that he, Stephen, must go at once to Chicago with a set plan which entailed a bold movement? He told himself that it was because matters were still too vague.

He began to go over in his mind all that he intended to do. A sense of increasing and powerful danger came to him. If it were not for Gunther, thought Stephen. Then he confessed to himself that Gunther was just the precipitating element, though an unknown one. Something, eventually, would have to be done about the Chicago Railroad System. He had known this, and had shrunk from it, hoping constantly that the inevitable might be delayed or eliminated. Now the time had come.

At length he did ring his bell. His clerk, a quiet young man of the utmost discretion, entered, and Stephen said in a low voice, "I am leaving the city for a few days. Please go down to the station and arrange passage for me to Chicago, in the name of— let me see— a Mr. Dawson. I don't want to use our private car. For reasons known only to myself."

"Yes, Mr. deWitt," said the young man respectfully. "But when you are on the train, the crew will know you are there."

Stephen smiled a little. "Yes, of course. But the train will be pulling out then, and news of where I am going won't be back in the city for several days. After that, it won't matter." He paused. "Naturally no one—and I mean no one at all—must know where I am when I am absent. You understand that, Gruger?"

"Yes, sir," said Gruger gravely.

"The twelve thirty-two, to-night, then. Hardly anyone will be about." He drummed his fingers rigidly on the desk. "And now, will you ask Mr. Rufus to come in for a few moments, please?"

When Rufus entered, smiling, he was struck by his brother's face and expression. Stephen was extremely pale; his eyes were fixed and still. He watched Rufus as the latter moved across the big warm room, and he thought: This is a stealthy and insulting thing I am doing, and I don't know what impels me. He said, "Rufus, I am leaving to-night on the twelve-twenty for Scranton. I have an opportunity to buy up some more potential coal acreage."

Rufus seated himself on the edge of his brother's desk and he turned his head alertly. "Anything I should invest in?" he asked with interest.

Stephen was silent. He was himself concerned with negotiations for what seemed to be a very promising two hundred acres. He sighed. He must give Rufus this opportunity. It was only fair, he considered regretfully. In some way he must atone to his conscience for this mysterious deceit he was practising on his brother. He said, "Yes, I think so. Of course, it won't be developed for some years, but I can tell you that I've seen no better possibilities anywhere. Have I your permission to place an option on it in your name? You could give me a small cheque. . . ."

If "grey Stephen" thought the possibilities were excellent, then they must be so, thought Rufus with excitement. He expressed his gratitude, made out a cheque, and gave it to his brother. After he had left the office, Stephen called his clerk and dictated a letter to his attorney in Scranton, and enclosed Rufus's cheque. He reflected that the attorney would be considerably surprised.

Rufus, back in his own office, did not go on with his work for some time. He remembered Stephen's face. Something was going on about which Stephen had not told him. But what? While Stephen was absent, he intended to inspect the files secretly.

Stephen was about to put Guy Gunther's letter in the latter's file, when he stopped, again assailed by that sense of danger. He finally folded the letter in his pocket. He called his clerk and dictated a letter to Mr. Gunther. He expressed his hope that Mr. Gunther would visit Portersville the next week-end, after he, Stephen, returned from some pressing business in Fort Wayne. Mr. Gruger took the letter with no change of expression, and made no comment when Stephen asked him not to place the copy in Mr. Gunther's file.

What they have done to me, thought Stephen with weariness. I am no man for chicanery and deceit, and it is thrust upon me.

CHAPTER FIFTEEN

FOR THE second time Rufus read the letter addressed to him from Mr. Guy Gunther.

"I am writing this to you, dear Rufus, as Stephen has informed me he will be in Fort Wayne for a few days. He did not mention the date of his return to Portersville. He kindly invited me to spend next week-end with you both, as I had written him on a matter of importance. I find next week-end will be impossible for me, as I will be moving about among friends until next Thursday, and cannot go to Portersville until then. Will you please inform Stephen of this on his return home? I hope my change in plans will not discommode the family."

Rufus thoughtfully laid aside the letter and scowled. So the "grey weasel" had deliberately deceived him. Why had Stephen not only deceived him but Guy Gunther in the bargain? Such deceit meant something of enormous import, something connected with Guy Gunther. Rufus, who had full access to all the files now, brought out the Gunther "dossier," and having learned Stephen's method of close study, however he derided it, he sat down in his office and minutely went over every item in the file. The first thing he noticed was that Guy Gunther's letter was not in the file. This was of such significance that Rufus fastened all his attention on every item, looking for a clue. His alertness became acute when he saw that there was no copy of Stephen's alleged letter to Gunther. The dog had secreted not only Gunther's letter to him but his answer.

There was nothing in the file to arouse Rufus's new suspicions to a higher level. Idiot clippings of Gunther's recent sojourn in Chicago among friends! Of what importance was that? Rufus noted the names of these friends, and not one of them concerned the Interstate Railroad Company at all.

Then Rufus caught his breath. The Chicago Railway System! The Interstate Railroad Company was invested, in a measure, in that concern. Feverishly now, Rufus re-examined all the notations about Gunther. There was no mention that Gunther owned any stock in the Chicago company, not even the slightest hint. If he did own any stock, Stephen would have known of it, and written it down. Rufus sat back in his chair. The Chicago Railroad System had "passed" only one dividend. It was a good company; it was planning to expand. Stephen had explained all this to his brother only recently, and had remarked on the threat to the Interstate Railway Company. Had the threat become more imminent?

Of course! And Stephen had gone to Chicago. Why had he not told his brother? Why had he distrusted him? Rufus's face flushed with rage. Was he not executive vice-president of this damned company? What had occurred, what slip had he made, that had aroused that ugly and latent suspicion in Stephen's

144

mind? Was all the slow and tedious work of years lost, then? For a few minutes Rufus was more disturbed over this than the deception practised on him by Stephen.

Rufus had the sort of mind that made lightning deductions and came to swift conclusions. But he had learned from his brother the art of verifying everything. So he shrugged on his greatcoat and put his hard hat on his head and left the office. He went at once to the railroad station, and sought out the superintendent, who adored him.

George Hassen firmly believed, as did all other employees of the company, that if it were not for Mr. Rufus there would be no railroad. He also believed that Mr. Rufus had been "done wrong." He was an old and precise man, who had loved Aaron and despised, and had always despised, the silent and reserved Stephen. "If that one's a railroader, then I'm a coal miner!" he would say contemptuously. "It's a shame, a rotten shame, that old Aaron could've done that to Mr. Rufus, who's a born railroader, and got idees."

He received Rufus with flattered delight, and led him at once into his hot and gritty office overlooking the rails. Rufus sat down in his jovial, democratic way and offered the old man one of the cheroots in his silver case. An engine was letting off noisy jets of steam just under the dirty window, and so neither man could speak, but just sat there smiling affectionately at each other. At length, with much clanging and grinding, the engine moved off down to the switchyard. Now only large wet flakes of snow splashed themselves against the window.

"Ain't seen you lately, Mr. Rufus," said Hassen, pulling on the cheroot with pleasure after Rufus had lighted it for him. "We miss you down here."

"Too much work at the office, George," Rufus replied in a tone of apology. "You know how I like to visit you boys. How is Jed Thompson's hand, by the way?"

"Well, the couplin' pin lost him two fingers, sir, but that's the way it is. The boys kind of expect it; it's a sort of badge of railroadin'. I gave him your fifty dollars, and he sure was pleased. Set him right up. 'Knew Mr. Rufe wouldn't forget me,' he said."

Rufus with amusement reflected that Stephen had sent five hundred dollars to Jed Thompson, had paid his medical expenses, and had ordered his pay to go on after the accident. But the superintendent, and doubtless Jed Thompson, too, had either overlooked this generosity, or had suspected, wrongly, that Mr. Rufus was "behind it." Rufus leaned to the latter conclusion, in which he was quite correct. "I never forget any of our boys," said Rufus in a deep tone, which so moved Mr. Hassen that his cloudy eyes moistened.

It did not need money, it did not demand compassion or mercy or gentleness, to make these dogs lick your hand, thought Rufus. All that was necessary was an engaging smile, a lying word or two, a rollicking laugh. Stephen was a fool, a stupid fool. His dollars and his pity and his great love of humanity could elicit nothing more than hatred and contempt.

"How are things here, and in the roundhouse, George?" Rufus asked. "Everybody satisfied and comfortable?"

"Yes sir, yes sir!" exclaimed the old man enthusiastically. "You won't have strikes here, Mr. Rufe. No labour trouble long's you're here! The boys know you're their friend, yes sir!" He scowled and leaned forward. "Long's you're here, Mr. Rufe," he added significantly.

The two men smoked in an atmosphere of affection and mutual esteem. Then Rufus said, "By the way, did Steve leave a brief case on the train a few days ago—when he left for Chicago?" It was part of his spurious democracy that he always referred to his brother and to the directors of the company by their first names, when speaking to even the humblest of employees.

"A brief case? No, Mr. Rufe. Did he lose one?"

Rufus shook his head, smiling. He said evasively, "Well, he didn't say he would take it, though it contained valuable papers. But I haven't seen it around the office, and I was worried. Did he take the nine thirty-five, so he'd have to change in Philadelphia, or the twelve thirty-two? Maybe the brief-case was on the other train."

"Mr. Stephen took the twelve thirty-two," said Hassen. "I didn't know about it, though I was here then. But one of the boys told me. He was surprised; there wasn't no reservation for Mr. Stephen, and he didn't ask for the private car." He added, "There wasn't any brief-case, Mr. Rufe. It's probably home somewheres."

Rufus looked impatient. "I'll have to search again."

He held out his hand in his bluff and friendly way, sent a message to Mollie, Hassen's wife, and left the station.

So, he had been right. Stephen was in Chicago. And it all concerned the Chicago Railroad System, and Guy Gunther.

Was there a clue here for him? Had the time arrived for action? Guy Gunther had been deceived by Stephen, so Gunther was a formidable threat in Stephen's mind. Suppose he, Rufus, sent a telegram to Gunther, a friendly telegram, expressing his pleasure at the coming visit, and then casually mentioning that Stephen was in Chicago, and not in Fort Wayne. Would that bring Gunther immediately to Porterville, appreciative of the subtle hint? Could he and Gunther then conclude something of tremendous advantage to Rufus deWitt? It was an exciting idea, and had its drama and colour.

But Rufus had painfully learned from Stephen that effervescent ideas, based on nothing but intuition and a desire for flamboyant action, were not only foolish but sometimes dangerous. Rufus also reflected that Gunther was a very astute man, and that he would soon learn, from a few artful questions, that Rufus was ignorant of Stephen's purpose in going to Chicago. Gunther, like Stephen, dealt in drab hard facts. His opinion of Rufus would not be enhanced by his becoming aware that Stephen had kept his brother in ignorance.

Seated now in his carriage, Rufus again became anxious about some possible slip he must have made that had inspired the sleeping mistrust of his brother. He went over and over, in his mind, all occasions where there had been a little danger. He could not remember that he had ever been indiscreet. But men like Stephen had a nose for duplicity, even though it was an unconscious sense.

The snow had come early this year. Rufus could not see through the carriage windows, which had become plastered heavily with a wet whiteness. Ahead, the carriage lights poured in an uncertain golden tunnel through the howling and swirling flakes. Rufus could feel the coldness of the night through the windows of his vehicle and through the fur robe which covered his knees. Fires would be welcome, and a glass of whisky near the hearth, and the excellent meal which his brother's new cook was now preparing. Then, of course, there were the children, the two little five-year-old girls who would cling to him, Cornelia shouting and demanding to be the first in his arms, and Laura waiting with her grey eyes shining in her wan face. Rufus sincerely loved children, and his bitterness against his wife invariably increased to a cold rage when he considered how she had deprived him of more daughters, and sons. There were occasions when he regretted that he had not accepted her suggestion for a divorce.

Stephen was due home to-night, or the next night. If this snow keeps up the trains will be very late, Rufus reflected impatiently. He could feel the lurching of the carriage, the pounding of the wind at the windows. His feet were becoming cold, and he did not like this riding through nothingness. He took a cigar from his pocket and lit it; the rich aroma comforted him, and the tiny coal lightened the darkness.

He continued, at intervals, to peer through the windows at the raging night, and it was with a profound sensation of relief that he finally caught a glimpse of the house high on its mountainside, its great yellow lights streaming out into the night. In a few minutes the carriage swung into the circle of the driveway, and the exhausted horses quickened their trot. Rufus, not waiting for the coachman, opened the carriage door himself, so eager was he to be inside the house, and safe from the blackness and the nothingness.

It was part of his theatrical instinct that had made him ceremoniously deliver up his keys to his brother shortly after Aaron's death. It had embarrassed and distressed Stephen, and Rufus had watched him with malicious pleasure. "Frankly," Rufus had said, knowing that Stephen would detect the "brave" lie, "I prefer to have the door opened for me. More dignity, you know. Besides, what are servants for?" So, Rufus, to-night, rang the bell as usual, and waited. The door opened almost at once, and Seth, the butler, admitted him with a smile of concern. "You were late, Mr. Rufus, and we were all worried."

Rufus glanced about the beautiful hall with satisfaction. For a man who loved change and movement and mobility, he was singularly susceptible to the changeless. In the business of running a railroad he was "progressive." In the business of living he was happily conservative. There were people who were changing candlelighted chandeliers into flaring gas globes, but Rufus preferred the chandelier in this white-and-gold panelled hall with its aureate flames. He loved the pale and delicate furniture, the fire on the small white hearth, the Aubusson rugs, the scent of flowers, burning apple wood and wax.

148

Never Victorious, Never Defeated

Seth relieved him of his bowler and his fur-collared coat and gloves. He paused for a moment to rub his hands near the fire; then, smiling, he entered the drawing-room and looked about him expectantly. As he had hoped, there was a rush of young footsteps towards him, and the hoarse, childish shout of Cornelia. Two little girls, Cornelia leading, raced in his direction, with outflung arms, Cornelia all red-gold and brilliance, pink-dimpled and laughing, and Laura, small and pale and gently smiling, with dark ringlets on her blue-velvet shoulders. It was Laura whom Rufus caught up first, though she reached him last, and he held her to him tightly, feeling the frail bones through the velvet, the thin and clinging arms. Perhaps he loved her alm' st as much as he did his daughter because he had saved her life, or perhaps in so many ways she resembled Lydia in her gravity, in her smile, in the large and quiet shining of her eyes. He kissed her tenderly, set her down, and then he picked up his tall and heavy little daughter who bossed him heartily. The thick curls almost smothered him, the strong arms choked off his breath. Crying out in laughing protest, he held her away from him, looking fondly into that round and highly-coloured infantile face with its radiant hazel eyes and big scarlet mouth. A beauty, his daughter, a robust, warm beauty, already charming and magnetic and spoiled, but delightful!

He put down Cornelia, took each little girl by the hand, and advanced into the room. Sophia was grimly sewing by the fire, and Lydia was reading. Both women glanced up at him, Sophia with a visible softening of her harsh face, and Lydia with her elliptical smile. Both presented a cheek for his kiss; Sophia clung to his arm for a moment, pressing it. "You're late, son," she remarked in her rough voice.

Rufus sat down on the yellow sofa near the fire, and the two little girls sat near him, as close as possible, Cornelia almost sprawling across his knees, Laura content to lie against his shoulder. He patted each head contentedly, and then talked of the storm to the women. Sophia listened to his pleasant comments as though each word was of absorbing importance; Lydia gave him her attention politely. The butler brought wine for the ladies and whisky for Rufus. The great fire blustered on the hearth, and the wind blustered at the windows. Lamplight threw golden pools and shadows on carpet, walls, and ceiling. Rufus felt almost at peace. Now, if only Lydia were truly his wife, and there were more children whose faces reflected the firelight and candlelight, safe here within these strong and beautiful walls from the night outside! Rufus was not one to be satisfied with half a loaf; he had too much vitality for compromise. Slowly, though he smiled at Cornelia and Laura, and talked with his mother and wife, his eyes became brooding. Once or twice they touched Lydia, and he thought: I should have let her divorce me.

As if she felt his thought, Lydia looked up, and her face was clouded with compassion and sadness. She turned to the fire and said to herself: Poor Rufus. He has so much life and power, and he has expressed it here only in one little daughter. I ought to have gone away; he would have forgotten me and there would be another woman in this house now, a woman as strong and as full of gusto as himself, who would have given him a home full of children, a woman all gaiety and as completely conscienceless as he is.

Why did I stay? I could have returned to my parents' house and have spent my life under those dreaming trees and in that timeless enchantment. Perhaps I stayed because I could not have taken Cornelia with me. Perhaps it was because of Laura, who would have been as lost here as her father. Or perhaps—and this made her start a little with profound wonder—I stayed to help Rufus himself.

"What can Stephen be doing so long in Scranton?" Sophia was asking with contempt. "He is always buying up worthless land there, and talking of coal. In the meantime, the land isn't being developed, and he pays taxes on it. He never did understand such things."

Rufus laughed shortly. "Don't underestimate old Steve. One of these days those acres of coal will be profitable. It's just a matter of time."

"If it weren't for you, son, ' time ' would eat up all our profits and the railroad would be in bankruptcy!" exclaimed Sophia with a toss of her head.

Rufus was bored; his mother's comments never varied. He had grown tired of tedious complaints against his brother, and had tired of fending them off with artificial laughter. He sipped his whisky, played with the strong red curls of his clamorous little daughter, smiled down at the quiet Laura. He frequently found adults tiresome; children always charmed him. He wished his mother would be quiet.

Never Victorious, Never Defeated

Lydia was unobtrusively studying her husband. He might yawn, might be genuinely bored with his mother, but there was something hidden and alert about him. Underneath his yawns, his tenderness with the children, his relaxation, something was moving restlessly. A faint but familiar sensation of alarm came to her.

Rufus was throwing back his leonine head in laughter at some remark of Cornelia's. As the child had not intended to be amusing at that moment, her pretty face changed into an expression of ferocity, and she began to beat on her father's chest with her pink fists. This further amused Rufus, and he swung her up high into the air where she kicked and punched impotently, and then dissolved into a shout of mirth. He let her down and hugged her, and smiled over the seething curls at his mother. "The little rascal," he said with fondness. "She makes up the most lovable lies, and when I catch her in them she is furious. But only for a moment or so."

There was sharpness in Lydia's voice. "Cornelia, stop laughing so madly. You'll be ill."

The child was instantly quiet, but she grinned affectionately at her mother, and Lydia could not help smiling in return. Cornelia then bounded off her father's knees and ran to Lydia, where she swarmed up on her lap. Lydia kissed her admonishingly. They were a charming sight, the dark thin woman in her maroon-velvet dress, and the sturdy little girl, all burnish and crimson silk, their faces pressed together, one slim and pale, the other blazing with life. Rufus, without jealousy, watched them, in content. But Sophia cried, "Cornelia! Come to Grandma."

Cornelia, even at five and a half, was too much of a diplomat to disobey. She might have a secret aversion for her grandmother, and resent the touch of her hard hands, but she immediately slid from her mother's knees and ran at once to Sophia, who gathered her up hungrily in her bony arms. Cornelia never forgot the scent of her grandmother, a scent compounded of camphor and peppermint and old flesh.

There was the sound of the hall door opening to the turn of a key, and then a gush of cold air raced into the living-room. Rufus straightened alertly. "It must be Steve," he said, and now he forgot both the children and stood up. Cornelia bounced from the arms of Sophia and cried shrilly, "Uncle Stevie!" and darted into the hall like a small image of flame. Laura, with a slight smile, climbed down from the sofa and followed Cornelia sedately and in silence.

A cold film flowed over Lydia's face, and she picked up her book again. Sophia and Rufus exchanged glances that were automatically significant, as they always did when Stephen was about to join them.

Stephen, drawn and grey, smiled at the little girls approaching him, one with a loud, bold demand for an immediate kiss, and one with a small hand held out. He came into the drawing-room, haggard and worn and stooped. His mother regarded him militantly, muttered a greeting; Lydia murmured courteously. But Rufus approached with a broad smile and held out his large warm hand, which Stephen shook lifelessly. The children hovered at Stephen's knees, looking up at him with eager attention.

"Welcome home," said Rufus amiably. "And how was Scranton? Did you buy that property for me?"

Stephen's tired features became more tired. But he fixed his eyes sombrely on his brother. "I sent your cheque to my agent in Scranton, Rufus. You now have the option."

Rufus raised his tawny eyebrows and waited.

Stephen sighed. "You see, I didn't go to Scranton after all. I went to Chicago. There was no sense in telling you before, because what I suspected might have been a delusion. It wasn't. It is a fact. After dinner, Rufus, we must go to the library for a long talk."

Rufus did not know whether to be profoundly relieved or disappointed now that his brother had told him of his true destination. So, he merely smiled. Stephen smiled also, a rueful ghost of a smile. "I didn't leave my brief-case on the train, Rufus," he said; and now, to Rufus's mortified confusion, Stephen's eyes actually danced a little as if with sad mirth and understanding.

The lamps burned yellow in the library until long after midnight. Stephen had stopped talking; he was running his hands wearily over his drained face. "So that is how it is," he said lifelessly. Rufus, who had listened without a word, stared at the fire. He was conscious of profound satisfaction and excitement. Then he thought: I've underestimated him, all these years. He is going to be very hard to overthrow.

CHAPTER SIXTEEN

RUFUS, WHO had learned much from Stephen, sometimes found his self-restraint frustrating. The bold stroke, the flair, the quicksilver drama, of which he was so fond, and which were part of his nature, must sometimes be subordinated to figures and quiet statements which were not only safe but profitable. Adventure had its place; but facts were insurmountable if tedious. Yet Rufus had to admit that when Stephen did move there was more weight and power behind his quietness, and even more drama, than in histrionic fanfares propelled by wind.

So Rufus, always ready with the flamboyant word, the eloquent gesture, remained almost silent during much of the conversation between Stephen and Guy Gunther.

The financier had arrived on a November day of bright snow and brilliant gales, and he said, when received at home by the two brothers, "I congratulate you for your decision to live here rather than in Philadelphia or New York. I never saw such glorious weather." He smiled approvingly at Stephen, gave a more cordial smile to Rufus. He went to one of the windows of the drawing-room and silently admired the blue mountains, the shining skies, and the white earth, and the turquoise river under its shell of ice. Privately, he told himself that this static quiet and immobility would drive him mad.

"Shall we have luncheon, sir?" asked Stephen in his low and unemphatic voice.

Mr. Gunther turned from the window, but he looked at Rufus, and what he saw pleased him. A few years ago Rufus would have joined him at the window and would have described the scene fully for him, in extravagant words. The new Rufus merely waited at his brother's side, smiling agreeably; yet he was watchful. Ever watchful, thought Mr. Gunther with admiration. He's learned very fast, and that shows a mobility of mind. He is becoming a very dangerous young man, and I need, and can use, dangerous men who are not all pyrotechnics and rainbow bubbles. Mr. Gunther went to the two brothers, linked his arms in theirs, smiled up at them, and said graciously, "Luncheon, of course."

He was a short and rotund man, with a full and benevolent face. Though he was only forty-eight, his head was almost completely bald. The remaining fringe of his hair was light brown. His really fine eyes were an innocent blue, without craftiness or guile, and below them were set a wide, pudgy nose and a full smiling mouth. His whole appearance, in spite of the fine black broadcloth of his clothing, the black silk cravat anchored with a conservative gold lover's-knot pin, and his plain white linen, suggested the unworldly cherub. He had a modestly charming manner, carefully cultivated, of spontaneous openheartedness and candour, and he conducted his sometimes deadly affairs with humour and a mendacious air of frank reasonableness.

At the luncheon table, seated between Rufus and Stephen (the ladies were not present), Mr. Gunther chatted pleasantly about his wife and family, told anecdotes that were so subtly ribald that even the haggard Stephen smiled, and related tales of Aaron that made Rufus shout with laughter. It was all part of Mr. Gunther's stage setting of prediscussion agreeableness, and it was so skilfully done that few ever suspected its deliberateness. Stephen was one of the few, and Mr. Gunther knew it, and admired him for it.

After the very excellent luncheon, which Mr. Gunther enjoyed fully, the three gentlemen went into the library. Stephen had brightened the gloomy room with rose-velvet draperies and fires and a few pieces of attractive furniture, and as he used it often, it was no longer musty and dreary. The high wide windows were like pictures set into the book-lined walls, all vivid with wintry landscapes. Brandy had been set out, and the butler, Seth, was waiting to serve the gentlemen. A lusty fire roared on the hearth. Mr. Gunther, honestly appreciative at having been served exquisitely in this "Godforsaken outland," settled himself near the hearth and sipped at the excellent brandy and beamed on his hosts. Very good, he thought; we're mellow. He liked mellowness, for business conducted in such an atmosphere rarely became raucous or angry.

He noticed that Stephen had only a little brandy, and he remembered that Stephen had drunk no whisky before the luncheon and had barely touched the wine at the table. Rufus was slightly watery of eye, but Gunther was pleased to see that the younger brother had not become confidential or indiscreet, as he had once done under the influence of alcohol. Definitely, I shall be able to use him to our mutual advantage in the future, thought Gunther.

"How was Fort Wayne, Steve?" asked Mr. Gunther. He puffed at a fine cigar which Rufus had given him. His small black boots glittered in the mingled sunshine and firelight.

Rufus watched his brother. Without colouring or flinching, Stephen said softly and calmly, "I'm sorry, Mr. Gunther. I changed my mind." He looked at the brandy in his glass. "I went, instead, to Chicago."

That was the way to do it, thought Rufus. No dramatic announcement. It is really effective then. Mr. Gunther was carefully putting down his brandy glass; his every motion was slow and thoughtful. And now he was regarding Stephen with mild surprise. The intensely blue eyes had become slightly narrowed and the smile that remained in them was the reflection of sunlight on mountain ice.

"Chicago? Well. And how was the weather there?"

"Very bad." Stephen gave a rather banal description. He spoke listlessly and without apparent interest. But Mr. Gunther's round and pudgy body had tensed. Stephen continued: "While there, I visited my friends at the Chicago Railroad System."

"A very ambitious concern," remarked Mr. Gunther. He chuckled. "Did they mention to you, by any chance, their still nebulous plans to build an independent line from Pittsburgh terminal to Philadelphia, which will carry all direct traffic from Chicago to Philadelphia and probably New York?"

"Yes," said Stephen quietly, "they did."

Mr. Gunther smiled tolerantly. "And did they reveal to you how that would be almost ruinous to your own road?"

Stephen sighed. "I didn't need their revelation; I knew."

Silence engulfed the library. During it, Mr. Gunther turned to Rufus, who was very serious, and whose hazel eyes refused to meet the eyes of the other.

Mr. Gunther was always delicate in his approach. He finally echoed Stephen's sigh. This amused Rufus, but he kept his face straight. "I should hate to see my old friend's company—injured," murmured Mr. Gunther in a distressful tone. "Is there anything I can do, Stephen?"

Stephen did not speak for a moment or two. Now there was a

flush on his sunken cheeks. He gazed at Mr. Gunther coldly and steadily. "No, sir," he said, and all his words were evenly spaced, "there is nothing you can do. Now."

Excellent, thought Rufus. Mr. Gunther had lost a little of his infantile colouring; the pleasant expression was a little too fixed.

"Well," said Mr. Gunther, spreading out his fat pink hands, "I'm glad you don't need my help, Steve." He waited tentatively, but Stephen did not reply.

Old Steve's left the way open to him to reveal himself, thought Rufus. If he does not, this will end with Guy in the extreme dark, and his visit will resolve into nothing. The next move is up to him; he can take it or leave it, and he knows.

Mr. Gunther was making up his mind rapidly. He disliked "coming to the point," himself. He preferred, by indirection, by suggestion, to force others into that position. But Stephen, apparently, was not going to be forced.

So Mr. Gunther said, with an open and blunt kindness, "You were always friendly with the fellers of the Chicago Railroad System, Steve. Can you tell me—confidentially, of course—if they are going to carry out their plans?"

"They are, Mr. Gunther," replied Stephen with some stiffness.

Rufus began to enjoy himself; he was not going to be completely deprived of drama after all. The financier leaned forward on the mound of his belly, and the cherubic features hardened and all his voracity stood avidly in his eyes.

"And—Steve—you can't stop them?"

"No, I cannot." Steve was beginning to show uneasiness, and Mr. Gunther contemplated him in shrewd silence. Have I underestimated him? he thought. Is he as intelligent and far-sighted as I believed? Mr. Gunther slowly turned his head towards Rufus, who had assumed a sober expression. Cautiously, Mr. Gunther extended that sixth sense of his into the atmosphere; something was happening, and he did not like it though he did not know what it was.

He sat back in his chair and looked reflective. He smoked calmly. Stephen was studying his boots as if completely uninterested. Then Mr. Gunther began to chuckle richly: "We can stop them, or at least delay them, if you wish, Steve," he said in a voice that almost purred. "And make ourselves considerable money in the process."

"How?" asked Stephen. His flush had returned. He was not a man for this cat-and-mouse game, even with Gunther. The sick softening with which he was so familiar began to gnaw at the edges of his ancient dislike of the financier. He could never learn to enjoy outwitting other men, liked or disliked; it gave him no exultation to demolish even an enemy. Always there was that damnable compassion of his, pouring like warm syrup over his sternest resolutions, blurring the stonelike edges of them in nauseous stickiness.

Before Mr. Gunther could answer his short question, Stephen put down his brandy glass so hastily that the liquid tilted and ran over his hand. He wiped his hand, and his voice was unusually quick and tremulous:

"Mr. Gunther, you, like so many others, play games. You do business, but you like the sharp pounce, the pleasure of the hunt, the stunning manipulation. I'm not like that. So, in my own fashion, which no doubt you consider drab, I'll tell you all you are angling to know."

Mr. Gunther was not taken aback, for he knew Stephen very well. But he was amused at what he saw in those hunted eyes now turned so desperately upon him. It was compassion for him, Guy Gunther, because he, Stephen deWitt, was about to "hurt" him. "What do I want to know, Steve? I confess I don't understand you."

"You do understand, Mr. Gunther, and that is why you are here," said Stephen. He was angered at what he had seen in Mr. Gunther's face, and wounded. It was the old old story; he extended compassion, or mercy, and it was received with ridicule and disdain. I never learn, he thought.

"You went to Chicago some time ago, Mr. Gunther," Stephen continued, speaking monotonously so that no emotion would betray him in his voice. "You went for one purpose: to discover all you could about the Chicago Railway System, and talk with your friends about that System, and to lay a plot against an honourable group of men. And then you saw that you needed us, the Interstate Railroad Company. You realised that we had an interest in the System, because you knew that we had some plans to lay a parallel line from Pittsburgh to Chicago, which would compete with the Chicago System. You knew that we were in much the better position, financially, than our Chicago friends."

Very slowly, as Stephen was speaking, Mr. Gunther forced himself to relax in his chair, though rage and consternation were gathering blackly in his mind. He managed one of his angelic smiles, allowing it to spread in tender light over his round face. Then it stood in his eyes, which sparkled.

"Assuming all this is true, Steve," he said gently, "how did you know?"

"I keep a dossier on everybody, Mr. Gunther." Stephen's voice was full of hard distress, and now he looked at the other man. "Your dossier is very detailed and extensive. I've never trusted you."

"I'm sorry, Steve," and Mr. Gunther's tone was deeply regretful. "You never understood about your father and me. I thought you had finally realised, but it seems that I was mistaken."

He's putting Steve on the defensive, thought the inwardly laughing Rufus. He saw that Stephen's fingers were clenched together, and that he was sweating with misery over what he was doing to Mr. Gunther. But Stephen, when he spoke again, spoke with quiet compactness: "You can't deceive me, Mr. Gunther. You can't make me feel guilty. I'm sorry you are forcing me to talk like this."

Mr. Gunther sipped at his brandy. Over the rim of his glass, his eyes were thoughtful. "Do go on with your—explanation," he suggested kindly.

"I am not 'explaining,' sir. I am merely trying to save you time, so you won't make the mistake of stalking me. You needed us; you knew we had an interest in the System; you knew that the projected new line of the System would injure us. So you and your firm thought we would accede to your carefully laid plan of depressing the stock of the System, and then buying it up and gaining control of that road. And then, in talking with your friends in Chicago, you discussed financing an independent line from Pittsburgh east. By that time, you considered, the System would be in the hands of your company, and the independent line would ruin our company. Perhaps you even contemplated seizing control of us. I am sure you did."

If Mr. Gunther felt horror, dismay, fury, and defeat, he did not reveal them. He continued to smile at Stephen, as at a precocious younger brother who had aroused his admiration by a particularly magical trick. "I am not admitting anything, my dear boy," he said. "I am only interested in your speculations."

158

Never Victorious, Never Defeated

"They are not speculations, sir." In spite of himself, Stephen's voice was becoming a trifle high and vehement. "They are facts, and you know it. Shall I go on?

"I went to Chicago to see if I could avert what you had in mind. I was not trying to 'outwit' you at your own game. I was concerned with keeping the System out of your hands, to the ruin of the stockholders, who never concern you at any time. I was concerned with keeping the company solvent, for they are friends of mine; and their projected line, though it would compete with ours, was not planned out of greed but only out of honest competition. Naturally, I was alarmed about the threat to the prosperity of our own Company, and so I made a very advantageous agreement with the System."

"Did you?" asked Mr. Gunther softly.

"I did, sir. Confronted with the fact that the System was planning to compete with us openly and honestly, but to our disadvantage, I brought to their attention how you were plotting to ruin them, and I asked the president to call his board of directors. I put the matter up to them frankly. I asked them to give us a 999-year lease on their right of way, guaranteed to pay the indebtedness on the line and a rental fee. If they did not accede, and remained blind to your plot, we would have to build a parallel line from Pittsburgh to Chicago, in sheer self-defence." He paused. "I have the lease, and all agreements, in my brief-case."

He leaned back, sickened and exhausted, and began to stare through one of the library windows. A new snowstorm was gathering: dark clouds massed themselves over the mountains. The earth became stark and flat under a lemon-coloured sky.

Mr. Gunther was silent. He had had some few defeats before, but never one so final, so complete, so humiliating. This yokel had manipulated matters with pure genius, which Mr. Gunther knew involved not only imagination and daring, but extraordinary power. How much had Rufus to do with this?

The astute Mr. Gunther said to himself: Rufus didn't know. He would have been all for my idea; he would have seen the immediate mutual advantage of an alliance with me. The long-range view is not his. It was done by Steve, and only by Steve.

His wrath and mortification were beginning to give him a violent headache, and he was vaguely concerned. The luncheon he had eaten was a mass of stones in his belly. But his face remained kind and open, and his eyes continued to smile.

"Your thesis about my devilishness is very interesting, Steve. I like the way you develop 'plots.' Naturally, I shall not either admit or deny the whole fabric. I'm a little flattered, though, about your belief in my omniscience. Let me congratulate you on a very fine piece of business. Your father could not have done better."

Stephen stood up abruptly, "I am afraid that I am going to make a rude request. I don't sleep well on trains. I am very tired. I must lie down for a while, so I beg you to excuse me, sir. Shall we meet at dinner?"

"Indeed, yes, my boy," replied Mr. Gunther solicitously. He stood up, and smiled at Stephen with creamy affection. "Have you a headache? I have some tablets. These business affairs are sometimes tiring, I know. Sleep well. And to-night I shall enjoy a pleasant dinner with your ladies."

He and Rufus watched in silence as Stephen went out of the room with his ambling and awkward walk. Then Mr. Gunther sat down again in his chair and resumed his smoking. Rufus stood before the fire and appeared to be very interested in it. Long moments passed. Wind rumbled at the windows.

Then Mr. Gunther spoke in the softest of voices: "Rufe, you and I, someday, must have a long conference. A very long conference."

Rufus turned slowly and looked down at his guest. Mr. Gunther was smiling, and there was a cunning twinkle in his eyes. Rufus smoothed down his mane of fiery hair and smiled in return. "I am hoping for that," he said gravely. "Yes, I am hoping for that."

CHAPTER SEVENTEEN

THE RELATIONSHIP of Lydia and Sophia had, over the years, congealed into polite hostility. When Lydia had come as a bride to the house on the mountain there had never been too much friendliness between the two women, but Sophia had respected Lydia's dignity and had never attempted any intimacy. The respect had grown over a period of ten years, so that now Sophia was sometimes afraid of her daughter-in-law, whom she intensely disliked. There was something else about Lydia, and that was the art of noncommunication, a repelling of any warmth or human approach. It is because she feels so secure as one of the "Fielding girls," Sophia thought with anger. She preens herself without reason. She is contented with the illusion that she is important, and probably does not know that some people laugh at her.

No one laughed at Lydia deWitt, in spite of Sophia's malicious belief. Like Sophia, they were afraid of this disinterested and beautiful woman, who courteously refused to become embroiled in social affairs except on rare occasions. They might whisper to themselves about Rufus's justifiable "indiscretions," but when they were with Lydia they fawned upon her and were eagerly grateful for her company.

During the past two years, Lydia had demonstrated, to Sophia's satisfaction at least, that her "queerness" was increasing. She had taken to long and lonely walks on the mountain roads at night. She would be gone as much as three hours at a time, and when she returned her face would be flushed, or very pale, and her eyes would either be too strained and bright, or brooding. Sophia noticed that these walks occurred only when Rufus was away from Portersville. When Rufus was home, Lydia dutifully remained there, the quiet but friendly wife. Once Sophia had mentioned those walks to Rufus, but he only smiled and shrugged.

Lydia's walks invariably ended in a spot she considered peculiarly her own. She returned always to the place which she had loved as a child, and which she would always love.

One approached it by leaving the mountain road, turning past a distant wood of ancient elms, climbing a knoll where dark spruces stood tall and thick against the sky, descending to a tiny valley where a stream flowed towards the river, then pushing through a thicket of wild honeysuckle and blackberry bushes. One emerged on to a hidden glade of thick soft grass in the centre of which was a mound shaded by silver birch trees. No one came to this spot, where, in spring, it was sweet with dogwood and wild lilacs, and golden with forsythia, all forming a towering hedge about it. A thin arm of the stream ran along one side of it until the hottest part of summer. Lydia would eat of the wild

L

strawberries which lay in the grass like rubies, and would break off the branches of the lilacs which seemed to her more intoxicating than those in the garden of Stephen's house. Wild roses grew in the thicket, and tawny field lilies, and tangles of black-eyed daisies. No cattle could wander here, and in so far as Lydia ever knew, no one ever visited its isolation.

Since her marriage she had rarely gone to the glade during the day. During her girlhood it had been her fortress in the hot summer noons, for the trees, shrubs, and thicket kept it always in blue shade. As she had grown older, and before her marriage, she had taken to visiting it at night, when, lying on her back on the low mound, she could fancy herself in an enchanted fairy ring, safe from any intruder, safe from any voice or laughter. She would look up at the sailing moon, or at the cool blaze of stars, and a sense of security would come to her which no house could ever give, and no walls could offer.

Sometimes, during the warm nights, she would fall asleep to the murmur of the little stream, the air scented all about her, the wind in the birches. She would awaken refreshed and renewed, able to resume the burden of a life daily growing more barren and dusty. She was never lonely here, as she was when at home, or among guests. Everything comforted her, the trees, the flowers, the trickle of bright water in the grass, the secret sky, the humming of insects, the quiet breezes. When autumn came, and the glade turned bronze and scarlet and gold, she would feel an intense sadness, a warning of banishment. If she looked towards spring impatiently, it was for the protection of her glade, her flight into herself. Hardly had the snows melted, and the ice thinned on the mountains, when she returned, careless of wet boots and skirts, and looking eagerly for the first blaze of the forsythia, the first violets in the grass.

It was two years ago that her shelter had been invaded.

She never forgot that night of leaping moon and scent and silence. She had gone there, and had seated herself on the mound with a sigh of deep content, the thicket walls closing behind her. A few dark clouds moved across the sky. The crescent moon, abnormally large and radiant, had suddenly plunged like a sabre into a cloud, only its shining upper edge visible. Lydia had watched, fascinated. Then, to her great alarm, she had heard the thicket snapping and crackling, and the shadowy figure of a very tall men had appeared, faceless in the quick gloom. She could see his mighty shoulders, his large bare head. He said nothing. He only stood there in silence. The moon withdrew its sword from the cloud and threw down a shower of pale light into the glade. Now everything turned a ghostly silver, trees, shrubs, grass, distant mountains, and the woman sitting in affronted and dismayed silence on the mound. The billows of her smoke-grey muslin dress foamed about her, and her bare shoulders glimmered like white stone in the spectral rays of brilliant moonlight.

She could feel the affrightened quickening of her heart, and she finally said sharply, "Who is it? What do you want?"

"Hallo, Lydia," replied the man in a rough and grating voice. He advanced towards her, his great body lumbering and slow like the body of a beast.

She recognised him now, for the moonlight revealed his face. "Jim," she said. "Jim Purcell."

Her heart, instead of quieting, began to race harder. He sat down on the mound beside her, and folded his big arms around his knees. He stared at the thicket through which he had come, and said nothing. Lydia had always believed that if she ever discovered that someone else had found this place it would lose its enchantment for her, that she would feel it had been desecrated and that she could come here no more. But no sense of outrage struck her now, no stir of disappointment or depression.

Crickets clattered loudly in the silence; there was a shrilling of insects in the woods beyond the glade. Now the fragrance of a disturbed earth, fecund, warm, and mysterious, rose up about the woman and the man who sat there so still together. The moonlight struck on the distant mountain peak and turned it into a cone of pale fire.

"How did you find this place, Jim?" asked Lydia, and her voice was gentle.

"Why, Lydia," he answered, "I always knew you came here. Since you were a kid. Remember? I used to follow you around, since we were knee-high to ducks." He reached in his pocket for a pipe, struck a lucifer. The orange glow illuminated his gross and pitted face, and Lydia saw it was full of gravity and contentment. She did not find him repellent; she had never found him so.

She could hear the sweet tinkle of her mother's voice: "But my darling, such a brute! So stupid, my love, and so poor. He shambles, love, and his boots are muddy, and he stares at you like an idiot, truly. How can you endure him?" Her father had said in his frail and patrician voice, "But my pet, Lydia cannot endure him at all. She is only sorry for the poor creature. He has trailed her for years, and she gives him a kind glance occasionally, as one would give a lost and mongrel dog."

I never wanted to hurt them, thought Lydia. I did not know, then, that it is sometimes necessary to hurt others if you are to save your own soul. She had told Jim Purcell not to come again, that her parents did not like him, and that she would never wound them. Now something began to ache in her like a desolation and an unbearable sadness.

"Guess you always did like me, Lydia, at that," Purcell rumbled. "Even now. It kind of gives me a comfort when you look at me across a room."

Lydia's eyes began to smart. She said, and her voice trembled, "How long ago did you find out that I came here, Jim?"

"Why, Lydia"—and his tone, though harshly accented, was almost gentle—"I've known all the time. I would be sittin' here, thinkin', and then I'd hear you rustlin', and I'd dive out the other side, and you'd sit down on this mound. For hours. And I'd be watchin' you." He turned to her, and the pits and swollen masses of his face became illuminated with a smile in the moonlight. "But I never let you know it was my place, as well as yours."

There was a tightness in Lydia's throat, and a tightness in her heart. The glade swam in dim shadow about her. "Why did you let me know—to-night, Jim?" she asked.

"Well, Lydia, I've come to the conclusion that things are gettin' out of hand with you. Thought you ought to know you have a friend. Don't know, yet, just what I can do for you, but I'm here, Lydia, any time you need me." His huge hard hand touched hers for a single moment, then withdrew. "A rude, uncultured man," he was privately called. "A dolt. How did he ever get so rich? But, of course, he's absolutely ruthless and without conscience. And viciously greedy and merciless."

Lydia knew that he was not "uncultured." If he spoke "rudely," it was because of the contempt in which he held the delicate mountebanks and polite buccaneers. If he was ruthless, and Lydia knew he was, it was an open ruthlessness, unlike that of her husband's. That was why she had never held Jim Purcell in aversion during these later years when he had plunged doggedly, and like an elemental force, towards wealth and power. If he was guilty of unethical machinations, and if he crushed weaker men, in his primeval passage, he did it with a contemptuous and potent honesty, with no feeble justifications, with no pious homilies and pretensions.

He was smoking placidly; the little red fire of his pipe waned and glowed. She could see his big shapeless mouth, the crudely fashioned nose, the small lightless eyes. An ugly man, a monstrous man, in a way. Yet, all at once, to the sudden racing of her heart, he appeared to her to be all strength and command.

"I think I always knew you were my friend," she said. Without volition, her hand lifted and touched his arm timidly. He did not move. His bulky legs were splayed without grace in the light of the moon; his shoulders were mountainous. The pipe continued to wane and glow tranquilly.

"How long are you going to stand it, Lydia?" he asked, not looking at her.

She folded her hands in her soft muslin-draped lap. Her honesty rose to meet his, with all simplicity. "I don't know," she answered. "I offered Rufus a divorce years ago. I have been thinking lately, of going to live in my own house." She paused.

"Well, why don't you?"

"Because he would never allow me to take Cornelia with me. And I must be with her, to do what I can."

He chuckled roughly. "Lydia, you'll never be able to do anythin' for that little girl, and you know it. She's just like her dad."

"But she's also a female," said Lydia, and her voice thickened with pain. "And women aren't usually as conscienceless as men. She's a very reasonable child, at times, and I love her dearly, and she loves me. I must do what I can for her,"

"Umph." He withdrew the pipe from his mouth and the smoke curled up, caught in a silver mist in the moonlight. "Yes, I suppose the kid does love you. I've seen you both, in your carriage, when you didn't see me. But you've got to remember that love doesn't change people's fundamental character, Lydia."

"I don't want her to grow up knowing her mother deserted her," said Lydia pleadingly. "Later on, many years later, she may use that as a hypocritical defence of any wickedness she does."

"And maybe she'll grow up despisin' a mother who didn't have the guts to save her own soul," said Purcell.

165

Lydia did not speak for a few moments. Her face had grown hot, and there were tears in her eyes. Then she said, "Cornelia's only seven years old. I must stay a while."

He knocked his pipe on a stone. He turned towards her, and she saw his enormous face and the piercing scrutiny of his tiny eyes. "That isn't the only reason, Lydia. There's old Steve. You're watchin' to see that Red Rufe doesn't do him in? Right, old girl?"

"Yes," she answered.

"H'm. But Rufe will do it, y'know. Maybe any day. He's a clever one, that Rufe. The panic's on, and it doesn't seem to be passin', and Rufe's busy. I've been watchin' him, myself, trying to guess what he's up to. But he's like a fast and expert dancer, and I just lumber a few feet behind. Well, anyway, he's movin' fast now. He's not sayin' anythin'; didn't say anythin' even when old Steve went right on payin' the workers' wages when there isn't much movin' on the railroads these days. But there he is, smilin' like a cat what's got its paws into the cream, and he's lickin' them." He added reflectively, "Interstate passed the last three dividends, and Rufe just goes on smilin'. He's been down to New York six times in the past two months, talkin' to Gunther."

"Why?" cried Lydia in desperate alarm.

Purcell shrugged. "Now, Lydia, that's somethin' I'd like to know, too. But Gunther's a big feller; he's not tellin' anybody anythin'."

Lydia wrung her hands together. "What can we do, Jim? Tell me what we can do?"

He put his hand on her bare shoulder, and in spite of her fear she could feel fire running down her arm, striking at her heart. "Lydia, old girl, you can't do anythin' for Steve. What could you do? And me? I can only wait around to pick up the pieces. You know old Steve. He wouldn't listen to anybody. He trusts Red Rufus, and that's like trustin' a tiger. I've tried to warn him, and he looked at me like I was dirt. Haven't seen him for weeks; he won't speak to me." He lifted his hand from Lydia's shoulder, and studied the palm as if in wonder.

"You could talk with Mr. Gunther," suggested Lydia in her despair.

He laughed loudly and hoarsely. "Gunther? He knows what I'd be tryin' to do. He's with Rufe in this. Besides, Gunther's

166

got an old score to settle with me. I can't get anythin' on him, if you know what I mean. Besides, it would do no good. Old Steve's the problem. You can't get around him. He's just got a conscience."

Lydia could only wring her hands over and over. Her beautiful profile was tense and wretched in the frail light.

"Steve, because he's Steve, and things in this country are too big for him, and he's got too many bad enemies, is going to be hurt, hurt bad, Lydia. So we just stand by when the inevitable happens. You can't help him by stayin' in that house. You might as well leave."

But she cried, "Jim! You can do something, I know you can!" She turned to him and the moonlight struck her face.

"Thanks, Lydia, for believin' that. I told you I'm tryin' somethin'. It's indirect. Look, old girl, I never asked nobody to trust me before. Never did care a damn, because, perhaps, nobody could trust me. But I'm askin' you to trust me now."

"Oh, I do, I do, Jim!" She spoke passionately. "I always did. I think I never trusted anyone at all, except you."

Purcell watched her in a deep silence, and an odd expression touched his muddy eyes so that they quickened with a stern tenderness. Lydia ran distracted hands through the masses of her black hair, and thick tendrils spilled over her cheeks and neck. Purcell picked up one of the tendrils and rubbed it slowly and strongly through his fingers. She became quiet then, her hands dropping to her knees.

He spoke as if nothing had happened, and dully, "It may take Rufe a longer time than he expects. Impatient feller, but somehow he's learned how to wait. And I've got to wait until he makes a move. Doubt if I'll be able to do anythin' then. But I'll do what I can."

Lydia spoke in the loud but toneless voice of a sleepwalker: "I've come to hate Rufus, because of Stephen, and because of all that he is."

"Well, now, Lydia, that's bein' kind of extravagant. That's the woman's way of talking. Rufe and I and Gunther would just call it all ' business.' Rufe's getting to be the better man, better than old Steve. Don't hold it against him. But Steve's not suited to the tear-and-eat school, though he's been doin' fine in an honourable kind of way. He's, well, I think they'd call him an ' anachronism ' these days."

Lydia began to cry silently, and then in the most natural way possible Purcell took his handkerchief, dabbed at her cheeks gently, then put the handkerchief in her hand. "Stephen's such a fool!" she wept. "Such a fool."

Purcell became very grave. "People think I haven't had much schoolin', but I have, in an uneven sort of way. I remember something that Pliny the Elder said, and I've always remembered it: ' I have studied much the philosophies of the old sages, and their dream of Demos and universal liberty, and the brotherhood of man. But still, labouring wearily in my mind, I am not convinced that such a dream shall ever emerge from the darkness of men's souls. Rather would I believe it possible that the sun should rise in the West, contrary to his custom, than that ever a single man should extend into reality a philosophy so at variance with all his instincts.'"

Lydia had hardly listened at the beginning, but as Purcell had gone on quoting she had straightened, listening intently, and a bitter look had hardened the contours of her face.

"The old feller was very bright, Lydia. You can't make the sun rise west. People bein' what they are, and what they'll always be. Got to deal with things as they are."

Lydia sighed. "How terrible it all is, Jim. It isn't only Rufus and Stephen. Portersville is changing, too. There's something ugly in the air, for the first time."

"Guess I can't be too romantic about that, either, Lydia. Let's say that Portersville was a sort of friendly and pleasant place, up to the last few years, because it was small-townish, and it was kind of in the family. Now there's all these immigrants comin' in, and nobody knows them, and they're queer to the folks in town, and the town's drawn together against them. Old human nature, to hate the stranger. That's how social castes are built up. What would you want to do, Lydia? Remake the whole damned world and damned human nature? You can just save yourself."

"I can't leave," replied Lydia. "There is Cornelia, and there is Stephen. And Laura, too. Too many to desert."

"H'm," commented Purcell. He examined one of his great boots in the diminishing moonlight. "Quixotic."

"And you despise me for it?" cried Lydia with some anger.

Purcell rubbed the mud from his boots. "No, ma'am, can't say that I do." He picked up his pipe. "I like to know it's there, though it seems damn foolishness to me. You don't understand me, eh?"

"Yes," said Lydia almost inaudibly. "I think I do, Jim."

He gave her his hand and helped her to her feet, and had stood looking down at her, smiling.

"You'll come again to this place, won't you, Lydia? I haven't frightened you away?"

She tried to smile in answer. "I'll come, Jim. I'll come."

Since that time they had met often, these past two years, from the first of spring until autumn. They had met casually and distantly in the homes of acquaintances. The fact that Jim Purcell was almost invariably present on these occasions was not even commented upon as coincidental, and no one noticed the sudden swift exchange of glances between him and Lydia or the sudden touch of hands in passing.

When spring would return, Lydia would come to the glade. She did not always meet Jim Purcell there, nor did he meet her. There was never, between them, any appointment for any particular night, never a promise given or received. There was never any love-making, except for a light pressure of hands, though at rare intervals, Lydia would lay her head on Purcell's shoulder in a gesture of exhaustion or in seeking for wordless consolation. More often than not, they would just sit side by side, listening to the cries of the night birds, watching the drifting of clouds over moon or stars, and sometimes they would part from each other after an hour or two with only a few words spoken.

It was the early spring of 1876, when the tragic panic was developing into acute and bloody violence all over America, that Purcell suggested to Lydia that she obtain a divorce from Rufus.

"I can't, dearest," said Lydia, with misery. "You know I can't leave Cornelia and Stephen and Laura. I know, as you have said, that there is nothing I can really do to protect any of them, but I'm like someone watching a man painting a steeple. You have the feeling that if you look away the man will fall." She continued faintly: "And in a way, I remain because of Rufus, vaguely believing that he needs me, too, and that but for me he might be worse."

Purcell considered this with some wryness. Red Rufus was fast coming to his planned climax, and bringing those associated with him into tragedy and despair. But Purcell, after some thought, decided not to tell Lydia.

He said, "You think you'll have to leave your girl. But you won't. You can get a divorce, and her custody." He pulled a sheaf of papers from his pocket, and by straining her eyes in the spring darkness and star-shine, Lydia could see that the sheaf was corded and sealed. "I've been havin' Red Rufe investigated—quietly, of course—over the past two years. Here are the names of all his lady friends, and their addresses, and where they meet. We can bring the whole business into court."

She said, "Oh, yes, I've known all about this for a long time. But it isn't Rufus's fault, entirely. He isn't guilty because he isn't what I thought he was when I married him. The delusion was mine, and I made him suffer for it."

"So you want to make him keep on sufferin', eh, Lydia! You won't let him go, and let him marry another woman who'll give him children? You won't marry me?"

Lydia moved a little from him and half turned her back. "It's also Rufus," she murmured. "Perhaps I'm a fool, but I think he refrains from some things because of me."

Purcell put his enormous hands on her shoulders and swung her fiercely towards him. "Lydia! You are a fool. He isn't refraining from a damn thing, as you'll find out soon. What then, Lydia? Don't you think I'm a man? Think I'm satisfied just sittin' here, year after year, holdin' hands with you like a kid at school? I want you in my house, in my bed. How old are you, Lydia? You're thirty-four, aren't you? Not too old for children. I want our children, Lydia."

But Lydia had caught only a few terrifying words from this rough diatribe. "What do you mean, Jim? Is Rufus——"

"I can't tell you things you wouldn't understand. And I can't stop them, either. But the day's almost here when Rufus will have the damned railroad in his hands. And the house, too, which Steve owns. And every goddamned cent. What then, Lydia? What then?"

"Stephen? Stephen?" Lydia's cry deepened to a groan. Purcell nodded grimly. "It'll be all up with him, Lydia. He'll find out, and it may kill him, findin' out. Steve's been ruined because he trusted: you'd call it bein' victimised, and may be it is. Well. There it is. What I could do now would be throwin' good money after bad. Besides, Steve doesn't know that the walls are about to fall on him."

Lydia seized his arm. "Jim, why don't you tell him?"

"He wouldn't believe it. He won't believe it until he sees it for himself. That's the kind of a fool he is. And you know it."

Lydia began to tremble, and after a moment's resistance, Purcell put his arms about her and held her against his giant's chest. He kissed her hair and her cheek and finally her cold lips. She clung to him and cried helplessly. "There, there, love," he mumbled. "Sweet love. My Lydia. There's some things you can't help; men kind of bring their destiny on themselves."

When she could speak, out of her pain and despair, she said, "If it happens, then I'll divorce Rufus. If I didn't, I think I should kill him."

CHAPTER EIGHTEEN

IT IS not true that one forgets sorrow, Stephen would think. No, there was no surcease of sorrow for him. The day of Alice's death ten years ago was as vivid and as terrible as though it had occurred only to-day. Her face and her voice, her sweet childish smiles, her gestures and her pretty figure and tender actions, never faded or blurred in his memory. They were always there, immediately remembered. To this day, if a door opened into his room, he turned expectantly. At night, he reached for her in his lonely bed. Sometimes, in his anguish, he pressed the knuckles of his hand tightly against his teeth and endured the waves of grief as a man, committing suicide, endures the waves of the sea into which he has deliberately walked. All the joy of the hours had gone for him, all the dreams he had ever had. He sometimes told himself that he lived for his little daughter Laura, now ten years old, but in truth he lived only for the day when she would no longer need him and he could die.

He did not believe that he would ever "meet" Alice again after death. The sorrow of his existence, and the blows which had been inflicted upon him by man, had obliterated any faith he had had in God and immortality. Despair had come to abide with him as a black presence which coloured all his days and his nights, and there was no hope to take its place and oust it from the stark and empty caverns of his soul.

The love he felt for his young daughter was, in truth, mostly constant anxiety for her welfare. He worked to conserve her holdings and her fortune in order to buy security for her, to make her safe from a ravening world. There was nothing in the child which reminded him of Alice. He never regarded her as needing him for any other reason except worldly security, and though he was invariably tender with her—for tenderness was part of his nature—and though he held her on his knees lovingly and stroked her dusky ringlets with a gentle hand, he never approached the farthest outskirts of her spirit.

There was only one member of his household who could provoke his rare smile or faint laughter, and that was Cornelia, his niece. Pert, saucy, and witty, and instinctively amiable towards everyone, she would climb unasked on his knee, as little Laura never did. She would smack him heartily, and then immediately ask him for some money. It gave him pleasure to put gold certificates in her grasping little hands, though Lydia objected. Her burnished young beauty, her consuming zest for life, her unabashed passion for living, warmed his cold hands and sometimes halted the constant chill shivering of his soul. Reticent himself, respecting all individual privacy, and bewildered, as always, by the mystery of other human beings, he never speculated on Cornelia's character or busied himself, with monkey curiosity, as to what lay behind her loud and husky voice, her boisterous and demanding, if endearing ways.

Sorrow and misery did not, however, free Stephen from his conviction that he was morally bound to relieve the sorrow and misery of others. In fact, his own despair drove him to excesses which ten years ago would have been unthinkable or which would have sensibly given him pause. His charities had risen to enormous heights, arousing both the wonder and the derision of the recipients, whether individuals or organisations. Stephen gradually came to be suspected of siphoning off money, in reality belonging to his "wronged" brother, for his own uses, and his charities seemed only a small sop to whatever meagre conscience he possessed. As an evidence of this, they pointed to Rufus's insignificant donations to local charities. A man so warm, so kind, so amiable and sympathetic as Rufus deWitt, would have been only too delighted to contribute largely—had he the means.

Never Victorious, Never Defeated

No one but Rufus and the directors of the board knew that Stephen drew no more from the Interstate Railroad Company than his very respectable salary, and it was to their interest that this matter not be given publicity. His coal acreage near Scranton was adding, as yet, little to his income. He could have developed it had he not invested the greater part of his money in trust funds for Laura, and in charities. The trust funds were irrevocable, and no one spoke of the charities. Of course, he retained the fifty-one per cent of the railroad stocks and bonds, but he hardly regarded them as his own property. And he had not received any dividends from them for over two years.

So it was that on a hot August Sunday, as he went over his accounts, the first stirrings of anxiety for himself came to him.

The panic, which had begun in 1873, and which showed, in 1876, little signs of vanishing, had hit the Baynes Locals very severely. Joseph Baynes now owed Stephen deWitt twenty-four thousand dollars. Virtuously, Joseph had insisted upon giving Stephen notes for this large sum of money. Once the notes had been given to the "affluent" Stephen, Joseph was rarely disturbed by the memory of them. He felt completely safe. Tom Orville, running into difficulty during the panic, might have lost his lumber business to the Interstate Railroad Company, had not Stephen given him ten thousand dollars, also secured by notes righteously thrust upon Stephen.

Stephen sat at his desk in the library, his haggard face sweating and grey with mingled heat and fear. His personal bank balance was less than twelve thousand dollars in cash. Rufus and Sophia did not contribute any money whatever to the upkeep of the great white mansion on the mountain. Stephen had refused Rufus's casual offer; it was all he, Stephen, could do, "under the circumstances." It never occurred to Sophia to suggest an equitable sum out of her own sound income, and it never occurred to Stephen either. Servants, food, household expenses, upkeep, and the support of the family came to at least seven hundred dollars a month. Stephen footed the bills for all the elaborate entertainment on which Sophia insisted. His mother had no intention of spending a penny of her own—all of which was bequeathed in her will to Rufus and Cornelia—even for her personal expenses and grand wardrobe. She would say to herself grimly: He's got to pay for what he did. Never a particularly extravagant woman while Aaron was building up his fortune, nor until the time of his death, she now was a prodigal. All bills coming to the house were addressed exclusively to "Stephen deWitt, Esquire," whether the bills were for the music lessons given to both Cornelia and Laura, medical bills for the entire family, or bills for clothing, coal, wood, or carriages. No bill was too small or too large to be placed on Stephen's desk.

It did not occur to Stephen that there was anything incongruous in Rufus refusing to accept a house key of his own, and Rufus's bills for himself and his daughter and his mother.

Twelve thousand dollars in cash, and six thousand dollars in bills since April! Of course, thought Stephen, rubbing his wet forehead, there was his salary. But he was committed to give twelve thousand dollars in September, November, and December to the Portersville Home for the Aged, the Portersville Home for Abandoned Children, the Retired Veterans of the Civil War, and the local hospital.

He thought: I could go to Philadelphia and borrow on my stocks and bonds. But how would I repay the loan, if things don't improve rapidly? Besides, his fifty-one per cent was a sacred trust, and he could not convince himself that in reality it honourably belonged to him. If there was only some way he could cut down, thought Stephen desperately. He went over the list of servants, and shrank. Sophia might not contribute a penny to their pay, but she regarded the servants as almost entirely her own and herself as the head of the household. She would have a fit, thought poor Stephen, and abandoned the matter. The carriages? There were eight vehicles altogether, and a corresponding company of grooms and coachmen. They could be eliminated to a great extent, but what would the poor wretches do at a time when employment was still rapidly declining?

There was no way out, except by borrowing. For a moment Stephen thought of bringing his financial troubles to Rufus, not to ask his brother to help with expenses (that would be unthinkable under "the circumstances"), but simply for consolation and advice about the mountainous dilemma. No, it would be wrong to force Rufus to share his anxieties. He must borrow the money very soon, giving a certain amount of his stocks and bonds as collateral. He reflected that the Chicago Railroad System was costing the Interstate Railroad Company an enormous sum of money these last few years, because it, like all other railroads, was suffering from the panic.

Stephen believed that his mounting troubles were unknown to anyone but himself. But Rufus knew; the bankers in Portersville were his friends. As he had suspected, Stephen's "weaknesses" of character were hurrying him into ruin.

It was not possible for Stephen to know that he was under any surveillance, nor would he have suspected it. He was on the best of terms with Rufus, and he constantly used the memory of Rufus's support of him in dealings with the board of directors as consolation when his personal troubles seemed to him insurmountable. Yet, during the past two years, some sixth sense had made him uneasy. He was like a man caught in a fog in a strange and dangerous country, not knowing from whence a deadly enemy might emerge. Lately his instinct would not be quieted; he would awake in the night, trembling and undone.

Now the periods during which his logic could drive off his nameless and faceless fear became shorter and shorter. On this hot August afternoon it seized him like the teeth of a great beast, and he got to his feet, looking about him in dread. He went to the western window of the library, which looked out upon the gardens slowly dropping in terraces over the side of the mountain. Upon the upper terraces grew tiers of mighty pines and elms, one above the other, sheltering the bluish-green grass which sloped below them. Here the shade, so clustering and cool, would permit no flower beds. But the terraces beneath exploded in scarlet, yellow, blue, white, rose, and purple, interspersed with winding stone paths, little brilliant fountains, and only an occasional tree. Three willows trailed their long green hair in the blazing wind, and caught pure glitter on their thin and delicate leaves. A group of birches turned copper under a sky of blue flame. A low white stone wall followed the garden down the mountainside, covered with interlaced rosebushes, dark green and thorny, with here and there a last late scarlet flower bursting forth from the mass like a rosette of fire. The far mountains loomed in mauve clouds in the distance, blending into the sky. Stephen, as he stood on the threshold of the windows, could feel the burning breeze on his face and could hear the raucous shrilling of the locusts. There was no other sound in the incandescent silence of the Sunday afternoon, no voice from the stables beyond the house, no movement of a servant or a member of the family through the corridors or in the rooms.

The garden usually brought a dim sense of peace to Stephen,

but it brought no peace to-day. He stepped feebly out on to the grass, began to wander distractedly along the narrow paths between the flower beds. He came to a tiny grotto surrounded by the willows. Now the wind was cooler here, and he sat on a marble bench, hidden from the house. Bees accentuated the stillness with their busy comings and goings. He heard the prism-tinkle of a fountain, the slumbrous chant of the locusts. A squirrel ran across the hot grass near his feet. Stephen felt for his pipe and lighted it, and sighed. The willows, which he loved, bowed and lifted, but they were no longer comforters. An evil enchantment had moved over the whole illuminated scene.

Without warning, a thought came to him: It appears hostile and removed from me because I fear it is no longer mine.

Stunned and distraught, he pulled the pipe from his mouth. Who could take his home from him? Rufus!

But Rufus was his brother, his reconciled and admiring brother. How could Rufus take from him what was his? I must talk with somebody, he thought desperately, someone who will ridicule my terror. But who?

Stephen got rapidly and involuntarily to his feet, as if impelled by an irresistible urgency stronger than logic. It was then that he heard the voices of his daughter Laura, and Cornelia, and he was stopped in his flight.

Cornelia's young voice was loud, laughing, and boisterous, but Laura's voice was soft and slow.

"Of course, Papa said I mustn't tell anybody where we were, when we were in New York," Cornelia was saying, and her voice came in jerks because she was jumping up and down in the excess of her ruddy energy. "Look, Laura, all those awful ants; they eat the flowers. Stamp on them. Here's another anthill just for you."

"No," said Laura. "Please stop, Cornelia."

"But they eat the flowers," protested Cornelia. "Do you want them to eat the flowers? They're harmful, the gardeners say."

"Harmful to whom?" asked Laura, with real wonder. "Do you think the world was just made for us? It wasn't; it was made for ants, too, and caterpillars, and crows and skunks and mice, and moths and butterflies and horses and trees. If any of them are harmful to us, we're harmful to them."

"Who cares? You've got only yourself to think of," said

Cornelia. "How tiresome you are, Laura. You talk like Mamma, sometimes. You even look like Mamma. Never mind, I was telling you about New York. It was so exciting——"

"If Uncle Rufus told you not to tell anyone where you went to in New York, then you shouldn't," Laura admonished with what Lydia would have thought an unnecessary righteousness.

"Phoo! I guess Papa thought it might make all of you jealous. What does it signify? You aren't going to run and tell Uncle Steve, are you, or Grandma, or Mamma?"

Stephen, halted in his rush from the grotto, sat down again. He had no desire, in his agony of mind, to encounter the two little girls hardly twenty feet from him.

"Well," said Laura, trying not to sound too eager, " let's sit down on the grass, and you tell me."

"Not until I stamp on this anthill, which I saved for you," replied Cornelia in a hurt tone. There were renewed sounds of vigorous jumping. "There. Pushed it right in. Look at the horrible little things running!" More stamping. "That will teach them not to eat our flowers, the horrid creatures." Stephen heard Cornelia throw herself down on the grass beside her cousin. He heard her draw a husky and reminiscent breath of delight. "It was wonderful in New York. Not like this awful Portersville, where nothing happens, and people just eat big dinners and go to bed. Why, it was lit up all night. I went to the windows, over and over, and there were gaslights, and the carriages rolling on the cobblestones, and people coming and going, and laughing, and all the ladies in their wonderful gowns. With bare shoulders! And you never saw such jewels. And you could hear the horsecars going right up to three o'clock in the morning. I just couldn't sleep. I didn't sleep a wink all the time we were there, and that was nearly a week. Papa didn't mind; he said I ought to see what would one day be my world." The child sighed blissfully. "Of course, I love our home here, and I'll always keep it, and never sell it, and I'll let you and dear Uncle Steve live here all the time and come back and visit you."

"But the house belongs to my Papa," said Laura with perplexity.

Stephen became cold and rigid in the sunlit glade.

Cornelia's common voice was affectionate and pitying. "But it won't be, when I grow up. Papa said so. He said it to Mr. Gunther. It'll soon be his house, and then he'll leave it to me. Never mind, Laura, I love you and Uncle Steve so much. You can live

M

here all your lives, and never pay me a single cent of money, and it'll be such fun coming home in the summer and on the holidays to see you."

Laura was touched by this generosity, though she was still perplexed. "Is my Papa going to sell our house to your Papa?"

"How can you be so ridiculous, Laura? Papa told Mr. Gunther that your Papa couldn't keep the house, and so as Papa is your Papa's brother, Papa will have it. Don't ask me so many questions. Anyway, I wasn't supposed to hear these things, and don't you dare tell anybody, hear? I was listening, sitting on the marble stairway in Mr. Gunther's house."

"Why, didn't you stay in the hotel in Murray Hill?" asked Laura.

"No. That's another secret. Papa had his post sent there, and telegrams from Portersville. But we stayed with Mr. Gunther, in his wonderful house on the corner of Thirty-fourth Street and Fifth Avenue. You think our house is fine? You should see Mr. Gunther's! It cost millions, simply millions, Papa said. It is all white marble, and it has pillars. He bought it from the Stewart family, when Mr. Stewart died. Marble bathrooms. And big marble fireplaces, though they have what they call central heating, too. And servants! Why, Mr. Gunther gave me a maid all for my own, and she combed my hair and drew me my baths, and helped me dress. Did I feel fine and royal! Like a princess. I bet Queen Victoria doesn't live in a palace like that, and have so many servants. It was the most wonderful house, better than Mr. Astor's and Mr. Gould's, and even better than Mr. Vanderbilt's. They have brownstone houses, and they're dull and dark, though big, too. And Mr. Gunther has such extraordinary furniture. Treasures, Papa said. From all over the world. Gilded chairs and tapestries, and rich paintings, and forks and spoons of solid gold!"

"Now, Cornelia, do you expect me to believe that?" asked Laura incredulously. "Solid gold spoons and forks! How you exaggerate!"

Cornelia was outraged. "Do you think I tell lies, Laura deWitt?"

Laura's sweet voice was tinged with amusement. "You quite often do," she observed.

Cornelia shrieked with good-natured and wicked laughter. "Well, the truth is usually dull. But I'm telling you the truth now, you picky thing. I haven't finished telling you about New York. We rode on the Pullman Elevated, and the floor had carpets on it, and the poor people rode in horrid coaches, and we just streamed over the city! And we went to the afternoon parade in Central Park, all down Fifth Avenue, in Mr. Gunther's grand carriage, which had two footmen as well as a coachman, all in red and silver uniforms. I tell you, I felt like a princess, or maybe a queen. And such ladies, all in bright colours, with bonnets with big plumes on them, and parasols just like flowers, all bowing to each other and laughing, and the horses prancing on the cobblestones and the silver harness shining. Such excitement. There was a band playing in the Park, and there was a pavilion, and you could be served China tea and little sandwiches with caviar and French cakes, and people would be out on boats on the lake.

"And then we went to Coney Island. We took a steamboat at the Battery and we sailed down the harbour. It was all so splendid. And people bathing in the sea. We even went to the amusement park, though Papa laughed. You'd love New York, Laura. Maybe your Papa will take you there some day, too."

Cornelia's voice became even more blissful. "Maybe, when I have a big house like Mr. Gunther's in New York, you'll visit me."

"I like my own home best," remarked Laura without envy. "I think I'll stay here with Papa."

"Well, you can, though it'll belong to me, then. But I've told you I want you and Uncle Steve to live here all your lives. Of course, you'll never marry," Cornelia went on with pitying confidence. "You aren't pretty, like me. Grandma calls you a mouse. You're a very sweet mouse. But you'll stay and take care of Uncle Steve, until he's a very old, old man. And read all the books. I"—Cornelia continued happily—"am going to marry Patrick Peale. We saw him in Philadelphia, working with his uncle, Mr. Alex Peale. You never saw such a handsome man as Patrick Peale!"

"I saw him a year ago," said Laura with laughing tolerance. "Anyway, you're only ten years old, and Patrick's a grown man. I expect he'll be marrying any day now."

Cornelia's voice took on shrill indignation. "That's not so! I asked him, and he promised to wait for me, so there." Her breath was loud in the hot silence. "And Mr. Alex Peale reminded Patrick, right there in their offices in the big bank, that he mustn't forget he was going to marry me, maybe in about seven years."

"There's Aunt Lydia, looking for us," said Laura.

Cornelia jumped to her feet. "Look at the grass on me! Remember, now, Laura, you aren't to tell a single living soul what I've told you. Papa didn't say why, but he was stern about it, and if he knew I even told you I'd never go with him to New York again. Cross your heart!"

"Very well," said Laura patiently. "There, I've crossed it. But you know I never tell anyone what you say."

Young feet pounded on the grass, away from the grotto, and Cornelia shouted, "Mamma, Mamma! I've just been telling Laura the fairy tale you told me last night!"

Stephen had not moved during this innocent recital. Now he was conscious that he was covered with cold sweat. Guy Gunther. Alex Peale. Astor, Gould, Vanderbilt. Secrecy. Rufus had returned only two days ago with Cornelia. Before leaving Portersville he had idly mentioned that he wished Cornelia to see New York, and that he might "drop in on a few old friends, if they aren't out of town." Nothing had been said about Philadelphia. When Rufus had returned he had remarked that New York was dull and empty. Everyone had gone to Newport. He had seen no one of importance, or interest.

Shall I confront him? Stephen asked himself in the extremity of his terror. But what shall I say? If I mention this conversation between the children, he will laugh it off, attempt to make me see it was nothing at all. And I'll finally believe him.

Stephen fell back on the marble bench. But what can any of them do? The fact remains that I own fifty-one per cent of the stock and the bonds, and I own this house, which my father left me.

Though the Interstate Railroad Company had passed many dividends, it was more solvent than its competitors, and no one could seize it, or force it into bankruptcy. Logic's voice became stronger in Stephen's mind. Now his cold trembling subsided. But though he could think more clearly now, he was aware of an overpowering sickness of both soul and body. His brother, whom he had trusted, was a sleepless plotter against him. This, finally, was the most awful thing to Stephen.

Lydia was sitting under a large elm near the house. Her light lavender silk dress, simply draped but exquisite, set off her slender figure. Her dark head and lovely strange face were bent over the two pretty little girls seated at her feet. She looked up, to see Stephen moving slowly and heavily over the grass. Cornelia uttered a scream of joy, jumped up, and raced towards her uncle. Her verve and vivacious beauty were like a sunburst in the brilliant light. Her red curls, set off with long blue ribbons, streamed behind her, and her white lawn dress, sashed in blue, fluttered in the hot wind. Scarlet mouth was open, teeth glittering, hazel eyes full of vigorous radiance. Laura, also clad in white lawn, but with pink ribbons, came to her father more sedately, her dusky ringlets a cloud down her thin back, her small pale face smiling shyly, her remarkable grey eyes shining.

Cornelia hugged her uncle vehemently, but Laura held up her cool little cheek for his kiss. She had a cleft white chin, a white arched nose, and brows like black and tilted streaks over her eyes. Stephen, still shaking and almost mortally ill, could control himself enough to kiss Cornelia briefly, and then Laura. For the first time he saw Laura fully and completely. His daughter. His threatened child, with the elusive innocence on her face, her delicacy, her mysterious, withdrawn quality! She was his charge, he, her protector. He lifted her in his weak arms and held her to him almost passionately, while Cornelia, a trifle puzzled, watched.

Still carrying Laura, and followed by the offended Cornelia, Stephen went towards Lydia. She waited, and when he was closer, and she saw his face, she uttered an exclamation and got to her feet with a silken rustle. She rarely spoke to Stephen, but now she cried out sharply, "Stephen! What is wrong? Are you ill?"

He forgot his own knowledge that his sister-in-law despised him—for some unknown reason—and he said, "It is the heat, Lydia. I—I just came from the house, for some air."

They stood looking at each other, and Lydia thought: He seems to be dying. He is holding Laura as if he is protecting her. Her heart began to beat with compassion and alarm. But before she could speak again he was gone from her, carrying Laura.

"You are not coming down to tea?" asked Rufus solicitously. His brother lay on the bed, drained and exhausted. "There are about ten people here now."

181

"No. No, thank you," said Stephen in a low voice. "I have a headache. Please ask them to excuse me."

He looked at Rufus, and his small, unassuming eyes became fixed and piercing, and there was a desperate quality of supplication in them. Rufus was smiling at him with sympathy, and his thick red hair was a glow in the twilight gloom. To himself, Stephen was thinking: If only I could be sure! Is it really possible that he is trying to betray me? His collapsed body yearned for reassurance, for a desire to know that he was wrong in order that he might be comforted and he might be enabled, through faith in at least one person, to go on living.

Rufus went down the stairs, whistling softly and reflectively. It wasn't possible for the poor fool to know anything. He, Rufus, had too much imagination. He chuckled richly at this self-flattery, and humming, re-entered the drawing-room, where Lydia was at the piano, entertaining guests.

Rufus smiled and twiddled his watch chain, and was tolerant. As he studied his beautiful wife at the piano, a burning attacked his heart. He could not get her out of his flesh; she was like a barbed and poisoned spearhead which never left him painless. Yet, he hated her for wounding his life. But she had been kinder to him lately, and her eyes sometimes regarded him with a sad pain of her own, as if she was infinitely sorry for him. She was almost thirty-five; she was more lovely and elusive than ever, more mysterious, and there was a sheen like a pearl over her face, a glisten on her lips, which reminded him of a Lydia of eleven years ago. She looked like a woman in love— A woman in love!

CHAPTER NINETEEN

LIKE A man dying of cold loneliness and starvation, Stephen began to visit his friend Joseph Baynes with desperate regularity. He wanted nothing from him but a sense that he was loyal to him, and had affection for him, and would comfort him in the unknowable and ominous future.

Joseph Baynes, now a man in his early sixties, had changed little in ten years. He was still neat and graceful; his delicate features had not lost their sharp etching in the blur of time. He and his wife and three children lived in an old stone house in the "wrong section" of Portersville. They had practically no friends except Stephen and the Orvilles, and desired none, for they were a suspicious and envious little clan. Stephen, in his innocence, thought them "discriminating," and in fact Joseph had often loftily remarked that he was "particular" about friendship.

Joseph always seemed to be delighted at Stephen's visits, as did his blowy pink-cheeked little wife, Elsa. They would stir up the fire in the tiny dank living-room, seat Stephen with solicitude, and offer him sherry. It was a very bad cheap sherry, but as Stephen sat by the fire with his friends and sipped at his glass, the wine became to him the liquid of consolation and Lethe. He did not notice that lately Joseph had assumed a too obvious and false hospitality, and that Elsa, as she pushed back the untidy masses of her light brown hair, would give him sly glances. The children, more outright, were scornful of their parents' hypocrisy. The girl, Flora, a pretty seventeen-year-old, and the boys, Duncan, twenty-two, and his brother Shaun, nineteen, would hardly glance at Stephen when he entered, nor would they rise. This made Stephen feel very humble and distressed. He gave the ancient excuse for them that they did not "understand," or that, naturally, they were bored with older people.

On a night in October, Stephen felt particularly beset. Uneasiness had become a restless fever in him. He walked down the mountain into the city, crossed the bridge over the black river, and entered East Town. The streets grew narrower and narrower, wound up and down small hills, descended into miniature valleys filled with a cool mist. Here the street lights were few, and reeked of oil. Above, a huge moon like a bronze plate stood in the sky of dark stone. The odour of smoke became thicker in the motionless autumn air, and dry leaves scuttled ahead of Stephen's hurrying feet, whispered on the cobbles. Occasionally a cricket shrilled insistently.

The Baynes's house lay on poorly tended lawns in a snarl of huge but half-dead trees. Stephen walked up the narrow grass-grown path towards the house, which showed only one yellow light. He lifted the stained knocker and struck it hesitantly. When Joseph opened the door and saw his visitor, he smiled happily, called out: "It's Steve!" He took Stephen's cold hand and pulled him into the house. Then, as Joseph divested Stephen of his greatcoat, Elsa entered the miniature hall, beaming. "Dear Stephen," she said, in her high and tinkling voice. "What a surprise." She stood on the tip of her pointed little boots and bestowed a sisterly kiss on his grey cheek. She was all curves and shapelessness and bulges, but Stephen thought her fat indicated a cheery and affectionate disposition.

A more cynical eye than Stephen's would have detected the falseness under the emphasised cordiality. But he was too hungry for kindness to look under the surface. He entered the untidy and shabby living-room and saw nothing but the fire. The children were there, glowering at their books, and did not glance up. This was nothing unusual. When Stephen greeted them timidly, they muttered something. Then, even before Stephen could take his customary seat by the fire in a battered wing chair, Shaun and his sister Elsa jumped to their feet and went rapidly out of the room as if Stephen were not present at all. But Duncan remained.

Duncan, the oldest of the three children, laid his book down on his knees, folded his arms on it, and stared furiously and silently at the fire. He was a short and stocky young man with a dark, alert face in which all the sharp features expressed an immovable sullenness. His black hair had been cropped closely, revealing a round hard head.

A glass of sherry was pressed into Stephen's hand by Joseph, who kept up a rapid and sprightly conversation. Stephen, who rarely noticed anything, saw, for the first time, that the glass was coarse and sticky and none too clean. The fire did not give out its accustomed warmth. There was wariness in the atmosphere, and in spite of Joseph's strong assertions that Stephen looked well, very well, indeed, and in spite of Elsa's loving expressions, Stephen became colder than ever. Perhaps it was that young man Duncan, sitting there so unfriendly, so engrossed in hard concentration on the fire.

Joseph, sitting opposite his friend to whom he owed so much, thought: He's only forty-two or so, but he looks over fifty. He's gone grey and sunken. He said, "I've never seen you looking so well, Steve. There's quite a colour in your face. Did you walk over?"

"Yes," said Stephen, trying to rouse himself from his uneasy contemplation of Duncan. "It's a nice night." He sipped at his sherry, and it nauseated him. He was suddenly obsessed with a desire for flight. He tried to control the desire; he had come to his friends for consolation. They would be hurt if he inexplicably ran away. He smiled feebly at them. Elsa had taken up her everlasting darning, but her plump face retained its automatic brightness and look of pleasure. She started to chatter about nothing at all, except that she occasionally mentioned the name of a neighbour. Then her laughing voice took on a high spitefulness and derision. Stephen began to wonder if she had always spoken so; he could not remember.

"Of course," Elsa was saying, "we never have anything to do with these vulgar people." She put down a thick sock and stared at Stephen with a blank brilliance in her brown eyes. "If only Joseph had been as successful as you, Stephen dear. If only he had had the opportunities! But Joseph is so upright and honourable. Joseph is a man of principle." She sighed, picked up the sock again and attacked it vehemently.

Joseph said with gentle admonition, "But Elsa, my love, Stephen never had anything to do with Mr. Aaron's machinations. Stephen, too, is a man of principle. And if Stephen has had wonderful opportunities, well then, it is just a matter of luck and the mysterious dispensations of the Almighty. We must not complain." He sighed, and gave Stephen a patient smile.

"But Rufus is not a man of principle," said Elsa. She threaded her needle with black wool. "As you've said, my dear, we must not complain. We are content with what we have."

She lifted her eyes to Stephen again, and there was a cold bright accusation in them. He was alarmed, and suddenly overcome with guilt. Yes, it was dreadful for poor Joseph and Elsa. He wondered, desperately, what else he could do for them to relieve his guiltiness at owning a splendid home. If only I had a huge private fortune, I could do something for my poor friends, he thought unhappily. But Joseph has been so unlucky with the Locals, and he is not a businessman at all. The Panic has hit him almost mortally, even with my help.

A painful colour came into his cheeks as his certainty of guilt increased. If he could obtain a sizeable loan on his stocks and bonds there was a possibility that he could indeed help Joseph and Elsa and their children. He began to smile. "I have some small ideas," he said gently. "Let me think them over for a little."

Duncan got to his feet clumsily but forcefully. He regarded Stephen with something like hatred. "You'll do nothing more," he said. "You've done enough to my poor father. Aren't you satisfied that you've kept him in a state of chronic ruin all these years, when he might have been retired now, on a decent income?

Or earning an excellent salary in payment for his knowledge and ability?" He approached Stephen as if to strike him. "Why did you prevent him from selling out years ago to your company, and accepting a salary? I know all about that twenty-four thousand dollars you claim he owes you. Owes you! Payment for a kind of blackmail, I call it! Biding your time until you can swallow the Locals whole, and keeping that loan as a club over his head! If you were a man of any feeling you would detest yourself." He knotted his fists. "My father ' owes ' you nothing, and if he had any guts he would tell you so."

Joseph and Elsa listened to this outburst in a state of appalled paralysis and horror. It was one thing for them to deceive their children; it was another thing for Stephen to learn of their treachery. Joseph cursed his son to himself in his frantic fear; Elsa turned white and her large full mouth dropped open on a gasp of terror.

Stephen could not speak; he could only regard the young man, aghast and stricken to the heart. A sudden awful silence fell over the room.

Yes, thought Stephen with almost overpowering compassion and sorrow, Joe told the boy that to preserve his pride in the eyes of his son, to keep his self-respect, to shelve up the crumbling walls of his ego.

His pity was like a crushing wound in his chest. He wished to say something to this angry and outraged young man, not in explanation, but in an attempt to keep his respect for his father intact. However, he could find no words, for he had no eloquence, and none of the oratory of deceit.

Joseph Baynes began to speak in the high and squeaking voice of demoralised panic: "Duncan, you don't know what you're saying! Old Steve here is my best friend——"

"Your best friend!" cried Duncan passionately. "The man who has kept you grinding away for years, paying illegal interest on his ' loan,' depriving you of the comfort and security you should have at your age!"

Joseph turned to Stephen pleadingly, his face silvery with sweat. "Steve, the boy don't—you must forgive him, Steve."

Stephen lifted his tired eyes to the other man, his mouth already forming words of comfort, his one desire to alleviate Joseph's distress. And then his vision cleared, and his compassion faded away and bitterness came to him. It was all very well for a man to excuse himself to his son with face-saving lies. But there was a limit to falsehood. Stephen heard himself saying in a stifled voice, "Joe, do you remember a time when you told me that you thought suicide was the only way out for you, and I——"

"You what?" exclaimed Duncan with a fresh access of rage. "Did you drive my poor father that far?" He clenched his young and meaty fists; his black eyes glared at Stephen murderously. "Why, you contemptible wretch!" he shouted. "I ought to kill you! If it weren't for the law . . . my God, Pa"—and he swung to the quaking Joseph—"you aren't going to keep this quiet any longer! This usurer and thief as you've called your friend all these years, this man you've been telling us about since we were children. . . ."

Usurer! Thief! Stephen thought of the non-interest bearing notes Joseph had virtuously thrust upon him against his protest. He thought of the day—the day that Alice had died alone because of Joseph's pressing problems—when Joseph had told him sombrely that death was the only possible solution for him, and he, Stephen, had rescued him. He thought of his honour that he had sacrificed for Joseph Baynes, when he had dealt with Senator Peale. And such a sickness came to Stephen that it seemed to him that he was drowning in black vomit.

Elsa had become frenzied; she began to weep convulsively. Joseph could only stand between his son and his friend, swallowing the salt water that kept rushing into his mouth. Then he stammered desperately, "Steve, Steve, don't blame the boy. . . ."

"I don't," replied Stephen gently. He looked at Duncan, and his huge compassion returned to him in a flood. "Tell me, Duncan, what you meant by what your father has told you ever since you were a child."

Duncan was silent, caught by the strange look on that grey face below him, that mournful and uncondemning smile. He was somewhat shaken. He glanced swiftly at his father, and now a horrible uncertainty came to the young man.

Torn between his fear and his shame, tears began to water Joseph's eyes. "You must forgive, you mustn't think, Steve——" he said piteously.

Stephen got slowly to his feet. He turned to the weeping Elsa; he glanced at Duncan, with his averted face; he looked at Joseph. "I know, I know," he murmured. "It's all right. I understand."

He went towards the hall and Joseph followed him. Once in the hall Joseph pleaded again, "Steve, you are my friend. Tell me you'll always be my friend. The boy is confused; he did not know what he was saying. I never——"

Stephen, in his mercy, lifted his hand. He could not endure it that Joseph should lie to him, should imply that his son was a liar. "It's all right, Joe," he repeated.

He touched Joseph on the shoulder, and the other man bowed his head and his whole body shook. Then Stephen went away, walking like an old man. Joseph watched him until he had disappeared up the street. Then he returned to his sobbing wife and harsh-faced son. He cried out in a tormented and womanish anguish, "Why did you tell him those things? What are you trying to do to me; ruin me? He was my guest, my friend, in this house, and you——"

Duncan stood up, and his strong limbs took on the contours of iron. An enormous loathing glittered in his eyes. "Why," he said, in a wondering tight voice, "you are a liar, aren't you? You lied all the time to us, didn't you? Why?"

Elsa broke in: "Speak to him, Joseph. Tell him you just tried to spare Stephen, though he doesn't deserve it."

Duncan waited, and then as his father did not answer, he smiled sombrely. "No, don't speak, Pa. I'll think better of you if you don't."

There is no place for me to go, thought Stephen, plodding weakly up and down the cobbled streets. No place to go. No surcease for a man. No comfort, no kindness. It was all lies; he had lied to himself all his life. No one ever had a friend. It was so plain now, the awful treachery that lived in every man's heart, the eager betrayal, the ravening envy, the greed, the pitilessness, the gloating joy at another's pain.

Step by step he passed under the high and lonely lamps, and his footsteps rang back dully to him. The houses had turned dark, had retreated into the night. Mists floated up from the damp cobblestones, twirled about the lamps, drifted off over silent lawns. Even the crickets were silent. The moon had dwindled to a round white ball, hard and compact as snow, rolling through streamers of black cloud.

All at once Stephen felt he could not take another step. He came to a horse trough and leaned against it, panting. He tried to call up some strength. He said to himself: I mustn't blame old Joe. What else could he do but lie to his children? But the agony would not release Stephen.

He did not even start when he felt someone grasp his arm strongly and roughly. It took all his strength to lift his head. Someone towered over him like a crudely fashioned dark statue in a bulky coat. "Saw you leave Baynes's house," said Jim Purcell. "Followed you to see if you might want a lift. Got my buggy here. Hop in, Steve." But Stephen had to be half-lifted into the scratched and battered buggy. He found himself lolling on the broken leather cushions. The buggy moved on and Purcell smoked silently. Then he said, "Cold out to-night. Why didn't you take one of those damn' fancy gigs or carriages of yours? What you need is a drink. Lots of it. We'll go to my house."

The buggy rattled and squeaked through the streets, the mists rolling about it. Stephen could make no sound; profound exhaustion kept him silent. It did not matter where he went now. He was only faintly aware of rumbling across the river. He had begun to shiver and his teeth were chattering. Purcell did not look at him; he drove his ancient horse, flapping the reins on its back, and clucking.

Purcell's house in West Town was as large a mansion as that of the Assistant Secretary of State's (formerly Senator Peale), and it was on River Road. But it was an ugly square house of yellow brick, the top story jutting out over those below in a curving ridge. Thin slits of windows with oval tops pierced it, the draperies invisible from the outside. So close together were all these windows, four stories of them, that they imparted a barrack-like look to the house, a staring, bleak, and contemptuous look. No trees softened the outline of the unprepossessing building, and no shrubbery gentled it with surrounding masses. It stood on its wide cropped lawns, and there was something stark about it, something implacable.

Stephen had entered this house a few times before, reluctantly. It revolted him, its enormous rooms badly furnished with mammoth mahogany furniture covered with dark tapestry or horsehair, its glaring mirrors hung without taste, its sprawling rugs of Brussels roses and green leaves, its marble-topped tables, its badly hung draperies of crimson or blue velvet, its velvet-draped fireplaces, its narrow halls and heavy doors and eternally burning great lamps. Purcell, who noticed nothing except human beings, and his business, was indifferent to any dust that gathered, and his servants took advantage of this.

Stephen did not notice the repellent furnishings of the library to-night. Purcell led him in there. He had the largest library in Portersville, and he had read almost all the books. A big fire fluttered on the hearth; it was very warm in the room, in spite of its vastness, its crowding windows, its walls of leather bindings. Purcell, above all things, insisted upon heat.

He pushed Stephen into a chair, opened a towering cabinet, and brought out two large glasses. He half-filled one for Stephen. "Here, drink," he said. "You need it." Stephen stared at the glass dully, and then his empty eyes wandered blindly about the room. He's had a shock, thought Purcell. I have some idea. He's found out something about that pious weasel, Baynes. Well, there was no warning him, the poor goddamn fool. "Come on, Steve," he said in his harsh voice. "Pour it down."

Obediently, Stephen's trembling hand lifted the glass to his lips. He suddenly thought of the antic Aaron, who had forced medicine upon him ten years ago. He said faintly, hardly knowing where he was or to whom he was speaking, "You remind me of my father. . . ."

"Good," said Purcell, throwing his bulky body into a chair opposite, and beginning to drink. "Your Dad and I had a lot in common. Well? Are you going to drink or not?"

"It's a great deal," said Stephen in his sick, courteous way. He drank the whisky suddenly, with deep thirsty swallows, while Purcell watched him out of the corners of his eyes. Stephen put the glass down. His long shivering began to lessen. He leaned towards the fire and stared at it with that blind and seeking gaze. Purcell drank placidly. He finally lit his pipe. He waited. From the hall came the loud and discordant clanging of a clock.

Purcell waited a long time, while Stephen's gaunt features remained fixed and expressionless in the firelight. Purcell said to himself: The world's too much for him; it's always too much for his kind. It gets them in the end. They get killed just as surely and ruthlessly as if a dagger was stuck in their backs. And you can never help them.

The whisky was taking effect on Stephen. He had never drunk so much before at one time, and in his weakened condition he was affected overwhelmingly. His pain receded; the fire enlarged before his eyes, became a conflagration. His body warmed, tingled; sensation receded from his feet and hands. His vision blurred, and he relaxed. He sighed over and over, and the piteous sound was loud in the bleak stillness.

"I don't remember coming here, Jim," he said, his tongue a trifle thick. He leaned back, very slowly, in his chair, and caught the arms, because he was swaying. "I'm very grateful. I—I was cold."

Purcell's grotesque face loomed closer and closer to him, and Stephen lifted his hand as if to ward off that impelling presence. Purcell merely sat and smoked. "I think," said Stephen, with a weak laugh, "that you gave me too much, Jim."

"I'll drive you home. Don't worry."

Stephen stared at him, glazed and confused. "Jim," he said falteringly. "Why did you bring me here? Why are you around me so often? When we were children—I don't know. I can't think clearly. You never said—say—anything very much. We—we don't have anything in common. I'm grateful. But I never understood."

"Maybe I just like to know there are people in the world like you," said Purcell, with one of his ugly smiles. "I don't know why, myself. Maybe your Dad liked to know it, too. Comforting."

Stephen attempted to focus; he frowned vaguely. "Comfort?" he repeated. "What comfort can I offer you? You are self—self-sufficient."

"Maybe," replied Purcell. "By the way, anythin' on your mind, Steve, that you want to tell me?"

Stephen's hands fumbled together; he wrung them again. "I think," he stammered, "that I'm afraid."

"Of what?" asked Purcell easily.

Stephen put one of his hands to his forehead. He was drunk now, but his nature halted any confidences. "I'm not sure. Perhaps I'm imagining things. A man does that, sometimes."

"We're all afraid of somethin', every damned mother's son of us," said Purcell. "If it isn't one—thing, it's another. Think you're the only one in the world with troubles? Look at me; I'm hounded by 'em. Can't sleep sometimes." He smiled at Stephen with gross humour. "That's why I drink whisky all the time; positively reek. You should take it up, Steve." He paused. "Want to tell me about it?"

But Stephen was mumbling incoherently: "My father—just like you. He would sit in the room—— He never liked me. And I only wanted a dog. I never had one. I don't want any now. The dog I wanted is dead a long time now. He was a pretty little fellow; he followed me around."

Purcell was silent. He took the pipe from his mouth and stared at it, glowering. Then he said, "What happened between you and Baynes?"

"Nothing," murmured Stephen. "It was the boy, Duncan. He didn't understand."

"Quite a lot of people don't understand, according to you, Steve. Kind of: 'Forgive them, Father, for they know not what they do,' eh? Well."

The words roared over and over in Stephen's drugged brain: Forgive them, Father, for they know not what they do. Father —forgive—forgive—forgive. . . .

"Yes, yes," said Stephen. "Forgive. I always keep forgetting that," he added apologetically. "I should remember." He drew a deep breath, and for a few moments his reticence was overcome. "The boy—thought—that his father was paying me interest. Twenty-four thousand dollars. You see, Joe needed the money for the Locals—there was the Capital trying to get them, and I think Rufus. . . . Duncan was very angry. Joe must have—must have—let him misunderstand. It was natural, of course; Joe had his pride. Poor Joe."

Purcell said, "I see. The world's full of 'poor Joes.' And they always get more 'poor Joes' to help them. Never mind. It's too late to tell you anything, Steve. There's somethin' from the Bible, I think; 'He that is surety for a stranger shall smart for it.' Proverbs."

"You think I am a fool?" asked Stephen with bemused pain.

"Well, naturally. But you can't help it; you're made that way. Goethe: 'So must thou be—thou canst not self escape.' Good things in those books yonder. If there's a God, I sometimes wonder why He made people like you. Like to think it over, myself, sittin' here by the fire alone. Almost came on the answer once—a damn fool answer that wasn't sensible. Look at you, Steve: you've been payin' all those railroad workers yourself, out of your own pocket. Been going on for a year, eh? Drainin' yourself. And who gets the credit? Red Rufe, the bleeder for his fellow man. The workers hate you because they don't have work, when the whole cursed country is out of work. They never think."

The roaring in Stephen's head was so violent that he put his hands to it; he sank deeper and deeper into his chair. He muttered, "It doesn't matter who gets credit for it. It's enough for me to know they aren't starving. The directors wouldn't let me pay the workers out of railroad funds; I suggested it once and they laughed as if I were insane. So, it had to come out of my personal funds. I haven't any money," he added, with broken simplicity. "The house costs me a great deal. I've got to borrow on my stocks and bonds just to live, and keep going on. I'm going to New York."

Purcell slowly raised himself in his chair and watched Stephen intently.

"It's the Chicago Railroad System, too—a great drain," Stephen whispered "I could keep our workers on my salary—but there are too many other things. Sometimes it all seems too much for me." Now his agony of mind gushed over the dam of his normal caution. "When things get better, I'll be able to redeem the stocks and bonds. They're bound to get better——"

"They're going to get worse before they get better," said Purcell raucously. "The Panic isn't over yet. And so, what will you do?"

Stephen rubbed his cheeks until they were burning. "I don't know."

"How much do you need, Steve, to go on living a while in the damn-fool way you are?"

Stephen murmured, "Forty thousand dollars, I think. I can't use what I'll borrow from New York on my stocks and bonds for purely personal expenses—and the workers. It wouldn't be right; the stocks and bonds are a trust; they belong to the road. So, what I borrow on them will be for the good of the company. But that forty thousand dollars. . . ."

"I'll let you have that forty thousand right now, my own cheque," said Purcell.

Stephen dropped his hands and stared at the other man incredulously. A slow light began to shimmer on his face. He cried out, "My personal note——!"

Purcell shook his head and replied with slow brutality, "Not good enough for me, Steve. I want your coal acreage—your real estate around Wilkes-Barre and Scranton. Outright sale, to me."

All light, all alcholic colour, faded from Stephen's face. Inch by inch, he pushed himself up from his chair. He caught the back of the chair in his sweating hands as he retreated behind it. Purcell watched him, unmoved and smoking, with interest and detachment. His pulpy features took on the contours of hardened concrete which had been discarded and left to dry without form.

"You got there first, Steve; one of the few bright things you've ever done. And I want that land. I'll develop it; you'll never have the money. What do you say?" His voice was loud and strident and beat implacably on Stephen's ears.

Stephen whispered, "I can't. I have to protect Laura. You brought me here, and gave me too much whisky, so you could ruin me, steal from my daughter. . . ."

Purcell shrugged. "Think what you want, Steve. I can't control your thoughts. You need forty thousand dollars. That's ten thousand more than you paid for that real estate. You're gettin' a bargain. I think you'd better take it. What else can you do?"

Stephen could make no sound; he could only crouch behind his chair like a desperate animal driven to a last cover. His breath came faster and faster, until he was panting. Then he said in a stifled and shaking voice, "I was told often that you were a wicked man. Joe and Tom told me. I've heard many stories—exploitation—mercilessness—cruelty."

Purcell raised his eyebrows. "Don't waste your time talkin', Steve. Do I get the land or not? Forty thousand dollars. Think of all the wages you can pay your fellers, even though there's no work for them. Goin' to let 'em starve, Steve?" He waited, watching those distended eyes, that open mouth, that gaping, stricken face. "Of course, you can stop payin', Steve. No weekly cheques, signed by Rufus, your executive vice-president, after you deposited your own funds in the railroad accounts. For the men. Evicted, that's what they'll be. Huntin' in the refuse for food. Kids not havin' any bread. Think it over."

Stephen looked up, his face aged and haggard. Purcell was sitting at his secretary, and the scratch of his pen was loud in the silence. He got up, waved the cheque before the fire for a moment, then extended it to Stephen. "I've written on the back of it: ' Received payment for real-estate acreage located in the vicinity of Wilkes-Barre and Scranton. Contract to be drawn within thirty days.' Put it in your personal account, Steve, so there won't be any gossipin' around. Then you can draw on it to be earmarked for your workers. The way you've been doin'. Puttin' it in the railroad accounts."

Stephen did not move. Purcell went to him, pushed the cheque in his hand. He thrust his hands in his untidy pockets, rocked back on his heels. "You're tired, Steve. Better go home and sleep. The whisky will help. I'm kind of tired, myself. I'll rouse up one of my boys and he'll drive you home. I'm goin' to bed."

Stephen glanced dumbly at the cheque. Then he raised his shattered face and looked at Purcell with agonised accusation. Purcell was apparently unmoved. He shrugged again.

"Rufe won't lend you the forty thousand, Steve. But he might offer to buy your land for about fifteen thousand. I'm bein' your friend, Steve."

"Friend, friend," Stephen repeated. His eyes dimmed. He turned away.

Stephen sat in a state of paralysis at his desk the next morning. He had just deposited the forty thousand dollars in his personal account, and then had immediately transferred twenty thousand of it to the railroad accounts in the bank. His workers would live again in some sort of security, until the Panic passed. But Stephen could feel only anguish and hopelessness. The fire burned strongly behind him; it could not warm his flesh.

His desk was piled high with the bills he had brought from his home that morning. They were like an inexorable demand, which must be met. He took up his pen, but it was a heavy rod of iron in his hand. His clerk entered, cleared his throat, and said, "Mr. Stephen, there is a young man here to see you. A Mr. Duncan Baynes."

Stephen shrank. His first impulse was to refuse to see young Duncan. Then he said feebly, "Send him in." He leaned back in his chair, bracing himself for further insults and upbraidings. He was certain of only one thing: he would not betray Joseph. Far back in his mind a voice was mocking him: "Poor Joe— poor Joe—poor Joe. . . ."

Duncan Baynes, half-belligerent, half-sheepish, came in, holding his hat in his hand. His round hard head stuck above his broad shoulders like a superimposed ball, and his strong features were grim. He said at once, "Mr. deWitt, I didn't know last night. I've come to apologise, and ask you not to blame my father too much. He didn't sleep; I heard him walking the floor. He's afraid you won't be his friend any longer."

Stephen tried to speak, out of his renewed pain, but could not. Duncan resumed: "I suppose you are holding it against my father. I wouldn't blame you, in a way. But my father is really your friend; he only lied to us to save his own pride. He's not much of a man, I'm afraid; he's weak."

Stephen's betraying compassion made him close his eyes with suffering and sympathy. "You mustn't blame your father," he said gently. "It isn't his fault there is a Panic. He will soon be able to recover himself. He mustn't worry about that money. I—I am not worrying. He'll pay it back one of these days. You must have confidence in him."

Duncan scrutinised that sunken face and closed eyes. He thought: By God, a good man! I never met one before. He said, "If my father can't pay you back, Mr. deWitt, we will."

Stephen opened his eyes. Some of the gaunt misery was gone from his face. He could even smile a little, and he said, in a stronger voice, "I understand all about it. Did your father tell you the truth about the whole matter, Duncan?"

Duncan hesitated. Then he lied: "He did, Mr. deWitt. He" —and the young man smiled ruefully, as if in remembrance of a stormy interview with Joseph—"raised hell with me. Now I understand everything." He eyed Stephen warily. "He said, my father, that if it had not been for you we'd have lost the Locals. He said you refused all interest, that you really wanted to give him the money as a gift, and not a loan."

Stephen smiled deeper, and he sighed as if some intolerable anguish were beginning to lift from him. "Your father told you the truth, Duncan. I refused his notes for a long time. But he insisted. He thought it more businesslike. So, to humour him— and he has much pride—I took the notes. But he told you all this, didn't he?"

Duncan's face darkened with something like hatred and contempt for his father. He was appalled. This was much worse than he had expected. He said gravely, "Yes. He told me. Mr. deWitt, you won't tell him that I came here to-day? He will think it presumptuous of me."

Stephen held out his hand, smiling at Duncan like a father. "Certainly, I won't tell him, my boy. I can understand your reticence. But don't hold anything against Joe. He is a good man; he is my friend."

Duncan took that cold and tremulous hand, and for the first time since he had been eight years old he wanted to cry.

CHAPTER TWENTY

THE GREAT crisis that was becoming obvious to a few thoughtful men as the intrinsic disease of the Industrial Revolution finally became dimly patent even in Washington. Enormous and unrestrained products of industry were not matched by a corresponding absorption. Foreign markets, depressed by aimless and insane wars, could not import American goods, nor could their own feverish manufacturers sell their wares to a penniless population. In America, thousands annually left the farms to "work on the railroad," or in factories, and acreage slowly became abandoned. The cities languished in a veritable paralysis of unemployment and starvation, while farmers exhausted themselves in labour with insufficient help. England, who had control of world markets, suffered less than did the United States and other nations.

Like a demented machine that could not stop itself, the mills and factories continued to pour out goods in spite of national inability to sell them. And, in grim secret, men of wealth who owned those mills and factories gathered together for discussion as to how to meet the crisis. It was agreed that only wars could stimulate the absorption of goods. It was noted that few nations, however, were at the present time interested in wars.

When President Hayes appealed to the new city-dwellers to return to the land in order to avert the industrial crisis, or to overcome its immediate manifestations, his plea met with resistance. At one time he said to a confidant, "Territory is no longer the goal of wars. Markets and destruction are the new objectives." He suggested a plan whereby new immigrants to America would consist almost entirely of farmers, who would take up homesteading or work good farms already cleared; he hopefully hinted that Congress might make it mandatory that the immigrants go at once to the land, under pain of subsequent deportation. His enemies, and a number of his friends, indignantly cried that this would be "dictatorship," and "against the principles of the Constitution." Wryly, then, he commented, "It seems that no one wishes to deprive an American, or an immigrant, of his sovereign right to starve." But, as he was a man of some ideas, he went on to suggest that if industrialists persisted in producing goods for which no one could pay, it might be an excellent plan to engage in barter with those nations who wished to buy American products but who had no money. "Medievalism!" cried his enemies. The President shrugged and decided that he would not be the Republican candidate in 1880.

Another crisis, unobserved except by a few, had arisen; the propertyless and rootless men of the cities, who dwelled in warrens, knew nothing of the land, and, in consequence, having no tangible stake in the nation, no contact with its roots, became creatures without honour or metaphysical identity with the source of their lives. Dignity had departed from them with the earth-soil from their hands.

The great Panic became even more terrible in 1877; the hungry and maddened people almost lost their minds. More and more mills and factories emptied themselves; the malignant machines and the open hearths were silenced. As railroads had become so dominant in the life of the nation, they were the chief object of resentment on the part of the farmers, who had discovered that when the cities had no money to buy bread and beef, they, too, suffered. Moreover, the railroads had succeeded in antagonising the farmers, because of their oppression. Most of them increased freight rates at whim, some so high that the farmer could not ship his produce. A powerful railroad lobby prevented the Federal or any State government from regulating them in behalf of the public, whether city or farm. Much of the best land in the West had been appropriated, at low prices, by the railroads; thousands of farmers, discouraged by this, declined to move to fresher acres and new markets. Hundreds of Middle Western farmers, it was learned by their Eastern brothers, were actually burning their fifteen-cent corn for fuel. In the East, corn was selling at one dollar, but the cost of shipping it to hungrier markets was made prohibitive by railroad rates.

The unique crisis in the world's history gathered momentum. Frantically, the city people looked about them for scapegoats. It was inevitable that they should find them in the wretched immigrants from Europe, "who work for almost nothing and are taking the bread from our children's mouths." It was noted that the immigrants created slums; the correlation between starvation wages and slums was not noted, or was ignored. The immigrant, as a person in himself, was the "cause" of the city worker's misery. Now racial hatreds, and especially religious hatreds, exploded through the abounding streets of the desperate cities. The starving and bearded little Jewish pedlar, with his pushcart of shoddy goods, the strangely accented Irishman with his "Popish" religion, were archetypes of evil presented to a frantic population. When the indomitable and courageous Irish immigrants, who worked for almost nothing in the mines and factories of Pennsylvania, formed their "Molly Maguires" in an attempt to raise wages generally, those "old" American workers, who should have been their stoutest and most eager assistants and supporters, found in this "unpatriotic and alien" union of desperate men a new source of hatred.

America, with millions of acreage undeveloped, with millions of bushels of wheat and corn unsold to the starving cities because of the high railroad rates, with industrial warehouses loaded with goods which few could buy, with tens and hundreds of thousands of farm workers leaving for the cities—there to collide with the battered and ragged streams of immigrants also looking for work which was not available—had reached the greatest crisis in her history, a crisis which was not to be resolved in the future except through deliberately planned wars to absorb the products of machines.

The railroads of America, having not been guiltless of this sooty conspiracy against the world, suddenly found themselves wallowing in it. The most appalling of the railroad strikes began in 1877.

The railroads had had a very fine and prosperous time since the War Between the States. They had taken fabulous profits for the operations of their lines; they had watered their stocks with a lavish hand. When the Panic became almost a way of life in America, the operators of the roads, to make up for a decline in income, resorted to such contemptible operating practices as building cheap bridges which collapsed with huge losses of life, neglecting maintenance, and reducing wages. They attempted to ban, through legislation, the Patrons of Husbandry; the farmers grimly began a long war against the carriers.

Never Victorious, Never Defeated

For a long time, through the deepening days of the Panic, the railroads went their happy way. The larger companies, as if demonstrating their scorn of the universal misery, continued to pay large dividends. The Central Pacific returned to its stockholders eight per cent on its stock, while reducing wages ten per cent. The New York Central did the same. Only a few railroads, such as the Chicago Railroad System and the Interstate Railroad Company, passed dividends, and, at the instigation of Stephen deWitt, did not cut wages. And finally the Interstate was the only road which did not seek to destroy the railway Brotherhoods.

For all these things, Stephen was doomed. He could not compete with men of evil. Singlehandedly he could not defy the darkening storm of the industrial crisis which was rolling rapidly over a whole world. He could not point out to all mankind that by debasing and deserting the soil for an open hearth and a machine it was degrading and enslaving itself. He could not say: "There is dignity and security in the land; there is only rootlessness and constantly threatening starvation in the mills."

Thus quickened the era of men without pride. And as they were men without pride they became the calculated prey of future malefactors in government. With an inner and prophetic eye, Stephen could dimly discern these things, and he sickened with his knowledge.

"Somewhere, he got the money to pay the dogs," Rufus said to Guy Gunther in New York. "It isn't a good deal, though he didn't cut wages." Rufus laughed. "The ironical thing is that the Brotherhood and the ' Molly Maguires ' hate him as a ' rich exploiter.' Well, such always happens to fools. But now we can move against him."

"Wait," said Guy Gunther. "A crisis is approaching. You've waited over ten years; you can wait a little while longer."

Throughout the Panic, the unemployment, and the cutting of wages, the railway Brotherhoods had been singularly patient, possibly because they had wise leaders who did not believe that strikes would immediately bring the millennium. But the action of the Baltimore and Ohio, in announcing as of July 16th a cut of ten per cent in wages of more than one dollar a day, was the gunshot that echoed through all the railway Brotherhoods. They decided to take desperate action. The B & O firemen at Martinsburg, West Virginia, struck, declaring that they would not return to work until the cut was restored. The mayor of the city immediately called out the police, who arrested the firemen. But the enraged citizens, who had witnessed the arrests and the resulting mayhem against the railroad workers, assaulted the police and released the prisoners. Infuriated at this attack on their fellow workers, the freight brakemen immediately struck, and no freight was permitted to run through Martinsburg. Over seventy-five freight trains, loaded and waiting, blocked all the lines in Martinsburg less than forty-eight hours later.

The carriers demanded that Governor Matthews of West Virginia call out the state militia. He responded at once, sending out two companies, with commands to shoot, if necessary, any intractable railway worker. But he did not know one important thing: the militia did not exist as a thing apart. It was bound to the strikers by blood relationships and local friendliness. The militia leaned on their guns and refused to act, and merely grinned at the strikers and their sympathisers. The governor, a man who loathed all "insurrectionists," called out the Wheeling militia, and took his place sternly at the head of it, marching upon Martinsburg. By the time he reached Grafton, however, he discerned that the whole area was in a state of dangerous fury, and with an eye to his political future he discreetly deserted his militia, and the pleased men wandered back to their homes.

Now the strike spread like wild flames. The B & O employees in Grafton, Keyser, and Wheeling struck. The alarmed governor demanded that President Hayes send Federal troops to "control this revolutionary disorder." The President debated. "They've brought this all on themselves," he commented with bitterness. He delayed heeding the governor's demand for a day or two, urging, meanwhile, that the carriers meet with their striking men. But the carriers contemptuously refused. The people violently sided with the strikers, and the temper of the whole state became dangerously heated. So the President, on July 19th, was forced to send part of a regiment of Federal troops. The situation became even more menacing when half-starved "scabs" took to running the roads in order that they might feed their families. They made up two trains, one to the west, the other to the east. They were protected by the Federal troops, who attacked the strikers with guns and bayonets. The troops also rode the trains, protecting themselves as well as possible from the stones and other objects hurled at them by a maddened populace.

Never Victorious, Never Defeated

Two days later the B & O was able to move fourteen trains out of Martinsburg. But the strike spread along the entire line into Maryland, where Governor Carroll called out the Fifth Regiment of the National Guard, but at Camden Junction the people drove the "scab" engine crew from the train which awaited the Guard, and the Guard complacently resigned itself to go nowhere at all.

The angered governor then sent three companies of the Sixth Regiment to Camden Junction, where they met a mob of nearly three thousand persons armed with clubs and missiles. In order to protect themselves, the militia fired into the masses of men, killing twelve and wounding scores of others. But from the Junction they were unable to proceed; thousands of men and women stood on the tracks and defied the trains to move. Federal troops rushed to the Junction, bristling with arms, and thirteen more men were shot and the wounded crowded the hospitals.

Desperate and hounded, the strikers formed a committee to call on Governor Carroll, offering once again to arbitrate with the carriers. But the B & O, sure of victory now, declined. More and more Federal troops poured into Camden Junction, and at length broke the strike. On August 1st, the strike was defeated. The B & O contentedly observed what they had accomplished and called it good. Guy Gunther and his friends in New York wired the company a telegram of congratulation.

Guy Gunther privately sent a telegram to Rufus deWitt. It contained only one word: "Now."

Stephen had been watching the progress of the strike and the suffering of the railroad employees with an almost physical agony. Anonymously, he sent a large sum of money to the Camden Junction hospitals to pay for the treatment of the wounded men. Engrossed as he was with his private despairs, and his despair over present events, he did not notice that there was an ominous silence emanating from his board of directors. When he, on August 15, 1877, was advised by his board of directors that they desired him to preside over an emergency meeting, he believed they were concerned only with an increasing decline in the company's income.

Usually warned by premonitions he felt none now. Exhausted and drained almost of his last strength, he met his directors in the board room, prepared for endless complaints and suggestions. He met his brother in the hallway to the room. Rufus smiled at

202

him sympathetically, and Stephen vaguely noticed that the younger man looked particularly warm and radiant. "Tiresome business," Stephen murmured. Rufus took his arm and replied merrily, "There is nothing more boring than men who insist on getting a return on their investments. Never mind; we've managed them before. We'll manage them to-day."

Rufus's obvious affection and winning sympathy to-day affected Stephen to the heart. He walked with his brother into the board room, where his directors sombrely awaited him, and he smiled at them timidly but with a sense of support. Rufus's soothing presence would sustain him in the face of a thousand scowls.

The late summer day was hot and sunless, as grey as ash from which a fire had only just receded. The mountains, clouds painted in grisaille, stood over the shadowless city against a livid sky. A heated and pearly reflection filled the board room, in which every face appeared colourless and harsh. The directors had never regarded Stephen with friendliness at any time, even before Aaron had died. Since Aaron's death, they had hated him, and he knew it. He looked at them now, these bankers, steel manufacturers, mine operators from Scranton, lumber merchants, representatives of various industries supplying the railroads. There were ten of them, and they stared at Stephen, not indifferently or coldly, as usual, but with motionless savagery. Among them was Jim Purcell, who shifted his eyes from Stephen and turned his doughlike face towards the window.

Rufus gave his brother a consoling pat on the arm and seated himself near Tim Brownell, president of the Portersville National Bank, who was his particular friend. He lit a cigar, winked with friendliness at everyone but Purcell, who ignored him. No one greeted Stephen, and this disturbed him. He stood hesitatingly at the head of the long table, examining each man, and each returned his regard stolidly. Finally his eyes fixed themselves on the massive profile of Purcell and lingered there, and his tired face tightened. He did not sit down. He said quietly, "You have asked me to appear. What is the business of the board to-day?"

It was Purcell who answered him in his loud, hoarse voice: "They want to reduce wages ten per cent, like all the other roads."

Stephen believed that the focus of this savagery he felt was in

Purcell, that Purcell was the spokesman to-day. This man had taken from him the fortune of his little daughter, had forced him, under vague threats, to part with what had been the fortress of his child.

"We can't reduce wages," said Stephen, and his voice thickened with panic.

The men stirred, glanced ominously at each other, returned their eyes to Stephen. Tim Brownell was a lean and gentlemanly man with a carved and patrician face. He said, with a banker's weighted intonation, "Sorry, Steve. We can, and must. We will be brief about all this, and come to the point. We've kept wages up, at your insistence, and have lost dividends. The railroads are in a hell of a condition these days. Every other line but ours, and the Chicago Railroad System, has reduced wages. We're being hated—by our friends, the other carriers. I'm not going into the matter of your paying the unemployed railroad men their usual wages." He smiled with aristocratic disdain. "That is your own doing—and your own borrowing from God knows where." He did not glance at Purcell, whom he feared and respected.

He went on with a graceful wave of his hand: "But, as of the 10th, we are going to have to cut wages ten per cent, to save our own necks, and to stop putting our friends in an embarrassing situation. Unless," he added gently, "you have the funds to make up for the cut, yourself." A chuckle broke briefly from his fellows, and then they were still again.

Stephen sat down. He placed his palms on the humid table, and they began to sweat. He turned his sick face from one man to another, and everywhere he encountered stonelike derision and hatred. He began to speak through a constricted throat:

"Aside from the fact that reducing wages from their almost barbarous level now, means we'll incur a strike, the B & O——"

"You forget," said Mr. Brownell with tender urbanity, "that the B & O settled that strike, with Federal troops. I don't think our own governor would hesitate at calling out the militia and demanding troops from the President."

"The people," said Stephen, "are dangerously aroused. They haven't forgotten the hanging of the 'Molly Maguires.' They haven't forgotten Martinsburg and Camden Junction. Something is moving through the whole country. You can't oppress men forever. If employers continue to do so, they'll reap the whirlwind, if not to-day then to-morrow. The oppressors will become the oppressed. Power has a way of shifting. I am afraid I am not making myself clear."

"No, Steve, you aren't," said John Schwartz, the biggest lumber merchant in the vicinity. "But I can tell you this: your coddling of our employees isn't getting you anything. They despise you, and they are losing respect for authority."

Stephen thought of the desperate dead and wounded in Martinsburg and Camden Junction. He thought of the starved wild faces, the hunger which had driven normally peaceful men into raging action. He said faintly, " One of these days the carriers will pay for what has happened. Bloodstains are never washed out."

He turned to Rufus, who was studying his clasped hands. Rufus was serious, his red hair flaming in the grey light. "Rufus," said Stephen. "Have you anything to say?"

Rufus sighed; he unclasped his hands, moved in his chair. He looked at his brother with a pathetic smile. "Steve, what can I do? I'm in the minority."

Every mouth in the room compressed itself to keep from smiling; eyes wrinkled; lips twitched. Then Purcell said casually, in his rough voice, "Well, I make another minority report. That makes two of us, then, Steve, and me." He shrugged. "Not that that will amount to anythin'."

Stephen was startled. He put his hands to his sunken cheeks, and pressed them. For the first time in almost a year he spoke to Purcell: "You, Jim? You're with Rufus and me?" He was incredulous.

"That's right, Steve. But correction, please. Just you and me. Rufe's not with us." He bent and spat into a cuspidor.

Rufus laughed richly. "Oh, come now, Jim. I know you don't like me. But please remember that I've always stood with old Steve here. You choose to ignore facts. For your own purposes."

Of course, thought Stephen. For his "own purposes." He was too confused and shaken to examine his disturbed thought. He could only think: Everyone knows what Jim Purcell is; I know, myself, to my own misery.

"We are wasting time," said Mr. Brownell, glancing at a thick gold watch. "Two clients are awaiting me downstairs at this very moment. We're going to be frank with you, Steve. You know that you've borrowed two hundred thousand dollars from Jay Regan, in New York, pledging twenty-five per cent of your stocks and bonds in Interstate. Of course, you did not feel it necessary to mention this important fact to your directors."

"Stop being so goddamn pious," interrupted Purcell with hoarse rudeness. "You're not superintendent of the Sunday School here, Brownell. Save the injured pieties for the little boys and girls who suck lozenges while you tell them all about God. Steve borrowed on his own stock—and that's his own business—and we've got our benefits. Our investments haven't depreciated, though the stocks and bonds of other companies have. Equipment's in fine shape. Come to the point. You want to reduce wages ten per cent. You're prepared to put down strikes with the state militia, and with Federal troops, if necessary. That's it, isn't it?" He glared at the blushing banker contemptuously. "Steve don't want any of that, neither do I. I think we can ride out the Panic. You don't think so, at least, you want dividends and you can only get them by reducing wages. Say it, and be a man, and not a parson."

Brownell, hating him impotently, gave him a suave twinkle. "I must congratulate you, Jim. You always come to the point, logically. Yes, that is what we want, and that is what we are voting for."

Stephen's confusion and anguish increased. Somewhere, there was a mystery he could not see. What Purcell had said was unbelievable; he was not a man to agree to passing of dividends; he was not a man to flinch at strikes and violence. Why, then, was he demurring now?

"I think," said Rufus gravely and with a look of sincere openness, "that Jim's afraid that a strike would result in damage to our property." He frowned, as if in distress. He spread out his hands. "Frankly, gentlemen, I am afraid I am not voting to-day. I cannot go against Steve; he is usually right. I am not prepared to say whether he is or not, at this time. Steve, you understand?" he added apologetically to his brother, and with a grieved smile.

"Yes, I understand," said Stephen confusedly. "And I'm glad you are refraining from voting, Rufus." He paused. Of course, Rufus was right: Purcell was anxious to avoid damage to Interstate property. He had no more magnanimous motive than this. Oh, God, Stephen thought, in his distraction: If only I had a lot of money! He stammered, "I'm sorry if I inadvertently offended any of the directors by not divulging to him that I borrowed on my stocks and bonds. I—I'm afraid I didn't think it necessary.

I'm paying the interest on my loan to Regan. I'm certain that I shall soon be able to redeem the stocks and bonds, as things improve. And do not be alarmed, gentlemen, that I shall pledge more of that collateral; I regard the Interstate as a trust——"

"A sacred trust," said Purcell solemnly. He spat again.

Stephen ignored him. "The Interstate belongs to all of us," said Stephen. He looked at them imploringly. "In many less tangible ways, it also belongs to our employees. We are not divisible. We can't betray our men. I believe the Panic is passing. Let us not alienate the men who create our wealth and make it possible to have a company at all. They are hard-pressed enough as it is. To reduce their wages would be to reduce them to at least semi-starvation. It would provoke a strike. You may be able to put down that strike, but the violence would leave its hatreds behind to boil up disastrously in the future. I am appealing to you as honourable and sensible men. . . ."

"Sorry," said Brownell. "This is not of our own choosing. We have our stockholders to consider. You are pleading for what you believe to be ' justice,' Steve. But you are forgetting that the stockholders ought to be given ' justice,' too. What is the vote?" he asked his fellow directors.

"Reduce wages ten per cent," said each man readily, with the exception of Stephen, Rufus, and Purcell.

The directors stood up and confronted the agonised Stephen. "That is all," said Schwartz. Stephen dumbly interrogated each set face in turn, then he averted his head and walked slowly out of the room. Purcell watched him go, alternately thrusting out, then sucking in, his thick lips. Then he said to his associates. "There'll be a strike, y'know. And we'll put it down, some way. Yes." He grinned sombrely. "First act, first scene. I know what you're all going to do—a little later. Can't say I blame you; Red Rufe here's the better man. Better for the Company. We'll get nowhere in the race a few years ahead, with Steve. Why didn't you ask him right away? Save him a lot of misery in the long run."

"Now, Jim," said Brownell affectionately. "For the life of me I don't understand you. We appreciate Steve's leadership; we are grateful——"

Purcell casually uttered an obscenity. "A thing I can't swallow's talking out of the side of your mouth. But a knife pushed into your guts with a smile, hurts just as much as a knife pushed in

without one; more so, in fact. Why don't you get it over with?"
He turned to Rufus, whose florid face had become dark and fixed.
He tapped Rufus on the chest. "Waitin' for your next orders,
eh? From Gunther?"

Rufus stepped back a little. But the other men laughed easily,
shook their heads, and left the room in groups. Rufus began to
follow them, but Purcell caught his arm. The two men regarded
each other in silence, Rufus's tawny eyes suddenly vivid with
hatred, Purcell grinning sardonically. They stood that way for
several moments, rigid and unspeaking. Then Rufus said, "Take
your hand off me, Jim."

"Have I got it on you?" asked Purcell, glancing down at his
hand with surprise. "Now, think of that. Always thought I
wouldn't touch you with a ten-foot pole."

He leaned against the board table and began to scrape out his
pipe, letting the refuse fall to the floor. "Got to sharpen this
knife, one of these days," he remarked. He peered at Rufus with
his muddy slits of eyes. "Always best to keep a knife sharpened:
never know when you might need to use it."

"What do you want?" asked Rufus.

Purcell blew experimentally through his cleaned pipe. He
nodded, as if satisfied. "Something you think you have, but never
had. No mind. I'll tell you about it someday. Maybe sooner
than you think."

"Your style of speaking is very literary," said Rufus. His
colour had become congested, and he clenched his fists. He moved
closer to Purcell, who was staring at him with interest. He started
to speak; the veins swelled in his temples and his throat became
swollen. "I congratulate you, though, on your subtlety."

"Do you now?" asked Purcell slowly. He snapped his knife
closed, and put it in one of his bulging pockets. He dusted off his
soiled hands—great and meaty hands—by rubbing them together.
The bulging areas of flesh under his sparse eyebrows knotted.

Rufus did not reply to him, but his breath became loud and
uneven in the renewed silence. He stood near Purcell, tall and
wide, and handsome as a lion about to charge. Purcell still leaned
negligently against the table, but his muscles tensed. What the
hell, he thought. Does he know? And how? Has he got a spy
out, or something?

"I'm not ready to deal with you yet, Purcell," Rufus said, and
he spoke almost inaudibly, as if he were strangling. "That can

wait a little. First business first. And let us not be subtle. You were about to say——?"

Purcell shook his head as if in wonder. "Who's bein' subtle now?" he asked, like a man speaking aloud to himself. He straightened, stood solidly on his feet. Rufus was tall, but not so tall as he. "And better watch out," Purcell continued. "Men of your colourin' are likely to get apoplexy. Shouldn't wonder if you had a stroke one of these days. And that would be bad—for the company. Expect big things of you in the future, Rufe. And I aim to go along with you. Nothin' can stop fellers like you, and I'd be the last to try. That's what I wanted to say, until you went—literary on me." He snapped his fingers in Rufus's face, but Rufus, becoming more crimson and congested even than before, did not recoil. For an instant or two he seemed about to lunge at the other man, and Purcell watched him.

Then slowly, moment by moment, Rufus forced himself to relax. His colour receded; his muscles slackened. Purcell observed this with admiration. Got to give the devil his due, he thought. He's smoothing himself out by will power and that's the kind of feller we need at the head of this business.

"You wanted to warn me about my health?" said Rufus, and now he was actually smiling a little.

Purcell nodded. "That's right, Rufe. And Steve's health, too. What you aim to do about him is all right. Better for all of us. But hurry about it. He can't stand the strain too long. Let him down easy. Or look for a few surprises you won't like. But then, I don't have to warn you. You're an expert at pushin' in knives so that the other fellow hardly feels it. Just remember to do that to Steve. No gloatin's, y'know."

"You mystify me," said Rufus.

Purcell sighed. "Well, now, Rufe, when you talk that way you kind of disappoint me. All I want of you is for you to keep on makin' Steve believe you're his friend."

"And if I don't?" asked Rufus.

Purcell lifted his mighty shoulders, then dropped them. "I hate to say this, Rufe, but you'd regret it. Yes, I think maybe you'd regret it to the last day you live." He scratched one huge ear. "No flies on you, Rufe. You know exactly what I'm talkin' about. Keep on rememberin'."

Rufus rubbed his upper lip with the knuckles of his right hand. He regarded Purcell with narrowed concentration.

O

"Regan's my friend," Purcell continued. "I could step in any time, and he'd never sell the stocks and bonds Steve put up to him, except to me. I'd hate to have to step in; you can bank on that. I'd rather let you go your fine way, for my own convenience and profit."

"I see," said Rufus. Angry consternation came to him. He was to be robbed of his dramatic triumph, a triumph for which he had lived. Gunther might be puissant, but Regan was king. Gunther would never forgive him if Purcell got word to Regan. He thought of the nights, the endless nights, when he had rehearsed what he would say to his brother on the final day.

"I thought you'd see," said Purcell approvingly. "Bright man." He nodded at Rufus amiably, and humming hoarsely under his breath lumbered weightily out of the room.

When he was alone, Rufus sat down suddenly, for he was trembling. He pulled out his kerchief and mopped his face. You won't get what you want, Purcell, he thought. And then he exclaimed aloud, with utter hatred and rage: "Lydia—Bitch!" He repeated the words over and over, and at each exclamation it seemed to him that something stabbed him viciously in the chest and something pierced his head with violent pain. He put his hand to it. Apoplexy. He must remember.

On September 10th, the employees of the Interstate Railroad Company were notified of a ten per cent cut in wages. They struck at once. That night, by torchlight, they hanged Stephen deWitt in effigy. They carried placards bearing lewd caricatures of Stephen, disfigured with a long predatory nose which the strikers believed represented Jewishness. The people followed them through East Town, cheering, carrying thick clubs.

On September 14th the governor called out the state militia, at the request of the directors of the company. On September 18th the President sent Federal troops. The trains moved, manned by gaunt men who shamefacedly averted their faces from the furious mobs in the switchyards.

It was the beginning of terror. And intermingled with it was the dangerous rise of racial and religious hatred. The people, detesting Stephen, turned upon each other. Riots broke out in the dingy streets. Strikebreakers were beaten, and their wives and children threatened. The trains moved, guarded by Federal troops armed with guns and bayonets. The turmoil and the frenzy grew in the city, and at least fourteen men were killed and scores more wounded. Miserable shacks were burned. The little Catholic church, standing humbly and shabbily on the edge of the city, was fired. The priest hid in the home of a friend.

On September 30th the strike was broken, violently and bloodily. The men went back to work, and all was calm. But Portersville did not forget.

CHAPTER TWENTY-ONE

THE LATE autumn evenings had become cold and sweet as a pear. But Lydia deWitt, as she forced her way through tall grass to the glade this September night, felt that all nature was overlaid with silent ominousness, abandonment, and desolation. The wedge-shaped moon, coppery and sinister, looked like a gleaming blade of an axe hurled into the heart of the black sky. A group of willows streamed with moonlight, appearing like great shrouded ghosts along the bank of the small stream. She saw Jim Purcell awaiting her on the mound. She saw the red coal of his pipe, and stopped near him, straight and tall and forbidding.

"I see you are here, finally," she said, with a hard intonation. "Four weeks——"

"Sit down, Lydia," he said, in his gravelly voice.

But she refused to sit down. "It's true I have no claim on you, Jim," she went on, without moving. "But things have been so frightful; I thought you'd be here at least once to tell me what is happening, and to give me some comfort." Now she faltered, as if fighting tears. "No one came to—him. Not a single one of his ' friends.' Lying there, after his collapse, watching his door. I saw him. You might have come. . . ."

"Sit down," Purcell repeated placidly. "Seems like we've got to have a talk."

Lydia, wrapping her cloak about her, sat down on the mound; but at some distance from Purcell. "Rufus—went to Philadelphia at least twice, these past four weeks, and to New York once," she said bitterly. "You must have known about it; you always do. But you never came. . . ."

He reached out and took her cold and inflexible hand. "Lydia, he didn't. Yes, we got to have a talk. Red Rufe didn't go out of town until last night. He was hiding out in the homes of some of his friends, overnight, every time he said he was leaving."

The hand weakened in his, and Lydia turned her pale face in quick surprise. "Why should he? He knows I don't care whether he comes or goes, or where he stays. If he wants to sleep over-night with—— He has done that before, and it was a matter of complete indifference to me. Why should he try to deceive me now, or give me false explanations?"

"Because, old girl, he's got on to us. Maybe he's known about us for a long time. Me watchin' him, and him watchin' me! Seems I'm gettin' slack as I grow older; I ought to have been suspicious about him, him bein' like a red fox."

"Oh, my God!" cried Lydia sharply.

"Now, now, don't get excited. I'm having him watched real close now. He's in New York all right, to-night. Wait a minute; I'll tell you all about it." Lydia listened and her face grew whiter, and she began to shiver.

She pressed her fingers over her face and bowed her head. "The children," she said weakly. "Cornelia. . . ."

"Now, you hush up, my girl. Think I'm a fool? When the time comes we'll rock Red Rufe far back on his heels, and you'll get what you want. Leave it to me; I've been around this world quite a while. Well, anyway, while he was waitin' to pounce on us, up here, and havin' his boys watchin' us while he was supposed to be out of town, I couldn't come."

"Loathsome," Lydia murmured, and shuddered.

"Most things in the world are, when you come up against them. Only way to have the world nice and sweet is not to be important, and live in back streets in a little house, and have no money. And maybe, too, Rufe thought he'd get a lever on me, to use for his brand of bluff and good-natured blackmail. Well, I fooled him. But let me tell you this: we aren't goin' to wait much longer. Maybe not more than a week."

He pulled Lydia's head down on his big shoulder with rough tenderness. "Things are movin' fast. And we're movin' with 'em. Now, tell me all about Steve."

"You knew he was ill," said Lydia. "You know everything." She tried to make her voice cold and forbidding again, though the strength of the arm about her shoulders comforted her wretched heart. "You never came."

"Well, I couldn't. Steve hates me now. Thinks I did him dirt."
Purcell then told her of the coal acreage. Once or twice she
stiffened, but the arm pulled her closer. "They'd have gotten
that away from him, too, the way they're goin' to get everything
else, except the trust funds for his kid. Thought I'd save somethin' from the wreck for him. When the time comes, I'll go right
up to him and say: ' Look here, Steve, I'm goin' to develop that
acreage damn fast. I'm puttin' my money into it, and you'll get
fifty per cent. And maybe you'll be able to buy back a good piece
yourself."

Lydia said, "Jim! Why don't you tell him now? It would
comfort him so."

Purcell shook his head. "That wouldn't be sensible, Lydia.
He never took care of himself. Know what he'd try to do? He'd
use any money I advanced him—and he'd ask for an advance—
for the railroad men. To help restore part of their reduced wages.
I've told you what he's been doin' for years, for them." Purcell
made a repulsive sound of disgust. "And look how they treated
him. But when Rufe does what he's goin' to do, real quick—
maybe to-morrow or the next day—why, there I am, helpin' to
pick up the pieces. Now, wait a minute, Lydia. I can't stop Rufe.
I haven't that much money; couldn't buy back Steve's stocks and
bonds. And wouldn't, anyway. Steve just isn't the man for this
business."

"The last blow will kill poor Stephen," said Lydia brokenly.

"Maybe," said Purcell, and now he was sombre. "The world
always kills men like Steve. Good old Christian world. Never
knew a man who did things for people who didn't get hanged
for it, or burned for it, or hated for it. That's human nature.
Two thousand years of Christianity, and look at the world.
No, sir. It don't pay to help anyone, if you want to live in
peace yourself."

Lydia smiled sadly. "But you've helped Stephen, though he
doesn't know about it."

"Well, yes, always did, though blamed if I know why. When
we were kids, there were young fellers always plottin' to make
him look ridiculous, or pull tricks on him. Once, when Steve
was about thirteen, I heard the nice lads makin' up a plan to
waylay him on the way home from school, and set some dogs on
him, and beat him. Why? A lady like you wouldn't know. But
I knew. You see, I always understood about this damn world.

213

It doesn't bother me any, no more than the wind does, or the snow, or the rain. It's just a fact, and you've got to deal with facts." He grunted.

"Well, anyway, I picked out the two ringleaders of the boys who were goin' to show Steve what the world was really like. So I kicked hell out of the two brawny lads, and laid down the law to 'em, and they left Steve alone." He smoothed Lydia's hair, then gently kissed her cold shocked face. "Why, old girl," he said with uncouth tenderness, "in some ways you're like Steve."

Lydia's cheeks began to run with slow tears. "His friends," she said. "That Joseph Baynes and Tom Orville. They never came once, after all he has done for them."

"That's natural," said Purcell mildly. "What did you expect? After all, he helped them, didn't he? Think they can forgive him for that?"

"But the Baynes boy came," said Lydia. "A dark, ungenerous-looking boy, with common features. He just sat with Stephen, and I don't think they spoke half a dozen words. I don't think Stephen was deceived this time; I don't think he thought Joseph Baynes sent his son. But he was comforted, just the same. It's strange that the most unlikely seeming people, the ones you'd never expect to show compassion, are the people for a crisis; while the soft-spoken ones, the ones with ideals about friendship and humanity, are the first to desert a man who's stricken."

"Well, of course," said Purcell indulgently. "That's very simple. Hypocrites, that's all. They know they're just as terrible as anyone else, and just as greedy and rapacious, but they kind of think it will elevate them in the eyes of other people by puttin' on a fine show."

"I think I feel a little ill," said Lydia.

Purcell kissed her again. "Come on, now, that's not like my girl. Not my girl who's goin' to stand up to Red Rufe very soon and tell him right out to his face what she thinks of him. Come on; give me a smile. Well, dreary sort of smile. Before we go on with this talk, you tell me why you love me. I'm nothin' to look at, no beauty."

Lydia laughed feebly. "I think I always loved you, even when I was a child." She put her hand on his misshapen cheek and love pulsed through her palm. He turned his head and kissed it, slowly and deeply. "I always knew what you were; yes, always,

Jim." Her pretty teeth glittered in the moonlight and her face softened with poignant emotion.

"That's wonderful," said Purcell, grinning. "Nice to know somebody appreciates my sturdy qualities, me havin' kept them hidden all this time, even from myself. But I want to know something, Lydia. How's Red Rufe treatin' Steve these days?"

Lydia became thoughtful. "I believe all you've ever told me about Stephen and Rufus, Jim. And so I can't understand. Nobody can be kinder than Rufus to his brother. He sits with him for hours at night, and, sometimes he's even made Stephen laugh. His solicitude is wonderful."

Purcell frowned, and he glanced at Lydia with sharp alarm. He said, "You know, sometimes I'm not very bright. Thought you'd have caught on, old girl. Knew things by intuition, or something. Made a mistake. You listen to me: I told Rufe that he must never let Steve know that he's the boy whose knife is in him, that he's plotted the whole thing, with a little side-help from his friends here and in New York and Philadelphia. Knew Steve couldn't be saved; but I wanted him to die as peaceful as possible, when the time came. If he got to know that it was all Rufe, Rufe with the smiles and winks and pats, Rufe he's trusted all these years, Steve would go out of his mind."

Purcell got up, and gave Lydia his hand. "A man always runs true to form. Almost always. Conscience? That's somethin' Rufe wasn't born with. Like bein' born blind. He can't help it." He brushed mould and leaves from Lydia's cloak, then took her in his arms very gently. "Don't you mind, now. I'm not a man with a conscience, either. I never tried to fool you, old girl. You know all about me. It's time to go."

Sophia said to Lydia irritably, watching her with fierce hazel eyes, "It's very tiresome. Stephen meets every crisis in his life by getting ill. I'm sure I don't know all the details, but Stephen is certainly a very poor-spirited man because he can't face the fact that the road had to reduce the men's wages. And surely, knowing how the strikers acted, and how they hate him and ridicule him, for doing simply what he had to do, he shouldn't have been so overcome. Every time he read the newspapers, and saw how the strike had to be put down with the militia and troops, and how the engineers and firemen and the conductors and such, tried to destroy our property, Stephen went to pieces. The doctor had to be called in the night, sometimes. It upsets the household dreadfully. Casts a pall over it, and that isn't good for the girls." Sophia's hard and raddled face twisted. "Rufus suffers too; he feels too deeply, and is too sympathetic. I don't know where he gets his patience from—having the burden of everything on his shoulders while Stephen lies in bed looking like a corpse and trying to escape everything by being ill."

The two women were having afternoon tea together, delicate China tea in frail cups. The drawing-room fire was lighted, and the amber light chased early evening shadows over the walls and the ceiling. Lydia dropped her hands in her brown-velvet lap, and the nails entered her palms. But she said calmly, "Stephen is returning to the office on Monday. You must remember, Mother deWitt, that the doctor said Stephen had suffered a slight stroke, or a heart attack. He can't help responding to stress."

"When Alice died," Sophia began, tossing her grey head.

Lydia stood up abruptly. She tried to control herself, but became very white. "You must not talk about my sister," she said in an unsteady voice.

Sophia stared, started to speak. Then she was struck by the tense and formidable expression on Lydia's face. She threw up her hands as if in despair. She said finally, "What is wrong with everyone in this house? Mad, absolutely mad. A person can't say anything! When I try to sympathise with Rufus, and deplore Stephen's weakness, he stops me and looks furious."

Lydia tried to soften her voice. "Mother, it is just that you don't understand everything. Neither do I." In spite of all that she knew, she felt pity for this impacable old woman in her black silk and fringes and gold chains and brooches and glittering rings. She sat down again and took up her cup and sipped it. "Forgive me if I was too brusque. We have all been under a great strain. You must remember that Stephen almost died once or twice. But he is better now, almost well. We must try to forget how wretched things have been."

Sophia was a little mollified, though she tossed her head again with an injured air. "Yes, things have been ' wretched,' as you say, Lydia. And you haven't helped them by going about with a very grim face. Sometimes your eyes actually flash—quite murderously. There are times when I feel that you actually—actually!—blame poor Rufus for it all." She watched Lydia cunningly, but Lydia remained impassive.

"You imagined it," said Lydia listlessly. "I—I have just hated the situation. I—I'm not blaming Rufus, if that is what you fear."

"The situation isn't Rufus's fault," said Sophia with umbrage.

Lydia was silent. She was well aware that Sophia had more than a slight knowledge of Rufus's plans and plottings, and her heart began to beat sickeningly with rage and disgust. But she slowly ate a piece of seed cake. She said, "I grant you everything. We can do nothing; we are only women. And now, if you'll excuse me, I'll see how the girls are behaving themselves at tea in their rooms."

She stood up, and Sophia gazed at her bleakly. Even after all these years she still resented Lydia's breeding and poise, the effortless grace of her head, her manner. The brown velvet of her dress was draped most simply, without fringes or shining buttons, and the bodice outlined her slender figure without artifice. She watched Lydia leave the room and muttered under her breath. No puffs or rolls or elaborate twistings marked Lydia's hair; it was smoothed back from her pale, quiet face into a thick knot at the nape of her neck. Not a morsel of style, thought Sophia, pouring another cup of tea for herself.

Lydia went slowly up the winding stairway, her gown flowing behind her. The afternoon was darkening steadily, this first day of October, and the rain rushed at the windows in wild gusts. Lydia paused at a window on the second floor and glanced out at the sombre mountains, purplish mist against a gaseous sky. She could see the terraced gardens below, the grass still almost unnaturally green, the faded and lonely trees.

Lydia hesitated at Stephen's door, knocked softly, then entered. Stephen was asleep. He lay on his bed like a dead man, his grey face turned to the window. Firelight shivered over his folded hands and ashen hair. Lydia waited, but he did not move, and so she closed the door softly again, a savage ache in her breast.

The children were alone. Their governess was a frail little lady, and Lydia had insisted that during this "tea-hour" she should rest in her own room. Lydia found this arrangement pleasing, for then she could speak to Cornelia and Laura as she wished. When she entered now Cornelia squealed delightedly, flung herself into her mother's arms and kissed her with exuberance. Lydia stroked the fiery curls fondly, touched the brilliant cheek with a tender finger. She knew all about this eleven-year-old daughter of hers,

217

but that did not decrease her love. Lydia believed that love had a powerful, gentling influence even upon those natively barbarous.

Laura had arisen when her aunt had entered, and waited near the table drawn up near the hearth. She smiled as Lydia came towards her, and accepted Lydia's kiss without a word. Sophia had remarked, on more than one occasion, and with malice, that "Lydia seems singularly uninterested in her own sister's child. A little unnatural." But Lydia and Laura understood each other without emotional displays, and a strange, silent, but eloquent love had grown between them. They were alike, and they were aware of it, and communicated only by a glance of an eye, or a faint gesture.

Lydia sat down at the table on a chair which Cornelia, with much briskness and considerable emphatic awkwardness, drew up for her. Everything that Cornelia did was done with emphasis, energy, and physical strength. This impressed people with her great "simplicity." But Lydia knew that the seemingly simple were not simple at all.

"What have you girls been doing all day?" asked Lydia. Cornelia beamed at her mother. "Miss Trenton's been telling us all about the telephone," she said. "Mamma, shall we have a telephone? Miss Trenton says that one of these days we'll all be talking to each other, way across the country, and maybe across the oceans, too! Won't that be wonderful?"

"I can't see why," replied Lydia with a smile. "I think we all talk too much as it is. Rather awful to think that we might be able, some day, to shout across continents and seas, breaking up the silences which, so far, are safe from our voices."

Cornelia frowned, somewhat puzzled. "But Miss Trenton says if we can ' span ' the sea and the countries and talk to each other, it will make the world smaller and then we'll understand each other and there won't be any more wars. And she says that some day we'll have big air machines, flying over everything, flying all around the world, carrying goods to everybody that needs 'em, and we won't be strange to each other any more, and will love each other, and we won't be fighting." Cornelia smiled at her mother wistfully, and Lydia suppressed her smile at this hypocritical ingenuousness. Then she was annoyed. "Miss Trenton is a dear little soul," she said in her most cool and practical voice. "But I'm afraid she is an idealist. She is wrong, of course. We'll just be able to murder each other more quickly and efficiently.

Never Victorious, Never Defeated

You remember the story of dynamite, Cornelia. That was supposed to make wars so horrible that no nation would dare attack another nation. The musket was supposed to do that, too, and the cannon. And the crossbow before them. No doubt the Greeks thought their fireballs, thrown from ship to ship, would bring peace to the world. But nothing ever brings it. Because man is a beast, you see!"

Cornelia's bright and eloquent face took on an expression of acute distress. This, too, was artifice, and was intended to inspire compassion in the adult Lydia for an innocent child who was being disillusioned. Lydia laughed shortly. "Don't pretend with me, darling," she said. "You are a little brute, yourself."

Cornelia, who had an intense sense of humour, broke out into loud and husky laughter. She hugged her mother with violence. "Mamma, you are so mean! You know people expect you not to be yourself. Why, you wouldn't dare!"

"That is true; not many people ' dare,'" agreed Lydia. "It is very wearing, and even dangerous, at times, to be honest."

"Well, I like people like me," replied Cornelia. "What's wrong with that?"

"Some of us are a little more discriminating." But Lydia smiled sadly.

Cornelia thumped herself down at her mother's feet, and began to smooth the velvet of Lydia's dress. She could be herself with her mother, and this was occasionally relieving. "If people like you, you can get what you want out of them," she said. The firelight flickered over her beautiful round face, which was full of laughter. Lydia put her hand compassionately on the head at her knee, and turned to Laura. "What do you think, my dear?" she asked.

Laura considered meditatively. Then she said in her low, sweet voice, "I don't care, very much, if people like me or not. I just don't want them ' touching ' me with anything. Unless I like them a great deal."

Cornelia was becoming restless, as she always did when she was no longer the centre of attention. She caught her mother's arm to attract her notice. "Mamma, why can't we have a tennis court? It's all the rage. Everybody has a tennis court. Tennis is so fashionable."

"You know why, dear. The grounds all slope. And I don't think Uncle Stephen ever takes any interest in tennis."

Never Victorious, Never Defeated

Cornelia studied her mother slyly. She began to hum hoarsely under her breath, a habit she had when she was indulging in secret and not very charitable thoughts. Then she jumped to her feet and exclaimed, "Let's play dominoes!" She made a clatter with the tea things, dumping them untidily on another table, and keeping up a loud and aimless conversation as she laid out the dominoes. Lydia watched her intently.

She played the game with the children; she played mechanically, for she was full of her own miseries and despairs. Where would they all be, a year from now? There were great boulders and chasms and gloomy, terrifying vistas before her, and thunders of violence. She, herself, could endure it all. What of Laura? Lydia looked at that small and reflective face bent over the dominoes. A stream of dark hair like a vapour fell over the child's pale cheek. Lydia saw the deep indentations about the full grey eyes: the stigmata of the sensitive and quietly impassioned.

"Why are you sighing, Mamma?" asked Cornelia curiously.

"It is a very depressing day," replied Lydia.

When she went down to the drawing-room later, Rufus was already there. He stood up when she entered, but he did not speak. Lydia sat down, conscious of her husband's concentrated regard. She kept herself very still, and said tranquilly, "The weather is bad, isn't it?"

"Yes," he answered, "it is." In spite of Lydia's efforts she could not refrain from glancing at him. He appeared drained and harassed, and he was strumming his fingers on the arms of his chair. "Something is tormenting him," she thought with sudden pity. "Something is driving him."

Rufus said, "I've just been up to see Steve. I believe he is coming down to dinner to-night. I'm very glad. There is—business—to do next week, and we need him." He shook his head. "Everything is very bad. Tens of thousands of dollars in damage to our property. The—rascals—burned up considerable in the yards. We're just beginning to discover the extent of the destruction."

Lydia was silent. Rufus did not speak again. He only sat there, staring at the fire and strumming. Moment by moment he became more absorbed in his thoughts, and they evidently did not please or comfort him. He is not thinking of the destruction and the strike, Lydia reflected. He is thinking of Stephen, and me. He hates us both now, and the hatred is not giving him pleasure. It is giving him pain.

Sophia came in then, sighing and complaining. She kissed her son and said, "My poor Rufus, how ill you look!"

CHAPTER TWENTY-TWO

"I SHOULD like to see the yards," said Stephen to his brother. His voice was very weak since his sudden illness, and more faltering than ever. Though the carriage was snug, and a thick fur had been thrown over his knees, a steady shivering ran over his emaciated body. Rufus had wrapped him in mufflers and coats; it was like draping a skeleton, he thought, without ridicule but only with a gloomy pity. It was stupid to feel pity for a poor fool like Stephen, who was better out of what had eaten away his life. But there it was. Rufus smiled at his brother easily. "It won't make you happy," he said. "Why not wait until you're stronger? This is your first day. And we're beginning to clean up the mess."

The rain had not stopped for five days; it lashed the roof of the carriage, shot long needles like quicksilver over the windows. The carriage swayed in the wind, and the restive horses ran like satin with water. "I should still like to see the yards," said Stephen; his cheeks had fallen in, his face had dwindled. His large grey moustache looked absurd in that diminished face. Yet it added to the pathos of his appearance. He was only forty-three; he seemed sixty or more.

"Very well," said Rufus cheerily, as he climbed like a youth into the carriage. But he was depressed. "Do it quick," Purcell had warned him. He was conscious of being hurried, not only by Purcell, but by this dying man beside him. He had no doubt that Stephen was dying. Lydia might have been incredulous had she known her husband's thoughts as the carriage began to roll gingerly down the hill, the wind screaming about it. I'll always take care of Laura, Rufus said to himself. A sweet child; I love her like my own. Somehow, I must make Steve understand that, at the last.

Never Victorious, Never Defeated

Stephen had no strength for speech during the long journey towards Portersville. Rufus had told him carelessly that the board of directors were meeting that morning but that it was about some "routine matter." What more can they do, than what they have done? Stephen thought. He was as cold as death; his muffled hands were icy. They'll probably be jubilant. But some way, I can alleviate what they have done. When I'm a little stronger I'll pledge some more of my stock for the men. The stock is rising; there will be dividends; I'll soon be able to redeem it. He glanced timorously at Rufus, who was gazing at the drowned mountain road and the dismal scene beyond it. The mountains surrounded them, sombre, drenched, and cold. Rufus, commented Stephen silently, seemed exhausted. He had much less colour; the flesh about his mouth kept twitching. Stephen murmured, "It has been hard on you, Rufus. I can't tell you how grateful I am that you stood by me."

Involuntarily, Rufus pressed his brother's shoulder. "Please don't," he said, and his voice was almost harsh.

They had almost reached the lower level on the grade to Portersville when Stephen, speaking with difficulty, and halting between sentences, told Rufus of the sale of his coal acreage to Purcell. "I had to do it; I needed the forty thousand dollars for the men. And the household expenses. And Joe Baynes had to have some to pay interest on the bonds he had pledged to Alex Peale in Philadelphia. And Tom Orville—he has such bad luck lately with his lumber mill. . . ."

Rufus heard this, aghast. He had counted on acquiring the coal for himself. For a moment he was enraged against this imbecile of a brother for depriving him. He said, and his words were heavy with hatred and anger, "Purcell! Forty thousand dollars! Robber! What a contemptible person! Why didn't you come to me, Steve?"

Stephen regarded him with dim surprise. "But you don't have forty thousand dollars, Rufus," he said.

Rufus caught himself. He shook his head despondently. "Of course I didn't. But I could have lent you some; we could have managed some way. But Steve! All that money for dogs who've been deriding and blaming you for weeks."

"But how could they know?" asked Stephen weakly. "I never told them; it would have been wrong, in a way."

Never Victorious, Never Defeated

"How much do Baynes and Orville owe you now?" asked Rufus, newly enraged.

Stephen hesitated. Then he said with apology, "Twenty-seven thousand dollars—Joe Baynes; twelve thousand dollars—Tom. But they'll pay it back some day, I'm sure."

Thirty-nine thousand dollars! A fortune. Rufus felt as a man feels who has been cruelly robbed; he thought again of the coal acreage. That coal ought to have been developed for the Inter-state Railroad Company. It would be bad news for the directors when they discovered that what they had intended to seize for the sake of the company now belonged solely to Jim Purcell. Now Rufus's wrath turned against his brother. What a fool this was! How completely incompetent and prodigal!

The carriage rolled through the cobbled streets of Portersville, and approached the railroad yards. Now it was with sincerity alone that Rufus said, "I wish you weren't determined to see the damage, Steve. It will only sicken you."

But Stephen, with a tremendous effort, pulled himself forward so that he might see all, and see it clearly. He saw the blackened hulls of the roundhouses, the repair shops; he saw the ebony skeletons of freight cars. Ties had been scattered; in a few places rails had been pulled up. The rain and the wind howled together over the desolate ruins. Stephen hardly saw the ruins, however; he was looking with passionate intensity at the men work-ing about the wreckage, grim-faced, gaunt, and shabby men shivering in the cold and dampness, their miserable clothing blowing about them. They worked in utter silence, not glancing at each other, not speaking. Stephen said, "Let us go on." He sat back in his seat and closed his eyes. Men did not destroy the means of their livelihood wantonly; men respected their tools. They had been driven to this madness only by hopelessness and hunger.

The worst thing of all, thought Stephen, who felt that he was literally dying in this resurgence of agony, is that now there will be a wave of punitive legislation against labour. It will probably be decades before unions will be of any force or importance again. In the meantime the people will suffer recurrent depressions, hunger, unemployment, and despair, without any redress. They will smoulder for many years, remembering.

Stephen's brain seemed to light up with a dreadful clarity. And when the people remember, he said to himself, they will become

223

as oppressive as the oppressors once were. There is never any charity in humanity, no reasonableness, no tolerance. They never say to each other: "Wrongs were committed against us. But revenge is no substitute for justice."

"We are here now," said Rufus, and he spoke gently. "Let me help you out." Stephen opened his eyes. The carriage was standing before the Portersville National Bank building, and the door was open. Moving like an old and stricken man, Stephen allowed himself to be almost lifted from the carriage by the coachman and Rufus. Leaning on Rufus's arm, he walked into the building. As he felt Rufus's strength and solicitude, Stephen thought: If it were not for Rufus I think I would drop dead, here and now, and I would not care.

"Rest a little in your office," said Rufus, helping his brother to remove his mufflers and coat and shawls and hat. Stephen sat down heavily, his breath hard and choking. He tried to smile at his brother, who was watching him with unguarded compassion. "I don't know what I'd do without you, Rufus," he said. "What do the directors want to-day?"

Rufus hung up Stephen's coat, and said, without turning, "Nothing important." He stood by the window and looked down at the wind-lashed park below, with its barren trees. The mountains were hid in mist.

"When I think what they have done," stammered Stephen. He wiped his wet forehead with the back of his hand. "They weren't starving, even if the dividends were being passed; our stockholders weren't in need. . . ."

Rufus still stood at the window. "I know," he replied.

"You stood with me," Stephen went on. "Loyally."

Rufus turned from the window, and all his colour was gone. Stephen shook his head over and over. "It is the only thing that has sustained me—your loyalty, Rufus."

Rufus said laboriously, "Let me help you into the board room." He lifted his brother to his feet, but he kept his head averted. Together they walked in slow step down the hallway to the room where the directors awaited them.

They were all there. They looked up when they saw Stephen and Rufus, and then, involuntarily, they rose. Each man examined Stephen's face, and then each man turned away, waited until Stephen was seated, then sat down. Jim Purcell's expression was morose and glum, and he stared at his swinging boot. Then every man looked as one at Rufus deWitt.

"I am sure that we are all glad that Steve is well enough to be with us again," he began smoothly. He waited, but no one answered him. Then Rufus said, in a louder and harsher voice, "Well, let us get down to business! I——"

"Feelin' the strain, eh, Rufe?" asked Purcell, and spat.

"I understand there are a few details," said Stephen, in his dim and deathly voice. "You wished to talk with me about them?"

"Not exactly details, Stephen," said Mr. Brownell. His aristocratic face was pale. "We have come to the conclusion that you aren't the man for a rugged business like this. We know you have been seriously ill; so we'll not take up too much of your time. What we have to say may sound cruel, but we believe it is for the best, not only our best but yours also. It is a hard thing to say; it must be said, and we regret it."

"Though the Sunday School has now come to order, we can still dispense with the pieties," said Purcell. "Come to the point, and let the man go."

But no one spoke. Rufus sat in his chair, his leonine face dark and gloomy. Stephen turned to one man after another, in silence; then he asked, "What is it? I am afraid I do not understand."

Purcell glanced about him contemptuously. "No one volunteerin' as the axe-man? Want me to do it, you bein' such nice kind gentlemen?" He received no answer. "You want me to be spokesman, eh? You haven't the heart for it now?" He paused. "Look at him, boys. That's what you did to him. Necessity, you said. He ain't the man for us, you said. But now you sit there and turn your palms up and examine them, and scrutinise your fingernails. All right, then. I'll give it to him, though it's not my place. That's his brother's job."

Stephen's heart began to beat very fast, and the anguished pain which had struck him a few weeks ago raced through his chest and down his arm. His breath caught in his throat, and he clenched his weak hands in an effort to breathe. He said to Rufus feebly, "What is it? Tell me."

Rufus was forced to look up, and he met Stephen's dying eyes, and flinched. A deep silence fell in the room. Rufus opened and shut his mouth, and then abruptly turned away. Purcell watched him cynically. "Well, well," he remarked. "You're not so bad

225   P

as I thought you, Red Rufe. Man like you shouldn't be president, maybe?"

"President?" murmured Stephen. Grey sweat stood on his forehead.

"No one is going to crash in, first off; so I'll start it," said Purcell. He leaned towards Stephen. "It's simple. They don't want you as president any more, Steve. Think you aren't fit for it. You gave Jay Regan twenty-five per cent of your stocks and bonds as collateral for a loan of two hundred thousand dollars. We went into that before. You can't redeem the stocks and bonds; short-term loan, three months. The three months are up. Regan's at liberty to sell the collateral on the open market now. Gunther and Gould and Vanderbilt want to buy it, and depress the Interstate stock. But they all had lots of meetin's, those fellows, and Red Rufe here. They kind of like him. In it with 'em."

"Wait!" cried Rufus, and now he jumped to his feet, his face congested. "Damn you, you wanted him not to know—you told me——"

"Changed my mind," replied Purcell. "He don't need you any longer, Rufe. He's got me. And he'll find out, anyways, in a few minutes."

Stephen's mouth was open, and they could hear his rasping breath. He put his hand to his heart. Rufus looked at him, and all his features sharpened with pain. He did not sit down, but supported himself by pressing his fists against the table.

"Well, let's go on," said Purcell, grimly enjoying the expressions on the faces of all the men. "All the fellers in New York, in their meetin's with Rufe, came to a very kind conclusion. They're helpin' Rufe buy your stock; they believe in him. Think they can use him in their manipulations when they take possession of other railroads, in a monopoly. Somethin' tells me that Rufe is going to fool 'em, after all, and so we're all in it with him, against the fellers in New York. But that's our secret.

"And there's the Chicago System. No funds in our treasury just now, with the Panic and strikes and all, to service the indebtedness to Chicago. But we're all gettin' together, and payin' in proportion out of our own pockets, to keep the Chicago out of the claws of the New York boys. Except Rufe. That's his game with New York. Sorrowful that the other directors worked behind his back. Gettin' the New Yorkers to help him buy your stock, while we watch in the background seein' that at the last minute we'll be able to repay their loans to him. Outfoxin' them. And Rufe'll have your stock, and we're behind him, and we're goin' to vote him in as president."

Stephen was no longer breathing audibly. He had become very still. The sweat ran down his temples and cheeks like tears. A strange dignity stood on his face. When he spoke it was with quiet strength: "I think I understand. But first I wish to say that Mr. Regan assured me he would not sell my stocks and bonds, so long as I paid the interest, which I have been doing." He was not looking at Rufus now, but only at Purcell.

"You have that ' assurance ' in writing?" asked Mr. Brownell in a hushed voice.

"No, I have not. It was only his word."

Purcell shrugged elaborately. "' His word,'" he repeated.

Stephen was gathering all his last resources together. "I am sorry if you consider me unfit to be president of this company," he said. "You will not, all of you, lend me the money to redeem my stocks and bonds?"

"Sorry, Steve," said one of the directors. "Jim, here, has explained the whole situation. But don't worry that the New York men will ever gain control of our company. It would be very hard for us to raise the money ourselves, as we have the Chicago System to consider, too. Rufus has managed very cleverly with Gunther and Gould and Regan and Vanderbilt. He'll hold them off for a long time. You couldn't have had our support. You haven't been well for a long time, and——"

"And you believe me incapable of directing the affairs of our company?" asked Stephen.

Mr. Brownell sighed. "I am afraid——"

"And this has gone on for a long time?"

No one answered him. Then, in an ebbing voice, Stephen polled them, man by man. "You, Tim? You, George? You, Stratton? You, Jim? You, Edward? You, you?" One by one they nodded, carefully avoiding his eyes. And then only Rufus was left, Rufus staring fixedly at the table on which he leaned.

"And you, Rufus?" asked Stephen gently.

Slowly, as if forced, Rufus lifted his head. Stephen smiled at him compassionately. "No, don't answer," he said. "I understand. You never believed in me, after all. Rufus, it doesn't

227

matter. You see, I have had an idea, for over a year. . . . But there is something else which I must say. You have plotted against me, and you've ruined me, and you've wanted my house and everything that is mine. You thought that it should all be yours. But there is one thing I shall always remember: you have been kind to me. You haven't willed it that way, but it happened. You began with treachery and hypocrisy; you ended it despising yourself, and with concern for me." He reached across the table and laid his thin fingers on his brother's arm. "I think perhaps you are right. I think you are a better man for this business than I."

Rufus regarded his brother in silence, and white clefts of honest shame and suffering carved themselves about his nostrils. If only he wouldn't smile at me, he thought.

Stephen's eyes were brilliant with his compassion. "Yes," he said, "a better man for this business. My father was wrong, and I knew it from the beginning."

"No," said Rufus, "he was right. I learned a lot from you, Steve. I learned how to be patient, and wait, and gather facts, and proceed on actualities and not on excited illusions." He averted his head. "I am sorry."

Stephen covered his eyes with his hand. "I wanted, from the first day, to give it all up to you. But something stopped me." He removed his hand and gazed apologetically at his brother. "I—I can't remember what stopped me. I suppose it is because I am very tired just now."

The great hollow of pain in his chest became wider. A silvery mist floated before his vision; there was a clamorous ringing in his ears. Now there was no sensation in his arms and legs. He made one last supreme effort. "There is an envelope in my desk, with a red seal. Would you bring it to me, please?"

Every man except Purcell immediately jumped to his feet as at the welcome offering of escape. But it was Rufus who reached the door first, and then the others merely stood about the room, not looking at each other. In a few moments Rufus returned and silently gave his brother the requested envelope. "A match, please," said Stephen, and his voice was now so far lost that only Rufus heard him. The match was lighted, and Stephen, with an enormous effort, applied the flame to the envelope. He let it drop into a large tray on the table, and watched it burn. The red reflections ran over his sunken features and over the sweat that dripped from his forehead and temples. Then, when the papers were consumed, he smiled.

"Those were Joe Baynes's and Tom Orville's notes, for nearly forty thousand dollars," he whispered. "Made out to me."

Rufus moved away a step or two, appalled. "But Laura!" he exclaimed, horrified.

"Laura—has the trust funds," said Stephen. He stared at Rufus mournfully. "And I have left the house to you, Rufus. You always wanted it. I made out a new will. . . ."

Jim Purcell, moving rapidly, came to the table, bent down and examined Stephen's face. "A doctor," he said roughly. "One of you damned fools go out and get a doctor!"

Four of the directors rushed from the room wildly, but Rufus remained, standing beside his brother. He muttered, over and over, "No. My God, no." There were tears on his thick red lashes.

Purcell gently leaned Stephen back in his chair. He folded the numb hands in Stephen's lap. He wiped the wet face with his own handkerchief. Then he peered up at Rufus. "Don't worry," he said in his loud, hoarse voice. "You'll get over it. In the meantime, bring me a glass of water."

When Rufus brought the water, Purcell pressed the glass against Stephen's ashy lips. But Stephen was beyond swallowing now. He opened his eyes slowly, and fixed them on Purcell speechlessly.

"Can you hear me, Steve?" asked Purcell, almost shouting. "Listen! That coal acreage—I'll develop it. There's fifty per cent for you, out of proceeds, or for your little girl. Hear me, Steve? Hear me?"

Stephen had no voice. But the death-filled eyes brightened for an instant, as with joy or wonder.

"I always meant it that way, you poor damn fool," said Purcell, kneeling beside the dying man. "To keep it out of the hands of these here other fellers. Saved it for you. Hear me, Steve?"

There was no sound in the room. The remaining directors and Rufus stood in distracted misery near the table. Then, suddenly, the silence was broken by one deep sigh, and then another. Rufus put his hands to his ears.

Purcell stood up, rubbing his hands together. "I hope he heard what I said. Kind of like to hope that. One of you better go out and meet that doctor and tell him it's too late."

CHAPTER TWENTY-THREE

THE MOON glared down at the snow on the mountains and in the narrow valleys, and the snow billowed in great white dunes so that the landscape might have been a scene on the moon itself. An absolute silence had sucked away all sound; not the slightest wind blew nor did the frost crackle or a tree creak.

It was midnight and Lydia was sitting alone with her husband near the fire. Sophia had retired an hour ago, but husband and wife had not spoken a single word since then. They might have been strangers, watching the fire, neither reading or moving.

At last Rufus said, " Well, you asked me to stay, after my mother left. What is it?"

Lydia looked at him before answering. He had lost considerable flesh these past two months, and much of his colour. Because of this, his red hair was more conspicuous than ever. Wrinkles had appeared about his eyes, and there was now a permanent cleft on each side of his mouth. If we have all suffered, he has suffered, too, thought Lydia with both bitterness and pity. She said at last, " I have wanted you to know that I don't blame you too much, Rufus. I know that you betrayed Stephen; I know that you have waited over eleven years to take what he had. You see, it wasn't you who really defeated Stephen, and killed him. The world killed Stephen, and his own nature."

Rufus's face changed. He began to rub his mouth with the knuckles of his right hand, and he turned to the fire again.

" You always knew that would happen," Lydia went on gently. " So you waited, and you worked, knowing your time would come. You were not deceived by the very paradox which amazed some other people: Stephen's sudden spurts of power and perspicacity and apparent ruthlessness. Yes"—and she smiled sadly as Rufus abruptly faced her—" I know so much more than you could possibly understand."

She waited, but Rufus, though he had flushed, still did not speak. She went on:

" Stephen never wanted to live after Alice died. In fact, knowing him so well now, I doubt if he ever wanted to live. Alice changed that a little, gave him something to exist for. Then she was taken from him. You see, Rufus, he told me about Mr. Gunther, and how he had been able to circumvent him. That was before Stephen and I stopped being friends."

"He told you about Gunther?" asked Rufus, surprised and deeply interested.

"Yes. I think he had to tell someone. He trusted me, and so he told me."

"Go on, please," murmured Rufus. The tenseness of his body was beginning to relax. *He had to tell someone.* He, Rufus, had long wanted to tell "someone" himself.

"So, even when he outwitted Mr. Gunther, it was no pleasure to him. It was a—sickness. He was always being betrayed by his compassion, and so, when he did what he had to do to Mr. Gunther, he was sorry for him. A paradox? But aren't all of us always being torn between our emotions and our reasons?

"Stephen was not fit to struggle with evil, because there was so little evil in him."

Lydia hesitated. She could scarcely bring herself to the final words she must say. She glanced at the ormolu clock on the mantelpiece. It was almost half-past twelve. Her hands became suddenly damp, and she wiped them with her lace handkerchief.

"Yes, you are right, Lydia," Rufus was saying.

"But there is something else, too," said Lydia in a lower voice. "Stephen also died when he came to realise that he had never had any friends, in spite of lies, hypocrisies, and affirmations of faithfulness. During the last few months of his life he would wait for Mr. Baynes and Mr. Orville, but they never came to him. They must have heard that he was ill, a month before he died, but they never came."

Rufus spoke with sudden bitter harshness: "He lent those rascals nearly forty thousand dollars, and to protect them he destroyed their notes! No, they never came, the righteous dogs. And I could have ruined them, and revenged Steve, if he hadn't destroyed those damn' notes! I could have taken over their——" He stopped abruptly.

But Lydia, as if she had not heard, went on: "What has a man to live for, except love, and personal ambitions? He can survive without ambition, but he can't survive without love."

She looked at Rufus, and now her face was stern and cold.

"Though you didn't have very much to do with Stephen's defeat—and I mean his spiritual defeat and death—you betrayed him in his emotions. The ' affection ' was an unnecessary cruelty. He came to rely upon it."

Rufus stood up very slowly but deliberately, and as if with purpose. "I've always thought you were a perceptive woman, Lydia, and an intelligent one. But in a way or two, you are stupid. ' Unnecessary cruelty.' I had my personal and exigent reasons for it, yes. I also knew poor old Steve well, and in the past years I came to know him better. What had begun on my part as ' hypocrisy,' as you would say, and for my own reasons, also became, a little later, and to my own surprise, a real affection for him. You see, Lydia, things are never as vile as you think they are, or as good."

He smiled at her sombrely, and she sat up straighter in her chair, staring at him. He nodded. "I never stopped hating the fact that he was president of the company, but I finally understood this served my purpose very well. The whole complex business would take too long to explain, and has too many ramifications. You never gave me any credit for being paradoxical, myself.

"I'm wandering from the point, though. Steve was not only a suicidally compassionate man, he was also intuitive. He was on his guard for a long time, and never was entirely trustful of me. But when I began to feel a genuine, if contemptuous, affection for him, he knew. He knew he never had a friend, except Jim Purcell, and he was always trying to beat down that knowledge because he detested Purcell's ethics. He knew you weren't his friend."

Lydia turned crimson. She stood up and faced her husband on the hearth rug. Then she paled, and her face took on the colour and naked shine of bone.

"You despised Steve, Lydia, because you considered him weak. That's the simple truth. As a woman"—and Rufus paused a little, his eyes shining maliciously—"you like strength in men. You call it cunning. You like open and brutal strength—like Purcell's."

The name lay between them like a weapon. Rufus watched Lydia, and laughed a little. "We'll come back to Purcell in a few moments. I just want to show you, my dear, that in your own clever way you are quite a fool.

"Steve loved this house. He knew that I loved it, too. And so, at the last, when he felt death in him, he left the house to me, though my father had bequeathed it to him and his heirs 'forever.' Naturally you never arrived at the truth when you thought about this. You probably considered it 'compassion' or silliness, on Steve's part. He did it because he wanted someone to own this house who cared about it as much as he did."

Lydia stood in stiff silence, very white, her black mourning silk draped about her slender figure.

"You don't love this house, my dear Lydia, nor does my mother; she is only proud of it, and she will live here all the rest of her life. Cornelia loves this house. No matter where she goes, she will always return to it. Steve knew that, too."

"You are imagining things," stammered Lydia. "You are trying to excuse your conduct. . . ."

Rufus was beginning to enjoy himself. He shook his head. "You are a very logical woman, Lydia. But logic is too rigid; it never bends or embraces, or covers intangibles. It is wonderful for syllogisms, but never admits that there is more to reality than it covers."

"No!" exclaimed Lydia. "I refuse to admit your premises."

"You'll never learn, I suppose, Lydia, that there is more to living than just premises. Do you know," he continued, eyeing her curiously, "I once thought you were a very subtle woman. You can be very subtle about abstractions, but realities throw you into a dither. Like little Laura, you are over-civilised."

Lydia gazed at him with sudden and intense astonishment. This made Rufus laugh shortly. "You are mortified to discover that I'm not as single-minded or as uncomplex as you thought I was. You'd much prefer to think I'm a very lively and completely ruthless villain."

He glanced at the mantel clock, checked it with his gold watch. "In about ten minutes, Lydia, your carriage will be here to take you down to Mrs. Townsend's house. Never mind how I know; I just know. Once there, with your friend, you intend to start suit for divorce against me, on some delicate ground. Then you intend to marry Purcell."

Lydia reached blindly for a chair, and fell into it, her great dark eyes fixed on Rufus. He was smiling at her with high amusement, yet he spoke gently: "There was a time when I would have fought all this, my dear. You see, I still loved you.

233

Perhaps, in a way, I love you still. But I intend to let you divorce me. You see, I am president of the company now, and I have the house. I need and want sons. It may surprise you to know I have already picked the lady who will be my wife.

"Cornelia is my pet, and my darling. But she might be in the way of my new wife, for a time. So, being a sensible man, and knowing that you are, in your limited way, a wise woman as well as a good one, I think it best that Cornelia go to live with you. And with Laura. You were made Laura's guardian, you know. I'm not afraid that Purcell will ' turn ' Cornelia against me. She is only eleven, but she has a mind. You are a just person; you will allow Cornelia to return home whenever she desires, on a visit, or whenever I wish to see her. And you'll never lie to her about me. You see how I trust you."

Lydia exhaled her held breath. Tears began to fill her eyes. When Rufus lifted her hand and kissed it, the tears spilled over her cheeks and she sobbed brokenly.

"Don't, Lydia," said Rufus softly. "Don't begin to think for a minute that perhaps you've been unjust to me. You haven't, in a large measure. I'm going to miss you like hell; I'm going to miss the girls even worse. But for what one gives up, sometimes, one gets a great deal more."

PART TWO

CHAPTER TWENTY-FOUR

ALLAN MARSHALL leaned on his hoe to stare for a considerable time at the great and beautiful white brick house high above him on its terraces. Hot sunlight struck its lower arches, its tall white pillars, its long and blinding windows. On this lower terrace the willows moved in constant light, bowing and blowing like green fountains, and oaks and elms sheltered tilted spaces of dark grass. Late roses were still blooming on the descending stone walls; paths lined with phlox, marigolds, sweet alyssum, summer lilies, and many other flowers whose names he did not know, wandered casually up and down the terraces and disappeared behind thickets of trees and shrubs. A mountain wind, carrying the scent of roses and pine, filled the shining silence all about the young man, and occasionally a bird sang suddenly, or, carrying radiance on its wings, darted up to the sky.

If I had a house like that, he thought, with mingled resentment, ambition, and envy, I'd never leave it for those damned places they go to—New York, Paris, Newport, and the Riviera. But he knew he would, for he was not only a highly intelligent young man, but a disingenuous one. He smiled to himself sourly. He wiped his sweating face, resumed his cultivation of the narrow garden on which he was working, and let his ambition take hold of him once more. He knew exactly where he not only wished to go but was determined to go. To dream was not enough; daydreams drugged a man's spirit and left him nothing at the last but the sick belly and hating nausea of envy and unproductive spite. He despised those who enjoyed fortunes for which they had not worked; but he despised, even more, those men without ability, intellect, or aspiration who hated the fortunate. He had to listen to them often. He knew he would need them, and that he would use them ruthlessly.

He saw the house, and what the house represented. Though he was the gardener and walked among beauty, and worked with it, he had no feeling for it and, in fact, hardly saw it. A tree was

237

a tree to him, and a damned nuisance, sometimes, when it had to be pruned; flowers were pretty, but they had to be staked and watered, and served no real purpose to a man who was on his way. He thought of the half-crippled and malign old woman who would occasionally, and with pain, lean on the arm of a manservant and stiffly walk around the gardens in the evenings. She rarely left the house and its grounds; she never went on the constant hegiras of the rest of the family. For her, these gardens bloomed and the trees blew and the paths must be kept well gravelled and trimmed. Allan suspected that she was as little moved by natural beauty as himself. The power of possession was enough for her, as it was enough for him.

He tore at some weeds with calm viciousness, ripping out the roots, tossing them aside. A weed produced neither beauty nor harvest, therefore it had no reason to live. He took pleasure in destroying the weeds, his young face intent. He thought of the men he represented, and he studied the weeds. These men were brothers to this worthless growth, but the men were necessary for what they could do for men like himself.

He wiped his face again, and then, on a higher terrace, he caught the vivid electric blue of a dress. What the hell, he thought, leaning on the hoe again. The old devil very seldom had visitors, and when those visitors did come they wore sober rich silks and not wild colour like this. Moreover, he had not heard the sound of a carriage winding up the mountain. Then he knew. It was the young girl, that Cornelia deWitt, the grand-daughter of the old woman. But what was she doing here in July, when her father, stepmother, and two little half-brothers were in Newport? She must have come last night.

The violent colour was slowly descending the terraces. He caught a glimpse of brilliant red hair between the trees. He had often seen Cornelia in her carriage on the streets of Porters-ville, during the brief weeks she and her family spent at home. He had thought her amazingly beautiful, except for her hair. He had no penchant for hair so blatantly red.

Unaware of him, she had begun to sing as she descended smoothly and easily. She had a hoarse and lively voice, and the song she sang was a popular one, vulgar, common, but vigorous. It suited her. Allan began to smile. He was averse to "unrefined" females, especially if those females were young; he preferred pale and gentle and silent young girls. However, if a girl was a

238

minx he believed it added to her jauntiness if she did not pretend to be otherwise.

Now Cornelia stepped out on a small area of velvet grass which sloped about four feet above Allan Marshall. She still did not see him. There she stood against the bright green background of grass and trees, unusually tall but with a youthful voluptuousness which was startling. She was only nineteen years old; she had the ripe figure of a woman in her late twenties. The blue dress, shimmering, skin-tight over the high full breasts, the narrow waist and the swelling hips, set off every attribute. Below the hips, the gown billowed into ruffles and draperies and ruchings. She was holding up considerable of it for the sake of free movement, and Allan could see her fine curving legs almost to the knees. Her slippers matched her dress exactly. Her flesh was as pale as a lily, enhanced by flutters of white lace petticoats.

A beam of light struck through the trees, and her masses of heaped red curls burst into fire. She blinked, but not before he had caught a glimpse of her tawny hazel eyes, full of life and vitality. They were lion's eyes, yet humorous, and seemed to possess a primordial zest. Her broad full face was coloured strongly, and her big full mouth looked like a poppy in full sunlight. Her slightly aquiline nose gave a predatory expression to a countenance that was otherwise good-tempered and gay. She was lifting her head, and Allan saw the long white lines of her young throat, and the roundness of her dimpled chin. She broke into another song more than slightly lewd and rollicking. She started to laugh. A red curl had fallen on her neck. She tucked it away, patting it lovingly. Then she saw the young man below. Her mouth fell open, showing the big white teeth.

"Hallo!" she exclaimed, and her husky voice was almost a shout. "Who are you? The new gardener?"

He smiled up at her, without respect. With enormous perspicacity, he understood people; so he knew that his lack of servility and humbleness would not offend her. "Yes, Miss deWitt. Or, at least, I'm one of them, working all through the summer when the spring work is done. I'm Allan Marshall," he added. He leaned on the hoe again, staring up at her with open admiration. She had not dropped her dress over her legs; she showed no maidenly confusion. After a moment or two, during which they smiled at each other, she advanced farther down the small terrace

239

to join him. He put out his soiled brown hand to assist her, but she was already leaping over the edge of the terrace in a shower of silk and lace. Once beside him, he could feel her tremendous verve and energy. She expelled a primitive force, utterly without any concealing elegance.

She was staring at him, pleased. She let her skirts drop, not as if conscious of what she had been revealing but simply as if it was no longer necessary to hold them up. "You don't look like a gardener, Allan," she said with candour.

"I'm not, really." He took out his pipe and calmly lit it while she watched him. "I'm reading law at night, in the offices of the Assistant Secretary of State, Mr. Peale. He's assigned one of his lawyers to teach me."

"That's wonderful," said Cornelia admiringly. "So you're going to be a lawyer. In Mr. Peale's office."

"Not exactly, Miss. I'm going to be a labour lawyer. My dad's an engineer on one of your father's roads. I know all about labour problems. They aren't going to be solved without lawyers. And I'm going to be one."

"Are you an anarchist?" she asked with interest.

He grimaced. "No, I don't think so. That's what the railroad owners call people like me. But I'm not. The future lies with the workers of America, and——" he hesitated.

She shouted with laughter, and pointed a ringed finger at him. "And you're going to be a part of the future! I know all about people, and you're really not part of the workers, and you don't groan for them. Not really!"

Her common but beautiful face glowed with mirth and happy derision. Her breasts rose and fell as she screamed in her amusement, and the bright blue of her bodice rippled and swelled like water. There was a scent emanating from her, a clean strong scent of atavistic youth and power, and her forehead exuded sweat in the heat of the sun.

For an instant or so, Allan was angry and nonplussed at her exposure of what he was. Then he was relieved. He leaned against the trunk of a small tree, crossed his legs, and smoked. What a damned vixen it was, and what a cunning one, too. He decided he liked Cornelia very much, but he was not prepared to trust her, for all her frankness and easy democracy. He suspected that they hid considerable hypocrisy and sly affectation. He waited for her to expend her gleeful and mocking laughter at his expense. At length she just stood and looked at him, her face simmering with enjoyment.

"I think I like you," she said at last. She studied him frankly, from head to toe, not with the insolence of the incalculably wealthy, but with the manner of one young creature scrutinising another. She was very tall, but he was at least six inches taller than herself, and thin and muscular, brown of skin, and very dark. He had a lean face, almost hawkish in profile, and quietly fierce black eyes. His black hair rose erectly from his tanned forehead like a mane, and curled at the back of his neck. Like Cornelia herself, he gave out an aura of immense strength, but his was less spectacular and more controlled and subtle.

Completing her scrutiny, Cornelia sank down on the grass in a swirl of petticoats. She sat cross-legged, revealing her calves. She kicked off her pointed satin slippers, and wiggled her toes with open relief. She squinted up at the young man humorously. "How old are you, Allan?"

"I'm twenty-six, Miss." She noticed again, and with pleasure, that he had a sonorous voice.

"I'm nineteen." She pulled up a handful of grass, and began to chew on one blade. "And I'm going to be married. I'm going to be married to Patrick Peale; he's in his uncle's bank, in Philadelphia. After we are married, he will help my father."

"That's nice," said Allan. "When is the happy day?"

The bright shine dimmed on her face, and she glanced away from him. "I don't know, yet. It—it hasn't been settled." She threw away the grass.

"Does Mr. Patrick Peale know?" he asked shrewdly.

She turned her face back to him, and now her eyes were narrowed and repellent. "Don't you think you are a little impertinent?" she remarked. Her mouth lost its fullness, and tightened, and she was no longer beautiful.

Allan shrugged. "If I'm presuming, Miss, you gave me the opportunity. I'm sorry." He picked up the hoe, moved away from her, and began to stir up the dry earth along the flower border. It was as if he had dismissed and forgotten her. He whistled thoughtfully to himself. She watched him intently. Then she smiled.

"Now you don't like me," she said.

"Is it important?"

"Well, yes, I like people to like me. It makes everything very comfortable."

He regarded her curiously. "But it's not because you like people, yourself."

She broke again into a loud shout of laughter. "I loathe them," she said. "And so do you." She tilted her head and studied him. "But we don't let people know how we feel about them. That would spoil everything."

"And we couldn't use them."

She nodded with delight. "You're very clever, Allan. I think you'll make an excellent lawyer." Her eyes glinted with mockery. "A labour lawyer."

He bowed ironically and continued to work. Idly, her eyes fixed upon him, she reached out to the flower border and broke off a cluster of small white blossoms. She tucked them in her hair, and she saw that he was aware of her careless gesture. "You don't like gardening, do you?" she said. "And how do I know? Well, we had a real gardener a year or two ago, and if any of us so much as looked sideways at his precious flowers he would have convulsions. I tore off these and you didn't so much as blink."

"They're your flowers, Miss," he answered indifferently.

She laughed. "If you were truly a gardener you would consider them yours, not mine. Tell me, Allan, what do you do in the winter?"

"I cut wood, clear away snow, tend horses, help my father when his firemen are sick, and many other things. I've been firing engines since I was twelve, to help me get some kind of an education." He spoke with no resentment. He turned his head and looked at her fully. "And I've done coupling; dropping the coupling pins between cars." He held up his right hand, and she saw that the middle finger was missing to the second joint.

If he had expected her to flinch or cringe or pale at the sight of his mutilation, he was disappointed. The gesture had had some measure of cruelty in it, some desire to shock. But Cornelia, though she stopped smiling, was more curious than anything else. She said, "My God, that's a damned shame."

"What language," he said. "I thought well-bred young ladies didn't use it."

"I've heard of the brakemen and such losing fingers," said

242

Cornelia, ignoring his comment impatiently. "I suppose it can't be helped."

"Oh, I have ideas," observed Allan. "Automatic coupler. I'm working it out. That's why I'm not going back to coupling on the railroad this winter. If I did, and invented the automatic coupler your dad could claim it, and perhaps I'd get an insignificant royalty, if anything. I don't want him to have it; I want lots of money for it. So, when it's ready, I'll look for the highest bidder among manufacturers, not railroad men."

Cornelia smiled craftily. "You want to be rich, eh? Good. I like being rich, myself. Clever people always make money; fools are born poor, live poor, and die poor. Of course, that isn't what the ministers say, but it's true. My grandfather was born poor, but he had the wit to become wealthy and had no patience for men without ambition. We have a great deal of money—millions, I think—and I want more. Why don't you ask me why?"

"Because I know." He bent and tore out another handful of weeds. Cornelia nodded. "Yes, naturally." She yawned, and he saw her pink tongue and almost all her teeth, for she made no effort to cover her mouth. Some of her hair had loosened and curled in moist ringlets about her damp pink cheeks. Allan looked at her with open admiration, and, seeing this, she winked at him. "Where do you live?" she asked.

"On Potter's Road, with my parents and my brother Michael. He is firing on the railroads regularly now."

"What are you, English, Scotch, Irish, or something?"

His dark face darkened grimly. "I'm Irish, Miss." She brushed some grass stalks from her dress, and her movements were slow and fastidious, and she bent her head. He nodded to himself. He added, "Catholic Irish, too, not one of your Protestants."

Cornelia got to her feet with one long fluid motion and threw back her hair. "What does it matter?" she asked without interest.

"I don't let my religion bother me," he said, but there was a congested expression about his nose and mouth.

"Who does?" said Cornelia. "Only an idiot would allow it." She shook out her flounces. "It must be almost four o'clock," she went on. "I promised my mother to have dinner with her and my cousin and Uncle Jim—he's my stepfather—and my sister Ruth. They don't go to Newport in the summer, as we do. They don't like it. Neither do I, particularly."

"But you go, don't you, Miss deWitt? I was wondering why you were in town at this time of year."

Her eyes widened as if with surprise. She turned and looked up the terraces at her home, and now her face softened, became almost tender and brooding. "I love my home, Allan. I can't bear to stay away from it. No matter how long I live, or where I'll ever go, I'll always come back. So, even in the summer, I must return for a week or two, just to be sure the house is still here." Her husky voice had become almost gentle. Allan, somewhat startled, looked up at the house also. The sun had left the arches of the first floor so that they had become flooded with a mysterious dusk, but the white pillars of the great piazza were incandescent with light and the upper windows blazed in the western sun.

"I'll have a house like that someday," Allan said. He was very grave and almost sombre. "I think I don't mind working here so long as I can look at it from any angle."

Something in his voice made her swing to him suddenly and regard him with a kind of intense wonder. They stood staring at each other for a long time. Then Cornelia's face became full of light and a kind of joy, and Allan smiled. A deep exchange of emotion passed between them, and Cornelia's lips parted softly in an answering smile. For one of the very rare times in her life she forgot who she was; she forgot who Allan Marshall was. They were caught up in a communication in which the two young people understood each other, and recognised each other. When Cornelia extended her hand to Allan it was an impulsive and entirely sincere gesture of fellowship. He took it at once, strongly but briefly.

He saw Cornelia's eyes, and now they were wide and golden in the sunlight, and humid. The hair he deplored was vivid and alive as fire.

Then Cornelia was laughing, not her usual boisterous laugh, but a gentle one. She caught up her skirts and bounded up the small terrace. Once there, she looked down at Allan and it seemed to him that she had, for an instant or two, concentrated the sunshine in herself and that she was pouring it down upon him. She waved her hand and flew up the higher terraces like an arrow of brilliant colour. He leaned on his hoe and watched her. An old woman, "the old devil," had appeared on the piazza, grim, white-haired, tall and bent, leaning on her cane. Even from the

244

distance below, Allan could see a change come over Sophia; her stiffness melted as she kissed Cornelia. Her loud harsh voice blurred into accents of mingled plaintiveness and affection. They walked around the side of the piazza together, Cornelia supporting the black-clad old woman.

Allan stood, gazing up at the house. For a young man so assured and compact of personality, he was oddly disturbed and shaken. Then he said to himself: Not some other house, but this. Not some faceless girl, but that one.

His thoughts did not seem vainglorious to him. He went on working, absorbed and intent, his black brows meeting over his eyes.

CHAPTER TWENTY-FIVE

Mr. Victor Drummond, yawning, closed the law books, winked at the blazing gaslights above his head, which flooded down on his silent office.

"I think, Allan, that's enough for to-night." He was a small and wiry man of fifty, with a bald head, a white moustache, and a peevish sharp face. He looked at his watch, yawned again, patted his waxed moustache, daintily thrust the books from him. "It's ten o'clock."

Allan Marshall stood up, piled the books together, folded the yellow sheets which he had been using, and on which were carefully inscribed many decisions in his hard small writing, and put them in his pocket. Under the brownness of his skin he was pale with fatigue. But the black glance he gave Mr. Drummond was indomitable. "I could go on all night," he answered.

Mr. Drummond, though he despised this "scum of the gutters," smiled, flattered. His position in Mr. Peale's office was a minor one; he did the more listless and unimportant research, but he was thorough. Nothing was too dusty for him, nothing too tedious for his meticulous nature. He said with kind condescension, "You will make a fine lawyer one of these days, Allan. I look forward to the day when you will join me as my assistant in research. There is so much work! I can use a young man like you. I believe that in another year or so you will be ready."

He added, "You owe considerable to Mr. Peale. You never did tell me how you approached him, and how you convinced him of your natural bent for law."

"I just walked into his office, when he was back from Washington, and told him," said Allan simply. This little grey mouse of a man! Let him have his condescending and pseudo-elegant ways. He was of immense use to Allan Marshall.

Mr. Drummond sighed blissfully. "Mr. Peale is a man of great democracy, Allan. How many gentlemen in his position would keep an open door for aspiring young men? He has what we call—uh—the ' common touch.' I well remember the day I first came to these offices. My parents"—and Mr. Drummond's pigeon breast swelled pompously—"had been able to send me to Harvard. Mr. Peale once told me that the office could not function without me." He laughed with a rich and modest sound. He patted his small stomach and sighed again complacently. The tips of his little fingers were dusty and ink-stained.

Allan kept his expression serious and attentive. He stood beside Mr. Drummond's scarred, roll-top desk in an attitude of respect, his brown cap in his hand, his old, short and skimpy overcoat tight over his broad shoulders. His boots were broken and dirty. Mr. Drummond was too dull a man to see the subtle contempt in the black eyes fixed on him. "Tell me, Allan," he said graciously, "why are you so interested in the labour legislation passed during the last ten years? Where do you expect to use all this information?"

"Here, perhaps," replied Allan. He smiled, and the smile was unpleasant. "Mr. Peale has a number of clients who are industrialists." The smile became even more disagreeable. "Besides, I can be of great assistance to my own people, you know—the workers. Making for fine labour understanding between employer and employees."

Mr. Drummond nodded seriously. "A very fine aspiration. One hopes there will be no more unpleasantness. Once your—people—are aware of the problems of industry, they will not be so eager to strike against their benefactors. And that reminds me: we have some little-used books on the subject. I will get them out for you on Wednesday. Elson's *Sacred Obligation of The Worker* and *The Bible's Admonitions to The Toiler*. In the latter is a chapter called, I believe, ' Essay on the Subject of Scriptural Exhortations to the Hewer of Wood and the Drawer of Water.' Very edifying. It calls for humility and gratitude on the part of the Man who Toils."

"It sounds very interesting," said Allan. His voice, deep, controlled, and full of eloquent inflections, filled the echoing office. Mr. Drummond listened; he scratched his chin. "Ah, yes," he murmured. He was not too stupid; something was making him uneasy. He pushed back his chair. "I believe my buggy has been brought from the stables," he said. "It is raining; very nasty weather this time of the year. You have a long walk, Allan."

He strutted ahead of Allan through the long dark offices where the fires had been banked. A chill permeated the unseen corners; a gas lamp from the street permitted the two men to wind their way through the litter of desks and chairs and files. Mr. Drummond carefully locked the doors and, leading the way as usual, with the shabby young man behind him, descended the two flights of carpeted stairs to the street. Quicksilver rain, cold and piercing, dashed against the walls of the buildings, and the autumn wind howled down the long and empty avenues. The river was rising; they could hear its hoarse voice against the thunder of the gale. Mr. Drummond's buggy was waiting at the kerb. He lived in East Town, as did Allan, and at least half of the journey was in the direction of Allan's home. It never occurred to Mr. Drummond to offer a member of the "lower classes" a lift behind the snug curtains of his vehicle. Allan watched the buggy roll briskly down the street; the wheels threw aside the sheets of silvery water which spread out from the gutters. He turned up the collar of his meagre coat, pulled his hat down on his untidy mass of black hair, and swiftly followed the buggy, picking his way indifferently through puddles in the cobblestones.

His long legs carried him rapidly and easily through the deserted streets. He kept his head bent against the rain, his hands thrust in his pockets. He went over and over, in his mind, the recent decisions against labour. Law was a double-edged sword. It was also a method of blackmail. "Justice" could be an avenger for the rights of man; she could also be employed to destroy the rights of man. "Justice" was the servant of the strong; she had a thousand hands, which could be bought. The highest bidder could be certain to have her, a docile slave, in his own employ. Law, thought Allan, should have been represented as a pool of

247

mercury, slippery and infinitely capable of assuming smaller and smaller particles.

The clock in the tower of the city hall clangoured. Half-past ten. Allan's father, Tim Marshall, would have finished with that dreary nightly rosary business by now. Allan could see his father, in his striped engineer's shirt, kneeling with his wife and younger son Michael, beside him. He could see the beads slipping through scarred old fingers in the light of the kerosene lamps. He could see his mother, prematurely grey and old, following the prayers, and that muddy clod, Mike, dutifully repeating. The cheap tin crosses would glimmer a little in the yellowish light, trembling in the devout hands. "Hail Mary, full of Grace. . . . Our Father, Who art in Heaven. . . ." How was it possible to teach fools that such humble gibberish was the incantations of their serfdom? Well, thought Allan, it is just as well they don't know. A stone was in his way. He kicked it and, with satisfaction, watched it sail across the street. As he stood there a moment, the rain running down his face, a tiny mouse darted from the side of a building and ran, confused, in front of him. He kicked it with as little emotion as he had kicked the stone, and it rose in the air with a squeal and dropped, writhing, in the drowning gutter. He went on, humming to himself. The mouse reminded him of Mr. Drummond.

He never forgot Cornelia deWitt. She was in New York now, in the fine mansion she occupied with her parents and her brothers on Fifth Avenue. He, Allan, had never been to New York except last summer, on a "long run" with his father. He remembered Fifth Avenue very well: the tall, square houses, the polished brass plates on the grilled doors, the silk-shrouded windows turned to the street. The carriages. The white steps. The gowns and furs of the women, their jewels, their parasols, their bonnets nodding with plumes, the rustle of their skirts, their silky laughter and pretty faces. The children with their nurses. The bright and vivid light on pale stone. He had found the DeWitt house, closed for the summer, and shuttered. He had stood before it and had told himself that one day he would live in that house, and it would be his own. Cornelia, in his imagination, walked with him, holding his arm. He was not dressed in patched clothing. He wore a brocaded waistcoat, his ankles in spats, his shoulders covered with fine broadcloth, a gold-headed cane in his hand.

He walked faster, now, through the poor, silent streets which led to his home. A matter of time. Perhaps not too long a time. He was nearly twenty-seven; he could not wait much longer. Three ten-cent pieces, one quarter, and a few pennies, jingled against one of the hands thrust in his pockets. He fingered them, rubbed them together. He began to whistle some old Irish air taught him by his father, and the sound was loud and sweet and strong in the rainy silence. He whistled to Cornelia, and now his whole body was filled with urgent lust and anticipation. It did not matter to him that he had not seen her for several months. He did not fear that white-faced dandy, Patrick Peale. For Patrick Peale was engaged to marry Miss Laura deWitt next June. Two ghosts together, thought Allan, chuckling. He made it a point to acquaint himself, now, with everything that pertained to the DeWitts, and he listened to all local gossip about them. There had been much malicious speculation about Miss Cornelia's disappointment in not "snaring" Mr. Patrick; Allan had listened to the light sneers in the Peale offices.

He doubted very much if Cornelia had been greatly "disappointed." Perhaps her vanity had been mangled a little, but he knew, vividly, that she had too much robustness and humour for real vanity, and too realistic a common sense not to understand, finally, that Patrick Peale was not of her kind, and antipathetic to her.

As he passed the blank and dripping face of an old warehouse, the wavering light of a street lamp struck on a fluttering fragment of a political poster. It was half torn from its position, wet and wrinkled. Allan stopped and examined it, and he chuckled again. He smoothed out the soaked paper, and it showed the features of a young man in the early thirties, a grave young man with a stern face and quiet, penetrating eyes. "Vote for Patrick Peale!" huge black letters exhorted. "U.S. Senate. Vote for the Man of the People! Justice for all, special privileges for none!" Allan ripped the poster from its last moorings, gave it to the raging wind. Old George Peale had done a great deal for that haughty son of his, with the subdued voice and the restrained manners. Allan had often heard Patrick speak at a political rally on a street corner. He had felt contempt for him. The imbecile actually believed what he had said with such fanaticism. At any rate, Patrick had been elected, though he had been an "unknown" up to five months before the November elections. He had put on an especially eloquent campaign,

249

tireless and sincere. But, of course, his father's fortune had helped him.

"Good luck with your old man, Pat," said Allan, watching the poster fly up against a wall, then settle in the gutter. "Something tells me you two won't be so happy together from now on."

So, Patrick Peale would not be the husband of Cornelia deWitt. He would not be part of the enormously powerful and wealthy Interstate Railroad Company. Allan went on his way, whistling an Irish air again. He said inwardly, and some of the old phrases of his parents returned to him involuntarily: "Mavourneen, it's not grievin' you are now, for grief is not for you, I'm thinkin'. Life and joy and food and money, but not sorrow. Wine and dancin' and shoutin' and laughin'. Sure, and it's a fine girl you are, and it's mine you shall be."

He remembered the very few times he had seen Cornelia deWitt since that day on the terrace. He had seen her only at a distance, in her carriage, rolling through Portersville. There was some rumour that she had decided to go to live with her father, and that she had left her mother's home permanently. It is the house that draws her, thought Allan. He remembered the last time he had seen her, in October, just as she had been about to climb aboard her father's private car. Her father and her stepmother, a pretty little creature, had been with her, and her brothers; but like a fire itself, she had been the centre of the group, her maid fussing with her furs and her luggage and twittering like a sparrow. Allan had descended from his father's cab and had leaned negligently against it, smoking a cigarette. He had not approached that group, surrounded as it was by lackeys and brakemen and conductors, all staring and eager to help. He had only stood there, willing her to look in his direction. She had; he would never forget the blaze of her robust smile, the lifting of her gloved hand, the mocking tilt of the head under the blue velvet bonnet. He had felt a proprietor's pleasure in being part of the engine which was taking her in the direction of New York. His own run, and his father's, stopped at Philadelphia.

She had not forgotten him. He had never believed she had. When, one day, a large mysterious parcel had arrived for him at his home, and he had unwrapped a huge set of leather-bound law books, he had only smiled. There was no message, but he knew. His parents had been overawed by the magnificent if

250

nameless gift, and had reverently touched the leather. It was Tim's conviction that the noble Mr. Peale had bestowed this expensive largesse on his son, and Allan did not undeceive him. It had shaken, for a time, Tim's conviction that the "big interests" (a phrase he used vaguely to define anyone who did not employ his hands to make a living) were uniformly malignant.

Cornelia would return home a few days before Christmas. Her family would join her a day or two afterwards, before returning to New York for the New Year and then the annual pilgrimage to the Riviera. Allan was not too gloomy about this brief visit. If he did not see Cornelia during it, she would remember him.

His invention was coming along very well. "Patent pending." His strength was without limit; he could work twelve hours a day and study law six hours a night, and feel very little fatigue. All in all things were going splendidly. But he must move fast now. There had been a silly and deliriously proud item in the local papers that Miss Cornelia deWitt was seeing a great deal of a certain middle-aged marquis in France, and that the patrician gentleman intended to visit America next summer for the purpose of continuing suit for the hand of the heiress. The marquis was described as a nobleman of immense wealth, which Allan doubted. Too many of the exquisite but impoverished noblemen were pursuing American young ladies of fortune these days, and marrying them. Cornelia was not the type for elegant Continental living, with its formality and restricted mode of existence, and Allan was convinced that Cornelia had the wit to see it. Still, Allan did not believe that any divinity looked on him with too much favour, and he knew that Cornelia was ambitious.

Snow began mingling with the rain, rapidly and thickly. The cobblestones were becoming slippery. He moved faster over them, whistling louder than ever. He turned down a wretched and narrow street which smelled of refuse and boiled cabbage. Once there had been no slums in Portersville. But now the slums were spreading like some evil fungus disease over small streets once respectably clean and neat. Allan knew that the "foreigners," which included his family, were being blamed for this deplorable development. The fact that the "foreigners" were paid much less than native labour did not occur to the hating inhabitants of East Town. Most of the area was owned by businessmen who had invested money in it, and the meagre rents were collected by agents who refrained from reporting on falling plaster, leaking roofs, broken steps, cracked windows, and leaning walls.

Potter's Road was no less wretched than the neighbouring streets. The small houses, mostly clapboard, had not been painted for many years. What trees had once been planted had died. The yards were full of household refuse and garbage. As the area was subjected to the soot of railroads and factories, the cottages were uniformly caked with soot, so that they were of one blackish-grey colour. The stench of decaying vegetation and acrid smoke hung in the cold wet air. Feeble kerosense lamps, glimmering dimly behind torn and ragged curtains, threw yellow blotches out on to the night. The Marshall house was distinctive; though Mrs. Marshall had to wash her curtains at least once a week, she kept them white and stiff with starch, carefully mended and patched. Tim had even planted a small elm tree on the tiny lawn, a thriving little thing, for Tim, at night, would take a basket and a shovel out on to the streets and gather horse manure for fertiliser, which he applied diligently. He had been able, in spite of the soot, to grow a small garden. All this was regarded with derision by his neighbours, much to Tim's bewilderment. He firmly believed, even in the face of overwhelming evidence, that the poor are noble, superior to those who possessed money, and of another species, entirely distinct from the "spalpeens who live in them houses by the river."

Tim had brought some red paint from the railroad shops and had painted the door and the window-trimmings last summer. This had provoked much hilarity among his neighbours. A man skilled with his hands, he had repaired his roof himself, had plastered cracked walls, had covered them with cheap wallpaper. As a result, the little cottage was neat and trim, a great contrast to the others. The neighbours, resenting all this prideful work, resenting the Marshalls for their self-respect, called them "those dirty black Irishers." When his "friends" were surly with him, Tim excused them on the grounds that they were tired and discouraged and "meant no harm, bless their poor souls."

Allan opened the red door and he could smell the wax his mother unremittingly used, and the soap she never spared, and the good scent of an excellent stew. The living-room and dining-room and kitchen were one, warm and humid this cold night from the heat of a great black range along the farther wall. There was no money for floor covering, but Mrs. Marshall kept the floor scrubbed white. An old brown sofa stood against another wall; a table, covered with a white cloth, was set for Allan. There were two ancient rocking chairs and two straight chairs scattered about near the stove. On one flowered wall had been hung a cheap and gaudy lithograph of the Sacred Heart, very violent and gory, which made Allan wince each time his reluctant eye touched it. The family—Tim, his wife, and his son Michael—were sitting around the stove, Tim's shoeless feet on the opened oven door, Mrs. Marshall knitting the family socks, and Michael poring, as usual, over some religious book.

Tim threw down his newspaper as Allan entered. "It's the boy!" he exclaimed with gruff affection. "It's the fine lawyer we have! And how are the law books, ye rascal?"

Mrs. Marshall lifted her lined cheek for Allan's damp kiss, and smiled at him proudly. Michael, twenty-three, looked in un-smiling silence at his brother. "The stew is hot," said Mrs. Marshall, getting stiffly and wearily to her feet, and limping towards the stove. "And the coffee is boilin'. Ye're late, to-night, Allan." Her thin body, clad in pallid gingham, was as curveless and worn as an old stick, and her masses of curling grey hair made the tired face below them almost corpselike. She was hardly fifty; years of endless deprivation, suffering, and grinding work, had aged her beyond her time.

"And how is that fine gentleman, Mr. Drummond?" asked Tim.

"The fine gentleman is—fine," replied Allan, looking at his stew-filled plate with pleasure. He moved aside the lamp to make room for the plate of bread his mother put near him. The coffee was poured into a cracked mug; Allan added bluish milk to it and one lump of cherished sugar. As food was considered too important to be spoiled by conversation, the family did not speak to Allan until he had finished the meal. Michael had returned to his pious reading, but Tim and Mrs. Marshall sat in docile silence, watching their older son with expectant love and complacency. He was their hero, their crusader, their deliverer; with his "law" he would free "the workers" from their ill-paid slavery. He would be their champion; he would use that deep and powerful voice of his against the mighty who exploited the defenceless. "A Clan-na-Gael it is," Tim would say with pride. There was nothing this lad of his could not do, eventually. Perhaps even the Senate, where he would fight for the rights of man. Tim beamed at his son, and then, as if ashamed of his pride, scratched his thick thatch of white and waving hair. For good measure, he rubbed his round and bristling chin, then tugged at his big nose. His striped engineer's shirt, always clean, crackled with the stiff starch his wife used. He stared at the stove, and his strenuous blue eyes brightened with eager thoughts. He was a small man, but he carried himself with dignity, and with high-footed determination. Not for him the dispirited slouch of his neighbours. He returned his eyes to Allan, and he said to himself: It's the voice like the harp he has, with many strings; it's the Irish voice he has. Our Lord made that voice, I'm thinking, for His own good work.

The possessor of the "voice like the harp" finished the large plate of stew and drank the hot coffee. His lifted eyes did not turn to his parents first; they turned on the "muddy lump" of his brother. Michael, who was as short as his father, gave the impression of complete brownness, from his thin and scanty hair and his large brown eyes to his skin and his hands. But it was a brownness like that of an autumn leaf, a fact which Allan never saw. It was the brownness of the patient and fruitful earth from which all life grew, and in which it flourished. His features inclined to roundness and sobriety and thoughtfulness. His hands were big and square and almost stiff with fire scars. Like his mother, he spoke very little. He had wanted to be a priest, but his mind was slow and too pedestrian and too wanting in force and anger to please those he had consulted.

Allan had a sort of contemptuous fondness for his parents. For Michael, the inconspicuous, the silent, the obedient, and apparently ambitionless, he had only disgust, and, strangely enough, a sometimes violent and nameless hatred. To him, Michael was the voiceless and anonymous prototype of the plodding worker, satisfied with crusts, respectful to employers, willing to live on a pittance as long as it permitted him to read his infernal religious books at night and to pray endlessly.

Now that Allan had completed his meal, his parents looked at him excitedly. "It's Mike we have to be proud of to-night," said Tim. "It's our Mike. The rascal did it behind our backs! He is joining the Franciscan brothers. It's off to missionary work he is, helpin' the good fathers in foreign fields."

"No!" laughed Allan, leaning back in his chair. Michael did not look at him, but he was blushing. "And what the hell can Mike do in those ' foreign fields '?"

Michael did not lift his eyes from his book, but he said quietly, "I can do any kind of handy work. I can cook and mend. I can nurse; I learned that taking care of the injured men, in emergency. I know a little carpentry. I can grow a garden of vegetables. I can do what God calls on me to do."

The vision of Michael in a cowl and a robe and with a rope about his round middle made Allan hilarious. Tim and his wife were affronted, but Michael calmly ignored the laughter. "The heathen Chinee!" exclaimed Allan. "Or maybe the lepers, eh? Or watching the blackamoors dancing around their fires in darkest Africa? A wonderful life."

"Yes," said Michael, "a wonderful life." His voice, low and without sonorousness, aroused his brother's inexplicable ire. "You haven't considered that your wages will be missed at home, have you?" asked Allan.

For the first time Michael turned his head, his brown eyes shining in the lamplight. And, in silence, Allan returned that strange and penetrating regard. Tim said angrily, "The wages! God guards His own. It's not missing the wages we'll be. It's the joy we'll have in our son."

Allan got up and shrugged. "That's very nice. But we'll be missing the wages for all that." He was annoyed that Michael, who lived so obscurely, almost forgotten at times by his parents, should to-night have acquired importance. He yawned, ran his hands through his hair. Tim and his wife watched him, hurt and baffled. They could not understand Allan's scorn and brutality at this fine news. "I think I'll go to bed," said Allan, yawning again. "I'm tired as hell, and I still have some studying to do."

Tim made an effort to overcome his anger against his favourite son. He smiled. "And ye'll be preparin' that speech at Union Hall, a week from Toosday. Sure, and it'll be the speech to set off the fireworks!"

Allan touched his father's shoulder carelessly, and smiled down at him. "The fireworks," he promised. He kissed his mother again, and left the room.

He shared a bare and tiny bedroom with his brother. The room contained only a double iron bed, a table heaped with neat piles of law books and papers, two kitchen chairs, and a single battered chest of drawers. A crude wooden crucifix hung over the bed; a curtain of faded gingham concealed the scanty clothing of the brothers. Allan lit a lamp; the room was deathly cold, though Mrs. Marshall had left the door open from the kitchen. Allan put a woollen garment which his mother had knitted, over his coat, rubbed his hands, and sat down at the table. He sharpened some pencils, examined his pen and ink. There was no sign of any of Michael's books in the room; he kept them in a corner near the stove.

Allan stared at the green and scarlet wallpaper, and thought. Then he drew a sheet of paper towards him, dipped his pen in ink, and started to write. The letter was addressed to Rufus deWitt, at his Portersville offices. It began: "Sir:——" Allan paused; he smiled grimly, and then his pen raced over the paper in his small, compact writing.

"I feel it my duty to inform you that a certain person with some education—a rabble-rouser—is to address the Brotherhood of Railway Engineers and other workers at Union Hall on December the eighteenth. He is a young man who has been encouraging rebellion among your men for some time; they have come to trust him absolutely, and to look upon him as their saviour. He is a dangerous character, for he has the gift of persuasion. I understand that his speech on that night will have repercussions, and might lead to another disastrous strike against your company. I suggest that you have some trusted employee, with discerning intelligence, present during the meeting, in order that he may report adequately and fully to you."

Allan re-read what he had written, then added, "Though the Brotherhood is not of much influence at the present time, as a result of punitive laws against labour in this Commonwealth, this person of whom I write now will urge the men to demand what they call their 'rights.' He will also demand that all the men be unionised. Are we to have the Molly Maguires again?"

He signed the letter, "An Indignant Friend." He put the letter in an envelope and sealed it. He slipped the letter into a pocket, and smiled again. The first quick step had been taken. He sat and contentedly listened to the wind and the rain, and the sounds of his parents getting ready for bed. The door opened and Michael came in. Allan frowned at him as an intruder, but Michael sat down on the creaking bed and fixed his eyes on his brother, not with his usual shyness and silence, but as if he knew everything and was sternly, if quietly, prepared to speak. The brownness of his face was somewhat paler than usual; he folded his hands on his knees, and Allan could vividly see him in the cowl and gown. A monk. That was all he was fit for, a drawer of water and a hewer of wood in the midst of some wide and endless desolation. Allan's upper lip rose. "Well?" he asked irritably. "What is it?"

"Is there something?" replied Michael gently.

Allan moved, and the envelope crackled in his pocket. "I have to study," he said. "You can go to sleep if you want to."

Michael smiled, and the smile was slow and sad. "I usually do, don't I?" But he did not move, and his eyes remained on his brother's dark and impatient face. "I have been thinking of your speech, Allan. Dad says the men are all talking about it to him. Poor fellows. They are counting on you to give them hope and courage, and to tell them what to do."

"Very encouraging," said Allan. "I hope we have a large crowd."

Michael nodded. The quiet hands on his knees did not move. "And our Dad has told us that old Dan Boyle is ready to back you with all the money you want. It will be a great day for you, Allan. It is a miraculous thing to have a voice like yours, and the ability to use it, and the knowledge to inspire it. In a way, it is a sacred thing, a gift."

"Thanks," said Allan.

"It can be a dangerous thing, too," added Michael thoughtfully.

Allan stood up. "What do you mean?" he demanded.

"Why, nothing at all," said Michael with extreme mildness. "What did you think I meant, Allan?"

"Are you trying to say that I shouldn't arouse the men to take action in their own behalf, and demand justice? Are you trying to say that I should just soothe them and urge them to wait for 'better days' in some vague future? And promise them a comfortable heaven at the end?"

Michael smiled again, and the smile was more sorrowful than before. "You know I don't mean that, Allan. I know when you are acting, and you are acting now."

Astounded, and enormously alarmed, Allan watched his brother remove his clothing and get into his long nightshirt. All Michael's movements were slow and prosy and deliberate. This had annoyed Allan before; to-night it infuriated him.

R

"Acting!" he said. "What the hell do you know about me, anyway?"

"A great deal, and what I know doesn't give me pleasure," said Michael. He got into bed and resolutely turned his face to the wall. Allan could see the broad and earthy mound of him, calm and immovable. There would be no more talk from Michael to-night. He fell asleep at once.

Allan sat down at the table and pulled a book towards him. His face was savage and intent. It was impossible for that mud-coloured fool to know anything, unless he had preternatural powers. He opened his law books, took out his yellow notes. Hour after hour went by. The windy rain battered screamingly against the windows. The lamplight wavered, sank, lifted again. Michael snored, as did Tim and his wife. A train howled dolorously through the darkness. There was no other sound in the room but the slow turning of pages. Allan pushed a book aside, took up another. This was a nightly search, dogged, unrelenting. It was not until almost three o'clock that Allan found what he had been seeking for many and almost hopeless months. Then he nearly shouted aloud in his delight, and he struck the page softly with his clenched fist.

Two years ago, in the tiny town of Flintsburg, an obscure and fusty old judge had rendered an opinion in the case of *The Grandon Smelting Company* v. *John Hillary*. He had died six months later. His decision, still valid, still a precedent, had been hastily consigned to oblivion, and had gathered dust. No lawyer, famous or unimportant, had discovered it in its limbo, or if one had known of it, he had never exhumed it. Yet it stood on that page like a concentrated flame.

John Hillary had tried to unionise the workers of the company. He had called them to a meeting and had aroused them. He had been arrested on the charge of "disturbing the peace of the people of the Commonwealth of Pennsylvania." The miserable little lawyer who had been hired by the pennies of the workers had apparently lacked all competence, and had probably been bribed. But Judge Seldon Timothy had said, "It is my opinion that the punitive laws passed against labour in this Commonwealth are unconstitutional. There is nothing in the Constitution which prohibits free speech and free assembly; in fact, it expressly emphasises these rights. Our punitive laws are a deliberate attempt to abrogate the Constitution, for no man is forbidden to form a brotherhood or a society which does not violate the precepts of the Constitution. Therefore, it is again my opinion that in bringing this man before me, true violence against the Constitution has been committed, for he has been arrested unjustly on a charge which attempts to abrogate the Constitution of the United States of America. It is further my opinion that any person or persons who attempt in any way to prevent the formation of a labour union or fraternal society are guilty of a violation of the Constitution and should be prosecuted. Case dismissed."

There was the precedent, and Allan laughed again, exultantly. The Law. The Law was a harlot.

Michael murmured in his sleep distressfully, and Allan turned with a quick movement towards the bed. The lamplight flickered, rose high, and struck the poorly carved figure on the crucifix, which hung over Michael. For an instant it glowed as if touched by lightning.

CHAPTER TWENTY-SIX

THE FREIGHT train lumbered, with screams and groans and squealings, through the narrow valleys and around and up and down the steep hills. Through sheer joy and pride and a sense of power, Tim Marshall pulled the cord and let the voice of the train, howling and echoing, race along the sides of mountains and go twisting through the valleys. The shrieking was not confined to demands for the right of way, or as warnings. Allan, his son, was firing for him, and, as usual, he was irritated by the irresponsible noise. But as usual Allan said to himself: Every man craves power. Small souls expend their craving in profitless clamour.

The pounding train thundered through small industrial towns, foggy and stinking with smoke and chemicals. Allan stood near his absorbed father, who was happily staring through the open window of his cab. The young man looked distastefully at the miserable little cities cowering under the December sky. Some day, he thought, people will demand the centralisation of industries into one area, crowded together where they can stink all

259

by themselves and allot one another space. And then about them there will be an open area like the circle surrounding a plague-stricken city, where no one will be allowed to live, and where only railroad spurs will be permitted. Far from the industrial centralisation, the people will build their houses, free to breathe unpolluted air, to cultivate their gardens, and to live in quiet. It will be a problem of transportation, but that will be solved if men put their minds to it.

Tim Marshall could feel his son, who was taking a short rest from the firing of the engine, standing near him, looking over his shoulder. He turned his head and grinned at the sweating and black-faced young man. Sure, and it was a fine lad, that Allan. A gentleman, as Mary always said. Even the filthy shirt, rolled to the elbows, the open collar, the soot and the patched trousers, couldn't take that look of gentry from him. But it's gentry the Irish are, I'm thinking, thought Tim proudly. Sons of kings. He began to roar: "The harp that once through Tara's halls!" His voice was a resonant bass, and it pleased him. He pulled the ear flaps of his cap down closer over his ears, for the bitter air stung; his face was bright red from the wind. He gave utterance to the train again; then, when the wailing died away, he shouted over the crash of his passage, "And so it's to Scranton ye'll be goin', with that patent of yours. Good luck, my boy. Your mither made a novena for ye."

Allan shouted back, "And when it's sold, and under production, you and Ma will be living in a mansion!" Tim laughed aloud. He could not conceive of any fortune, in his simplicity, and so he said, "The poor lads, losing fingers now, and ye'll be the cause of savin' 'em."

He was happy. A train was a beloved and living thing to him, a yelling monster answering his will. What more could a man want, except, perhaps, a decent living wage—not much, but enough for contentment, a pint of beer on a Saturday night, and solid food in the pantry. A new dress at Christmas for Mary, and a bit for the collection plate of a Sunday. Tim sighed, but not too discontentedly. A man had much with a wife like Mary and two fine sons. He shouted again, "And it'll be off with Mike after the holidays! And ye'll be marryin'."

He heard the raucous scraping of the shovel. His frown was not only to squint his eyes against cinders. Twenty-seven, that Allan. A lad that age should be married to a nice colleen, and there should be grandchildren. A little girl with black curls and a smile. Tim pulled the whistle again; steam and smoke poured from the smokestack. The train was hurtling itself through open country now, before approaching Scranton.

Allan paused to wipe the blackened sweat from his face with the back of an equally black hand. He stood again near his father. The December sky, remote and cold, was the colour of blue steel, adrift with layers of white cloud. Below it, the dim aquamarine hills circled a small valley in which lay a small lake like frozen and pallid silver. The heaving and nearer land had taken on a dark bronze tone, flecked in crevices, by veins of snow. Along the right of way spruces coated with glimmering ice stood in ranks of pale crystal. There was something wild yet static in the scene, something of desolation. Tim was seeing it also. "Not like the ould country," he said. "After twenty-seven years, it gives a man's heart no comfort." He looked forward. The grime of Scranton blurred the painted colour of the sky, and Tim was relieved.

Allan's Sunday suit, and a clean shirt and a black cravat and his best boots, had been carefully wrapped, that morning, by Mary Marshall. Over the newspaper bundle Allan had thrown his working coat to protect it from soot and sparks. He would wash in the station. He went back to his firing, for the last spurt to Scranton. Tim was singing again.

The great murky bulk of the Interstate Iron & Steel Company stood like a fire-breathing and black-smoking dinosaur in the midst of tiny ramshackle cottages and gaunt, impoverished double-family houses, all grimed with soot, every window coated with dark film, every brick or wooden walk gritty underfoot, every stoop overlaid with the lave of cinders. The monster chimneys roared and spewed with flame against a lead-coloured sky that seeped filthy moisture; a heavy stench mingled with the smoke. No one had considered the welfare or health of the inhabitants of the region when this stupendous mill had been built some eight years ago, a subsidiary of the mighty Interstate Railroad Company. Had anyone suggested that the company build beyond the confines of the city, indignation would have been expressed: "We need a constant water supply, and the Interstate Railway Company should have easy access to its own freight yards."

"The imperious needs of our hugely expanding country, and, in fact, the needs of the Public, come first," Rufus deWitt would have said virtuously. No one had suggested that the inhabitants of the area were part of "the country," or had any relationship with the "Public." The relationship existed, however; many of the men who lived in the immediate area of this gigantic volcano worked within its smouldering walls. They coughed and sweated around its open hearths and its pits, and they coughed and shivered in their broken little houses at night. The river which ran near the mill was discoloured with purple, yellow, sickly blue, and reddish blotches, its banks throwing up the skeletons of dead trees, its margins smeared with slime and the residue of chemicals, so that no living thing could grow there.

The yards about the mill were filled with man-made hills of slag and coke. They steamed, and they grew daily. Three spurs of the Interstate Railroad Company entered the yards, and the clanging engines and the belching smokestacks contributed to the noise of the area and the foulness of the air. A tall wooden fence, pointed and almost invulnerable, surrounded the yards and the mill, and at each of the four entrances armed guards, truculent and forbidding, stood in small booths, permitting only carefully scrutinised visitors or bona-fide workmen to enter. There had been threats of "labour troubles" recently, and so the guards were doubly watchful, scowling and threatening.

Allan Marshall approached one of the gates, his cap pulled over his forehead, his old greatcoat fastened tightly over his Sunday suit. He glanced above the fence and saw the firelit and bellowing chimneys. He pulled the bell rope beside the gate, and immediately a guard slid aside the cover of a small opening in the thick wood and glared out at him. "No help bein' hired!" he shouted contemptuously, noting the obvious poverty and low estate of the young man outside. He slapped the cover back over the opening. Allan nonchalantly rang the bell again. The cover flew back and the guard's face, savage and swollen, appeared. "Get the hell out of here if you don't want a bullet in your yeller hide!" he screamed.

Allan smiled and extended an envelope towards the face. He said very gently, "You'll be looking for another job to-morrow, Cerberus, if you don't read this and let me in at once."

The guard's eyes, black and piglike, stared at him with inhuman rage. The two dirty fingers appeared beside the face and the envelope was snatched from Allan's hand. The fine dirty rain sifted down, and as the sky darkened, the fiery chimneys brightened. Allan could see only the bent cap of the watchman now; the man was slowly and painfully reading a letter signed by Thomas Angers, Superintendent of the Interstate Iron & Steel Company, and addressed to Allan Marshall, 3 Potter's Road, Portersville, Pennsylvania. Then the cap disappeared, the opening slammed shut with a violent clatter, a key grated in a lock, and the heavy gate swung open with loud creakings and groanings. Allan stepped inside, and the gate fell back, and was locked. The watchman studied Allan with the hatred of all small men who have been humiliated. "Who'da thought it?" he jeered. "In them clothes, too!"

"Not any worse than yours, my good man," replied Allan.

"And my name ain't Ceri—— or what the hell you call it!" said the guard with a fresh glare.

"It fits you," said Allan. "Which way to Mr. Angers's office?"

Another guard, gnomelike yet powerful of body, appeared at the door of the booth. "Watch the gate: I'm takin' this fine gentleman to the office," said the first guard sneeringly. He beckoned to Allan with his head, then trudged towards the mill, his boots grinding on gravel and cinders. Allan followed, whistling. The sweet strong sound pierced through the clamour and the roar that beat through the heavy and sodden air. The faery Irish theme was like a nostalgic memory in purgatory, sad yet hopeful. The guard stopped, turned his head, and the brutal face changed. "Irish, eh?" he growled. "So'm I." He trudged forward again, looked back. "You don't believe it, I'm thinkin'." Allan continued to whistle, as if he were alone in some dreamlike green glade drifting with fragrant mist. "You think I like this job?" said the guard belligerently.

"Why not?" asked Allan. "You make a living at it." The guard stopped as if struck, swung about and glowered. He studied Allan for a long moment, squinting at him. Then his heavy features became sombre. "I can see," he said, and walked on. "And it's a favour you'll be doin' me to whistle somethin' else."

The walk seemed interminable to Allan; the two men wound around the steaming hills of slag and coke and coal. Now tiny streams of black water ran through the cinders, and little pools reflected back the scarlet vomiting from the chimneys so that they formed puddles of fire on the dark and broken earth. The mill and its subsidiary buildings loomed like gushing mountains in the near distance. A very good facsimile of hell, thought Allan. To the side, somewhere, engines screamed, and freight vibrated on some unseen tracks.

Now they were on wet brick walks, which skirted the mill. They were suddenly in a clear place, devoid of hills of slag, and the unbearable noise became more bearable. Allan's whistling became louder and clearer. The guard was pointing in silence to the front of a building with a grilled door. He thrust Mr. Angers's letter in Allan's hand, and after a long and bitter look at the young man he turned away and trudged back, leaving Allan alone. Allan watched the squat and ungainly figure recede, and he smiled. He went to the grilled door, rang a bell. The door opened and a thin and white-faced man, obviously a clerk, peered at him from under a green eyeshade. Allan gave him the letter.

In a few moments he was in a quiet corridor, gaslighted and clean and bare, lined with closed doors. The roar of the mills was almost obliterated here. Allan followed the silent clerk, turned a corner in a corridor, and found himself walking on crimson carpet. This new, and shorter, corridor was obviously private, and now Allan could hear subdued voices, assured and rich, and once he heard a man laugh confidently. At the end of the corridor there was another door, and this the clerk opened with an obsequious bend of his head directed not at Allan but at those who sat beyond. "Mr. Marshall," he murmured.

Allan saw before him an immense firelit office with panelled walls, on which hung an excellent painting. Crimson curtains shut out the desolation beyond the windows, and an Oriental rug covered the polished floor. A glittering chandelier, ablaze with light, hung from the tall ceiling and shone on brown and blue leather furniture and on a broad carved desk in the exact centre of the room. At the desk sat a slender, middle-aged man, and beside him, smoking a very fine cigar, sat another man, ponderous, clad in broadcloth, with a florid face and a mane of grey hair streaked with red. Rufus deWitt! thought Allan, and for a moment he was taken aback.

The slender man said quietly, "Come in, Mr. Marshall." He indicated a chair opposite Rufus with a movement of his white and elegant hand. As Allan walked to the chair, Mr. Angers's eyes, calm and almost colourless, scrutinised him without personal interest. He possessed the stillest face Allan had ever seen; it seemed carved and moulded out of ivory, without a line of character, without a wrinkle, without expression. His pale hair was coated exactly over every contour of his narrow head, and his bloodless ears lay flat against his skull. Here, thought Allan, as he carefully removed his greatcoat, is the most impersonal face I have ever encountered.

Rufus deWitt was an entirely different matter. His great muscular body had lost its heroic outlines, had softened to a mass of round suet. His thighs, in the black broadcloth, bulged tightly and thickly; his big belly swelled out the maroon-brocaded waistcoat, upon which hung a sparkling gold watch chain. His shoulders were mounds; he had lost his neck, and so his large rectangular head sat on his shoulders without division, with hardly a glimpse of white linen and broad black-satin cravat fastened with a diamond pin. His face was pulpy and of too bright a colour, some of the protuberances accentuated by purplish-crimson wrinkles; his chin rested on the cravat, a swelling fold with a somewhat oily sheen. His hazel eyes nested in hollows of fat, sparkling like topazes. His mouth was too smooth and red, and gave a sensual look to his face. But his smile was genial, and the big white teeth gleamed between his lips in the friendliest manner possible. Diamonds glittered on the pudgy fingers, which sprouted red hairs. He might have lost the violent hue of his hair, but the hair itself remained luxuriant in spite of its greyness, and was carefully arranged. He emanated a bulky vulgarity, an animal vitality, and a limitless and unfastidious appetite. The fact that he was here to-day excited Allan; the occasion must be important.

Rufus beamed at the shabby and youthful visitor, and extended his jewelled hand in a gesture of democratic cordiality. Allan deliberately looked at the hand, bowed stiffly, and seated himself. The two gentlemen were immediately aware, then, of a kind of man they had certainly not expected, and for the first time the gelid eyes of Mr. Angers focused on Allan, and tightened at the edges. As for Rufus, he withdrew the cigar from his mouth and studied Allan; a peculiar expression appeared on his face, something akin to surprised recognition.

Mr. Angers spoke with a low languidness: "Mr. deWitt was passing through Scranton to-day and stopped in to see us. He became interested in your patent."

Allan smiled, raised his thick dark brows politely, inclined his head again in Rufus's alerted direction, and waited.

"I am glad you thought of us," said Rufus. His voice had acquired a round unctuousness with the years. "We are always grateful when our employees remember the company, and show their loyalty."

"Loyalty," said Allan gently, "has nothing to do with it. I am not one of your regular employees, Mr. deWitt. I sometimes assist my father, who is an engineer on your road, by firing for him when one of his firemen is ill. I am only a casual employee, if you can call it that. I," added Allan, "do not do coupling at all."

The swiftest glance passed between Rufus and Thomas Angers. Rufus then settled in his chair more comfortably, but his eyes narrowed.

"I came to the Interstate Iron & Steel Company for one reason: I believe you are more prepared to manufacture my automatic coupler than any other company." Allan crossed his lean legs and smiled at each man in turn.

"I am glad you thought of us first," said Mr. Angers ironically.

Allan was not diminished by the tone of the other man, "I think you will be even more pleased, later, Mr. Angers," He became thoughtful. "Naturally, I am not a patient fellow. I came to-day for your decision. If you decide against making my coupler, I shall at once approach other companies." He paused. "In fact, I have already approached two others, who are very interested. They, too, have received copies of my patent."

Rufus smiled disarmingly. "You are the son of one of our best and most valued engineers, Mr.—Marshall. I have often ridden with Tim. I should like to believe that old Tim influenced you, in a way."

"He did not." The three words were cold and flat. "No one influences me. You gentlemen understand that I am reading law in Mr. Peale's office. Law is my first objective; I have become quite an authority on labour laws. But I am not averse to making a fortune while"—and Allan let his pause become significant— "I study those labour laws to discover how best I can help the workers to whose class my father belongs."

There was a silence in the room, while the fire pulsed on the hearth and the smoke of Rufus's cigar curled upward. Mr.

Angers began to study the drawings on his desk. Rufus sat very still. An impudent, impoverished, and probably hungry young devil, full of arrogance and impertinence, he thought. But he is also fearless, and in some ways he is a threat.

So Rufus said pleasantly, "I never underestimate my fellow men. I have no doubt that you'll make an excellent lawyer, young man. Labour laws? I am interested in them very much."

"As an employer, you should naturally be interested," said Allan, with an extreme courtesy. He withdrew from his pocket a single sheet of paper, and now he looked only at Rufus. "I have here a decision made only two or three years ago, in the little town of Flintsburg. An obscure decision, but it can be—shall we say—potent, sir? It took me a long time to find it, but I eventually did, though I doubt if most lawyers know of it, and even if a few know they are careful not to disinter it."

Mr. Angers raised his head and regarded Allan with icy affront. But Rufus nodded agreeably and held out his hand for the paper. Allan gave it to him. Rufus smiled as he read, but the pulpy features became a trifle fixed towards the end. In silence, he then handed the paper to Angers, who read it carefully. Now a change came over Mr. Angers. His slim and elegant face stiffened. He put the paper on his desk, and one slender hand covered it as if to hide it. He waited for Rufus to speak.

Rufus gazed at his cigar as if abstracted with enjoyment. Then he said, almost detachedly, "The Assistant to the Secretary of State, Mr. Peale, is an old friend of mine."

"Yes, I know," said Allan, looking at him fully, and smiling. "And Mr. Peale has the reputation of being greatly concerned with the problems of—exploited—labour. In fact, he was elected several times to the Senate on the platform. And his son, Mr. Patrick, has just become a senator on that platform, too. With this difference: Mr. Patrick is sincere."

I was not mistaken, thought Rufus, who continued to smile with affectionate tolerance. The threat is not only real, it is ominous. And this young rascal has his price, if I'm not mistaken. A very large price.

Allan added, "I haven't, as yet, brought this decision to Mr. Patrick's notice. He is a very earnest young gentleman, and he has extraordinary integrity. But you, Mr. deWitt, know that very well. He is to marry your niece, Miss Laura deWitt. If Mr. Patrick should learn of this decision—and I have discovered he doesn't know of it—he would utilise it in behalf of the working people of Pennsylvania."

Mr. Angers, coldly annoyed and contemptuous, asked, "May I ask why you haven't sent it on to Mr. Patrick before this? If it is so pertinent?"

But Allan did not glance at him. He only smiled silently at Rufus.

Rufus asked in a rich and gentle tone, "Do you intend to bring it to Mr. Patrick's notice?"

Allan shrugged. "I haven't as yet decided."

Rufus laughed comfortably. He lifted the paper from under Mr. Angers's hand and studied it again. The red lips puckered. Then, very slowly, he tore the paper into pieces, his bright hazel eyes smiling at Allan. "I think," he remarked, "that we understand each other, my boy." Mr. Angers turned his eyes from Rufus to Allan, and then back again, and a slight cleft appeared between his brows. Rufus went on: "No doubt, Mr. Peale and the young senator have a high regard for you, Mr. Marshall. And I am sure the regard is justified. Sometime, soon, perhaps, we must discuss the whole matter."

In spite of his self-possession, Allan had been secretly tense. These were men of power and wealth and position. He himself was nothing compared with them, except that he had knowledge, and he was ruthless. He had been prepared for smiling indulgence and condescension and, at the worst, a complete and patronising rebuff. The fact that Rufus had recognised Allan for what he was, and had not underestimated the danger he personified, not only made Allan relax his tense muscles but increased his respect for the older man.

Mr. Angers spoke indifferently. "Mr. deWitt employs a staff of very learned and competent lawyers. Even if this miserable little decision were brought up, they could deal with it effectively, and induce a prominent judge to create a new precedent."

"Perhaps," acknowledged Allan. "But in the meantime, the decision is there." He spoke impatiently to the other man. "And first of all, there would have to be a pertinent case brought up; it would have to be argued in the light of this first decision, no matter how obscure it is. Mr. deWitt: you have heard of old Dan Boyle? He was once an engineer on your road. He lost two sons and a son-in-law in the '77 strikes in Portersville. Since then, he has made a large fortune in coal. He is a very bitter man. He is my godfather, and has offered me anything I desire. He has suggested Harvard to me. Why I have so far refused his help is of no importance at this time. Should Mr. Boyle know of this decision he would hire the best lawyers in Pennsylvania to bring it to public notice. He would spare no money at all. And no effort. He is, as I have said, a very bitter old man, and he is out for blood."

"And you have refused his help, you have so far not brought this decision to his notice, for your own reasons?" asked Rufus with more affection than ever. "May I ask why, considering that he is your godfather, and you are so concerned about labour? May I suggest that you have not availed yourself of all this because you have another object in view?"

"Your suggestion is correct," answered Allan.

Rufus nodded. "I knew, of course. If I am curious about all this you must forgive me. Mr. Marshall, I think you'll go very far." He smiled contentedly. Then, grunting a little, he pulled a small cheap handbill from his pocket, badly printed on yellowish paper. "You are the Aloysius Marshall who is mentioned here, I assume."

Allan inclined his head. Mr. Angers, with a disdainful and suspicious glance at the young man, picked up the handbill, which cried: "Grand Meeting of the Brotherhood of Railway Engineers! All welcome! December 18, 1885! Union Hall, Portersville! Seven o'clock in the evening! Don't fail to come and hear our great Speaker, Aloysius Marshall, Worker and Workman's Friend, son of our Brother, Timothy Marshall! He will deliver a Speech, Arise Sons of Labour! Come one, come all!"

Mr. Angers tossed the handbill from him with a gesture of loathing. Deliberately he wiped his delicate fingers on a fine white handkerchief. The bones stood out in his fleshless face as he regarded Allan with disgust. "A rabble-rouser," he said. He added more quickly, "Young man, in all fairness I think you should be warned that if your—speech—is inflammatory and disturbs the public peace, you will be summarily arrested."

"In that event, Dan Boyle will rush a bevy of highly-paid lawyers to my assistance, and I shall present them with the John Hillary decision." Allan spoke calmly and without any signs of consternation or fear.

Rufus lifted his plump hand in loving admonition to both the other men. But he spoke to Mr. Angers. "Thomas, I have no fear that Mr. Marshall will do any real rabble-rousing. Am I correct, Mr. Marshall?"

"You are correct, sir," said Allan politely. "As of this day, at least."

For the first time, Mr. Angers lost his contempt for this wretched upstart, this alien and hungry intruder. "I am beginning to see, I think," he murmured, and now he actually smiled, a chill and understanding smile. He eyed Allan with reluctant respect and surprise. Then he recovered himself. "You have a slight—brogue—Mr. Marshall. Are you an Irishman?"

"I am an American," replied Allan.

Rufus leaned back in his chair and he suffused an atmosphere of immense satisfaction and brotherhood. "Shall we now go into this patent matter? That was Allan's purpose in coming here, wasn't it? Very fortunate that I should have dropped in on my way home." He gave Allan a benevolent and paternal smile, and tapped the sheets of drawings on Mr. Angers' desk. Two hours ago he had said to Mr. Anger. "This is the most remarkable concept of an automatic coupler I have ever seen; it is unique and invaluable. The man who invented it is a genius, and he worked as a coupler on our road, and is now a fireman. But genius or not, he is probably a dull and plodding ignoramus, in so far as business is concerned, like all his benighted class. Who worked up the drawing for him I do not know, but it was an expert draughtsman. We shall offer this Marshall one thousand dollars for his patent, and five hundred extra for his draughtsman." Rufus had laughed comfortably. "A man who makes two dollars a day, or less, will regard a thousand dollars as a fortune. We can dispose of him in five minutes."

Now he said to Allan, "May I ask who made up these excellent drawings?"

"I did," said Allan.

Even Rufus could not dissemble his astonishment. "You did! And where did you get your knowledge of mechanics, and your ability?"

"Dan Boyle," said Allan, smiling into Rufus's eyes, "financed my draughting education in Scranton, in the offices of Boyd, Lynch & Company, for four summers, for over five years. You see, Dan—my godfather—lost four fingers when he was employed as a coupler for your company, many years ago. When I told him I wanted to invent an automatic coupler, he was very enthusiastic."

"I see," said Rufus thoughtfully. His russet brows drew together as he studied the drawings again. "You know we use the Janney coupler, and the Westinghouse air brake now. We have found the coupler eminently satisfactory, though we do not employ it on all freight trains."

"But trains are becoming heavier," said Allan. "The Janney coupler is inadequate. My patent is practical for any weight, as I have shown here." He pointed to a third drawing. "Incidentally, Janney is interested in my coupler. You will notice that my invention consists of throwing up the flange on the knuckle hub, engaging the coupler lug, and relieving the knuckle pin from side strain. This permits a reduction in the leverage in the knuckle by carrying the fulcrum point farther forward. It was necessary, for your own couplers, to change from malleable iron to steel. But you've found that more strength was necessary, and that has been your problem. My invention has solved this problem. The knuckle pin is loose, and is removable when the knuckle is under pressure." He paused. "Men are still being killed or injured with your Janney coupler in spite of it being a very great improvement. As loads become heavier, your coupler, in its present form, will become less and less reliable. It couples by impact, and the knuckle unlocks without trainmen going between the cars, but the swinging of the knuckle into open position still has to be done by hand."

Though Mr. Angers and Rufus had thoroughly studied the drawings together for over two hours before Allan's appearance, they kept their expressions judicious and doubtful. Seeing this, Allan smiled disagreeably to himself. He said, "I talked with Mr. Patrick Peale about my invention, after he was elected. He told me that he would work, in Washington, for a law making automatic coupling compulsory. He is very dissatisfied with the Janney automatic coupler as it is now. After I explained my coupler to him, he said he would bring it to the attention of the Master Car Builders Association. When I informed him that some company was going into its production, he said that any railway adopting my coupler would be hailed by him, and his colleagues, as a benefactor of man."

"Mr. Patrick is a very humanitarian person," murmured Rufus, still studying the drawings.

"And he is going to marry your niece, sir, who owns considerable Interstate Railroad Company stock."

Rufus glanced up quickly at Allan, but Allan's dark face was very bland. Rufus chuckled richly. "Mr. Patrick is not concerned with the railroad, Allan. He is going to practice law in his father's offices, when he is not in Washington."

Allan inclined his head. Rufus became uneasy. He personally detested young Senator Peale, and his relief, when it had become evident that the senator preferred Laura to Cornelia, had been profound. He wanted no more "grey Stephens" in his immediate family. Such a man, a politician and a lawyer, would not disturb him when married to his niece. But such a man, interested in Rufus's company, was dangerous. Rufus repeated, "He is going to practise law in his father's offices, when he is not in Washington. He can have no real interest in our road, except, perhaps, in the stock dividends!" He chuckled again. Allan remained grave.

"When it comes to a matter of life and limb, I think dividends will take second place with Senator Peale, sir. He is an idealist." Allan looked directly at Rufus, and his strong black eyes flickered with contempt.

This young scoundrel will use anything, or anybody, to further his ends, thought Rufus, with mingled anger, uneasiness, and admiration. He has a very subtle command of the art of blackmail.

Rufus gave the young man his most magnetic and affectionate smile, and a slight wink. "I can see, my dear boy, that you do not hold idealists in very high esteem."

"On the contrary, sir, they are very valuable. To men like myself."

"For your own purposes?"

But Allan only smiled in answer.

Rufus turned from him then and exchanged a long look with Mr. Angers. Allan scrutinised that look, and was satisfied. But he held himself alerted. When the silence became deliberately oppressive between Mr. Angers and Rufus, Allan said quietly, "I assume you must have more time to consider my coupler. Shall we say two days?"

"Impossible," said Mr. Angers coldly. "We cannot be sure your invention, young man, is practicable. We shall have to consult——"

Allan shrugged. "Mr. Angers, you have had considerable time to consult, as you call it. I am willing to extend the time for forty-eight hours, in deference to the Interstate Railroad

Company. But, in the meantime, I shall write to the two other companies interested in the patent, notifying them of a quick decision on my part in the very near future."

Rufus lay back in his chair, his fatty hands clasped together over his belly, his thumbs twiddling rapidly. He studied Allan with sharp intensity. The scoundrel might be a blackmailer, but he did not bluff. Whatever battle he entered, he would not come inadequately armed. He would be certain of every step he took, every weapon he used. As a polished blackmailer, himself, Rufus recognised an even better artist. Rufus came to a quick decision. He changed his expression to one of confidential fondness.

"I cannot tell you, Allan, how much we appreciate your consideration of the Interstate Iron & Steel Company. I should like to feel—and please don't disillusion me!—that it was inspired by loyalty to us. Suppose, now, that we take an option on your patent for six months, giving you, as of this date, a company cheque for two thousand dollars?"

Allan's eyes narrowed. Then he slowly shook his head. "The option, if you wish to take it, must run for only two weeks. I am sure someone in this company has already studied other patents." He stared at Rufus very hard.

Rufus pretended he had not noticed that implacable stare. He slapped his hand roundly on the desk, and smiled so widely that almost all his teeth showed in the brilliant light of the chandelier. "You are a difficult young fellow to deal with, I must admit. Well, then, two weeks. In the meantime, terms concerning royalties will be considered, and we shall consult you." He motioned to Mr. Angers, while not removing his smiling gaze from Allan. "Thomas, you will make out the cheque and the option papers for this boy at once."

"I might as well inform you, Mr. deWitt, that the royalties will have to be adequate." Allan withdrew a slip of paper from his pocket. "Here is Janney's offer." He gave the slip to Rufus, who looked at it. Rufus was appalled. "This is preposterous!" he exclaimed, honestly shocked.

Allan stood up. "I could ask for a bigger offer from you, Mr. deWitt. But I am only asking what Janney has offered. I believe that extraordinarily fair, considering that Janney has not merely offered me an option."

The two older men regarded him with outrage. But Allan smiled down at them. "I suppose your unspoken question is

273

why, then, I have not accepted Janney's offer, and why I have bothered to come to you. The answer is my own, and I don't intend to tell you. I can only say that I don't mean to live on my royalties. These will only be a source of a fortune. My business is law—labour law."

Only Rufus understood. "I see," he murmured. "As I said before, Allan, we must have a talk, a very long talk, confidential and intimate." He forced his face into a florid amiability again.

When Allan had gone, cheque and option papers in pocket, Rufus said to Mr. Angers. "Thomas, that is the most dangerous, and most admirable, and most valuable young devil I have ever encountered. I am full of respect for him. And that is why, perhaps not too long in the future, he will join us."

Allan ran through the dark of the early evening, the rain pouring into his face. He was hot with exultation and triumph. He reached the yards, swung on to the caboose. He felt his heart pounding, and it was not with exertion. He had won his first major engagement. He would always win, to the end of his life.

CHAPTER TWENTY-SEVEN

THE SMART phaeton drove up the gravelled driveway of Jim Purcell's house, and a young man in his early thirties alighted as the gleaming white door of the mansion opened. The young man remembered this house from his childhood. It had been large but untidy, full of dust and mould, unkempt and "a disgrace to the neighbourhood," as the neighbours had protested sullenly among themselves. But Mrs. Purcell, who had once been Mrs. Rufus deWitt, had changed the picture gratifyingly. The house might still be ugly externally, and expressive of bad architecture; however, what had been bleak yellow brick had acquired a soft golden patina, glimmering through thick ivy which, mercifully, blurred the uncouth lines. Jim Purcell, "the miser," had permitted his wife to do whatever she wished, even to the discarding of his appalling furniture. He was proud of her taste, though he grumbled he did not understand it. But secretly, it gave him pleasure.

Never Victorious, Never Defeated

There had been considerable whispered scandal when Lydia had quietly divorced Rufus, and then, in due time, had married Jim Purcell. The scandal did not reach Purcell's ears; the gossipers were careful about that. He was a dangerous man, and never forgot injuries, and he had become more dangerous and powerful through the years. When Mrs. Purcell gave parties, the élite of Portersville thronged to the house eagerly. It was noted that she was less elusive since her second marriage; she had more warmth and kindliness, and her remarks were not so elliptical or mysteriously turned. If she was still reserved in a large measure, the reserve could be melted by a sincere reference to her little daughter Ruth, who had suffered "the paralysis" in her early childhood and who now limped cheerfully if pathetically. Ruth was seven years old; there had been no other children.

As the young man mounted the low wet steps to the door, he was, for the first troubled moment that night, conscious of the brilliance of the white December moon and of the voice of the river. Another sound struck him as he entered the white and walnut hall. Laura deWitt, in the distant music room which Lydia had so exquisitely decorated and furnished, was playing Debussy. The shining notes seemed to sparkle in the air, trembling with radiance, at once meditative and unearthly. The young man forgot the servant standing by the opened door. He stood and listened, one foot on the top step, his head turned to look at the stark black trees on the lawns, and the whitened river flowing under the moon.

The young man, disturbed as he was, wished he could stand here in lonely silence for a little longer, letting the notes drop about him while he let the night console and calm him. But the servant, however patiently waiting, was still waiting, and the air was sharp with cold. "Good evening, Senator," said the old man, smiling at the visitor with genuine pleasure. "Good evening, Gratz," replied the other, and gave the butler his hard bowler hat, his white scarf, his well-cut coat and his cane. "The family is in the music room," said Gratz, and Patrick Peale nodded and went down through the hallway, which extended from the front door to the rear, and entered the music room through a wide archway.

Two blazing gas-lighted chandeliers dropped like stalactites from the carved white oval ceiling, and shimmered over white, ivory, and gold furniture. On a raised platform stood Laura's white and gilt piano, which faced the archway. Jim Purcell was sprawled on a gold-coloured velvet sofa, with his little daughter nestling close to him. Lydia sat by the monster white marble fireplace working at petit point. Laura saw Patrick first, and she smiled at him quietly while her fingers wove out the last pattern of music on the keys. No one as yet, except Laura, had noticed the slight young man in the arched doorway, a grave young man with inflexible brown eyes, wavy light-brown hair, and a compact figure. And, though conscious of the other inhabitants of the oval room, he really saw only Laura, a thin and graceful girl in a blue-velvet dress that outlined her figure and displayed her pale narrow shoulders. Her dark hair, fine and silky, was like a vapour about her almost colourless face. But her eyes, large, grey, and radiant, gave an exceptional beauty to small features which otherwise would have been too inconspicuous and indefinite for loveliness.

Patrick had known that Cornelia deWitt had desired him, but the thought, instead of flattering him, had been distasteful and almost humiliating. And yet, because she had loved him, he was almost compassionate for her, and had extricated himself from the situation so tactfully, so expertly, over a long period, that he had left her pride intact.

Lydia Purcell glanced up as Laura concluded her music, and she smiled welcomingly at Patrick. Her black hair was winged with white, and there were lines in her face, but her body, in dark green velvet, was as graceful as Laura's. Her dark eyes touched him luminously, and Jim Purcell turned his gross head and nodded without speaking. His little daughter was sleeping in the shelter of his big arm, her bright golden ringlets on his sleeve. His hair was a shock of untidy grey on his great round head, and the years had made his rude features more repulsive than ever, and had hardened them into masses of stone.

Laura rose from the piano, stepped down from the platform, and gave Patrick her hand. She led him into the room, and he sat down opposite Lydia, with Laura beside him. They began to speak in low voices, because of the sleeping child, who ought, thought Patrick, to be in bed. It was long after ten o'clock, and Ruth was frail. But Purcell found it hard to part with his daughter. Somewhere in the house, there was a portrait of young Alice Fielding, and Patrick often remarked that Ruth bore a striking resemblance to her dead aunt, which gratified Lydia.

Jim Purcell noted that Patrick was unusually serious. So he muttered in his hoarse voice, "Well, how did that talk go which young Marshall gave to-night?"

Patrick frowned. "There was something strange about it. I can't lay my finger on it, but there it was. As usual, it was eloquent—he has the most remarkable voice, and he can play any tune with it. And it was full of threat."

Purcell smiled sourly. "His speeches usually are."

Patrick shook his head, as if baffled. "Yes. And this talk was no less threatening than the rest. 'The bosses.' 'The exploiters of labour.' 'The oppressors of the people.' 'The despoilers of the workers.' 'The serfdom of the masses.' 'The dumb patience of the toilers.' All the usual things. The men listened, and their mouths and eyes were open, and they hardly seemed to breathe. When he had finished they became hysterical, and mobbed him, and threw their arms around him, and many of them cried. It was very moving." Patrick paused. "But still, I was uneasy. Something was wrong."

Purcell smiled again, and the smile was darker, if indulgent. "Look, now, Pat. Don't go cryptic on me. Let's have facts, not imaginin's. What the hell is it all about?"

"I don't know," said the young senator slowly. "But I did notice something. Duncan Baynes—you know, Mr. Rufus's local assistant superintendent—was there, and listening to every word. He kept well in the background, and tried to hide his face with his hand."

"What's wrong with him bein' there? Labour trouble comin' up, we all think. Maybe Red Rufe sent him to get an idea of the men's tempers."

"It could be," agreed Patrick thoughtfully. "But I'm not satisfied. Why should he send Duncan Baynes, who's too important for spying? Baynes is a very ruthless and clever man. . . ."

"Maybe it needed such a feller for the job to-night. Think you're gettin' too vapourish, Pat. Looking for bogiemen. Is that the only 'fact' you got to offer?"

Patrick moved uncomfortably on his chair. "Just the quality of the speech. I felt that Marshall was showing off his power; I felt that his threats were definitely focused. It was as if he was

277

warning someone in particular, and exhibiting what he could do. He was particularly showy to-night, and I think it was for a purpose." He tried to smile at the contemptuously glowering Purcell. "It's the purpose that is worrying me."

Purcell snapped his fingers. "I told you, I don't deal in intangibles. If Marshall was threatenin', or showin' off, or warnin' anyone, it was for the sake of the men. Mind you, and I've told you this a dozen times, I don't like Marshall. He's a trouble-maker, and I hate trouble-makers. I'm not sayin' the men are gettin' a livin' wage, and I'm not sayin' I wouldn't vote for more money for 'em, but I got no use for the Marshalls. And I think Marshall is just out for himself."

He pointed a hard but shapeless finger at Patrick: "And what's wrong with a man usin' other men? If he uses them, and gets somethin' for them, sort of a by-product to what he gets for himself, who's to get all indignant and fired-up?"

Patrick coloured. He met Purcell's derisive smile angrily. "Allan convinced me, for over four years, that he was dedicated to helping his fellow workers. I believe that some men are honestly devoted to the cause of others." He hesitated, then added, "I am. I believe I am."

"That's because you can afford it," said Purcell. "What can young Marshall afford? It's true that he's sold his automatic coupler to Interstate Iron & Steel Company, and will probably make a fortune out of his royalties. But so far he's got only five thousand dollars on it. Maybe the coupler will bring him in a lot of money in a few years. Yes, maybe. In the meantime, he's readin' law in your father's offices, and from what I hear he's goin' to make a mighty smart lawyer. Well. He's goin' to make a fortune for himself, and he's goin' to be a labour lawyer." He rubbed his big chin, which was bristling with mingled black and white whiskers. "If Rufe's disturbed about him, he's got reason."

Patrick was silent a few moments. Then he said, "I was convinced to-night, and I admit I might be wrong, that Allan's not concerned, and never was concerned, about the plight of his class. And so I don't think that Mr. Rufus need be afraid of him. I think it is others who should be afraid."

Purcell laughed jeeringly, but carefully, in order not to awaken little Ruth. "And who was it who was all enthusiastic about that young jackanapes in the beginnin'? You, Pat. And comin' down to facts, again, what have you against him gettin' somewheres? You want others to carry the burden for you, while you live in your fine house, and go to Washington with fanfares? Come on, don't glare at me. I'm not throwin' sneers at you. I'm just remindin' you that if Marshall don't want to be a martyr for anybody, no one can blame him."

"I have no objection to a man ' getting somewheres,' as you say, Mr. Purcell," said Patrick coldly. "But I do ask that he not be a hypocrite and a liar, and I do insist that he not use others, who trust him, and who are helpless, to further his own purposes."

Purcell chuckled. "Fine sentiments. But only rich men can afford 'em." He shook his finger at Patrick again. "Not that I like hypocrites. If a man's a scoundrel, and if he's thinkin' only of himself, let him be open about it. Seems as if all your worries is because you've convinced yourself Marshall's a liar and a hypocrite, and a scoundrel to boot. Throw him out of your office, if you don't trust him any more."

Patrick got to his feet and began to pace up and down, slowly and uneasily. "What good would it do if I acted on impulse, and threw him out? He has money now; he'll have more. And he can finance his own law education himself. No, it's better to have him under my eye, I think." He stopped in front of Purcell, and his normally composed face was disturbed. "I believe he is preparing to sell the men out."

Purcell shrugged. "Maybe. But that's just your idea. Comin' back to me, I'd rather he was on our side than the other. You've known that all along; I never fooled you."

"But you're not a liar, or a hypocrite," said Patrick. He laughed a little uncomfortably. "You are, at the very least, neutral. You wouldn't advance the cause of the workers, but you wouldn't oppose it."

Purcell grunted, but made no answer. Patrick sat down again. "I'm marrying Laura in June. My business is politics, and law. I've never taken any interest in the railroad business, except the labour problem. But now I want some information. The Interstate Railroad Company is as rich as the New York Central now. But I'm hazy on the extent of it."

"Oh-o," said Purcell, and grinned. "Well, that's easy. Five years ago it absorbed the Capital Railroad Company here in Pennsylvania, and then the Chicago Railroad System. Goes clear to New York, now. Absorbed the old Baynes Locals, too, when old Joe went bankrupt after Steve died. Has a lease line to St. Louis, from Chicago. Big business. Rufe's responsible for all that. We're mighty lucky to have him.

"I think I know what's in your mind, my bucko. Steve, quite a while before he died, pledged twenty-five per cent of his fifty-one per cent holdin's in the company to old Jay Regan; he needed the money for a lot of damn fool schemes, for your precious workers, and others. After Steve died, Gunther purchased the stock from Jay Regan, but arranged with Rufe that he would vote his stock to approve the election of Rufe as president of the road, and arranged with our beamin' friend that he would sell the stock back to him at a prevailin' price each year, five per cent of it, until Rufe had gained back the whole twenty-five per cent, provided that at no time Gunther should suffer any loss in his original investment. So, Rufe now has fifty-one per cent."

He grinned cantankerously at Patrick. "You don't like our Rufe. But let me tell you that I respect him. He's brought us a fortune. He's made the road what it is. Steve would have kept it nice and conservative and maybe've run it into bankruptcy. Could be you prefer bankruptcy to dishonour, but you'd be a lone young feller in this world, and the sooner you learn that the better. You're goin' to have to deal more and more with the world as it is, especially now you're in politics, and politics stink to high heaven.

"You know that Laura here has sixteen per cent of the stock in her name. Steve had twenty-six per cent before he died. But he owed a pile of debts. Stupendous, that's what they were. It was necessary for the estate to sell ten per cent of the stock to liquidate his idiotic debts, and Rufe, who was one of the executors of the estate, sold Jay Regan that ten per cent, with the condition that it would be resold to Rufe upon payment, interest, principal, and a bonus. That's how he cornered his fifty-one per cent."

Purcell lifted his sleeping child into his arms and cradled her, brooding over the gilded head on his shoulder. He added grumpily, "You're wonderin' why Gunther and Jay Regan did all that for our Rufe. I can tell you. They like him. You wouldn't think that men like Regan and Gunther would slaver over charm, would you? They love our Red Rufe. Even murderers like those two sharks soften up with Rufe. They'll do things for him they wouldn't do for their own brothers. And they know he's able as hell. They might laugh at what you call virtue, but they never laugh at ability, even in a competitor." He squinted at

Patrick sardonically. "You ain't poor, yourself, Pat, my boy. But Laura's not a Cinderella, either. Thanks to Rufe, she's a mighty rich girl. You should be grateful."

Patrick stood up again, stiff and unbending. "Thank you," he said. Purcell smiled furtively at the young man's tone, but waited. "I'm thinking of Laura's sixteen per cent, sir. Mrs. Purcell and Mr. Rufe are her guardians. Mr. Stephen stipulated that when she was married her husband would become her guardian."

"Well?" Purcell said, carefully getting to his feet.

"I want to be in the railroad company," said Patrick with firm bluntness. "With that sixteen per cent."

Lydia and Laura gazed at him with mute surprise.

"H'm," said Purcell. "Better get out your law books and start to study up on the subject."

"You wouldn't object to me as a director?"

Purcell turned his huge, rocklike head and contemplated the young man. He scowled. Then after a few moments, he grumbled, "Must I, in my old age, stand another idealist?"

"You won't help me then?" said Patrick.

"I'm not sayin' I will, and I'm not sayin' I wont," Purcell muttered. "When the time comes, I'll decide. Gettin' too old to have any more idealists foulin' up my business. Well, good night. I'm takin' this child to bed, and I'm not coming downstairs again." He studied Patrick's stern face intently. Then he shook his head. "Guess, maybe, you're not like poor old Steve, after all."

He marched out of the room, a giant with a fairy in his arms, and the three watched him go. Laura said gently, "Uncle Jim will help you." She linked her arm through Patrick's. They were almost equal in height, for she was tall. She smiled into his face.

Lydia sighed, and folded up her work. "When I was young, there was only right and wrong in the world. Now I'm not so sure. No man is a devil and no man is a saint."

She rose to her feet with a movement as lithe as a young girl's. She put her hand on Patrick's shoulder and gazed earnestly at the young man. "Once Stephen told me that good is always defeated, but so is evil. Neither wins, permanently. I don't know, but I feel he is right." She added, more lightly, "Don't forget that Rufus is giving a large reception for my Cornelia on Christmas Eve. We are all such civilised friends, you know, even though I divorced him. It scandalises everybody; but business, as Jim would say, is business, and no grudges. Besides, Rufus and I parted so amiably, and when Cornelia is here he often calls on us." She laughed somewhat bitterly. "Cornelia hasn't confirmed it even to me, her mother. But I understand that Rufus is to announce her engagement to the Marquis de Fontaine-bleu. He will be Rufus's house guest, and everyone is coming, even business associates from Philadelphia, Chicago, and New York. It will be a very grand affair."

"You are happy about it, Mrs. Purcell?" asked Patrick coldly.

She turned away. "Cornelia hasn't been very close to me since I divorced her father. Oh, she is gay and loving. But she eludes me, in the merriest way possible. Cornelia is very like her father." She continued sadly, "If Cornelia wants to marry this young Frenchman she will know what she is doing. She always does."

Later, when in her room with her husband, Lydia said despondently, "Patrick has all the virtues one could desire, of course. But there is something unbending about him, something which will never compromise. That may be very worthy, I suppose. And it is an excellent quality in saints. However, for some reason, I don't think he is a saint." She laughed wearily. "He doesn't like me, Jim; he looks at me very oddly sometimes. Ah, you are laughing at me, but I do wish he wasn't to marry Laura. I have a sense of foreboding. . . ."

CHAPTER TWENTY-EIGHT

THE PHILADELPHIA HOUSE in Portersville was considered the most "genteel" of residential hotels: conservative, quietly luxurious, and established. The families and bachelors who lived there permanently were people of solid wealth and "refined" tastes, many of them retired and elderly, with sedate habits. To be admitted as a resident of the Philadelphia House was to be tacitly admitted to Portersville's "society," and to be regarded as a person of consequence, character, and importance.

The lobby, all in green and crimson plush and heavy mahogany, and with rubber and palm plants in huge brass pots, and dotted with brown marble pillars upholding a carved white ceiling, was never the site of any hilarity or loud voices or brash costumes. The thick crimson carpet hushed every footstep; decorum ruled at the desk; conversation was muted. Rich silk might rustle, but it did so discreetly. The employees of the hotel, in uniforms of brown with very light touches of gold, were mostly elderly and of long service; they showed their aristocratic pride in their establishment, and their demeanour was less obsequious than dignified. Only lately had the House marched with progress and gaslights been installed. Even these, however, flared dimly, as if in apology. Guests, meeting in the lobby before dinner in the vast chill dining-room beyond the plate-glass doors, would murmur about the weather, their health, any coming holiday, their minister, politics or business, all with a vague, disinterested manner as if these things were of no particular importance.

A few elderly ladies and gentlemen, waiting in the lobby for their carriages this dull and sombre December 21st, spoke with reserve of a new resident. A very old man wondered what "the House is coming to, admitting that person." An old lady fluted that "he seemed very gentlemanly, and was quite personable." A younger lady, not more than sixty, tittered gently and mentioned that she understood "he was well on his way to an unbelievable fortune," though she, of course, deplored "trade." The junior of the very old man, a short stout gentleman of about seventy-two, suggested that "we all wait and see. After all, times change." "But Irish, I understand!" exclaimed the very old man with distress. "And a Papist, it is said. What will Mr. Ivers say?" "A protégé of Secretary Peale's. Mr. Peale would not endorse him if he were not entirely respectable and worthy."

"Hush," whispered the younger lady. The object of this uneasy conversation had appeared in the dim precincts of the lobby on his way to the door. His carriage, undistinguishable from all the other carriages owned by residents of the House, was waiting at the kerb. He walked across the crimson carpet in a properly stately manner, head high, his motions slow and correct. His air might be sober and preoccupied, as befitting a "Resident," but the uneasiness of the elder lady and gentleman increased. There was something "peculiar" about him. He did not appear in the least subdued. However, no one could quarrel with that conservative bowler in the gloved left hand, or with the ebony,

283

gold-topped cane in the right hand, nor with the fine black broadcloth of his suit, the broadcloth greatcoat with the fur collar, the restrained white linen and black cravat and the excellent boots. The quarrel, if any, was concerned with his curiously fierce and restless black eyes and the intent sharpness of his features. Real gentlemen were not so distinct and clear-cut as this young man; he lacked unobtrusiveness. As no Resident had as yet spoken to.him, he had not attempted conversation either in the halls or in the lobby, or in the dining-room. He had been covertly watched at table; he had displayed no gaucheries. It was noted that he read only the most approved newspapers and periodicals. Inclusion was almost imminent in his case, and some of the old residents even began, very secretly, to think of unmarried nieces and granddaughters.

As he passed the elderly group in the lobby he glanced at them swiftly. To the alarm and disapproval of the other, the younger lady nodded just a little. The young man bowed very slightly, went on without a pause. They watched him leave the House, and enter his carriage. "How could you, Elsie!" said the very old man.

Once in his carriage, the new Resident burst out laughing. "The damned old fools!" His coachman, an old man, stiffened his shoulders in silence. The carriage rolled off down the streets in the direction of the Portersville National Bank building. The young man began to whistle, "Come Back to Erin. . . ." He leaned back against the leather cushions and lighted one of the deplorable new "cigarettes," and he puffed with the swift intensity which was characteristic of him. He pushed his bowler back on his head, and sent up clouds of smoke. He picked up his cane and admired the gold head. He turned it about in his gloved hands, and now the laughter went from his face. I've come a long way, thought Allan Marshall. I go on from here, and it must be fast. To calm some turbulent emotion, he began to sing, and even the coachman listened, unwilling, but enraptured. The song might be unfamiliar; the voice was rich and full and of great dramatic power.

The carriage rolled smoothly over the cobblestones, drew up before the bank. Allan climbed the stairs to the second floor, to the branch offices of the Interstate Railroad Company. During the past eight years, the company had come to occupy the whole of the second floor, though now the main offices were in Philadelphia. Smaller offices had been thrown together to make larger offices; a private door shut off passers-by to the third floor and the less affluent offices of local businessmen. Allan discreetly rang the bell at the second-floor door, and it opened to show the serious and elderly face of a black-clad man with a formal air. "Ah, yes, Mr. Marshall," he said, opened the door widely to admit Allan, and bowed. Allan, led by the guardian, traversed a carpeted corridor to the glass door on which was printed, with flourishes and bars, the name of the president of the company, Mr. Rufus deWitt.

Only one desk remained in this office, which was comfortable and snug with fire and leather and velvet and bookcases. Rufus sat at the desk, and now, as Allan entered, he rose graciously and extended his hand to the young man. "Well, well," he said, genially, "I'm glad to see you, my boy. And pleased that you accepted my invitation for a little consultation this afternoon." He beamed on Allan fondly, offered him a chair near the desk, sat down, and increased the beam to a ruddy glow. He implied that he was proud of his caller, and held him not only in the highest esteem but in personal affection. Allan smiled to himself, kept his face grave, and sat down. He did not lift up the tail of his coat; he merely loosened the buttons, and revealed a black-brocaded waistcoat cut in the most conservative and elegant manner, and the chain of a gold watch.

"I want to thank you, sir, for recommending me to the Philadelphia House," he said.

Rufus locked his hands together over his broad belly. "Ah, yes," he said richly. "I thought it was just the place for you, Allan. A rising young gentleman, the famous inventor of our automatic coupler. By the way, our subsidiary is going into production at once. The Master Car Builders have already placed an enormous order. You are well on the way, it seems, to be a millionaire, though, of course, the royalties won't be rolling in in any large quantity for at least a year. However"—and again the beam brightened—"you have only to mention the fact and the Interstate Iron & Steel Company will be happy to advance —anything—you need."

Allan said, "I think, then, that I shall ask them for six thousand dollars, say about January 2nd."

"A lot of money," murmured Rufus, cocking his head in a paternal way. "But then, you are young, and I believe you are a boy who doesn't intend to let life go by without living it. Frankly, at your age, I was exactly the same." He made a note on a piece of paper. "Six thousand it is, then. A cheque will be sent you in January."

I must be very careful; I'm playing for the highest stakes in my life, Allan was thinking. One hand rested lightly on the top of his cane; his gloves lay on his knee. He watched Rufus as keenly as Rufus watched him; he must not miss a single flicker of an eye, the slightest gesture. Rufus opened a silver box on his desk. "A cigar, Allan?" Allan hesitated; he loathed cigars. However, he inclined his head, accepted a cigar. There was an instant's pause, then Rufus, beaming like the sun, struck a match and lit the cigar for his visitor. *The first round,* Allan said to himself, *was won.*

"And you like the Philadelphia House?" asked Rufus lovingly. He put a little anxiety in his tone. "It suits you?"

"Very much, sir. It is just my style," said Allan. "The flamboyant isn't to my taste."

Rufus, whose delicate little wife sometimes complained that he was "flamboyant," did not care much for this. His eye sharpened suspiciously on Allan. He laughed. "It isn't to my taste," he said. "It's somewhat like a mausoleum, full of old relics. But eminently respectable. Very important—for a young man on his way up."

"I'm very respectable myself," said Allan. Then they burst out laughing together, and both relaxed in a sudden swell of good-fellowship.

Rufus said, "By the way, did you receive our invitation to Miss deWitt's Christmas Eve celebration, Allan?"

Allan met his fatherly glance, and immediately understood that no invitation had been sent at all, and that the idea was an entirely new one and decided upon only this very instant. "I'm afraid I have not seen it as yet, sir. But doubtless it is in my box; I did not call for the post before I left." *Another round won!*

"Well, matters are a little rushed," Rufus apologised. "Not all the invitations have been sent out as yet, though the time is growing short. We expect to announce our daughter's engagement to the Marquis de Fontainebleu that evening. He is our house guest, you know."

"I saw something about that in the newspapers," replied

Allan. His fingers tightened on the head of his cane. "It is quite settled, then?"

Rufus smiled disarmingly and allowed himself to show a little ruefulness. "Our daughter is not definite," he said. "Candidly, I should not like her to live in France, though we go abroad every spring. Cornelia and I are very close; she is much like me, they say. And, after all, she is all I have."

Your wife? Your two little sons? thought Allan, amused. His fingers loosened on the cane. He barely controlled a loud breath of desperate relief. "So," continued Rufus, with a genuine sigh, "I am not altogether pleased."

An atmosphere of the deepest intimacy now prevailed in the office. For some reason Rufus's guardedness abated. He studied Allan for a long moment or two, and he said to himself: He's almost a gentleman. Good brains there; no fool. Allan said respectfully, "Perhaps Miss deWitt will change her mind, even if she ever had any idea of such a marriage."

As this exactly met Rufus's hopes, in spite of the sweet, shrill urgings of his wife, and her raptures over the "magnificent honour," Rufus gave Allan one of his sincerest smiles. "Ah, yes," said Rufus. "Well, it is growing late, and so I really think we must come down to business. Allan, I have a suggestion to make to you. An offer, if you will."

Allan evidenced polite and serious interest. "As you mentioned before, my boy, in Scranton, law is your forte, and you do not intend to live on your royalties, enormous though they will later be. We are all very proud of you. Well, then. How long will it be necessary for you to continue reading law in Mr. Peale's offices?"

Now, thought Allan, keeping his expression unchanged. He said quietly, "I believe until about the first of February."

"And then?" prompted Rufus gently.

"My decision to concentrate on labour law is unchanged," replied the young man. There was a paler tint about his mouth as he studied Rufus.

Rufus smoothed his chin with his right index finger, and his tawny eyes glowed on the younger man. "I hear you are a very forensic speaker," he remarked.

Allan smiled. "I am glad you think so, sir. No doubt Mr. Duncan Baynes told you about it. I noticed him at Union Hall on December 18th."

Rufus was not confused. He chuckled. "I sent him," he said with charming candour. He lifted a letter from the desk, and chuckled again. "You did not write this by any chance, did you, Allan?"

Allan glanced briefly at the letter, and his only answer was a reserved smile. Rufus laughed heartily. "Your object is very clear to me." He waited, but Allan only lifted courteous eyebrows. Rufus leaned back in his chair and regarded the young man most benevolently. "You and young Pat Peale have been very good friends, have you not, my boy? It happens, as you know, that he is to marry my niece, who is like a daughter to me. She mentioned that Pat was disturbed about your speech at Union Hall, and is beginning to—well—shall we say that he found it somewhat ambiguous?"

"Ambiguous?" Allan frowned. "In what way? I noticed, a week or so ago, before Mr. Pat returned to Washington, that he was a little cool to me. The Peale offices are not the most important in Pennsylvania. I'll finish reading law there. I am going on with labour law, as I said. If Mr. Pat does not like that, I am sorry, but I don't intend to give it up."

Rufus grinned slyly. "Don't be disingenuous, Allan. You may speak to me as to a father, or at least an older brother. You know very well that Pat is deeply concerned over more favourable laws for labour."

Allan shrugged. "I also know that he is backing a bill for the regulating of railroads, sir. He has considerable support in the Senate."

"And you approve of the regulation?"

"At the present time, sir—and you must forgive what might appear to be rudeness—I am not in a position to say." He fixed his eyes on Rufus and now they sparkled with open ferocity. "It all depends on a number of things."

There was a sudden silence in the office as the two men's eyes met and held, hard and knowing. Then Rufus glanced away, played with a pen on his desk. "You have been unearthing labour decisions, and other matters, in assisting Pat. He told my niece all about it. He said you were invaluable. Have you told him yet of—ah—that obscure decision you mentioned in Scranton?"

"No, I have not."

"May I ask why?" Rufus's tone was tender.

"It is all part of my plans, when I finally make up my mind."

Nothing could have been happier than Rufus's smile. "You are a young man who is not only out for money, but for power. I know all the symptoms; I've had them myself. My dear boy, would you like to join my legal staff here in Portersville?"

Allan puffed lightly on his cigar and gazed at the fire. He appeared to be considering. Then he shook his head. "Thank you, Mr. deWitt. But no. I want more than to be part of a legal staff. I have been thinking of politics, in conjunction with my legal work."

The challenge was thrown down between them, and they looked at it, Rufus meditatively, Allan without perturbation. After the silence had prolonged itself, Allan said softly, "With my knowledge, my training, and my money, I think I could do very well in politics. Labour, all over Pennsylvania, is looking to me. Only to-day I received a letter from old Dan Boyle. I am thinking of running for senator, myself."

Rufus heard the deep and implacable threat in the young man's expressive voice. Rufus hid his suddenly violent consternation. This young devil would not be seduced by benevolence, flattery, or a show of affection. He wanted what he wanted. There was a smell of danger in the warm and placid air of the office. Rufus tapped his fingers slowly on the desk, and his reddish brows drew together in a hard knot of concentration. He pondered his reply, then came to the shrewd conclusion that Allan saw through all pretence and was waiting for a blunt statement.

"Well, Allan. What do you want? What is your price?"

Allan lifted his gaze to the ceiling. "If I should let my political ambitions go, I should want to be head of a legal staff, not part of it. I assure you, sir, that I am quite capable."

"In other words, my dear boy, you want to be head of my legal staff in Portersville, which already contains some of the best minds in the Commonwealth—old, experienced minds, well seasoned. You would also want to be called into consultation in our offices in Philadelphia."

"I think, sir, that you have summed it up very clearly."

"You are a very formidable young man," said Rufus benignly. "And I think you would be most invaluable to us. Shall we say ten thousand dollars a year? Beginning March 1st?"

"Ten thousand dollars a year," repeated Allan thoughtfully.

T

"That is more, I believe, than the present head of your legal department is now getting. It must be understood, sir, that that salary is just the beginning."

Rufus drew in a deep breath of relief and complacency. It was ridiculous that, confronted by this man not yet thirty, he, Rufus deWitt, powerful and invincible, should experience such emotion. But Rufus never underestimated others.

"Mr. Patrick Peale is not going to like this," said Allan, after he had satisfied himself that he had won a complete victory. He laughed shortly.

Rufus joined him in the laughter. He extended his fat hand to Allan, who shook it. "Nor will your other friends," said Rufus cunningly.

"I have no friends," said Allan.

Rufus lit another cigar and took some time about it. "My brother, Mr. Stephen, remarked that before he died. But he said it bitterly. You aren't bitter, Allan, are you?"

"No, sir. I am a realist." Allan began to put on his gloves without hurry. "In fact, I've discovered no man has any friends."

Rufus chuckled deprecatingly. "Now, now, Allan. You do sound bitter. I think you and I will be very good friends indeed."

"Yes, indeed, sir," said Allan gravely.

"And you had all this planned, from the very beginning?"

"From the very beginning."

Rufus nodded with deep content. He began to accept Allan warmly, as he always accepted potent and single-minded men. "What do you think, now, dear boy, since you have gotten what you wanted?"

"I think nothing in particular, except that it was inevitable."

Rufus was intensely amused. "But what if I had refused?"

Allan grinned briefly. "You were not in a position to refuse, Mr. deWitt. Moreover, you saw the immense advantage to yourself. I never offer anyone something which will not benefit him, in exchange for what I want. I think, sir, that we have both made an excellent bargain."

He stood up. He had undergone a frightful strain this past hour; he had gambled; he had won. But now his knees started to tremble and there was a dampness between his shoulder blades.

There was a brisk knock at the door, which immediately, and without ceremony, flew open. Cornelia entered like a blaze of sun and wind, and shouted huskily, "Papa, when in the world

are you coming downstairs? I've been waiting in the carriage——"
She stopped when Allan turned to her, and her mouth fell open.
But her surprise was very brief. She began to smile, widely and
with knowing delight. She advanced rapidly to the young man
and thrust out her hand. "Well, if it isn't—our gardener!" she
cried, her yellowish eyes filled with mocking points of radiance.
"Papa told me all about you. Is it too late for congratulations?"

Allan took her hand. For a moment or two he was quite
unable to speak. He could only look at Cornelia and tell himself
how beautiful and vital she was, and how tall and abounding.
A swift lust for her almost overpowered him, a deep and ravening
hunger that was an overwhelming appetite. She stood and
laughed in his face gleefully. Her father stood up and came to
stand beside her. "Not too late, my pet," he said richly. "I have
just made this dear boy here the head of our Portersville legal
staff. You may congratulate him."

"Well, well!" boomed Cornelia, not withdrawing her hand.
Her fingers curled about Allan's. She looked over her shoulder
at her father and laughed again. "I deserve the credit for discovering Mr. Marshall. I met him in the gardens last summer,
and then I sent him a very fine set of law books."

"Indeed!" said Rufus. His cordial smile became a trifle fixed.
His hand was on his daughter's arm, and he mechanically stroked
the snow-white ermine sleeve of her short jacket. His gesture
was possessive and jealous, and his gaze roved over her slowly
and anxiously. A round white ermine hat perched on the top
of her red curls, and she held a small muff of the same fur. Under
her hat, her face was all malicious and buoyant light, her cheeks
bright scarlet from powerful health, and cold, her big mouth
grinning and her splendid teeth glittering. Pearls shimmered
in her ears, and there were diamonds and pearls on her fingers.
The turquoise-blue velvet frock she wore enhanced her natural
vividness of colour. She sparkled with electric magnetism, so
that even while she stood there, laughing, she appeared to be all
movement.

"Oh, yes," said Cornelia, in her bold and common voice, as
she continued to twinkle on Allan. "I recognised the genius
immediately. Did you ever know, Mr. Marshall, that it was I
who sent the books?"

"I knew at once," he said. His throat felt very thick. He
released her hand and she stood back on her heels, as her father

always stood, and surveyed him with pleasure and jeering friendliness. The colour in her cheeks became more emphatic, and for an instant she glanced away in unaccustomed confusion. Then she laughed again. "Who else but I?" she demanded gaily. "Who else could understand all about you?"

"Very perceptive of you, my love," said Rufus. "But then, we are both perceptive, aren't we?" He withdrew his watch, glanced at it, affected to be astonished at the time. "We must really go. We have guests for dinner, and it is getting dark. By the way, Cornelia, Allan is attending your party."

"Wonderful," said Cornelia. "There are so few handsome men in the world." Deliberately, and openly, she examined Allan's clothing, her head cocked; she wanted to annoy and embarrass him. He stood before her stiffly and in composed silence, and she flashed him a derisive smile as she took her father's arm affectionately. She knew Rufus had become vaguely uneasy; so she said, "Mr. Marshall and I have so much in common. We must find time for a little talk at the party." She dropped her father's arm, flung herself, almost sprawling, into a chair, and tossed her muff on the desk. "Just as you, Papa, and I, must have a talk right now, before we go home."

Her sideways glance was impudent and dismissing. So Allan bowed coldly, shook hands with Rufus, and left. Cornelia watched him go, and chuckled. Rufus came back to his chair, frowning. "My love, that was indiscreet, sending him those books. He might have misunderstood."

Cornelia hooted. "He never misunderstands—anything. Quite the gentleman, now, isn't he? Or, almost a gentlemen—just as you, dear Papa, are almost a gentleman. Now, don't glower. I'm not a lady, either. Not at all like our dear Estelle." Her voice lowered with contempt.

"I wish, Cornelia, that you wouldn't sneer so at your step-mother, or so obviously dislike her," said Rufus. His warm pink flesh crawled with discomfort.

"Dislike her?" exclaimed Cornelia, her eyes widening. "I don't at all. Besides, dislike is wasted on Estelle. She believes she has people deceived with her sweet face, and her innocent curls piled on top of her darling little head, and her sweet smiles and her damnable sweet voice, and her idiot dimples and exquisite little ways. What a fraud she is! Not good, healthy robust frauds like you and me, Papa. Just a sugary hypocrite, Estelle, positive that she's diddling everybody with her sympathetic, gentle voice, and her aching heart for the ' poor and downtrodden,' as she calls them, when all the time she is simply the most avaricious and greedy little bitch——"

"Cornelia!" ejaculated Rufus angrily.

His daughter waved her hand airily. "Oh, Papa. I'm not refined, I admit. Now, as we were discussing Estelle: no one objects to anyone liking money—except fools—but your dainty little wife pretends it is of no importance. Yet she goes over the household bills with an eye like a buzzard's, and she has as much mercy in her as a stone. But we've talked about dear Estelle's character too much in the past. I only bring it up to-day for a very particular reason."

"Well?" said Rufus, still uncomfortable. His daughter stared at him with real love and a kind of coarse tenderness. He could not resist this, so he laughed half-heartedly. "What a rascal you are, Cornelia. I can't remain angry with you. What is it now?"

"Nicki had a talk with Estelle this morning. She came up to me and reported it, all chittering and sweet little grins and flutterings. Full of delight. It seems Nicki wants one million, five hundred thousand dollars to marry me, cash on the line, and a nice fruity block of Interstate stock."

The fire crackled. Cornelia and Rufus regarded each other in a grim silence. Then Rufus moved ponderously in his chair and faced the fire. He said, "That isn't so—excessive. In exchange for the title and a mouldy castle or two, and a big château on the Riviera and a large house in Paris, and assorted vineyards and such. If that is what you want, Cornelia."

"I don't," she said roughly. "I never did want it. I like Nicki; he's so finished, and has such manners. But I never seriously considered him as a husband. Imagine being married to that mixture of pomade and sophistication and—well, what we call depravity. Have you noticed Europeans much? Elegant corruption. We aren't corrupt, in that special meaning. We love life, they merely perfume it, and pervert it."

"Dear me," said Rufus, with genuine alarm, "where in the name of God do you get your ideas, Cornelia?"

"I just look," replied Cornelia equably, and in a reasonable tone of voice. "We're a nation of *entrepreneurs* and throat-cutters and pirates, and what Pat Peale calls ' robber barons.'

We have no culture either, thank the Lord, if by culture is meant the Continental variety. But at least we aren't diseased."

"Diseased?" repeated Rufus with consternation. He coloured violently. Cornelia studied him with high amusement. She then dropped her eyes demurely. "Disease of the mind, I mean, Papa. What else did you think?"

Rufus got to his feet and stood before the fire, his hands in his pockets. "For a girl brought up as nicely as you were, Cornelia, with a finishing school, and everything, and all the refined advantages, your conversation is extraordinary."

"So you've remarked before, Papa." She stood up and went to him, and put her arm coaxingly in his. She stood on tiptoe and kissed his heated cheek. "Papa, I'm being honest. Damn it, I can only be honest with you, so don't expect me to pretend anything else."

He patted her hand abstractedly and continued to look at the fire. "What did you say to Estelle? And stop swearing; it's unheard of in a young lady."

"I told her to tell Nicki to go to hell," said Cornelia roundly. "And, of course she had hysterics, and I had to call her maid and there was smelling salts. Poor Papa," Cornelia continued, with real concern. "How our little angel-face bullies you! Mamma never bullied you like that."

Rufus's face darkened with pain and anger. Almost roughly, he pushed Cornelia's hand off his arm. "Let us not discuss your mother or Estelle. Let us get down to facts. You made your stepmother ill. That was to be expected. And I hear about it half the night. Is she in bed?"

"Certainly. She was when I left. But she'll be all scent and ruffles and fringes by the time we get home. We have house guests, remember, and ' one must never reveal one's emotions. It is vulgar.'"

Rufus sighed. "You make life very difficult. Well. You don't want to marry Nicki. I never wanted you to. You know that, Cornelia." He chewed on his lower lip. "The guests at your party are expecting an announcement. It is going to be very awkward."

"Not at all, Papa. Estelle gave Nicki the bad news this afternoon and he is leaving to-morrow morning. Awkward? Who cares? Our guests anticipated staring at the Marquis, and they'll find nothing to stare at." She continued offhandedly: "On the way down here I stopped in at the newspaper offices and asked them to insert in a society note that the Marquis de Fontainebleu has been called home to France on urgent matters—by cable."

"My God!" shouted Rufus. He turned to Cornelia, then he paused. Helplessly he began to laugh, and she burst out laughing with him. She threw herself into his arms and he hugged her furiously.

CHAPTER TWENTY-NINE

THE SNOW blew up in clouds like brilliant fireflies in the lamps of Allan's carriage. Swift scarfs of white gossamer swirled over the cobblestones, and a rising gale made the carriage vibrate and sway. The horses, feeling the savage wind in their manes and tails, bent their heads and moved rapidly. The sonorous shout of the river, stirred to violent action, filled the bitter air like an imminent presence. The dark of the early evening threw a vagueness like fog over the city, in which the yellow street lamps struggled dimly.

The gates were down at the railroad crossing. The carriage, and its restless and uneasy horses, drew up, waiting. Allan had no need to glance at his watch to know what train was approaching down the glimmering rails, its polished bells clanging furiously against the storm, smoke and sparks pouring out of its gigantic smokestack, lines of fire spurting from its wheels. It was "old Sixty-Eight," and Allan sat in his carriage, his face pressed against the window. He had believed that the railroad had been a necessary evil in the life of his family, but now he knew he had resented it only because it had not been more significant. He was aware, as the train bellowed closer, of a strong excitement and exhilaration, a sense of belonging to the power which sent these monsters to cities and over plains and mountains, and which battered their fiery heads against closed dark wildernesses and primeval fortresses. What they opened became the property of man; what became the property of men sounded with life and commerce. The burning smokestacks of the engines were torches lifted to civilisation in the gloom of wastelands. Behind them marched the men of industry, the builders of cities, the whores, the teachers, the judges, the murderers, the poets and the writers, the architects—and the soldiers.

Who was driving old Sixty-Eight to-night? Thursday was "change-over" day. It could be any engineer at all. And then Allan, squinting from his carriage, saw that the engineer was his father, Tim Marshall. The wavering street lamps at the crossing flickered on Tim's face, which had recently aged, become drawn and despondent under the striped cap. The engine was slowing rapidly, and now, as Allan looked at his father from the shelter of his carriage, he heard a difference in the clangorous bells. They were no longer exuberant, as when Tim usually rang them. They had a mechanical and almost dolorous note, listless and without life, and the eyes that followed the passage so carefully no longer had in them the old pride and exultation.

Allan sat in his carriage, frowning. Sightlessly, he waited while the long line of freight rumbled by. He put the head of his gold-topped cane against his mouth. The old fool!

Allan was still a very young man, and in spite of his ire and impatience he could feel sadness for his father. He had been fond of his parents in a way he had considered compounded of indulgence, superiority, and superficiality. His sadness increased his impatience, and he was in a bad humour by the time the last winking red lights of the train had receded into the distance. The carriage rolled on, clattered over the stones, rounded corners, and climbed hilly streets. It finally reached the Philadelphia House, which was discreetly lighted, a genteel bulk in the darkness. Allan entered the quiet lobby, where a few pre-dinner groups of elderly men and women, with a scattering of well-bred and very drab young ladies, were chatting in soft and elegant voices. Allan's entrance caused them to become silent, while they studied him covertly. The dark silks and velvets of the women, their decorous and colourless faces, the black broadcloth of the men, the whole air of studied quiet and gentility, suddenly made Allan think of a funeral. This thought restored his good temper as he advanced towards the single creaking elevator of the House.

"Ah, Mr. Marshall," whispered the ancient clerk at the desk, sibilantly. Allan halted. The clerk leaned across the desk with a conspirator's air, at once dubious and confidential. "There is a —a gentleman—waiting over there near those palms. He asked for you. He has been here an hour, I believe, and did not give his name."

Allan turned. A short, somewhat plump young man in shabby brown was reading a newspaper calmly under a prudent cluster of gaslights affixed to the panelled wall. Allan's face tightened; he hesitated, then walked with ungenteel rapidity towards his visitor, conscious of the following eyes and curiosity. "Well, hallo, Mike," said Allan, holding his cane squarely across him with both gloved hands.

Michael was smiling up at him, his fine round brown eyes shining pleasantly. "Hallo," he said. "I've been waiting for you."

"So I heard. Shall we go up to my rooms?"

Michael rose, the paper crackling noisily in the warm quiet. He had been smoking his pipe, probably unaware that the rules of the hotel prohibited gentlemen from smoking in the common meeting ground of the lobby. His wrinkled clothing was covered with ashes and flecks of tobacco, and the pipe, in that pure atmosphere, stank abominably. Allan began to smile, though pricked with some embarrassment.

The elevator had risen to respond to a bell on an upper floor, and now it was descending with muffled creakings and groanings. Allan saw the ladies and gentlemen emerging, greeting those already in the lobby with measured smiles and little bows. He touched Michael's arm and advanced to the elevator, murmuring "pardon me" as he was forced to find his way through the thickening groups. The ladies and gentlemen divided to let the two young men through, and they stared in affront at Michael's plebean appearance, his rough brown greatcoat and mud-stained boots. A working man, a rough labourer, a coachman! And with that young Mr. Marshall who had been on the point of being accepted! One old gentleman murmured to another: "I don't know what the world's coming to. I never thought, in the Philadelphia House—we must really speak to the manager—insulting to all that the House represents—incredible. . . ."

Serenely unaware of the general disapproval, Michael, who had a slight waddle when he walked, trundled at his brother's side. Allan was frowning again. He marched into the elevator with Michael, and in silence, the two were slowly wafted to the third floor. Allan fumbled for his keys as they emerged into a dimly lighted and carpeted corridor. The floor silenced their footsteps and the gaslights flared in a draught. Allan opened a dark mahogany door, and the young men entered a firelit sitting-room, small but warm and intimate, all crimson and dark blue velvet, monolithic furniture, and heavy draperies. The fire chuckled under a mantelpiece of black marble. On the walls hung some very fine but dreary engravings, and everywhere, on the furniture and the curtains, fringe dripped and rippled. An opened door revealed a bedroom as sober as the sitting-room, with a walnut headboard which touched the high yellow ceiling and with a dresser and commode weighted with brown marble.

Allan turned up the globed lights on the walls. "Sit down, Mike," he said. Michael obediently sat down in a red velvet chair which folded itself about his rounded contours. Allan threw off his fine coat, tossed it on to a huge blue sofa, hurled the cane and his hat after them, and removed his gloves. As always, he glanced at his mutilated middle finger. Then he put his hands in his pockets and stood before his brother. "Good to see you," he said ungraciously. "After all, it's been two weeks, hasn't it? How are Dad and Ma?"

Michael smiled, and his plump and ordinary face lighted up affectionately. He replied, "They're in good health. They miss you, of course. You look quite the gentleman." He smiled directly into Allan's eyes, and added, "Aloysius."

Allan grunted. "Why ' Aloysius ' ? Or are you being nasty? It took me five years of steady punching and kicking to make our playmates call me Allan. Even Dad and Ma haven't called me by that damned name since I was twelve years old."

Michael was suddenly sober, and he sat in his chair and stared at the fire abstractedly. "Never mind," he said. "I wasn't being nasty, so forgive me. I was just trying. . . . Never mind. It's very nice here, Allan. Very genteel, and everything else you always wanted."

"Is there any reason why a man shouldn't want things?"

Michael's face showed a very real distress. "Did I say he should not?"

He laced his short fat fingers together, leaned forward, and studied them. Allan fished in his pocket for his new and expensive cigarette case, which was all silver curlicues and glitter. He opened it. "Have a cigarette? Or are you too holy, or old-fashioned? Tailor-mades," he added. The cigarettes had his name engraved on them in discreet gilt. Michael regarded both case and cigarettes with unfeigned admiration, and gingerly lifted a small white cylinder. Allan thrust a taper into the fire and lit the cigarette for his brother and another for himself. Michael puffed distrustfully and carefully for a few moments, while Allan, leaning against the mantelpiece, the cigarette held with the proper elegance in his left hand, watched him.

"They're very good," said Michael.

"Turkish," said Allan. His face was half-turned away and so he did not see Michael's glance of compassion and pain. He continued: "I suppose you had some reason for coming, not connected with mere brotherly solicitude."

"Yes," admitted Michael hesitatingly. "I did. I came on my own, too. I wanted to know if we could expect you at home on Christmas Eve for dinner, and if we'll all go, as usual, to Midnight Mass. Together."

Allan threw his cigarette into the fire. "I can't," he said flatly. "I have been invited to a very grand ball at the home of Mr. Rufus deWitt." He turned to Michael in order to catch his brother's expression of incredulity and awed amazement. But Michael's eyes had become dark and sorrowful; he was again studying his clasped hands. "That will hurt our parents terribly. We've never missed a Midnight Mass—the whole family together. You always extended them that consideration before."

Allan's voice rose angrily: "What nonsense! Yes, I humoured them, because it was Christmas. But you know damned well I've never believed—anything—for years. Did you hear what I said? I've been invited to——"

"I heard you." Michael spoke very softly. "And you have my congratulations. I'm not surprised; I've always known you would be very successful some day. I just wanted to be able to tell Dad that you would be with us, as usual. After all, I soon leave them, forever, and you and I probably won't meet again. It will be a lonely life for them, after this last Christmas; I'd like to know that you and they had become reconciled and that they had one son left to console them." He added: "It will be a comfort to them, if you are with them."

"Sentimentality," said Allan. "Black Irish sentimentality. Have you forgotten Dad's thundering when I told him I was moving here, and when I offered to buy him a decent house out of the city, away from that stinking neighbourhood?"

"He has his standards," said Michael mildly.

Allan's eyes were glittering irately. "What did he expect me to do? Bank my money, and continue to live in that rat hole with what he calls his ' people? '"

"He believed what you have always led him to believe—that you were exclusively concerned with labour, and that you were its spokesman. I think it was not just your leaving which broke his heart. It was something else." Michael lifted his eyes, and they were very bright and steadfast. "Dad, you see, is a very simple man, with very old and simple standards."

Allan's mouth became furious. "And what are his standards? He innocently believes that all wealthy men are malefactors, and all poverty-stricken wretches, by very virtue of their poverty, are saints. If a man by effort and imagination and work and intelligence manages to lift himself from the gutter, he becomes, *per se*, in Dad's eyes, a kind of traitor and rascal. But you think that, too, don't you?"

"Did I say so?" asked Michael.

Allan stared at him. The fire flickered in silence. "But you believe it," said Allan at last.

Michael shook his head slowly. "You are wrong. Men are the same, whether rich or poor. They differ only in degree. I agree with you that few understand this, and that is why the world wallows in envy and hatred and malice. Our neighbours are no different from Mr. deWitt, for instance, except for money. And those who tell them lies to the contrary are trouble-makers, and dangerous. Such men are the real ' enemies of the people.'"

Allan's eyes narrowed vindictively. "You are speaking of me, of course."

Michael nodded. "Yes, of course." Michael regarded Allan straightly. "You see, you never deceived me at all."

"You are a fool, as you always were," said Allan. "A man employs the material at his hand to get what he wants."

Michael said thoughtfully, as though Allan had not spoken. "In some way you exploited those poor wretches. You won't tell me, I suppose. Dad understands you employed them but he is as ignorant of the method as I am. You wouldn't care to enlighten me?"

Allan walked rapidly into the bedroom and returned with a bottle of whisky and two small glasses. He put them on the table near his brother. He smiled darkly. "Will you have a drink, Mike?"

"I like beer," said Michael. His plump face was full of sorrow. "But I'll have a drink with you." He noticed that the bottle was half empty, and a little knot of flesh thickened between his eyes. "You like whisky now?" he asked, as Allan filled the glasses.

"Yes. It's not a ' gentleman's ' drink. Sherry is." He lifted his glass in a brief toast, and the whisky, at one gulp, disappeared down his throat. Michael watched him, slowly sipping, the pain deepening on his face. "Whisky," he said, "is an Irishman's drink. At least, so I've heard. And it isn't the best thing in the world for him, above all other races."

Allan grinned. The whisky had loosened the tight lines of his face. "I'm an American," he said.

"It was the great German poet Goethe who said that a man cannot escape the mould in which he was cast," said Michael.

Allan laughed shortly. "And it's the poet we are," he said. "And it's proud of my brother, I am. I never knew he was so educated."

" You never knew very much, and probably never will," replied Michael almost inaudibly. "That is your greatest misfortune. The ignorant man despises his fellows; the comprehending man pities them. How is it possible to live in the world," he continued with a kind of tragic wonder, "and not see what there is to be seen?"

Allan filled his glass again, threw back his head, and swallowed the whisky. He set the glass down with a thump, leaned his elbow on the mantelpiece, and stared sombrely into the fire.

Michael said musingly, "It is when we are children that the world is a magic place, where anything can happen, when there is a marvel over the hill and an enchantment in the morning and the end of the world at sunset. It is when we are children that we glimpse the blinding core of life and guess all the other mysteries. We lose that when we leave our childhood behind us. But there are a few of us who were never children, and so, not even in our young years did we have any understanding."

"Meaning," said Allan, "men like me."

"Yes," said Michael.

Allan was silent. He glanced at the bottle of whisky again, then glanced away. Finally he said, "You speak with authority, Mike, but what do you know about me? I think you're arrogant and presumptuous, and what Father Tom calls ' vainglorious.'

Isn't that a sin, eh? Remember to include that in your next confession." For an instant his jeering eye glinted on his brother.

Then he thought suddenly, and without warning, of an incident which he had not consciously recalled for many years. Now it was illumined, not only in the fresh and vivid colours of that long-ago warm and early summer day, but with the apocalyptic and sinister lightning of later adult comprehension.

He had always been a fiercely proud and lonely little boy, the son of immigrants tormented by the sons of equally bewildered and hungry immigrants. He had learned to fight for himself, and even when very young he had been fearless, ever ready with his fists, fighting fairly but without mercy. His brother, more placid and complaisant, or, perhaps, more gentle and tolerant, had escaped much of the childhood persecutions inflicted upon Allan.

Truculent, imaginative, and contemptuous of weakness and ignorance, Allan had been feared, finally, by his schoolmates, and left alone, never invited, for dread of his eloquent scorn and his fists, to engage in any play or adventures. Though so young, his solitude had forced his thoughts to grow into larger dimensions; he borrowed or stole books which gave him insight into the lives and drives and purposes of men. By the time he was ready for his First Communion, it was a man, rather than a child, who approached the altar, in a mood of resistant cynicism, indifference, and disdain.

"I was never religious; I never believed in anything," he said morosely to Michael, and this time he did not glance at the whisky bottle. He lifted it and poured another drink for himself and drank it down. Then he stood by the fire and stared emptily at his glass.

"No?" said Michael gently, leaning forward with his hands on his round brown-clothed knees.

But Allan did not hear him. He was still in his memory of that day. The present was dissolving in a blur of alcohol.

He had impatiently learned the catechism, and had absorbed the pre-Communion teachings of old Father Gallacher, not because of interest but for fear of the strap. And then that Sunday had arrived, all golden warmth, sweet young trees, gleaming sky, and quiet. Portersville was not as yet overhung with the clouds of industry, cinders were not so numerous underfoot, noise had not yet invaded every crowded street. It was still a rather provincial city, lying below its amethystine and blue-green mountains. In spite of himself, Allan had been stirred by the peace and tenderness of the day, which had further been enhanced by a new pair of knee britches, black cotton stockings, and cheap shining boots.

He knelt with his young enemies and acquaintances. He listened idly to the priest. The hot sunlight fell in a coloured cataract through the few cherished stained-glass windows of the shabby little church, and each small face became a moving prism. Father Gallacher, a thin and wizened man with fiery and earnest eyes, spoke gently to those children at whom it was his custom to roar in discipline. They knelt before him, and his sentimental heart was touched and saddened. He said, "Dear children, you wish to-day for the first time, to partake of the Table of the Lord. Before you are admitted, I demand your profession of Faith. . . ."

Allan was bored. He moved his lips silently as the children recited the Creed and the Our Father. The warmth and slumbrous peace in the church, the flickering of the candles, the shadowy corners, the chorus of mechanical young voices, induced a sleepiness in him and a yawning ennui. "Do you renounce Satan, and all his works, and all his pomps?"

"His pomps"—what were they? The great houses along the river, the carriages that glittered as they rolled through the streets, the pretty faces under umbrellas, the genial complacency of the gentlemen, the fine boats and the sailboats, in summer, on the water? Allan became interested, and began to listen. "Do you believe in Jesus Christ, His only Son Our Lord, Who was born in this world and Who suffered for us?" Did the Lord "suffer" for the fabulous ladies and gentlemen in those houses, the people who strolled on rolling green lawns and laughed under dark trees that sparkled in the sunlight? The young Allan began to sneer inwardly, and then all at once he said to himself: Yes. This new and intriguing thought sobered him, and Father Gallacher saw the hard eyes of that "black Irish rascal" fix themselves on him with passionate intensity. The old priest was namelessly stirred, and he spoke even more earnestly. "Will you always live according to the Faith you so solemnly profess to-day?"

"We will," said the children, and the loudest, the most emphatic of all, was the voice of Aloysius Marshall.

Father Gallacher prayed: "O God, Heavenly Father, mercifully look down upon Thy little ones here prostrate before Thee. . . . We commend them to Thy Paternal care and love. . . . Divine Redeemer! through Thy love these children are children of God —Thou art the truest Friend of children, and on earth didst love to be with them. . . ."

Allan, enormously uplifted and excited, glanced sideways at the faces of his youthful enemies and all the hatred left him. In its place there was exaltation and something strangely close to love. He would not challenge them any longer; he would not strike or despise them. He would extend friendship to them, convince them that he could become their friend. He would forgive them their persecutions of him; like a vague cloud it came to him that only the unhappy persecute others, and he was filled with pity. They, too, were aliens in an alien land, children of immigrants, derided by those who could boast of a longer ancestry in this country.

"It was stupid," said Allan to Michael, who was watching him piercingly. His eyes were ablaze with mingled alcohol and rage and gloom.

Michael could not know his brother's thoughts, but he said in that same gentle voice, "How could you judge?" Something was happening to this brother in his sleek broadcloth, with the gold chain across his brocaded waistcoat, this elegantly barbered brother who leaned against the mantelpiece.

The taste of the bread and wine was still on his tongue as Allan emerged from the church into the light of the street. He began to run as if his thoughts drove him. He must tell Michael, the despised little brother, what had happened to him to-day. He must find a quiet place in which to examine what he had experienced.

"But I really experienced nothing," said Allan. He looked for the whisky bottle with glazed eyes. It had disappeared. In a fog, he automatically began to look for it, while Michael watched him with profound compassion. In the midst of his fumbling search he forgot the whisky. He forgot that Michael was there. He stood on the hearth before the fire, his back to his brother, his hands thrust into his pockets, and the fire lighted up his tense dark features and his bitter mouth.

He was running through the hot streets again. He would be a priest! That would make his parents happy. Dad would rejoice as

he cut up the tough Sunday chicken. They would go together to
Father Gallacher. . . .

Allan had raced down Potter's Road, dusty, sun-swept in the
Sunday quiet. He heard a sound of crying, and stopped. Little
Michael, even then brown and plump and gentle, was sitting on
the kerb, surrounded by four hulking boys, slightly older than
Allan. They were laughing at him, threatening him, thrusting
dirty fists under his fat little chin.

"In a way, it is all because of you, Mike," said Allan in a
thickened voice.

"Tell me," said Michael with pity.

But Allan was approaching the group at the gritty kerb, and
now his hands were tightening into fists and the glory receding,
and all the understanding and joy. There was a black seeping
into his heart, and his scalp prickled. No one saw him as yet. He
listened to the voices: "You dirty Irisher! What you doin' in
our country? Where's your brudder? Thinks he's so smart!
Well, he ain't here now, and when we get through with you . . ."

"Worship idols, don't you?" jeered another boy, rubbing his
knuckles hard against Michael's wet cheek. "Think you can take
over our country, don't you? Well, we'll fix that, and right here
and now."

Children of God! These grimy and dirty wretches who were
frightening a very little boy! Unhappy, were they? Their faces
were alight with evil laughter and gloating.

"And it's still there, all of it," he muttered. His hands clenched
in his pockets.

Allan had been outnumbered, and he was not a boy who fought
with all the odds against him. He had learned guile in the barren
streets of the slums. As he came closer to the group he began to
whistle, that peculiar sweet and tuneful whistle of his, so familiar
to hostile years. The boys started, drew away from Michael,
regarded Allan in his new clothes, with fear and hate. He had
smiled at them broadly. "Looking for a fight?" he had asked in a
soft voice. "Well, I like fights, too." He had smiled at them with
open friendliness as they stared at him with glowering caution.

"Tell you what," said Allan. "I've got a new big red ball.
For my birthday. There's four of you fellows here. Just suppose
you divide up, picking your friends. Then two of you fight the
other two. And then the winning two fight, and who wins
gets the ball."

Four pairs of eyes began to gleam suspiciously and with avarice.

"And I'll referee," offered Allan grandly. "You know I'm a fair fighter, and I got all the rules."

The big boys would have preferred to attack Allan in a body. But there was that red ball. The avarice brightened in their eyes and they wet their lips. Their hatred was less than their greed.

"It always is," commented Allan dully, thrusting at a burning coal with the toe of his boot. "It is always greater than anything else—greed."

But in some deep and intuitive way Michael understood that his brother was not thinking of himself, and he sighed.

The boys, shouting eagerly and excitedly now, had picked their partners. In a moment the street was a brawl, the Sunday peace gone. Allan had dodged about the fighters, admonishing, threatening at an unfair blow, laughing aloud at the sight of blood. Michael crouched on the kerb, still whimpered softly, the tears still on his cheeks, his eyes, preternaturally horrified and aware, fixed on the combatants. But he looked at Allan more than anyone else, Allan dancing lightly on the balls of his feet, Allan with his young face gleeful and alert, his black curls tumbling on his wet forehead. There was a gleaming look about him, a sort of brilliant vengefulness.

The fight was soon over, the bloody victor stretching out his hand demanding the ball. Allan nodded, raced into the little house of his parents. His father and mother had not as yet returned; every small room echoed to his pounding footsteps. He found his ball, ran out again into the street where four boys were wiping away at their gory noses and scowling at each other. Allan looked at them, grinning, for a long moment, then tossed the ball to the winner. It flew through the air like a great clot of blood, catching the sunlight. The winner caught it, grunting with satisfaction, and the others crowded about him, pleading for a chance to throw it, forgetting their fighting rage in mere slavering desire to touch the fruit of battle. He was no longer an enemy. He was one to beseech, for he was rich.

"Damn their souls," said Allan. "They're always like that." He turned from the fire and his eyes focused on his brother. "I learned my lesson that day. And I've put it to good use. You wanted to know my ' method.' That was it. Divide and rule."

306

Never Victorious, Never Defeated

Michael watched the tormented face of his brother, and he thought: He has gone a long way back, into hell, into disillusion, into hatred. And he has returned with it, and perhaps he'll never forget. "Where's that damned whisky?" asked Allan, but he did not move from the fireplace.

"Perhaps I will remember to include my ' vaingloriousness ' in my next confession," said Michael almost humbly. "There is so very little I understand."

Allan smiled gloomily. "Especially about those you and Dad always call the ' robber barons.'"

Michael laughed a little, lifted his hands in a surrendering gesture of resignation. "Well. They steal prodigiously, on a grand scale. But nearly everyone is a thief, one way or another. The small thief envies the big thief secretly, and so he berates him righteously."

"What talk for a coming monk!" said Allan.

Michael became serious. "The Church does not deplore personal wealth, if gotten by honesty and hard work and intelligence. She is just alarmed when that wealth becomes more important to a man than his immortal soul."

Allan uttered a contemptuous sound. His eyes were not so dulled now, and Michael was emerging from a blur. "Do you remember Dad telling us how he and Ma, and hundreds of other Irish people, were not permitted to land in this country for a long time, but were shifted about from port to port, starving, sick, and cold, until the gracious authorities finally allowed them to come ashore into a grudging land? Like cattle they were, the immigrants. Ma lost her first child, then, on shipboard, in the stinking underdecks. On a dirty bunk. She almost died. But who cared?"

Michael thought with vivid understanding: I wonder how often a man's success is revenge?

Allan's thoughts, though intense, wandered still in the cloudy haze of whisky. "I want you to listen, Mike. I'm just on my way. And do you know? I am going to marry Cornelia deWitt."

He waited for Michael to exclaim, to laugh at him incredulously. But Michael was silent. He was torn by his compassion, and there was the weight of tears behind his eyes. A sharp and bitter sword it is, my brother.

Michael's hand furtively touched the top of the whisky bottle that he had hidden in the depths of the velvet chair near his thigh.

He sighed. It was folly to say to a man: Don't you care what happens to you, in the drink? Michael understood that a man drank to excess for the precise reason that he did not care what happened to him. A man who hated living used any method to destroy his thinking mind, and his body.

He answered Allan at last: "Yes, you will probably marry Miss deWitt, if that is what you want. You always will get what you think you want."

Allan's thoughts veered. "And the house for Dad and Ma. They must have a decent place to live. . . ."

"Tell them about it," said Michael quickly and eagerly. "Come to dinner Christmas day. A fine dinner it will be, with a goose."

Allan frowned. Then he threw out his hands. "Yes. I'll go. If Dad"—and he smiled—"doesn't kick me out when he sees me."

He added abruptly: "Where is that damned whisky," and he stared about him with bleared eyes. Michael stood up. "It's food you'll be needing, and wasn't that the bell I heard?"

Allan was bemused with the whisky and the emotional storm through which he had battered his way. So he offered no resistance when Michael took his arm affectionately and led him to the door, and then out in the corridor. Some last few groups were gathering for the entrance into the lofty dining-room, with its chill silver, its cold plates, its white walls, white table-cloths, and austerely painted gold and white columns. Allan said, "You must dine with me, of course."

Michael smiled obsequiously, and said very loudly, "Thank you for the offer of the job, Mr. Marshall. I'll think it over, but I don't believe I'll suit."

Allan stared at him blankly. Michael, in the approved fashion, pulled his brown forelock, bowed, and holding his hat meekly in both hands, and keeping his head bent sidled away. Allan's mouth dropped open. He watched his brother creeping across thelobby, and he was dumbfounded. But when Michael reached the door and glanced back, Allan had begun to smile, a dark but understanding smile.

The little group of ladies and gentlemen had paused at the doors leading into the dining-room. They were exchanging glances, and then they looked at Allan and smiled faintly. A very old and venerable man with a white beard said with gracious reserve, " A bad storm, isn't it, Mr. Marshall ? I am Mr. Blakely, and these . . ."

Yes, thought Allan, a bad storm. He was bowing and acknow-ledging introductions in the best manner, and murmuring.

CHAPTER THIRTY

ONE BLIZZARD after another had assaulted Portersville during the last few days, until the city's houses and buildings resembled monstrous heaps of snow pierced by jagged patches of windows and narrow tunnels. The railroad yards steamed with idling locomotives, and the men smoked in the roundhouses restlessly, and other men, with fires, tried to thaw out frozen switches. The mountains rose above each other in chains of immutable whiteness. Only the river, sheathed here and there with ice, moved in sullen blackness through the valley.

But on the day before Christmas the blizzards stopped. The mountains flamed in alabaster incandescence under a cold and blazing sun set in a pale blue sky. The river ran, a bright cerulean passage, through the white land. The air became crystal, and shining with light.

On Christmas Eve the stars crackled and pulsated in a dark purple sky. Every great house along the river, and on the moun-tains, throbbed with yellow light. Roads had been cleared, and Cornelia deWitt, who had been afraid for her party—which had no particular purpose now except festivity—rejoiced. The guests would not be prevented from coming.

Singing loudly and hoarsely, she allowed her maid to add the last touches to her toilette, and then she stood and surveyed herself in her long pier glass. She smiled with satisfaction, then hummed as she pirouetted and bowed and gestured in utter unself-consciousness. Her Worth gown, bought in Paris last spring, a triumph of silvery grey velvet, was draped lovingly across the front and looped richly at the back, caught here and there with clusters of velvet violets. It fitted her superb figure tightly, half-revealing her full white breasts, and completely revealing her strong white arms, shoulders, and throat. She wore her father's gift, a heavy collar of yellow gold twined with pearls, diamonds, and aquamarines, with huge ear-rings to match. Golden slippers, glittering at the tips with diamonds, peeped from the gown as she walked. Her red hair had been elaborately dressed in a new Parisian style, all bouffant curls and fringes at the top, with one long roll over her right shoulder, and it, too, glittered with pins set with brilliants. She was quite aware that her delicate stepmother considered her "common." But that, of course, was sheer envy. Dear Estelle considered colour and strength vulgar, especially when displayed by a lady. "I am not," sang Cornelia, almost in a shout, "a lady, a lady, a lady! Thank God! I am a woman, a woman, a woman!" As the words were sung to the tune of a sacred hymn, the elderly maid was shocked.

Cornelia gaily patted the thin shoulder, bent and kissed the wrinkled cheek. "Sally, it's Christmas Eve," she said. "Don't wait up for me. Go upstairs and say your prayers, and don't forget me in them." Cornelia sailed out of her room, which was all lamplight and firelight and warmth, shouting another song: "Damn you, Merry Gentlemen!" She tramped down the quiet hall to her father's apartment, waving her jewelled arms in time with her singing. She banged on the door of Rufus's bedroom, singing still other, and blasphemous words to the tune of "Hark the Herald Angels Sing!"

"Come in," called Rufus irritably. He was standing before his marble dresser, and his man, sweating, was trying to tie Rufus's evening cravat and not succeeding to his master's satisfaction. "I wish," said Rufus, "that if you have to sing so damned loud and raucously, Cornelia, that you wouldn't offend others with loose and inappropriate words—— You aren't doing that right, John, for God's sake!" He tried to glare at his daughter in the mirror.

Cornelia waved aside the valet. "Run along, John. I'll tie Mr. Rufus up. I'm clever at it."

The valet scuttled from the bedroom, while Rufus stood irately with the cravat dangling around his thick neck. Humming, and peeping at her father coquettishly and with obvious teasing love, Cornelia expertly caught up the end of the cravat and deftly tied it. "There, my pet," she said, standing off with her hands planted on her hips, and critically studying Rufus. "You look grand. Really grand. Handsome as all hell."

Rufus turned and peered at his mirror exactly as his daughter had done in her own room, while she watched him fondly.

"You do well at the cravat business," he admitted grudgingly. He patted the satin lapels of his evening coat, and scrutinised Cornelia. "Isn't that the gown Estelle says is entirely too sophisticated for a young, unmarried girl?"

"And isn't it the gown you helped choose for me?" asked Cornelia, kissing her father's ruddy cheek.

He scratched one eyebrow. "I paid for it, anyway. It's Christmas Eve. Perhaps something in white—simple, girlish." His eyes began to beam with pride and adoration. When Cornelia laughed boisterously he laughed also. "Still," he said, "as this is also Estelle's birthday you might have tried to please her, instead of annoying her."

"She's always afraid I'll outshine her, Papa." Cornelia lifted the back of her gown candidly, showing her legs, and threw herself into a chair. "The devil with Estelle. Let's sit down together, and you may tell me what is going on. And you may give me one of my cigarettes, which you are always trying to hide from me."

"You know very well that it's abominable—it's risqué—for a lady to smoke," protested Rufus abstractedly, while he opened a drawer in a gold and mahogany chest and brought out a small box of cigarettes. "You're a scandal, Cornelia."

She nodded lightheartedly. "Of course. We both are. And now, tell me all about it. I thought it was all settled, but you are worried."

"What makes you think I'm worried?" Rufus, lifting the tail of his coat, sat down with his daughter before the fire and lit a cigar.

"I always know. Don't we always know about each other? Isn't it always just you and me?" In her tone was a dismissing contempt for her stepmother and her two little brothers. Rufus did not protest. He had some affection for his wife, whom Guy Gunther, the astute, had frankly suggested to him. ("You may be a rich and coming man, Rufus, but you need a certain social éclat. All of us are rolling in money these days. However, many are called but few are chosen. Society can afford to be discriminating in America now. I have just the lady for you, somewhat ripe, about thirty, or even a little more, but impeccable as to family. You can't do better than pick a Main Line Norwich woman. Best in Philadelphia; good as the Biddles. In fact, they're related to them. They'll overlook divorce, in spite of their propriety, when it's coated with cash. Estelle Norwich.")

Cornelia continued: "I haven't seen you for three days, and there was no time at dinner for talk. So, here we are. Out with it, my boy."

Rufus grumbled and glanced at his watch, shifting bulkily to do so. "It's nearly half-past nine. We have to be downstairs at ten. Half an hour. Well." His smile was gone, and he was frowning. Cornelia smoked lustily, and with enjoyment, and waited. She crossed her silken knees, and gently swung her glittering foot.

"It's still that damned bond issue," said Rufus, beginning to relax. "We've got to have that heavy, latest type of locomotive. New York Central's buying them hand over fist. They move longer freight and passenger trains, as you know, and they expedite traffic, and so save fuel. But I'm still not sure about the financing. Yes, yes, I know we've all discussed that, to your satisfaction, if not mine. But you know that whatever funds there are in the treasury are always being distributed to the stockholders and officers. . . ."

"The bonds wouldn't mature for twenty-five years," said Cornelia patiently. "And they'd bear a low interest rate. And our credit has never been better. Don't be so cautious in your old age, Papa."

He smiled at her narrowly. "If we issued common stock, dear little daughter, it would reduce your profits on that block, worth over a million dollars, which I gave you on your eighteenth birthday."

"Naturally," she agreed. "And I wouldn't like it. And neither would the other stockholders. No, we must float the bond issue. And no more common stock just yet; dividends are dividends."

"There is always a bad chance——" began Rufus.

Cornelia waved her hand. "Papa, you didn't talk that way, at one time. Chances were your glory. Well? Do we issue the bonds, or not?"

Rufus was piqued. "I'm not senile!" he shouted. "I've taken more chances than any other man! What the hell are you talking about?"

"But you've started to eye Mr. Gunther and old Mr. Regan, those darling buzzards, very carefully lately, Papa."

Stung at this truth, which he had considered his own secret, Rufus flushed an unhealthy scarlet. "I know them better than you do, you little fool!" he exclaimed. "All right, we float the issue. I hope you won't be sorry."

"I won't." Cornelia grinned at him, waved her cigarette with a frolicsome gesture. "What do the directors think? Not that it matters."

"It matters a lot, you idiot," Rufus paused. "They think the bonds are all right. Purcell is all for it."

"And he is sweet Laura's guardian. Papa, I suppose a little brandy——"

Rufus got to his feet. "None for you," he said emphatically. "You're not going downstairs smelling like the gutter." He opened his closet door, reached in, and brought out a brandy bottle. He glanced at Cornelia over his shoulder. "You're a scoundrel," he said. He produced two little silver and crystal glasses. "One of these days your whole past will be public property, and who the hell would marry you then?"

"Anybody," said Cornelia, taking her glass. She sipped, smacked her lips. "An English duke, if I wanted one, which I don't. Besides," she added, "I'm in love. That's why I kicked out the little marquis."

"What?" cried Rufus.

"You haven't poured yourself a drink yet, Papa. Here, let me help you."

But he waved the bottle at her threateningly, and some of the contents splashed on his knee. Cornelia rubbed at it with her lace hankerchief. "Your arteries, Papa. Do you want apoplexy? There, it will dry in an instant. Let me have the bottle." She took it from her father, poured his glass full, set down the bottle with a bang. "Drink it up, child," she urged sweetly.

"I suppose," bellowed Rufus, after he had obeyed, "that it is a secret, this 'love' business? And I suppose it is none of my affair who the honoured gentleman is?"

"How can I tell you just yet, when the 'honoured gentleman' doesn't know, himself, at this time?" asked Cornelia. "And I hardly know him. In fact, I've seen him exactly three times." Her face, mocking and rosy, suddenly changed.

"I never heard such infernal nonsense," said Rufus. "May I have a hint, myself? Do I know him, and his family?"

"Oh, yes, Papa, you know him." Cornelia smirked happily. "But you don't know his family. But come, have another sip of brandy. Don't look like a thundercloud. When I am sure,

I'll tell you. You know I've been in love hundreds of times."

Rufus began to shake his head. But he was greatly relieved. Cornelia was not serious, of course, about this unknown man. He wished his daughter to marry someday. And there must be grandchildren. But not yet, he repeated silently. As frequently happened, he began to hate the man who would some day marry Cornelia. "Yes," he said with weighty sarcasm, "you were in love with the marquis, and you sent him packing. Estelle hasn't forgiven you; she cries about it at least once a day. People think he jilted you."

"No doubt Estelle gave them that idea," said Cornelia.

"Never mind Estelle," said Rufus angrily. "Why can't you two women—— It's all you, Cornelia. You're a baggage. Well, who's the man lurking in the portières?"

Cornelia laughed loudly. "Maybe he isn't there," she said. "Let's talk about something more immediate. And important. What do you think about Pat Peale's last speech in Washington?"

Rufus's jowled face swelled with rage. A few days ago young Senator Peale, speaking in behalf of the bill to regulate railroads, had said to a packed gallery: "Never in human history was the creation of material wealth so easy and so marvellously abundant as now, its consolidation under the forms of vast units of power for the benefits of a few so dangerous to the whole country. These monopolies absorb and withdraw individual and independent rivalries. Herein are dangers it will behove us to contemplate gravely and consider what forces shall be summoned to counteract them."

"He's an ass," said Rufus wrathfully. "Monopolies! Doesn't the half-wit understand that a great nation can't expand as efficiently and as rapidly as it is doing now under a system of millions of little individual owners who don't have the money and the capacity to run great enterprises? Little men think in little terms. What is good for a small country is not practical for a huge one. We have made America the monster industrial nation it is. And how did we do it? By consolidation, by pooling inventions, by initiative, imagination, boldness, risk capital—all giant necessities. All things the whining little protesters, and their whining little politicians, don't understand."

"Papa, you don't have to orate to me," said Cornelia. She smoked meditatively. "I'm thinking, in connection with Pat, of Laura's sixteen per cent of Interstate."

"What of it?"

"Papa," said Cornelia, "there might be a way to draw Pat in on the ' powerful monopolies ' he deplores so feelingly."

"What?" roared Rufus.

"It's something to think about," said Cornelia. "He might be persuaded, after he marries Laura, to become a director, or something. First-hand knowledge. And then——" She drew a finger across her throat and made a clicking sound with her teeth.

Rufus glared at his daughter. "You talk absolute nonsense," he said slowly.

"There's just one thing you can do with a politician—buy him," said Cornelia. "I don't know how it is, but I have some intuition which tells me that he is already thinking of joining us. Laura called me, quite nervously, to-day, and wondered if you would find time to-night to talk with Pat quietly. Well, Pat's rich, but where is the man who ever had enough?"

Rufus examined the brandy bottle on the table near him. He hesitated. "You and your intuition," he muttered. He continued to think. Young Patrick Peale, in the opinion of Gunther and Regan, had become a "menace." He was one of a bloc demanding regulation of railroads. "It is only the beginning of regulation for all industry," Mr. Regan had said.

What was it old Steve had said so long ago? "There is nothing wrong with great centralised industry, in itself. An enormous new nation needs its genius. But there is the threat that it will become more powerful than the government, become a government within a government, stifling younger and smaller industries, or absorbing them. It can drain off the resources of a nation for the production of limitless goods, and for all these it will have to make world markets. And in search for world markets it must inevitably come into conflict with other industrialists in other nations, notably Germany and England. Owning lawmakers then, it can induce wars to eliminate foreign competitors and to control world markets. That is my fearful prophecy for the future," Stephen had said.

"You and your intuition," repeated Rufus, but this time he was speaking to his dead brother. He swallowed the last of his brandy. He saw that Cornelia was watching him with that strange look which sometimes appeared in her eyes. It was a kind of blank innocent savagery.

"If Mr. Pat Peale wants to talk to me to-night . . ." said Rufus sullenly.

"Be serious, but coy, Papa." She repeated, idly, but smiling. "Where is the man who ever had enough?" She threw the remains of her cigarette into the fire, and stood on the hearth, tall and splendid, all colour and lustiness, and Rufus stared at her enchanted. "You should have been my son," he said. He laughed shortly. "But it would be very uncomfortable for a man like me to have a son like you."

She stared down at him again. "Yes, it would," she agreed. She rubbed her foot on the silken carpet. "Papa, haven't you poured enough into that charity you created, The Stephen deWitt Foundation for the Children of Railroad Men Killed in Accidents? Two hundred thousand dollars this year alone!"

Rufus thought of Stephen's face on the last day of his life, when the two brothers had driven by the blasted ruins of the local station.

"Not even Commodore Vanderbilt ever thought of such a thing," said Cornelia.

"We aren't a ' bucket railroad,' " replied Rufus irascibly, shaking his head as if to rid himself of his memories. "Vanderbilt may have a good line, but we're the soundest railroad in the country, and the greatest carrier in the United States. We were never in difficulties; we've made enormous fortunes. We can afford the Foundation, you greedy young miser. Besides, it gives us a talking point in Washington. My father was wise, too. He always had some thumping charity to pull out of his hat to confound the shabby politicians." He smiled reminiscently. "When my father and Vanderbilt were called to a legislative committee of investigation, shortly before Papa died, Vanderbilt infuriated the little men with his remark: "I was at home, gentlemen, playing a rubber of whist, and I never allow anything to interfere when I am playing that game. It requires, as you know, undivided attention." The question that had been put to him deserved that remark, but it was impolitic. When the same question was put to Papa, he said very gravely, stroking his beard, ' I cannot answer that readily, for I was, at that time, soliciting my friends for contributions to my charity, The Fund for the Widows of Ex-Mayors of Pennsylvania.'"

"And?" asked Cornelia, chuckling.

Rufus leaned back in his chair and chuckled, too. "What

316

politician can resist a rich man who is concerned about the welfare of relics of ex-politicians? Well, Vanderbilt built up his fortune by manipulation, and though we—we—have done a little buccaneering ourselves, we've continued to be known as a railroad, a carrier of goods and people, a service to the state and the nation. The politicians harassed Vanderbilt; they left my father alone, and they left me alone, too." He shook his finger at Cornelia. "Never try to swallow everything at one gulp. Leave considerable for public effect."

"H'm," said Cornelia. "How astonished Uncle Stephen would be to know what you've done."

For some obscure reason, it always annoyed Rufus when Cornelia spoke lightly of his brother. "Don't forget, you minx, that your uncle was one of the finest railroad men America ever produced. And our father was the best chief engineer. He built solidly. When Erastus Corning started the Central in August, 1853, he was a scheming politician. But not a railroader, and neither were his associates. They were merely lawyers and investors, and raffish speculators. Our family," added Rufus, a trifle ponderously, "built for the future, not only ours, but the country's."

He glanced at his watch, and swore. "It's almost ten. I must go to Estelle at once. How you talk, Cornelia!"

She put her hand on his arm. "Just one thing more, Papa. The new bridge over the Ohio River at Pittsburgh."

Rufus fumed. "Our directors don't look too kindly on long-span bridges, as you know. Just at this time, when 'monopolies' are being investigated. Especially now. We own a majority of the stock and bonds of the Hubert Hamilton Bridge Company. It'll come up for discussion later, when things die down a little."

They left the room together, and, arm in arm, went to the door of Estelle deWitt's apartments. Before Rufus could knock, Cornelia flung open the door of the bedroom and they stood on the threshold, looking at the pretty woman sitting before her dressing-table mirror, her maid at her side.

She was absorbed in her reflection in the mirror. There was something narcissistic in her pose, something reverent. A little woman, with a charming full figure, she wore a gown of mauve velvet, very décolleté, very tight at the short and slender waist, and all asparkle about the low shoulders with brilliants. Her neck was clasped with a collar of diamonds, and diamond bracelets were like imprisoned stars on her little plump arms. Her fine hair, of undistinguished brown, had been piled in exquisite curls on the top of her small head, and held in place with diamond pins. She had a childlike heart-shaped face, large brown eyes which beamed radiantly and tenderly, a short retroussé nose, and a pouting red mouth which expressed, almost constantly, the utmost engaging sweetness.

She smiled at herself, not with satisfaction but with adoration, and her small teeth glimmered in the soft lamplight. She began to stroke her left cheek with loving fingers, the strokes of an idolising lover who could touch only with humble worship. Her fingers arched, trembled, almost with a sensual vibration of self-love and homage. There was, to Cornelia, something indecent in the movements of the fingers, something repulsive and voluptuous. Estelle began to moan ecstatically, "Oh, oh!" in tempo with the rather shameless self-caressings. "Oh, oh," groaned Cornelia, in the accents of one unbearably and sexually stirred.

It was typical of Estelle that she was neither flustered nor embarrassed at this intrusion. She did not catch Cornelia's coarse mockery. She pretended to start prettily. "Why, Rufus," said Estelle in a high sweet voice. "And Cornelia, dear. I am so glad, Cornelia, that you like my new gown and coiffure. Aren't they adorable?" But Rufus had turned red; he gave his daughter a rather vicious glance of understanding, and advanced into the room. Estelle was regarding Cornelia with gratification. "Isn't the gown charming, my dear?"

Cornelia sauntered in, all red and grey and violet and gold and scarlet. Immediately, Estelle became a pale little lump of a woman in an unbecoming gown, the jewels garish upon her. "I think," said Cornelia demurely, "that you'll be the belle of the ball, and not I, Estelle."

This reminded Estelle of something, in spite of the compliment in that jeering voice. The smile faded. She picked up her mauve and jewelled fan and fanned herself pettishly. "' Belle of the ball,' indeed," she said petulantly. "There really isn't room for an impressive ball in this little house. I can't see why, year after year, we must come here for Christmas. So provincial; country-like. Our house on Fifth Avenue, where we should be right at this very minute, like other people of our class, would be ideal for this holiday celebration." She added, "What is the use of this elegant gown, and my jewels, when we must entertain people who are, for the most, insensitive and ignorant clods?"

Her sense of outrage mounted. Cornelia grinned at her. "This is a damned big house, and it's in perfect taste, and Papa and I love it, and it's our real home, and so here we are."

Estelle became pink with indignation. "It is certainly not appropriate for us. I can't understand why you won't sell it, Rufus. 'Perfect taste!' Why, it's practically a cottage."

Rufus, who could endure everything except disparagement of his beloved house, scowled at his wife. He stood at her shoulder. "You forget my mother, and her age. She wouldn't go to New York. And, as Cornelia has said, it is our home, and here we should be at Christmas."

The rosy lips parted, sweetly if tightly, with an open malice. "Dear Mother deWitt," she said. "It would be splendid for her in New York. She would be excited by the ships and Central Park and the crowded carriages."

"You know that isn't true." Rufus was scowling more blackly. "Please oblige me, Estelle, by not speaking of it further."

Lydia had sat at this dressing-table, with her pale and aristocratic face, her dark hair, her distinction and quiet pride. She had been reflected in this gilt and crystal mirror. She had emanated a scent of sophisticated freshness, and not this exotic and cloying odour from Paris. Lydia, to-night, perhaps, would be wearing a gown of misty silver, and there would be silver jewellery on her long neck and on her arms. Rufus could see her vividly in the lamplight, hear her cool, calm voice. The Norwich girl! She looked like an overdressed frump in all that velvet and in all those jewels.

Little pots with garnets and aquamarines and emeralds crowded the dressing-table, mingled with gold mirrors, combs, and brushes. (Lydia had kept the table austerely uncluttered.) The thick perfume began to nauseate Rufus. "Shall we go down?" he asked abruptly, offering his wife his arm. Cornelia was insolently smelling of the flagons and pots, one of which was filled with a bright scarlet paste. "Why don't you mind your own business, Cornelia?" asked Rufus irately.

"Of course, Rufus darling," said Estelle, with exaggerated docility. She rose, and the Worth gown swirled about her. She glanced at Cornelia, and her whole face became unpleasant, and was touched with hatred. "Oh, Cornelia! You look so—so—

gaudy! That dress will never do; so old and improper. And you ought not to be showing your—your bust—like that, and with your arms and shoulders so bare. Indiscreet for a young girl, to say the least."

"I," said Cornelia in her deep voice, "am not a young girl, and never was."

Estelle took her husband's arm, and paused. It was impossible for her to pursue any thought for longer than a moment or two, no matter how disturbed she was. (She has a mind like a firefly, on and off, Cornelia had once remarked.) Another idea had struck Estelle, and she exaggerated her pause until Rufus looked down at her impatiently. "It is such a humiliation about the marquis," she wailed. "How can I face our guests?"

"Our guests," Cornelia began rudely, " can go——"

Estelle pulled her hand away from Rufus and pressed it with delicate drama to her ear. "I shall not go down. I shall simply not go down, Cornelia, unless you promise to use more genteel language. Isn't it enough that I——"

Rufus's face had begun to turn purple, so Cornelia, in alarm, said quickly, "I won't swear. I'll be very proper. Our guests are arriving; I just heard a carriage." She waited until Estelle, whimpering softly under her breath (mewing sounds, thought Cornelia in disgust), had placed her hand once more on Rufus's arm and started to glide daintily towards the door. Then Estelle glanced up with a tender appeal at her husband.

"The darling boys, Rufus!" Her breath caught with loving pathos. "It is Christmas Eve, and they are so excited, and they always expect their mamma to tuck them in. We must go to them at once."

"Estelle," said Rufus, somewhat stifled, " let's not be so precious to-night."

His wife's large brown eyes widened tragically. "I must, I must. It is Christmas Eve. Do not deprive me, Rufus." She could be as obstinate as a tree stump, and as easily moved, when she desired. Cornelia made a disgusted face, nodded at her father, and the three progressed farther down the hall to what Estelle fondly referred to as " their little nest." This had once been the south bedroom where Stephen and his young wife had lain between cold sheets, held in each other's arms.

The little boys, Jon, seven, and Norman, five, were still awake in the warm dim bedroom, which was lit only by firelight. Their governess, a quiet and intelligent young woman of about thirty, sat, half-sleeping, in a chair by the fire. She was not permitted to have a lamp, Estelle had decreed, for she might "neglect the boys" for reading. ("She must always be on hand until the little monsters are fast asleep," Cornelia had observed contemptuously to her father.)

Jon and Norman sat up instantly with shrill and complaining cries when their parents entered. Miss Schultz started in her chair. "Are you asleep, really?" asked Estelle in a sharp voice. "When the boys are still awake?" She gathered the children broodingly in her jewelled arms, as if protecting them from some awful threat, and her glance at Miss Schultz was malevolent. The girl rose, pale with exhaustion. "I am sorry, Mrs. deWitt," she murmured. "But it has been a tiring day."

"No doubt," said Cornelia. "These kids are completely undisciplined." She gave Miss Schultz a ribald grin, and her magnetism flowed from her like palpable force. "I took care of them one day last summer, and I know. I finally used a club on them; wonderful argument, a club."

The boys were bouncing about in their mother's arms, shrieking meaninglessly, glaring with the distended eyes of spoiled and unruly children. "We waited, we waited!" screamed Jon, and he struck his mother's bare shoulder with a clenched fist. "You promised, you promised!" yelled his younger brother.

Rufus was silent. These were the sons he had passionately desired, these rather undersized little fellows, too dainty, too effeminate, too like their mother with their thin brown hair, their pointed faces, their small noses and stubborn mouths. Had he had so little vitality, then, that he could not produce a boy in Cornelia's mould? Estelle called her sons "patrician." Whenever she simpered so, Rufus would think of the antic vitality of his father, the strength of his mother, the stern if muted power of his brother, the blaze of his daughter.

"What did your mother promise, boys?" he asked, and his voice was harsh and loud.

"A Christmas story, a Christmas song, to put them to sleep," replied Estelle yearningly.

"For God's sake!" shouted Rufus. "Why didn't you get in here before, then, Estelle? Why wait until our guests arrive? 'Put them to sleep?' What imbecility."

The boys feared their father, even in the presence of their

mother, and they subsided, squatting on their beds. They began to snivel. They turned their eyes, huntingly from side to side, and they finally rested on Cornelia, who had advanced to the beds. She smiled at them affectionately, shook her fist. "And here's big sister just waiting to pound hell out of you, if you make a single sound," she said. She reached out and pushed Jon's head, and then Norman's. They held, for Cornelia, mingled malice and dislike. But she was an excellent and romping playmate. "I'll break every one of your own presents with my own hands, if you don't behave," she threatened, and lifted Norman and threw him down among his pillows.

"Throw me, throw me!" shrilled the older boy, bounding excitedly. Cornelia obliged, her big white arms like marble. The two children screamed with joy. Estelle watched this with jealous affront.

Rufus turned to Miss Schultz and smiled kindly. "You seem very tired, my dear. Go to your own rooms at once, and a tray will be sent up to you."

"But the boys!" cried Estelle. "They cannot be left alone, awake."

"And who will hurt them in this house? Don't be a fool, Estelle."

"But they've never been left alone, until they slept."

"They are beginning to-night. Go, Miss Schultz." Rufus's face had become very dark with congested blood.

It was curious that whenever her husband rebuked or reprimanded her, Estelle's eyes turned automatically to Cornelia, or if Cornelia was absent, her thoughts so turned. Cornelia was quite accustomed to that gleam of pure malignance, and it amused her. She left the room, after a gay wave at the reconciled boys, and Rufus and Estelle followed her. Rufus silent, Estelle's head bent in meek and suffering submission. And so it was that Allan Marshall, the first and only guest waiting below, saw Cornelia descending the curving stairway alone, like a pillar of fire and smoke in the form of a woman.

Rufus and Estelle had not yet reached the top of the stairs. Cornelia stopped, half-way down, and Allan looked up at her. All at once there flashed between them something intensely powerful and magnetic, something of profound recognition. Cornelia seemed struck into immobilisation, and her lips parted. Involuntarily, Allan came to the foot of the stairway, and his right hand lifted towards her. Then, slow step by step, she moved down to him, her eyes fixed on his, like one responding to a mesmerist.

She was on the last step when she gave him her hand, and as he assisted her down, and they stood there in that silence, looking at each other. Their hands did not part until Rufus and Estelle descended.

What a strange person, Estelle thought. Really not a gentleman, though I cannot just put my finger on the difference. Perhaps it is because his evening clothes are a trifle too fashionable, a trifle too well-tailored. There is such a peculiar air about him. She simpered at Allan as she graciously acknowledged the introduction. "Mr. deWitt has told me so much about you, Mr. Marshall. Such a genius. You are quite famous, aren't you? An inventor!" She managed to give the word an intonation of superiority and aristocratic condescension.

Rufus patted Allan's shoulder heartily. "More than that, one of the finest young lawyers in the country, and we'll be proud to have him on our staff." He beamed at the young man proudly.

"Are you the first here, Mr. Marshall?" asked Estelle sweetly, conveying her opinion that a guest who came on time, and was the first to arrive, was not entirely acceptable in polite society. Allan's black eyes hardened upon her. "I once heard that punctuality is the courtesy of kings," he replied quietly.

Estelle fluttered her fan before her lips. "Really?" she murmured vaguely. She was not offended. Her mind could not remain upon others for more than an instant or two, and her conviction of her importance made her invulnerable to any rudeness. She did notice that Rufus was smiling slightly, and Cornelia broadly.

Allan had learned the trick of keeping the fingers of his right hand always slightly bent, so that the mutilated middle finger was not obvious. As he talked with Rufus, he was all surety. The interior of the house, though it had aroused his deep admiration and pleasure, had not overwhelmed him. He felt that he had come home, and that this house belonged to him, and that some day he would take full possession. He stood answering Rufus's fond and paternal questions about his progress in the Peale offices in a voice without strain or embarrassment. Cornelia, standing near her father, had become grave again, and she listened intently. Her calloused young heart was beating with unusual speed, and she felt a prickling dampness along her hairline and in the palms of her hands.

As Allan glanced at her, and smiled a little, her heart beat even faster, and a soft humidity came over her eyes, and the lusty face melted into a strange tenderness and excitement. She regarded him breathlessly, and she said to herself: He is splendid. He is fierce. He is strong. He is ruthless. He is like me. Why, I have been waiting for him all my life.

Now, what's wrong with the girl? Rufus thought. He had been telling Allan a very good joke, and Allan was laughing. Cornelia, who always appreciated her father's anecdotes, had not responded at all. She was a little pale, and her mouth stood apart foolishly. That damned brandy, Rufus told himself with irritation. He took Cornelia's arm and said loudly. "This is only an informal party, Allan. Nothing grand. We are having hardly ninety guests; just old friends who'll like to meet you. Shall we go into the living-room?"

"The main drawing-room, Rufus," said Estelle with a quick frown, and then a smile. She took Allan's arm; it was necessary for her to charm everyone, and she peeped up at him. "Dear Mr. deWitt is so sentimental about Christmas at home. However, we shall be in New York for New Year."

Rufus, a few steps ahead with his daughter, glanced back. "And by the way, Allan, we shall expect you there, also." His decision, instantaneous, had been prompted by his wife's lilting attempt to patronise the younger man.

Sophia, "the great grey hag," as Allan had always called her to himself, was already waiting by the bounding fire in the beautiful living-room. She sat there, grim, stiff, and offended. "I have been here half an hour, Rufus," she said in her abrasive voice.

Cornelia went to her quickly and kissed her cheek, and immediately the livid face softened. "Why are you always so prompt, Granny?" she teased. "No one is here yet but Mr. Marshall, of whom Papa has told you so much."

"Indeed," said Sophia haughtily. She smoothed her rich black lap with wrinkled hands heavy with gems. She studied Allan, without offering him any further greeting. A foreigner. She could always tell these foreigners, with their sharp dark faces, penetrating eyes, and hard mouths. Marshall. Of course, when they gained a little success, they changed their names. She added, "I hope you will enjoy yourself, young man."

Allan bowed respectfully and said, "I expect to, Mrs. deWitt." Sophia looked more keenly at him. Rufus had been discreet in his accounts of Allan to his wife and mother. A young inventor, a rising young lawyer, who was about to join the legal staff of the railroad. This was a ticklish moment for Rufus. His mother rarely, if ever, forgot a face. Sophia's lofty expression was already becoming thoughtful. She played with the subdued necklace of pearls and jet that encircled her strong if wizened throat. "Haven't I met you somewhere before, Mr.—Marshall? You seem very familiar."

Only in your garden, you old witch, thought Allan. He bowed again, with a properly deferential smile of regret. "I am afraid not, Mrs. deWitt," he murmured. "Or at least, not that I recall."

"Of course, I don't go to Philadelphia often," said Sophia, pleased with him in spite of herself. There was something familiar, yes, about this young whippersnapper. Then she thought suddenly of Aaron. The look in the eyes, the sudden mobility of the mouth, the bow which had a touch of the ironic in it— Aaron. "You remind me of my dear departed husband, young sir," she said, and her hoarse voice was actually quavering. "Not that you resemble him in the least physically. I think, perhaps, it is character."

Rufus was surprised. "I thought so, too," he said, and glanced at Allan with real affection. "A gay old party, my father, but full of steel. Perhaps gayer than you, my boy. There is something a little too sombre about you." He patted Allan's shoulder.

To some extent, Sophia was still overawed by the name and position of her daughter-in-law. But this usually expressed itself by irascibility. "Isn't that gown a little too young for you, my dear Estelle?" she asked. "Light mauve velvet?"

"I am not very old," responded Estelle coldly. "And speaking of age, don't you think, Mother deWitt, that Cornelia's gown is too extreme for a young girl?"

Sophia chuckled in a way that Estelle considered very common. The old woman took Cornelia's hand, held her off, studied her. "Extreme? No Why should she hide her shoulders and arms like these? Ah, me, she looks exactly as I did at her age. If she were a man she would be the image of her father at twenty.

By the way, have you been drinking, child?" She gave Cornelia a haggard grin.

Estelle's eyes began to widen with horror, but at that moment many guests arrived, and Rufus thankfully went to the threshold of the room to meet them, firmly grasping his wife's arm. Cornelia, standing beside her grandmother, winked at Allan. Sophia, who in her old age was given to even more bluntness than in her youth, said, " I am glad to see eligible young Americans here again, Mr. Marshall. Did you ever meet that marquis? A dreadful fortune hunter. I despised him, and was very happy when our Cornelia gave him the mitten."

Cornelia shrieked with laughter. Her face was bright with excitement, and her eyes turned to Allan, sparkling, malicious, yet oddly shy. She stood perfectly still, but again, as he had noticed before, she gave the effect of iridescence, of constant and unrestrained vibration.

The guests were pouring into the room, elegant, glittering, talking animatedly, and accompanied by their host and hostess. The ladies swirled over the fine old rugs, the gentlemen at their sides. Among them were Patrick Peale, Jim Purcell, Lydia, and Laura. Allan turned to them politely. He met the grave eyes of Patrick in the manner of a stranger waiting for an introduction. If Jim Purcell regarded him with a muddy blank stare, Allan was not too disturbed. He knew the older man slightly, for the latter had, once or twice, come into the Peale offices late at night. He recognised Lydia and Laura from the photographs he had seen of them in the local and Philadelphia and New York newspapers. He immediately dismissed them as pale and uninteresting women, for all their height and grace. Cornelia dwarfed and extinguished all other women, no matter how jewelled or gowned they were, or how pretty.

More guests were arriving, and Rufus and Estelle again moved away, leaving introductions to Sophia and Cornelia. Purcell grunted, shook hands briefly with Allan. Patrick murmured, "We have met," and retreated. Allan smiled to himself disdainfully. He had not missed Patrick's reproachful intonation. I love these lovers of mankind, he thought. They'll do anything for the "common man" except meet him on equal ground. He feels, this Peale, that I have "betrayed" something, or at least he believes he feels it. But the truth is that he is hurt because he has been forced to accept me socially.

Never Victorious, Never Defeated

Cornelia was talking above the voices of the other guests:
"We have a wonderful surprise to-night. The great Metropolitan
tenor, Giovanni Monetti, is going to sing for us. He arrived this
morning, and immediately hid himself in his rooms, primping,
no doubt, and doing all the other things tenors do."

Cornelia twinkled on her guests. The marquis had jilted her!
They were peeping at her with furtiveness, and she almost burst
out laughing. Some of the ladies were of her own age; she had
played with them as a child. They wore smug expressions which
did not annoy, but only amused, Cornelia. She also saw that they
were much attracted to Allan and spared him some discreet
glances of interest. When he spoke to them, his voice held them,
and quite a number of young eyes melted. Cornelia was pleased.

More guests were pouring in, and the room, warm and filled
with lamplight and firelight, became even warmer and weighted
with scent. Fans fluttered; white arms flashed; white necks
arched flirtatiously; jewels shone and dazzled. The gentlemen
moved about in seal-like black, bowing, laughing decorously,
complimenting, greeting. Sophia sat rigidly by the fire and
looked only at her granddaughter.

The men were curious about this stranger. They had heard of
him from Rufus, who had been very careful. They could not
"place" him. They could not remember whether Rufus had told
them he had come from Philadelphia or New York or Boston.
His accent was definitely not Philadelphian, nor did it have a
New York intonation. There was something "odd" about it.
Boston, no doubt, thought one of the gentlemen. But where
had he heard that particular inflection in Boston? Irish! Only
a faint flavour, but unmistakably Irish. The gentleman said to
Allan, "You are of Irish extraction, I believe, sir? I have
friends. . . . You must pardon me. . . ."

Allan inclined his head. The gentleman wandered away,
reflective. The Irish were invading the sacred groves of Boston
these days. Fine old houses were filled with lamentations. But
the Irish, a few, were becoming quite wealthy. Not socially
acceptable, of course, though some of them were approaching
the periphery with their charities to approved causes.

Allan was enjoying himself. He was very cautious. He
generalised. He avoided answering tentative questions about his
origins with the utmost deftness. When he did not catch a
reference, he did not improvise. There was too much danger in

327

that. They spoke of music, and he replied to them in matching words, for his vocabulary was tremendous, the result of his enormous reading. Within less than ten minutes, in spite of his "strangeness," he had attracted much approval from both sexes. He dexterously evaded the subject of politics, on which some of the men became quietly vehement. And he listened; everlastingly, he listened. In the background Lydia and Laura watched him uncertainly; Purcell grunted and said nothing; and Patrick, a little white about the lips, was silent.

Delightful strains were issuing from the smaller drawing-room beyond. Servants were beginning to circle with silver trays of champagne. Allan sipped at his glass. Cornelia was suddenly beside him, full of elation, her eyes dancing with mockery as she looked at him. As she began to speak, he felt a touch on his arm. He turned to see Patrick Peale. Patrick bowed to Cornelia, and her broad smile disappeared in an expression of unpleasantness. "Forgive me, Cornelia," said Patrick. He glanced at Allan.

"Could I have a word with you, please? Just for a moment?"

CHAPTER THIRTY-ONE

"WHY?" ASKED Cornelia. She put her glass to her lips, and over it her stare was bold and fixed. This puny creature with his big solemn eyes! This meagre man with whom she had thought herself in love even as late as the past summer! Her humiliation thickened her throat; she wound her arm through Allan's and repeated, "Why?"

Patrick was extremely distressed. "I'm sorry, Cornelia. It is only a matter of business." He paused and regarded the girl closely. Her cheeks were crimson; had she drunk too much champagne? She had never stared at him before with this particular dislike. Since his engagement to Laura she had shown him an offhanded and indifferent affection. He began to colour. Cornelia smiled, and tightened her hand on Allan's arm.

"Business?" she repeated. Her voice was more than a little slurred. "Mr. Marshall was about to dance with me, and it is Christmas Eve. No time for business." She turned to Allan. "You do dance, don't you?"

Allan had been watching the two closely. He had nothing to fear, now. If Patrick was embarrassed, if he believed that Cornelia still loved him, the more fool he. Allan put his hand over the hand on his arm, and looking at Patrick he replied to the girl. "Yes." He continued with more deliberation: "Yes, I do dance. I have taken daily lessons for over three weeks. I can waltz very well."

Cornelia threw back her head and bellowed mirthfully. Then her face changed, became almost ugly. She tilted her glass towards Patrick and said, "I'll spare Allan for a moment. But Pat, if I were you I wouldn't mention Allan's origins to anyone."

"I don't understand," Patrick answered, his colour deepening.

"Oh, yes you do. I saw the wrinkle in your fragile nose to-night, when you saw him here. Papa and I won't like it in the least if you try to disparage Allan."

Patrick looked quickly at Allan. But Allan displayed nothing but pleasure. Cornelia was patting his arm; some of the champagne had spilled over her grey velvet dress. "Go on, Allan, let the little boy tell you his story." She tossed her head and went off followed by many glances of admiration.

Patrick regarded the floor for a moment, and then in a low voice he said, "In the far corner. Near the Christmas tree. It isn't lighted yet, and no one is near it." Allan shrugged, and the two young men, murmuring regrets to those they passed, reached the comparatively secluded spot where a giant spruce, brilliantly decorated, candles still unlighted, waited for the stroke of twelve. Allan stood with his back to the tree, and Patrick stopped before him. "Well?" said Allan. He fumbled for his cigarette case automatically; then, noticing that no other man was smoking, it came to him that it would be improper among the ladies. He dropped his hand. A servant came by with another tray of champagne, and Allan reached out and captured a glass. He put it to his mouth.

Insolent, thought Patrick. Allan was drinking the champagne a little too fast, but his eyes were intent.

"I haven't seen you for nearly three weeks, Allan," said Patrick.

"I just returned from Washington two days ago."

Allan was silent. He emptied the glass, then held it negligently in his hand. Should I congratulate him? wondered Patrick miserably. Should I even mention the automatic coupler? He

329

was always difficult. "Our staff has missed you, since you—you decided to read law with the Interstate staff, and leave us."

Allan thought of the last time he had been in the Peale offices. The news had just got about, about "our new and famous young inventor, Mr. Allan Marshall, who is reading law with the staff of our Assistant Secretary of State, Mr. Peale, and his son, Senator Patrick Peale." He had gone there to collect some forgotten notes. It had given him a disgusted and angry pleasure when the staff had received him with eager subservience, and with many respectful questions. Patrick, anxiously studying him now, saw the bleakness on his face. He knew that Allan had forgotten him, and he said, "I'm sorry. We'll send you our certificate. . . ."

"Thank you," said Allan.

Patrick sighed. "I can't tell you how surprised and disappointed I was to hear you are going with Interstate."

"Is that so? I can't imagine why you were. The staff at Interstate is much larger, and more—shall we say—specialised than the Peale staff." Allan raised his black eyebrows.

"Yes, specialised," said Patrick reflectively. "That is just the trouble." Allan waited, smiling slightly. Then Patrick knew that subtleties were not going to force Allan into argument. He said, "I was under the impression you were going to be a labour lawyer." Now his voice was sharp. "To assist the people with whom you have worked, and who still work with your father. Wasn't that your original idea?"

Allan expertly removed still another glass from a passing tray, and let Patrick wait until he had sampled it with the air of a connoisseur. He said, "I can't afford it. You can afford to be a ' labour ' senator, and perhaps, some years hence, when I have a fortune, too, I will be able to afford a similar luxury."

"Allan." Patrick became almost despairing. "I had such hopes of you. I believed in you. I never thought you would betray——" He stopped.

But Allan was not disturbed. "Betray whom?" he asked, as if in surprise.

"Those who trusted you," said Patrick bitterly.

Allan laughed. "Trust me, Pat? Who ever trusted another man? And, coming down to it, who is worthy of trust?"

"I thought you were," said Patrick.

"I never thought you were," Allan rejoined. "You see, I gave

330

you credit for more intelligence than you seem to possess. Or perhaps you are just a hypocrite. You are in politics, aren't you?" He touched Patrick on the chest with the knuckles of his left hand. "Law is a harlot, but politics is a pimp."

Patrick glanced hastily over his shoulder for fear someone had overheard, for Allan's voice had not only thickened but had become forceful. Allan followed his glance. And then he saw, at a distance, the pale and troubled face of Laura deWitt gazing at them. The champagne had sharpened his vision. He could plainly see the pure radiance of her large grey eyes, the shining whiteness of her forehead, the set of her gentle lips, the vapour of her dark hair. He forgot Patrick; he forgot everyone else in the room. It is the face of the Blessed Virgin, he thought; it is the face of a saint.

She met his eyes and stood there, poised, graceful, and calm in spite of her anxiety. She did not smile. Across the great room politely clamorous with voices, shining with gems, aglow with colour and with the movement of men and women, they looked at each other. Then, very slowly, her head bent as if in distress, Laura turned away.

Patrick was speaking to him again; Allan heard the voice but not the words. He had seen something infinitely beautiful, steadfast, and merciful, something of unspeakable tenderness, directed not at him but at the whole world. Now, from the valley below, above all those voices, above the new gale raving out of the sky, he heard, or thought he heard, the sound of church bells, thin and sweet, striking on his heart with nostalgia and sadness.

Cornelia's voice soared out: "It's midnight! Merry Christmas. Merry Christmas! The tree!"

The guests turned towards the tree, Rufus, ruddy as the sun, was approaching. Allan pressed his knuckles again on Patrick's chest. He said, "*Finis coronat opus.* The end crowns the work, Pat."

The church bells sang closer to him, insistent, calling. He could feel the throbbing of the church; the candles were burning, their tips sheathed in golden flame. There was a smell of incense, and then someone was chanting, "*Gloria in Excelsis Deo! Gloria—Gloria. . . .*" The organ was rising like a sea.

Rufus was beside them, a jewelled box of matches in his hand. "We must light the tree," he said exuberantly. "Allan. Pat."

He struck a match, and the guests, laughing in anticipation, crowded about him. Patrick looked long at Allan, and said, "But you won't forget; you'll never really forget."

He retreated and stood with the others. The match was glowing in Rufus's hand, and his eyes were narrowed on Allan. "What did he say?" he muttered under his breath. What was wrong with the boy? Was he drunk?

Allan said, "Nothing at all. He said nothing at all."

Sophia had greeted Lydia with stately aloofness. It was frightful that "that woman dares to enter this house; it is a scandal." Sophia often repeated that to her friends, though she knew in her shrewd heart that to antagonise Jim Purcell would not be to Rufus's advantage, even though Rufus was now far wealthier than his old enemy. However, as she said, the situation was almost untenable. In some confused way she had come to identify Laura with Lydia, and there were times when she spoke of Laura as being "that woman's daughter." As she grew older, she began to forget, at increasing intervals, that Cornelia was Lydia's child, and would speak to Cornelia of "the contemptible person." Cornelia, much attached to Lydia, had nevertheless, at an early age, come to accept the comments good-humouredly.

Sophia, who had a keen eye, in spite of the vague confusions of her old age, knew, as no one else, not even Cornelia, knew, that Rufus had not forgotten his first wife. She would watch him with pain when he greeted her so magnanimously and kindly as the wife of an old friend and a director of his company. She would see that misery stood in his eyes, and that his smile was taut with longing. She would never speak to her son of this, for that would be mortifying to Rufus, but she hated Lydia in consequence, and despised her fervently. In her mind she called Lydia "that adulteress." Though not usually on easy terms with Estelle, she could approach an intimacy when discussing Rufus's first wife in the privacy of her own apartments.

Estelle paused now, on the way to the small "ballroom," to speak a word to Sophia. She was in a bad temper. Not only had that execrable Cornelia paled her own appearance, but Lydia and Laura, with their height and poise and grace, had rendered her insignificant. Sophia was still fixed by the fireside, acknowledging the presence of guests with a queenly manner, inclining her head with dignity. Estelle, fanning herself vigorously, murmured, "Mamma deWitt, when will those awful people leave, the Purcells? Really, it is humiliating to have to receive them. The gowns those women wear—so without style or fashion."

Sophia glanced about her. Lydia and Jim Purcell were evidently preparing to leave, Patrick Peale beside them. But Laura was nowhere in sight. "The girl's a born old maid," she muttered. "Laura. I doubt if the marriage will ever take place. Wretched creatures. They always leave after the lighting of the tree, Estelle. They have a little decency left, it would seem, for they never stay for the festivities."

"In Philadelphia, such a thing would not be permitted," said Estelle, with increasing ill-nature. "But what can one expect of so outlandish a place as Portersville?"

This vexed Sophia. She aroused herself, and said maliciously, "The Fieldings were always received well in Philadelphia. Their parents were old society there, and their grandparents, when, I believe, my dear, your family was tanning hides." Her hazel eyes lit up her craggy face for an instant.

This infuriated Estelle. She said in a shaking voice, "My ancestors prepared leather for the kings of England . . . royal grant—commissioned. . . ."

Sophia was very pleased with herself. "A horse," she intoned, "is still a horse, and a hide is still a hide."

Estelle, with a gasp, swirled away, and Sophia smiled happily to herself. There were so few times when she could "put Estelle in her place." It invigorated her. She had endured too much from the delicate ways of her daughter-in-law, and the latter's assumption of haughty superiority to everyone and everything. "Who does she think she is?" she muttered aloud. "What has she ever done, personally, to put on such airs?" She was quite content now (and as if she had scored some great personal triumph) to rise and leave the room and go up to bed. As she passed the door of her grandsons' rooms she did not even glance at it. Sometimes she forgot they existed.

"What is keeping Laura so long?" Patrick asked Jim Purcell restlessly. "I can hardly endure this house. The singer Rufus imported from New York is already tuning up."

Purcell smiled sourly. "Laura must be havin' quite a time persuadin' her Uncle Rufus to permit you to become a director," he said. "Give the girl a few more minutes."

333

"I think it would have been better for Patrick to have seen Rufus, alone, in his office," Lydia said, flushing. "It is such an ordeal to be here, under any circumstances." Purcell patted her shoulder tolerantly. "A few more minutes, old girl," he repeated. "I'm in a hurry, too. I promised Ruth to carry her downstairs no matter what time it is, to see the tree." He turned to Patrick. "Saw you talkin' to that Marshall feller. Well?"

"It was no use," said Patrick. "I've tried to catch him over the last few days, but never could. We only had a minute or two. He laughed in my face when I tried to remind him of his duty."

"Duty," repeated Purcell with reflectiveness. "Funny how a lot of folks, who won't be hurt if they do their ' duty,' are always urgin' it on others who would be hurt. Now, now, Pat, I'm not criticisin' you." He chuckled. "Can't help thinkin', though, that I'd have done exactly what that feller has done, in his place. In fact, I did, though the circumstances weren't exactly the same."

Rufus, in the meantime, had shut himself up in the library with Laura, his niece, and had carefully locked the door to prevent intrusion. She sat there, near the great walnut desk, her hands in her blue lap, and she was blushing with embarrassment, though her grey eyes were all earnestness. Rufus sat on the edge of the desk and regarded her with genuine love and pleasure. He had saved her life, he thought, as he listened to her gentle and stammering voice. Such a charming young thing, so aristocratic, so contained. Her eyes actually radiated light. For some reason, the fact that he had helped to snatch her from death had always held him powerfully to the girl. If it were not for him, she would perhaps be dead, and not sitting here gazing at him with the affectionate pleading of a daughter, with the utter trust of a daughter.

He had listened to her for a full fifteen minutes, and had not interrupted except to ask her a fond and benign question. He had pretended to ponder everything she had said, judiciously and with affected indulgence. Slowly, moment by moment, he allowed her to gather that only her importunities were moving him, against his will. He would frown, pluck at his ruddy lip, scratch his chin, sigh, look meditative. He would play with his watch chain, simulating a little distress. He could almost hear

334

her innocent thoughts: I think I am persuading him, dear Uncle Rufus!

She looks like Lydia; she might have been Lydia at her age, Rufus said to himself, and the old pain twisted in him. I could never deny Lydia anything. Even if this matter of the young Peale fellow weren't exactly what I wish, I'd have a hard time refusing Laura.

"Patrick said he could contribute so much," Laura was saying, twisting her handkerchief in her hands. She smiled at Rufus anxiously. "Am I presuming, Uncle Rufus?"

"You could never ' presume ' with me, my love," he answered. He reached out and stroked the fine dark hair which always seemed to float in spite of anchoring pins. His hand was very tender. It dropped to her chin and lifted it, and he bent and kissed her cheeks, which had been touched with the softest and sweetest powder—Lydia's own scent. Rufus's hand slipped away, and he stared at her, overcome with a strange pain and jealousy. She is, in every way, my own child. She belongs to me.

He took her hands and pulled her gently to her feet, then held her in his arms. She clung to him, and put her head on his shoulder. "There, there, my dear," he said. "Don't worry your little mind. If your boy is actually serious, and it will make you happy, let him come to see me next week, before I leave for New York." He held her off from him and studied her with pride. "Of course, I'll have to call a board meeting, and nothing can be done, really, until after he marries you in June." He added, again with jealousy, "You love him very much, don't you, my darling?"

Laura was very astute, and she smiled at Rufus with a tenderness equal to his. "But you, Uncle Rufus, will always be first with me."

Rufus swelled with triumph. Purcell had not been able to replace her uncle in her mind, though she was fond of him. Rufus kissed the girl again. "Of course," he said. "You are always my girl, and you always will be. So, run along now. I must get back to my guests."

Laura went joyfully to Lydia and Patrick and Purcell, gave them the news in a voice quivering with delight, and then they all prepared to leave as inconspicuously as possible. Purcell alone was thoughtful. He knew of Rufus's attachment to Laura, but that would not be enough to interfere with Red Rufe's

335

business. There was something else. H'm, thought Purcell, and he began to smile to himself. The future appeared to promise considerable entertainment.

They found Estelle bubbling with some friends, her saccharine smile pulled tautly over her small and greedy teeth. She fanned, and she preened, and in every affected gesture there was revealed her enormous contentment with herself, and her vanity. The smile grew slightly congealed as the Purcell group approached her. Then, with a catch of her breath, and a flutter, she put her hand on Patrick's arm. "Dear Patrick," she said, "I cannot tell you how much I applauded your speech in the Senate recently! I understood! I agreed! It was marvellous! And you are working so hard for labour. . . ."

A passing servant accidentally brushed her arm with a tray, and she said viciously, "How careless of you, George! You have not done well to-night; I must speak to Mr. deWitt about you."

"I'm sorry, ma'am," murmured the young man, whose thin face was white with exhaustion. He had been working steadily since six that morning, in preparation for the party, and his hands were tremulous. Before Patrick could speak, and before he could control his indignation enough to speak, Estelle was trilling again: "Servants are so impossible! So stupid! And so ungrateful, aren't they?"

Patrick's face became stern; Jim Purcell took his arm and led him away. "That woman!" muttered the young man. "The DeWitts. . . ."

Purcell laughed. "Oh, old Rufe isn't so bad these past few years. D'you know, I think he's mellowed. That's what money can do for a man: make him kinder to his fellow men."

Estelle, who had tactfully convinced the society of Portersville that she, a Norwich, born and bred in Philadelphia, knew all that it was possible to know about culture, skilfully herded her guests into the small ballroom. She had thought it shameful that the room was not large enough for more than four musicians. "It gives such an air of poverty," she had told Rufus with petulance. The musicians were grouped at the end of the room, near the piano, and their expressions conveyed their excitement that they were not only to play for the later dancing but were to accompany the famous tenor Giovanni Monetti. They peeped at the great man, slender and small in his impeccable evening dress, and they almost grovelled at his glances of rage at the slowly gathering audience. He stared furiously at his watch; his mighty chest, so out of proportion to the rest of his figure, swelled out grotesquely. He was insulted. When he appeared on the stage of the Metropolitan Opera House, he received ovations before he could sing a single note. The guests, seating themselves on small gilt chairs, and chirping and laughing, hardly gave him a look. Peasants! Santa Maria!

The guests were now seated on all the gilt chairs available, and the overflow of gentlemen were standing against the wall. Monetti surveyed his hostess; no charm, no grace, no cosmopolitanism. Then his gaze wandered, and stopped.

That young man there, leaning against the wall, his head bent a little, with the lady of the fiery red hair beside him—a most extraordinary face, that young man's. An *Italiano?* No, it was too cold, too fixed. Yet, it had an anguish—definitely an anguish. It was a face one did not forget; it was a face of passion. Monetti decided to sing to it, to stir it out of its ice, to melt and move it. The first song would decide if he, Monetti, was a fool.

The murmur, laughter and flutterings in the room continued. Ladies leaned across gentlemen and twittered. Their powder and their scent choked the singer. He coughed loudly; he moved deliberately from his place, walked back and forth, and exhibited temper. This finally caught the attention of the guests, and at a dignified gesture of Estelle's, they sank into silence. Monetti waited impressively, his leaping eye cowing each it touched.

Allan knew nothing much about music except the sacred variety which he had heard in his youth. Neither old Father Gallacher nor his present successor, Father Tobin, had been able to afford a good organ for their little church. The choir had been lamentable at all times. Only once had it been distinguished, and that had been during the one year when Tim Marshall had forced his older son to become a member. The only other songs Allan knew were Irish ballads picked up from his parents. He had never had the money to attend the very infrequent "concerts" held in Portersville, and concerts in Philadelphia had been out of the question. Yet, he had an instinctive ear for fine music, and the tenor had sung hardly five notes before Allan's head jerked up.

Though Monetti was a cynic, he had given an Italian's courteous glance at the date, and was now singing his own arrangement from Gounod's "Messe du Sacre Coeur." He was certain that Gounod would not be annoyed, but rather flattered. (Had not the great composer congratulated him enthusiastically only a year ago?) As he sang, he looked directly into Allan's eyes, and something about those eyes made him involuntarily add a greater depth to his voice, a pure and reverent and urgent splendour. Tears moistened his eyelids; his own heart palpitated mysteriously. He had not been wrong; Monetti was never wrong.

Someone had touched Allan's arm, and he pulled away with unconscious wrath. He did not know he was trembling; he did not know he was staring blindly at the singer. But all at once, and after what seemed to him a great passage of time, he was aware of silence followed by the discreet patter of hands—like the tinkling of icicles—and a blur of coughings, murmurs, creakings, rustles, and dainty chirpings. He looked about him, dazed. Several of the gentlemen were sliding along the wall to the door, and ladies were rising to accompany them. Now more and more of the audience were moving doorward, and the little platform where Monetti had stood was empty even of the musicians. The chandeliers flooded into Allan's eyes, and he blinked.

"I believe you were sleeping, Mr. Marshall!" cried a husky voice beside him. He glanced down at the flaming head which was rising up to his shoulder, then passing it. Cornelia was laughing at him mockingly, but there was a curious expression, half hard, half affectionate, on her face. Suddenly he thought of a large and amateurish painting he had seen somewhere, too highly coloured, too crude, too full, too polished and glazed. No, it had not been a painting; he had once wandered in New York, into a wax museum where all the female figures had a hard bright glossiness over tints unnaturally brilliant, and had been clothed in gowns of a theatrical gaudiness. One of them had hair like this, and he had furtively touched it and had been repelled at its springing harshness.

Cornelia was watching him, and something in his intense regard made her uneasily offended. Of course, he had drunk too much; champagne was too rich for his stomach. She touched him lightly, again. "Intermission," she said.

"Intermission," he repeated automatically. It was ridiculous for him to feel that he had said something momentous. He followed her out of the room into the colourful turmoil of the one adjoining. No one was speaking of Monetti's voice, but only of Rufus's generosity in engaging the tenor for entertainment this evening. A few of the ladies hid yawns behind fans. Gentlemen wandered away into the library for a smoke with their host. The Christmas tree shimmered in unnoticed light in the corner; the fire blew up boisterously on the hearth. Suddenly Allan was conscious of exhaustion and emptiness. The laughing voices of men and women became unbearably clangorous to him, the scent of powder, perfume, and burning wood intolerable.

"Can't we go somewhere where it is quiet?" he muttered to Cornelia. She laughed at him, tilted her head, and scrutinised him mirthfully. "Somewhere cooler?" she suggested. "The hall, then."

The hall was unoccupied; the fire on the white hearth burned low, and the beautifuly curving stairway was full of shadows. The candles guttered in the chandelier above. Allan stood there, looking about him at the elegance and delicacy of the furniture and the damask walls. His breath came slower now, and easier. "I think you are drunk," Cornelia said, in a matter-of-fact and indulgent voice. She added, without a moment's thought, "I think I am, too."

Intermission, thought Allan. Intermissions were all very well, but a man had his life to live. In this half light of fading candles and dying fire, Cornelia was less strenuous in appearance, softer, and she was gazing at him strangely, gently, as if very moved and hesitantly eager. They stood and looked at each other, and moment by moment their eyes took on questioning intensity. I love her, he thought, and she loves me. He could see the faint glitter of the jewels about her throat, and now they appeared to be agitated. Her immense vitality, somewhat muted, flowed out to him as if to draw him into itself, and something restive in him melted and surrendered. He lifted his hand and touched her throat in a tentative gesture, and she did not move away. He let his fingers remain on the smooth warm flesh, and then, not retreating, she covered his hand with her own and pressed it harder against her throat. Her tawny eyes became humid, and then she was trembling. "Yes, yes," she said, and her voice was a whisper. He put his arm about her, bent his head, and kissed her lips. They were, for an instant, firm and cool, then they softened and became warm as all youth and living. He pulled her roughly to him, and her white arms were about his neck, her full breast crushed against his stiff white shirt.

339

She was murmuring against his mouth, and clinging to him, and he held her tighter. One by one the candles guttered out and the fire sank lower. "I love you, I love you," Cornelia was saying, over and over, until he could not remember when she had begun speaking, and this moment was one with the moment of summer in the blaze of the sun.

When Rufus came looking for his daughter, he found her alone before the fire. A manservant was lighting new candles, and as he did so the shadowy hall brightened and the walls gleamed out of dimness. "Where the devil have you been?" demanded Rufus. He stood beside his daughter, and she looked up from the golden velvet sofa where she was sitting. "Out here alone! That singer's starting again. And where's that Marshall fellow?"

Cornelia smiled at him. She took his hand fondly. "Mr. Marshall? Oh, he left about five minutes ago. I said good night to him."

Rufus frowned. "Why didn't he speak to me, and Estelle, before leaving?"

Cornelia studied a ring on Rufus's hand reflectively, the ring her grandfather had given him many years ago. "He wanted to steal away, or something; not disturb anyone, I suppose." Suddenly she flung her father's hand away, laughed loudly, and jumped to her feet. "Didn't you know, Papa? He's the man in the portières!"

"No family, no breeding, no background!" moaned Estelle to her husband at three in the morning. She had refused to be undressed; she had refused to go to bed. She sat at her dressing-table watching Rufus pacing up and down the room. "Who is he? Where does he come from? Who knows him?"

This had gone on for long over an hour. Rufus stopped beside his wife. His face was drained and grey. "I can't stand any more of this. You'll have to shut up, Estelle. She is my daughter, and, by God, my daughter can marry any damned—— Will you be quiet? 'Family?' 'Background?' 'Breeding?' Let's look at this baldly. I haven't any, either, and you were cursed glad to get me, weren't you? An old maid, a Philadelphia old maid. I'm brutal, am I?"

His features became gross, thickening under an unusual pallor. "No, no, you've talked enough; I am talking now, and when I have finished that'll be the end of it." Estelle got to her feet, assuming a half-swooning position, one hand supporting her body against the table's edge. "None of your delicate ways with me now, my dear. I'm not even going to get your smelling salts for you. And you're not so damned delicate! The great-grand-daughter of a groom, and an indentured servant at that, has no business being so fragile."

His breath was hard and painful, and there was a heavy pain in his chest. Estelle's head had fallen and he could see nothing of her face except her shaking chin. Her careful curls had become straggly, and for the first time he noticed that the hand which was supporting her whole weight was not the hand of a "lady." Flesh was flesh, and it always revealed itself in its nakedness during moments of stress. Curiously, a kind of relief and triumph came to Rufus, a feeling of conquest.

"I'm not going to repeat what this Marshall feller means to me and my business," Rufus continued. "He's not the man I'd have picked for Cornelia, but she could do worse! By God, she could do worse, such as your mincing marquis! And you're going to behave yourself, and hold your tongue, and stop your sweet lies about my daughter. I've heard them for years, and I've heard you speaking them to others, too. She is my girl; she was always first and last with me." Colour was coming back into his face, and suddenly he struck his clenched hand against the table near his wife's hand. "Sweet, malicious lies, Estelle, calculated to separate me from my daughter. But nothing ever shall. Nothing ever shall!"

CHAPTER THIRTY-TWO

ALLAN LEFT his carriage some three streets away from his father's house, and went the rest of the way on foot. He had done this in consideration of his parents, but as his polished boots slipped on the black ice over the plank footwalks he cursed. The champagne of the night before had done him no good, he reflected. It was responsible for the cold pain in him, for the sense of desolation. It made the squalor of this neighbourhood meaner, closer, more stifling. It caused the stench hanging over the houses to sicken him. He concentrated on the champagne he had drunk and would permit no other explanation.

The ghostly moon stared at him blankly; the mounds of snow along the walks were leprous and pitted with black grit. A bitter wind stung his face, and he pulled the fur collar of his fine greatcoat closer about his neck. Suddenly he was angered against his family; it was ridiculous that a man like himself, dressed as he was, should be picking his way through this foulness. But when he came to his father's house, so neat, so small, so painted, so different from the squalid shacks about it, he felt a pride. He paused to examine the red door with something like affection, and then he knocked. It immediately opened and Michael stood there, the yellow lamplight behind him. He touched Allan's arm and whispered hastily, "I think it is all right. Dad will behave himself, until at least after dinner. He promised Ma."

Tim was sitting before the great black stove, absorbing its heat, and Mrs. Marshall hovered over the lids, stirring and tasting critically. There was a splendid odour of roasting goose in the clean, poor room, and a fragrance of boiling onions. Mrs. Marshall, her worn face more lined than ever, looked up eagerly as Allan entered, and she came to him and kissed him. Tim glanced at his son and muttered. Then he said sarcastically, "Merry Christmas." In spite of himself, however, he boyishly eyed the packages Allan was carrying. "And what did my gentleman do with himself last night, when he should have been with his family? Praying, I'm thinking."

"Now, Dad," said Michael. He pressed Allan's arm, and Allan remained silent.

Tim turned fully, and elaborately examined his older son. "And it's the fine clothes he's wearin', with the gold watch chain and the boots like mirrors. It's forgettin', he is, where he came from."

Allan drew a deep breath and smiled. "No," he said. "It's because of where I came from that I have the watch chain and the boots and the clothes. It is because of my parents that I had the brains and the ambition to do what I have done."

"It's the Blarney Stone he's been kissin'," said Tim.

"Now, Dada," said Mrs. Marshall. She patted Allan's shoulder. "It's proud of him we are."

Tim turned a purplish crimson, and he half rose from his chair. "Proud!" he shouted. "Desertin' his people, turnin' from his people . . . !"

"Don't be a damn fool, Dad," said Allan, placing his parcels on a corner of the table. He was determined to keep his temper in the presence of this old idiot. "I'm not going to argue with you, and I'm only going to say this. I can do more for those you call 'our people' than I can from the outside. I believe it's called 'infiltrating the ranks of the enemy.'"

"It's the liar you are," said Tim. His bushy brows drew over his furious eyes and the purplish blush rose higher. Allan shrugged. "Believe what you want."

Tim subsided, but Allan had instilled a doubt in his mind. He continued to glare at his son and rumble under his breath. Michael and Mrs. Marshall gathered about the packages. The poor woman's hands were trembling and her thin body was rigid. "Look, Dada," she wheedled. "A package for you, from our Allan." She laid the package on Tim's knotted and restive knees, and turned away. "I want nothin' from the spalpeen," he said. "Not to go to Midnight Mass with his family, and not to-day either, I'm thinkin'. Holy Day of Obligation, and all. He'll be ponderin' on it all when he's in hell."

Allan ignored him. "Open your package, Ma," he said. "Let me help you; it's heavy." He lifted the lid of the bulky box, and Mrs. Marshall cried out joyfully. "A coat, a wonderful coat!" she cried. "A warm and lovely coat, with fur! A beautiful black coat."

"Broadcloth with mink," said Allan, and helped his mother to put it on. He was still young; he could feel the lurch of his heart as his mother stood before him, lovingly touching the cloth, reverently feeling of the fur. Over the splendour of it her ravaged face became young and tender and full of eagerness. Tim watched her, and began to blink suspiciously. "Ah, Mary," he murmured. "Ah, my colleen. It is a girl ye are, and it's a failure I am, that ye did not have it sooner."

She bent and kissed him shyly. "Not a failure. We have our sons, Dada."

Tim immediately became wrathful. "It's no heart in him that he brings this. It's mockery at us."

Michael regarded him with serious reproof. "You are wrong, Dad. Allan is not the man to waste his time mocking unimpor-

343

tant people. If he had not wished to give us pleasure, he would have abandoned us completely, and forgotten us."

As Michael, about to become a Franciscan Missionary Brother of the Sacred Heart of Jesus, had taken on almost a supernatural quality in Tim's mind and so was almost infallible in his judgment, Tim fell silent. His face remained stubborn, but his fierce blue eyes began to soften. He fumbled with his own package, and Michael gently helped him. The father muttered, "No doubt velvet britches to wear in my cab." But the small package produced a large gold watch, a repeater, and a gold chain. Tim stared at it, dumbfounded. He jerked his hands away; he dared not touch this wonderful thing. Mrs. Marshall exclaimed with awe, "It's gold, it is. To wear on Sundays." The watch glittered on its satin bed, and all at once it sweetly tinkled the hour of six. Tim drew in his breath. Mrs. Marshall turned it over reverently. On the back was inscribed: "For my father, Timothy Marshall, from his loving son, Aloysius." Mrs. Marshall read it aloud and began to cry.

"Aloysius," repeated Michael, smiling at his father, whose features had begun to twitch. "It's ashamed of yourself you should be, Dad."

"I'm ashamed of nothin'!" shouted Tim. But he took up the watch and held it as a priest holds the Host. "And where would I be a-wearin' of it? On my runs?"

They ignored him. For Michael, Allan had bought a Missal and a Bible, bound in the most silken leather, and stamped with gold, with his name upon them. Michael gave Allan a silent look of gratitude; and it came to Allan, for the first time, that this formerly despised younger brother of his had acquired stature, dignity, and authority in this household. Tim leaned from his chair and scowled at the books. "And what'll we be givin' *him*, after all these fine things?" he growled. "He'll be throwin' it in the gutter, I'm thinkin', on the way to his elegant hotel."

Mrs. Marshall timidly produced the family's gifts for Allan: a coarse black scarf she had knitted herself, a cheap silver rosary with imitation pearl beads from Michael, a thick and modest pocket purse from Tim. Allan studied them in silence, while they watched him anxiously, and with embarrassment. Then Allan said gravely, "Thank you. I'll always keep them." He put the scarf about his neck, the rosary in his pocket, and some silver in his purse. All his actions were careful and sincere. Even Tim could find no fault.

"And this reminds me," said Allan, after a proper interval had elapsed. He withdrew a slip of paper from his wallet. "A cheque for five hundred dollars for Father Tobin. Saint Joseph, in the church, has been peeling badly for years. It's a disgrace."

"He'll want no money from you," said Tim, but his growl was weak. "And what's the matter with the statue? From Italy. It's many a prayer we made at that altar. . . ."

"A new statue, a good one, will cost only about three hundred dollars. Father Tobin could use the rest of it to buy himself a chicken once a week, or some good pork chops or a rib of beef," said Allan good-naturedly. He pushed the cheque closer to his father. "I'm sure Father Tobin won't refuse this righteously. The money was earned, not stolen."

"Wasn't it, now?" demanded Tim with exaggerated irony.

At that moment there came a great crash, and a tinkle of glass, and Mrs. Marshall screamed and her hands flew to her mouth. Tim started to his feet. A cold blast of air gushed into the room, followed by a shout: "Dirty Irishers! Goddam Irishers! Git out of our country!" There was another crash, and a tinkle, and a second heavy stone fell on the floor. Mrs. Marshall moaned, fell into a chair, and covered her face with her hands. Michael stood frozen and aghast.

Tim started for the door, but Allan thrust him violently aside. He opened the door and ran out. Two large young men, shabbily dressed, stood on the walk laughing loudly. One of them had another stone in his hand, ready to hurl. The wan street lamp glimmered on their uncouth faces. Allan recognised them at once.

Then they saw Allan on the doorstep, and the laughter choked in their throats and their faces paled. They had not reckoned on Allan's presence here to-day. The rich "gentleman" was not likely to be with his poor family.

"Well, well," said Allan softly. "Georgie Stevens, Johnnie Lind. Good evening, boys. Having a nice time breaking the windows of decent people, are you?"

Michael and Tim had crowded to the threshold. "Watch it!" called Michael. "There're two of them, Allan, and one of them has a rock."

But Allan was leaping lightly from the doorstep, and for an

instant Michael saw his face, white and smiling. It was a savage and lustful face, and Michael cried out. Stevens and Lind stood paralysed, their mouths open. Allan was on them in an instant, and in an instant he had caught them both by the collar. He shook them swiftly, like a cat, and then he brought their heads together seemingly without an effort. A loud dull crack resounded through the street. The heads came together again and again, and the young men began to scream and twist in Allan's hands. For a time, which appeared endless to Michael, the head-cracking went on without Allan's uttering a single word.

Then Allan flung both limp bodies into the running and icy gutter. Without compunction, he kicked both solidly in the ribs, his boots glittering dully in the lamplight. The young men groaned and lay still, dazed, their mouths running with blood. Allan stood over then, and he laughed aloud.

"The next time," he said, "I'll kill you. You understand that, don't you? I'll kill you—you swine."

He was hardly mussed. He straightened his sleeves, shot his cuffs, shrugged his shoulders. He stood on the kerb, smoothed down his hair. Slender, nonchalant, exuding power, he surveyed his work, and was pleased. He added, "Remember me to the rest of the boys, Georgie and Johnnie. I'd like to meet them again, like this. It's always a pleasure to have this kind of talk with you."

He gave himself a last fastidious dusting-off and turned back to the house. His father and brother let him enter, in silence. Allan went to his mother and stood beside her. "Stop crying, Ma," he said gently. "We'll have those windows mended to-morrow. In the meantime, if we can find some cardboard, or planks, we'll cover them up."

Tim closed the door very slowly. His seamed face was sombre. He said in a slow and foreboding voice, "It is you who brought this on us. The men know you—you left 'em, deserted 'em. . . . It's a punishment on us all."

"Hell," said Allan easily, but his fierce eye brightened bitterly on his father. "I suppose that is why they broke our windows two years ago, and a year before that, too." He tried to control his rage. "Do you know what is wrong with them? First of all, it was your painting of the house, and Ma's keeping it clean, and your respectability. Then it was our religion, and you being an immigrant, you old fool. And now it is even more

346

unpardonable: they're envious. Envy is always like that, murderous and hating and full of malice." He remembered the men in the gutter, and he began to laugh.

"It's envy it is, is it?" bellowed Tim, purpling again. His fists knotted. "It's the poor souls rememberin'. . . ."

Allan uttered an obscene word half under his breath. Tim advanced upon him. But Michael put himself in his way, and laid his hand on his father's shoulder. He was smiling broadly, though his eyes remained serious.

"Allan's right, Dad. It is only envy. One of the deadly sins. Perhaps the most terrible of them all."

Tim stopped, his head bent and lowering like a bull's. He hesitated. His new awe for Michael halted and silenced him.

"You should be proud again of Allan. What a fighter he is, an Irish fighter! And it was you who taught him, Dad. Aren't we a race of fighters?" Michael began to laugh. "Think of it, two against one, and he fought them down!"

Tim's lower lip thrust out. The grimness stayed on his face but his blue eyes sparkled. He said, "Fine talk this for a Brother, I'm thinkin'. Fine Christian talk."

But Michael was convulsed with his laughter. He bent double. Mrs. Marshall began to smile wanly, and her hand stole to Allan's arm. Tim stared blankly at his younger son, then all at once he melted and he started to shake with deep and rumbling mirth. He went to Allan and sheepishly struck his shoulder with his clenched fist. "But ye don't kick a man when he's down," he said.

Allan smiled. "I didn't have an appetite before. I have a splendid one, now."

Mary Marshall busied herself about the stove while father and sons found flat pieces of wood to nail over the broken windows. Allan worked at one, and it was while he was doing so that he noticed the family's old crèche standing nearby. One of the thrown stones had fallen on the Infant Jesus in His cradle, and the head was smashed. Allan, hammer in hand, stood and looked at it. Suddenly, out of the depths of him roared a black rage so intense that he became weak, and all that was still hesitant and doubtful in him, all that was still young, died. He began to hammer, and every stroke was a blow.

347

CHAPTER THIRTY-THREE

ON MAY 30th Michael Marshall wrote to his brother. The letter began humorously and quietly, an account of his new life. Then he had written:

"The letters I receive from Dad and Ma are full of misery. . . . I understand the break between you is complete, since your coming marriage to Miss Cornelia deWitt has been announced for June 5th. Our parents cannot overlook the fact that you are marrying out of the Church, and I understand from Father Tobin that you have not approached him. For Dad and Ma to have grandchildren not brought up in the Faith will be a grave sorrow and anguish to them."

For God's sake, thought Allan with disgust. He tore the letter into small pieces and threw them away. Medievalism. He walked up and down his pleasant if somewhat ponderous sitting-room in the Philadelphia House, and as he did so he sipped a glass of whisky. Here he was, about to marry the heiress of a great railroad empire and, his ridiculous parents, and brother were distressed over the "Faith!"

He sat down near an open window, this early May afternoon. The sky was blue and warm, and the sound of traffic below very soothing. Head of the Portersville legal staff of the Interstate Railroad Company—Allan Marshall. Called into consultation with the Philadelphia staff, who greatly respected him and who fawned on him. A long jump from last May, Allan reflected. But not far enough—not ever far enough. His thoughts, becoming golden, meditated on the future, and he forgot his brother, the monk, and his parents. He refilled his glass, glanced at his watch. There was a dinner to-night, at the home of the Brownells. He must begin soon to dress.

He thought of Cornelia and smiled. He recalled the warmth of her, and the springing youth, the ebullient spirits, the sly ribald laughter, the wit, the beauty. "We shall honeymoon in our home in Newport," she had told him. "Before the family descends on us. Papa is giving you a yacht, and this is a secret.

348

Never Victorious, Never Defeated

Shall you call it *Cornelia*, darling? But, of course. Or *Corallan*, perhaps. Yes, that is much better. *Corallan*. Kiss me, dear. Do you know how much I love you? Look in my eyes. I never loved anyone, not even Papa, as much as I love you."

He had looked indulgently into her eyes and had seen the quickening yellow fire in them, and then her arms had been about him hungrily, and her lips on his.

Hunger, he thought now. My Cornelia is a devourer. The glass paused at his mouth. He stared through the windows for a long time. Then he threw the whisky down his throat and said aloud: "Damn." Cornelia was only a young girl of twenty; he was nearly twenty-eight. He was a match for any young lioness, and besides, he loved her. How could she threaten him in any way, she who was so full of humour and tolerance and gaiety, who wanted nothing but to be petted and stroked and admired?

No one could be kinder to him than Rufus deWitt these days. Rufus was proud of him. His salary was enormous. His position was assured. He remembered the magnificent ball given for him and Cornelia last January in the DeWitt mansion in New York. There he had met the owners of fabulous names; the Gunthers, the Regans, the Vanderbilts, the Whitneys. He had conducted himself with reserve and elegance, and Cornelia and her father had chuckled, pleased. He had liked Mr. Gunther, who had discussed the automatic coupler with him admiringly.

Newport for a few weeks. Then home again to Portersville, to that beautiful house on the mountainside, where, only a year ago, he had been one of the gardeners. Then New York again, then the Riviera and Paris, and London and Berlin. The honeymoon, interspersed with hard work at home, would last a year, Rufus had said. Allan shook his head, and for a moment he was dizzy. Then he was overcome with such an enormous excitement that he could sit no longer but must begin his rapid pacing up and down the room. There were times when he could not believe what had happened to him, so swiftly, so surely. A man prepared for endless hard years of poverty and hardship, working alone with only his own faith in himself to sustain him. He worked in silence, closed in by cold walls; he walked dirty streets in shabby clothing. His stomach was never entirely filled. His hands were hard, calloused, and gritty. In the winter he shivered under inadequate blankets. The smell of cabbage and dust and coal gas choked his nostrils. There were raucous voices about him, and the heavy stampings of patched boots. In the midst of it all he worked alone. And then one morning it was all over, and the fruits of his work, the golden apples in the golden basket, were given to him in one generous and overwhelming gift, not one by one, grudgingly, but all.

The wedding was to be held in the First Presbyterian Church in Portersville, the "family church," Rufus had informed Allan seriously, with not even a twinkle of an eye. Allan had agreed, just as seriously. He knew very well, from Cornelia, that though the family supported the church, and had its own plush-upholstered pew there, Rufus and Cornelia rarely, if ever, attended any religious services. They never spoke of religion; it did not exist for them, just as poverty and fear did not exist for them. They were as "godless" as fine wild animals in a jungle where they were kings. To call them anti-religious was absurd, for God was only a name to them and had never been a part of their lives, or even a subject of speculation.

One matter had made Rufus uneasy, for his wife had mentioned it over and over, hysterically. So one day he said to Allan, "Your parents, my boy. They—they will, of course, be present at the wedding."

Some strange malice had impelled Allan to pretend to hesitate gravely. Then Allan had said, "I hardly think so, sir. You see, I am marrying out of the Church."

Rufus had stared at him blankly, completely baffled at this remark. Allan explained. Rufus wrinkled his brows and his eyes, so like Cornelia's, had opened wide with incredulous laughter. Rufus said, "Well, well. How very odd. Really odd. Do you mean, my boy, that there are people who actually. . . ." He had shaken his head and laughed again. But he was immensely relieved. It would have been impossible to have Allan's parents at the wedding. Tolerance could go only so far.

Rufus had had much less trouble with his mother about the coming marriage. She, like Rufus, was more concerned with "losing" Cornelia than with Allan's background and family. "The only child!" she had wept, completely forgetting her grandsons. She had relapsed into maudlin pity for herself and her son, and it was not until Estelle (protesting wildly against "this most improper and outrageous marriage with a man who is little better than a labourer") had described Allan's personality in terms which strongly suggested Aaron deWitt to his widow, that Sophia had risen, battling furiously for the young people. And she fought not only with fury but with pleasure, for in this way she could completely frustrate her daughter-in-law.

With Cornelia, Allan had visited the Purcells on a few occasions. It was hard for the young man to believe that Lydia was Cornelia's mother, and he was incredulous at the affection for Lydia, for when she was certain that Cornelia loved him, she had accepted the situation graciously and coolly. She had long ago come to the sound conclusion that no one had a right to interfere with another's life, though there were times when she said to her husband, "Cornelia will always be the victor in any situation. I am beginning to worry about young Allan, however. There is something mysterious about him, something that can never be touched. He has the capacity to suffer enormously." To her surprise, Jim Purcell agreed with her. He said, "The feller thinks he's ruthless. That's different from being ruthless." Only Laura had appeared distressed, and she would not explain. When Allan and Cornelia arrived, she usually managed to be absent. Sophia had suggested a double wedding, and Laura had been unaccountably disturbed by the suggestion.

All in all, Allan found matters very satisfactory. If sometimes he awakened in the night with a sensation of fear and foreboding, he explained this to himself easily. Things had happened too fast, and in too great a profusion. A man needed time to adjust. He would light a gaslight and take up the fine miniature of Cornelia, painted on ivory, and look into the smiling eyes and at the alluring jocose mouth, and he would be reassured. He would say to himself: "Even if I did not love the wench I'd marry her." Sometimes he found it necessary to take a drink if he was to fall asleep again.

He paused now, beside the miniature, and took it up in his hands and returned the smile. "Minx," he said aloud. He put down the miniature and lit a cigarette and smoked it rapidly. He was sweating a little. All this excitement—all these arrangements— all these parties. And the working pace. He glanced at himself in the mirror; his black and curling hair was damp along his forehead. His features had sharpened; his nose appeared longer and keener. His eyes were feverish. His clothing was fitting him too loosely, and he impatiently supposed that it was because even the best of food no longer interested him. Suddenly there was a stiff cold shaking in him, in spite of the warmth of the evening. It was as if his very bones were chilled. He poured another drink for himself. When someone knocked discreetly at his door he jumped and cursed. An elderly hotel clerk stood outside and obsequiously informed the young man that a certain gentleman, a Mr. Boyle, wished to know if he could come up for a few minutes.

Allan frowned. He had almost forgotten old Dan Boyle, and he had no desire to see him again. That ignorant old boar, that ancient railroader who hated the "interests," though he was actually one of them now! The interview would be violent or unnerving. Allan said, "Please tell Mr. Boyle that I am not——" He was interrupted by a bellow from behind the clerk, and there stood Dan Boyle, squat, broad as an old tree trunk, fierce and red of face, flat of nose, fiery blue of eye, and with a big splayed mouth that suggested furious purpose. He held a wide black hat in his hand, a senator's hat, and the top of his round head was covered with a tangled mass of white curls. He wore the richest of black broadcloth, but his brocaded waistcoat, flowered and vulgar, was reprehensible, and from his watch chain, as thick as a man's thumb, dangled a number of seals and other miscellaneous objects. The cigar in his mouth was huge and stinking. He shouted, "My bhoy! Aloysius! The divil with ye; it's comin' in I am."

He shouldered his way past the quaking clerk, whom Allan tipped and hastily dismissed. When Allan turned to his unwelcome guest, Mr. Boyle was critically studying the sitting-room. "Sure, and it's a long way ye've come, ye rascal. Let me look at ye." He scrutinised Allan, and the choleric blue eyes narrowed. "Hemph," he commented. He lowered his short bulk into a chair and kept his disconcerting gaze on the younger man. He was so stout that he wheezed constantly. His eyebrows, white as snow, jutted far out over his big face like a hoary cliff.

"A drink?" asked Allan somewhat lamely. Mr. Boyle grunted, and Allan poured a glass of whisky. Mr. Boyle drank it almost in one gulp, not once glancing away from his host. He put the glass on the table slowly, pursed up his lips. "And what would be the matter with my godson?" he asked. Now the choler was leaving his eyes.

"Matter!" asked Allan, sitting opposite the old man. He smiled easily. "I'm glad to see you, Dan."

"It's the liar ye are," said Mr. Boyle, but without rancour. "I'm

352

here because I wanted to tear you limb from limb, and beat hell out of ye." He shook his head. "But not now, I'm thinkin'." He stared at the whisky bottle and again shook his head. "I've been talkin' with your dad."

Allan was silent, and his face closed. "Ye'll be wantin' to know about thim," said Mr. Boyle, ignoring Allan's expression. "It's a fine actor ye are, but not good enough for old Dan. So I'll tell ye now that your dad is a poor bewildered man and your mum will have nothin' said against her bhoy. So there's no harmony in that house, and it's missin' they are the Franciscan son, with his oil on the waters.

"The mother has a cough since February," went on the old man. "So I'm lendin' thim the money for a little house in the country." He eyed Allan shrewdly. "It's what you wanted, Aloysius, and the poordad said no. So ye'll be makin' me out a cheque for two thousand dollars to-day, so ye'll have the satisfaction. Nice house, with a garden it is, and someday ye'll be a-tellin' of thim that ye bought it with your own money."

Allan's eyes quickened. "Thanks, Dan," he said.

Mr. Boyle smiled sadly. "Ye'll not be waitin' too long, I'm hopin'." He paused a moment, and his red forehead crinkled. "Ye are bein' called a hypocrite and a deserter by the workers. It's said ye've used thim. Maybe ye did, in your crafty way. Yes. But I know somethin' they do not. It was I who offered to send you to school years ago, for the studyin' of the law, the labour law, so ye could be a-helpin' of the lads. And ye refused. Ye preferred to work your own way, ye who come of the good family in County Mayo. Worked till your hands was raw. Why? I know now. It was not in your soul to accept a man's money for a lie." He smiled again at Allan, and there was something of paternal love and understanding in that smile. "It's a good bhoy ye are, Aloysius, and someday ye won't be ashamed of it."

Allan's mouth tightened irritably. "Let's not be sentimental, Dan. It's true I wanted no help from you; I'll never take help from any man." All at once his eyes brightened with ferocity. "I've always hated the ' workers,' as you call them—from my childhood. There is no more good in them than in any other classification of men." He stopped a moment, and the ferocity deepened in his eyes. Then he told Mr. Boyle of the Christmas episode, and the smashed figure in the crèche. The old man listened soberly, and nodded his head from time to time. Yet,

353   z

there seemed a profound satisfaction in him, which Allan saw, but could not understand. When Allan had finished, Mr. Boyle broke into a bellow of laughter and slapped his knees. "Ah, that is a fight I should have seen! A noble fight." He put up his fists and shadow-boxed in the air with delight.

Allan refilled Mr. Boyle's glass and his own. Mr. Boyle fell into silence and watched Allan drink, and he was grave again. At last he said, "So ye're takin' to the bottle. A man does that when his soul is sick and there's no hope in him. And ye're not the lad for drink, Aloysius. Me, I've been drinkin' hard all me life, but it did no hurt because even in the worst days I had no despair. And perhaps ye'll be tellin' me now why ye're desperate."

"You make me sound like a drunkard," said Allan contemptuously. "Again, don't be sentimental, Dan. It's the pressure on me. When it is over . . ."

"Never will it be," interrupted Mr. Boyle. "It was in you as a lad. Now it is worse. Why?"

Allan turned the glass in his fingers. "A man grows older," he muttered.

"Sometimes a man grows up," said Mr. Boyle. He was watching Allan with keen sorrow. "What is it ye cannot stand, godson? What is it that eats at the soul?"

"Did you come here to inquisition me?" asked Allan with increasing irritation.

"Why, yes, that is what I did," Mr. Boyle replied. "It's angry I was with ye, but not for what you thought." He waited, but Allan did not answer. "I promised at your baptism, that I would guard you," he continued. "Keep ye strong in the Faith. Could it be that ye are desperate because somewhere on your way ye lost God?"

Allan shouted with laughter. But Mr. Boyle became more sorrowful. "So that is it," he said. "Ye lost God because ye came to hate men. It's the feelin' soul ye have, and such souls make men devils or angels. What hurt ye so, somewhere in your life, Aloysius?"

Allan took out his watch and frowned at it. "Dan, you should have been a priest. And now, you must excuse me. I have to dress."

But Mr. Boyle continued to sit and watch him. "A confirmation it was to ye, of your opinion, when the Infant Jesus was

354

smashed. Aloysius, ye cannot understand, but I am leavin' lighter of heart than when I came." He stood up, and went to Allan and put his hand on the young man's shoulder. He could feel the broad thin bones under his fingers, and he sighed. " I'll be rememberin' you in my prayers." He pressed Allan's shoulder heavily.

Allan shrugged off his hand, went to his desk, and wrote out a cheque, which he gave to Mr. Boyle. The old man tucked it away. Then Allan said maliciously, " Perhaps, Dan, I'll be as rich as you someday. I hear it's a fine house you have in County Mayo, in spite of the English landlords."

Dan struggled to keep from smiling, then he confessed: " A whole village, Aloysius. The damned Sassenach was bankrupt, though he squeezed the poor folk. And now we have a school for the little ones, and a chapel, and the roofs don't leak, and they bless the name of Dan Boyle. For what else does a man live?"

He walked slowly to the door, his mammoth head bent. Then he stopped, his hand on the latch, and turned to Allan. " It was in the newspapers that I read a little poem. On Monday. I cannot remember all of it, but only the first:

> ' *Now, was it Abel, was it Cain,*
> *Who suffered death, who suffered pain?*
> *Who dealt the blow that killed the other?*
> *Now, was it Cain?   Was it his brother?* '"

CHAPTER THIRTY-FOUR

THE EARLY September day was very warm and very still. The trees appeared to be larger and greener, and more filled with light, and flowers seemed to be more profuse and vivid. Yet, there was such a silence. Allan Marshall, the town-bred, felt the silence uneasily. When the locusts suddenly and fiercely shrilled he heard them with relief. He had found his way to Stephen deWitt's beloved grotto, secret and hidden, and he was sitting on the marble bench. Clover heads studded the bright grass, and bees hummed from one to the other in the drowsing brilliance. Allan watched them abstractedly and thought: How long does it take for a woman to give birth? This has been going on since dawn. . . . I can't stand much more of it.

He thought of Sophia deWitt, "the great grey hag." She had died only two months ago, very suddenly. He had come to have a kind of love for the furious old woman, who had shown him an almost vehement and pathetic affection since his marriage to Cornelia two years ago. He had finally realised her loneliness and misery, and he had been able to comfort her. The fact that he had developed a malicious affection for Rufus, and had somehow revealed his increasing love for Cornelia and his devotion to the business of the family, had disarmed the mistrust she had felt for almost everyone. Sometimes she had addressed him as "my son." And she had confided in him, telling him of Stephen with a strange lostness in her voice and a distant look in her eyes. "He believed in mankind," she had said once, wonderingly, and she had turned to Allan as if expecting him to explain this incredible thing. "Except at the last. And that killed him, my poor Stephen." She had added faintly, "Now, how did I know that?"

Only he and Cornelia had been at home when Sophia had died. The rest of the family had been in Newport, as usual, but Cornelia had refused to accompany them. "I want the baby to be born here," she had said, "where I was born, and in the same room." Allan was only too glad to please her in this. Newport bored him, except when he was alone and was standing on the wild rocks bordering Narragansett Bay and observing the blue and savage sea roaring in. Then watching the arching breakers at full tide, something was assuaged in him. He would turn from them at sunset, and, with regret and a sense of desolation, go back to the great reddish stucco house on its bluff overlooking the waters.

Sophia had died shortly after luncheon on a late July day, all heat and humidity. She had gone to her rooms to rest, and then her maid had come down screaming, and Allan had run upstairs alone. Cornelia was napping, as prescribed by her doctor. When Allan reached the bedroom, Sophia was already dead. The family had returned at once from Newport, and there had been an enormous funeral. Cornelia had been utterly disconsolate. She had clung to her husband desperately, and only he could console her. It was during those days that Allan had acquired a deep tenderness for his young wife, and he spent hours stroking her coarse red hair and wiping away her tears. He had been enormously touched to discover that Sophia had divided her huge fortune between him and Cornelia.

Allan glanced at his watch. Only fifteen minutes had gone by. In another ten minutes or so the family would arrive from Newport in response to his telegram. Jim Purcell had called him an hour ago and had told him that he and Lydia and Laura and Patrick would be with him and Cornelia after dinner. Lydia, too, had spoken gently to her son-in-law, assuring him that all would be well, and that he must not expect matters to hurry with a first child. She had left a loving message with Allan for her daughter.

Allan lit another cigarette from his last one and smoked restlessly. The doctor had returned to his rooms, leaving Cornelia with her two nurses. He, too, had reassured Allan; the child would not be born until about midnight. He pointed out to Allan that Cornelia was doing excellently; why, she would not remain in her bed, the dear girl! And Cornelia, who only winced occasionally, and only scowled and swore a few times, had indulgently ordered her husband to go for a walk in the garden or do something, damn it. She had kissed him, her eyes twinkling, and had literally pushed him from her rooms with her strong young arms. "Come back, just before dinner, and we'll have a toast together," she had said, and her voice had boomed.

They treat me as if I were an idiot, thought Allan. He looked at the great house above him; the upper windows were one sheet of flame in the sunset. No one had drawn the curtains on Cornelia's windows. The house and gardens slept under the golden sky. I was wrong, thought Allan, in his tiredness. She is not the zestful lion cub I thought. She is the very fiery heart of the family; there is a kind of terribleness about her, for she is like a force. She cannot be blamed for that any more than the sun can be blamed for burning, or the sea for rolling. She is elemental and full of natural power.

He thought of his first startled shock and realisation when he had accidentally overheard Cornelia and Rufus talking together one evening. Rufus and his daughter were discussing business matters, and Cornelia's voice was firm and hard; her husband had hardly recognised it. Allan incredulously listened to Cornelia's suggestions, and the respect Rufus accorded them. Stocks, bonds, investments, subsidiaries, policies—Cornelia discussed them all. It was impossible that so young a woman should know so much, and so surely. Never had she discussed these things with her husband, and Allan had been mortified at his own puerility and at the implicit slight to him. And then he had become frightened. The lovely young wife who was so gay with him, so full of verve and laughter and teasing, so ardent and occasionally so tender, stood on an almost equal footing with her father.

Then Cornelia had seriously spoken of her husband, and her voice had become gentler and more thoughtful. "He does what he does because something drives him, and that something is nothing we can understand, Papa," she said. "If ever that 'something' leaves him, he won't be the man either of us knows. Yes, he does drink a little too much, and that is part of the strange thing we'll never know."

Nor will I, Allan had thought with angry humiliation as he had turned away. He felt exposed, and it was all the worse that his exposure had come from a young girl whom he loved as a husband, and whom he had believed to be inferior to him. Intelligent, yes, but a female intelligence. From that day on he began, very cautiously and tentatively, to discuss legal and business matters with his wife. She had listened at first, as a mother listens, with sweet tolerance, to a story she has already heard. It was not so now, Allan thought, as he viciously ground his cigarette in the grass. He was satisfied that Cornelia had finally admitted him to the congregation of the inner family, and that he was no longer an intellect and a force to be manipulated and used, and a man only to be loved.

He decided he could not endure the silent and golden peace of the gardens any longer. He went back to the house. Muted noises from the servants, as they came and went through the rooms, annoyed him. There was a faint clatter of silver and dishes in the dining-room. He would eat alone to-night. He went to the library, opened a cabinet, and took out a bottle of whisky and a glass. Then he looked at them with distaste. At last he took out another glass, and carrying the bottle under his arm, he went upstairs. Cornelia's door was open so that the cooling evening air could wash away the warmth of the earlier day. Cornelia was laughing, and her laughter was followed by the titter of the nurses. Downstairs the telephone rang stridently in the dimming stillness. Those damned reporters again, thought Allan, and he went into Cornelia's room. Now church bells began to ring faintly and sweetly from the valley below, for it was Sunday, and Allan thought of the Italian campanile singing across the hot blue waters of the Bay of Naples.

Cornelia was sitting at her dressing-table and her maid was brushing her long and vivid hair. Her turquoise dressing-gown flowed lightly from her shoulders to her feet and billowed on the soft tints of the Aubusson rug. She turned her head and grinned in welcome at her husband. "Back again? Why, you've been gone only half an hour or so. Tell me, who is having this kid? You or I?" She kissed him heartily as he bent over her. There was no pallor in her face, no sign of pain, though there was the slightest crease between her eyes, coming and going every few minutes. "I've decided something," she said, as her maid braided her hair deftly and the fatuous nurses looked on from their chairs. "I'm going to have twins. I always said so."

"Where is Dr. Schwartz? Why isn't he with you?" demanded Allan angrily. Cornelia shrugged and laughed. "He's all worn out, poor old man. He said he'll have a tray in his rooms. Anyone would think," she added, "that I was giving royal birth or something. I see you have your bottle, and two glasses." Her smile remained, broad and good-tempered, but all at once she winced and cringed a little. "A large drink for me, please." Her voice, for an instant, was a trifle faint.

One of the nurses, the young and stout one, came forward and spoke timidly: "Do you think it best, Mrs. Marshall? Don't you think we should consult Dr. Schwartz?"

Cornelia had recovered, and she waved her hand. "Nonsense. I know what is ' best for me.' Go on, Allan," she said, as Allan hesitated. She tipped the bottle in his hand as he poured, and took the filled glass even though he protested. Then she turned to her nurses and maid and suggested they leave her alone "for a few damned minutes at least." They left, not offended, but only anxious. Cornelia's spurious democracy, so like her father's, commanded their utter adoration.

She put her glass to her lips and her eyes shone with merriment at her husband. "To the twins," she said, and tossed down the whisky smoothly. Allan frowned. He had never known a woman who drank anything stronger than wine, except the poor drabs in the slums who were addicted to gin. But Cornelia drank like a man, easily and naturally. He supposed it was all right—for Cornelia. She said, raising her thick red eyebrows, "You aren't drinking, my pet."

Never Victorious, Never Defeated

"I think your drinking is disgusting," he said sullenly, but he refilled her glass. She laughed at him. "I've been drinking with Papa since I was eighteen, or younger." She put down her glass and stretched her arms, and the folds of the blue and gauzy material fell away; her arms were large and had the perfection of heroic marble. She yawned contentedly.

"You are certain you are well?" Allan asked, going to her again. He drew her head to his chest in a need to give her tenderness. She looked up at him mischievously. "Perfectly wonderful, except for those twinges. I am supposed to count them. Am I disappointing you, darling? Should I be howling my lungs out and fainting?" He left her and returned to his chair. "If you hadn't kept prowling into my rooms this morning, you'd never have known I was even awake." Her mocking face changed, and now it was suddenly warm with affection, and the ebullient eyes softened into seriousness.

"How hard you take things, Allan," she said. "I doubt I'll ever take things hard for very long."

Childbirth, Allan reflected apprehensively, sometimes brought death to the mother. However, it was impossible to think that this glowing young woman, all health and strength and bounce, could be in any danger. He saw that she flinched and bent over with a grunt, and he started to go to her. "For heaven's sake," she said, when she could recover her breath, "do relax, Allan, No child is born without a little bother."

"We should have had the best doctor in New York," said Allan.

But Cornelia only smiled indulgently. "I could get along with a midwife, I think, or nobody." She glanced at her jewelled clock. "That was over a five-minute interval. The whisky did me a lot of good." Recovered from her spasm, she yawned again and displayed all her glistening white teeth. "Tell me, Allan, what do you think of this baby, or babies?"

"I want them, or it, of course. What man doesn't? And your father is practically incoherent all the time with joy." Allan smiled wryly. "He keeps forgetting he has two sons of his own."

Now the expression he was becoming accustomed to, and which at first had startled him, came over Cornelia's face. It had derision in it, hardness, and a kind of amused cruelty. "It's not their fault they are miserable wretches. It's Estelle's. And I think Papa thinks of them as Estelle's children rather than his. If you are worrying about them, my angel"—and the expression changed to one gently jeering—" Estelle has a lot of money of her own, and Papa won't forget them in his will."

But an incredible thought had come to Allan. He stared at his wife. " Do you mean, Cornelia, that it isn't taken for granted that Jon and Norman will be named by your father, in his will, as president and vice-president, with the voting stock. . . ."

She stared at him in her turn, disbelieving. Then she burst into a roar of laughter, and slapped her thighs. When she could get her breath she shouted, "Oh, my God! And you didn't know! You didn't know that you are his heir, and I. The company is ours when Papa dies, with the fifty-one per cent of the stock." She stopped laughing suddenly, and gazed at him in astonishment. " What else did you expect, may I ask? I am my father's daughter. I have been in consultation with him since I was fifteen years old, or even younger. I know all about the business. I thought you understood that." Again her face changed, became charged with power and implacability, and from her sprang an aura of indomitable force.

Allan, fascinated, could not look away from her. His heart was thumping heavily. He had thought that very shortly he would be named a director of the board. He had come to see himself as chairman, eventually. He stood up, swept to his feet by a wave of dizzy exultation. President of the Interstate Railroad Company! The prize was only a heartbeat away. He could not hide his exultation from Cornelia, and she saw it with cynical contentment. " But, in your heart, my darling, weren't you aiming for it?" she asked.

Yes, thought Allan, I see now that I was. Nevertheless, to escape the smile in Cornelia's disingenuous eyes, he went to the window and looked out.

The western skies had become a bright lake of green, changing to sharp scarlet over the tops of the hills. Early frost had already struck at the mountains: here and there the crimson glow of a maple burst forth from the emerald green background. As the slopes fell to the valleys they floated tenuously in misty heliotrope. The river was a vein of fire winding through the narrow purple land. Allan had never been able to accustom himself to this stern and silent grandeur, for it inevitably aroused in him a deep melancholy and pervading desolation. He started when Cornelia came to his side and looked out with him. He saw her profile, and he was taken aback, for she was grave as she was rarely grave, and even pensive. She leaned against his shoulder, and some of the greenish light from the sky lay on the predatory nose, in the sockets of her eyes, and on the roundness of her chin. She said abstractedly, "And what shall their names be?"

"We never talked of that," replied Allan, putting his arm about her. He spoke with surprise. "I wonder why?"

"Because we always talked only of us," she answered, and she was smiling again. "Well?"

He hesitated. "I thought—Dolores, if it is a girl. And—Timothy, if a boy."

She reflected. "Suppose your choice should stand, if a girl; and mine, if a son." She went back to her chair. "I think I'll make a dreadful mother. I don't care for children. But it doesn't matter. If I don't dote on mine, they will be better for it. One has only to look at my little brothers. I do hope Estelle has the sense not to bring them back from Newport to-day." She glanced at her clock again. "They're late. There was a time when everything was cleared for our private car, but Papa has become meticulous these past few years."

Her maid and nurses returned with the news that the family had arrived.

Rufus informed Allan that they had all decided to dine not in their car but to keep him company at dinner. Estelle, the boys, their nurses, and their governess were with him, to Allan's vexation. On this special occasion they would dine with "everybody." Allan, sitting at the candlelit table beside Estelle, was forced to listen to the shrill clamourings of the little boys. He wondered if only he knew that Jon and Norman hated each other jealously, and were in constant competition for their mother's sole attention. Norman, the younger, had a loathsome habit of leaping on Estelle's lap when she was talking in her bubbling tones to Jon, and fastening his mouth over hers to prevent further conversation. Then he would snuggle babyishly in her arms, his head on her breast, and listen smugly to her endearments, watching Jon the while. His brother was little better. In Allan's opinion, there was something secretly obscene in the rivalry of the boys.

Estelle, who always managed to listen in spite of the uproar of her own children, gave Rufus a vindictive peep. "Jon is talking to you, my dear," she said. Rufus, forced out of a joyous brooding over his daughter, turned in irritation to his son. "Yes?" he said impatiently. Jon's light brown eyes narrowed on his father, and he said petulantly, "I want to go back to Newport to-night. Eddie Glynn's having a birthday party to-morrow. Why can't we go back. Why did we come?"

"Because something more important than you, or your brother, is happening here now," said Rufus coldly. "I think I'll go up to see my daughter, if you'll excuse me."

Allan smiled to himself, and seriously ate his dessert. Estelle was silent; he could feel her hating eyes upon him. "You seem less concerned about Cornelia than her father, Allan," said Estelle at last, in a venomous voice.

Allan shrugged. Then he regarded Estelle curiously. "I think this child means much to him," he answered. "Perhaps more than any of us realise."

He knew that Estelle had never ceased to detest him, and that in the past two years and three months she had come to fear him. It was very seldom that she permitted her thoughts to reveal themselves, except by the flash of her warm brown eyes or a curl of her pretty red mouth. But now, disturbed and frightened by what her husband had said to her sons, and enraged by Allan's half-smile, she glared at him with open hatred. "More important" than her boys, her lovely aristocratic boys—that rowdy and vulgar hoyden with her red hair and execrable manners and rough voice! "More important," too, perhaps, this intruder, this nobody, this "foreigner," this Irishman, and his child, who would probably be a monster! Jon and Norman turned their attention upon her suddenly, and what they saw excited them, as all wild things are excited by primeval emotions.

"Shut up, shut up!" screamed Jon, and kicked out his leg at Allan. But Allan deftly caught it, twisted it enough to make the boy howl, then stood up. He and Estelle exchanged one violent look, and then he left the room without a word of apology. He went into the candlelit hall just as the Purcells and the Peales arrived. They thought him extremely pale and agitated, and this made Lydia smile at him with affection. She gave him her cool cheek to kiss, and her enigmatic eyes were concerned under the rose velvet bonnet with its grey plumes.

Laura Peale, her niece, resembled her so closely that she might have been her daughter. Her dark blue taffeta frock had been contrived so cunningly that one was hardly aware that she was about six months pregnant. Like Lydia, all her movements were unconsciously perfect. Her forehead, under her blue bonnet, had a peculiar glow of its own, like an inner light of intelligence and purity. Allan was always fascinated and humbled at this, for he was, innately, a superstitious man.

Jim Purcell never changed, except to grow more monolithic in appearance. But Patrick, nearly thirty-five, was already grey at the temples, and his face had acquired stern and unbending lines. He hated Allan with a zealot's hatred, and he never saw him without saying to himself: I have never wanted to kill anyone, except this man.

Jim Purcell said, "What's the matter, Allan? Things going all right?" He shook Allan's hand and grinned at him knowingly. He had a profound respect for this young man, who let nothing stand in his way. Pat could rave about his "lack of ethics," and smoulder silently when Allan's name was mentioned. But Jim Purcell was only roughly amused. He did not know exactly what had happened a year ago between Allan and Patrick, but, as he told Lydia, "I'll bet it was considerable, and murderous."

Allan was recovering himself. He was angry that he had permitted an insignificant, false woman to annoy him, especially to-day. However, Estelle was perhaps the one person in the world who could enrage him, childishly, with her bubbles, her smirks, her sweetness which was so cloying, her "ideals" which were greedy lies, and her artificial effervescence. He knew that Estelle disliked and resented all the family except Patrick Peale, whom she had succeeded in convincing, at long last, that she possessed a humanitarian soul, full of selflessness and enthusiasm for the "common man."

Allan informed the newcomers that Cornelia was doing well, that her father was with her, and that nothing seemed imminent. Lydia went upstairs with the nervous Laura to see her daughter, and the three men remained alone in the hall below. Jim Purcell lit Allan's cigarette, and put his pipe in his mouth. "Let's go into the library, or somewhere, until you're called," he said. He took Allan's arm, and the two, followed by Patrick, went into the library where the lamps had already been lighted. Jim surveyed the lamps and said, "I'm putting in electricity, myself. That feller Edison. He'll light up the whole world in a few years. You'll see. And his electric cars are better for our streets than our old horse cars. Progress." He sat down and winked at Allan. "Anything for your guests to drink, eh?"

"None for me," said Patrick curtly. He stood by the window and looked at the featureless darkness. Allan brought out a bottle and two glasses, and filled them to overflowing. Jim Purcell lifted his glass and said, "To the mother and babe, and may it be a boy." He watched Allan gulp the liquor. Allan spoke grittily in the voice of a man who has drunk too much. "She says it will be twins."

"Cornelia's never wrong," replied Jim emphatically. "Always a girl for good judgment." He grinned. "Didn't she marry you? Hear you're goin' to bring your hell-fire to the board of directors soon. And Red Rufe told me you've invested in the new oil wells near Titusville, and Idaho's gold mines. Got right in on the ground floor, when everybody else, includin' me, was laughin' their fool heads off."

Patrick always avoided speaking to Allan whenever possible, but now he turned with a jerk from the window and his muted face was greatly disturbed. "The board of directors?" he said. Allan refilled his glass. "Yes," he said coolly. "Any objection—from another member of the board?" Patrick did not reply. He went to a distant red leather chair and sat down. His hands clenched on the arms, and the fanatic's gleam was flashing in his eyes. Jim Purcell had once remarked, "No wonder you're so het up all the time, and so full of nerves. No vices. A good vice or two're necessary for a man to keep his perspective."

Jim was intensely curious about what exactly had happened between the two young men a year ago, but no one, not even Allan who trusted him, had enlightened him in spite of wide hints. However, Jim Purcell derived considerable amusement from the savage tension between the two, which seemed to crackle openly. He said, "D'ja hear Pat and Laura have just bought a fine piece on the mountain, about half a mile from here? For a new house? Tired of living with us old folks." He chuckled.

Allan knew that Patrick and his father, the former Secretary of State, were on bad terms, in spite of the pathetic attempts of the older Peale to conciliate his son. Mr. Peale lived alone in his great house, to which he had returned after he had had a stroke in Washington. Patrick rarely visited him, and never took his young wife on those infrequent visits. And he, Allan Marshall, was responsible for this. Sometimes he felt compassion for the old man in that empty mansion on the river, who could no longer go even to his law offices or accept dinner invitations. What he, Allan, had done, had had to be done. If an "anarchist" like Pat Peale made his own father the victim of his virtue, it was no fault of Allan Marshall's. He began to think of what had happened a year ago.

After months of long debate, consideration, and weighing, large carriers such as the Interstate Railroad Company had come to the conclusion that government regulation of railroads might have its advantages, provided that the regulation did not go beyond construction, inspection of equipment, and the maintenance of the roads. The railroad industry was one of the mightiest industries in America, and no longer operated in the sort of lighthearted, catch-as-catch-can, and haphazard methods which had distinguished them twenty-five or thirty years ago. As the frontiers shrank, and the railroads ran like vital veins through the body of the nation, the industry gained not only in incalculable wealth but in prestige and importance. In 1887, however, there were still some "privateer" little railroads scattered through the communities, with which the great carriers were forced to connect if they wished to serve those communities.

"There is no longer a place in America for small business to compete with large," Rufus had said to his officers. "There must be the sound uniformity which only the large industries can afford."

There were irreconcilable individualists who insisted that the devouring of the small businesses by the large was a threat to liberty. Rufus had smiled urbanely at this. "Liberty? What has progress got to do with liberty?"

Allan, who had the Celt's innate horror of any sort of regimentation or control by government, disagreed with Rufus. Once let government into anything, he would think gloomily, no matter how apparently unimportant, and it will soon find a way to occupy the whole premises. He attended conferences between the presidents of the great carriers, and while he openly acquiesced, he frowned inwardly. He was not sentimental about the "small" man. He was only concerned with the dangerous principle involved. "Let a beggar be oppressed, and the man with the diamonds on his fingers will not escape," he thought.

In his prophetic alarm he had even suggested that the great

carriers assist the little ones to bring up their standards. Rufus had stared at him, astounded and full of incredibility. "My dear boy," he had remarked, embarrassed before his associates, "we want those small roads ourselves, and if the government is inadvertently willing to assist us in this, why should we object?" He had added, "Not having the money to meet government standards, they'll have to sell out to us. Yes, this proposed regulation, I see, has its tremendous advantages for us, and for the public, who deserve to be safe in their persons and their goods on any line."

Then the carriers and the investors and the manipulators quietly informed their representatives in Washington that they were withdrawing their objections to the proposed law. They were exceedingly unhappy however, when some independent enthusiasts in Congress, taking advantage of the "capitulation" of the great carriers, rapidly introduced an amendment to the law governing rates of passenger and freight traffic. But the "sound" politicians took advantage even of this menacing amendment. It would be impossible for the small carriers to meet these new rates if they were high enough. They became high enough. The large carriers acquired the small roads.

Patrick Peale, the young idealist, having missed the directors' meeting at which the decision had been made, had not in his single-minded blandness understood that the "capitulation" by the Interstate and the other great carriers had been voluntary, for their own reasons. He believed a "victory" had been obtained by the "forces of democracy" in government. He believed that the time had come for a tremendous "revolution" in "behalf of the common man." He was convinced that in a nation, still young and expanding and individualistic, it was possible to pass laws in the name of "human rights," to destroy individualism. He did not fear government, believing that if it contained only men like himself (and he believed it could) it would bring a new heaven upon earth. He was never aware that all men are intrinsically tyrannous and dangerous, no matter what their position in the world. And only Allan Marshall knew that men like Patrick, who honestly believed in their transcendental theories, were the sinister and ancient threat of the ages.

He, Allan, had talked this over with Rufus and with Guy Gunther and the others, and they had gazed at the young man with mighty respect. They agreed with him that Patrick and his friends in the Senate should be "watched." While Allan wished him watched for any ominous signs of incipient tyranny, the others wished him watched for any indications which would affect their pockets.

To Patrick, the undeniable misery of most workers in America in the eighties, the oppression of labour unions, could all be swept away in one government edict. He did not know that sound progress in human affairs was a matter of the slow awakening of the public conscience, and the painful application of the religious principle that every man is spiritually responsible for the well-being of his brother. Patrick, the believer in the rights of man, had a subconscious contempt for mankind, a trait he shared with all reformers and fanatics.

It was Allan's ability to see "bogeymen" that made him the unsleeping enemy of Patrick Peale. Let Rufus and his friends "watch" Patrick and his friends, for the preservation of their wealth and power. He, Allan, would watch him for more terrible reasons. Many years later he was to think to himself: My metamorphosis began with my comprehension of Pat Peale. I thought I was driven by self-interest. But it was much deeper than that, unknown even to myself. I think I began to see when I found out that he possessed all the works of Nietzsche, and read them constantly. Every fanatic is a disciple of that insane philosopher, whether he knows it or not.

Mingled with all this was an ingrained personal hatred for Patrick Peale, which he would not acknowledge too often. Patrick had married Laura deWitt.

Carried away by the delusion that they had "forced" capitulation on the great carriers, Patrick and his colleagues believed the time had come to strike for even larger concessions. Patrick proposed to introduce another amendment to the bill regulating railroads: it demanded that the government include in the act a section giving to the government means to supervise working conditions on the roads, enforce minimum wages, control working hours, compel all carriers to recognise unions to be set up by an arbitrary and to-be-formed governmental agency, force the carriers to build homes for their workers at their own expense, provide free medical attention to the workers, build schools for the worker's children, divide profits with the workers, limit dividends paid to stockholders, erect hospitals, at the carriers' expense, for all railroad employees, subsidise food in special railroad shops so that the workers would not need to buy expensive goods in the open market, and "enlarge the horizons of all workers and their families so that no longer should they absorb the opium of the people—religion."

"If we can win on this, over the railroads—and we can win if we are dedicated—we can impose this law on all other industries, too," Patrick told his colleagues, who shouted their enthusiasm at him.

When the proposed amendment came to the knowledge of the carriers, there was great hilarity among them. The young feller was insane. Let him talk and "get it out of his system." No one would take him and his friends seriously. After all, he was the son of a rich man, and a director, himself, on the board of the Interstate Railroad Company, and owner, through his wife, of sixteen per cent of the stock. When Allan, appalled, declared that it was precisely because of all this that he would be taken seriously in Washington, they patted Allan's shoulder and spoke again of bogeymen. Only Rufus, after long arguments with Allan, ceased to smile, and began to listen.

"That Allan of yours is right on every count," Jim Purcell had said to Rufus. "But all the rest of you are muttonheads."

"The amendment must not even be introduced," said Allan. "Pat must withdraw it at once, and be forced never to mention it again. Of course, it would be thrown out, anyway. But news of it would get into the papers, and the poisonous idea would spread slowly but surely among the people, to the eventual destruction of the Constitution in some later decade."

Greatly alarmed now, Rufus asked what Allan could do. Allan said, with a dark smile. "There is a skeleton in the closet of every man, even men like Pat Peale. It's only necessary to find it, and rattle it in his face. And I'll find it. It will cost a lot of money."

Rufus had considered this, and then he had laughed soundlessly, his eyes sparkling and rounded. Then he said severely, "We must move fast. There has been too much delay as it is." And he had given Allan a glance of paternal reproach which had made Allan burst into bitter mirth. Allan had then gone to New York and had engaged the services of the entire staff of a private investigation agency and had told them that money was no object. Important information would be rewarded with incredible sums, especially if they were prompt.

In three weeks, the head of the agency reported to Allan with immense satisfaction. Allan had immediately gone to see the senior senator from Pennsylvania, a good and devoted friend of the DeWitts, an intelligent, able, and conservative man who owed his election to the family.

Then Allan had asked Patrick Peale to see him privately, and at once, on a matter of the most extreme seriousness. Patrick, who was at home, agreed in spite of some disdainful hesitation, and asked Allan to come to his secluded office. The senior Peale, now the Secretary of State, was in Washington, and there would be no interference. Patrick was much annoyed, and taken aback, when Allan arrived with the senior senator, a Mr. Horace Thornton.

Allan had come to the point at once. " Mr. Thornton has come with me because he is disturbed by the amendment to the act regarding the railroads that you propose to submit during the next session."

Patrick had raised polite eyebrows and had bowed to his senior. " I am sorry," he said, " but I intend to do what I believe is right."

" The amendment will be laughed out of the Senate," said Mr. Thornton. " You know that, Patrick."

" Possibly it will," returned the younger man, frowning. " It is very revolutionary," and, candidly, I do not believe it will be adopted. However, the people will be fully informed through the papers of what we have in mind, if not immediately, then for the future. Public sentiment, especially among the workers, will be aroused. And public sentiment, at first nebulous, can become later an irresistible force."

" True," said Allan, looking at Patrick with fierce eyes. " And that is why you are not going to propose this demented amendment."

Patrick gave Allan a faint, aristocratic smile. " Who is going to prevent me ?" he asked.

" You are."

The two young men looked at each other in a sudden and vibrating silence. Then Patrick laughed a little, gently. " Are you going to attempt to bribe me, Allan ?" His voice was disbelieving, and even contained a trace of the pity which men who believe they are superior reserve for those whom they are convinced are inferior.

" Bribe you ?" Allan had shown all his teeth in a genuine smile. " I wouldn't dream of it. I am just going to present certain facts to you which might force your resignation from the Senate, and which will make every word you say quoted with ridicule and contempt in the newspapers. It is only regard for the family, and for your wife, who is the niece of Mr. deWitt, which prevents me from giving all my facts to the newspapers now without offering you an opportunity to withdraw your amendment voluntarily, and keep silent about it forever after." He added, "I'm being generous. Don't press my generosity too far, Pat."

Patrick Peale became deadly white. Anger flared into his eyes, then increased to rage. His first impulse was to order Allan out of his office. But normal human curiosity, and something like dread, halted him.

"Are you trying to blackmail me?" he demanded, incredulous. "And if so, with what? There is nothing in my life . . ."

"That is true," Allan conceded quietly.

"Then you can do nothing," said Patrick with another faint smile. His colour was returning. He glanced at his senior colleague courteously, ignoring Allan. "I am sorry, sir, that you are so strongly opposed to my amendment, but I cannot help that."

Senator Thornton sighed. "I, too, am sorry, Pat. And for you. I think you are dangerous—please forgive me. However, I feel it my duty, in my sworn capacity as a defender of the Constitution, to warn you that should you continue on your disastrous path, I shall bring up—certain matters. . . . I loathe the idea; I sicken at it. But sometimes a man must use a dirty sword to protect his country."

"I do not understand." Patrick's voice was stifled. His new colour was fading again. "My amendment—what do you mean, ' warn me? '—a ' dirty sword? '"

"We are not here to debate your amendment with you," said Allan. "You wouldn't be moved by any argument; you are too much of a fool. You are, in your way, even an evil man. But that's too subtle for you." He smiled at Senator Thornton, who looked momentarily confused. "An intangible, sir, and a very vital one." He returned to Patrick. "It is true, as I admitted, that there is nothing in your life which could disgrace or ruin you. But there is in your father's life—your father, the Secretary of State, and held in national esteem. I understand you have a great attachment to your father."

Patrick half rose in his chair, and now his face was a blaze of

371

wrath and powerful repudiation. "How dare you speak of my father! You! What has my father to do with this?"

He was outraged and aghast, and Allan understood why with answering rage. These fastidious and expensively educated idealists were all the same, nursing in themselves a secret contempt for the "self-made" man, despising the life-force that had catapulted him from his original low estate because they knew they had no such dynamism, and though they prated of the "majesty of labour and the nobility of toil," they disdained the vigorous men who had had to acquire position by hard work, and knowledge by sheer determination. Allan had come here with the resolve that nothing would provoke him, but he said now, "You are a white-handed hypocrite, Peale, a moral snob, a liar who does not know he lies."

"My dear young men," said Senator Thornton in dismay, as he saw the violence in the two faces. He said to Allan, "You are unjust to Patrick."

"No," said Allan, still staring at the man he hated. "I just detest, and know, his kind. He reaches intellectual conclusions, which never include human imponderables. He's arrogant, and an egotist, and so he'll never be reached by anything except something which strikes at him through those qualities." He leaned towards Patrick, who gazed at him in pale and formidable silence. "I came to use a weapon against you, and I didn't like the idea. But I do now."

"State your business and get out," said Patrick in a constricted voice.

Allan leaned back in his chair and took his time lighting a cigarette. "I'm going to refresh your memory. Two years ago an under-secretary at the French Embassy shot and killed his wife, then committed suicide. She was a pretty woman, Madam Giroud. Perhaps you met her."

"I did." Patrick shifted, and his mouth was carved contemptuously beneath his sharp nose. "No one ever knew why it happened."

"I do," said Allan. "I think the matter was dismissed, as the French say, as a *crime passionnel*. It was. But the other man in the triangle was never discovered. Until three weeks ago."

Patrick laughed slightly. He picked up a pen and played with it. His brown eyes rested on Allan as they might have rested on a servant who was being insolent. "Well? Should I be interested?"

372

"You should. He was your father."

Patrick did not speak. The pen fell from his fingers, rolled a little, then dropped to the floor. It made a small click in the silence. All the life was leaving Patrick's face; slowly, it was becoming deathlike. His jaw bone, sharp under the flesh, gleamed white.

Allan, watching him and speaking musingly, said, "Your father—he is about sixty, isn't he? And Madame Giroud was only thirty, her husband thirty-eight. A very attractive and amiable pair, and popular. Washington was shocked. So was Paris. It was quite a scandal, nationwide, for they were the favourites of the President, who entertained them frequently." He laid a thick packet on the desk near Patrick's stiffened hand. "Newspaper clippings, from all over the country. Some as recent as three months ago, commenting on the ' mystery.' It isn't a mystery any longer, at least to the three of us in this room. The Secretary of State—and the Girouds."

"Slander," whispered Patrick.

"Not slander. The truth." Allan laid a thinner packet on top of the other. "I have had it all thoroughly investigated. You might take these papers to your father, and ask him, yourself."

"You are trying to destroy my father, who gave you your first opportunity." Patrick was still whispering.

"I don't want to hurt Mr. Peale, and I don't intend to. It's in your hands. Just in those hands of yours, there. If I give the matter to the press, it is you who will have forced me to do so."

"Lies," said Patrick, and with an uncontrollable gesture he pushed the packets to the floor. "You are a liar."

Allan's mouth tightened. "I think not."

"If you dare—I know the law—you will be arrested." Patrick was having obvious difficulty in breathing.

Mr. Thornton spoke reluctantly. "Then you'll have to swear out a warrant for me, too, Pat. If you force Allan to act, I'll have to mention it to the senators. It's a moral obligation. After all, I voted to confirm your father's nomination as Secretary of State."

The white Puritan! thought Allan. But Puritans are proud, and jealous of honour. If he were a normally ambitious man, a realistic and expedient man, he would tell me to get the hell out of here, and his father be damned or take the consequences of his own acts. But personal honour is another matter.

373

Allan stood up. "I suggest you take this information and show it to your father. In Washington. I'll give you four days. After that, it'll be too late, no matter what your decision is."

"Merciless devil," said Patrick.

"On the contrary, I'm merciful. I haven't given out the news to the papers. Whether or not I do rests entirely on your own decision."

Mr. Thornton got wearily to his feet, and he was full of pity for the stricken young senator. "Believe me, it's all true, Patrick. I'm sorry you had to know. And it may seem strange to you, but Allan is acting on principle, and not on mere self-interest as the son-in-law of Rufus deWitt."

"Principle," repeated Patrick, with sick emphasis.

"Yes," said Allan. "Principle. The upholding of a system of government which protects all Americans from men like you. But you'll never understand that. It's beyond your ability."

Patrick left for Washington that night. Two nights later the Portersville papers had black and excited headlines. The Secretary of State, Mr. Peale, had suffered a sudden stroke, which had paralysed his right side. His son had been with him when the calamity had occurred, and when Mr. Peale was able to travel his son would bring him home. Young Mrs. Peale had left her Washington house to be with her husband.

Allan had received a telegram from Patrick. "I have withdrawn the amendment."

"What was it that you used as lever?" Rufus had asked his son-in-law avidly. "I love a scandal, what else is scandal for?"

But Allan never told anyone. He knew he could trust Mr. Thornton. He was honestly disturbed about Mr. Peale, whom he had respected and whom he had liked. He hated Patrick, now, with an implacable hatred. The cursed Pharisee must have given the old man a very bad time.

At midnight, Cornelia, with a minimum of pain, gave birth to a boy and a girl, as she had prophesied. They were thin and pretty children, with hair like silver, and with large blue eyes. Cornelia had yelped boisterously when she had seen them. "Changelings!" she had cried, pretending to reject them. "They look like my sister," Lydia said. "And like my little Ruthie." "But where is my red hair, and Allan's eyes?" Cornelia had jocosely demanded. She had actually sat up to stare with amusement at the babies. The first kiss she had received was not from Allan, but from her father, who radiated pleasure and warmth like the sun. He was proud and delighted, and was unwilling to move aside either for his daughter's mother or for her husband.

He said, "My boy. My girl. I am going to deposit one million dollars to-morrow to their personal account. One million dollars!"

Estelle came in in time to hear this joyous announcement. She had given Rufus two sons, yet he had done nothing for them like this.

"And a million dollars' worth of stock for me," Cornelia said with complacence. "After all, it was I who gave these rascals to you." She added, "Really, Papa, the nurses have to take them away now."

Dr. Schwartz was rewarded with a staggering fee and much emotion from Mr. deWitt. It was not for two hours that Allan was remembered by his father-in-law.

In due time the babies were christened in the church where their parents had been married, and by the minister who had married them. The girl was called Dolores, the boy, Rufus Anthony Marshall. Newspapers all over the country gave a prominent place to the arrival of the new heirs to the DeWitt fortune and position. Allan's parents gave no sign. But Michael wrote to his brother: "Let me quote a letter written by Fra Giovanni in 1513: 'I salute you. I am your friend, and my love for you goes deep. There is nothing I can give you which you have not got; but there is much, very much, that while I cannot give it, you can take. No heaven can come to us unless our hearts find rest in to-day—— No peace lies in the future which is not hidden in this precious instant. Take peace!'"

CHAPTER THIRTY-FIVE

THOUGH ALLAN had had some idea of the vast interlocking management of a great railway company, he realised, as the years passed, that his original conception had been very restricted and narrow. Each railroad was an empire, complete in itself.

There was the president, the treasurer, and the secretary (now himself, in 1895). Below these personages was the board of directors, elected by the stockholders at annual meetings. There were seemingly endless departments, interlocking yet independent, each under the charge of a vice-president. The operating department was headed by a vice-president and general manager, to whom were entrusted the maintenance of ways, structures, and equipment, the operation of yards, trains, and stations. The traffic department was directed by a vice-president and traffic manager, empowered to fix rates and solicit traffic. Allan remained the head of the legal department, which furnished advice to the officers of the board, the president, and all other officers of all other departments, dealt with the regulatory authority, instituted any legal proceedings, and handled claims against the company. A vice-president headed the department of accounting and finance, assisted by one or two general auditors, and a treasurer. This department had full control of funds and made disbursements drawn by authorised officers and approved by comptrollers. Purchasing agents, storekeepers, general managers, comptrollers, chief engineers, assigned to construction and the formation of standards and instructions governing maintenance of ways and structures, were part of the beehive which created the golden combs of the company, not to mention vice-presidents in charge of personnel, an executive in charge of public relations and the study of the views of changing politicians.

These men were the hierarchy. But the Insterstate Railroad Company, like its sister railroads, was divided into districts, for operating purposes, and each district was partitioned into divisions. So there were general superintendents and division superintendents, division engineers, division master mechanics, trainmasters, station agents, and yardmasters.

This tremendous structure was almost self-operating, and needed Rufus deWitt's attention only occasionally, for authority was delegated and assigned only to the most competent men. However, as head of the constantly expanding legal staff, Allan as secretary, was the keeper of the corporate records, and attended meetings of the board and the annual meetings of the company. Grimly conscientious as he was in matters of business, it was hard for him to delegate responsibility, and his natural mistrust of the intelligence and integrity of others prevented him from enjoying the lighter aspects of personal living. Though never underestimating the perspicacity and power of Rufus deWitt, it seemed to him that his father-in-law was sometimes unduly casual about the empire he controlled, and he often found it hard to arouse Rufus to any anxiety or alarm.

"But, my dear boy," Rufus would sometimes say with indulgence, "we have a veritable kingdom here, run by princes and nobles and lesser men. I can't keep my finger on every damned yardmaster and little lawyer or vice-president or chief engineer or general manager. When my father started out, with about two dozen men, and when I was a boy, things were simpler. You could be everywhere at once. Everything was under your eye and your hand. It is different now." He would twinkle at Allan. "Suppose, for instance, I examined every little voucher for whistles or bells. Suppose, for instance, I scrutinised every small decision by our immense legal staff, and consulted with you on every item? You see how absurd it all is! Important decisions? We have important men handling them. When it comes, however, to major matters, I am right there, as president of the board. Are you trying to kill yourself, by any chance?"

In 1894 Allan had a collapse, and was ill for three months. He was ordered to Europe for a long rest, and "complete relaxation." He went—for six weeks. When he returned, Rufus noted that he appeared to have gained "some sense." He drove himself, as always, but he had become more indifferent to details. This determined attitude was, in itself, a strain on his temperament. "You are only a man," Rufus said affectionately. "You will notice that the railroad did not disintegrate during your absence, and that while some of the more important legal matters awaited your return, the country did not fall apart while they waited."

"An organism without a head will sometimes decay," Allan replied.

"But not a hydra-headed organism, each complete and self-operating. Remember that every man we have is working solely for his own advantage, and in doing so he is working expertly for the company. That is the unassailable structure of free enterprise, and that is why privately owned industries will always be run efficiently, and as economically as possible. Each man working as best he can for himself inadvertently works best for all other men. Self-interest leads to universal improvement.

This is the most irrefutable argument against those idealists and irresponsibles who declare that men should be, and can be, induced to ignore their own immediate interests in favour of what they call ' the welfare of everybody.' The profit motive, the self-interest motive, has given us what civilisation we possess. Man must always have inspiration to accomplish anything, and if he has no rewards he will have no inspiration. And that brings us, as usual, to Pat Peale. You will notice that though he is a member of the board he does not usually challenge anything which would change his own fortune."

"At one time," said Allan doubtfully, "he was a selfless reformer and a fighter for what he calls ' human rights ' as opposed to what he calls ' exploitation.' I wonder what happened to him?"

"You did," said Rufus, smiling. "You exposed to him his fundamental self-serving, which is natural to all men. And that is why he hates you."

"I'm glad he is out of the Senate," said Allan, nodding. "But he broods now. He is becoming increasingly silent and sullen and arbitrary. His children detest him. And Laura . . ."

"Ah, yes, Laura," said Rufus, his ruddy face darkening. "She is not what I would call happy. I have asked her. She says Patrick has ' changed.' He is bad-tempered, at times, dogmatic and immovable, sometimes rigid with the children, sometimes maudlin." Rufus began to laugh. "I remember the occasion when he was orating about ' the people,' and you brought to his attention the fact that he too, is one of ' the people.' He was offended and outraged, and denied it. You never told me. . . ."

Allan only smiled. "By the way, sir, you know he is backing that radical newspaper in New York, called *The Proletariat?* Is that another example of his desperate attempts to evade reality, and evade acknowledging he is no better than other men? Or is it vindictiveness?"

"It is both of them. You will notice that though he heads charitable organisations, and works for them, he gives little of his own money. He hounds other rich men for contributions, however. I have noticed, too, that he has become much more phrenetic since he withdrew that old amendment to the act regulating railroads. It was a long time ago. I suppose you won't tell me . . ."

Allan smiled again wryly. "Well," said Rufus, "he never goes to see his father any more. The poor old man. I am glad you are kind to him, and visit him."

"Pat," said Allan, "is full of vengefulness. You may laugh at him, sir, but I think of him as a volcano. He might, sometime in the future, become desperately dangerous."

Allan Marshall loved his children wisely as well as devotedly. If he had a favourite at all it was the girl, Dolores. Cornelia regarded her two sons and her daughter with mingled amusement, good-temper, impatience, and affectionate dislike. She found them, in her self-centred lust for life, boring and uninteresting. "I'm not fascinated by prattle," she would say. "I have enough of it from Estelle, who grows more childish as she grows older, and then, of course, I had my brothers. Read the children fairy tales, if you want to, dear Allan, and talk to them, and drive them about the whole damned country. But don't try to inspire devotion in me for them. Incidentally, though Dolores is only seven she has all the delicate, angular, and little gestures of a born old maid. She will probably cost us a couple of million dollars to marry her off. And Tony is almost as bad as she. I can stand DeWitt easier than I can stand the twins."

DeWitt, five years old, sometimes made Allan uneasy. He was small, very dark, quiet and penetrating, and very cold and peremptory. There was a stiffness about him, a certain sharpness, which Cornelia would declare he had inherited from his father. Black-eyed, possessed of straight black hair and pointed features, sceptical even at his very young age, disdainful of his older brother and his sister, whom he called "softies," he was hard, at times, to love.

Rufus Anthony, or Tony, was brilliant and discerning, and had a subtlety beyond his years. He might be a little too gentle, a little too devoted to his twin sister, a little too grave about his responsibilities to others, a little too prone to be hurt by a casually brutal word or act. But he was not effeminate; he was not too bookish, though at seven he read many adult books, and he was an excellent scholar. Too, he was tall, slender, strong, and healthy, and when his rights were challenged, he could fight, and win over, any of his playmates, of whom he had many in Portersville and New York and Newport. Other boys respected him and courted him, and admired his mastery over horses and boats and his skill at sports. His amazing good looks never inspired envy, which was a remarkable thing, for he had softly

379

curling hair the colour of old silver and beautiful eyes of so pale a blue that they looked crystalline in sunlight.

Dolores, his beloved twin sister, was so like her brother that only her long and flowing hair, only the slight dimple in her right cheek, only her feminine ways distinguished her from him. Allan would hold her in his arms, fondle her almost fiercely, murmur incoherent words of adoration into her ears. Though he loved DeWitt (with conscious effort), he was frequently angered by the little boy's contempt for Dolores, against which she had no defence.

As usual, Allan and Cornelia and the children always spent two or three weeks in the summer in the house at Portersville. Allan worked furiously during this time, but he gave many hours to his children while Cornelia visited, sat in the gardens, planned her wardrobe for the season in New York and on the Riviera, and wandered through the rooms of the great house with all her childhood affection. If she happened on her children accidentally, she would hurry away as fast as possible. She went often to the Portersville offices of the company, and sat in on the drowsy summer meetings of the board of directors, and in a common-sense and practical way, gave her opinion, which was invariably received with the deepest attention and respect. It seemed to Allan that she was treated even more deferentially than he, but he had to admit that she had an astuteness at times beyond his own. There she would sit in a tall chair, a little back from the long table, flamboyantly beautiful and stylish in her white linen suits and high lace shirtwaists, her red hair partially covered by wide flower-filled hats, her gloved hands tense on her purse, her hazel eyes quick and discerning and blazing with life and intelligence. There was nothing she did not know about the company. Her remarks and suggestions were incorporated into the minutes of the board, and usually acted upon. Her loud voice, when she spoke, dominated the men. If, at twenty-nine, her features had become harder and more predatory, and if there was a sharp line between her eyes, she was still striking and full of fascination and power.

She listened to Allan with thoughtfulness and attention, and if she disagreed, it was a disagreement between equals. He knew that sometimes she was secretly amused by him, as was her father, though he never knew why. He had also discovered that his wife and his father-in-law would sometimes glance at him warily, and again, he never knew why. These were his only complaints against his wife.

On Sunday afternoons in Portersville during the summer he would take his children for drives, while Cornelia napped at home or went over papers concerning company matters. A favourite place of call was the Purcells', where Grandma Purcell would listen with loving concern to her grandchildren, and where Grandpa Purcell could always be relied upon for a joke, a surreptitious handful of chocolates and cakes, a game, or a rough story. To the twins, lame and gentle and lovely Ruth Purcell, now seventeen, was the most important member of the family. Between the girl and the children there was an unspoken understanding and sympathy.

For DeWitt, at least, the most interesting place to visit was the home of Patrick and Laura Peale. All the children called Patrick "uncle," and Laura, "auntie." DeWitt, who knew that Patrick and Laura found him incomprehensible, and who looked at him with some coolness, was great friends with the Peale children— Miles, seven; Fielding, six; and Mary, four. Here the pretty twins were held in some scorn by the younger Peales. Here DeWitt's remarks and opinions were received with approval; here he was the leader, though younger than the other two boys. It did not annoy him that "Daddy" was not so welcome in this house as he was at the Purcells'.

On this hot Sunday in August, Allan was besieged by his children. It was almost two o'clock. When were they going for their drive? And what house first? Dolores saw that her father appeared to be unusually tired to-day, and she nestled against his arm, looking up at his face concernedly. "Do we have to go see old Ruth?" asked DeWitt. "I like Grandpa Purcell, but Grandma isn't so nice, and I hate Ruth. I hate lame people. Let's go see Miles and Fielding and Mary. They've got a new pony."

"What does it matter if Ruth is lame?" asked Tony admonishingly. "She told me she'll have some new books for us to-day."

"Pish on your old books," said DeWitt. "Besides, they're not good stories she reads. Silly ones. And Dolores looks silly, too, sitting on Ruth's knee like a baby. Daddy, let's go to the Peales'. Besides, they won't be here next week. They're going to the seashore, they said last time. They don't go to Newport like us."

Allan reached out to rumple the black hair of his youngest

child, but DeWitt pulled away. He loathed having anyone touch him without his consent, and his small dark face, so concentrated and alert, darkened still more with resentment. He smoothed down the hair, which Allan had not touched, and he threw up his little head angrily. All his slight body stiffened. He repeated, "Let's go to the Peales'."

"I think," said Allan judiciously, "that DeWitt should have his choice this week."

This seemed fair to the twins, who, however, found the Peale children wearying and unfriendly. So Allan and the three children rolled away in one of the victorias, open to the hot wind and the sun. Tony and Dolores laughed and chattered with their father. DeWitt, as usual, was almost completely silent, his eyes raking the countryside with their accustomed pouncing look. He thought the babble of his brother and sister about the grandeur of the mountains, the glimpses of wild creatures in the woods, and the view of the city falling away below them, eminently foolish and pretentious. He could not imagine himself becoming ecstatic over a field of buttercups, or the blue flash of a jay among the dim boughs of a tree. When the twins begged that the carriage be stopped so that they could look closer at the silent flitting of a doe and a fawn among the trees, he uttered a low rude sound. DeWitt nursed a small animosity against his father. There was something about Daddy which invariably aroused annoyance and impatience in the little boy, and something close to contempt.

Allan, though he smiled at his children, was abstracted. He leaned back in his carriage, and acknowledged to some misery and more than a little weariness. He said, "I wish there was some other place to go, somewhere interesting, where we've never gone before."

"Where?" asked Tony eagerly. But Dolores pressed her face against her father's arm with sympathy. Allan raised his hand, and the coachman drew up the horses on the mountain road. "Let me think," said Allan, frowning. He looked off into the radiant haze of the trees, and then far off into the mountains. He rubbed his chin thoughtfully. He started to speak, then stopped. No, it would not "do." The whole idea was sentimental and ridiculous. Why should he have thought of it to-day, when he had not thought of it for years, and had not even cared? He had been working too hard this week. In fact, the past two years, which had included the Panic of 1893, had been almost too much for any man. His burdens and responsibilities had been increasing steadily. It was his exhaustion which had given him that absurd idea. . . .

"Where?" repeated Tony, and now even Dolores asked.

"Somewhere to play?" asked DeWitt, interested. "If it's new, I don't care."

Allan looked at his children. The golden dust was slowly settling about the carriage, and the sleek black horses shrugged in it and tossed their heads. The hot and windy silence of the heights stirred the woods on either side of the road, and the mountains stood against the hot pale sky in vague green and purple. As Allan considered, and gazed at his children, the horses moved impatiently and their harness clattered in the quiet. The coachman sat like a statue with folded arms.

It was absurd, thought Allan, even to think of it. Cornelia would stare, round her eyes with amusement, and shrug. Allan could endure her rare but savage tempers with equanimity; he could quarrel with her, and even, on occasion, let her have her way without a loss in his own self-esteem. But her amusement, covert as it always was, and only revealed by a hazel twinkle, never failed to enrage him. He said aloud, "I don't think we'll go, after all. If we did, it would have to be a secret, and secrets . . ."

"A secret!" cried the twins with delight.

"A secret," repeated DeWitt with slow and sinister pleasure.

For the first time the difference in intonation between the twins and DeWitt came forcibly to Allan's attention. Now he looked only at the youngest child, and he frowned. "Secrets aren't always good," he said somewhat pompously. DeWitt brightened. "This wouldn't be, would it, Daddy?" he asked. His black eyes shone with anticipation.

"I didn't say that, DeWitt." Allan became irritable with himself and the little boy.

Dolores said, "If it's a nice secret, and it would be fun . . ."

"There aren't any ' nice ' secrets," said the precocious DeWitt scornfully. "Who would want them then, you silly old thing?"

"It's not a secret," said Allan, annoyed. "I didn't mean it in your way, DeWitt. You're too sharp for your own good, young man."

The small eyes narrowed on Allan cunningly. "Oh, all right, then. We'll go to the Peales'. They've got a new pony Who wants a secret anyway, except girls?" His little sallow hand played indifferently with the buttons of his jacket. "The last time, Miles kicked Dolores and made her cry, and Mary put pepper in old Tony's lemonade. It was awfully funny. I have lots of fun at the Peales'."

The twins were depressed at this recollection. Dolores hesitated, then said, "Daddy, we'd like to go to see the secret place."

DeWitt laughed his quiet and derisive laughter. "Fielding hates old Tony, too. He puts burrs on his chair. Lots of fun at the Peales'. They like me and I like them."

"I think they're awful," said Tony. His fair face was already flushed with sun and heat, and now it flushed deeper. "Sometimes they play all right, but most of the time they're nasty. Daddy, let's go to the secret place."

De Witt smiled and said nothing. Why, the little devil gets what he wants almost all the time! thought Allan wrathfully. He said, "We'll go to this new place, but it isn't a secret; at least it isn't from your Mamma. Is that understood?"

"Do we have to tell her?" asked DeWitt, still smiling.

"Not if you don't want to," replied Allan. He leaned towards the coachman and gave him instructions. The carriage was driven to a wider place in the road, then carefully turned about. Allan continued: "I haven't been there, myself, except to drive by it."

The carriage rolled down the road in the warm and golden silence. Portersville rose slowly up to meet it, its river a sparkling flash dividing East Town from West, its houses and factories dun-coloured in the sunlight. Now the carriage began to roll down a long and winding road away from the city, and green fields sloped into the valley. "Winston Road," said Dolores wonderingly. "We don't know anyone on Winston Road." Allan did not answer. He was excited, dubious, and uneasy. It might all turn out very disagreeable for everybody, under all the circumstances. DeWitt, the little fiend, had goaded him into it. Allan glanced at the child, and was angered to see that his son was watching him with a speculative gleam in his eye.

Allan leaned back in the carriage and closed his aching eyes. Perhaps he hadn't recovered completely from his "collapse" of a year ago; perhaps it was returning. With some fear, he recalled the weeks previous to his breakdown: the insomnia, the nightmares, the sense of smothering and choking even when working quietly at his desk, the cold trembling of his bones, the nausea, the increased necessity to drink if he was to meet people with any composure, the nebulous but awful forebodings which struck him without warning, the consciousness of some enormous loss which was without a name, the sedatives which finally could not calm the sick and unconscious dreads, the restlessness which tormented him and made him aware of every curling nerve in his body, and finally the total inability to think and concentrate.

He became aware, now, that he was sweating, and that his sweat was cold in spite of the heat. Good God, he thought, not again! His fear made his throat tighten. If only, his thoughts continued, I knew what the hell had caused that damned collapse, and why it is threatening again. I have everything I ever wanted; no man could want more. He felt a gentle touch on his arm and opened his eyes. Dolores was gazing at him with concern. "Don't you feel well, Daddy?" she asked anxiously. He put his arm about the child and tried to smile. "Not very," he admitted. And then, without thinking, he added, "Perhaps that is why I thought of going to—this place."

His own words startled him. He pondered over them. I'm losing my mind, he said to himself. What have they got to do with it? I haven't given them a passing thought for years, except, perhaps, at Christmas, when I've sent them gifts. And I wouldn't have sent them at all, if it hadn't been for my mother.

The carriage was bowling rapidly down the suburban road. Handsome houses gave way to those less pretentious, and finally the green spaces were wider and wider and cornfields appeared, clusters of straggling woods, meadows yellow with wheat and oats, grey farm houses, fences, and cattle. Bridges over summer-shrunken streams were crossed smartly; the mountains hovered in the sky like mauve clouds. Dogs ran out from lanes, barking at the carriage. The Sunday silence seemed to have absorbed all motion from the landscape.

"We're coming to Laketon," said Tony. "Are we going to a farm?"

"No," said Allan. "We are going just two miles beyond Laketon. You've never been there."

The carriage went through the small village, emerged on to a country road overhung with ancient elms tangled and cool against the sun. The children were sitting up straight, watching.

Never Victorious, Never Defeated

"What little houses," said DeWitt scornfully. "Poor people's houses."

"I think they're pretty," said his sister. Her pale hair, moistened by perspiration, curled about her beautiful young face, so classically perfect in all its features. Her white frock, billowing yards of voile with insertions of real lace, enhanced her delicacy. She had perfect legs; the sunlight glanced from her alabaster calves and patent-leather slippers. Allan sometimes found it incredible that Cornelia was her mother, Cornelia who sometimes appeared larger than life-size, all colour, all blaze, all movement. Allan looked at her twin brother; her replica, he thought with tenderness. All at once these two children were dearer to him than all life, dearer than himself and Cornelia, dearer than anything he had gained in all his years.

"I never told you," said Allan. "I have a father and mother, too. That is where we are going—to see them."

Tony and Dolores stared at him with astonishment. He could not meet the crystal shine of their eyes. He tried to smile at DeWitt instead, who could be depended upon, Allen knew now with some bitterness, not to be surprised at anything. DeWitt was smirking. But Tony stammered, a little aloofly, "Daddy, you never told us you had a father and—and a mother."

"You're such a ninny," said DeWitt, and pushed a sharp elbow into his brother's ribs, not so much with malice as with disgust. "Why shouldn't he have? Everybody has."

Dolores saw the colour creeping over her father's thin face, and said quickly, "Maybe Daddy had a reason."

"Oh, maybe he had," DeWitt said. And he turned the narrow glitter of his eyes jeeringly on his father. "Everybody's got a reason, don't they, Daddy?"

Tony regarded his brother sternly. "Perhaps people have, DeWitt." It was seldom that the kindly boy could bring himself to rebuke anyone, but when he did, he received respect, even from DeWitt. "And it's nobody's business but Daddy's."

"Look here," remarked Allan uncomfortably. "There's no mystery about it. I had a quarrel with them a long time ago."

"What was it?" DeWitt, after a sullen glance at Tony, looked interested.

Allan did not answer. The carriage turned up a short country road, emerged on a broader stretch. It was windier and brighter here, and the two boys clutched at their stiff straw hats and

386

brushed the dust from their blue serge jackets and short trousers. Tony's broad white collar was somewhat crumpled, because heat affected him adversely, but little DeWitt looked all neat edges and unperturbed nattiness. Dolores, who was becoming excited, fluffed out her dress and rearranged her sash and shook back her flowing hair. "I hope they like us," said Dolores.

"My darling, they could not help it," said Allan gently. Tony was silent. His profile, so like his sister's, was more than a trifle severe, but DeWitt had a gloating look about him.

Allan knew that the farm had only eighteen acres, but it was enough for a cow, a horse, a few pigs, and some chickens. The fields were rich and green; Timothy Marshall had a "hired man." Here was a stretch of glittering ripe wheat, and another of oats, and a stand of yellow corn. Here was a good wood of first-growth timber, and a brook, from which a very fat cow was drinking contentedly. She raised her mild brown eyes as the carriage twinkled past. All was shining silence in the August sun; trees stood in utter quiet, crowned with light, under the pale hot sky. The carriage turned a slight bend in the road, and now the farmhouse came into view, white and snug and neat, with green shutters and a red-shingled roof. A garden of flowers sprawled before it, and a box hedge outlined the scattered flag-stones leading to the green door, which stood open. Behind the house stood the red-painted barn, tidy and large. Beyond the buildings and the sweet-smelling acres the mountains rose in warm and deepening purple and green.

"Here?" cried Dolores eagerly, as the carriage stopped at the walk. "Here," said Allan, and sat uncomfortably, watching the open door. He saw no one beyond it, though the small hallway glimmered with sunlight and the polished wooden floor was like a brown mirror. He did not know what to do now. He became aware, after a minute or so, that his children were watching him and waiting, Tony and Dolores with surprise at the delay, and DeWitt with knowing interest. Then just as Allan was about to give the order to turn about and drive away, his father appeared in the doorway, smiling, with his wife behind him. For a moment Tim paused, beaming, unsurprised, his thick white curls bright in the sunlight, his square face contented and happy, his blue eyes sparkling. He wore a very respectable black Sunday suit. Mary, his wife, was dressed in thin black silk, with a golden cross hanging on her flat bosom. In that clear light Allan could see her distinctly, could see the slight flush of colour on the cheek bones. She seemed younger and even more gentle, though time and illness and trouble had scribbled her calm face over with fine wrinkles.

Timothy, so amazingly unsurprised, burst from the doorway and came at a trot to the carriage. He shouted, "You're late! Two hours late, and the tea waitin'! Aloysius, my boy, and these are the young ones, I'm thinkin'!"

Allan was stupefied. He could only sit among his silent children and stare at his father. "You were expecting us, Dad?" he finally asked, as Tim completed his joyous survey of his grandchildren. Tim did not answer at once. He was looking at Dolores, and the blue of his eyes was dimmed with tears. Then he took the little girl's hand, and she bent over the side of the carriage and kissed him. He put his arms about her and lifted her down to the ground. Mary was at his side now, and she knelt down on the stones and embraced Dolores, murmuring into the silvery curls. Tim next turned his attention to Tony, who was smiling uncertainly. "Ah, a fine lad, and a twin it is," said Tim. "Come to your granddad, my lad. Ah, the good face, the good eyes, the good mouth. Sure, and he and his sister look like the angels out of the holy pictures. Not a kiss for me, but the hand? No, a kiss it will be from the little gentleman. And here's the grandma waiting."

"You were expecting us?" asked Allan again, feebly.

But still Tim did not appear to have heard him. He had become silent, and the trembling smile was seeping out of the rugged folds of his face. He was looking at DeWitt, who returned his gaze in cool dark silence. Tim's calloused hands suddenly gripped the side of the carriage, and old man and child studied each other. Then Tim said, as if to himself, "And this little one—it is the stranger." He opened the carriage door and DeWitt, composed and fastidious as always, climbed out and set his small polished boots on the ground. It was then that Tim turned his attention to his son.

He saw everything, and what he saw evidently grieved him. He smiled again, a forced smile. "'Expectin' us,' he says. Sure, and why not? Didn't I have the letter from Mike in North Dakota, among the wild Indians, only the other day, sayin' ye would all come on Sunday? And is not Mike the saint, and does he not know?"

388

Never Victorious, Never Defeated

He extended his hand to Allan, and the smile became deep with pity. "And was it not Mike who wrote us ye had bought this fine place for us, Aloysius? We never knew, till then, for even old Dan Boyle was not tellin' us, even to the day he died, and left me the twenty-thousand dollars. But come in, come in. The tea is gettin' cool, and your mother made the wonderful cakes for the children. Come in. My son."

There were too many years between; too much had happened for conversation and reminiscences, except the most casual. So Allan's parents accepted the situation as though they had never been parted from their son. They appeared, in their tranquillity, to have known all about him in these years, and Allan began to suspect that they did indeed know. He walked about the small house, genuinely admiring what his father had done to make it charming and beautiful. Pridefully, Tim showed his son the fine furniture he had made himself, the simple polished pieces of black walnut and maple. It was he who had made the brick kitchen, with its rows of gleaming copper kettles hanging on the walls. He had added the two small bedrooms upstairs, with their bright floors, their four-poster beds, their solid walls clothed in paper roses and lilies. Almost single-handedly, he had built the red barn and put up the few necessary fences. "You'll be knowin', I'm thinkin', that I've not been the engineer for three long years," he said. "I lost the heart in it. But the good acres fed us and comforted us." He put his hand briefly on Allan's arm. "It was hard, but it was good, with God's grace. And now, look: we're lace-curtain Irish!"

The children were with them in the tour of the house. Tony and Dolores listened in pleased and respectful silence, earnestly studying everything.

DeWitt, so withdrawn, so dignified, made no remark, glanced at the things presented without interest.

Tony said, "Grandpa, what is ' lace-curtain Irish?'" He stood beside Tim and looked at him with shy affection. Tim put his arm about the boy's shoulder, and winked at Allan. "It is what we are, and what your Dad is. Irish with a little money." He put his other arm about Dolores, for whom he seemed to have a special tenderness, and the two children regarded him with their beautiful Renaissance faces upturned trustfully.

DeWitt spoke for the first time, with cool hauteur. "We have more than just a little money, sir. And we're not Irish—foreigners. We're Americans."

"So are we all," said Allan with annoyance. "Your governess tells us you are a very sharp boy, DeWitt. But I think you are a little fool."

DeWitt did not move; he only gave the impression that he had removed himself. He stood there, slight for his age, reserved and distant, and silent. Allan was immediately contrite. A peculiar little boy, but his child. He reached out his hand, but DeWitt automatically stepped back to preserve himself from any undesired caress or unsolicited touch.

DeWitt remarked, without impudence, "You talk funny—Grandpa. We don't talk like that."

Tim bent, his horny hands on his knees. He smiled at the boy. "You'll learn, child. There's more than one tongue in the world. But it's the baby you are, and it's not hurt by your words I am."

Tony said severely, "Your manners, DeWitt." But DeWitt ignored him.

"It's not bad manners he has, Tony," said Tim. "He's not the lad to have bad manners, ever. A gentleman. Never the one to have tempers, without a purpose, and never will the purpose be a little one, but calculated. Our Lord makes many different kinds of people, and sometimes it is a wonder to us simple folk."

Allan was disturbed. "They say DeWitt resembles me," he remarked.

Tim shook his head. "It is the colouring. But not the soul. But we should not be talking about the child in his presence. Though I doubt it will ever hurt him. He is a law to himself." He studied DeWitt somewhat sadly. "Does he ever smile?"

DeWitt answered composedly: "Yes. When there's something to smile about. Should I smile now, sir?"

"You see," said Tim, still smiling at the boy, but speaking to Allan. "There must always be a purpose in everything. Even for love."

It had never occurred to Allan before, and now he thought: DeWitt loves nobody. And yet, and yet, Allan's disturbed thoughts ran on, when Tony is stern with him, when Tony reveals something strange to him, something, perhaps, of integrity and inner power and character which can't be shaken, then he regards Tony with respect and gravity. Perhaps it is the unconscious homage the unrighteous involuntarily tender the righteous.

Never Victorious, Never Defeated

The bedrooms blew with hot wind and sun. Tim was lifting a photograph from a tall chest of drawers, and Tony and Dolores were waiting courteously to be shown. DeWitt stood apart, his eyes on the floor, his small pale underlip thrust out, a mannerism he had when thinking secret thoughts which Allan doubted were childlike. Allan said in a low voice, "Don't sulk, DeWitt." There was a plea under his words.

"But I'm not sulking, Daddy," replied DeWitt with genuine surprise. He suddenly smiled, and the sallow face became, for an instant, almost engaging.

"And this is your Uncle Mike, Brother Michael it is," Tim was saying, showing the photographs to the twins. "See, among the Indian children, teaching them, caring for them, in their wild heathen country, where the government keeps them. See how they gather about his knee, the little ones, listening to his stories."

"But why does he wear those clothes?" asked Tony. He held the photograph in his hands, and showed it first to Dolores and then to DeWitt, who had moved silently to his side. It never seemed to surprise Tony that DeWitt, in spite of his usual derision and his hostility towards his brother, should still manage to be with him, unsought and uncalled.

Tim did not glance at his son. He only said, "It's the holy monk he is, a Franciscan brother. A man in the service of God. You'll be knowing about God, I'm thinkin'?"

"Oh, yes," replied Tony, puzzled, and examining the photograph closer while Dolores peered over his shoulder. "My tutor and Dolores's taught us the Lord's Prayer, and we say it every morning, and we have Bible stories and history. But how is— Uncle Mike—in the service of God?"

"He gave up his life to God. But that is a story your Dada must tell you. You see, my loves, there are men who would rather work for Our Lord, among His poor creatures, than work for themselves. You must ask your Dada." Tim gazed down at his grandchildren with sorrow and anxiety. He took the photograph and extended it to Allan, who examined it without expression. Michael radiated peace and happiness upon the young Indians grouped about him; a small child sat upon his knee. He was the earth and holiness and all repose, and the bend of his stout body was implicit with protection and love. Now Allan saw why he had seemed ridiculous and plebeian in the clothing of ordinary

391

men. The habit he wore gave him stature, was part of himself, and it had permitted that which was in him to emerge with grace.

He looked down and saw DeWitt scrutinising him with an odd mixture of amusement and curiosity. He felt naked under that wise old regard on a very young child's face. He turned away. He had imagined what he had seen; five-year-old boys were still hardly more than infants. They did not have Satanic eyes. There was something wrong with a father who believed they had.

Tim led the way into his and his wife's bedroom, and proudly exhibited the chests he had made. On one of them was an object which Allan recognised, for he had given it to his parents two Christmases before. It was an alabaster statue about sixteen inches high, made in Italy. The image stood in an arched grotto, the wall of which was carved with a minute rosebush. It was a lovely thing, and light poured through its luminosity. Before it burned a candle in a red glass. Tony and Dolores exclaimed with pleasure as they stood before it. "Our Lady of Lourdes," said Tim. Again, he did not glance at Allan. "Your Dada gave it to us. You must ask him about it."

Tony looked over his shoulder at Allan. "But who is she, Daddy?" he asked. Allan hesitated. Tim said very gently, "She is the Mother of God. She is your mother, too. She loves you very much."

Tony asked no more questions. I should never have brought them here, thought Allan. I was a fool.

They went downstairs to the brick kitchen with its cool floor of yellow stone, its wide windows, homely table, black stove, and rocking-chairs. They could see the trunks and branches of old elms and oaks outside, dappled and streaked with sun, the pleasant dim lawns, the wide fields, wide sky, and far mountains. There is a difference between the mere absence of sound, and encompassing peace, thought Allan. His mother was pouring hot water from a copper kettle; it was like a small patch of sunlight in the kitchen. She had kept the teapot he had given her when he had been twenty years old, a dark brown thing with little clusters of white porcelain flowers scattered over it. She had set the table with a stiff white cloth, thick and unpretentious china, thin polished spoons which she had brought with her from Ireland, little sandwiches of watercress and ham, and the cakes which her family had loved, plain fat circles with a rich taste. She smiled timidly and shyly as the family came in, and with a gesture of her worn hand, she indicated places at the table.

His mother had never seemed full-bodied to Allan. He had thought of her as a shadow in the background of his life, always gentle and loving, but retreating. He could not recall that she had ever advanced an opinion; for the first time he wondered if she was able to read or write, for there was no memory in him of a book or a newspaper in her hands. Yet, thought Allan, I never knew it until now: she was all comfort and serenity, all through the damnable years of poverty and hunger and pain and fear.

He was glad that his children had been trained not to chatter. Jon and Norman, Estelle's boys, though seventeen and fifteen respectively, babbled like very young children when they were home from their school. They skylarked, pouted, had tantrums, shrilled, stamped, and ran like colts through the house—and competed for their mother. They appeared like giant but retarded infants, when with their nephews and niece, a ludicrous contrast painfully evident to Rufus. Yet, they were not really stupid young men; they led their classes at Groton in all their studies.

Tony, Dolores, and DeWitt sat sedately at the kitchen table in Tim's house, and Mary Marshall smiled faintly at them, her brown eyes softly beaming. She did not speak; she only passed cups and plates; she seemed to notice nothing. She listened to her husband as he spoke to her son of crops, of old Dan Boyle, of Michael. His voice was hearty and warm; occasionally he would run his rough hand tenderly over Dolores's long hair, smile at Tony, and glance with troubled question at DeWitt. Speech was not an urgent matter to Mary; she rarely found it necessary to talk. A smile was a substitute for a laugh, and when she smiled her tired face became radiant and alive.

Mary saw and understood everything. If there was pain in her as she gazed briefly and intermittently at her son, she revealed no sign of it. There Allan sat in his long, thin elegance, his striped white-and-blue blazer open over his lean body, listening with absent respect to his father. She refilled his half-empty teacup and appeared not to notice that he was eating nothing. But she thought to herself: He is not yet forty, my son, but there is a whiteness at his temples, and an agony in the lines of his face, and his shoulders are tired and his hands tremble. He is old with suffering.

Allan broke in on his father's confident boasting about his land, unaware that Tim had been speaking. "What is this letter from Mike?" he asked. "It sounded very mysterious, his knowing we were coming."

Tim's broad red face lighted up. "Ah, it is the saint he is! He knows everythin', our Mike." He fished in a pocket of his black coat and proudly produced a crumpled letter and gave it, with a flourish, to Allan. "I could tell you many things he wrote to us; it is the second sight—a miracle, he has."

Allan recognised the round neat writing of his brother on the cheap paper. The first page or two recounted his life in North Dakota among the Indian children, whom he taught and nursed and loved. Then there were family items, the thanking of his parents for the clothing for the parents of his charges, the food they had sent him, the prayers they had said for him, the money given to his Mission in his name. He promised to send them a "spiritual bouquet" from the children very soon, and he prayed for them constantly. He prayed for his brother, he wrote with simplicity. He charged his parents to do likewise.

Then the short and homely sentences ended. Michael wrote: "We were taught to love God and man, for if we love God and not man our prayers are unacceptable to Him. If we love only man, and not God, then we have fallen into the error of mere 'humanism.' However, I find it infinitely easier to love God than man, for one has only to look about him in the world of nature, the world of sunsets and sunrises, the cry of a bird in the forests at twilight, the springing of a flower in thick grass, the white winter hills under the moon, the glitter of a tree in the noonday sun, the scent of fields in midsummer, the blaze of lightning cracking asunder a black and stormy sky, to see and know God in all His Majesty, to adore Him with humility, rapture, and awe. He is All-perfect, and He less commands our love than inspires it. By His excellent works He is manifest. And that is the trouble.

"For it is by man's works that we find it hard not to detest him. At the altar, love for God comes to me in a flood, effortless, without struggle, a grace given to me freely and by no special merit of my own. But observation of man can easily lead to impatience, weariness, anger, loathing, and despair. The visible and the invisible God is there for him to see and to know and to worship. Yet he is blind, not with a physical blindness, but with a spiritual one. Man, the conscious, the aware, cast in God's image, has the darkness of hell in his soul, and almost everything he does is sinister. He is the relentless enemy of his brother, the tyrant of his brother, the oppressor of his brother. He is the sword lifted eternally against his fellow man. He is the hunter who craves blood; he is the creator of war, the burner of cities, the despoiler of the fields. He is forever in conflict with the world and the creatures of the world, and where he treads all things flee from him in terror. He, little lesser than the angels, is the only ugly thing in the spaces of Creation, for he shapes his spirit with his thoughts, and his flesh reflects the distortion."

Allan held the letter in his hands and thought: Yes, yes. He no longer felt the sheets in his fingers; he felt the roundness of a precious ball leaving them, sailing through the sunlight into the hands of a gross-faced enemy who had been bribed not to inflict pain. Tim was watching him, forgetting the children and his wife, and he thought: There is something terrible in the heart of my son.

Allan continued to read.

"These are the thoughts which come to me, unbidden at my prayers, unsought at my studies, uncalled at my work. I had no power, at first, to resist them. I prayed feverishly for delusion, for a blindness that I might not see what man is, for an illusion which would reconcile me to my brother. At last, I spoke to my Superior of it, without hope. And he told me there was a key to the black door which I had shut, in my knowledge, against my brothers. But I must find the key myself, with the grace of God. ' He who does not know that man is evil will never understand him, or love him,' he told me, for he had travelled this wasteland of rejection himself.

"So I prayed without rest, without sleep. I fasted; I prostrated myself. I wept to the silences. For I knew that without enlightenment I could not rid myself of my bitterness and grief. Once it came to me confusedly that I had once possessed the key, and had lost it. In a simpler day, when I did simpler work and had less contact with men, I had had the key and had not known that it was valuable beyond everything else to me. I had heard it a thousand times, turning in its lock; I had seen it imprinted on the pages the saints had written; I had seen it shining on the altar at Mass. Without knowing, I had watched its bright flicker in the eyes of tired Sisters, and priests, and unlettered men, in the eyes of my mother.

"Its name is compassion. A simple key, it is said. But it is the heaviest of all objects, the hardest to hold, the most painful to use. It can move a world; it can slip through the fingers like a straw in an angry moment. It has the power of an army, the fragility of a butterfly's wing. It is the way to all knowledge; the way of the saints. It is the imprimatur of God, set on the book of life. Without it, man is a devil; with it, he is an angel.

"I have found the key. But I must pray constantly, in dark moments, that I may not lose it again. For to lose it is to lose faith, to be shut out from the presence of God, to be an exile forever at war with all things."

Allan thought: To whom was this written? To me?

There was only a short ending to the letter, but it came vividly to Allan's eyes.

"On the next Sunday Allan will come to you, with his children, at about two o'clock in the afternoon, I think. Expect him, Dad, and be kind, as if he were a frequent visitor. He has not forgotten you, just as you have never forgotten him. There is a furious river between you, which began to flow when he was a child. You never understood, and neither did he, but I am beginning to know."

Very slowly, Allan refolded the sheets and laid them on the table. He stared at the floor, controlling himself, for the cold sweat was on him again, the trembling of his bones, the sense of weakness all through his body, the horrible depression and hopelessness. He had a sudden and awful craving for alcohol. He passed his damp hand slowly over his face. Tony and Dolores were watching him with anxious foreboding, but DeWitt was eating a cake. Allan had the conviction that his younger son had been regarding him closely for a long time, and that he was derisive.

"A very good letter," said Allan dully. He must have a drink; he must have it at once. He never drank in the presence of his children; he believed Tony and Dolores were unaware of his driving addiction, but he was convinced now, no matter how careful he was, that DeWitt knew. "A very good letter," he repeated. He stood up, and Tim, greatly alarmed, saw the sweat on his son's forehead. "May I see you alone a moment,

Dad?" asked Allan, and without waiting for a reply he walked from the kitchen into the small parlour, where early twilight, luminous and blue, was already filling the corners. He looked about him, alone for a few moments, at the round table his father had made, at the horsehair furniture, burnished into a soft glow, at the little fireplace ready with logs of apple wood, at the crude holy pictures on the violently flowered walls, at the oil lamps. Through the windows, carefully draped with his mother's lace curtains, he could see the mellowing fields, the first stain of scarlet in the sky over the darkening mountains. Now the silence was sweetly disturbed by the voices of birds, the movement of a cool breeze against the shutters, the cluck of fowl, the lowing of the cow coming home to her barn.

Tim entered the room, and he was carrying a bottle in a napkin, and a glass. He stood for a moment and he and his son regarded each other without speaking. Then Tim put the glass on a table and opened the bottle. The tawny whisky splashed noisily into the glass, and Tim did not control his hand. Still not speaking, he extended the liquor to his son. Allan took it, and his fingers were so eager that he almost dropped it; he put it to his lips and drank it all, without once pausing to breathe. Tim watched him, his face heavy with sorrow and understanding.

Tim lifted the bottle questioningly as Allan looked into the empty glass. "Another?" he murmured. Allan hesitated. A deep colour came into his face, settling into the emaciated hollows of his cheeks. But finally he extended the glass speechlessly, and Tim refilled it. This time, standing in the centre of the parlour, Allan drank more slowly and gratefully, keeping his eyes averted from his father.

"I always have a drink or two at this time of day," said Allan. "It—it gives me a lift when I am tired." He paused. Tim said nothing. "You don't know how damn' tired I get," Allan went on. "So much responsibility. . . ." He glanced furtively at the older man. "Aren't you having a drink with me?"

"Sure, and I am," said Tim. His voice was slow and old with grief. He went back into the kitchen and returned with another glass. "A man should never drink alone. It is a sign of despair, and despair is one of the mortal sins." He set his short bulk on a stiff chair, and his belly rolled out. His blue eyes were strong and bright in the shadows. "And won't you be sittin' and joinin' me?"

Allan sat down on the small horsehair love seat, and it pricked him through his clothing. But the trembling had stopped; the spasms had left his stomach; his brain was no longer fiery; the depression had begun to warm away. He sipped at his drink now, in order to prolong his sensation; he drank it as one drinks an anodyne. Slowly, one by one, his taut-strung muscles relaxed, and the aching in his neck and shoulders soothed itself into nothingness.

Embarrassed now, Allan said with an attempt at lightness, "You never kept whisky in the house, Dad, except at Christmas. Are you taking to the bottle?"

Tim swirled the liquor in the glass and answered in a low voice, "No, my son. But I knew you were comin' and I knew you'd want it."

Allan began to laugh a little. But Tim did not look at him. Silence came again to the room, like an observing presence. They could hear the children talking with Mary in the kitchen. Even DeWitt was speaking, and asking a question, and Mary's voice, tenuous and gentle, answered. Allan's laughter stopped abruptly. He put his empty glass on the table.

Then he said very softly, over and over, "Oh, my God; oh, my God, my God, my God."

The children talked little on the way home through the purple and crimson twilight. The twins seemed unusually thoughtful and perceptive in their attitude towards their father as the victoria rolled through the dimming landscape. Dolores held Allan's hand. When DeWitt said, "I don't think I like that place," Allan did not hear him, and only Tony's stern look quieted the little fellow.

They were almost to Portersville when Tony said, "Grandpa told me you have a fine voice, Daddy. He said you could sing like the angels, and when you talked everyone had to listen. I never heard you sing. He said you knew old Irish songs that told stories."

"Eh?" said Allan, turning his dulled eyes on his son. "Oh. Yes, I used to sing, when I was young. As you grow older you find less and less to sing about, and then you stop altogether. Long before you're dead, you are mute."

It was late when they reached home, and Allan climbed heavily up the stairs to his wife's rooms. Cornelia was sitting before her crystal, gilt, and silver dressing-table, which was softly lighted. Lamps bloomed on French tables and glimmered on the pale gold rug and white walls and carved white ceiling. Her chaise longue, heaped with coral pillows, showed where she had rested in the afternoon; beside it was a heap of papers, and her own special brief-case. Windows opened on the darkening chaos of mountains and river. She turned her head and smiled affably at Allan when he entered. "Late, aren't you, darling? Did you have tea at the Peales' or at the Purcells'?"

"No," he replied. "We didn't go to either place." He sat down on one of the gold-velvet chairs, and his body sagged. Cornelia inspected him more closely. She said quickly, for something had both startled and disturbed her, "Allan. Where did you take the children?"

He told her, speaking as if to himself. She listened, without interruption, to the lifeless recital, which was brief. Slowly, towards the end, she began to smile, her eyes round and mirthful, her mouth opening over her glistening teeth as though what she was hearing was both childish and ridiculous.

He lifted his head when he had finished, and when she saw his face she became grave. There she sat on her rose-satin stool, her mauve dressing-gown falling away from her heroic white neck and shoulders and arms. Her breast, half-revealed, had a pearly sheen in the lamplight, and her flowing red hair, cascading to her hips, gave her a gaudy appearance that was yet striking and magnetic.

She said, and her voice was light and bantering, "Well, it was a change, wasn't it, for the children?"

He was vaguely surprised. "You don't mind?"

"Good heavens, Allan, why should I?"

He knew by now, all about her mendacious democracy, and so he was more surprised to see that she was absolutely sincere in her exclamation. "Am I a snob like Pat Peale, or a pale aristocrat like my mother, or a carrier of Christmas baskets and clothing to the poor like Laura? Or a hard, simpering fool like Estelle?" Her voice was genuinely impatient. "I know all about my ancestors, the DeWitts. I think they were a sturdier race than the Fieldings, my mother's. They lived. I suppose your parents do, too. It's time the children learned there was something else in the world besides ' blood,' as Estelle calls it. Blood!"

He stood up and went to her, and put his hand on her shoulder;

she gazed up at him with her usual expression of mockery and deep love. Then, after a moment, she turned her head and kissed the back of his hand lightly. After this, she pushed him away with good humour. "What an idiot you are, my pet. I believe, in your own way, that you are a snob, too, like that awful Pat. I, personally, wouldn't give a cent to charity, nor does my heart bleed over the blessed poor, nor am I horrified at the thought of slums of unemployment, nor would I ever visit an orphanage or a poor farm or give a rag to cover any beggar's nakedness. Every man for himself. That's a law older than milk-sop charity. But, good God, what is wrong with your children seeing their grandparents, who are doubtless self-respecting and decent? Your father was an engineer; he might inspire Tony with some interest in what will be his holdings one of these days."

He put his arms about her big shoulders and pulled her head to his chest. He stroked the coarse and vital hair. "You make me ashamed," he said. "I think you are a more worthwhile person than I."

Again she pushed him away and laughed in his face. "Oh, no I'm not! I'm not a sentimentalist."

Her face glowed and shimmered with her mockery, and he caught, again, that puzzling wariness gleaming in her eyes, that derisive flash. But she only remarked, "I can smell that your father gave you something to drink. I suppose the children didn't guess; they missed the lovely odour of your peppermints. Change to another flavour, one of these days, my child."

He moved away from her, humiliated and sickened, and she watched him in the glass. He began to wander about the room, in his speechless and helpless shame. He paused by the chaise longue and picked up a few of the neatly-piled papers. Stock reports, quarterly reports, dividend reports, policy—he dropped them and they fluttered from his hands like old dried leaves. Dry and dusty, he thought, all at once. I am filled to the lips with dust; every crevice of my life sifts grey powder. I sleep with silt on my pillow; the air I breathe is grey. My footsteps crackle on old mortar fallen from the bricks of my hopes. He said unsteadily, "I am ashamed, but I must have another drink. No, I can't leave it alone. It helps me to . . ."

"What?" asked Cornelia softly, as he hesitated. She rose and went to him and pulled him to her with strength, but his arms hung by his sides. "Allan," she said urgently. "I love you.

You, and Papa, are all I have. Isn't my love enough? Isn't your work enough? Isn't your position, and all that you have done, and all that you do, enough?"

He felt the warmth of her large arms, but they brought him no comfort. He looked into her eyes and he was too beset to be moved because they were full of tears. "I know you love me, my dearest," he said. "But it isn't enough, Allan?" She dropped her arms and regarded him with deep consternation. "What is it you want?"

He appeared very ill, with the livid shadows under his high cheek bones, with the heaviness of his eyelids and the anguish of his mouth. He thought over her question, shook his head slowly, over and over. "I don't know, Cornelia. I want some meaning in my life, perhaps. You see, when I joined your father's company, the empire was already made, consolidated. All that can be done now is some more monotonous expansion, more improvements, more piling up of money. Your father— he has a sort of splendour about him, for he was an *entrepreneur* when he was younger. He built the road which I can only help him conserve. He has memories full of excitement; he battled on equal ground with giants. I am not the kind of man he is. I don't have the love for living he has. Once, I thought power was enough. I didn't know, then, that it would never be enough for me, even if, and when, I become president of the company."

She was frightened as she was rarely frightened. She repeated, with an edge of fear in her loud voice, "What is it you want?"

He turned away from her and whispered, "I don't know. God help me, I don't know."

He became aware that she was silent, not with her usual vibrating silence, but with a sort of stillness. The dinner bell rang with muted music through the house, and they did not move. He went to the window and leaned against it and saw the great white crescent of the moon standing like an uplifted sword on the black mountain below it. "Forgive me," he muttered wretchedly. He looked at his wife and saw that the high colour had left her face and that her features had a pinched look, "Cornelia, what is it you want? Tell me; perhaps it might help."

"I want what I have." She paused a moment. "I find almost every hour wonderful and exhilarating; I never let myself become bored. Life itself is enough for me."

2C

He listened with wonder as if to an astounding philosophy which he would never understand, which astonished him. He pondered on what his wife had said, then shook his head in bafflement. "I hear you, but I don't feel a single response to it, Cornelia. I never enjoyed living, I am afraid. Nothing excites me; nothing is an adventure." He did not speak for several long moments, then answered in a low tone, "Life is not enough for me."

"I was afraid of that," she said, and now her voice was full and hard in the room. "I suspected it, these last few years. And so did my father. You see, in a way, we are simple people, not complex, like you."

Cornelia was laughing now, and the laughter was not sympathetic. "Damn it, Allan, take off that infernal blazer and dress for dinner. You see, after all, one has to eat."

PART THREE

CHAPTER THIRTY-SIX

CORNELIA WROTE to her son Rufus Anthony in March, 1905: "We are all well, and the Riviera has been unusually warm and pleasant, and has done your grandfather a great deal of good. He has almost entirely recovered from his pneumonia, which he had in Paris. He appreciated your somewhat frantic cables, my dear, but really, they weren't necessary; he was never in much danger. Of course, he is seventy now, and one has to be careful. He hopes to be with us at Groton, when you are graduated this spring. Incidentally, we hear very seldom from DeWitt, but as he is with you there, I assume he is in good health.

"Jon and Norman are spending two or three weeks with us at our château here, or, I should say, they are spending them with their mother. She says she is quite exhausted over your grandfather's recent illness, but we had a very grand soirée last night. Jon invited quite a number of his weird friends from Paris, young American painters all supported by indulgent parents in America, and French painters who are being supported by the young Americans. His friends are ' *avant-garde*,' he says, and I am at a loss to know what he means. If it means daubing, striking poses, letting one's hair grow long and shaggy, arguing on peculiar political points of view, and hating everybody, especially those with money (including parents who support them), and deriding the great painters of the past, then these young gentlemen are indeed ' advanced.' And perhaps it is ' modern ' of them to dislike girls, and prefer each other's company. That is a subject, I believe, about which ' well-bred ' people do not talk, or write; one just ignores it and pretends it does not exist. Well.

"Norman has not patched up his old quarrel with Jon. He is becoming more and more the lap dog for Grandma Estelle. He seems happier since Jon has gone in for ' art,' and spends less time with his mother. Jon is twenty-seven, with an aversion for women, and Norman is twenty-five, and has an aversion for everybody except Grandma Estelle. There is a famous Austrian doctor visiting here, a Dr. Sigmund Freud, who has written several weighty books about strange mentalities, and I precipitated a furious row with Grandma Estelle when I suggested that her sons visit him for treatment. Now she complains to your grandfather that I have spread the scandal that her sons are 'insane.' This is quite untrue; my private thoughts are my own. The more one knows of life, the more amusing it becomes; sometimes it is hilarious.

"I am sorry that you still don't like Miles, who is in your form. After all, he is your second cousin, and you do like your Aunt Laura. Miles always seemed to me to be an especially intellectual and realistic young fellow, and I had hoped he would have a good influence on you, my dear, for there are times when you go off into dreams that have no substance. You do not mention Fielding, but, of course, you young men despise those in lower forms. You speak of Mary Peale's affection for you, and you sounded annoyed in your last letter. Well, the child is only fourteen, isn't she? And very pretty, too. You are both very young, but I am still hoping that you and Mary will come to an 'understanding,' as we said in my day. Possibly three or four years from now.

"I was more than a little surprised to gather from your discreet letter that you are disillusioned with Uncle Pat, of whom you were once so fond. Frankly, I was not censorious about this; I laughed. I know all about Patrick Peale, and he has grown more difficult with the years. But you still love Aunt Laura, and I am glad of that.

"We are sorry to hear that Grandpa Purcell has shown no improvement since his stroke last Christmas. But, after all, he is in his middle seventies, and one has to expect these things. You are always too hurt about too much.

"I know you miss Dolores, but she is doing very well in her school in Switzerland. We saw her a month ago, when she ran down on a holiday. She is very anxious about you, naturally. As she is seventeen, I have been seriously looking about for a suitable husband for her, preferably one with a title. I know this will make you angry, but I am more and more convinced that, because of her old-maidish, shy ways, she will cost us a pretty penny to marry off. I agree with you that she has some sort of beauty, but noblemen in Europe want something more than

406

that, preferably American dollars. When she was here we had a house guest, Lord Gibson-Hamilton, who is a distant relation of King Edward's. A rather birdy young man, with no chin and a big nose and a feminine Oxford accent, but a great catch, with a castle in Scotland, another near Windsor Castle, shooting boxes, a huge crest, distinguished noble and royal ancestors by the gross, and some sort of honorary position at Court. Forebears teeming under the floor of Westminster Abbey, too. He writes poetry, but that can be overlooked. Dolores dislikes him, and your father is quite violently opposed to him. These are small difficulties to overcome, and I never allowed difficulties to get in my way.

"And that brings me to your father, about whom I am considerably anxious. No, he is not ill, and shows no signs of another breakdown, though he drinks as much, or more, than ever. He was always moody, as you know; he is becoming moodier. He goes off on long walks. When he is not walking, he sits in his rooms overlooking the sea, and reads constantly. I can't imagine what he finds so absorbing in his books, for they are all about, or by, queer foreigners with such names as Hegel, Kautsky, Marx, and Engels. Jon has a similar library, and that is understandable, he being what he is. But why your father reads about those creatures is beyond me. Dinner sometimes becomes intolerable; he and Jon often engage in the most savage and obscure quarrels, which I confess bore and irritate me. Jon takes the stand that these writers are ' messiahs,' and he looks at your father in a very sinister way, as if your father were responsible for something which Hegel and Company appear to denounce endlessly in their books. Once he called your father ' the prey of superstition, a product of oppressive centuries.' Your father threw wine at him, not in the gentlemanly tradition of a mere glass, but a whole bottle! I almost collapsed with laughter; it was really very funny, and I was delighted that Jon suffered an enormous purple lump on his forehead as a result. Grandma Estelle had hysterics.

"Your father sometimes charges into your grandfather's rooms, armed with the books, and goes off into harangues in which the word ' danger ' occurs frequently. Fortunately, Grandpa has a sense of humour.

"I have written you at great length because I loathe letter-writing, and this makes up for the many weeks you have not heard from me. And it will have to last you until we go home to America in time for your graduation. Now I must really return to the huge stack of business papers which have just arrived."

A man adopts a philosopy suited to his own personality and needs, thought Allan Marshall. Now what, in God's name, has spewed up these philosophies, and these personalities, in the past fifty years or so? The red flags of warning fly from every page of these books, but those who should be terrified smile with wondering smugness at me, and yawn. If and when the bloody dawn stands up over their grand houses, it will be too late. I may be dead then. Why should I care? Possibly because I am an Irishman, and above all things I hate slavery and love freedom. Rufus calls them "abstracts," and when I read to him certain pages in these books, he looks at me as if I were not only amusing, but more than a little insane. He does not seem to understand that a fire lighted somewhere in Europe could devour the whole world. This is no longer an insular planet, and contagion spreads by wire, by the movement of peoples.

He sat upright in his chair, and suddenly remembered what Rufus deWitt had said only to-day, and with a comfortable and indulgent smile: "My dear boy—and you still seem only a boy to me—I am sure that if any of these philosophies ever engulfed the world, which you appear to believe, we, as very wealthy and powerful men, could come to terms with the propounders of them. We always do, all through the world's history. Do you remember what Frederick the Great said? 'I take what I will. There will always be enough professors to justify me.' And there will always be enough greedy madmen, in any kind of government, to protect us—if we grease their palms sufficiently."

Allan had cried, "But what of those who are not so powerful and so rich? What of the world of men who might be ruled by devils?"

Rufus had not answered immediately. He had only narrowed the still lively hazel of his eyes on his son-in-law and had contemplated him in a very strange silence. Then he had lifted his afternoon glass of port and had sipped at it reflectively. Finally he had said, "You have changed considerably, Allan, during the last ten years or so. I am not complaining of your work and your magnificent contributions to our company. Recall what you have just said: 'What of the world of men,' and so on. At one time you, yourself, would not have cared. Don't explain; explanations are tedious, and never tell the whole story anyway." He had sipped again, and again he had given Allan that curious long look. "You never knew my brother, who died when you were still a very young man. But you remind me of him, in some disturbing way. My brother Steve was a very good man." Rufus had laughed heartily. "I hope you won't become a ' good man,' too. I'm afraid, at my age, that I would find it overwhelming."

"We won't be spared; we won't ever be able to come to terms with these madmen," Allan had answered grimly. "For you see, it is a kind of religion to them, and nothing shakes a man in his religion."

Rufus had closed his eyes, affecting weariness. "Granting some of your wild premises, what have these foreigners to do with America?"

Allan had stood up, and he said slowly, "A great deal. Your son is one of their disciples, your son Jon. And there are thousands of young Americans, just like him, absorbing this poison in Europe, taking it home with them."

Rufus had opened his eyes, and he had stared at Allan incredulously. "You never gave him any religion," Allan had gone on bitterly. "You never taught him respect for his country, but only respect for money, which, never needing, he derides. A man has to have some religion. . . ."

"And what is yours?" Rufus had asked in the softest of voices.

But Allan had not replied. He had only left the room. When he had closed the door, he had heard Rufus chuckle.

The DeWitt château, on the vast wide promenade overlooking the ocean at Cannes, was situated between two enormous hotels, surrounded by exotic gardens and palms and bright green grass, the garden walls overflowing with the cool lavender of wistaria. In architecture, it was a felicitous blend of both Spanish and French, jalousies protecting balconies against the sun, the white mansion reflecting back the pure light from the sky, the red-tiled roof brilliant as a rose. All floors were of coloured tile: yellow, pale pink, soft blue or green, set in intricate designs and covered, here and there, by small oriental rugs. A white stone and marble staircase, fully twelve feet wide, curved massively from the circular hall to the three upper floors. The mansion had originally belonged to an Italian prince, and so the furniture, dark and heavy, shimmered with green and old gilt overlays in elaborate design, against brown, gold, or pink marble walls, upon which crests and enamelled shields and fine oil paintings and tapestries had been hung.

The whole effect, to Allan, was singularly oppressive, in spite of the narrow but blazing shafts of sunlight which shot through the pointed windows from noon to sunset. Property no longer impressed him in itself; there were days when the very thought of the hugeness of the DeWitt mansions gave him a crushing sensation, with the exception of the house in Portersville. The immensity of the DeWitt holdings had the effect of disorienting his mind, so that there were times when his skull felt empty and loneliness invaded the very bones of his body. Sometimes, in a despair which was huge but amorphous, he would say to himself: I have come to my end. He was never quite certain what he meant.

Though all the family walked every afternoon for hours along the gay promenade before the château, he rarely accompanied any of them. Sometimes he would excuse himself by wryly declaring that he could not endure the sight of the red-faced, sun-starved Englishmen grimly taking their constitutionals with tightly rolled umbrellas held in their hands as if in suspicious defiance of the Mediterranean sun. Cornelia would laughingly accuse him of being a provincial Irishman, and intolerant, and he would permit her to believe it. It was much less wearing than trying to explain to her that something was brewing in the world, something terrible and devastating, which he sensed with his uncanny Celtic intuition. Once, at a dinner in the mansion, he had committed the unpardonable offence of insulting a guest, a ponderous English nobleman, who, while smacking his lips over the after-dinner port, had elaborated on the growing industrial might of "The Empire," and had paused, graciously, to give a condescending bow in the direction of America. Allan, drunk as usual, had struck the table with his fist and had shouted, "Wake up, you fool! Why don't you read, instead of talking? Don't you know we are all on the verge of wars that will destroy all of us, if we don't begin to work at once?" Without waiting for reply, he had rushed upstairs and had brought down some of his books, and he had spilled them on the table before the alarmed guest, scattering silver and glasses in every direction. "It's all in there!" he had exclaimed. "Devastation. Ruin. Slavery.

Never Victorious, Never Defeated

The overthrow of constitutional governments. Through carefully calculated wars. Damn you, why don't you read?"

Allan's shunning of the promenade, the gardens, and human company, rose from his despair and his growing fear and the unknowable sorrow which afflicted him constantly. He hung the black coat of his depression on every insignificant hook. He worked, with Rufus, on the daily accumulations of business papers, which arrived with almost every post. His last break-down, which had occurred eight months before, could not be shaken off. He lived in a world pervaded by nightmares. Some-times he was aghast at the apparent changes in his personality over the years, and sometimes he had an inkling that there had never been any change at all, and that his soul had been immutable and fixed from birth, and that only youth and ambition had obscured, temporarily, the real drives and urges of his spirit. Now youth was gone; ambition had been fulfilled over and over with enormity, and there was nothing left—but himself . . . and the alcohol and the sedatives which briefly obscured that self from his agonised awareness.

If any place at Cannes gave him enjoyment, it was the balcony which ran before the windows of his apartment. At sunset, he would roll up the jalousies and sit in solitary sombreness on the balcony. He could forget the promenade before him; he could forget the phrenetic gaiety of Cannes, Juan-les-Pins, Nice, Antibes, Monaco. He could even forget Allan Marshall.

To-day, after his latest talk with Rufus, he went on to the balcony and sat down in a cushioned rattan chair. Exhaustion fell over him like a desperate illness, and his hands dropped over the arms of the chair and the fingers trailed on the tiles of the floor. He said aloud, "Defeat. I am defeated." Church bells began to ring over mountain and sea, and they were not sweet and entrancing to him, but a tolling.

The arm of the mountains to his right, grey-blue blurred shapes, extended itself over the flat and dimming waters. The faded coral of the sunset spread cloudily above the sea, brought into more distinctness the shadowy quicksilver of a promontory to the left, tumbling with the golden-beige, white and pink and terra-cotta of villas perched on its slopes. All stood in utter silence; the voice of the ocean was muted. Then, as Allan watched, the low metallic sun strode from the tinted clouds, and a broken pattern of copper ran over brightening water to a crimson horizon, limitless and cold. He sat there, not moving, vaguely aware of the church bells that seemed the articulation of his own anguish. Slowly, the sun dropped to the edge of the world, the copper and restless path was extinguished, the sea fell away into colourlessness, and its voice rose with the sound of unquiet. Moment drifted into moment. Now all was only a painting in silvery and diffused greys, the sea liquid ash, the mountains pearly and without substance. On the horizon, a single red spark quivered for a minute or two; a single scarlet beam struck the mist. Then, this too was gone.

Allan could not move, could not lift his fingers from the chill tiles. It was some instants before he became conscious that someone was knocking smartly on his door. It was a dreadful physical effort for him to speak in answer. It was even more of an effort for him to rise and go into his ponderous sitting-room, which was steadily darkening. He struck a match and clumsily lighted a gilt wall bracket as his door opened. He began to shiver, and his clothing and body felt clammy with the evening dampness.

"Well!" exclaimed Cornelia, on the threshold. "Aren't you dressed yet, Allan? How tiresome of you. I saw you sitting on your balcony nearly an hour ago, from the garden. Have you been sitting there all that time?"

"All that time?" repeated Allan dully. "I thought it was only a few minutes."

Cornelia said with brisk impatience, which hid her anxiety, "It was nearly an hour. Really, Allan, you should be dressing now for the dinner at the Sainte Germaine's. Where's Antoine, for God's sake?"

"I told him not to come until I rang for him," Allan, though still not yet fifty, moved to the bell rope like an old and feeble man, and pulled it listlessly. Cornelia compressed her lips, took up the box of matches and quickly lighted the lamps, which immediately flooded the big room with soft light. She said, "And sitting there in the evening chill in just your shirt sleeves. Do you want to be ill again?"

He did not answer. He only stood on the dark red and blue oriental rug, surrounded by the weighty gilt and polychrome Italian furniture, and ran his hands through his thick grey hair, dishevelling it. He was very thin, and his broad shoulders drooped with chronic weariness. He dropped his hands, and they hung at his side, tremulous and twitching. "I'm sorry," he muttered. His emaciated face glistened like a skull in the lamp-light. He tried to smile. All the fierceness of his black eyes had vanished years ago, had been replaced with cinders. Only his bony and aquiline nose, large now since his loss of flesh, still jutted arrogantly from the ruin of his face. It was, thought Cornelia, like the slender marker on a grave, which testified that here had once been a man. For an instant her own fine body sagged with the nearest thing to despair she had ever experienced. She went, with a rustle of silk and a waft of perfume, to Allan's carved Italian desk and put her hand on the neat mound of papers. "You've had too much of a burden lately, my darling. But Papa is well enough again to take up considerable of it. I'm proud of you. All this to-day! When you are supposed to be enjoying yourself."

"I never enjoy myself. I never did," said Allan.

He's in another of his moods, thought Cornelia with alarm. She made herself smile indulgently, and came close to him, her head tilted sideways. Before she could speak, the French valet entered discreetly. "Go away," Allan commanded. "Come back in five minutes."

Cornelia pointedly lifted the lid of her jewel-encrusted watch on her breast. "All right, Antoine. Just five minutes." She sighed.

She waited, but Allan stood there in silence, forgetting her, distractedly rubbing at his head, staring at the floor. At thirty-nine, in the gentle lamplight, she appeared not to have acquired years. She wore a soft cream-coloured gown of old silk and pale yellow lace caught tightly at the narrow waist with a stomacher of intricate gold and yellow canary diamonds and opalescent pearls. The stuff floated about her splendid figure like the garments of a goddess. Her throat gleamed with yellow diamonds and pearls, and there was no line on its smooth surface. The still violently red and springing hair stood above her forehead in a blazing pompadour, glittering here and there with diamond combs and pins. From her there exuded the indomitable vitality that could never be quenched by time, for it sprang from her spirit.

She carried a big fan of yellow ostrich plumes on her wrist, and she lifted it abstractedly and fanned herself for a moment as she studied Allan. The gaslight near which she stood flickered, then brightened, revealing her face vividly. Her face was tighter,

413

more strongly chiselled than in youth, harder and more astute, cynical lines about a mouth which depended these last few years on paint rather than on young blood for its colour, her cheeks rouged expertly but lacking their original roundness and the flare of natural tint. However, nothing could extinguish the power, the light, the indomitable passion of her character fully revealed in her eyes. Nothing but death would ever quiet or subdue them, or drain from them their bawdy gleam and strength.

Allan said, as if to himself, "Why do we have to go out?"

"Let's not be disagreeable, dear," replied Cornelia in a coaxing voice.

"You talk as if I were a child," Allan answered, and his voice rose on a note she dreaded. He looked at her with a recurrence of his wildness, and the burned eyes became alive again momentarily. He reached out and seized her gloved hands and held them fiercely. "Cornelia, what are you? Who are you? Tell me!"

Oh, God, she thought hopelessly. Is it beginning again? She made herself answer tenderly, "Why, darling, I'm Cornelia deWitt Marshall, your wife. You've asked me that so often."

He threw her hands from him. "But you've never answered me." He sat down in one of the gilded monsters and averted his head.

Cornelia had become familiar with this sudden quiver about her heart, which annoyed her. She knelt before her husband and put her jewelled hand on the arm of the chair. She made herself smile widely, conscious of the inexorably ticking watch on her breast. "I have; over and over. But you've never listened, my dear. And coming down to it, and being a little metaphysical, which I loathe, how can anyone answer such questions, not knowing the answers?"

He listened with an alertness which gave her hope. He regarded her with sudden astonishment. He reached out timidly after a moment and touched her neck. He said, "Cornelia, I never knew you had such thoughts, that you : . ." His feeble smile was pathetic, his eyes eager and seeking.

Damn, must I have another role, too, in addition to all the others I have taken on? thought Cornelia with amused ruefulness. Must I be yearning and significant and soulful, implying all sorts of weird spiritual nonsense?

Despite her impatience and secret amusement, and because she loved him with an amazing depth, she made her head droop. She sighed. She bit her lip theatrically. She forced her broad shoulders to sag. She was a picture of a beautiful and invincible woman undone by an assault on a hidden and sensitive spirit concealing itself beneath jewels and rouge and silk and feathers. "I am very proud, my dear," she murmured. "I never believed it was fair to inflict one's moods and uncertainties and fears on another, especially not on one you love." She was repeating, verbatim, lines from a very emotional and flamboyant play she had seen in Paris, but which fortunately, Allan had not attended.

Allan's hands were on her shoulders now, desperately gripping, and she winced. She thought: I must stop this nonsense immediately, or I'm going to be in for endless years of soul-searching and soul-moods and soul-communion and other ridiculous things, and one of these days I won't be able to keep from laughing right in his poor face. "Cornelia!" Allan cried. "You do understand." He lapsed into rapid incoherence, the words stumbling from him. "All this time. You see, in the beginning, there was the illusion, or perhaps the reality. I had union with the work; it was something my hands could do, something my feet could stand in! There's a story about the Titan who had to keep in touch with the earth or he'd lose his strength—his existence. Contact. You do see? Now it's monstrous." He paused for breath, strangled, and coughed, still holding her. She could feel the pulsing of his blood, frantic, struggling, as he fought for expression. "In the beginning, it was a thing I could handle, even when I first came in. But not now. It's sucked away my identity. If we all died to-morrow, it would go on, like a nightmare Frankenstein monster, clicking away, rolling, steaming, unaware we were dead. We aren't needed, your father and I, or anyone else."

As Cornelia was intelligent and shrewd, she had some awareness of what her husband meant, and she became thoughtful, looking up into his face. But the sense of power in her was only stimulated and made exultant by his words. And she also had her suspicions that this was not the whole story of his agony.

She had no need to pretend, for she was no longer amused. This was serious. She was convinced that subtle action at this moment might result in new health of mind for her husband, a lifting of the horror which was crushing him, and which existed only in his own imagination.

She took Allan's face between her firm palms and looked into his eyes. "I said you were selfish, my dear, and I repeat it now. You are selfish. Most of us are incapable of expressing ourselves. But, out of decency, out of consideration, we hold our tongues, and try to make a living of smooth and pleasant surface so that life can be tolerable for all of us."

He wound his fingers about her wrists and gazed at her with such naked despair, and with such intense lostness, that she was shocked. She glanced away, almost ashamed. The fingers tightened about her wrists, and when she looked at him again she was even more ashamed. His face had changed; it had lightened with tenderness and compassion and with something that was like joy. "I'm sorry, darling," he said, as if controlling some inner weeping. "I've been callous. I never understood you."

She said quickly, "You can help me and help yourself, by not speaking of this again." She laughed a little. "We have others to consider, too."

He bent his head and laid his cheek against hers with a gesture of hunger, and she forgot herself and held him tightly in her arms. One did not mock, unnecessarily, the pain of a child, no matter how a damned watch was ticking on and no matter how imminent a dinner hour. She loosened herself from Allan's grasp, and rose, shaking out her silk and lace. He sat, looking up at her so tenderly that his expression, to her, was practically fatuous. "You are right, Cornelia," he said, and there was new firmness in his voice. "I've been selfish; I never knew."

Lightness, in this "understanding," was now a necessary touch. But even while she began to smile, to speak, Allan's valet, a small, rapid man, came into the room hastily, carrying a yellow envelope in his hand. He bowed to Cornelia, and said to Allan with excitement, "Monsieur! A cablegram! From America."

Allan, bemused, took it. Cornelia said, "Business, no doubt. Don't bother about it now. We are so late."

But Allan, his hands no longer tremulous, the muscles of his face no longer twitching, was already tearing open the envelope. "But business is business," he said, and he actually laughed. "Just a moment, Cornelia."

Idly, she leaned against him to read. The cablegram was from Tony, their son. "Please return home at once. Doctors advise it. DeWitt has infantile paralysis. He is at Portersville with me. Paralysed in right leg, very ill. Love."

Cornelia uttered a sharp loud exclamation. Her first thought was; Papa. Her second: We shall miss Paris in the spring. It was only when Allan rose, his face ghastly, that she remembered that it was his son who had been stricken, his peculiar, unlovable, and unknowable son. And it was even later that she remembered that this was *her* son, also, possibly dying in Portersville.

The vesper bells had long ago died on the black sea, but Allan heard them again, a jangle, an imminence, a roar and a pounding in his ears. There was nothing else in his ears but the bells, and through them, piercing them, cried one agonised voice: "Lord, have mercy upon us . . . Lord, have mercy upon us . . . Christ, have mercy upon us . . . Christ, have mercy upon us . . . Lord, have mercy upon us. . . ."

CHAPTER THIRTY-SEVEN

CORNELIA HAD acquired a good-humoured tolerance and respect for the little fat monk who was her husband's brother. She found herself, to her humorous surprise, actually confiding in him when they walked together through the grey-green April twilights, pausing now and then to admire the golden buds of the daffodils leaning against the cold spring wind or the red stars of the maples standing against the greenish sunset sky. Brother Michael was such a "quaint" person, his head hardly reaching to her shoulder. He was kind; he was understanding. He was gentle, and sometimes he joked and made her laugh. But more than anything else he emanated calm confidence and serenity and a kind of wry wisdom which Cornelia appreciated. Estelle might complain that their friends would consider his frequent presence very queer, and "truly, we have worked so hard not to let others know of Allan's background; so Popish, so vulgar, so unacceptable." Cornelia enjoyed Michael's company, and Rufus frequently asked for him. There was an earthiness in father and daughter which responded to the earthiness of the little monk. To Allan's amazement, there was even a kind of rapport between the three. He could not comprehend it.

Upon returning from Europe after twelve days of endless travel by rail and by ship, the family had found Michael assisting the nurses in the care of young DeWitt. Tony had quite simply informed them that he had asked his uncle to come. In the confusion of the homecoming, the consultations with a battery of physicians from New York and Baltimore, the comings and goings of teams of nurses, no one had thought to ask Tony why he had sent for this smiling, brown-faced monk, and why Michael had responded. It seemed quite natural to everyone, except Estelle and Jon and Norman, for him to be present. After all, was he not a species of nurse, himself? He came each day, travelling in a dusty trap, and it was not for some days that anyone gave a thought to sending for him in one of the DeWitt carriages, with two black horses and silver harness, and coachmen.

He must return to the Dakotas in two days, he informed Cornelia to-night. And then it was his hope that he would be sent again to foreign fields. He spoke tranquilly; his life and work were at God's disposal. Cornelia paused to admire a clump of narcissus and to bend to look into their fragile golden hearts. She said, "The only time I think there might be a possibility of God is in the spring." She touched a red tulip gently as she went on. "An uncomfortable thought. God can quite ruin one's private life if you permit Him to enter. And I'm very satisfied with my private life."

Yes, thought Michael, you are. He conceded, with unhappy surprise, that there are actually people in the world who have never felt a need for God, or mourned at His absence in their lives, or were even aware of His presence.

"Well," said Cornelia, examining a cluster of lilac bushes with spears of closed buds, "it is a great relief to all of us that DeWitt is getting better. I need not tell you, Michael, that the last report that he'll never walk again has been terribly upsetting, particularly to his father. DeWitt is such an odd boy, but he is my favourite, though I don't become as emotional as Allan does about his crippling. DeWitt will always find a way to dominate his world, even from a wheel-chair." She smiled down at Michael. "Do you think I am an unnatural mother because I don't go around weeping and wailing?"

"I never judge anyone," replied Michael. "No, you are not unnatural, Cornelia. You are just yourself. However, I don't concur with the doctors. DeWitt will walk again, either on crutches or with canes. I'm sorry he doesn't like me, but when

418

I told him this morning that he would walk, he said he was glad there was someone around him who had some sense."

Cornelia smiled. "He was always a boy with a lot of will. I suppose," she added meditatively, "that something good comes out of every calamity. A foolish aphorism, I always thought. But Allan has recovered amazingly from his last nervous break-down since DeWitt was taken ill and we returned home. I simply don't understand him."

They walked on. Michael was silent for so long that Cornelia was about to speak of something else. Then Michael said in a low voice, "Allan is the kind who is at his best in the most desperate crises, and when he is fighting something tangible."

"Business takes an enormous amount of his time," said Cornelia. She hesitated. "All these breakdowns, four of them in ten years, and dreadful! I never understood. I thought it was overwork. But they usually occurred when any crisis had long passed."

Michael waited. He looked up at her with his calm brown eyes, so clear and so unreserved. Birds were lacing the darkening sky; their sweet calls and insistent shrilling filled the mountain silence. Now from the earth rose an almost overwhelming odour of passionate life. "Tell me," said Michael, when Cornelia, with a movement of restlessness, was about to move away.

"I detest dramatisation, emotionalism, stripping yourself or others naked and begging the world to look at your nakedness," she said. "It—it is almost obscene. It makes me very un-comfortable, and I am embarrassed by——"

"By Allan," said Michael, when she paused.

"I love him, believe me. And, though we would not agree, I understand him very well. We knew all about each other. I thought it was enough; why isn't it enough, for God's sake?"

"Perhaps what Allan attained was not his real aim," said Michael. Cornelia turned on him with astonishment, her grey flannel skirt whirling about her, her red hair rising above her head like a fiery crest. Then she cried vehemently, and with hoarse anger, "Then what, in God's name, *is* his real aim?"

"I'm afraid he doesn't know what it is, consciously, and neither do I."

Cornelia stood there against the sky, large and lusty, and Michael could see the uncertain hardness of her face. She began to tap her foot on the wet grass. Then she laughed shortly, and shook her head. "Nine months ago, when he was very ill, the doctor drugged him heavily, and he didn't know where he was, or even what he was. He began to talk to the doctor in the voice and words of a child. He said, 'I am going to be a priest, Dada. I knew it this morning, after my First Communion.' Michael, what is the matter? Have I said something . . .?"

The brown of Michael's face had paled to a luminous pallor. "Please," he begged in a stifled voice. He moved off a few feet, and stood with his head bent. Cornelia approached him after a few moments and said anxiously, but trying for lightness, "Something changed his mind. Children get odd ideas, but discard them. There is nothing to be dramatic about, is there? As Allan grew up he wanted something else, apparently."

"I am wondering what changed his mind; I am wondering what happened to him," said Michael. He clasped his hands across his black-robed pudgy belly, and the knuckles whitened. Cornelia studied him narrowly.

There was no avenue to this robust and vital woman, so far as he was concerned. She lacked sympathy, sympathy in the real meaning of the word. Besides, there was an agony in Allan which would forever be beyond her capacity to comprehend. So he chose a more superficial explanation, which would be acceptable to her and which contained some truth.

"Let me put it this way, Cornelia. Most young men who attain sudden success, an overwhelming success, as Allan did years ago, inherited the means or position to attain it. They have had a background of fine schools, fine homes, money, leisure, other diversions, pleasure, and interests. Once attaining great power and position they accept them naturally, for no real strain or striving has been attached to them.

"But those *entrepreneurs* like Allan had nothing in their backgrounds but poverty, almost satanic ambition and determination, and lust for power. Nothing was of any other interest; gracious society, recreation, the company of secure people, the pleasant joys of relaxation, travel, pleasure in sheer living—these had never been in their lives, and when these things entered they were not attuned to accepting them and enjoying them. They were even, to these men, an irritating waste of time." Michael stopped, and sighed heavily. "And when their goal was obtained, they had only two choices before them: gaining even more power, world without end, or dying of frustration when they consciously, or unconsciously, realised that this was not what they had wanted at all, that it gave them no delight, and the world they had attained was empty of everything. They had narrowed their existence; like a projectile, they were trained on only one target."

He walked on, and Cornelia followed, lifting her skirts from the cold dew. "I can offer no advice except patience, Cornelia, and kindness, and love. If you can't understand, at least pretend you do." He wondered if he should talk to Cornelia about Tony, but decided against it. This was a resolute and inexorable woman, and Tony was only seventeen, with an almost abnormally developed sense of duty. He did say, however, "Tony has been a great comfort to my father since my mother died two years ago. He always visits Dad in the summer and on his vacations."

"Tony is a very serious boy," said Cornelia absently. She was aware that Michael had been telling her very portentous things, and she was grateful for his kindness. But she was more impatient with Allan than ever. Something had not been conveyed to her by this plump and gentle monk, and she suspected that it had been withheld in mercy. This annoyed her, and humiliated her.

"I have decided to begin walking. Now," said DeWitt to his mother on a day in late November, after the family's return from Newport.

"Good. It's about time," replied Cornelia briskly.

She did not believe in pampering the sick; she never entered DeWitt's room for the sentimental reason of comforting, cheering, or amusing him. She went on: "I've been coming into this room just waiting to hear from you when you are going to walk. And, incidentally, I'm not going to help you."

DeWitt was not wounded by this statement. He sat up in his large bright room overlooking the mountains, propped up in bed by many pillows. Against all that whiteness, his dark and gnomelike face, his sharp features and his piercing black eyes, his delicate black skull and his brown hands, were thrown into strong relief. He had suffered almost intolerably for several weeks, but only the tightly-drawn skin on his small face, the short deep line between his eyes, betrayed the pain he had endured in silence and resentment. Cornelia, studying him with a friendly smile, thought: He was never a little boy at all. Even as a baby he was an old man. At sixty, he will look almost exactly as he does now, at fifteen. He is ageless.

As DeWitt was incapable of loving anyone in the full meaning of the word, he did not love his mother. He thought her gaudy, too large, coarse, and common. Nevertheless, he sensed that in her was a power that could never be quenched or overthrown easily. He was well aware that he was her favourite child, a favouritism mixed not with real maternal love but with a kind of respect for him for being what he was. They understood each other perfectly.

"Well?" said Cornelia, smoothing her violet-velvet thighs with her big white hands. "When do you start?"

"Now," he repeated in the low flat voice that was one of his characteristics. He threw back the silken quilts and fixed his old eyes on his mother. She regarded him with calm curiosity and made no movement. His nurse had been sent from the room; they were alone. Cornelia said, "You know, of course, that that leg is shrivelled and shortened, and weak, though you can move it a little. You must allow for that."

He did not reply, but he smiled his small and saturnine smile of contempt. "Don't start pitying me," he said.

"Don't be a fool," answered Cornelia without rancour.

He swung his left leg to the edge of the bed; his right followed with a feeble and jerking motion. He regarded it with detestation. Now he just sat there and concentrated on the miserable member, and Cornelia watched. The boy did not move, but slowly his sallow forehead became moist, his yellowish mouth tightened, his thin nostrils flared. Cornelia was filled with admiration, and she became a trifle breathless. Will was in action, almost visibly. She leaned forward, not speaking.

In complete silence, DeWitt slipped towards the floor, his tense little hands gripping the side of the bed. A long shaft of wintry sunlight struck through the wide window and enveloped the boy, lay redly in the folds of his white nightshirt, fell across one taut cheek, bathed his legs. Now the small dark feet were on the floor, the right wrinkled and bending. All DeWitt's concentration was turned upon it, all his will commanding it to support him. Some moments passed. Then, almost imperceptibly, the foot straightened out, wrinkle by wrinkle. Its dead sallowness became infused with living blood. The knee became rigid, instant by instant. The sweat on DeWitt's forehead began to run down his face like tears, gathered in the corners of his mouth.

Now DeWitt was pushing himself away from the bed with his hands, inch by inch. Then he was standing, unsupported. Cornelia held her breath. Her son stood there, swaying, livid, his hands clenched and held away from his emaciated body in order to balance himself. Cornelia said very quietly. "Good." He lifted his eyes, so fathomless and yet so flat, and looked at her, and she smiled.

He continued to sway and his colour was frightful. His mouth was so compressed that the lips disappeared and left only a wide and narrow slit in his face. He was giving his next command, and his leg was frantically trying to obey. He took one short step, tottering, not with his strong left leg, but with the right. He staggered, fell sideways, and caught at the bed. He pushed himself away from the bed, stepped forward with his left foot. This gave him more balance. Then, step by step, limping, bending sideways, he moved into the centre of the room. He spoke for the first time: "I'll need a cane. The leg is too short." His tone was uninterested, as if speaking of another person and not himself.

"Your grandfather has a dozen or more," said Cornelia. "There's one with a gold head, wide and bent. Old Mr. Regan gave it to him years ago. He must have been in a sentimental mood when he had it inscribed in Latin: ' Not even hell can prevail against the human will.'"

The boy stood in the centre of the room, weaving, sweating, the shrivelled leg straight beneath his nightshirt. Short of stature though DeWitt was, bearing all the marks of long suffering, thin and yellowish and contracted of face, unprepossessing, even ugly, there was yet about him a profound dignity. He said, "Yes. I'd like that cane." He smiled at his mother, and she smiled back broadly.

He turned slowly and made his way back to his bed. He climbed into it. He did not permit himself to fall in exhaustion against his pillows. He wiped away his sweat, folded his handkerchief neatly, and laid it beside him. He pulled the quilts over him, arranging them as neatly as he had arranged his handkerchief. He commanded his environment, and it fell into sharp and angular folds about him.

Then, as if he had not performed something close to a miracle, he said, "How is Dad these days?"

"Splendid," replied Cornelia. She went to the window and looked down at the tumbled blackness of the mountains heaving against the crimson sky. "He evidently can't stand what he calls ' idleness.' In some way, Portersville is his base of operations: he thinks he is really working when he is here. Like," she added, remembering that conversation with Allan in March, "a Titan needing to touch earth for his strength. Perhaps"—and she turned and looked at DeWitt curiously—" we also have our own delusion."

"It operates handily for us," said DeWitt. He picked up a glass of water and sipped it. Cornelia, with pleasure, noted the pronoun and was gratified. He was not unconscious of the flattery he had extended to his mother, and he nodded at her. "Why do you haul him around, all over the world? Let him stay here. Grandpa is failing rapidly, and I"—he paused and looked again at his mother—"am still only fifteen."

Cornelia burst out into one of her loud and boisterous laughs. "You are forgetting Tony," she said derisively.

"Tony," repeated DeWitt. He lifted his folded handkerchief and contemplated it. Then he tossed it from him delicately. "Don't you know about Tony? He isn't interested in the railroad. Does he ever go down to the switchyards or accept invitations from Grandpa to visit our offices here, in Philadelphia, or New York, as I have done? I think he is interested in something else. While I was"—he paused to consider his illness with distaste and disgust—"incapacitated, he would have long walks and talks with our monk-uncle. I could see them from my window, and hear them muttering downstairs, very cosy."

"What are you trying to imply?" asked Cornelia.

"I think he's influenced Tony for a long time, since they first met about ten years ago. Tony's ' got religion,' as the quaint saying is. While we were at Groton together, he attended some Romish church every Sunday. One of the fellows told me."

Cornelia was alarmed and dismayed. "What does that matter? Of course, it would be ridiculous. . . . I never interfere with the religion of others, and if any of my children should want to be a Buddhist or a Mohammedan, or a Roman Catholic, that would be none of my affair. Anyway, what has that got to do with the railroad, and Tony's interest or lack of interest in it?"

DeWitt permitted himself to lean back against the pillows. "It's my opinion that Tony wants to be a priest."

Cornelia gasped. "Don't be an idiot, DeWitt!" She stood there, lushly shaped and magnificent in the violet velvet of her gown, her red hair catching the last light of the sun. How over-coloured she looks, thought DeWitt fastidiously. Like a florid painting by an Italian amateur who has gone mad among his paints. "Why get in Tony's way, Mother, if that is what he wants? You are always so tolerant, you know." He squinted at her. "Some of the best people, I understand, are Catholics these days. Or"—and he stopped to study his mother—"are you afraid of some kind of upheaval in my father?"

Why, the little monster! thought Cornelia. He puts his monkey hands right down into your vitals and tears at them. He knows too much.

She said, "DeWitt, have you been giving Tony some of your hypocritical encouragement, for your own ends?"

"I?" he asked disdainfully. "I've always admired him more than anyone else in the world, but the compliment isn't returned. I have seen Romish books in his room, and when I asked him about them, he would not answer me. Why don't you ask him, yourself, when he comes home for Thanksgiving?"

"I certainly shall," replied Cornelia. She scrutinised the sick boy, and her smile was ugly. "Quite a little schemer, aren't you, angel?"

"Thank you," said DeWitt with the utmost gravity. "It runs in the family, doesn't it? And now that we're talking frankly, Mother, don't you think I'd do better than Tony, anyway?"

She walked to the door with a rich rippling of her skirts. She paused on the threshold and turned her head over her shoulder. DeWitt was smiling. In spite of herself, and her anxiety and dread, she could not prevent herself from smiling in return. "That was quite a display this afternoon, and I admired it."

"You know, Papa, that you are allowed only one cigar a day," Cornelia said to her father as she sat with him in his room before dinner. Yes, Rufus was failing; he was almost visibly losing flesh. Wrapped in a soft quilt, and still dressed in a silk robe, he had not as yet prepared to go downstairs after his afternoon nap. But as he leaned back in his chair, smoking with pleasure and care, his vitality still seemed immortal. His white hair was still thick and rose crestlike on his head, and his eyes sparkled with golden youth and virility. When he smiled, his smile was still ripe and urbane, and there was none of the slow infirmity of age about him, no vagueness or weariness of mind, no difficulty with memory or reflection.

He waved his hand affectionately at his daughter. "Never mind my cigar, dear. A *non sequitur*, after what you've just been telling me about DeWitt. He has a measure of us in him, combined with something else. Cold. Almost vicious. He doesn't take the joy we take in scheming and planning. He lacks the capacity for pleasure—not Allan's lack, which comes from his never having had pleasure in his young years, but a kind of despising of lightness and gaiety." Rufus chuckled, still richly. "Allan, if I am right, wanted power to satisfy some hurt in him, some vengeance. But DeWitt wants it just as a thing in itself. And he'll get it, mark my words."

He exuded a huge fog of smoke. "Yes, he'll get it. It comforts me to know that I'll have continuity in this boy. But he's not my favourite. Not any more. Tony is the one, and I want him with me to my last day. A wonderful boy. Now about this priest matter. I don't believe it, Cornelia."

Cornelia opened her jewelled case and took out a cigarette. She tapped it on the back of her hand, and leaned forward for her father to light it. "I noticed something remote in Tony this time, something withdrawn. And he is becoming thin and pale. He doesn't want to hurt us, but he's being pulled somewhere."

The sky over the mountains had turned a deep purple, slashed with brilliant yellow and rose. Rufus contemplated it. A strange, faraway look settled on his face, a kind of transparency. Seeing it, Cornelia was frightened. She put her hand over her father's; the fingers were cold. She got up and poured two glasses of brandy, and gave one to her father. "Damn the doctors. Brandy always was our specific." Rufus took the glass with an absent smile and began to sip. Cornelia waited.

"Suppose the worst came to the worst, and Tony did become a priest," said Rufus. "I'm too old now to worry about any reaction among our alleged friends. I'm too old to tell a man he is a fool if he is drawn to any religion. I only ask of him that he doesn't annoy me, fanatically, with his convictions. A priest in the family even amuses me in a way, except for the fact that I don't

426

want to lose Tony's company, though he'd never leave me until . . ."

"Don't talk like that!" said Cornelia with such a sharpness in her voice that her father looked at her.

"Well," he said, and his voice was moved. "In the way of nature . . . I won't speak of it if it distresses you. But, my darling, it isn't so much Tony you are worried about. What is it?"

Cornelia got abruptly to her feet and stood by the fire. "Allan," she said almost inaudibly. "It would shatter him."

"He was once a Catholic, child."

"But he isn't, now. He thinks he is not, but he is a churning chaos of emotions, and it is getting worse all the time. When we heard about DeWitt, in Cannes. . . ." She stopped and drew a deep breath. "You can't shake off your childhood. It comes roaring in on you, with everything terrible that ever happened to you, under stress. I read about it in a book by that doctor named Freud, and though I discounted it, I was struck by certain things about Allan. . . . Thank God, my childhood was pretty much what my life is now, and it is all of one piece. That's not so with Allan."

"I see," said Rufus very quietly. Then, as always, he was stung with jealousy. "You love Allan very much."

CHAPTER THIRTY-EIGHT

WHILE LAURA PEALE waited for her husband to answer, she watched him, and her thoughts, distressed and melancholy, became rapid and confused. He is four or five years older than Allan, but in some ways he appears much younger—fifty-two, white just at the temples, hair still thick and brown and curling, face lined and seamed; yes, but the lines express so little, as if put there by accident—— Why did I never see it before? He looks like an ageless Puritan, fanatical, frustrated, and made coldly fiercer by his frustration. I should not be thinking so, my husband. . . . It is his small stature which makes him seem so much younger than—but no, he actually appears old—I am full of confusion. . . . He is a stranger to me; we were always strangers; did I ever love him? Yes, I think so. But not for a long time, a very long time; he has no heart, no real heart; I never knew. . . .

They were sitting in Patrick's library in their house on Mountain Heights, some few miles from the DeWitt home. The house had been furnished by Patrick; Laura's suggestions had been ignored. I should have known, then, that he had no respect for anyone but himself, thought Laura, now. He is, to himself, the rare human being incapable of making mistakes. A tyrant. Dogmatic. He should never have been in the Senate. I am glad he was defeated the last time. Yet, so blameless, so righteous. The house resembles him; thin, cold, austere, with windows that seem to repel even the hottest summer sun or spring warmth; I have never been comfortable here, in spite of the furnaces and the fires. I have always hated this house, the dusky, lean furniture, the tapestries, the dim draperies, the faded old rugs which were never brilliant even when new, the sombre paintings. All the corridors are narrow and ghostly, and filled with echoes. A Pharisee's house; the mirrors seem to hold only his own image.

"There is no need to become emotional, my dear," said Patrick. He wore a crimson velvet smoking jacket, though he did not smoke, and his elegant feet were stretched towards the fire this cold November day. Spectral drifts of grey snow blew across the windows; the chimney howled with wind, and the grey mountains stood at a distance in the grey air.

"I thought I was discussing all this very quietly," said Laura. Her fine black hair was a shadow on her cheek and neck. She regarded her husband without expression, and her large grey eyes were very still, her folded hands motionless on her knee. Patrick, watching her for signs of "weakness" so that he might reprove her, shifted in his chair. He would never have admitted it to Laura, but it annoyed him that she looked much less than her forty years. It was Patrick's opinion that his wife had small mental capacity, very slight and superficial emotions in spite of an occasional tendency to womanish "hysteria" over the most insignificant things. He was aware that for over half their married life her presence had made him uneasy, that the curious way she had of "staring emptily" at him was a source of vexation, and that her silences, after he had delivered himself of an eloquent attack on the faults, stupidities, malevolences, plots, lack of

428

integrity of neighbours, relatives, friends, or colleagues, provoked him.

"Don't you think this discussion is very premature?" he asked. "After all, the man has been in his grave only a week."

Laura's eyes became even larger and darker. "'The man,' as you call him, Patrick, was my dear Uncle Jim. You never liked him, did you? You thought I didn't know. But I always did."

"I disliked his lack of morals, his expediency, his heartlessness," said Patrick coldly. "How emotional you are, Laura. I remember many things about Jim Purcell of which you are unaware. No matter. I don't pretend to attachments if I do not feel them."

Pedantic, pompous, thought Laura, and allowed herself the first unrestrained bitterness against her husband. She smiled suddenly. "You are so right, Patrick, you never feel attachments."

How like the poor creature to catch only part of anything I say, Patrick commented to himself. He sat up straighter in his chair, like a schoolmaster. He began to speak, but Laura interrupted softly: "Once, you were so different, Patrick. I remember. I adored you, as a child, as a young girl, as a young wife. But something changed you, somewhere, some time, or, perhaps, somebody."

His thin cheeks reddened. He said with dignity, "Don't be so flighty, Laura. We were discussing your untenable idea of asking your Aunt Lydia, and Ruth, to come and live with us. It would be impossible for many reasons. One, for instance, that she would not consider it."

"We can at least offer, Patrick." Laura's voice remained mild. "I think Aunt Lydia would appreciate that."

"I never make offers about which I am not sincere, Laura."

She did not answer, but looked contemplatively at her folded hands. "Besides," he added with irritation, "I find Ruth repugnant. She is twenty-seven years old, and has never married. Her limp would not have kept away eligible suitors, for she is rich. An heiress. And she has considerable stock in the railroad, now. . . ." He paused, and the muscles of his face quickened. "Four per cent."

"And I have sixteen," said Laura. He turned to her. But no, he thought, she is not intelligent enough to have made a subtle or derisive remark. He said, "I have five." He waited, but she made no further comment. "It is not that I object to Ruth, *per se*. A charming woman, for all her disability. Strange, is it not, that

DeWitt has a similar crippling? The susceptibility must run in the family. If Miles were twenty-seven instead of seventeen I should even consider . . ."

Laura said very quickly, "Then I must not make the suggestion to Aunt Lydia?" There was a white circle about her lips.

Patrick judiciously folded his right index finger over his mouth and frowned. "She has a very fine home of her own, and she has her daughter. She would not consider coming here, not for a moment. Your aunt and I have not had much in common. But I once thought her a woman of honour—in spite of many things."

Laura's face became bright as if touched by the reflection of steel. "You did believe in the brief scandal about her and Uncle Jim, didn't you?"

"I don't like your tone of voice, Laura. It sounds very strange."

Laura stood up with an impulsiveness unusual with her. It came to Patrick, not for the first time, how much she resembled her aunt. Laura was speaking again, in that "strange" voice: "You want to believe it. You'd believe it even with full evidence against it. Why, Patrick, why?"

"You go off into the most ridiculous tangents, Laura," he said, affronted. "Why should I ' want ' to believe anything so repulsive about my wife's aunt? You insult me." He waved his hand forbiddingly. "I refuse to discuss it further. I think we were speaking of your aunt and Ruth coming to live with us. I cannot make the offer with sincerity. But, if you wish, you may do so, and I promise to look pleasant."

"Aunt Lydia never changed. She is what she always has been, Patrick." Laura was somewhat breathless. "The finest person I have ever known. Uncle Rufus still loves her; even Cornelia is fond of her. And Allan. . . ."

She bent her head. Now she was overcome with pain so intense that she was overwhelmed and astounded. She grasped the mantelpiece and her lips whitened to complete invisibility. Patrick, flooded with the red hatred he had never felt for anyone else but Allan Marshall, was preoccupied with controlling himself. He said faintly, "You know we don't mention that man in this house unless absolutely necessary. We don't have contact with him, except on occasions when the whole family meets, or I am compelled to talk with him at board meetings."

"I know!" exclaimed Laura. "You've always hated him; I never knew why. But he frustrated you at one time, didn't he?

He stood in your way when you wanted something. That is something you can't ever forgive. You'll never be satisfied until you've revenged yourself." She gazed at him with that curious, almost elated, scorn.

Patrick got to his feet slowly. "We don't discuss Allan Marshall. . . ."

But Laura, for the first time in her married life, laughed in his face, a high and shaking laugh. "We do, this time. You and I—we've never been honest with each other; we've pretended from the first day. I should never have married you, Patrick. I had fallen out of love with the illusion I thought was you even before our wedding day. . . ."

"You're hysterical, Laura," said Patrick, sharply. He winced at the blow to his ego. "I can overlook it, for you were much attached to Jim Purcell, and you've been brooding since he died. And at your age . . ."

But Laura was laughing again. There were tears in her eyes. She clasped her hands against her breast in a convulsive gesture. "I should never have married you; I should never have married you. It was wrong from the beginning. You can see it in our children. They despise both of us. They laugh at us; I've heard them! And why not? Aren't they justified?"

He grasped her shoulder, and shook her with a fury that had in it something demented. "Stop! This hysteria—it's shameful. Haven't you any pride? Even if you have no intelligence, ordinary decency . . ."

Laura was sobered by the rageful hand on her flesh, by the awful expression on her husband's face. She had seen that expression before, but never had it been so terrifying. It was compounded of anguish, despair, and hatred, and she felt them in herself with appalled sympathy. She thought with a clarity like a stunning light: He hates himself above everyone else. He has never done anything wrong, but still he is loathsome to himself.

She began to speak quietly, compassionately, as he still grasped her shoulder: "Patrick. Patrick. We must be out of our minds. The strain, perhaps. We must forget we ever spoke like this. We must forgive each other. Forgive me, Patrick."

His hand dropped like lead from her shoulder. Now the frenzied expression drained from his features. He turned away, looked about him as though he were a bewildered stranger in a house he

431

had never seen before and which he had not been aware of entering. Then, not speaking again, he walked out of the room.

Laura put her hands over her eyes and wept without sound.

Laughing silently and gleefully to himself, Fielding Peale tiptoed down the misty upper hall, his ski boots as quiet as velvet. He knocked discreetly at his sister's door, opened it, and popped in his head with what Cornelia Marshall often called his "jack-in-the-box way." Mary was yawning over a book near a lighted lamp in the dusk. She looked at her brother eagerly; he was waving his long arm at her, beckoning. She jumped to her feet with the swift bound of a kitten, and followed him farther down the hall to Miles's room. She did not know what was making him laugh so widely and soundlessly, but she was certain it would be worth hearing. With an air of conspiracy, Fielding opened Miles's door, his sister at his heels.

Miles was smoking and reading. He quickly snuffed out his cigarette. His father, who detested anyone's smoking, had "exploded" when he had discovered that his son "indulged in the dirty habit"; so Miles's rapid gesture was an irritated reflex. However, when he saw his visitors, he relaxed in his chair and put down his book on the neat pile beside him on the table. "You've got to stop bouncing around on those cat feet of yours, Field," he said in his light voice. "How you manage it with your big clodhoppers, I don't know. Ski-ing again? You'll break that giraffe neck of yours. Hallo, Mary." He gave his sister his most charming smile.

Though all three of the Peale children had a close affinity for each other, they seldom met for friendly conversations, except for those inspired by malice. So Miles looked expectant. As Fielding was sixteen, his giggle was somewhat falsetto still. He could not control his giggling now; he gave in to it, threw his long and awkward body in a chair, and slapped his bony knees. He was the only definitely ugly member of the family, and in spite of his great height he gave no promise of ultimate dignity. Cornelia had once described him as "all of one colour—tan." There was considerable truth in the description; his mop of straight hair was of the lightest brown, his small eyes of the same hue, his skin rough and yellowish, his angular lips without the slightest hint of youthful rosiness. He had a large and crooked nose, light brown and straggling eyebrows and lashes, and a

432

knobby forehead. "Lantern-jawed," Allan had once remarked, also with truth, for the boy's chin was long and jutted out below his mouth.

He sat and laughed with a whinny, clad in what Miles considered the most repulsive garments in the world: tightest trousers thrust into enormous boots, brown wool shirt, and woollen jacket. He had "picked up" ski-ing on a visit to the Austrian Tyrol last spring, a sport which Miles derided as he derided all strenuous and vigorous exercise. Fielding had even added a knitted woollen cap with a tassel, another monstrosity, according to Miles.

"The old man and lady just had a mad dust-up in the library," he informed his brother and sister with delight. "I heard them; I listened at the door, and then had to duck into the second drawing-room as the old man jumped out, tearing wild. I'd just come in and heard it all. It was good! Not one of their usual refined, genteel fights. But a humdinger. Maybe the old man slapped her or something," he added, relishing his tale.

"Oh, no!" cried Mary, clapping her hands and rocking on the window seat. "I don't believe a word! Tell us more. What was it about?"

Miles, who was sometimes patronising with his brother, lit a cigarette, waited with interest. "Well," Fielding went on with enjoyment, "I didn't get all the first part. There was something about old Aunt Purcell and that horrible Ruth coming to live with us, and I can tell you, it made me sick at my stomach. But Pa wasn't for it. And then, somehow he was." Fielding frowned, trying to remember it all. "Ma got kind of hysterical when he said he would be 'pleasant,' and talked about Ruth and her stock in the railroad. I don't know why." Suddenly he was overcome and laughed and laughed, slapping his knees again. "Do you know what? Pa said if you were older, Miles, he would consider your marrying old Ruth! Wouldn't that kill you?"

"No doubt," said Miles without indignation. "But it sounds like Pa. All nobility and piousness—until it comes to the railroad. What he wouldn't give to get his hands on it. Even something insane like my marrying a woman old enough to be my mother."

"Hardly; just almost ten years older, that's all," said Mary with happiness. "But do go on, Field."

"And then the row burst out, with Ma screaming something about Uncle Allan doing something to Pa. She shrieked; honest she did. And making a mistake about marrying Pa, and laughing out loud over and over. But things got really exciting when she said we kids laughed at them."

"Well, don't we?" cried Mary. "But how did she ever guess? Maybe she isn't as stupid as we think she is."

"I never thought her stupid," said Miles.

He shook off some ash from his cigarette. "I've never told you kids, but she's always been infatuated with that furious Irish madman, our dear ' Uncle Allan.'"

"No!" breathed Mary, fascinated.

"Well, maybe Miles is right," said Fielding, awed by his brother's insight. "Uncle Allan's name seemed to set him off. Look, is Uncle Allan returning the compliment?"

"Of course. You can see him doing it, if you watch."

"What a perfectly delicious scandal!" said Mary, hugging her rounded knees. "I wonder if anyone else knows."

"Aunt Cornelia does. That's why she'd love to cut Ma's throat. But you kids mustn't hint a word of it, I warn you."

"Delicious!" exclaimed Mary again. "But such old people. They ought to be ashamed."

Miles smiled at this childishness. He waved to his brother to continue. But Fielding was staring into space, with gleeful pleasure. "Does Pa know?" asked Mary. "It would be just too exciting if he did."

"He hasn't the sense," replied Miles disdainfully.

Fielding went on: "And there was something about a scandal and old Aunt Liddie; and Ma accused Pa of believing in it, and wanting to believe in it."

"I shouldn't doubt it," said Miles. "I've noticed that these ' lovers of mankind ' are always ready to think the worst of it. And to exploit it, too, in a fashion normal men haven't learned as yet. Ma was crushing our father's toes, apparently, when she accused him." Miles smiled his exceedingly beguiling smile again. "We can't keep help around here, though Pa pays more than anyone else, as a kind of bribe. He's too demanding, too autocratic, and while he talks to us about ' labour,' as if it were some kind of ineffable species, he treats our help like dogs. Ma tried to explain it to me a couple of years ago; Pa, she said, in that foolish, gentle way of hers, wasn't always this ridiculous. He used to believe in what he spouted; he used to put his own words into action. Something changed him; something left him with

434

the oratory and paralysed the rest of his body. It's my belief," said the astute Miles, "that nothing 'changes' anybody, intrinsically."

His brother and sister listened to him with respect. He sat in his chair, at ease, and spoke with that authority which comes solely from never-wavering contact with reality. Unlike the gawky Fielding, he was small, relieved only from daintiness by an aura of dominant masculinity, implicit for all the delicate formation of his body, his hands, and his feet. He was elegant and graceful; an exquisite. He possessed what is called in women "style" and distinction.

It was all this, and his face, which made him practically irresistible to ladies of any age. When dour and disgruntled maids gave their notice to Patrick in outraged indignation, Miles, when at home, could invariably soothe them and persuade them to remain. They murmured in the kitchen that he had the character and the face of a "holy cherub." He had a small and ethereal face, a rounded chin with a dimple, a perfect nose, and, to quote the ladies, a "rose-bud" mouth. His eyes were an absolute blue in all lights and under all conditions, and were unusually large and brilliant, shaded by astonishingly long dark lashes. His forehead was wide and high, and crowned by dark auburn hair which curled all over his round head in silky ringlets.

He had used his own lavish pocket money to refurnish his rooms at home. Tasteful and artistic, he had, over a period of five years, thrown out the gloomy furniture his father had bought and had replaced it with either original French furniture, or admirable copies. Everything in his rooms was light and airy, yet strong, like himself, and perfect, from the blue and gilded chairs to the soft draperies at the windows. Patrick, offended, had declared the rooms full of "frippery."

Miles had determined to marry his kinswoman, Dolores Marshall. This, too, was his secret. At seventeen, he was not youthful; he was a man. Dolores's coldness to him did not discourage him in the slightest. For he had acquired for this girl, since he was fifteen, an authentic passion and desire and love which sometimes astonished him. There was no reasoning with it, no explanation. She was beautiful, but he had seen girls as lovely. She did not parade her sex, nor was she a coquette, a fact which made many of her masculine acquaintances indifferent to her.

It was his opinion that his sister, who adored him, was a wanton at heart. There she sat now, regarding him with adoration, a petite girl with a delightfully-rounded figure and his own grace and daintiness of movement and gesture. The rose-velvet frock set off the hanging masses of her curling black hair, her huge black eyes, so animated and full of sauciness, her broad white cheek bones and pointed white chin, her fleshy pink mouth with its malicious expression. Everything about her was piquant and suggested a forgotten strain of Latin blood. Like Miles, she gave an "air" to everything she wore, everything she did.

"Coming back to old Aunt Liddie," said Miles. "She's a very rich old girl, and she won't forget us, I hope. Mary, I've often wondered why Uncle Jim didn't leave any of us money, except you. Have you any idea?"

She shook her curls and grinned at him as if keeping a secret, though, in fact, there was no secret at all. Jim Purcell had found her amusing, and Ruth was fond of her for some unknown reason. "You must have played up to him," said Miles knowingly. But Mary merely shook her head again. Miles began to muse. "Ma is very rich, herself. She has stock in the company, and she'll leave it to us. Our grandfather was Stephen deWitt, and he was once president of the company. By the way, would you kids mind getting out now? I'm studying."

"Always studying about railroads," said Fielding, trying for disdain but glancing at his brother with admiration. He stood up to his full and awkward length, and yawned. "Want to be president some day? And how are you going to manage it, with Tony and DeWitt, not to mention Uncle Allan and Aunt Cornelia, and Uncle Rufus, who's still on the premises?"

"Did I say anything about being president, or anything?" asked Miles. Fielding lounged to the pile of books by his brother's chair and picked up one of them. He scratched his yellowish cheek and frowned. "Patents. Uncle Allan's got three in here, all by himself. He must've been a bright boy when he was young. I mentioned it to Pa once, and he got mad."

"Pa doesn't like plebes, or people without background or family, or men who get where they want to go by their own efforts," said Miles languidly. "It offends his ingrown sense of what is ' proper.' Once I heard him say that he despised men who tried to ' rise above their station.' He forgot himself that

436

time, and then tried to explain, and it came out gibberish. Just another symptom of his 'idealism.' Now, will you get out?"

Mary had been staring into space as if entranced, forgetting her brothers. She said suddenly, "Do you know what? I'm going to marry Tony."

Fielding howled with laughter, but Miles did not even smile. His blue eyes narrowed thoughtfully on his sister. He said seriously, "No, my dear. He won't marry anybody, I think. Least of all, you. You might try for DeWitt, though; he's sweet on you, and someday, perhaps five or six years from now, it can be a match." He became more serious than ever, and studied his sister as though she had appeared to him in a new and important light. "DeWitt. What if he'll always walk on crutches or be in a wheel chair, or at best, use canes? He's a DeWitt."

Mary was angered, and her eyes flashed. "I think DeWitt Marshall is detestable. Oh, we all had fun together when we were kids, but now I can't stand him. I'm going to have Tony. It's true he isn't very bright about a lot of things, but just look at him! He makes my mouth water. The girls at school rave madly about him. And he'll have your precious railroad one of these days, too."

"No he won't," said Miles softly. He ran his hand over his silken auburn ringlets. "DeWitt might. Don't glare at me; I know what I know. Get after old DeWitt. You will, if you have any sense."

Mary, in outrage, flounced to her feet, and the rosy skirts swirled about her in the perfect circle of a dancer's costume. "Don't tell me what to do, Miles Peale! I know you're soft on that horrible Dolores, but she won't look at you, not for a second! Besides, there's that English nobleman, or something, and you can be sure that Aunt Cornelia is getting up a sweat working on it. And did you ever hear of Aunt Cornelia not getting what she wanted?" She laughed at Miles, who made no reply but pointedly took up one of his books.

"Ever hear of Miles not getting what he wanted, either?" asked Fielding, coming to his brother's aid. "And you're wrong, Mary. Who would want old Dolores? Looks like wax, with all that light hair. The family's got millions, but even the hungry boys let her be a wallflower at dances."

Miles never lost his temper visibly. So he smiled with superior

437

kindness at his brother. "Yes," he said. "Who would want Dolores? And again, do I have to throw you kids out?"

When they had finally left him, he closed his book over his finger and gazed at the fire, and those who knew him would have been astonished to see the intensity of his expression and his monumental concentration. He finally got up, lifted a book from its narrow shelf on the wall, and from behind it withdrew a letter he had received that morning. No one had ever violated his privacy, but he distrusted all human beings. He re-read the letter, which was from Jon deWitt. It was a very thick and rambling letter, written in cramped handwriting, and here and there it was incoherent. It was full of lyrical and frantic devotion to this seventeen-year-old youth, and Miles smiled in an ugly fashion as he read on. ". . . . dreadful time at Cannes, which I loathe—miss you, dear boy. . . . You are such a child, but so beautiful. Even when you laugh at me, I forgive you because of your face and intellect. . . . You don't understand these things —the purity, the loftiness, the classic. . . . But you've given me some hope . . . do not despise me—the pain, the longing. . . . There is no one like you. I am losing interest in my French friends—they pretend to a subtlety they do not have . . . just want my money. I am ten years older than you, but I know you would understand if you would allow me to explain. . . ."

Disgusting obscenity, thought Miles. He tapped the papers against his teeth. Then he continued to read: "Lonely—lonely— lonely. . . . I remember that discussion I had with you last summer. Let me talk with you again, I have so many new books on the subject. When one looks at Allan Marshall, and my grandfather, for that matter, one is filled with hatred for them. Cruel, greedy oppressors of better men. Monopolists of the worst kind, but they always manage to evade the anti-trust actions against them. What do they know of the suffering of the exploited, the people? Do they ever hear the clatter of the tumbrils at any time? But they'll hear them, one of these days! Did you read the last translated pamphlets I sent you, which were smuggled out of Russia? The hour is coming! In this respect you are so perspicacious, so perceptive. You, like me, know that the day of the robber barons is finished, that the day of the Proletariat is approaching with thunder. . . ."

I wonder, thought Miles, sitting down near the fire again, if there is anything to my suspicion that unspeakable people like

Jon deWitt are just naturally, and inevitably, drawn to ideas like the "Day of the Proletariat"? Their perversions? Their dementia? Do they hate successful men, and so try, this way, to destroy them? Is that their revenge?

Miles had met some of Jon's New York "friends." He remembered the zealot's glare in their eyes, their shrill denunciatory voices, their clenched fists, their piercing and insistent arguments, their womanish malignance and airs, their passion for "oppressed groups and the Masses." Degeneracy—and perhaps the light of burning cities to-morrow. The fragile but spiteful banshees of doom. Miles wrinkled his nose as if offended by a foul smell. One or two of the "friends" were men distinguished for literature, for obscure, beautifully written, frail poems or novels. Their work had the scent of putridity about it, for all the exquisite phrases and the general excellence. Moreover, they wrote almost exclusively of men—masculine, dominant, warlike men—and they wrote voluptuously.

Miles rolled the letter tightly together, and pushed it between the coals of the fire. He watched it burn, and his smile was cryptic. Jon deWitt. Rufus deWitt's son. He could be useful, very useful. Miles began to think of the letter he would write to him. A cautious letter, harmless and unintelligible to others, significant to Jon.

CHAPTER THIRTY-NINE

As THE family sat at breakfast on the morning of Thanksgiving Day, Tony Marshall felt that he had at least one reason for humble gratitude to God: his father was looking strong again, the life had returned to his eyes, his air of concentrated potency, which over the years had appeared to deteriorate slowly but steadily, had returned in its full power. Still very thin, and with grey hair, he was, for the first time in a long while, giving the impression that he was in absolute control, thought Tony, the feeling that he was "present."

Because he had such sensitivity of feeling, Tony knew that the seemingly trivial have a stupendous place in the lives of men. Allan, in his youth, might have had a contempt for his parents;

439

nevertheless, his acceptance by his father in these later years had comforted him. He was needed by his father, that old man, so serene, so belligerent, so affectionately blustering and kind and simple. Tim's wife was dead, but he hardly grieved. "Sure, my lad, herself is just dustin' up the new house and settlin' the furniture for me," he had told Tony. "It's lookin' out of the window for me she is, right at this minute." His filmed eyes had smiled at the young man. "And it's not surprised, I'd be, if some of the blessed angels didn't drop in for a cup of tea sometimes, and one of her tarts."

This highly unorthodox view of the hereafter had not disturbed Michael. He had said softly, "And when you get there, Dad, don't forget to keep a chair brushed off for me." This was before he had left for India. He, as if he knew Allan's need, wrote constantly.

Tony pitied Estelle and her two sons, Jon and Norman, but in spite of the imperative Command he could not love them, and this worried him sometimes. Estelle, in her early sixties, looked much younger to the casual glance, though the thin skin of her sweet face was cobwebbed with time. She never appeared, even during slight illnesses, without the bloom of expertly applied rouge and powder, and her luminous brown eyes were still distended with a synthetic enthusiasm. She had no need, even at her age, to resort to the dye pot, as did Cornelia. Estelle's soft curls were still brown, if thinned, and she wore them like a crown on her head. She had kept her youthful figure, her artificial eagerness of expression, and her saccharine quality. But malevolence had pinched and sunken the corners of her mouth, had driven pits around her nostrils, had shrivelled the area about her eyes.

He also disliked, in spite of earnest effort, her two sons, who resembled her so closely. Norman was his mother's courtier, a young, brown-haired, brown-eyed man who gave the impression of having no "body." At twenty-five he was a perpetual youth, and always would be. Adolescence was part of his spirit; it was his livery. Sometimes he was even guilty of clapping his hands in delight over some trifle. Yet, though he was interested in no woman but his mother, he did not give off that certain effluvium of disease and ominous distortion which hovered about his older brother.

Even when he had been much younger, and much more

innocent of life, Tony had recognised that Jon deWitt was unhealthy in both personality and soul. At fourteen, Tony, who had always called Jon by his Christian name, simply, was instinctively impelled to call him "Uncle Jon." (What had occurred to cause this change was almost blotted from his memory, but he retained the impression that it had threatened him and that he had fled from it in horror and loathing.) At any rate, the firmly enunciated title had changed Jon's former interest in his nephew to cold and spiteful hate.

There were times when Tony, though only eighteen, had a mature man's perceptiveness; and it came to him at irregular but fully enlightened intervals that if there was some awful fate which had deformed Jon, and had kept Norman in infancy, that fate was their mother.

Tony did not know that Rufus, over the years, had come to recognise his sons for what they were, and now shuddered at one and regarded the other with the unthinking aversion one extends to the unknown. His last will left them some amounts in cash, but no stock or bonds in the railroad. Their mother had increased her own original wealth in the stock market.

Rufus, though he had lost much flesh lately, still retained his hearty appetite and joviality. He had insisted on joining the family at breakfast, for the company of his daughter and his grandchildren, Tony and Dolores, had become a necessity to him. Allan, since his revival of mind and health, sometimes became tedious to the old man; he wanted to "talk business" all the time, as Rufus complained to Cornelia. "I never thought the day would come when I wouldn't be predominantly interested in our company, above anything else," he would admit. "Would you mind telling Allan, in a very subtle way, of course, that I'm 'not what I was,' or something?" Cornelia, therefore, would tactfully move the conversation from a business discussion when her father and husband were together. "For God's sake," she would say, "there's something else in the world besides locomotives and stocks and bonds and directors and patents and rights of way, especially at breakfast and dinner."

The morning was disquietingly showing every indication of making life miserable for human beings. Snow had fallen heavily all night; it lay in greyish and mounting heaps on the mountains and in the valleys. It seemed to be determined to do much more. Vision through the windows was limited to curtains of whiteness, torn apart by a thunderous gale. "Roads will be blocked," said Cornelia. "I do hope that Mother and Ruth won't have too much difficulty; they won't if they use a sleigh. I must call them. Remind me, somebody. The Peales, unfortunately, will get here. Patrick becomes more intolerable all the time. Why isn't it permissible, on regulated occasions, for a woman to poison her husband?"

Rufus laughed heartily. But Allan, who had been about to ask Rufus his opinion of a newly invented automatic switch, did not smile. His face darkened and he put down his fork. Cornelia watched him intently from under her tawny lashes, and for an instant she was completely ugly. But she went on: "Mother didn't want to come, considering poor Uncle Jim's recent death. I became quite the wounded daughter; she knows all about me, of course, and she laughed a little. She understood, though, that we really wanted her."

Estelle glanced up. "Do we?" she asked sweetly. "Frankly, as you know, I never cared much for Lydia. She is completely neglecting herself; she looks like an old woman."

"None of us are young," said Rufus. He regarded his wife with a hard gleam in his eyes.

Cornelia said, "Thank you, Papa. I do feel decrepit. Honestly, these large gatherings-of-the-clan on holidays bore me. But it's my turn. Thank God we go back to New York next week, after Tony returns to Harvard, and DeWitt to Groton." She complained, "I never thought the Peales would make me want to leave home, but they do."

"There's nothing wrong with Miles. And Mary," said DeWitt in his unaccented voice. His face, so sharp and dark, flushed a little. His mother, beside him, patted the small hand on the table, and he shrank away, rebukingly. "Never mind; we all know you like Mary," she said. "And why not? Such a darling girl. Miles? A terrible rascal, of course."

Estelle furtively patted her curls. "I must say that Lydia seems to take Jim's death very calmly, and they always appeared to be so devoted."

"There's more to grief than emotionalism," said Cornelia, accepting another large slice of ham from the platter the butler was offering her. "Or don't you know, Estelle?"

"Now, now," murmured Rufus with enjoyment.

"I, for one, will be happy to get back to my apartment in New

York," said Jon, in his feminine voice, precise and lyrical. "Dull, here in the country. I think I'll make it a little earlier than usual. Papa, it won't be necessary to order out our private car for me."

Rufus held a piece of toast in his hand. "I won't," he replied. "What's wrong with our Pullmans, anyway?" He put down the toast as if he had suddenly sickened of it, and he turned to his left, where Dolores sat. Immediately he was warmed. "Why do you have to go back to that school in Switzerland, my love?"

"I don't," she answered with a tender smile. "I'd much rather stay here with you, Grandpa."

"Now don't encourage her, Papa," said Cornelia with boisterous vigour. "You know she has to finish. And we'll be on the Riviera again, before you know it."

Rufus smiled ruddily but did not answer. His daughter fixed all her attention on him, and her heart, usually so invulnerable, contracted. Allan turned to her, caught her eye, and smiled with affection. She responded to it, but under her thick and robust application of bright rouge her skin paled.

What complacent, wicked, or dull fools they are! thought Jon deWitt with such violent revulsion and hatred that his vision became distorted for a moment, and all objects and the people about the breakfast table drew together in tall and jagged lines before him, coloured only in white and black. He was familiar with this phenomenon, and with its accompanying sensation of extreme nausea, intolerable head pain and plunging heart. There had been times when the stalklike and glittering lines had fused as one, glimmered like lightning, and had then disappeared in a total darkness which had lasted for several terrifying moments. He was afraid it was going to happen again, and he forced himself to breathe slowly and steadily, to swallow methodically, as he had been taught.

There sat his father, that oppressor of the workers, that battener on the lives of humble men! No doubt he still fancied himself as a Jove, thought Jon, a benevolent Jove, with all his condescending charities, his chairmanships of "welfare" organisations. Too late, too late! Jon went on in himself with raging satisfaction. Too late for anything, you damned, twinkling, chuckling liar, who have made my mother's life a hell since the day you married her. And that daughter of yours, that loud-voiced brazen bitch with her gusto and her shouts of laughter and her way with men! Pollution, corruption! Allan Marshall! Thief, conniver, plotting Irish rascal. Low-bred scoundrel. I thought you would die the last time you were ill; if I believed in any God I would pray that you would die.

Jon picked up his glass with trembling fingers and drank. The ominous flicker of darkness was touching the corner of his right eyelid. He made himself look desperately at his mother as a distracted peasant kneels before a wayside shrine. Her dear, sweet, shining face. Her young and eager eyes. The adorable curls, the dimpled chin. He had been choosing her clothes for many years now; his gaze lingered on her blue morning robe with its froth of white lace about her neck and flowing from the wide cuffs. He sighed. He looked at his brother and was stabbed with jealousy. Norman was leaning against Estelle's arm and was smiling up at her like a dependent child. Jon smiled virtuously to himself. He knew what he knew about Norman; he had taught him. Norman's emotions might be those of an adolescent, but there was a mind behind the prattling, the clapping of hands, the apparently senseless laughter. A voracious and calculating mind, capable of absorbing the new and flowering philosophy of the common man. The family would have to reckon with both of Estelle's sons.

He studied the rest of the family. DeWitt. Cold, clicking away in the depths of him, ignoring that repulsive crippling as if it were an irrelevance. One could hear him ticking, tabulating, adding up, endlessly, sleeplessly. But the mind of a man could defeat a machine, however intricate. Besides, the ugly, black-faced little monster was only fifteen.

Jon came now to Tony, and for a few seconds he was completely blinded with hatred, and with something like terror. Had he ever told anyone, his mother, his father, his grandfather? It must be so, otherwise he, Jon deWitt, would not be so avoided and treated with such open aversion.

At last, Jon came to Dolores, so like her brother. Positively repellent, thought Jon, despising her. All that pale light hair curling about her Renaissance face, those empty eyes, that delicately swelling figure. In some way, she appeared to him even more of a threat than Tony. He glanced at her breast, and shuddered, and at her white throat, and shuddered again. With what grossness of body the animal could be seduced! Her rose-coloured lips, smiling so gently at Rufus, nauseated Jon.

Never Victorious, Never Defeated

Rufus was speaking in that rich voice of his: "We always believe that our lives and our thoughts are marvellously unique, our calamities beyond the understanding of others, our hopes higher and nobler, our despairs deeper, our aims purer, our comprehensions more refined, and that the things which happen to us, whether for good or for bad, have never happened before to anyone else. Do you remember, Allan, what the Pharisee said: ' I thank Thee Lord, I am not as other men are '?" He laughed. "I've never done a thing which hasn't been done before thousands of years ago in exactly the same way by millions of others."

Estelle, who had been trying to break into a conversation of which Jon had been oblivious until this moment, said eagerly, "Why, yes, in a way. Nothing new under the sun." Rufus nodded his head at her with kindness; Estelle might be obvious and shallow, but one had to acknowledge her existence occasionally.

Jon said abruptly, "You are wrong, Papa. There *is* something quite different in the world to-day, a new and growing philosophy —beyond selfishness. . . ."

"I know, I know," said Rufus, bored. "I've heard about it, here and there." He glanced with a twinkle at Allan. "But it isn't new at all, my boy. It's as old as sin; it was conceived in sin, or ignorance, thousands of years ago by the cave man. I hope the world won't revert to barbarism, Jon. I doubt it will; the age of tyrants has passed. The new philosophy you talk about is fossilised."

Allan's black eyes sparkled with furious irateness at his wife's half-brother. "We haven't outlived selfishness, and I hope we won't, for it has its good facets. Such as self-esteem, self-respect, responsibility, ambition, and the drive to self-betterment. Held in control, as all human emotions have to be, they can benefit society as well as the individual."

He pointed his knife in a "low-bred" gesture which he sometimes could not restrain.

"You, for instance, Jon. There is some emotion in you which is carrying you to dangerous extremes."

"Why does any family discussion always end in personalities?" murmured Estelle in despair.

Cornelia came to her assistance robustly, "Estelle's right. Allan, do put down that knife; you really aren't going to stab Jon, are you? I read somewhere that gestures directed towards

445

others are sometimes subconsciously hostile, and have the real and original intention behind them."

Allan smiled grimly and put down the knife. "Possibly right, Cornelia. But why can't your brother argue or talk about anything else but his infernal obsession?"

Jon's face flushed intensely. "You are afraid," he said, and it was as if he was spitting at the other man. Allan regarded him scornfully. "Of what?" he asked. "Men like you?"

Rufus put in hastily, "'The times are out of joint.' I suppose you think that, and believe that, Jon. But they always were. Time has smoothed out the long past behind us, made it almost featureless, levelled out the volcanoes, turned the wild rivers into quiet streams. . . . And after we, ourselves, have been forgotten, and our children's children, too, millions of men will look back on our times, and, in the midst of their own confusions, wars, and events, will say, perhaps enviously, 'How peaceful the old days were, how leisurely and pleasant and good and tolerant.' And it will be a lie, what they say, just as what we say about the past is a lie."

"But we have to deal with the present just the same, and with the idiots the present spews up!" exclaimed Allan.

Cornelia rose briskly. "And now that the day has started out in its usual normal fashion for this family, and nothing agreeable has been said to disturb the customary pattern, I think I'll go upstairs with Allan for a little consultation about some matters."

Tony, rising, laughed with Rufus and his father, and with Dolores, but his eyes were troubled. He took his sister's hand and went with her out of the dining-room. He whispered, "I must talk to you, dear. I want your advice." She gave him a sad and fearful glance, and nodded.

The butler drew back DeWitt's chair, and the youth put one hand on his cane, one hand on the table, and pushed himself slowly but surely to his feet. Allan waited. He dared not offer assistance. He tried to make himself invisible as he followed the painful progress of the crippled and gnomelike figure across the heavy carpet. DeWitt ignored him, and it came to Allan again that DeWitt had not spoken a word to anyone but the servants. Was the boy retreating more and more into his silences, or was he, as usual, only observing? If I could only reach him, thought Allan, slowly moving behind his son. But I never could, and no one else has ever succeeded either, except Tony.

Never Victorious, Never Defeated

DeWitt crept over the floor, his hand whitening on the cane, his small features compressed with almost superhuman determination. If he saw his father behind him, it was not evident. Estelle was standing with her sons close beside her, and was looking up at them in speechless communion, and with an air of touching helplessness.

"I think to-day would be best," said Dolores to her brother, as they sat in the snowy dusk of her small sitting-room. "Daddy is feeling and looking so well lately, though he has not stopped drinking." She sighed mournfully. "Then the family is coming for dinner, and I've noticed that he doesn't do too much drinking before parties, except that he can't stand Uncle Patrick and is sometimes—careless. Then, having to appear on holidays, at dinner, he is restrained by not wanting to be a spectacle before his own children."

"But we understand," said Tony.

"Yes, dear. However, he has his pride to consider, and he still believes he is hiding it from us. So, even if you disturb him, he won't—he won't . . ."

Tony pressed his hands over his eyes and his face with a slow movement of distress. "What if our father should be thrown back into what he was, by me? I can't have that on my conscience."

Dolores smiled sadly. "Nobody really throws anyone ' back.' You can only precipitate what was already there, and waiting. And you have yourself to consider, too, and your whole life." She touched his shoulder again comfortingly. "For good or evil, we are always influencing someone, every day of our lives, and they are influencing us. Do you remember telling me how you first knew what you wanted to do? You were walking along a back road in Cannes, and you suddenly came upon a white wall covered with magenta bougainvillæa, and the sun struck it and you stopped, and all at once you knew. The light on the flowers— it was just a precipitating factor."

Tony stood up, put his hand lovingly on his sister's fair head, and she looked up at him with gravely smiling eyes. He nodded, and left her. The corridor outside shifted with greyish light from the raving sky. Everyone would have luncheon in his room; so the servants could lay the table for the Thanksgiving dinner. Tony could hear no one about upstairs. He walked soberly down the hallway, then stopped at the door of his brother's room. He hesitated, then opened it. DeWitt was resting on his bed, reading. He regarded Tony with dark coldness, and retained the book in his hands. "I didn't hear you knock," he said.

"If I had knocked, you wouldn't have said ' come in.' You would have said, ' Who is it ? ' And if I'd told you, you would have answered that you're ' busy.' And I would have had to go away, and I don't want to go away."

The nearest grimace to a smile which DeWitt ever allowed himself glimmered about his tight lips. He put down the book. "All right, sit down, make it brief. I suppose you've got something to tell me."

Only the lamp by the bed had been lighted, and it threw golden shadows on the white ceiling, shadows which were joined by the crimson shafts of the fire. Tony sat down near the bed and gazed silently at his brother.

The fire fluttered on the hearth and the windows moaned with the wind. The two young men regarded each other without speaking for some time. Then Tony said, "I hope you won't think me mad or something, but I am going to be a priest."

He waited. DeWitt's expression did not change in the least. He merely put down the book beside him. "Do you think that is news?" he asked. "I've suspected it for over a year. And, incidentally, Ma knows, too. I told her."

Tony was incredulous, and DeWitt gave his small grunt of laughter. "She didn't believe it, and she laughed, and made some sort of coarse comment, I think, but she wasn't disturbed. I have reminded her once or twice since the first time, and now she is beginning to accept it, in her sort of way. But she is afraid, I'm sure, that it will upset darling Papa."

"Do you think she has told Grandpa?" Tony was still incredulous.

DeWitt shrugged. "Doesn't she always tell him everything?"

Tony was so astonished at all this that he blurted, "Do they know I am a Catholic now?"

DeWitt thought this naïve. "Possibly. They aren't fools, you know. Besides, she's just found out that there are Catholics in that pecky Englishman's family, and, best of all, a bishop in the background. A wealthy bishop, with a title in his own name."

Tony said, "But of course, Dolores isn't going to marry Dicky."

DeWitt yawned. "Does she know that? Ma doesn't. And that's all that matters."

Tony got up, immensely disturbed, forgetting his own troubles. He used a poker on the fire, swept up some ashes, walked to the windows for a moment, then returned to his chair. He repeated, "Dolores isn't going to marry him. I know. She dislikes him very much. And she isn't a weakling."

DeWitt smiled his saturnine smile and made no answer.

Tony's thoughts were distracted, and he tugged at his ear. His brother watched him, his small black eyes faintly curious. "I suppose," said Tony, "that you wouldn't like to know my reasons for my decision?"

"Not particularly."

But Tony clasped his knees with his hands and stared at his brother with deep earnestness. "I've got to tell you. I want to be of some use in this world; I want to serve God."

"Good," said DeWitt, with not even a hint of irony in his voice.

"You really don't understand. I have a vocation. I've known it for years. There has to be a call, to serve Him."

DeWitt shifted on his pillows. "I suppose you believe so. Who am I to judge?" The curiosity became sharper in his eyes, but Tony saw that the boy was not ridiculing him, as he had feared.

"I wish," he said very softly, "that there had been some religion in this family."

"Why? Why should we delude ourselves, if we don't want to?"

"Delusion? DeWitt, it's the only reality."

DeWitt again shifted on his pillows, and now his whole diminutive body expressed impatience. "That's your delusion, Tony. My reality is my own. I'm not going to talk metaphysics with you: you'd only bore me. I'm old enough to choose who shall bore me, and you aren't my choice just now."

In spite of himself, Tony laughed. The odd rapport which had always existed between the two established itself, and after a moment, DeWitt laughed also. Then he became gloomy. "Tony, I've always believed you were the only honest person in this damned family. You never pretended, out of sickly affection or slyness. At any rate, I've always respected you. It's sometimes necessary for everyone to be with someone honest, if only for a unique experience."

Tony laughed again, got up, and rumpled the fine dark hair on his brother's head. DeWitt did not automatically shrink as he did from a touch from others. In fact, he sat very still, and it was not until Tony had seated himself again that he fastidiously smoothed down his hair. The line of pain between his eyes disappeared, and he looked thoughtfully at the fire.

"You aren't as bad, or as sophisticated, or as contained, as you think you are," said Tony, affectionately.

"I never dissect myself," replied DeWitt. "Don't be soulful, Tony."

But Tony said, "Don't forget me, kid."

DeWitt turned his head and regarded his brother with a peculiar expression.

" I shouldn't have been any good in the railroad business," Tony went on. "But you will."

"Certainly," said DeWitt.

"I hope others will agree with you."

"You won't have a hard time convincing anyone about your decision, except our dear Papa," DeWitt remarked after a short pause.

Tony sighed. "I wish I could hope you'd comfort him, DeWitt."

DeWitt glanced at him out of the corner of his eyes, and for the first time Tony thought of evil, and he was shocked. He leaned forward to study his brother. Was it possible that DeWitt hated their father? Envy, resentment, the scorn of a self-sufficient and narrow soul for a man who could never be self-sufficient and who was a tumult of dynamism, emotional storms, and upheavals? Tony said, "So few understand Dad. He is a giant of power and genius, and no one can oppose him when he makes up his mind to something. Men like him are sometimes ridiculed by those whose own experiences have been superficial or uneventful or fortunate."

DeWitt clasped his thin fingers together and let them drop off the sheet. He made no comment, though Tony waited for a long time. Then the young man said, "DeWitt, our father went through hells no one knows about to get where he is."

DeWitt was speaking: "And now you've come to your own conclusions. About me and our father. You want me to ' comfort ' him. I can promise you this: I won't disappoint him. Is that enough?"

"I suppose it'll have to be." A sense of sorrowful frustration overwhelmed Tony. He stood up. "A man can't promise to do what he can't do. But there's something else I wanted to say to you. You're only fifteen, and it will be years, yet, before you can take over from Dad. In the meantime, there are others. . . ."

DeWitt looked bored. "You mean Miles and Fielding."

Tony was surprised, and this made DeWitt smile. "It's so obvious, Tony, that it almost hits you in the face. Uncle Pat is out for blood—Dad's blood—and always has been. And how can he ruin Dad, and with what weapons? His sons. They are the grandsons of Stephen deWitt, and the stories about our great-uncle still circulate. Oh, it is all very righteous in Uncle Pat's mind; just retribution or something. He's had years to think it all out. By the way, are you afraid of them, for me?"

"Why, yes," stammered Tony. He blushed. "Uncharitable, perhaps, but I know them. And I know what stock they have. I'm thinking not only of you, but of Dad."

DeWitt raised his black eyebrows. "Did you know that one move in the game is Dolores? Miles not only wants her, because he wants her, but he also wants the future Marshall heiress."

He nodded at his speechless brother. "Don't worry about that too much. Ma dislikes him, and so does Dolores. But he's still dangerous, I admit, and so is Field. I've got a card against them, though. When we're old enough, I'm going to marry Mary."

Tony shook his head, dazed. "You can't," he muttered. "I'm afraid to go away."

DeWitt was amused. "And what could you do? By the way, weren't you going to see someone else this afternoon? Better hurry; it's already four o'clock, and the Peales are coming at six."

He smiled into Tony's startled eyes, and picked up his book again. "I think you're beginning to bore me. Run along."

Tony went downstairs in the warm dusk, looking for his father. He could see the thundering greyness gathering force against all the windows; a grey and spectral light glimmered through the snow, but not sufficiently to give any signs that beyond the house lay anything but crepuscular mounds and drifts. The doors of the dining-room were shut, and from behind them came the comfortable sound of silver and china being laid, a reassuring sound in a silence otherwise unbroken except for the booming of the wind against the house and the wail of it under the eaves. Every room had its fire blazing and roaring, and scarlet shafts fell intermittently over silent furniture and coloured rugs and white walls and ceilings.

Allan, Tony knew, was nowhere upstairs; Cornelia was napping and so was her father. So Tony glanced into the drawing-room downstairs, and even in the breakfast-room. He wandered through the halls. There was one door he had not yet approached, but he knew it was shut, and he shrank from it: the library. Over and over he told himself that his father was doubtlessly working on business papers, as he usually did when at home, and that there was no occasion to worry. However, there was something ominously familiar about that shut door, some emanation which Tony caught. He knocked softly. Allan's voice, dull and lifeless and thick, came to him. "Who is it? What do you want?"

Dear Mother of God, help me, prayed Tony, and answered as lightly as possible, "Tony, Dad. May I see you for a few minutes? It's very important."

The wind rose on a howling note and the great house trembled. Tony waited, praying feverishly. Then he heard a chair pushed back, and Allan's voice was nearer: "Go away, Tony, I'm busy."

"I know," said Tony. "But this is very important, Dad. I can't talk about it later. Please, Dad."

From behind the door he heard a groan, then there were slow and dragging footsteps, the shooting of a bolt. The door opened and Allan stood there in his shirt sleeves, his tie unknotted, his hair dishevelled. Tony could, very dimly, see his face, dark and distracted and tensed, and he could smell the odour of whisky. The boy's courage was shaken; this was very bad. It had not been so bad for a long time. He went into the library. There was no light but from a dying fire, and a glass and a bottle of whisky stood on a table near the hearth.

"Why do you want to talk to me now?" asked Allan in the harsh voice of a man filled with shame and despair. "Yes, that's whisky. Damnable day, all that yelling of the wind. And thinking of Pat Peale always drives me to the bottle." He tried to smile. Tony smiled as if he understood and it was all very amusing. Allan fell back into his chair, and his hands clutched the arms as he tried to control himself. "Well, well," he said indulgently. "Want a drink with me, to toast the weather and hope nobody will be able to get up here, to-day?"

He was watching Tony suspiciously through his bloodshot

eyes. Tony said, "To tell the truth, I would like a drink. I thought I might share your drink, and have a talk, just the two of us alone. Got any brandy down here?"

Allan tried to rise, then shook his head as if dizzy. "Right there, right-hand compartment, in the breakfront. Glasses, too." Tony opened the bottom door and took out the brandy and a small glass and concentrated on pouring. The firelight struck the books on the walls, the draperies, the ghostly windows. The boy sat down on the other side of the hearth and began to sip. Was this the wrong day? Was this the time? Other men were made amiable and complaisant by alcohol, but not Allan. Irascibility and intolerance were the least effects of his desperate drinking. But Tony was impelled to speak, in spite of his fears and doubts.

"Dad, it's about my future," he said.

"Good God, is that all?" exclaimed Allan, almost infuriated. "I thought it was something important, and immediate. Your future! Isn't that all settled? Harvard, then the office. What else?"

Tony held the small glass tightly in his fingers, and prayed again. His grief for his father was like a dark and scattering wind among the bright straws of his prayers. "Dad," he began, feeling his way, "there is something else. I should have talked to you about it a long time ago, but you were ill, and I didn't want to disturb you."

Allan suddenly became sober, the alcohol lingering in his brain only as a stormy and waiting emotion ready to break out disastrously. "Well?" he said, and Tony was alarmed at that quiet word. Allan's eyes were fixed on this most beloved son, but there was no expression of tenderness in them now, but only a look of furious waiting, of gathering together, of a catapult lifted.

"I can't go back to Harvard, Dad," said Tony, looking away from that picture of violence. "I can't go into the railroad business."

Allan did not speak. He poured his glass half full of whisky and drank it thirstily. He put down the glass and stared at it. "I knew all the time, I suppose," he muttered at last, just when the silence was becoming intolerable to the younger man. "It was in my bones, the knowing. Sure, and it was in my bones like an aching."

What little remained of Tony's courage sank away. His father did not revert to this brogue and this phraseology of his childhood except when under insupportable stress. But Tony had to say, "Yes." He tried to smile into his father's eyes. "We always know about things not spoken of, we Irish, don't we?"

Allan threw up his head, pierced again in a wound which had never healed. His face subtly changed. Again he watched his son, and he licked his lips. Tony said gently, and with a tone of loving mirth, "We shanty Irish, grown up to be lace-curtain Irish. You and I, Dad."

Allan's dry lips fell open. "Tony, you never considered yourself ' Irish ' before, did you?"

"Yes, Dad, from the day you took us to see your parents."

Allan said, "I should never have taken you. It was wrong."

"Why? I'd never have known them, and Uncle Michael."

Allan got to his feet and began to wander up and down the room, distraught. He made pointless gestures; he knotted his fist and rubbed the side of his thin face with the fierceness of despair. Aimlessly he walked about, while Tony watched him with profound and miserable compassion and yearning.

"I learned so much from them. I learned about the victims of intolerance and cruelty and malice. They told me of the Irish Rebellion; they told me of the Famine, and the ships we wouldn't let into our harbours, and the degradation inflicted on hopeless men, and the social contempt, and the persecution of the Faith not only in America, but in Australia and England and many other places. They told me of the oppression of other men, too. . . ."

Some word had immobilised Allan. He stood where he had been walking, and all his body had become stiff and paralysed, caught in the midst of a gesture, a turn of the head. He said, huskily, "The Faith?"

Tony got to his feet and went to face his father. "Yes," he said very gently. "The Faith."

"You?" whispered Allan. Then he cried, "No! No!" He began to curse savagely, striking his fist into the palm of his left hand. "I knew it was wrong, taking you! Wrong, wrong! They influenced you, behind my back, treacherously——"

"No, Dad, no. They gave me a heritage, roots. They gave me something to hold to. I had never had it before. I never had any frame of reference, or anything to be proud of, or to identify myself with."

With a disordered upflinging of his hands, Allan threw himself away from his son. He shouted, "It's always the same, everywhere! The children reproach their fathers, and the children's children reproach their fathers, world from the beginning, world to the end! ' You never gave me—you never did this for me—I asked, and you didn't answer! '" He stopped abruptly, his hands on the back of his chair, and he glared into the fire as if struck by some blinding thought.

Tony, almost weeping, said, "I'm not reproaching you, Dad. You see, you didn't have anything to give. You lost it before I was born."

"It's always the same," Allan repeated feebly. Inch by inch, he crept around his chair and then fell into it. Tony came to stand beside him. I have made him worse; I've done something awful to him, thought the boy, distracted. After a long time Allan lifted his head and looked at his son. "I lost it," he said. "It was a long time ago; a June morning. A red ball. My First Communion. Mike. A long time ago."

He spoke as if speaking to himself, and it was like looking on nakedness. Tony glanced away. There was something here of supreme agony, which the most gentle hand dared not touch.

The fire fell away into dull crimson embers and the gale soared up into renewed ferocity as the earth dimmed outside. Then Tony, sunken in his own wretchedness, heard his father speak almost normally: "Give me another drink, Tony. Half a glass."

The young man obeyed, and his father took the glass from him and drank just a little. The firelight danced on the amber fluid and the tendoned hand holding it.

"Never mind," said Allan, overpowered with weariness. "What you've done is your own doing. I have nothing to say, no questions to ask. I'm too tired, and all at once it doesn't seem to matter. The railroad: you don't want to be part of it. Never mind. There's always DeWitt. I'm too tired. What do you want to do?"

Tony's lips parted, and then he could not speak. He sat down near his father, and he was very afraid. Allan began to study him, moving the liquor in the glass. The wind screamed at the windows, howled in the chimney. Now everything in the room retreated in the dusk.

"Well?" said Allan, not angrily or impatiently, but with sudden tenderness. "Don't be frightened, Tony. Tell me."

Tony sat there in all his blond splendour and strong young

manhood, but his face was anguished. "Dad," he said, "we've always been so close." He faltered. "Dad, I want to be a priest."

The glass fell from Allan's hand and crashed into firelit splinters on the marble hearth. Allan clutched the arms of his chair, began to rise. Then he dropped back as if he had received a blow which would kill him. He said, stammering weakly: "You came here—it's mocking me, you are. You know—sure, and you've been knowing all the time—to strike me down."

"I don't know what you're talking about, Dad, before God, I don't know!" cried Tony in simple terror. "What are you trying to say, Dad? What have I done?" He jumped to his feet, wavered, then collapsed on his knees before his father. He took one of Allan's hands, and was horrified at the cold clamminess of it. Allan's eyes burned down on his son, and his breath was raucous. But he was otherwise silent, looking deeply, listening.

All at once he was very still. His body relaxed like that of a dying man. Tony's head was bent, and now he began to sob dryly. He pressed his forehead against the wing of the chair, near Allan's head, and he cried like a child.

Then, to his incredulity, he felt Allan's hand on his head, a comforting hand, the hand of a father. Allan's fingers began to move down his son's face, turning it to him so that he might see the tears. Allan was smiling, an exhausted but loving smile.

"It's crying, the great boy is," he said. "It's crying, the boy who's wanting to be a priest! And what will he do, the great boy, when he has a parish, or is in foreign fields, and must see all the pain, and administer the Last Sacrament, and console the bereaved? Will the tender heart of him break, then?"

Tony, disbelieving, sobbed and stared at his father. Allan smiled into his eyes, and his mouth was shaking. Then, with a loud cry, Tony flung himself into his father's arms and they held each other in a convulsive embrace.

CHAPTER FORTY

"BOURGEOIS" HAD become Estelle deWitt's most contemptuous epithet, under her sons' secret tutelage. To her superficial mind it meant not only a class of people whom one did not invite, of course, to dinner or tea, but the whole DeWitt family. Uneasy about her own background, she had fortified her self-assumed position as an aristocrat by dainty sneers and simpers at those she stigmatised as "soulless grubs" and "coarse and vulgar boors engrossed only in their trades and businesses." Allan, to her, was the very archetype of the "family-less" and low-bred scoundrel with no interest in life but money.

So, after breakfast this Thanksgiving Day, she had sighed with sweet resignation and had said, "I must now consult with our country servants—such creatures!—to be sure that they will be careful with the china and count the silver and not overdo the turkey. I feel quite the middle-class wife in Portersville!"

Accompanied by Norman, she sailed into the pantry. Jon went up to his rooms, still chaotic with rage against Allan and his father. His loathing for them made his ears ring and his eyes blur when he tried to read by the fire. Middle-class swine! Who had permitted that class to emerge from their gutters? Before 1840, an aristocrat, a man of wealth and position, was the sole king in his world, a world composed of meek farmers and craftsmen living under the benign rule of the enlightened patrician. Then, with the revolting industrial revolution, had arisen the merchants, the tradesmen, the shopkeepers—the bourgeoisie, the employers of city labour. They had expanded industry to its present disgusting levels, had seized power from their betters, had built their bloated houses, and had piled up wealth which they did not deserve.

They had invaded "business," had seized it from white and gentlemanly hands and turned it into a vast empire. Their sons hammered at the gates of the genteel professions. Their shouts were enormous in the cloistered places, and their fat faces leered at the marble gods. They shouldered aside the dethroned and ancient masters of men.

They must be destroyed. Only then would power revert to the proper custodians of it—the aristocrats by birth and tradition—and only then would farmers and artisans and shopkeepers, and the "little" man, be returned to their ancient state of innocent happiness under the rule of their natural leaders, joyously content and obedient.

Jon and his friends in America and Europe were very careful not to be honest with each other about their real aims. Most of them were not even honest with themselves. Their one

457

passion was hatred for the middle class, the "exploiters." Though the bourgeoisie were responsible for compulsory education of the masses in Europe and in America, and though this same bourgeoisie had shown an insolent interest in building hospitals and art galleries and orphanages, and though they had regarded labour unions with a more or less friendly eye and had even assisted in their formation, this was never admitted by Jon and his friends. The fact that they were vehemently and proudly patriotic, whether American or English, French or German, was another manifestation of their "vulgarity."

The "aristocrats" were few, and helpless. The battering ram they needed to force the iron-hinged doors of the bourgeoisie was "labour." And labour could not be made one single battering ram unless it was convinced, in these burgeoning times of both the middle class and labour, that it was "exploited" and dispossessed and enslaved. Labour needed a voice. They had first heard that voice in the works of Voltaire and Rousseau; they had heard it more thunderously in Marx and his contemporaries.

It was odd that Jon and his friends did not count among the bourgeoisie the men who had amassed fortunes beyond credulity in the earlier days of the industrial revolution, and who now lived, apart from trade, in châteaux in France, and in mansions in Scotland, and in great houses on Fifth Avenue, and who now were aristocrats in their own right. Many of their memories had become very tenuous. Their lusty ancestors had emerged vague and patrician-coloured in their minds, delicate figures moving in a mist of spinet music and soft-scented air, intellectuals, patrons of the arts, gentlemen, administrators of law, grand seigneurs.

There were times when Jon deWitt's mind was torn open by his hatred of men like Allan Marshall, and then he saw the truth and saw it clearly. But this only increased his hatred. Nothing was too mad to say, to write, to do, so long as it clouded over reality and relieved the painful tumescence of truth, and promised power.

He threw aside the book he had been attempting to read, and snatched up a New York newspaper to reread a large item on the society pages which had, this morning, infuriated him. "Mr. and Mrs. Rufus deWitt have returned to the family home in Portersville, Pa. for Thanksgiving. They were accompanied by Mr. Allan Marshall and Mrs. Marshall, daughter of Mr. deWitt, and Rufus Anthony and Dolores and DeWitt Marshall, children of Mr. and Mrs. Allan Marshall. The family intends, as usual, to remain in Portersville until after the Christmas holidays, when they will return to New York."

At the very bottom of the article were a few insignificant lines: "Mr. Jon deWitt and his brother, Norman deWitt, sons of Mr. and Mrs. Rufus deWitt, are at present with the family in Portersville for the holidays."

It was these lines that so enraged Jon. His egoism, always touchy and sensitive, writhed at the yawning indifference. He might deride "those fools who love to get their names in print for the delectation of the drooling and imbecile public," but the fact remained that his insignificance in the eyes of newspapers struck violently at his self-love and his belief in his own importance. He said to himself vengefully, as he flung the paper into the fire: One of these days they'll notice me. One of these days they'll fawn on me and write of me with servility and terror."

When his luncheon tray arrived, the very sight of the food sickened him, and he left it untouched. So secretly convinced of his own lack of potency, so secretly nauseated by himself for all of his rationalising, the appearance of sustenance for his body, which was necessary if he was to exist, revolted him. All at once he wanted to talk with his mother, who was so sweetly understanding, and in whose comforting arms he could feel dominant again, and a man. He waited for over an hour, sitting by his windows, watching the crepuscular sky, the rising grey mounds of the desolate snow, the grey shadow of the deathly mountains. As he waited, he shivered. Once or twice he glanced at a table on which lay an opened letter he had received yesterday from Miles Peale. A kind, short letter, discreet and full of hinted promise. He could see the words again in his mind: "We must have a long talk. So many things are unresolved in me, but after all I am only seventeen, and you are so much wiser and experienced."

When Jon had received the letter he had been much aroused, and his heart had beat very fast. Now, as he looked at the letter, he could feel nothing but revulsion. He finally stood up, stretched wearily, and went in search of his mother. He expected to find her resting after luncheon, her pretty robe spread over her chaise longue, her youthful head pressed against satin pillows. But she

459

was not in her perfumed bedroom, all pink and white ruffles and pink draperies and rosy carpet, nor in her sitting-room, all gilt and blue and bright pink. Someone had stirred up her fire, and her scent was everywhere. Jon wandered about, touching lengths of silk and damask and ruffles lingeringly, opening her wardrobe doors to admire her gowns, picking up a small satin shoe to hold lovingly against his cheek. Then, in the dusk of the late afternoon, he sat down in a corner and waited.

It was some time before he heard her trilling girl's laughter, and a response from his brother Norman. Jon uttered an angry oath, then subsided. Probably Norman would merely conduct Estelle to her rooms, or remain only a few moments. Jon pulled himself smaller in his chair as the door opened. Estelle sailed in, giggling, with Norman beside her. She immediately sat down at her dressing-table, and Norman lighted the candles about it. She watched him, then said, "How ridiculous! We still have candles in this dreadful place, and oil lamps. So anachronistic, not even gas! How wonderful it will be to get back to New York where one has only to press a switch and every room is flooded with electric light! But I suppose we have to humour your father and Cornelia, who like to think of themselves as simple countryfolk."

Norman leaned over his mother's shoulder and admired her in the candlelight. "But you look so pretty, darling, in this flickering glow."

She preened, gave him a flirtatious look which was reflected to Jon in his hidden chair. He saw the look, and all at once it seemed monstrous to him, and not endearing as once it had appeared. He saw his mother's eyes well with light, as the eyes of a mistress might well in the company of an unacknowledged lover. So his mother had always been with him; he had never really known that his brother was also the recipient of these glows; these lambent glances, these arch touchings of arm, hand, and cheek, these tiltings of head, these conscious or unconscious slipping of a robe on a shoulder. To him, they had been "lovely," reserved for him alone in a secret and lonely communication of kindred spirits, untainted by ugliness, lighted only with tender beauty.

Norman's hands were moving slowly but firmly over his mother's shoulders. He bent his head and kissed her full on the lips. She murmured, "Such a sweet darling. I don't know what

I'd do without you, dearest. You are such a comfort." She patted his cheek and her distended brown eyes fixed themselves on her son. "The only one who understands me, in all the world."

Norman drew his hand yearningly over the sprightly curls on the top of Estelle's head. "Yes, I know. Everyone else is so gross. Even Jon."

Jon moved in his chair. Norman was laughing lightly. "Jon. He and those unspeakable friends of his in Paris. They talk of ' revolution ' and the ' rise of the proletariat ' and their modern art, and the ' new world.' But they're only babblers, really. The work which must be done will be done by men like me, and though we'll use the—the——"

"The what, darling?" asked Estelle innocently.

Norman smiled. "Well—odd—people, like Jon. Don't bother your beautiful head about it, Esty. We have to employ the strangest characters, and we will in the future, too. Any means to the good end."

Estelle was genuinely puzzled. "Jon is not exactly ' strange.' He does run off at tangents, I admit. But he's my boy, too, you know, though not as close as you, sweetheart."

Her face darkened, and the soft hands on the table clenched. "Oh, I do wish things could move fast, Norman! Men like your father, and that dreadful Allan Marshall, should be taught, finally, that they are no longer the masters of the world."

Norman's smile was indulgent. He repeated, "Don't bother your beautiful head about it. Well, now, I suppose I must leave you to rest. That goddamned awful family! I can't bear Thanksgiving Day, or any other holiday, when the clan gathers and glowers at each other."

"I do hope Jon won't precipitate another fight, as he did this morning," said Estelle crossly. "He only antagonises his father, and each time he does so, I see Rufus making another will, leaving him less and less. You, dear, have better sense. You agree with everybody, and never quarrel with anyone. So discreet."

"Don't worry," said Norman. "After all, it won't be Jon who will be in the thick of things. We move quietly, without noise, behind the scenes. We have a plan, now, about the schools, which we won't be able to put into operation, probably, for a few years. I've already had many long talks with educators . . . but there, I'm boring you, and you must rest."

He gave his mother another kiss, and left the room. Alone,

461

Estelle deliberately relaxed her taut face. She stood up before her mirror, ran her fingers lovingly over her whole torso. She began to make soft and cooing sounds to her image in the mirror, the murmurs of a lover. Jon watched through his frightful sickness of body and soul, and his mouth and hands and feet were cold and numb. All at once he could no longer endure the sight of his mother. He said over and over to himself: Bitch, bitch, ugly, perverted bitch. Treacherous, self-loving bitch. His body became slack and weak and immovable.

He had known that he had always been in competition with his brother for the sole affections of his mother. But he had not known this, this deliberate setting of brother against brother for a shallow woman's vanity. He had thought himself the chosen one, the confidant, the protector, the guardian. He had thought of Norman as an eager and docile student of an older brother's teachings, a follower, a somewhat childish and petulant demander of a few maternal kisses. He and Estelle had often laughed fondly together about all this, as they had sat cosily together in this very room. Estelle had sometimes complained about Norman's "immaturity," and Jon had soothed her with remarks that time would take care of that.

He was not enraged, now, against his brother. He saw himself and Norman as victims of this woman's conceit, repulsive superficiality of soul, and resentment against all the other members of the family. They were her coming revenge against the DeWitts and the Marshalls; they were her secret weapons which she sharpened with murderous words of love and incitement in the seclusion of her rooms. And while she sharpened these weapons she must destroy her sons, too, in her devouring greed for power.

Estelle rang for her maid, and her tug at the bell rope was vicious. She went into the bathroom, and Jon, gathering what remained of his volition, slipped from the chair, ran into the sitting-room, and let himself out into the dark corridor. His one instinct was flight, and he went into his rooms and pulled on his fur-lined overcoat. He fled down the stairs only five minutes ahead of his nephew Tony, and went outside into the roaring chaos of wind and snow. It was hard, walking against the gale and the heaped snow of the unshovelled walk. He did not stop until he was panting and his chest was a painful constriction. He stood near an enormous spruce, which was already so weighted with the dull greyness that it bent sideways. The softly-lighted windows of the house rose some distance behind him, its outlines blurred against the ghostly sky.

The fierce cold penetrated through the fur, and Jon was one long trembling. Suddenly he began to retch. He grasped one of the prickling branches of the spruce in his bare hand to support himself. Acid poured from his swollen throat; it seemed to pour from his very soul in a burning stream. He did not try to restrain it; it was as if he were purging himself of poison.

His shoulders, his uncovered head, whitened dimly in the howling gloom. His mouth was filled with fire and sickness. He put his hands in his pockets and stood with bent head. But his shivering became a constant spasm all through his flesh.

Too late for me, he thought. I can never be a man again. Never a man. She has killed the manhood in me; she has turned me into a—a thing. Perhaps it was latent in me, but without her it might never have come to the surface. I could be a man, now, with a wife and with children. I could be a son of a father who respected me, and who wanted my help. I could stand with Allan, without his sneers. There could have been health in me. I could never have been used by the hating whisperers in London and Paris and New York, for I would have been a man.

The gale shrilled through the spruce. Too late, too late! He listened to the dolorous words, and knew they were true.

Die. He caught the wounding spruce branch again, and stood very still, his body still heaving. Die. Of course. Somewhere, deep in him, had lain the awful alternative to what he was; it had lain there ever since he had been a youth.

He pulled out his watch and strained to see it in the falling darkness. Almost five o'clock. In another hour the family would be arriving. Jon closed his eyes convulsively. The time had arrived for what he must do. He went back to the house, struggled against the heavy door, let himself into the warm hall with its fire-shadows on the ceiling. He closed the door, and stood panting. He shrank when he heard the door of the library open. Tony was crossing the soft-coloured carpet, deep in some engrossing thoughts of his own. Without willing it, Jon whispered his name.

Tony, startled, came to a halt and peered at his uncle in the dusk. Jon saw that he was unusually grave. When Tony identified Jon, he coloured, and began to turn away, but Jon followed him and caught his arm. "Tony," he muttered. "Listen to me, just for a moment. I'm asking you to forgive me. Forgive me, forgive me."

Tony stiffened, then turned fully to him. His eyelids were red, but he studied Jon earnestly, and in silence. He saw the snow on Jon's shoulders; he saw the blueness of his hands and the strange set of his face. He said very gently, "But I already forgave you, a long time ago. Don't think of it, Jon. Try to forget it."

He drew his arm from Jon's grasp, nodded, smiled kindly, and went up the stairs. Jon watched him go. He thought: If he would just turn once, and smile at me again, and let me know he forgives me. . . . But Tony, preoccupied with his own urgent problems, did not look back.

Jon, climbing the stairs after his nephew, and moving like a dying man, fixed his thoughts on only one thing. In his rooms, finally, he rang for a servant and said that he would not be down for dinner, did not feel well, and would ring when he wished a tray. But the family must not be informed until they were all assembled at the table, and Mrs. deWitt must be begged "not to bother" until after dinner. Mr. Jon had "one of his headaches" and would join the family later. Jon had no fear that his mother would come anxiously darting to his room, for he had given many messages like this before, especially on days like these. She would excuse her son prettily. He could see her now coquettishly tilting her head, smiling her sweet and avaricious smile, her brown eyes shining with that artificial ardour of hers, her manner bravely buoyant to cover the inconvenient whim of a son.

He closed the door after the servant, to whom he had spoken very quietly. He neatly hung up his coat and shut the wardrobe door. He brought out a set of keys and unlocked a drawer in his chest. There, among perfumes he used for his own delight in his rooms, and other miscellaneous objects, was a small box. On the lid he had written, many years ago, in a light mood of bravado and fond amusement at himself: "For future reference." How quaint, he thought. How damnably quaint I was, how naughtily droll and sophisticated! His disgust for himself renewed his sickness. He glanced at the mirror on the chest and saw his face, drawn, cloven with lines of suffering, contorted with self-revulsion.

He opened the box and looked at the deadly little grey tablets in it. When he had been twenty he had strained his back in some absurd way, and had had considerable pain. "Warning: one tablet every eight hours." The tablets had relieved the pain, had bestowed delicious drowsiness on him, had enabled him to sleep. Sleep, he thought. He went into his bathroom, drew some water, and swallowed all eight of the tablets. Then he returned to his room, stirred up the fire, and sat down.

How long would it be? A deathlike calmness had come to him. He hoped that the tablets had not deteriorated with time. He would dislike to hang himself, or cut his throat. Melodramatic, and ridiculous, and sordid. He laughed silently in the warm stillness of the room. The storm was rising in ferocity. The draperies swayed out a little from the windows; the fire crackled hungrily. One had only to wait; he leaned back in his chair and closed his eyes.

Then, without warning, a most appalling loneliness took hold of him, a desolate sorrow, keen and piercing. The locked door of his room seemed symbolic. He was alone. He had always been alone. He would be alone forever. Imprisoned in the earth, the suns and the centuries would mean nothing to him. The earth would be blown into chaff and would whirl in its empty orbit, and he would not know. Soon he would drop into the tunnel of blackness, and all that he was would be lost until the end of time.

All that I am. But I am nothing, nothing. I was never anything. For the first time he thought of his father, and the sorrow became more poignant. His father had been cheated—first by wives and now by a son. He said aloud, "But it's better for you. I never thought of you before; I saw you through the eyes of my mother. I am not sentimental, and I do not say you are a good and injured man. You are no better, no worse, than others. But you are better than I. I've seen you shudder at me, and you had a right to shudder. I could not wrong you by dying; I could only wrong you by living. You'll know that, for I don't believe you ever lied to yourself. Forgive me—for having been born."

Loneliness had him in advance of death. It was a parching on his lips, a grievous aching in his bones. It was a despair in his heart. Slowly, a numbness began in his feet and crept upwards, but his thoughts became more intense. Men were born alone; they lived alone. But most terrible of all, they died alone. And died impotent. The impotence was worse, in the last hour, when a man realised that his life had been one endless insult against life and nature and his fellows. Then there was no consolation. There was only the looking down into the abyss. For this loneliness, there was no hope.

The numbness had reached his knees, and suddenly he recalled the cherished letters from his friends which he had kept in another locked drawer. He remembered that the police would come, as they always came at a hint of unnatural death. There was also his diary, with damning names garlanded with an affection like rotten flowers. There was Miles Peale's letter on his table. He could do one decent thing. He would burn it all, so that what he was and why he had died would not permanently mar others and throw filth upon them. His mother's name was in the diary. That, too, would vanish. He forgave her with a rush of pity that was like a convulsion in him. He, alone, was guilty, however much she had cajoled and perverted him. At the end, each man was guilty of what he was.

He tried to stand up. The numbness had taken his knees. Crawling, then, like a wounded animal, he pulled himself to his chest of drawers. Curiously, it seemed a long way, acres away, retreating into mists. His desperate fingers sank themselves into the carpet, which had become a yielding rubber floor. The sweat of dissolution was on him now. He could feel death rushing at him on black wings, a buzzard eager for decaying flesh. His eyes were filming; coils of wispy darkness floated before and about and over him. They were winding themselves in his throat, and stopping his breath. Inch by tortuous inch he dragged his body over the carpet. The chest was becoming a tiny object, infinitely far off, dancing on its legs. He whispered aloud, "God, help me to get the letters, the diary. Don't let me die until they are burned."

His breath had so diminished that he had to stop, weaving his head back and forth to clear it. God. But there was no God. Had not he and his friends laughingly and contemptuously agreed to that? Superstition; the mumbo jumbo of a church which used God like a whip to subdue the masses. God was a materialistic and mechanical force, mindless, sightless, operating like a gigantic machine whose end was inevitable in a storm of cosmic dust. He gasped, and his voice was stronger. "God, help me. Only a short way. Help me."

His breath had returned a little. The numbness had engulfed his thighs; he dragged them behind him, for they were already dead. His thoughts became confused. He had been crawling for æons; he had never done anything else in all his life but crawl, crawl like this on his belly. Caverns opened in his brain, caverns full of emptiness and noise. Was that the sea he was approaching? It was pounding in his ears; it was surging about him. Mother sea, lightless depths of her, cloudy deeps of her, moonless and bottomless. He reached out his hand to touch the water, and touched the chest. His thoughts cleared again. He struggled against the chest as Hercules struggled against mountains. The letters and the diary were in his hand. Now he was breast-deep in the breakers. "I must throw them, before the waters wet them." He said again, "God help me," and strength was in his arm and he threw everything into the fire. The numbness retreated though the ocean was frothing about him, surging into his throat. The table was nearby, and grasping it, he reached Miles's letter, and then it, too, was in the fire which danced in its joy of feasting.

The last and dying strength went from him. He lay down on the rug. Combers rolled over him; he could hear them hissing. He breathed deeply of their substance, drew it into his lungs. Now they rolled him about, tossing him back and forth strongly yet gently. They hummed and thundered with music, wild and majestic music, and he thought of God again as the sea took him with love. The sky was without a moon, but a beautiful milky light poured down on him. It flowed through the waters in which he was sinking. He thought: There really is no horror in it. But there is God. How does one address God? Words from his childhood, taught briefly in forgotten years, returned to him. Only a few; he wished he knew them all; he could see the bright tails of them slipping away fish-like in the cold curl of the breakers. "Our Father, Our Father . . ."

"Our Father," prayed the sea, and sucked him down.

He lay on the rug, curled in a fetal position, the fire on his drained face and open eyes. And they were full of peace, the peace of a child who had reached home after a terrible journey among monsters in a twisted jungle.

CHAPTER FORTY-ONE

CORNELIA GLANCED furtively at her watch. Half-past seven, and the dreadful yearly dinner almost over. In another hour and a half, perhaps earlier, considering the storm, the "family" would be gone. So far, she thought with relief, though there had been the customary tensions, the half-hidden glowers, the ambiguously sarcastic words, the meaningful glances and smirks —as usual—there had been none of those "explosions" which had sometimes broken out during and after such dinners. One of the "triggers" was absent, of course: Jon deWitt. Everyone seemed somewhat distrait and unusually silent, which was a blessing. Allan hardly spoke; though she knew he had been drinking, he had appeared at the table in complete sobriety. Lydia Purcell, straight and slender as always, though her hair seemed to have whitened perceptibly, spoke only of the most ordinary things, smiled at everyone with her characteristic cool and kind aloofness, did not mention her dead husband, and murmured about the storm, which had become worse during the past hour or two. No one ever really knew Mamma, thought Cornelia, and thought this, too, was a blessing, and very considerate of Lydia. There were no people more tedious than those who insisted on baring their souls to you, preferably in antagonistic or sneering or maudlin voices.

Laura, Cornelia noted with pleasure, looked less attractive than ordinarily. Pinched, thought Cornelia. Like her aunt Lydia, Laura had the decency not to become confidential or "warm" at any time.

Cornelia did not want to know in the slightest why everyone at the dinner was so quiet and indifferent to everyone else. It was enough for her that they were. But she had her own inquisitiveness, which was, however, very mild and fleeting. That dreadful Pat Peale looked sick and broken; good. Cornelia's half-sister, Ruth, was silent near Allan, her translucent face grief-stricken over the death of her father. Such a pretty thing, but such an old maid, thought Cornelia idly. Ruth's head was bright yellow silk in the candlelight, and she kept it bent over the table. The "children," Tony, Dolores, DeWitt, Miles, Fielding, and Mary, had nothing to say to each other, though Tony and his sister sometimes exchanged gentle glances of some secret understanding about which Cornelia was not curious. She did, however, smile at Mary Peale affectionately when she caught the girl's vivacious eye. Mary had "common sense," and a high and mischievous humour. She would be excellent for Tony, who was too grave.

Estelle, dressed in baby-blue silk, and jewelled and perfumed, prattled. She was the only one not caught up in her own thoughts. It did not matter to her very much that the others merely muttered or murmured at her foolish remarks. She was all radiance. Let the surly DeWitts simmer in their bad tempers; she alone knew that a hostess, and her guests, should be "enthusiastic" about anything and everything. Beside her sat her courtier-son, Norman, watchful of her every beam and glow.

Cornelia was happy to see that her father, Rufus, seemed almost his own self, affable and with quite a good colour. But he, usually so loquacious, confined himself to looking after his family and guests. He smiled and smiled, benevolently. Cornelia did not catch his occasional long and yearning glance at Lydia, his former wife.

The servants were bringing in the ritualistic pumpkin and mince pies, and there was also a flaming plum pudding. The butler was discreetly placing a bottle of port on a silver tray with glasses already waiting. This was for the "gentlemen," Rufus, Allan, Patrick Peale, and Norman, after the "ladies" had retired to the drawing-rooms and the "children" had gone upstairs to talk briefly together. Lydia Purcell saw the tray; a fifth glass was missing. Her grey lips twitched once or twice, then became quiet again.

"The storm is getting much worse," said Cornelia hopefully. "I pray none of you will find it difficult to get home."

Lydia smiled at her with understanding affection. She said, "I'm afraid we'll have to leave almost immediately after dinner. Cornelia, that green velvet and lace is very becoming. I haven't seen it before."

Mahogany gleamed back from its polished surface; the silver twinkled; the candlelight fluttered, the fire snapped heartily. The gold-banded china on the white lace cloth shimmered, and the crystal glasses winked in and out. How handsome we all look, and how gracious, thought Cornelia, laughing maliciously to herself. A wonderful picture of a loving family gathered about the Thanksgiving board. I wonder if all family gatherings are like this, charged with hatreds and resentments and malevolences and griefs and envies. No doubt, she added. Something should be done about "family dinners." They should be abolished in the name of peace.

No one had spoken for a few moments, then Estelle sat up very straight in her chair, her prettily-rouged face intent. "I thought I heard somebody cry out, or something," she said, giving her husband an anxious look. "Do you think it might be Jon?"

"I heard nothing," said Rufus.

"His terrible headaches," murmured Estelle. She put her hands on the arms of the chair. Should she excuse herself and go up to see Jon? No, that would be discourteous and ill-bred during dinner, though the DeWitts would never understand that. She subsided, then became conscious that Tony was regarding her intently. "I thought I heard it, too, Aunt Estelle. But it seemed to come from outside, or nowhere." He added, "Probably just an animal, captured by an enemy. It didn't sound—human."

All at once he thought of Jon deWitt, and he shivered. He would go in to see Jon. There had been something very wrong with the older man. I felt I should turn, on the stairs, he thought.

As Estelle so thoroughly despised Tony, she discounted what he had said. Her anxiety left her. She fixed her attention on the slicing of the pudding. Why could not servants in the country do anything with style? But then, nobody here cared.

The pudding was eaten in a thick silence, broken only once or twice by Rufus's gracious remarks about its excellence. Patrick merely moved his serving on his plate; Allan watched him. He was getting indigestion again, as he always did when Patrick was present. Moreover, he wanted something to drink, very urgently, another symptom of his detestation for the other man. Port! An old man's drink; it merely stupefied one.

The ladies retired, their skirts murmurous behind them. Rufus bestowed his sunlike smile on the gentlemen. "Any who would prefer brandy?" It was a polite question, and was always answered politely in the negative. But this time Allan said abruptly: "Whisky and soda for me, please." Rufus raised his eyebrows, then ordered whisky. Patrick smiled very darkly, for Allan's benefit, and sipped at his port. Norman smiled his open and deliberately silly smile, and took the glass of wine. As always, he prepared to listen acutely; his expression was a boyish camouflage.

"I know this is a holiday," said Allan, in the aggressive voice which he helplessly assumed in the presence of Patrick, "and I know I shouldn't talk business . . ."

Rufus put up his hand benignly. "Then, please don't, my boy."

"But we are to have a directors' meeting Monday, and we are here, and there is just a point I want to emphasise." Allan spoke doggedly. Patrick sipped his wine, looked weary; Norman grinned inanely. "All right, what's the point?" asked Rufus. He wore a small plaid shawl over his shoulders, against draughts, and he pulled it closer.

"It's that damned Pullman Company again," said Allan. "It's not only the manufacturer of sleeping, dining, chair, and club cars, but I've heard a rumour it is gradually buying up other companies manufacturing these cars. It services all of its cars, and it charges us a nice penny. I think it would be an excellent idea for us to buy up some of their stock so we'll at least get back some of our money, and if we bought enough stock to have a voice in the management, we could get preferred treatment in so far as our road is concerned."

Rufus considered this thoughtfully. He motioned to the butler for a forbidden cigar, had it lighted for him, and puffed. Now he lost much of his elderly appearance, and his old ruddy colour brightened, and his eyes sparkled. "They're quite a monopoly," he said thoughtfully. He laughed. "Monopolies sometimes hurt other monopolies. Well, I'm not very worried about them, the Pullman people. They're very ambitious, and ambition is looked upon with suspicion by government these days. If they become too—ambitious—we can always get our friends, the senators, after them. It's too early yet, however, for us to be virtuous about the Pullman monopoly. I should say a few years —then we may be able to buy and own our own Pullmans, and service them. Allan, my boy, make a note of that for the future —your future, not mine. In the meantime, of course, we could buy up as much of their stock as possible. Patrick, you as one of our directors—what do you say?"

"I shall give it thought, sir," said Patrick coldly. "I am not prepared to give my assent to our company buying it. Perhaps as

471

individuals, private individuals. . . . I can't say I'm particularly interested, and I'm against monopolies. . . ."

"Don't buy up all the available stock early on Monday, before I have time to get around to it," said Allan contemptuously. "With Laura's money, and yours, and your influence on Ruth . . ."

"Now, now," said Rufus. "Didn't someone say this was a holiday, boys? Thanksgiving; festive family board; gathering together in a spirit of gratitude and good fellowship." He enjoyed the violence of the long look Patrick turned on Allan.

Allan was also pleased at that look. "Well, I'm going to propose that the company buy as much as possible, too. On Monday."

Patrick drew a deep breath; some of the port splashed on his fingers. He said in a suppressed voice of rage, "I resent your insinuations. I have no 'influence' on Ruth Purcell. Her mother, and her lawyers, manage her estate."

"But she is such an innocent soul," said Allan. "She is the last remaining member of the family who believes in you, Pat. I hear she gave you twenty thousand dollars for one of your pet charities in Philadelphia."

Patrick turned a sick crimson. "There's no secret about it."

Allan was almost happy. "Yes, there is. I'm the only one who knew. Congratulations, however. It's a worthy charity." He held out his cigarette for a light, and the butler sprang to attention. "Poor Ruth," meditated Allan, with a malefic side glance at Patrick. "Too bad there isn't a man in the family available for marrying her, such as one of your own sons."

Patrick put down his glass, his small hands clenched on the table, and he looked at Allan. The latter was immediately alerted, his Celtic intuition stirring. No, it wasn't possible! The pallid Pharisee wasn't actually plotting, back there in his immaculate greedy mind . . . It would be a disaster, all that power in those bloodless hands, a disaster for the company. All that stock, that money.

Rufus, watching, slowly tapped his cigar in a silver tray. He saw that Allan and Patrick were regarding each other fixedly, the hatred and suspicion darting like lightning between them, almost visible. "Too bad," repeated Allan softly. His black eyes jumped under his brows.

Then Patrick turned to Rufus. "Sir, you are our host. Am I to be insulted this way?"

Rufus smiled urbanely. "Are you children exchanging blows, instead of middle-aged men? Should I reprove one of you? But Allan, Pat is our guest. It is becoming tiresome, always having to remind you. Shall we change the subject?"

You killed my father, when you told me about him, thought Patrick, remembering the terrible scene between himself and the older Peale so long ago. It had never occurred to him that he had not needed to tell his father what he knew; he believed it had only been "just" to do so, to throw his bitter accusations in the old man's face, to scorn him, to display his enormous anger and disillusion. He felt no guilt that he had neglected his father in his age, nor any shame that Allan had been, at the last, the one comforter of a man who had only been human.

Allan, having struck at Patrick victoriously again, abandoned him. He had to have these victories to assuage his own lifelong pain. He gave his attention to Rufus. He filed away the thought of Ruth Purcell for future reference. He removed a clipping from his coat pocket. "I read this in a London paper yesterday, sir, and I kept it for you." He began to read: "'The United States is like an enormously rich country overrun by a horde of robber barons, and very inadequately policed by the central government. This situation can become dangerous for the rest of the world. . . .'" He threw the clipping on the table, then lifted it and burned it down to ash with the aid of a candle. "Do you know, sir, what they really mean? They are frightened that we'll invade what they call their 'traditional' markets. We, and particularly Germany, are already doing it."

"Yes?" said Rufus. "And if we and Germany are?"

Allan slapped his hand on the table. "Germany is still the greater threat. She is as busy as a bee, all over the markets of the world, selling superior goods at lower prices. The Kaiser is encouraging all this, and German industry is given every assistance by the German government. Nothing restrains it. No price fixings, in a gentlemanly way, as in England. No cosy little agreements among manufacturers."

"Well?" said Rufus.

"Don't you see?" asked Allan impatiently. "We've been in a new era since the middle of the last century. Before that, wars were fought for territories and peoples or to settle private national grudges. Now they are fought for world markets. It really began, though most people don't realise it, with the Civil War."

Never Victorious, Never Defeated

"War?" exclaimed Rufus. "Now, really, dear boy, you are using your imagination. Do you think England—and Germany —would actually engage themselves in a war for world markets?"

"I do." Allan's voice became excited. "That is what is being plotted, now."

"Plot?" repeated Patrick with disdain. "Are you out of your mind?"

"No insults, please, no personalities. Allan, you are incorrigible." But Rufus was disturbed. "It is true that the history of the world is the history of hunger. . . ."

"Look at the agricultural acreage of the world," said Allan, becoming more and more excited. "It is retreating. Industrial cities are expanding, becoming bloated. Wealth isn't based on agriculture any longer, but only on goods. Hunger remains, however, and it will increase as long as industry expands uncontrollably. A man can get along without a machine, but he can't get along without bread. That's something we'll all have to learn, and we may have to learn it written with blood. England hasn't learned it, and neither have we, nor any other nation. In the meantime, wars will be fought for markets for goods, while agriculture declines and men begin to starve. Famine will eventually destroy our cities, and our city industry."

But Rufus came back to the one alarming word: "War? Who says so?"

"The English are already preparing. I have books you must read, sir. And Germany is beginning to smell what is brewing in England, among all the polite words of diplomats and the peace-mouthings at The Hague. And we'll be in it, eagerly looking at world markets, too, to avoid panics—panics in our industrial cities."

"Incredible," murmured Rufus. "Are you sure your fertile Irish imagination . . .?" He thought, characteristically, not of his own sons, but of his grandson Tony, and Tony's children. And the children of Dolores and DeWitt.

Patrick smiled with cool contempt at Rufus, but Rufus was frowning. "Why do you suppose," asked Allan, "that Congress is considering, again and again, against the wishes of the people, a Federal income tax? We've gotten along very well without it, but now politicians in Washington are agitating for it, and jabbering about it. How can a nation conduct a war unless it has vast revenues? Each time a Federal income tax is suggested, the people protest angrily. But they grow tired of old issues. It is my prophecy that within a few years we'll have that tax. And then we'll have a war. For markets. And to avoid panics in the country, and to devour the products of our machines."

Rufus tapped his fingers agitatedly on the tablecloth. "It's very strange," he mused, "but long ago, a long time ago, my brother said almost the very same thing. I laughed. . . ."

"Do you really believe, sir," said Patrick protestingly, "that England would kill off her young men, and acquiesce to a war merely for markets? If war comes between England and Germany —and I reject the monstrous idea—it will be a war of principles, for England invariably has conducted wars on the noblest of principles. . . . She must maintain the loftiness of Anglo-Saxon culture—our own culture, by the way."

Allan turned to him wrathfully. "Our own culture? Have you forgotten that over twenty per cent of the American people are of German stock, and that we have millions of Americans of Italian.stock, and other racial origins? Anglo-Saxon culture be damned!"

"You speak, of course, as an Irishman," said Patrick with an almost feminine malice.

Rufus lifted his hand to restrain a vehement movement on the part of his son-in-law and said to Patrick, with the utmost mildness, "Allan speaks as a rational man, for he speaks of facts. Sorry, Pat. But, Allan, I am certain we shall never have a Federal income tax."

"We shall," said Allan, nodding his head grimly. "And look for us to be in a war shortly thereafter. A peaceful nation, sir? We are an industrial nation."

Smiling disdainfully, Patrick examined his hands. "Would you have us return to an agricultural economy?"

"Yes," said Allan. "Or rather, if I had the supreme power, I would keep an equable ratio between industry and agriculture, and remembering the warnings of Patrick Henry, I would forever prohibit the Federal government from taxing the people. The Federal government, again quoting the warnings of Patrick Henry, and George Washington, would then never be in a position of power to destroy the liberty of a nation through wars and taxation."

Norman deWitt had not spoken, but had only smiled. Now he looked at Allan and his eyes narrowed viciously. Allan was shaking a finger in Patrick's annoyed face. "I tell you, there are men hoping and plotting for wars in order to enslave the world! Freedom is hateful to them, anywhere, for a free nation frustrates their lust for personal power."

"Really, this is ridiculous," said Patrick with aversion. "America shall never engage in any wars, for any reason. But let me propose a hypothetical question: what if we are ever attacked?"

Allan turned from him slowly and fixed his eyes sombrely, as if seeing something at a great distance. "I feel, I know it in my very body, that we'll never be attacked. We may be *told* we have been attacked, but it will be a lie. Unless—unless . . ." and he looked with the deepest gravity at Rufus, "we invite the attack, or arm a nation to attack us. It could happen. It is already happening in Europe. The munition makers of France are arming Germany, and the German munition makers are arming France, with full knowledge and consent of their respective governments."

"That is mad!" exclaimed Patrick.

Allan stared at him for a long moment. "I will send you some of the books I have been reading. Among them will be books by Karl Marx and his contemporaries. You should get an idea from these books about the kind of men who are plotting against all mankind. Wars are their opportunities." He shook his finger again at Patrick's face. "The Spanish-American War was a testing ground for new weapons, not a mere *opera bouffe* written for Teddy Roosevelt."

He knows too much, thought Norman. He burst into a high, giggling fit of laughter, then clapped his hand over his mouth and gazed at the three affronted men like a naughty schoolboy, his eyes brightly shining and rounded. He dropped his hand and simpered. "I was thinking of Teddy in his Rough Rider hat," he apologised.

He had effectively broken up a conversation which he considered dangerous. Rufus was ashamed of him, Allan looked as though he should like to strike him, and Patrick glanced at him coldly. "Shall we join the ladies?" asked Rufus, and prepared to rise.

"Just one moment, please," said Allan. All mirth vanished from Norman's face. Allan hesitated, and his cigarette trembled in his fingers. He put it between his lips in an agitated gesture. "I suppose I should speak about this when we are alone, sir, but this is the family, isn't it?" He paused, and dropped the cigarette on a tray. "Tony is going to be a priest. He told me this afternoon."

"Incredible," said Patrick angrily. "You, of course, refused to permit it."

Rufus lost his new colour, but he smiled at Allan affectionately. "I suspected it, my boy. Were you afraid to tell me alone?"

Allan was silent. Then he asked, "Does Cornelia know?"

"She suspected it." Rufus sighed. "Don't you know yet, Allan, that Cornelia is fond of you and will be quite happy about Tony if you are happy?" He waited. But Allan did not speak. Rufus added, "You are happy, aren't you, Allan?"

Allan looked only at Rufus. "I am happy," he answered. He smiled with gratitude. "I am still here, and there is DeWitt."

Tony, in the upstairs living-room, was not happy. He was afraid of the young Peales, even though Miles showed him interest and respect. Fielding was awed by Tony's proficiency in sports, and constantly consulted him, and admired him for these talents, at least. Mary was open in her preference and fondness for him, and could make him laugh even when he was the most grave. Yet in the moments he was most entertained by these young relatives, his fear was the strongest. He sat near his sister to-day, and his fear was more insistent than ever. It made him reach out his hand involuntarily to Dolores and hold her hand tightly. The grey storm and the dark night pressed against the windows and the sound of it filled the chintz-bright "children's sitting-room," and the imminent presence of it seemed to dim the lamplight and threaten the fire.

Miles had been discussing their instructors at Harvard, and Tony had been listening with interested attention, as if the subject were important to him and as if he would return to Harvard after the Christmas holidays. Miles was witty and charming; he could pinion some hapless teacher with a few words; he could, with a word or two, a gesture of his eloquent hands, paint a hilarious and vivid picture of some timid and learned professor. DeWitt, who rarely laughed, laughed now. Mary shrieked with mirth. Dolores smiled in spite of herself. Tony, though inwardly distressed, also smiled.

Mary sat on the hearthrug, petite and very fetching in her scarlet-velvet dress with its lace collar, her black hair tumbling in fire-crested waves down her back. Next year, she would "put up her hair," but she was not in a particular hurry for this sign of adulthood. She knew that her dusky curls added to her winsome prettiness, and as she was not young in heart, they gave her a look of false innocence which she shrewdly suspected disarmed others, to her advantage. Her large black eyes were full of light, and her mouth was a ripe plum in her pointed face. When she glanced at Tony, sitting in almost complete silence next to his sister, her expression would soften, yet grow even more animated.

As she covertly watched Tony, so did her brother Miles watch Dolores's angel face topped with its waving mound and escaping tendrils of pale but shining hair. He thought he had never seen so exquisite a girl, or one so happily quiet, or so dignified. Her dark blue silk, cunningly fashioned to enhance her purity of character, was like a postulant's uniform with its small white collar. To the superficial, Dolores had no "personality." But Miles was not superficial; his love and longing for this girl made him intuitive about her. When she glanced at him reluctantly, as he spoke, he saw the crystalline glimmer of her light blue eyes, and he would think in the very midst of some clever remark, that there would never be any other woman in the world for him. As much as was possible for the worldly and intellectual Miles, he reverenced her. Her smiles at some of his sallies were genuine, and not forced as were Tony's, and Miles was quite aware of this. He was careful to keep any hint of salaciousness out of his word-pictures and ridicule of his teachers, even though gay lewdness usually distinguished his speech when with others.

As she was so much under the influence of her brother, Miles was respectful with Tony, while he secretly hated him for that influence which stood in his way. He knew that Tony would urgently and sternly object to any marriage between Miles Peale and his sister, and Tony's opinion was important to Rufus deWitt and Allan Marshall. Cornelia, who disliked Miles, as she disliked all the Peales except Mary, was determined on an international marriage for her daughter. She would stand with her father and husband against him, for her own reasons. Miles, the realist, never discounted the odds operating in his disfavour, nor was he of a particularly optimistic nature. The way to Dolores appeared almost impregnable.

DeWitt watched everyone, as he sat, so small and dark, by the fire with his cane beside him. He was coldly diverted by all the currents in this room, and relished, in advance, the coming frustrations of his companions. He had already dismissed Tony, who was no longer a rival in love or in ambition. Miles, married to that silly Dolores, would be half-disarmed in a war. Mary could flirt her curls at Tony, and tilt her head and look at him through those thick eyelashes, and it would come to nothing. In the meantime, he, DeWitt, could enjoy her prettiness and think of a future marriage with her. He was the only one really at ease in the room.

Fielding had been coached in ski-ing by the obliging and good-tempered Tony, and when Miles had delivered himself of a last sally about his instructors, Fielding eagerly began to discuss his favourite sport with Tony. Tony stirred a little in his uneasy apathy and fear, and suggested a new Alpine wax for skis, about which he had learned a few weeks ago. Then his interest dwindled. He was thinking again of his uncle, Jon deWitt, and the look on Jon's face in the dusk at the foot of the stairs. I should have gone back, he thought. I shouldn't have given in to my dread of him, and my disgust for him. These are not emotions a future priest should have; it is like a doctor wincing away from sores and pulsating ulcers instead of treating them. Something had happened to Jon. Perhaps if I had gone back I could have helped.

Miles, who ridiculed his brother's ardent preoccupation with sports, pretended to listen with attention to the conversation between Fielding and Tony. He yawned inside. Children's jabberings. It was incredible to him that Tony Marshall, who topped him in honours at college, should actually be interested in attempts to break his neck on steep and snowy hills. Miles, smiling with fixed politeness, passed his hand over his mahogany ringlets, and drifted off again into thoughts of Dolores. Mary yawned like a kitten, showing all her small white teeth. She stretched, lay back on an elbow on the hearthrug, and listened to Tony's voice if not to his words.

Fielding, who was no fool, quickly guessed that Tony had lost interest in ski-ing. His long and yellowish face became affronted. He said, "How about ski-ing with me, to-morrow?"

Tony hesitated.

It would be exhilarating to fly down a white and shining slope, with the sun hurling your shadow after you and the pines

479

throwing up a spume of snow as you hissed by like the wind. The brilliant loneliness of the mountains, the scent of resin, and the wild purity of the cold air! It was best to be alone when you ski-ed, even if dangerous. But the danger of loneliness was its own intoxicant. Tony looked at Fielding, who was waiting eagerly. He was just a "kid." It wasn't good to let him ski alone. Tony said, "Well, all right. But first I'll have to see if the snow has packed down enough. I'll call you." He asked, curiously: "Why do you like to ski, Field?"

Fielding raised his yellow eyebrows. "Why, it feels good. A kind of power. You go fast; nobody can catch you. And there they are down there, in the valley, on the roads, in their silly sleighs, and there you are up there, going ten times as fast, and laughing at them."

Tony made no comment, but Miles quickly turned to his brother and studied him thoughtfully. He rubbed a knuckle over his chin as he reflected. Slowly, he took out a packet of cigarettes, put one in his mouth and lit it. "A kind of power." It was disquieting to have to reckon with Fielding in the future, Fielding of the ridiculous skis and boats and balls and rackets and punching bags and golf clubs. One either reckoned with a man as a competitor or one got him to join forces with you. The latter course was the most astute and profitable.

"What's the matter, Miles?" asked DeWitt mildly. He rubbed the head of the cane in his hand, and something like secret amusement glinted for an instant over his dark face.

"I think," said Tony, "that I'll go in to see Jon."

Miles, ignoring DeWitt, turned his attention to Tony. "Why? He usually gets peevish when the family is all together. Detracts attention from him, and his ideas, and he can't monopolise the conversation. He's just sulking in his room, waiting for Mamma to come to him." He puffed at his cigarette. "Loathsome kind of a creature—Jon." He glanced at Tony out of the corner of his eye, and the firelight made a vivid blue flash of that glance.

The young people stood up, Mary rising in one quick swirl of scarlet, DeWitt concentrating on his cane. The top of Miles's head reached only to Dolores's eyebrows; yet he did not appear small beside her. He touched the back of her hanging hand, and she did not recoil. He smiled up into her face. "I'll take you down," he said, and his voice was very gentle. "I'll wait for Tony," said Mary, "in the hall."

Never Victorious, Never Defeated

The ladies waited for the gentlemen and the children to join them. This is the most dismal family gathering we have had to date, Cornelia thought. Thank God for the storm; they'll be going soon. A maid stood at her elbow while she poured coffee into the little gold cups. "Sugar, Mamma?" I always forget. Fresh logs had been thrown on the fire. The softly beautiful room danced with light, and the lamps defied the primordial howling at the windows.

Lydia, all grey and black and white, accepted her cup from the maid. She found it almost insupportable to have to speak at all, and tried to substitute faint smiles for conversation. Ruth was sitting in Jim's usual chair near the hearth, drooping and pale. But she only knew him for twenty-seven years, thought Lydia. I knew him forever; the whole world has become empty for me and there are no voices left anywhere. The snow was drifting high and steep over Jim Purcell's grave. The gales were screaming over it. My dearest, thought Lydia, wait for me.

Cornelia thought: Mamma looks so old, and yet she still seems as serene and elliptic as always. She is smiling to herself, the first real smile since Uncle Jim died. What is she thinking? Of Uncle Jim, of course. It must be frightful to lose your husband. Cornelia glanced at the doorway and wondered impatiently why the men had not yet joined them. She poured a cup for Laura, her cousin, and forgot to ask about cream or sugar. Laura sat in her own silences, but, to Cornelia's vexation, the firelight was giving her face a bloom and radiance. She, too, was glancing at the doorway, and now Cornelia's hard-coloured face became ugly. "Have you forgotten me, Cornelia?" asked Estelle sweetly.

Damn you, you'd never let anyone forget, said Cornelia to herself. "Sugar?" she demanded contemptuously. Estelle sighed and smiled. "Oh, my dear, you know I don't."

Cornelia poured her own cup half full and deftly added brandy to fill it. She leaned back in her chair and began to sip with enjoyment. But one of her crossed legs swung back and forth. Her red hair was a blaze against the green velvet of her chair. She reached for a gilt box on the table beside her, took out a cigarette and lit it. Lydia watched her fondly, and smiled again. But she was also afraid. The strong profile was more predatory than ever, and the red lips were hard as coloured plaster. We are what we are, thought Lydia. From the moment of our conception we are what we shall be. Free will? I do not know. If we struggle, however glimmeringly, however faintly, is that enough? Is the struggle, no matter how brief, the only importance? I should like to believe that Cornelia has those lightning-like pauses. I doubt it. She is aware of neither good nor evil.

How trivial, or coarse, they all are, thought Estelle, smiling brightly at nothing. She said, "You must really see our new Picasso! It is hung in the first drawing-room in New York. Such colour, such meaning. . . ."

Cornelia made a rude sound. Estelle blushed, shocked. But Lydia, for the first time since her husband's death, laughed a little, and Laura smiled. Cornelia described the painting with more than a hint of obscenity, and Estelle listened with horror. "We met the man in France," Cornelia concluded in her loud and domineering voice. "Utterly impossible. He maunders about something he calls the 'Coming People's Revolution.' I tried to get him to become more specific, but he merely looked mysterious."

Estelle's wide brown eyes glittered with cunning, and she thought with pleasure of her sons. Lydia said, "I agree with Allan that something evil is stirring in the world. I could feel it in Europe last year before—before . . ." She paused, to swallow painfully.

Ruth, in silence, looked timidly from one face to the other. She always tried not to think exclusively of her father, for her mother's sake. Her golden hair was a crown of light and her lovely face, though so pinched now, was like the very shadow of innocence. She faltered: "I should like to work with the Quakers in Europe. At The Hague. I had thought . . ."

"If you want to, darling, you must do so," said Lydia. "Next summer? I'll go with you." She smiled at her daughter, and the pain caught at her throat. Then she gave her attention to Laura, Laura who was Alice's daughter. Laura had not spoken in this room. Her grey eyes studied her cup, which she held in the palms of her hands. "I heard you and Patrick were going to Europe next summer," said Lydia. Laura started, put the cup on a table. "Oh, no, I don't think so," she murmured. She brushed at her cloud of dark hair vaguely with the back of her hand, and averted her face. The women waited, but she said nothing more. Cornelia's eyes glinted. She had once been fond of her cousin; she had hated her for years now. Cornelia's long leg swung a little faster.

The men came into the room, Allan's hand under Rufus's elbow. "Well," said Rufus cheerily, "I hope we weren't too long. Such an interesting discussion." Cornelia looked at them alertly. Allan was in one of his "solitary" moods, she observed with anxious impatience. Patrick walked a little apart, a walking corpse, thought Cornelia disgustedly. Norman was smiling his wide and meaningless smile, and he went to his mother at once and perched on a foot-stool near her knee. Allan assisted Rufus into a chair, and the maid entered with fresh coffee and glasses. Rufus picked up the brandy bottle and studied it critically. "Glad you left some for us, Cornelia," he said. "I can't get that Napoleon in any quantity these days."

Cornelia poured coffee for the men. Allan, who had been hovering uneasily near his wife, waited until the maid had gone on her rounds. Then he bent over Cornelia and said in a low voice, "I'm sorry we are late. We had something to discuss." She looked up at him, and then her face softened. But he did not smile in return, and she saw that he was extremely nervous. "Well?" she said. Rufus had stimulated some conversation, and husband and wife were covered by voices.

"It's about Tony," said Allan.

Cornelia lifted her cup to her lips and drank a little. "Well?" she repeated at last. "Has Tony been annoying you, or worrying you, in any way?"

"No." Allan hesitated. He wished Cornelia would not look at him so directly. "You know he's never caused us a minute's trouble." He hesitated again. "No, he isn't worrying me. It is something he wants to do. My only worry is about how you will take it. . . ."

"I can 'take' anything," said Cornelia. She lifted her large white hands, glittering with jewels, and touched Allan's cheek briefly. Why couldn't the dear idiot understand that her children were nothing to her compared with him? "If he wanted to become a butcher or a trapeze performer or a sword swallower or a travelling preacher it wouldn't matter to me, so long as it didn't matter to you."

Allan's hands clenched on the back of Cornelia's chair. He said, "Tony wants to be a priest."

Cornelia's hazel eyes moved, the corners hardening. She stared at Allan; he was wretched, she saw, and almost undone with dread. "A priest?" she muttered. She stared at Allan again. "Absurd, of course." Allan did not reply, and her lips curved in a sardonic smile. "What about the road?"

"He doesn't want to be part of it." He moved restlessly, still watching her. "It's very hard to explain—to you. . . ."

"Granting the foolish premise for a moment, if he should be —a priest—what would you think of it, Allan?"

He leaned against her chair as if exhausted. "I—I think I should like it, Cornelia." How could he make her understand? How could he prevent her from assaulting Tony with furious and contemptuous words? And Tony . . . Allan started, for Cornelia was rumbling with laughter. He could not believe it. Her eyes jumped with mirth, and her teeth shone in the firelight. She was reaching up, and now she had taken his hand and was pressing it.

"Dear, dear fool," she was actually saying. "What does it matter? You are happy about the ridiculous idea. Haven't you learned yet that what makes you happy makes me happy, no matter how silly or incredible? What is Tony to me, or Dolores, or DeWitt, when it comes to you?"

Rufus was laughing with the others over a joke he had just told. But never for an instant had he been unaware of his daughter and Allan by the fire. He knew the subject of their conversation, and had deliberately withdrawn the attention of the others from them. When he saw Allan suddenly bending over his wife and kissing her full on her mouth, and when he heard her laughter, he smiled with ruddy content.

Then he saw that Allan was apparently distressed again. He was whispering in Cornelia's ear, and she was looking both astonished and wildly amused.

"You won't understand, darling," he was saying, "but for Tony's sake you and I will have to go somewhere, very quietly, in some out-of-the-way place, and be remarried by a priest." "No!" exclaimed Cornelia with high delight, and she was laughing again. "All right; don't look so—— I'd do anything for you."

Estelle asked, "Where are the children?" She stroked Norman's hair and told herself that this had been the dreariest holiday ever.

"They'll be down soon, I'm sure," said Laura. She did not glance at her husband, sitting apart in his white silence, as if the others did not exist for him. Then, as always, her eyes were drawn helplessly to Allan Marshall. He was still bending over his wife, and he was holding her hand, and they were chuckling gently together. Laura's heart constricted, and she turned her head aside.

Tony was entering the room alone. Allan, seeing his son, beckoned to him, and Tony came at once. When he reached his parents they were struck by his pallor. He stood beside them and could not speak. Cornelia lifted her eyebrows at him and said, "Don't look like death, Tony. Your father has told me, and it is perfectly all right, if you want to make a fool of yourself."

But Tony only gave her an agonised glance, and his mouth opened speechlessly. Allan, alarmed for him, put a hand on the young man's shoulder. "What is it?" he demanded sharply. "What is wrong?"

Tony whispered, "I went in to see him—you see, this afternoon he had gone out into the storm—I was downstairs—I should have turned back to speak to him—I might have prevented it. . . ."

Cornelia wet her lips. She lifted herself straight in her chair. She, like Tony, whispered, "What is it? For God's sake, what is it?" Her hand caught at Allan's arm protectingly.

"Jon," said Tony, and his eyes filled with tears. "He's dead. He must have killed himself—there was the box on the table . . . poison. . . ."

CHAPTER FORTY-TWO

ALLAN MARSHALL had once told Cornelia bitterly: "A witticism is an unpardonable answer to a cry of pain."

But there are times, thought Cornelia, when a witticism is the only answer to maudlin sentimentality and self-pity. She sat in her sitting-room overlooking Fifth Avenue, facing her desk, and with a pen in her hand. She had begun to write to her son Tony, who was now in his seminary.

"You are such a damn' fool, my dear," she wrote, on the third page, "and apparently your ' superior ' thinks so too, considering his advice, though he would hardly be so blunt as I. Why do you torment yourself so, and brood over something which was not your fault, and accuse yourself endlessly until you become a bore to everyone?

485

"You know as well as I do that the autopsy showed clearly that the tablets which Jon had stupidly swallowed had not caused his death at all. The drug had become, over all those years, completely deteriorated and ineffective. He could have taken a hundred of the same without a single bad effect. The verdict was ' death from natural causes.' But you know all this. Who can say what brings death about in such cases? It is true there were no signs of any organic defect, but who can truly and dogmatically declare that there is nothing to the theory that a man can will death for himself? I am sure Jon did. It is quite possible that his death was a mercy for himself, and for others. I doubt very much that if you ' had gone back,' as you have repeated *ad nauseam*, that you could have helped him in any way.

"Your grandfather is still in a state of partial shock since Jon's death, and this is a tremendous worry to us all. He has been out for a drive only twice since we returned to New York, and now that he fully realises that you have permanently removed yourself from the family, and the affairs of the family, he is very depressed. If you MUST feel guilty about something, you could begin with your grandfather. He can do very little now about the road except when some extreme emergency comes up, and even then your father tries to spare him. This means added burdens and responsibilities for your father. He, too, is beginning to realise what it means to all of us for you to go away; for eighteen years he has thought of you as his natural successor. Here is another point about which you may feel guilty, if you wish.

"Your ' Auntie Estelle ' does nothing to raise the horrible gloom which surrounds us; in all truth she appears determined not to let a single ray of light intrude through it. It was only two weeks ago when she got up from bed and decided to hold mourning court for her friends in one of the drawing-rooms instead of her bedroom. The murmurs and sniffles and sobs over the tea, every day, day in and out, infuriate me while they distress your grandfather. I have literally had to lock her out of his rooms because she made a habit of invading them nightly to scream at him and reproach him for having ' treated our poor child so.' The house is a bedlam, and big as it is there is not a corner which does not echo with moans and sighs and the rustling of black silk and the subdued clink of teacups and the foolish comfortings of morbid ' friends.'

"Instead of indulging yourself in self-pity and squalid ' regrets,' you might help me with Dolores. We had hoped to announce her engagement to Dicky this spring, in Paris, but now she writes me very impudently that I may as well put the whole matter out of my mind as she had definitely decided against the marriage. He is one of the greatest catches in Europe, though not very well off, and a most estimable young man and with a most desirable title. Dolores could never do better; in fact, I don't think she'll ever have another offer. Why don't you write her and put some sense into her head? If something is not done —and I haven't given up yet—she will become one of those appalling old spinsters who spend their sterile lives in what we used to call ' good works.' Your father does not particularly care for Dicky, either, but he is slowly coming to the conclusion that Dolores is in real danger of spinsterhood, as she takes no interest in young men except as casual friends. And she will be nineteen in September.

"I am glad that you went to Groton to see DeWitt, but I had to laugh at your bewilderment at discovering that he didn't need sympathy at all, but was doing very well, thank you. It's nice of you to pray for him. I assure you he will get along splendidly without a single prayer in his behalf. He is that kind of a boy, and is the only hope your father has. Are you feeling a little guilty? Good; I hope so.

"You might be interested in hearing that your father has promised Miles a sound position on the road when he is graduated from Harvard. I was against it, but now I approve. Miles is a very serious boy, and has convinced even me that he will be an asset to the company. He is a genuine ' railroader,' which surprised me very much. And after all, his father is a director and there is considerable stock in that family. I did not like Miles, for I've always believed he was a schemer. I still believe it, but I have began to like him for very sound qualities I did not suspect he had. I cannot look at my own children, except DeWitt, with any pleasure; it is ironical that I find pleasure in one or two of the Peales. Mary had quite a shock when you went away; I had hoped there would be a match between you. But she is turning her interest upon DeWitt and visited him a short time ago, and he writes me, in his usual reserved way, that he ' enjoyed' seeing her. I hope the ' enjoyment ' will turn into something important in a few years.

Never Victorious, Never Defeated

"I have had only one letter from my mother. She is not at all well since the grippe she acquired on her way home that awful Thanksgiving Day. After all, three hours in the terrible storm in a sleigh, though full of fur robes, was an ordeal for a woman her age. She and Ruth never speak of those hours when they were lost on the mountains, and when the horses could not force their way through the drifts. I would appreciate it if you could spare a few minutes from your sickly preoccupation with Jon to write to her regularly. Ruth is of no particular use to her and whines, in her letters, about wanting to go to The Hague very soon to ' study ' with the peace missions. She seems all wrought up about something, and her letters are full of black suspicions about ' coming wars,' which is all nonsense, of course. She even hints she is writing a book about it all, and she goes off for days at a time, leaving her mother, to consult with the Quakers in Philadelphia.

"You see, we have troubles and anxieties, ourselves. Your imaginings seem very trivial and exasperating to me. Do whatever you do in a seminary with every bit of vigour you have. I really won't forgive you for everything until you become at least an archbishop, or better, a cardinal."

Curse it, thought Cornelia, and threw aside her pen. She was invariably angered when "the family" forced itself implacably upon her attention, and compelled her to write letters. She stood up and went to the windows overlooking Fifth Avenue. It was snowing heavily, and slush was gathering on the sidewalks and the streets. Brown and white houses floated insubstantially in wild blows of grey-white snow. Traffic choked the streets: omnibuses and drays and carriages, and a few red automobiles that steamed in the cold winter afternoon. She could hear the blatting of the horns even high up here, and even through the silk-shrouded windows. Black and brown figures thronged the walks; umbrellas tilted and blew; street lamps were already being lighted by little scurrying men, and the yellow glow of them was almost obliterated by the blizzard. The old excitement that had always filled Cornelia when looking down at Fifth Avenue did not come to her. She and Allan were to attend a Vanderbilt ball that night, and she had chosen a turquoise satin with a train to wear with her magnificent pearls and aquamarines. It was, as the newspapers said, "an occasion." Estelle had made a most deplorable and screaming fuss about the matter: the family was in mourning; it was unspeakable and common to attend social gatherings so soon after Jon's death—hardly three months. Cornelia, who rarely quarrelled with anyone (for the reason that quarrels bored her), had fought exasperatedly with her stepmother. She and Allan, she said, were not in mourning for anyone, and if her half-brother had chosen to die, it was certainly not her affair.

Damn her, thought Cornelia, letting the golden silk of the draperies drop into place, shutting out the wintry scene below. If anyone killed Jon she did. She is not going to stop us from going, even if she chokes to death, which would be the only intelligent thing she could ever do. And this time I am going to be firm with Papa, too; we have given in too much to Estelle's rages, in order to let him "have peace."

In spite of her unquenchable buoyancy, Cornelia could not shake off her depression. Her gilt and jewelled clock on her bedside table chimed half-past four. She compared it with her watch. Allan should have returned from Philadelphia by now. Doubtless, the train had been delayed by the snow. And Allan and I must have at least an hour to dress, she thought, fuming. Well, as this ball is to be given in our honour, I'll simply have to leave without him, if he doesn't return in time. She rang the servants' bell, and then sent for Rufus's "man."

He informed her that he would, indeed, lock all his master's doors and keep guard over them and admit no one. Cornelia suggested her father's customary sedative a little earlier than usual. The valet then informed Cornelia that Mr. Marshall's carriage had just driven up, and, with immense relief, she ran down the circular marble staircase in the dusk to meet her husband, the valet hurriedly switching on the electric lights like a flare behind her. He reflected that for a lady of "Mrs. Marshall's age" she was certainly uncommonly fleet-footed and active; he noticed that she lifted her skirts very high as she flew down the stairs and that she had long and robust legs, like a youth's, and that she did not touch the balustrade in her passage.

The butler was just opening the glass and grilled door as Cornelia reached the marble hall with its vast areas strewn with too many oriental rugs. Now the hall bloomed with myriad electric fixtures fastened to the crimson damask walls, and sprang out in the white arms and hands of the fine old statues of Greek gods and godesses standing in distant corners. A monster white marble fireplace fluttered with the burning of monster logs, and the glimmering white floor reflected sheets and lances of red fire. Yet the great hall was cold, and as Allan entered with his heavy brief-case, a cloud of snow flies entered with him, dancing and whirling. She ran to him exuberantly, shouting that she had been worried about the train, and throwing her arms about his shoulders and kissing him heartily. He held her to him briefly, warning her of his dampness, then put her aside to rid himself of his coat and muffler and derby. She saw at once that he was desperately tired and preoccupied.

He stood for a few moments before the hall fire and rubbed his cold hands and tried to smile at his wife. There was a strained pallor under his dark skin. "Something's wrong," thought Cornelia, and braced herself for it. She put her arm in his and drew him to one of the enormous drawing-rooms. "We'll have a drink at once," she said. "You're chilled. I don't know why you did not use the private car. The Pullmans are always draughty—and in this weather!"

When Allan, as a young man, had wandered on the outside of this house and had lusted for it, he had believed that to live within those formidable walls of stone and glass and grills and copper doors would be the ultimate of human desirability. Now he loathed the mansion, with its music room and gilt chairs, pipe organ, and monolith of a grand piano; its Chinese and bronze urns overflowing with exotic plants; its drawing-rooms hanging with precious ancient tapestries; its archways draped in silken velvets; its Louis XVI and old Spanish brocaded chairs; its golden or painted ceilings flowing with nymphs and cherubs; its pier glasses; its giant marble and ebony chests; its Renaissance paintings on the damask walls; its rare tables and crystal, marble, painted, or golden lamps; its Persian rugs and murals and palms in Chinese tubs; its cloisonné vases on teakwood stands; its statues and statuettes in every niche and corner; its automatic elevators with velvet seats; and its dining-room which could seat seventy-five people at the Italian refectory table in thronelike Italian chairs. It had, he thought, the crowded magnificence of a museum; millions of dollars had erected and furnished it, and it was without taste, though not without grandeur, from the glittering ballroom to the marble bathrooms fit for Nero.

He pulled back on the threshold of the tremendous first

drawing-room, shivering. Despite a very efficient heating system, and the constantly burning fire, the room was chilly. "Let's go into the library," he said. Cornelia agreed. The library was only a trifle smaller, but the thousands of books on the walls (rare volumes and folios) gave a false sense of seclusion and warmth to the room. Here, too, in a black marble fireplace, a lusty fire roared. The dark blue velvet draperies had been drawn over the ceiling-high windows, and the blue-velvet rug shim. mered like thrown silk in the firelight. A maid in smart black and white was turning on the wall brackets and the red and blue lamps, and she curtsied as Allan and Cornelia entered, the butler at their heels. Cornelia briskly ordered whisky and soda, and husband and wife sat down near the fire on the blue-leather chairs.

"We can only waste half an hour," said Cornelia, lifting her skirts frankly so that the warmth could reach her legs. She reached for a cigarette and the butler lighted it and offered the crystal box to Allan. "Remember? The Vanderbilts to-night. And we must dress and then go in to see Papa for a few minutes before leaving."

"My God, I'd forgotten," said Allan wearily.

"We're the guests of honour. What a day! I'll certainly be glad to leave for France next week." She smiled at him encouragingly, bracing herself again. Her eyes sparkled and her rouged face was vital in the lamplight. She raised her glass. "Here's to us, pet."

He drank thirstily, and she watched him. He looked about the library, at its long mahogany table and dark chairs, at its walls of books and paintings. He said, "What a damned gloomy house this is." As he had said this so often in the past, Cornelia ignored the remark. She waited for him to go on. The butler had been dismissed, and Allan rose and refilled his glass. Cornelia frowned. She said, "Not too much, please, dear. I know you're cold, but we do have to go out." He sat down and again drank, still thirstily.

"How was Portersville?" asked Cornelia. "Damn it, I wish we were there. I hate this house, too."

"We've just finished probating Jon's will," said Allan. He looked into his glass. He had pulled up the legs of his damp trousers, and his ankles, very slender and neat in their black silk, moved Cornelia to tenderness. "He left all his money to Miles, every penny of it. A very curious will."

Cornelia stared. "To Miles Peale? How extraordinary!" Her eyes narrowed and her painted mouth twisted. "I wonder why?" She gave a short laugh like a bark. "I can't believe there is anything wrong with Miles!"

Allan's head was bent; he looked at his wife, and below the black irises of his eyes a white area glittered. "There isn't. But that wasn't Jon's fault. He tried. Anyway, I suppose there'll be whispered and tittering remarks behind hands, and I'm sorry for Miles. 'To my dear and beloved kinsman, Miles Peale, I hereby bequeath——' Well, that kinsman business takes some of the curse off it."

"How much?" demanded Cornelia.

"One million, eight hundred thousand dollars."

Cornelia said, "One million, eight hundred thousand. Not an enormous lot, but considerable. Invested?"

"Half in Carnegie. Miles is going to keep it invested that way. He has a good mind."

"Estelle isn't going to like this."

The preoccupation remained on Allan's face. He put down his glass. "I think," he said, "that you'll soon be a director of the road, Cornelia. The directors are getting over their original outrage. Only one, to-day, muttered something about the 'New Woman.'"

Cornelia roared, "I'll bet anything you wish that he was Pat Peale!"

"You'd win the bet." He picked up his empty glass, glanced at Cornelia, and put it down heavily. He clasped his hands between his knees and looked at the fire. Cornelia snapped open her watch. "Ten minutes," she began. Allan jerked upright. "Damn it, Cornelia! What the hell does time matter?" His voice was a shout of rage, and Cornelia gazed at him thoughtfully, without answering. He jumped to his feet and began to pace up and down restlessly, his hands in his pockets, and Cornelia said to herself: Yes, it's something, and it's bad, and he's afraid to tell me, and he's distracted. She folded her hands on her knees, and waited.

Allan stopped by her chair, and put his hand on her head. She stiffened, forced herself to smile. "I'm sorry I disturbed you about the time, but we are the guests of honour, you know. Hell itself wouldn't prevent me from going."

Allan's hand dropped from her head, and he turned away.

492

Cornelia's fingers wound themselves around the short pearl necklace which enclosed her high-boned collar. She repeated, "Hell, itself."

Allan said desperately, "Cornelia. . . ." She lifted her hand and broke in pleasantly: "I wrote to Tony to-day. Very tiresome. He's still worrying about Jon, and blaming himself. But you read his letter of a few days ago. I thought Tony had some intelligence."

"I saw my father to-day," said Allan, as if he had not heard her.

Cornelia let out a small exhalation. It was only his father, then.

"He's very old now, and he wanted to go down to the road-house to talk with the ' boys.'" Allan's voice was lifeless, and Cornelia caught her breath. It wasn't his father. "How interesting," she said politely. "After all, he *was* an engineer, and I think you once said that he hasn't been down to the yards for years. Did he enjoy it? And, by the way, how was the weather in Portersville? As bad as here?"

"It didn't begin to snow until we reached Philadelphia." Allan had moved down the room and was pretending to study a land-scape on the wall between two windows. "Cornelia, there's a panic brewing. You can feel it."

"So you've been saying for two months, dear." She stood up, rustling. "Perhaps you are wrong. I think we've finished with panics."

"You forget the Regans and ' young ' Gunther, and the rest of them."

Cornelia shrugged. "Sometimes, dear, you talk about our friends like Jon did. After all, they're financiers, and financiers do what financiers are born to do, if one believes in fatalism, which I'm inclined to, myself. And now, please excuse me. I must dress, and I'd advise you to do the same."

She walked serenely towards the door, her hands clenched tightly in front of her. She had reached the threshold when Allan cried out, "Cornelia! There's something I must tell you. . . ."

Tony? she thought, stopping in the doorway, but not turning. DeWitt? Dolores? No, she would have heard. It was someone in Portersville; it could be no one else. She said in a loud hard tone, still not turning, "Allan. I am going to the Vanderbilts', and you are, too, unless you want to humiliate me by letting me go alone."

He came to her rapidly and caught her shoulder, and she looked at him steadily. He could see her face, and he thought it as cold as painted marble, and as impervious. "Allan, my father is still very weak, and whatever you have to tell me must wait until to-morrow, for I feel it will affect him, too; and if you tell me now I may think I must go to my father, and that I shall not do. To-night."

"Because of the Vanderbilt dinner?" he asked bitterly.

She was slowly turning white under her rouge, but she answered with composure: "Because of the Vanderbilt dinner, and because of my father."

"Then you have an idea?"

"I have no ideas at all. I am just wondering if that fool of a maid of mine has laid out my proper gown." Her eyes contemplated him and they were like bits of amber, as remote from him as from a stranger. "I shall be ready in an hour."

She moved her shoulder under his hand, and he stepped back, releasing her. She went on, and he stood in the doorway and watched her mount the marble stairs, lifting her skirts and not looking back. She knows, he thought. She always knows everything, almost immediately. Does she care? I wonder. I've been married to her for many years and I never knew her. She lied to me last spring at Cannes. She lied to help me, or because I was boring her with my misery. I very often do.

He went to the library table, wrote out a telegram: "Dearest Ruth, Cornelia and I will return to Portersville to-morrow afternoon and will remain with you for some time after your mother's funeral." He lifted his pencil, and hesitated, then continued: "Cornelia is broken-hearted and in no condition to travel to-night. She has not yet told the news to her father, for he is still ill. We send you our love."

He leaned his head on his hand and thought of the desolate young woman who had been deprived of both parents in only a few months. He thought of the silent house on the river, and the girl who wept without sound, and the voice of the river raging against the shrouded windows, and the woman lying in her coffin among flowers and candles. And he said to himself: There are times when I hate Cornelia, because nothing will ever stop her. I was stopped, a long time ago.

494

Never Victorious, Never Defeated

The great ebony clock boomed through the white and dusky areas of the hall, and its echoes bounded back sombrely in every room, Allan started, and thought of the Vanderbilt dinner and drearily reminded himself that he must dress. He rang for his valet, and when the man entered the library Allan said, "Please prepare my bath. No, I'll have no time for it. Just lay out my clothing; I'll be in my rooms in a few minutes."

He stood up and looked with dull anxiety around the book-lined walls, as if he had become aware of them for the first time. Then he went out quickly and ran up the stairs; he was always forgetting the elevators in this house. The house was lighted from top to bottom and was filled with silence. Allan paused on the second floor; a very fine Aphrodite, which had first known the brilliance of a Grecian sun, stood near the landing, and in her white cupped hands glared an uninhibited electric bulb. The stark light flared upwards on her serene and smiling face, and Allan looked away as if he had encountered an obscenity. He went down the marble hall swiftly, knocked like a conspirator on the door of Rufus's apartments. The door opened very cautiously for a few inches, then widened as his identity was established. Allan nodded at Rufus's man and went through the warm sitting-room into the bedroom, where Rufus was resting in his ornate French bed before his dinner.

"I had just begun to worry about you, my boy," said Rufus, lifting himself away from his orchid-tinted satin pillows. "I was going to send to inquire where you were." He held out his hand, so thin and transparent now, and smiled fondly at Allan.

"I had a talk with Cornelia first," replied Allan, seating himself precariously on a purple satin chair near the bed.

"Bad weather," commented Rufus, letting himself fall against his pillows again. His smile had gone; he looked, now, what he was—an old sick man, dwindled and very tired.

"How are you, sir?" asked Allan. "You look a little stronger to-day."

Rufus smiled again, and glanced at the fire. "When I was a very young fellow, probably about four, I told myself that I must always give a cheerful answer to every damn' thing. I found that it spared me tedious questions and had a nice effect on other people and gained me popularity." His face became very serious and more tired than ever. "Now I don't care a damn. So, in answer to your question, whether it bothers you or not,

495

or depresses you or not, I will say, 'I feel like hell. I am certain I am going to die very shortly.'"

Allan did not laugh. He said, "I hope you aren't going to die 'shortly.' I'm sorry you 'feel like hell.' I know you do. And do you know, I think that dying is the least unpleasant part of living, and probably the most relieving."

Rufus turned his head and studied Allan reflectively. After some moments, he said, "It's really incredible, but you are reminding me more and more of old Steve every day. Steve was the right man in the wrong place; I always believed, and sometimes still do, that you are the right man in the right place. And at other times I think you are the wrong man in the wrong place. Something happened to you. But I thank God you never told me, and still have the decency not to tell me."

He folded his hands over his sunken stomach and again studied his son-in-law. "Tell me about Portersville," he said. "No; not business. Just about the city and the house, and . . ."

"We are going to the Vanderbilts' dinner to-night, sir, and Cornelia is already dressing. We'll be late; not that it matters very much. This is more important. I went to see my father this afternoon; he's old and failing, and I haven't seen him since Christmas. He wanted to go down to the yard and talk with 'the boys.'" Allan paused and looked at the floor.

Rufus said, "Yes, yes, I understand. I also want to talk with my own 'boys.' It's very natural. Tell me."

What could Rufus deWitt, mighty president of the Interstate Railroad Company, have in common with an old and weary Irish engineer who had merely loved his engine? Allan glanced up and understood all at once that these old men had everything in common.

He began to talk, avoiding a single look at the clock on the mantel over the shouting fire. He had driven out to his father's farm early this day, and was pleased, as always, to see that Tim Marshall was being more than adequately cared for by the comfortable middle-aged couple who ran his farm and coddled him outrageously.

To-day, he had seemed very frail, for he had only just recovered from a severe grippe. Yet he boomed as usual at Allan, kissed him heartily, pounded his back with his fist, shouted for tea, "and mind you heat the pot first and put it on the fire afterwards," and then had sat with Allan to talk about Michael and Tony.

Michael, in India, was very happy at Tony's decision to become a priest. He was writing Tony regularly; he himself was very well. The old man went on and on, proudly, about his son and grandson, and his round Irish face had turned scarlet with his pride and enthusiasm. Then he had stopped and had peered at Allan intently.

"And here's my fine lad, with all the money, and all the things he has done, and with the president job coming up, and it's stupid, I am, not asking him what he is doin', and tellin' him that I am proud of him, too." He said to himself with a pang of sorrow: And it's looking like death, he is, my boy, and with the agony in him he does not know about."

"I think I am to be president after we return from France," said Allan, and he said this without pleasure or satisfaction.

"Sure, and that is fine, but it's afraid ye are," said Tim gently. "Afraid all your life, I'm thinkin'. You mustn't mind an old man who loves his children, and prays for them," he added hastily, rubbing his thick mass of white curls. "And who is not afraid? There is our young priest, who's that confident, and visitin' me almost every day, and bouncing in like a schoolboy, and with the cheery voice, and his talk about the Fathers ' gettin' closer to the people and understandin' their problems,' and all the time the great blue eyes of him are scared. And I says to him, and me a man old enough to be his granddaddy, ' Father, and what is the fear in ye, a fine young lad like you?' And he says, 'Tim, it's not fear I have, for that is a sin, and Our Lord cherished us all.' And I says to him, crossin' myself,' Be that as it may, and it's sure I am that it is true, but we are all frightened, even as babies at our mothers' breasts, and the fear gets stronger and stronger every day we live, and when we are old we are more frightened than ever. And why is this, and meanin' no offence, Father, that we are all so afraid? Is it because we don't trust our fellow man, or maybe knowin' him too well, and ourselves, too!' And I says, 'I have had the time to read all these years, Father, history and such things, and sure, I have seen that men have always been afraid, and that, at last, livin' becomes a weariness because of the fear.'"

"And what did Father Dugan say then?" asked Allan, not indulgently, but with intense seriousness.

Tim rubbed his chin, blinked his eyes, which were as bright as in his youth. "Well, now, it's a very curious thing. The

boy just sits where you're sittin' now, and it's thinkin' he is
that he should just quote what he's been taught, and answer like
a priest. And then all at once he's just a young feller talkin' to
his granddad, and there's tears in his eyes, and he says, ' Tim,
fear is the absence of God, may our Blessed Mother forgive and
pray for me!"

Allan thought of the ancient legend of Sisyphus, condemned
forever to roll a monster stone up a hill, only to have it roll
down again as he approached the summit. He could not remember whether the man had ever fallen, in his exhaustion,
and had been crushed by the stone. He said, "This isn't a very
cheery conversation. Would you like to go out for a drive for
an hour or so?"

Tim had then expressed his desire to go down to the yards.
"And perhaps for the last time," he had said. "I've been readin',
and thinkin' very strange thoughts, and I want to see if what I
have been fearin' is true."

They drove down to the yards, a long distance, in Allan's
carriage, under a grey-brown sky which pressed close over the
barren earth and the shut fields and seemed to touch the dun-
coloured roofs of the lonely farmhouses. Tim sat beside his son,
swathed in the fur robes, and looked out at the grey silence and
was silent.

When they reached the yards, and Allan was about to order
the carriage to approach the roundhouse, Tim stopped him.
"No, it's just lookin' at the lads I want, or maybe just to speak
to a few that pass us. They are strangers to me, and they don't
know me, and so we'll sit and look at them and I'll see if it is
true what I've been fearin'."

He had not been here for years, and he regarded the great mass
of buildings with wonder, but without admiration. The yards
were full of giant engines, bellowing and steaming and ringing
and clanging; long freights pulled out, alert young or middle-
aged engineers looking ahead, their hands on the throttles, their
striped caps surmounting sharp and hardened faces. Fire ran
along the grinding wheels; the pistons thrust and recoiled in
titanic gestures of force. Hundreds of men ran about the yards;
there was a constant bustle and calling, a constant marking on
records, a constant coming and going. The men consulted each
other briefly, not smiling, not talking casually, not pausing to
look at the monsters they serviced without pride or contempt.

Never Victorious, Never Defeated

No groups of young firemen stood about in knots, chewing or smoking or laughing or telling each other ribald jokes, or arguing vehemently, or shaking fists, as in the days Tim remembered. All was efficiency, timed movements, cold precision, and disinterest. Signals flared down the glistening tangle of rails; smoke rose in tremendous exhalations to the bitter winter sky; hands were raised, not in greeting, but in signals. More and more lights came on in the buildings, not with the slow mellow warmth of oil but with the violent blare of white electricity. A freight pulled in, slatted cars holding scores of cattle that groaned and called in bewildered voices of fear and pain. A passenger train, all light and length, glided into the station, the Pullmans gleaming. Conductors alighted on to steps placed at the doors by coloured porters in trim uniforms; the trainmen, with eyeglasses and set faces, looked only at their records, and glanced only at their watches. The youthful engineer in his cab yawned, and looked at his watch, and did not call out to any of the men on the platform, nor did they call out to him. Passengers came briskly down the steps, carrying brief cases and small bags, and their faces were preoccupied. They had come a long way, safely, drawn rapidly by the locomotive ahead, yet they gave it not one affectionate smile. They were not even aware of it.

Allan, sitting in silence beside Tim, suddenly saw the great station and yards through his father's eyes. It was as if he had been given another vision, superimposed on his own. "Not like the old days, eh, Dad?" he asked, and tried to smile.

"No, and it's not," Tim replied. An engineer was passing, huddled in his thick coat, and carrying a sheaf of papers. Tim leaned out of the opened carriage window and called to him, and the man stopped. "Is that old Thirty-eight just pulling in now, and would ye tell me?" he said.

The man was impatient, but he looked long at the fine carriage with its two black horses and its coachman, and his eyes lowered sullenly. He said in curtness, "Yes, it is. You makin' it?"

"No," said Tim, "I am not."

He rolled up the window and stared heavily at the yards; the engineer shrugged and went on, muttering. Tim folded his hands in the fur robe and his head drooped. Allan said impatiently, "Well, Dad, would you have the old days back, with their inefficiency and their bad schedules and their rattling cars,

499

and their danger and raucousness and discomfort? And the casualness of the men. . . ."

"I am thinkin'," said Tim, "what all this is doin' to the men. I am thinkin', too, of the great factories, with men like these at their machines, which go crash-crash and never stop, and the men movin' their arms and their legs, themselves like machines. I am thinkin' of the faces I am seein' now, out in the yards, and I say it is bad, very bad. It is worse than I thought; sure, and it is worse."

He went on, as Allan did not comment: "It was in the papers the other day. Old Sixty-two ran on a straight stretch of track near Ada, Ohio, and made three miles in ninety-two seconds, and there was much hurrah in the papers about the new record, and much talk about the future, and the speeds, and I says to myself, as I am reading, ' And where will they be goin', all the people, that they must go so fast? The people with their faces with no light in them, and with their runnin' feet, and no time to live?' And I thought of that fine future they talk about, when all God's sky will be full of the flyin' machines, and the people going faster and faster to more and more places, and not stoppin' to see where they have gone, and not carin' just so they can go faster and faster and see less and less. Ah, and it's the modern age acomin', the papers say, and I say it's the age acomin' when men will not have time to talk to each other, and comfort each other, and pray with each other. And when that day comes, I says to myself, then men will hate each other because they hate their lives, and there will be terrible wars in the despair which will have men by the throat."

Allan still did not speak. Tim turned to him, and the brogue was thicker on his tongue. "Sure, and it's strikes we had in the awful past, and the people starvin'. But there was a conscience growin' in the big men, and it is growin' all the time, and soon there'll be no starvation and no miserable wages, and maybe there'll be what Mr. Ford says in the papers, that every man will have his automobile and run over new roads, and there will be comfortable houses for everybody, and no man will sit by his stove and wonder if he'll starve in his old age. But there'll be strikes, strikes such as old men like me never knew, I'm thinkin', and the hate will be worse than in the seventies. And why will there be strikes? Because men will have no pride in their work, and no pride in themselves, for they'll think of themselves only as machines, as their bosses will think of them; and the heart of man will not be able to stand it, for men's hearts are not steel but only flesh and blood. And a man's heart cries out for more than just good wages; it cries out for pride in itself, and in the work of hands, and fellowship, and the knowin' that it has accomplished somethin' each day. For a man is a spirit; he is a soul, and he must have the satisfactions of the spirit, Aloysius, and there is no room for man's spirit in the world to come, which is dawning to-day."

Allan lit a cigarette, and the red flame lighted up his thin dark face with its fixed eyes. But he said gently enough, "And what would you do, Dad?"

Tim said, "I would tell the men, in those days, about the God they have lost, somewhere among the machines and the fine trains and the flyin' machines and the automobiles. I would tell the children every day, in all the schools, about God; and I would set the priests and the ministers to walkin' the streets every day, and stoppin' the people, and tellin' them; and I would ask the newspapers to tell them; and I would have all the churches open all the time, day and night, with the candles burnin', and a priest or a minister in them every hour; and I would light up the crosses on the steeples against the night skies, as bright as the sun."

He turned to Allan and cried out, "When ye make a man into a machine, it's the heart and life ye are taking from him, and when ye count the hours of a man's life as ' man power ' ye have sinned against God Himself! And when ye have made of all men only machines, then there will be an evil day such as the world has never known."

"So," said Allan to Rufus, who had listened without a single remark, "I sent Dad home in the carriage, and took the train back to New York."

He stood up, then paused when Rufus held up his hand and said, "Just a moment, my boy." He regarded Allan in a long and serious quiet. Then, in the kindest of voices, he went on: "Allan, though you think you have a remarkable gift for it, you are really a very poor liar. You don't have the bland features to make your lying convincing. You see, from the very moment you came in here I knew that something out of the ordinary was bothering you, and upsetting you. It wasn't that drive with your father. Tell me; I've heard enough bad news in my life and it's too late now, for anyone to try to ' shield ' me. I don't need it."

Rufus continued, even more kindly: "Your first really awful lie, which convinced me you were lying, was when you innocently said you sent your father home in the carriage and you immediately took the train back to New York. That would be old Thirty-eight. In that event, you'd have been here two hours before you actually arrived, in spite of the storm which began in Philadelphia. I'm not a curious man," went on Rufus, settling himself deeper in his pillows. "If you had any private—affairs— it would be of no importance to me. But the fact that you tried to deceive me has convinced me that whatever it is you are hiding might be important to me, or ' hurt ' me in some way. It isn't business; it's something personal. What is it, Allan?"

"Nothing," said Allan. "You're imagining things, sir. It's true there is something else, but I can tell you to-morrow. You've been ill. . . ."

Rufus shook his head slowly. "Haven't you learned yet that the worst part of bad news is wondering what it is, while fools try to ' protect ' you? That's adding the torture of apprehension to the coming blow. What is it, Allan? Who, for instance, died in Portersville? There's no one there whose death would affect me very much, now, except——" He pushed himself upward, painfully, and his broad face, through which the large bones had begun to project lately, turned ghastly. "Allan? Is it—Laura? No? Lydia!"

Allan was sick with his alarm. He sat down again and rubbed his eyes, and could not speak. Rufus said gently, "When? How?"

Allan threw up his hands. "I tried to tell Cornelia; I think she suspected something. But she wouldn't let me tell her. There's the Vanderbilt dinner for us, and she said that bad news could wait until to-morrow. I think she's very sensible in a way. . . ."

"When? How?" repeated Rufus inexorably. "Speak up; I can't wait until to-morrow."

Allan surrendered. "Cornelia will . . . You mustn't let her know I told you. I did send my father home, just before the Thirty-eight left. Then, at the station, I called up to find how Mrs. Purcell was. Ruth couldn't answer; a servant did. Mrs. Purcell—she had rested after lunch, and when her daughter went to have tea with her, she found her—in the bed." He sighed. "I immediately went there, and tried to do what I could, which was nothing. Ruth was quite calm; she was crying, but not making any noise, just the tears running down her face as she talked with me. She wanted to be alone in the house with her mother—until to-morrow. I had to respect her wishes, though the idea was morbid. . . ."

"I don't think so," said Rufus in a normal voice. "I think it very natural. That is the way it should be: the first day one should be alone with one's dead."

He glanced at a distant table. "Will you give me a glass of brandy, please, and do have one for yourself."

Allan obeyed. Rufus's hand did not tremble as he took the fragile glass and began to sip. Allan gulped his drink in a gesture of desperation. Rufus said, "You don't appreciate good brandy, Allan. You drink it as an anæsthetic. I've never needed an anæsthetic, for anything."

He leaned his powerful grey head back against the abominably tinted satin pillows, and closed his eyes. He began to talk, as if to himself: "Lydia hasn't been my wife for almost thirty years. In fact, she wasn't my wife since Cornelia was born, and that is about forty years. Forty years. Much happens in that time; you bury your dead in every sense of the word. Except that I never buried Lydia. To me, in spite of a second wife, and—two sons, I never had any other wife but Lydia."

He sipped at the brandy again, tilted the glass so that the firelight was reflected on the liquid. "So 'Mrs. Purcell' died quietly in her sleep. Even if I were—well—I wouldn't go to her funeral. Lydia wouldn't want it; she hated funerals. You and Cornelia are the only ones who could go—properly." He laughed soundlessly at the last word. "I've found that propriety is a very useful thing. It saves a lot of wear and tear on the emotions. I won't even send Lydia a flower. So I'll just lie here and pretend she and I are young again, and I'll be in the mountains with her." He glanced at the clock on the mantel. "You are due to go, I think, in about two minutes."

Allan walked slowly towards the door. When he was almost there, Rufus said, "Do you believe in life after death, Allan?"

Allan did not turn, but he said dully, "No. No, I don't think so."

"Some people think if you don't have that faith you are without comfort. I, personally, am of the opinion that's balderdash. Who would want to live, after living in this world, no matter how comfortable or successful a life you've had? I like the idea of nothingness very much; I like the idea of not being any longer. That comforts me."

Then Allan did turn, but Rufus was smiling at his brandy again, with complete serenity. "You'd better leave, Allan," he repeated. "And don't tell Cornelia to-night; she didn't want to know, anyway." He added quite strongly, "I'm going to think of what your father said to you to-day. I believe he is right. You see what old age does for people!"

When Allan had left Rufus put down his glass carefully and began to think. He had believed that he would think exclusively of Lydia, but now he could only think of Cornelia, his daughter. He said to himself: I, too, would have refused to listen to bad news when an important matter was imminent. Cornelia, as I was, is all immediacy. That is the source of her strength. No permitting of life to intrude. Cornelia is even stronger than I was; there were times when I couldn't sleep, thinking of old Steve. Cornelia would have done the same to him as I did, but she wouldn't have lain awake a single moment, afterwards. Neither Lydia's death, nor mine, and probably not even Allan's, will disturb her for more than a day or two.

He thought of his earlier days of marriage with Estelle, and now he began to remember things he had not thought he had even observed. Cornelia, laughing disdainfully at Estelle's simpers, and goading the older woman, and ridiculing her to her father when she and Rufus were alone. She was always managing to be alone with her father, even as a child. Estelle was a fool—yes. She was a *poseuse*—yes. She had very little intelligence—yes. She was artificial and "radiant" and dull— yes. All that could be admitted.

But Cornelia saw her as a threat to herself, thought Rufus with wonder. A threat to what she would inherit; a threat to her own power. She deliberately manœuvred Estelle into situations that would make her appear ridiculous in my eyes, and in the eyes of others. I can remember—I can remember. . . . I laughed, and so all possibility that Estelle and I could become friends, and I could draw her away from her foolish ways into full womanhood, was destroyed by me and Cornelia's laughter.

And when the boys were born. . . . What did Cornelia call them? "Plucked little robins." I began to think they were not mine at all! Cornelia was always there, when I held them, making fun of them. They weren't really ugly; I just saw them through Cornelia's eyes. She used my love for her—for she was so like me that I couldn't help loving her more than anyone else—to make my sons appear too absurd and stupid and colourless for my serious consideration. She hated them because they would naturally be my heirs, too.

I can remember—I can remember. . . . I was sitting in the garden in Portersville, and the little fellows were running all around me, and tugging at me to play with them, and shrilling in the excitable voices they had. I was smiling at them and thinking, for perhaps the first time, that they were nice little creatures. And there came Cornelia, almost a young lady, so beautiful, so full of colour and vitality, with her parasol over her head, and I forgot the boys. And she said to them: "Run away, monsters. You're bothering Papa. Go and play with your mother." She sat down beside me on the swing, and kissed me, and I forgot all about my sons. . . . So many similar episodes, with only one thing in Cornelia's mind as she stroked my hair and talked with me. How witty she was, and also so good-tempered and full of humour. There were even times when I wished she were not my daughter. . . .

And just as Cornelia said, I let my sons "go and play with their mother." They were Estelle's, as Cornelia had told me a thousand times. Estelle brought them up; my only wish was that they wouldn't intrude on me, because they bored me, as their mother bored me. But who told me that they and their mother "bored" me? What was it that Lydia said to me, Lydia who was so wise: "I think you should send Cornelia far away for a few years, to school. It isn't good for her to be home so often, and it isn't good for the whole household." I should have listened; if I had listened my son Jon would not be dead now, and Norman would not be a smiling stranger to me.

My sons. Estelle made them impotent—and dangerous. Because they really had no father who cared for them, or had an interest in them. Because Estelle was hurt, she revenged herself on me through our sons. She adored them, but she used them against me. Everything that they were, and that Norman still is, was my fault.

Rufus reached out and refilled his brandy glass. His right arm and leg were curiously numb, and there was a severe pain in the left side of his head. It is the brandy, he told himself. I remember when Norman, who was four, had scarlet fever, and was very restless. He was calling for me, and Estelle rushed on to the terrace at Newport and shrieked that I must come. And Cornelia looked at her as one looks at a repulsive spider and said, "Tell the nurse to bathe him again. She's such a lazy person; I can't imagine why you keep her, Estelle." We were talking about the road just then, and I became impatient with Estelle and said, "Yes, go bathe the boy. I'll go in to see him before dinner." Estelle crept away, and Cornelia watched her go and said, "How Estelle dramatises everything! Norman is being difficult, that's all. Just look at Estelle! *East Lynne* in person, moving across the grass as if you had beaten her or something." And we laughed together. Norman never called for me again.

There was Jon. I recall now, that he wasn't a "grinner" like Norman. A very earnest little boy, even if Estelle had spoiled him abominably, because I wasn't there to stop her. He was always reading, though he was so hysterical and shrill and had a way of running heedlessly up and down in a sort of blind way. I can see him, running, with his eyes distended as if he didn't see anyone, and Cornelia finally catching him with such good nature, and sending him off so he couldn't "bother" me any longer. I remember how he began to scream, over and over, as Cornelia pushed him away; he screamed for a long time, even in the house. He never had a father. Cornelia managed it so he never had.

Year after year fluttered mustily through Rufus's memory. The pain was heavier in his head, but he was hardly aware of it. How clever Cornelia had been! My sons learned to hate me, for Cornelia had taught me to mock them in a fond sort of way. Their ideas were always puerile; who told me that? Cornelia. "But then, one must remember their mother is so prettily— childish, Papa. It really is quite feminine to be childish, like Estelle; no wonder you fell in love with her. I'm not feminine in the least, am I?" But she was; she is. She has a terrible kind of femininity, the very essence of it. She persuaded me she did not; she wanted me to believe she was more manly than my sons. She wanted me to think she was in every way my "son," and the only child I had who would ever be interested in the road. . . .

Jon. Why did you die? It wasn't the poison, for there was no poison. Did you die because you couldn't stand what you had made of your life? But you didn't make your life, not entirely. Cornelia helped you, though you never knew it; your mother helped you, and perhaps you understood. But a death is never simple, not a death like yours. There are a thousand agonies. A man kills himself, and a hundred people are guilty of it; but no one ever punishes them, no one ever cries out to them, "Cain, where is thy brother, Abel?" Rest in peace, Jon. And if you still live, forgive me.

I practically disinherited my sons. Why? Once Cornelia went over the stocks and bonds and savings which Estelle has. She was so laughingly surprised at the amount of money Estelle possesses. "Why, the boys could do us a lot of damage, Papa, if they only had the brains! Or, at least, they could do me such a lot of damage." How could I let anyone "damage" my girl? And so I left my sons practically nothing.

Norman. Rufus moved on his pillows with a spasm of pain that was more mental than physical. He remembered that he very rarely "saw" Norman, even when that young man was with the family in Portersville, Newport, New York, or France. What was there to "see?" All at once he "saw" Norman as he must have seen him hundreds of times, not the boyishly smiling full face of him, not the mediocre profile. He saw a Norman he had never noticed consciously: the featureless stern embryo, the high withered forehead, the gnarled and shrivelled cheek, the long neck, the thin, sloping shoulders. Where had he seen ghostly outlines like that before? It was terribly necessary for him to remember. Ah, yes, he had it now. The "intellectual" friends of Jon, in New York, London, and Paris! Full face, they appeared alert, even brilliant, even thoughtful and discerning. But from another view there was the betrayal of their emotional paucity, their spiritual immaturity, their meagre grasp of life and the meaning of life, their fetal lack of contact with the world and their fellows. Unfinished, and never to be finished, these poor, sapless, and sinister men. Their Marxism, their Socialism, their Fabianism—all their isms—what were these things but the expression of their ominous ignorance, their umbilical attachment to the placenta of unbirth? Norman was one of them, one of the unborn, secretly and silently poisoning the body of his host.

Frantically, now, Rufus tried to sit up, to call. But his right side was heavy as lead, and immovable. The brandy, he thought confusedly; I have drunk too much of it. I'll wait a little and then I'll send for Norman. Surely there must be a way to bring him into life, even now.

I must talk with Allan, too. Allan. Rufus closed his eyes; it was too much of an effort now, to keep them open. What made a man drink as Allan drank? He was a frantic and desperate man. Of what was he afraid? Of the demands upon him? Who made those demands? Cornelia? Cornelia, who despised weariness and weakness, who must always be a-doing, who had such inexhaustible verve, who endlessly took and gave nothing?

Yes, Lydia, thought Rufus, I understand so much now. It is very kind of you to come and stand beside me and smile at me. Yes, I know you must leave very soon. It is very foolish of me, but I thought I remembered you with white hair; a dream. You are so young, and wise. I'm glad you have forgiven me for not being what you thought I was. Laugh; I love to hear you laugh. Will you sit near me for a while? Good. I want to talk to you about . . . No, I only want to talk to you about us, and Steve, and Alice, and my father and mother. Then we'll go downstairs together and join them before the fire. Your hand is so cool and firm on my forehead, and it has taken away the pain. The pain? But it was as much outside me as in me. I am an old man, and I have had years to remember, and to think. . . .

Cornelia whispered to Allan, as she stood beside her father's bed, "He has such a very good colour, hasn't he? Almost rosy."

"He's flushed. I think he has a fever or something," replied Allan uneasily. "And he's making a very loud noise, breathing."

"Snoring. All old people snore," said Cornelia. "Besides, it's very warm in here." She lifted her aquamarine ostrich fan, and an aura of rich and spicy scent flowed about her. "Let him sleep, poor dear. We'll just tiptoe out; he hasn't slept well recently. Do come, Allan; we're very late."

They went into the sitting-room beyond the bedroom, where Rufus's man was just entering with a tray. "Mr. deWitt is sleeping," said Cornelia. "Don't wake him."

PART FOUR

CHAPTER FORTY-THREE

FROM THE very first, Allan Marshall had hated Washington. Later visits, through the years, had increased this hatred, as they had increased his knowledge. Unlike most Celts, he had no affinity for politics, and his father's enthusiasm for politics in any form had bored him. Perhaps, he would admit to himself, Patrick Peale had "soured" him on governmental activities, or perhaps his contacts with politicians over the decades had convinced him, as they had convinced Thomas Jefferson, that that government is the best which governs least.

Senator George Woodland was a short, big-bodied, pale man with a large face and a large bald head and a pair of cold, shrewd eyes and a wide mouth. An expert and subtle politician, he knew that his canny mixture of uncomformity and conservatism pleased both the "progressive" and "laissez-faire" members of his constituency. Each group was certain that he represented it to the full, and that its word was law with him. It would have discomfited both factions to know that he represented only what he himself believed best for his country. He was neither a scoundrel nor a fool, neither an actor nor a believer in "causes." How, then, asked his colleagues, did he return so constantly unchallenged to the Senate?

The answer was one no politician would ever accept: the people are more intelligent than their governments. The people, at times, feel that they can afford to send one or two honest men to Washington. The population of the Commonwealth of Pennsylvania had permitted themselves this luxury for many years in the person of Republican Senator George Woodland. As there is an organic humour always present in humanity, they also permitted themselves the extra luxury of sending a colourful blackguard to the Senate in addition to Woodland, for the people must have their wily clowns as well as men of integrity. "Old George," they would say, would "keep an eye on that damned Washington, and no nonsense, and Old Jim will regularly raise hell with Wall Street, and dance around on the floor, and give us some fun." But the people saw to it—being so much wiser than their government—that "Old Jim" did not "get out of bounds," and that "Old George" had their hearty support whenever he called for it, particularly when he disagreed with "Old Jim."

"Let's go outside; it's pretty mild for January," said Senator Woodland to Allan, whom he had known for many years, and whom he liked, though in the main he distrusted men he suspected of being "volatile." He lived in a fine and quiet house on Massachusetts Avenue, a house which he had bought a number of years ago. White and reserved, it stood back from the street on a long if narrow lawn, and had an excellent garden which he cultivated himself during his stays in Washington, and which he reluctantly delegated to gardeners in his absences. Having a great admiration for the admonitions of Benjamin Franklin, he "kept his fences high," living fences of thick tall evergreens against stone walls. Here he could sit, on warm nights, and no neighbour could peer at him curiously, and better still, could not seek him out to invite him to a dull party. He opened the door this afternoon to the terrace overlooking his gardens, and contemplatively put his big pipe in his mouth. He appeared to forget Allan; his eyes roved about the trees, looking for premature buds. "Those Japanese maples," he mused. "I think they'll pull through all right if we don't have too much sleet." He leaned against the door of the house and smoked, and the pale blue smoke rose through the wan sunlight. A brilliant blue jay flashed through the branches of a bare tree, and the senator gazed after it with the nearest approach to warmth he ever displayed.

Allan was not interested in Washington or its weather. He looked at the cool brightness of the sky, and at the backs of nearby mansions. He thought of the wide avenues of the city, its beautiful circles, and his unfathomable loathing rose in him again. His name for Washington was "the black pit of the black politicians," and all its whiteness, its long stretches, its lovely parks, expressed to him the very essence of corruption. Acquainted with the capital cities of Europe, Washington seemed no capital to him. It was a small country town, grossly swollen, secret in its vices, scurvy in its plottings, dominated by rascals who must be endlessly watched lest they do a mischief to the country. Little men came here to do little evil deeds, to plot against the Constitution, to connive together to enrich themselves at the expense of America, to compromise for profit when compromise was wicked, to scurry and whisper and wink in cloak-rooms. What would the stern and blameless Wilson do with all these, after his inauguration in March?

The senator said, "You voted for Wilson, didn't you, Allan? I think I heard it rumoured that you gave a large donation to your party during the last elections. And that brings me to a point: what did you come here to see me about?"

Allan shifted uncomfortably. He said, "Well, I've always been a Democrat; Jefferson, these many years, has been a hero to me."

The senator laughed shortly. "Any resemblance, now, between the Democratic party of to-day and Thomas Jefferson, and between Abraham Lincoln and the Republican party, is purely coincidental. I'm a Republican, and so is my colleague, Jim Norcott. Two good Republicans together. Do you bracket me with that prancing oaf, ' the enemy of Wall Street? '"

He put his hands in his pockets, moved his broad shoulders to a more comfortable position against the door, and let his large belly protrude. His pipe hung from his mouth, and he regarded Allan without curiosity. He looks so damned sick, thought the senator with genuine if hidden sympathy. "How old are you, Allan?" he asked. "I'm not really interested, and you needn't answer if you don't want to."

"I'm nearly fifty-six," said Allan. "Why?"

The senator shrugged. "I'd have thought you older. But you've got a lot of responsibility on your hands, and you're the kind to take it seriously. You didn't come to me to talk about the road, did you? I own a lot of stock in it, and I hear it's going down again since Wilson was elected. Never be what it was in the Panic of '07, though, I hope. Is it the road?"

Allan became irritable. "We got through the Panic, all right, though I'm under the impression you sold a lot of our stock during it, Woodland. Didn't you believe in us?"

"I believed more in old Rufus," replied the senator bluntly. "You did fine, and I congratulated you, I think. I heard, from my father, that Rufus went through many such things in the hoary past with a kind of *élan*. By the way, Cornelia has that *élan*, hasn't she? She must have been a big help to you during the dark days."

513   2κ

"She was," said Allan gloomily. "She'll always have it. Though," he added, with involuntary resentment, "she's going on forty-eight."

"Never would have believed it, if I didn't know, myself. She looks hardly forty. Plays the best damn' game of tennis I ever saw, for a woman. Nothing ever bothers Cornelia. I heard she's quite a power and a terror on the board; read the last newspaper account of her only a week ago. And yet she's not one of those suffragettes, is she? Well? What are you doing here in Washington? Especially considering you've never supported my party in any way, and gave a nice sum last year for the campaign of my Democratic opponent."

"I came because I know you for an honest man, and even though I know now that you can't do anything about what has happened. I mean the coming adoption of the Sixteenth Amendment on February 25th—the cursed Federal income tax."

Again, the senator shrugged. "I worked hard enough against it. But the states ratified it. Want to blame it on me?"

"Don't be a fool," said Allan. "I know how you tried. It's just that I want to discuss it with you."

The senator's broad shadow became sharper on the white wall of the house. "Go ahead, discuss it," he said. He glanced about his garden again, but a deep line appeared between his eyes. "Have you talked with Jim Norcott?"

"No, that ass," replied Allan, his voice rising. "I found out that a year ago, while he was the most vociferous about having this Amendment adopted, he put all his very considerable cash into what will be tax-exempt securities. Want to keep that in mind, George, when he comes up for nomination again?"

The senator grunted. "Remember? He's a Republican, too; stands high with the party. I've been in this game too long to start target practice at a member of my own organisation, except when it will do some good for the country generally. However, you're a Democrat; bring up Jim's dark background if you want to, when it will hurt the most." He added, "Well?"

"You'll think me a fool," Allan began awkwardly. "Perhaps you won't understand why I came to you to-day; I don't quite understand it myself, to be frank, except that I have a feeling you can be helpful in the future. It's not just the unconstitutional Federal income tax—and a thousand Supreme Courts can pass on its constitutionality and it still wouldn't be convincing--it's the implications for the future that worry me." He hesitated. "Ever read anything about Karl Marx and Engels, and the rest of them?"

The senator said nothing; his eyes had suddenly fixed themselves on the distant wall of his gardens, and they remained there.

"Well," said Allan, more and more awkwardly, "I've been reading their sinister writings over a period of many years. One of the things Marx advocated, in order to destroy capitalism and bring about a communist revolution, was the graduated income tax. So now we have put into our Constitution a Marxist philosophy. Oh, the tax is very insignificant as it stands now; it will only be a nuisance—as it stands now. I'm not thinking of the present; I'm thinking of the future, when this Marxist measure really gets under way. I'm thinking, in connection with the Federal income tax—the Communists' first measure to destroy freedom—of another outline for the destruction of freedom, as advocated by the Marxists: war, on a world-wide scale. Are you following me, George?"

But still the senator did not speak, nor did his eyes move.

"I have documents, secret reports, from Europe," stammered Allan. "Too much to go into now, but I could send you an outline of it if you wish. There's a war brewing there; been brewing as far back as 1908. A war for markets and for profit, between England and Germany. This war, which will come almost any day now, has been carefully plotted by the enemies of freedom; they've been plotting it for decades—the disciples of Marx and his contemporaries. They know that great wars will undermine capitalism, free enterprise, constitutional government, and will bring about power for them. And they're everywhere, George. You think I'm talking gibberish, don't you?"

"Go on," said the senator quietly.

"But it's the deadly truth," said Allan, and his voice was louder and more vehement. "And that's where our Federal income tax comes in. A nation can't wage wars without vast revenues. How have the European nations raised revenues for wars? By a personal income tax, a tax alien to America, and conceived in European minds for European purposes. It's true we had an income tax during the Civil War, but it was quickly ended after the conflict, and we had a short taste of it during the

Spanish-American War. But our presidents understood that this was a European policy and had no right to exist, except in dire emergency, in America. It had no peace-time reason for existing in America. Yet, now we have this Sixteenth Amendment. So we can engage in a war plotted for the whole world, in order to destroy the existing order of the world."

"Go on," said the senator briefly.

Allan lifted his arms in a gesture of desperate defeat. "I believe, and I feel I am not alone in so believing, that many of the advocates of a Federal income tax in America are part of the world conspiracy in behalf of socialism, or communism, as it is beginning to be called. In spite of George Washington, then, and his warning against 'foreign alliances,' we'll be manipulated into the European war which is rapidly brewing."

The senator slowly turned his head and scrutinised Allan, but made no comment.

"The war, and wars after it, are not only plotted by the enemies of liberty everywhere, but the tyrants who will arise as the result of these wars, have also been plotted for. The American people, who have been so blandly indifferent to the Federal income tax, won't understand until it is too late. Millions of them believe that it will be only a tax on the very rich, and a light one at that, for what is already being called 'the general welfare.' But the day will come when the people will understand that 'the general welfare' means slavery, and that the Federal income tax is being used not only for deliberately plotted wars to overthrow existing governments but as a personal instrument of coming despots in America. How can a free nation be subjugated from within by domestic criminals in league with the world-wide conspirators? By crushing personal taxes, by designed inflation, by confiscation of the people's labour in the form of taxation, by attacks on the Constitution, by debasing the currency, and by centralising power in the State. George?"

"I am still listening," said the senator.

"We'll see European bureaucracy coming to pass on a grand scale in America," Allan went on hopelessly. "We'll see the fears of Thomas Jefferson—the absorption of State rights, a prodigally spending State devouring the labour of the people, and European entanglements—all be fulfilled. The plot against America, and against free peoples everywhere, did not begin with this Sixteenth Amendment. It is being culminated in it."

Never Victorious, Never Defeated

The senator lifted himself from against the wall, went to the edge of the terrace, and emptied the contents of his pipe on the sodden wintry grass. He said musingly, "Did you think you were the only one who knew, Allan?"

"You know?" exclaimed Allan. The senator smiled grimly, and nodded. "The enemies of us all, down in Washington, also know," he said. "Don't believe for a minute that any one particular party is guilty of what has happened, and will happen. I see you don't fall into the error," he added, after another scrutiny of Allan's face.

"My God," said Allan in a dull voice.

"I'm afraid it's too late now, to stop the first act, or perhaps even the second and the third and the fourth," the senator went on. "Yes; we'll be in a European war, and in others. Yes, everything will happen as Thomas Jefferson feared. But we, the elected representatives of the people, will be able to do nothing until the people themselves understand the plot against them. And then may come the bloodiest day the world has ever known, in all its history, perhaps." He made a distasteful grimace. "Much as I, personally, would like to see the coming tyrants and their cohorts openly massacred in the streets, the idea is too European. I'd prefer to see the American people rise and rid themselves of the monsters at the ballot boxes." He lifted his large bald head and looked at the sky, and smiled again, this time triumphantly. "And they will, they will! In the meantime, we can only keep them aware of what is happening, by constant reiteration, by constant warning."

For the first time he regarded Allan with affection. He raised his meaty hand and put it on the older man's shoulder. "The battle will be for men's souls and minds," he said. "And I have faith, not only in the American people, but in the people of all other nations. What will come will be the last mighty stand of the despots against their peoples. And the despots will lose." He patted Allan's shoulder before removing his hand. "Depend on it; they'll lose, no matter their strength, no matter how many socialists and communists they'll have with them, everywhere."

"By the Grace of God," said Allan.

The senator said, nodding, "By the Grace of God."

They went into the house. The long and narrow library glimmered with the pallid sunlight that fell from the wintry sky, and a fire of cannel coal burned richly on the black marble hearth. Here was a kind of ugly, masculine comfort, full of old draperies, worn rugs, and black leather. The two men sat down, and Allan looked at his watch while the senator poured glasses of whisky and soda. Mr. Woodland watched Allan as the latter gulped his drink; he himself sipped with enjoyment. He peered at Allan's seamed face and large narrow nose, and grey hair which was turning white at the temples. "Tell me," he said, sitting on the arm of a chair, "what's changed you, Allan? You were the *entrepreneur* type, bless their memory, for they pushed back the frontiers, opened the mines and the oil wells, and filled the ranges with cattle and the cities with their smoke. I've been reading of your talks to other railroaders all over the country, about a balance between industry and agriculture. And now you are all steaming about a threat to American liberty. Something changed you."

Allan cradled the glass in his hands and sombrely puckered his pale lips. "Perhaps I never really ' changed,'" he said. "My brother, who is a monk, once wrote me that. I don't know."

Allan went on: "Above all things, my dad hated oppressive governments. He'd had experience with them. And like all Irishmen, freedom seemed to him the only climate in which humanity could live without dying of suffocation. I used to laugh at him when I was young. I don't think, however, that anyone ever forgets what his parents teach him, in spite of laughing."

"In other words, your father was a very intelligent man," said the senator. "Do you know, one of my constituents, who is a labour man of much intelligence, and who has given his life to the organising of unions and in fighting for reasonable wages for everyone, recently told me that he fears that in the future labour will become ' big business,' and that in that event, it will become dangerous."

"A monopoly?" said Allan incredulous.

The senator nodded. "I've been around a long time, politicking, and I don't trust my fellow men worth a damn. And I don't trust the silent hordes who are now lining up behind Wilson, our Minority President. He's a good man, an austere and even noble kind of fellow, but he doesn't know who is getting ready to use him. Things are going to be pretty horrible in the future, I'm afraid." He got up to poke at the coal, which flared vehemently at the touch of the poker. "Anything too ' big,' whether business or labour, can be used by despots, taken over by them." He went back to sit on the arm of the leather chair. "Let's talk about something more pleasant, and less sinister. Such as your family. I hear you are a grandfather now. A grandson?"

Allan's expression darkened. "Yes, Dolores. They named the boy after me; at least, that is one of his names. Alexander Beaumont Allan Richard Gibson-Hamilton. His father is Richard, Lord Gibson-Hamilton, as you know."

How had Dolores come to marry the "Sassenach?" Allan did not know. The year after Rufus's death in February, 1906, had been a year of dreadful confusion and clouded and desperate hurry, for Allan. It had been a year of grief and strife. There had been no time for his children, not even for his darling, Dolores. The Panic of 1907 had come fast on the heels of all the other events. Dolores's young and beautiful face came through dimly to her father now, shadowed by those years. She had come to him, very quietly, one night, in the very midst of his inner and outer turmoil, and she had told him that she was going to marry Lord Gibson-Hamilton. He, Allan, had been overwhelmingly exhausted and harried. He had said, "Why?" It was a question in a nightmare-ridden dream, and he had thought: I'll think about it to-morrow. Somehow, to-morrow had never come. He remembered protesting vaguely to Cornelia, who had kissed him and had declared that all was well, and Dolores wished the marriage after all. There had been two million dollars given to the young couple as a wedding present, composed of cash and stocks, and there had been a wondrous marriage full of fanfare and much lyrical newspaper reporting; and then all at once Dolores was gone, whitely smiling, with a last kiss for her father, and a touch of her hand.

How often had he seen Dolores since late 1907? He could not remember. Four times, five? He could not remember. He had not as yet seen his grandson; he and Cornelia would visit the new parents on their way to the Riviera next month. What had happened to prevent more frequent visits in the past six years? "Everything," he said aloud to the senator, in a tone of distraction, "has always been in such a hurry. I was against the marriage from the very start, when Cornelia was all for it. Nothing against the man, personally, though."

"You've forgotten I was one of the guests, at the church in Portersville," said the senator with hidden pity.

"Yes, so you were. I don't know," added Allan. "Dolores writes she is very happy and contented. I'll find out for myself. I'm going to give myself more time."

"And Tony?"

Allan began to smile, and some of the distraught darkness lifted from his face. "Oh, Tony! He was ordained last year, you know. And he's Father Dugan's young curate, in the very church where I was baptised! Funny. It's been rebuilt, the church, and is very impressive now. I think there are two curates. I donated a lot of money to the rebuilding, and to the Sisters' Hospital. Tony's very happy. He wasn't pleased with Dolores's marriage, though. But he and Dolores drifted apart, and there was nothing he could say or do."

The senator thoughtfully filled his pipe. He said, "And how is your boy DeWitt since he married that pretty Peale girl last June?"

Allan laughed softly. "DeWitt is a natural-born railroader. And he only twenty-three! He's taken a lot of burdens off me lately. By the way, Mary is 'expecting,' too. How time passes. Children yesterday, men and parents to-day. It's confusing. You know, of course, that Miles Peale married Ruth Purcell, very quietly, two years ago last September? It surprised everybody, except Cornelia, who has taken quite a liking to Miles. I thought the marriage unsuitable, myself. Ruth is nearly ten years older than Miles, but then he is very mature for twenty-five—twenty-six? Just about Tony's age. Miles is doing very well; one of our best superintendents. He moved in with Ruth in old Jim Purcell's house near the river. I took on his brother Fielding as Miles's assistant. Fielding's going to marry old Brownell's granddaughter—the banker."

Allan's face had become black, though he had talked casually enough. The Pharisee, Patrick Peale, had succeeded. His sons were in the Interstate Railroad Company. One of them now was in control of the Purcell money and the Purcell railroad holdings. Patrick had his own control, and through his wife Laura, even more dangerous control. (I wish to God he'd die, thought Allan. Perhaps I'll get my wish; he looks like death itself these days.) Allan thought of Ruth, thirty-five years old, with a pang. A sweet and innocent woman, for all her age. She adored her young husband, and there again was a danger.

The senator considerately puffed his pipe and did not look at Allan. "By the way," he said, "I understand that your brother-in-law, Norman deWitt, has made quite a stir in literary circles with his book *Design for the New Order*. Read it myself. Have you?"

Allan stood up; he lit a cigarette. "Yes. He's one of the enemy. I thought his brother Jon was, but it was he all the time. Funny. He always seemed to me to be a youth, soft and without shape, just smiling and hanging around his mother, and never a thought in his head. It just proves that you never know. Lives in London a lot of the time, talking Fabian socialism. And he with all that damned money he is scheduled to inherit when his damn'—I mean, his old mother dies. He's got a lot of his own, too. You can be sure those socialists are very miserly with their cash; he lived somewhere in the neighbourhood of Soho, in a run-down house practically in the slums. 'The wealth of the world should be justly shared,' the imbeciles like him say. But they don't mean their own wealth, which they hang on to with both hands. They just mean yours, and mine."

"He never married?"

Allan said viciously, "No. You see, he couldn't marry his mother."

He refilled his glass automatically, with invitation. "Sometimes," he said, "life gets too much for me. I'd like to move off somewhere. I can't recall a single day, during the past twenty years or so, when I've known an hour of peace or happiness. A man of my age surely deserves a little quiet once in a while, a time to think. But things move faster and faster. . . ."

He smiled with difficulty at the senator. "I suppose they always do, for men like me. I'm not the kind old Rufus was."

CHAPTER FORTY-FOUR

ALLAN AND Cornelia and Estelle did not arrive in England until late in May.

Allan was acquainted with London, which he reluctantly admired for its mighty feeling of power and strength, and which he disliked for its all-pervading stench of coal gas. The south of England, where his son-in-law Lord Gibson-Hamilton had his country seat, was unknown to him. He and the two women left London on a particularly warm and humid day, went by train for a considerable distance, and then were picked up by a huge black limousine, with a chauffeur and assistant chauffeur, at a country way-station, where all was wind and rolling sky of vivid blue and brilliant white. Allan watched the little English villages fly past, with their quiet and curving streets and little crowding shops, thatched roofs, and brick or cobbled roads. The limousine rolled cautiously up and down country lanes sunken far below neat fields walled with earth thickly overgrown with ferns and buttercups. He caught glimpses of towering purple rhododendrons and the pink candles of chestnut trees. Then the hot sun poured down like a flood of light on the plushy green hills of Devon, studded with trees like a great park. Here and there an ancient farmhouse with stone walls stood alone on the moors, and golden gorse sprang from the spring earth like twisted torches.

The moors, green, brown, and russet, particularly interested him; and their wild and isolated hills, on which roamed the famous untamed horses, called to some deep instinct in him. The party wheeled over old stone bridges, which cast their shadows on blue and green water. They stopped for a luncheon at a hoary inn, reputed to have been patronised by Drake. Then the limousine swung along the silent countryside, winding its way through dim green lanes between high banks, and passing woods spotted with sunshine, and clumps of lilacs in full bloom, and copses of plane trees. Now, occasionally, the sea flashed into view like a purple mirror. "It is more like the South of France than England," said Allan with pleasure. He was amazed when he

522

saw an occasional cactus and a lonely palm tree, as they rushed south.

"It's England, all right," said Cornelia dryly. "This happens to be a fine day, but it's likely to be as cold as death to-night, and to-morrow. I wonder if the cacti and the palms really grow here, or are they set out in tubs?"

She was just as cynical about Cockington, with its winding streets and thatched whitewashed cottages and antique smithy. But Allan was charmed. While Estelle remained in the limousine, he and Cornelia walked up a sweet-smelling lane to the little church of St. George and St. Mary, mouldering softly under the sun. They strolled through gardens unbelievably beautiful, up and down long paths about which gigantic rhododendrons bloomed in all shades of pale and dark lilac, magenta, and rose, and great twisted trees stood at a distance in gauzy and dreamlike light. Allan became more and more entranced by the gently dim and fragrant lushness of the country; he stopped, with Cornelia, at The Ponds, sheets of still water in which the rhododendrons were reflected in masses of colour, and on which floated tame ducks who came nearer to inspect the visitors with inquisitive and fearless eyes. England's green and pleasant land, thought Allan, and he came to believe in the old stories that this was once a merry land also, full of legends and lusty men, castles and strange forests heavy with silence and spectres, Merlin and King Arthur and the Knights of the Round Table. What remained was a mysterious memory, hanging in space, without sound, while the mills of Lancashire roared over the horizon of dreams, and the mighty heart of London beat incessantly in some far distance.

"But still," said Allan to Cornelia, "the English respect their land. In America, we do not respect it. We ravish it, as if with greedy contempt."

"Dear, let's not talk about your obsession concerning agriculture again," said Cornelia, slipping her gloved hand into his arm affectionately. "Remember, our resources in America are practically inexhaustible, while here they must conserve everything."

"No," said Allan obstinately, "our resources are not inexhaustible. And we'll learn that we, too, must conserve, perhaps when it is too late. Think of the lumbermen who are destroying our forests. . . ."

"Estelle will be getting impatient," said Cornelia, and twinkled indulgently at her husband. "We have no respect for the earth," Allan repeated, but Cornelia did not answer him.

The palms became more numerous as they went on, though Allan had to admit to himself that they appeared a little unhappy and unhealthy in this country. The long English twilight was setting in. Estelle drowsed under a robe, Cornelia yawned and drowsed also. But Allan watched with an eagerness he had not felt for a long time. A lovely country, he thought, a beautiful land. He smiled at the villagers, pink-cheeked men and women and children, who stopped to gape at them as they passed down the lanes and through the quiet little streets. They smiled in return, and one old man waved his pipe in salute, and an old woman curtsied. What had changed the English? Allan asked himself. Of course, they say that they must have industry, and export, or they will starve. But what had become of their legendary spirit, their boldness, their wine-drinking hilarity, their fearless men? Have they all died in the factories and the mills and in the bleak and dreary streets of their industrial cities? Or is it all waiting there, asleep, for some trumpet call? Will King Arthur ever gather his knights about him again, and will Merlin weave spells, and will these green and silent lanes ever hear the tread of brave men once more, and the laughter of full-bodied wenches? Will there ever be another Elizabeth to move poets and set great fleets on the seas and make the inns resound with the thump of goblets and the courtyards ring with horses?

They were closer to the sea now, which had turned to a grey mistiness under a sky of faded rose. The woods had become cloudy, and wisps of fog curled on the flowery banks along the lanes. The hills drifted in mauve and heliotrope. The limousine bowled along a sea-lane and the quiet became an intense and present thing. Then they were turning from the ocean and entering through high iron gates opened for them by two countrymen, who removed their caps in a servile gesture which Allan found irritating. Now they were in a green and rising parkland filled with monster oaks and larch trees and rhododendrons, the grass almost covered with tiny white daisies, dreamlike vistas opening everywhere and coloured with flowers. They seemed to go on forever. Allan said, "Is this all part of Dick's land?" Cornelia nodded. "You've never seen a real English estate before," she said. "This is only one small section of it. He has a huge farm, too, at some distance."

The land rose steadily, and there, on a low hill, stood a great mansion of grey stone, turreted against the sunset sky, its battlements floating in mist, its high and narrow leaded windows flaming with scarlet. Again, Allan was entranced, though he thought wryly to himself that the Interstate Railroad Company had probably restored the castle to habitability, and was responsible for the fine condition of the park.

But he was really happy that his beloved daughter lived among such beauty and in such splendour, and he was glad that he had made it possible for her. When the bronze doors of the mansion opened, and servants appeared, he looked for Dolores anxiously, for he had a "plebeian" idea that she would be there to greet him at once, with her child in her arms, her pale blonde hair blowing about her face. However, there was no sign of the family as Allan and the two women entered a massive stone hall whose walls were lined with armour and pennants and banners, and which was lighted with candles set in a huge iron chandelier. He smelled mustiness and an indefinable odour of antiquity and felt a chill which a fire, burning briskly in a grey stone fireplace, could not banish. A broad stone staircase, ponderous and dim, wound upwards into growing dusk.

The candlelight winked back from old dimmed armour, and the banners lifted a little in the breeze that came through the yawning entrance. The house echoed spectrally as the party was conducted upstairs. All at once Allan was overpoweringly depressed, and he was afraid for his daughter in this mass of stone and iron, in this cold silence overlooking the grey sea and the dreaming, unreal park.

But the suite of rooms assigned to Allan and Cornelia was pleasant enough, all big old furniture and tapestried walls and fires and lamplight. "Damned old fashioned and inconvenient," said Cornelia, discovering commodes and accompanying china. "But then, it's the country. Smell those lamps! Shades of my childhood!"

Allan said nothing, for he liked these rooms. He examined the enormous old bed in his bedroom, with the black posts carved intricately, and tested the hard mattress. He rubbed his hands before the good fire. It could be peaceful, he told himself, as a neat maid entered with a copper pitcher of hot water and extra towels.

Never Victorious, Never Defeated

I have a feeling they know how to live, Allan thought, washing his face and hands. His spirits rose a little. It was possible that Dolores liked all this, after all. He momentarily forgot that she wrote very seldom, and then in the most impersonal manner. As he wiped his hands the house suddenly vibrated to the sound of a brazen bell, the announcement that it was time to dress for dinner. Its echoes remained, and once more Allan was depressed. While a valet deftly unpacked his bag containing his evening clothes, Allan went to the leaded casements and pushed them open and looked out beyond the park to the darkening sea. A lighthouse blinked on a pile of rock; a wind blew in scented with grass and roses, and ivy rustled on the old walls. Where is my daughter? thought Allan, with the perfumed dampness on his face. And he repeated despondently: Where is my daughter? The distant sea answered dolorously, and again he experienced fear.

It was not until three in the morning that Allan fell into the sharpest and uneasiest of his dreams, in spite of the fact that he had drunk heavily before going to bed to loosen, without result, the awful tension in him. Within half an hour after he had fallen into this nightmare-ridden doze, the kaleidoscope of bodiless faces and shifting images which had printed themselves on his closed eyelids faded away, and he dreamed clearly and sharply. He was walking down a rain-driven street again, with the gutters awash at his right and the dripping walls of lonely buildings at his left. He could see the misty lamplight on each corner of the street, glistening faintly on the steel lines of the rain slanting away from it. He was young again, and he was whistling "Killarney," and the sweet and piercing music rang back from the closed walls he was passing. There was a tattered election poster on a wall, and he tore it loose and looked at it. But it was not the young Patrick Peale's face now; it was the face of a man of sixty, a sick and broken man with white hair, haunted features, and fanatical yet vulnerable eyes. "You should not have done it," said the pictured face to Allan sadly. And the young Allan, in his shabby and streaming clothing, replied, "There is so much each man should not do to another."

The poster was torn from his hands and it fled down the street like a tattered ghost, and Allan called after it, "Lord have mercy upon us both." A man's voice began to sing in the darkness: "Now was it Abel, was it Cain—who suffered death, who suffered pain?"

526

I must hurry, thought Allan. He shook his head, which was aching unbearably. The mouse ran across his path, and he kicked it and it flew in the air. In its passage it looked at him; it had his own face in miniature, his face as it was in his middle years, and it cried out in a loud and bitter voice. It fell in the rushing gutter, and Allan watched as it was borne away in the murky water. He said again, "Lord have mercy upon us." He began to run, and the walls closed in upon him, and he was in a crevice and he shouted desperately for help. But the walls narrowed until he could not move and they rose far up into the blackness towards the sky, and he was trapped and he knew he would never be free again, not until he died.

He struggled against the horror of the dream, in which loneliness seemed the greatest terror of all. He panted and gasped, and then he was awake in a ghostly flood of moonlight and in a torrent of dark wind gushing in through the casements from the sea. He was sitting upright and his silk nightshirt was soaked with sweat and his heart was beating wildly. "Christ, what a dream!" he said to himself. He could not lie down again. He fumbled for his slippers and robe, and they were damp. He went to the casements and leaned on the wide ledge beyond them. The sea, flowing almost silently, lay beyond the dusky gardens, and it was a plain silver, breaking here and there into silver fire. The moon floated over it, cold and calm, and the wet air ran over Allan's shivering body like water. He closed the casements tightly, and locked them to shut out the wind and the eerie sound of the whispering ivy, and he lit a lamp.

There was a pigskin case on his dresser, and he opened it, seeing all his movements in tall and spectral mirrors. He lifted the bottle that lay within the case and put it to his mouth and drank long and deeply. He wiped his mouth with the back of his hand. The fire had long since died. There was a dank chill in the big room, like a cellar, and Allan pulled the rose-silk eiderdown from the bed, wrapped it around him, and sat down with his bottle of whisky. Everywhere, his image was reflected back to him, and the shadowy light of the lamp; he saw himself huddled in the eiderdown, and he was sick with pain.

He could see his daughter Dolores as he had seen her only a few hours ago, a daughter he did not know. There she had sat, in pale satin the colour of ice, her white shoulders and throat bare, her light blonde hair braided in a coronet on her small, high head, pearls and diamonds glistening about her neck and falling on to her breast. She had sat beside her father, and she had given him frequent faint smiles and sometimes had glanced at him with shy love. But when he had looked into her eyes it was like looking into blueness behind glass, utterly without expression. She talked of her child, little Alexander, and she spoke of the races she and her husband had attended, and of the gardens and the gardeners, who were Scotsmen, and of the King and Queen who were so gracious to her at their garden parties and in the Palace. She talked of everything, and talked of nothing. There was no colour in her smooth cheeks, and only the faintest of rose in her lips, which were tight and very still in repose, like the lips of a statue. The huge chandelier above the dining-table glimmered and flickered with candles and crystal, and the fugitive light ran over the classical outlines of her face.

Allan, as usual, had drunk too much, and during a moment's pause, he had leaned towards Dolores and had whispered, "Don't you remember me, darling? I am your father, and I love you." She had turned to him and had smiled vaguely and gently. He had then said, "Dolores, it is too late, but why did you do it? You aren't happy. . . ."

It was then that she had looked at him fully, and for the first time the glass slipped away from between them and she was gazing at him with an expression of intense and unfathomable amazement, and her mouth had opened on a startled sound. And then a look of affront—to his greater surprise—passed over her face, and she had turned to the man on her left and had not spoken to her father again at the table. I have lost my daughter, thought Allan. But where and when I do not know.

He drank again now, pulling deeply at the bottle as a child pulls at the breast. The whisky ran through him, quickening his blood, slowing his shivers. As moments passed, his brain began to warm in the familiar and soothing incandescence, and he could remember everything. There was Cornelia at her son-in-law's right hand, the candle-blaze full on her face, and it was a large face, coarsely painted on coarse canvas, the powder and the rouge and the crow's feet and the dyed red hair making her look like a gay, indomitable harridan, surging with cunning and strength and an incredible lust for living. She blinked, and her eyes were the eyes of a lioness caught in vivid daylight, a predatory lioness whose eagerness for hunting and flesh would never be satiated.

Her throat and half-covered breast were white as milk, and so intense was the life-force in Cornelia that her body seemed to palpitate. She was wearing her favourite colour, a kind of electric blue, and the lace and silk showed off her narrow waist and swelling hips superbly. The diamonds in her hair, about her neck, and on her wrists and arms and fingers, coruscated with coloured fire in the shifting light. Never had she appeared so fearful and so powerful to her husband, and he winced at her loud hoarse voice booming in the vast room with its ancient table and buffets and cabinets and princely chairs, its stone walls and tapestries and dusky paintings. She joked and howled with laughter, and her son-in-law regarded her affectionately, for he was not offended by her vulgarity but rather appeared fascinated by it. His guests, a confusion of faces that Allan never attempted to sort out, or to know, appeared equally entertained and fascinated, and listened with enjoyment.

Allan had long ceased to dislike the little wiry man who was his daughter's husband. He even liked him, reluctantly, and sometimes was sorry for him without reason. The birdlike profile, with its great hawk's nose, was not the profile of a bird of prey, but gentle and thin and almost timid, the receding chin defensive, the sloping forehead retreating to a small and balding head. All his features, and his hands, and his body were patrician, and attenuated, and his tiny avian eyes, bright and kind, kindled with intellect. Though he spoke courteously to his guests, and listened to them, and was anxious for their comfort, and scrutinised the wine labels carefully, his gaze invariably came to Dolores. There it melted, sought, shone with tenderness. Dolores, in turn, seemed unconscious of the presence of her husband.

Lord Gibson-Hamilton was even considerate and patient with old Estelle deWitt, and would listen when no one else paid her any attention. He would let her prattle, and would bend his head towards her with an attentive smile, caring for her desires. She had dwindled these last years, but her wrinkled face still simpered inanely, and she still strove for "radiance," and her thin white hair was still piled in coquettish curls on her pink skull. Since Rufus's death she had dressed invariably in black, but with many pearls and other gems, and her puckered hands were heavy with rings. As her mind was so immature and commonplace, her brown eyes were the full and distended eyes of a very young girl, and they beamed happily to-night in such distinguished company.

What had been said at that dinner? Allan, swimming with alcohol, could not remember. He was engrossed with his own wretched thoughts, and the tall waxen image of his daughter beside him. Occasionally Cornelia's resounding voice irritated him, and he wondered at the genuine laughter she invoked.

There had been something said about riding early in the morning, and Cornelia had shouted her approval. No matter how late she went to bed, she was always up by six o'clock in the morning, eager for life, bursting with vitality. She had suggested tennis later in the day, and Richard Gibson-Hamilton, with admiration, had assented. Allan shuddered, and Cornelia had said in her rallying way, "Don't expect anything of Allan. He hates the morning, and always has. He hates sports, too, and flinches at the sight of a horse or a tennis racket."

The wine was excellent and Allan had drunk much of it. One of the butlers was almost continually behind his chair, pouring. Cornelia had frowned once, staring pointedly at her husband with her hazel eyes, then had shrugged. She had hoped that he would not "make a fool of himself, as usual," or grow morose or quarrelsome. Allan, she thought privately, simply had no capacity for alcohol in any form.

Later, the family had the first glimpse of the baby, Richard's son and heir. The little man had taken his child in his arms and had held him tightly, kissing him with the tenderest hunger. He had to be reminded by Dolores that perhaps her parents might wish to hold the boy for a few moments. He had apologised, looked about him anxiously, and then, as if by instinct, he had given the baby to Allan, who was already swaying slightly.

The child was slight, yet had a long body and an alert and sensitive face, full of curiosity and friendliness. But his light brown eyes were grave, and he had inspected Allan closely before smiling. Wisps of fine brown hair spread out in an aureole about his head, and he had a firm dimple in his chin. The warmth of him in Allan's arms suddenly penetrated to Allan's exhausted heart, and he held the baby close to him with so vehement a gesture that the nurse moved forward in alarm. But little Alexander did not cry out. He let himself be pressed to his grandfather, and he was very still.

"Why, the little spalpeen!" Allan had said in a blurred and

shaking voice. "It's the fine lad he is, sure, and it is a fine lad, and it will be a fine man, I am hoping. And praying. It's the face of my mother he has, the saint's face, with the holy light in the eyes."

Estelle was embarrassed, Cornelia amused and annoyed. Allan was always "far gone" when he relapsed into the brogue of his childhood, and she began to scheme how to whisk him away before he made himself objectionable and insulting. She thought Allan very dramatic, clutching the child like that, a very ordinary-looking child in her opinion, and nothing to elicit charmed exclamations. His only asset was that some day he would inherit his father's title and estates and position in international society. With a grin of good humour, she took the boy from Allan's straining arms, and held him out at arm's length and scrutinised him. "Well," she said, "a nice baby, I suppose. At least he doesn't squall and struggle."

The warm nursery swam in firelight and lamplight before Allan. Dolores was a tall shadow nearby. Richard watched his father-in-law, and something tightened in his meagre breast, for Allan was engrossed with the baby, and trembling. Estelle simpered, "Why, I do believe the little darling looks like my Norman! Yes, the same——"

Allan turned on her so suddenly that he staggered for a moment. His dark face became livid. He cried, "And may God forgive you for the lie you have said, woman! The wicked, wicked lie it is. . . ."

Cornelia swore emphatically under her breath. She caught Allan's arm in a firm grip, a thin tense arm under the black sleeve. "Now, now, dear, Estelle only meant something very nice. You've frightened her. You fool," she added in a whisper. She smiled brightly at her daughter's smooth and expressionless face, at Richard's quiet eyes, at Estelle, shrinking with elaborate and affected fear from Allan's vicinity. The nurse stared enraptured, and thought of the servants' hall where she could tell this incredible story about the "heathen" Americans and their ill-bred ways. "And I assure you, Sally, I heard that Mrs. Marshall swear like a hussar, and her husband—drunk as a lord! And little Mrs. deWitt looking all gone, that she did, and his lordship so gentle and kind."

Somehow Allan found himself in his rooms, with the valet in attendance, and Cornelia leaning against the polished mahogany door and expressing herself without reticence. "I don't know why you have to be such a damnable boor after you drink too much," she said.

"You'll never know, Cornelia, why I drink too much, as you say," Allan had replied in a voice so faint that he was barely audible. Then he became excited again: "That cursed woman—Norman—that child—my grandson. . . ."

"Oh, shut up," said Cornelia, beginning to laugh. "You're a fool, my darling. I wonder what these people are thinking of you now? However, who cares? We're the monstrously rich DeWitts and Marshalls, and I never saw even an aristocrat pale with disgust at the thought of money. However, I only hope to God that they merely think you eccentric. Estelle is doubtlessly explaining to everybody that you're Irish, and that will settle things in their minds. Don't tug at your tie like that; you'll strangle. By the way, do you know I think that Dicky would have married Dolores without the money? He actually loves the poor cold thing. Funny, isn't it? Do go to bed, and I'll trip downstairs and try to cover up for you."

She had blown him a gay kiss and had gone. He had permitted the valet to undress him. He had found his box of sedatives and had taken three pills. Then he was in bed, with the low light beside him, and he was alone. He had turned out the light and had lain on his pillows and had begun to think.

The thoughts were familiar, and sharp, in spite of all the whisky and wine. Cornelia. How long ago had she begun to look at him with the rounded eyes and the rounded mouth of mockery? How long had she indulged him, drawing him away not only from guests and hosts, and taking him home, but drawing him away from board meetings with light words, smiles, and winks at directors? How long had she been treating him as an irresponsible person, and how long had she been inviting others so to treat him? For several years, at least. And this was the reason that his directors listened to him more and more impatiently, or exchanged amused glances, and later consulted Cornelia in private? Who was imparting the suggestion that he was a fool, a bad-tempered, excitable fool, sometimes talking incoherently? Cornelia.

But why? He had the power. He was the president of the Interstate Railroad Company. By incredible work and effort he had prevented the road from suffering too much during the

Panic of 1907. The company owned his four exclusive patents, about which authorities had written numerous books. The wealth of the company had doubled since 1900, when he had relieved Rufus deWitt of practically all responsibility. He had given all his heart and mind and energy and inventiveness to the company. He had been regarded with majestic respect by the presidents of other roads. Even the president of the New York Central and the Pennsylvania had conceded that Allan was a "railroader" in the greatest tradition of genius. He had averted strikes on his own road when other railroads were paralysed by them. The railroad Brotherhoods spoke of him with affection, while they spoke of other roads with sullen rage. All this he had done, in spite of "the drink," in spite of his innate fear and moments of terror and uncertainty. Why, then, did Cornelia treat him as an unpredictable and dull-witted child, and why had she, during these past years, attempted to impart this opinion—which he did not believe she actually held—to others?

Envy.

But I am her husband, I am her father's heir, and she loves me.

It is power that Cornelia wants, thought Allan in the darkness. She cannot, as a woman, be president of the company. But she wishes others to believe that she is the real power behind the apparent power. How can she do that to me, she who loves me, my wife?

He lay there and felt utterly abandoned and alone and betrayed. He turned on his pillows and sighed groaningly. He began to doze. It was then that he had had the nightmare which had awakened him.

And now he was sitting in this great dank bedroom, drinking desperately, while the sea, coming alive, blew its restless voice against the leaded windows and the moon sank in the black sky. Allan muttered, huddled in his quilt, "Lord have mercy upon us, Christ have mercy upon us. . . ." He was startled into silence. He had not spoken voluntarily. His eyes began to sting, and he thought of his son Tony, and he put his forehead on his hand and did not resist the awful despair that swept over him. What have I been looking for all my life? he asked himself. I don't know what it is. I only know I am defeated.

The whisky could not calm him. He fumbled to his feet and went to the windows again, throwing wide the casements to the wild and perfumed air of very early morning. He looked to the east; the sea still ran in darkness, but upon it stood broken mountains of dull fire, and the sky above the cloud-mountains tumbled in dark green and purple. Light fog rose from the gardens and park below like ghosts twining into nothingness before the threat of the coming sun. An unearthly shadow began to gather in the topmost crests of the great trees, and now the birds broke into vehement song which blew up into the greying light like a tuneful explosion. Doves cooed; thrushes threw their sweet voices to the sky. Larks cried in angelic voices. But the house remained wrapped in entranced silence, except for the murmur of the ivy·

Allan's eyes were burning, his head aching violently. He began to sweat, in spite of the coolness and freshness of the air. He looked down at the ground, and he saw a slight figure standing there, its face upturned to his. He started, and remembered the stories of spectres which were supposed to haunt these old mansions; his Celtic blood stirred and a chill ran along his nerves. Then he heard a low and tentative voice: "Sir? Is it you?" He stammered, "Dick? Why are you up so early?"

"I never went to bed," replied Lord Gibson-Hamilton. "May I come up to your rooms for a few moments?"

Allan opened his door, sat down, and waited. He looked at the whisky bottle, had a thought to remove it, then shrugged in his awful weariness. Let his son-in-law know the worst, if he wished. He probably did, anyway. In a few moments the younger man came into the room on silent feet, and took a chair opposite Allan. The lamplight made the shadows in the corners of the room more unreal yet more intense. Richard looked at the bottle of whisky and asked softly, "May I?"

"You don't have to," said Allan, suspecting profound courtesy.

"But I wish to," said the other, smiling sadly. He picked up the bottle and, to Allan's amazement, he drank a long and thirsty drink. Richard held the bottle, then, in his hands, and said, "Sometimes I have to do this. Not very often, you know, but sometimes, especially when I have not been able to sleep."

Allan did not reply. They regarded each other as if sharing a terrible and mutual secret. Then the young man sighed and put the bottle down. "There are times when life seems impossible," he said. Again he looked at Allan, and added very gently, "You know, sir, that I love your daughter, and always have?"

"I—I think so," said Allan.

Richard's smile was sadder than ever. "Did you know that she doesn't love me in the least?"

"I suspected that, to-night. But why did she marry you, then, Dick? I admit I opposed the marriage. It had nothing to do with you, honestly; it was just that I believed she didn't want you. Then, all at once, she changed her mind, or something. At that time everything was confused for me," Allan went on, a little incoherently. "Things were pressuring; old Rufus had died; there was so much to do. I'm not the man he was; we had different backgrounds. I, you see, panic sometimes. It's something I don't understand, not clearly. So, I was in a panic, though I knew it would always happen. You wouldn't understand, with your background. My family was poverty-stricken; I got out of the gutter by—efforts—broke me in a way, I suppose. . . ." I'm talking gibberish, he thought miserably. He can't understand.

Richard nodded gravely. "Yes, I know. I can't tell you how much I admire you, and men like you. We don't have many of your kind in England. Once we did, but not now." He sighed. "But you were asking me why Dolores suddenly changed her mind and married me. I don't know. I was so happy at that time, for I'd given up hope of her, and I didn't question." His kind and birdlike face was touched with shy light.

He clasped his thin hands between his narrow knees and studied the floor. "Were you worrying about Dolores? Don't, please. She is very—competent, in a most wonderful way, and seems to enjoy herself very often. She likes England. But it's as if she has grown a glass shell."

"She was always such a sweet little girl," said Allan. He reached for the bottle and took another drink. "But from the time she was about fourteen she began to slip away. . . . I didn't see her very often. Schools, and things. Somehow, she was always away from me. More than other girls are away from home, generally. And when she was at home, in Portersville, there were parties for her, and she was gone, and all our walks we used to have together—there was no time, or something. . . ."

He stopped and looked at Richard, and his dark and pallid face paled even more. His mouth dropped open. Cornelia. It was always Cornelia, whisking the girl away from him, sending her to house parties, taking her with her, smuggling her off.

But why? Allan stood up distractedly and clenched his fists. It was my fault, he thought with agony. I never took the time, or never had the time, to stop and think of my daughter. There was always something. If Cornelia did what she did, I could have stopped it. But why did she do it?

Richard stood up and pushed his hands into his pockets. He still wore the evening clothes he had worn last night, and they had a bedraggled air. He went to the window. "I've been in the library, reading, and then I walked in the gardens. I like to see the dawn come up." He turned to Allan. "But Dolores isn't the only reason you couldn't sleep, is it? You are worried by so many things." He laughed apologetically. "Is there anything I could do to help you, besides offering you my sympathy?"

"There're a thousand things wrong. Most of my friends laugh at me when I tell them. They think I'm going out of my mind or indulging a fantastic imagination. They won't see; maybe I *am* obsessed, as Cornelia is always saying. I don't think so. You've met Norman deWitt. He's part of what I mean. Perhaps you think I'm mad, too."

The younger man sank into his chair and gazed at Allan with intense seriousness. He said, after a long moment, "I'm a member of the House of Lords. No, sir, I don't think you are 'mad.' I've been talking as you've been talking, for the past few years. No one listens. Except the ones who know only too well. I've watched their faces. They laugh at me, too, but it's jeering laughter as much as to say: 'There is nothing you can do to stop us.'"

Allan was astonished. "You know!" he exclaimed, and his voice shook. "How many of—you—know?"

"Quite a number, sir. Only recently I was talking with Sir Edward Grey." Richard stretched out his hand and turned the lamp down, and the room swam in grey light. Then the little flame died, and there was nothing. "That is what is about to happen to Europe, to the world. All the lights going out, and no colour left anywhere, no men left, only shadows." He regarded the unlighted lamp with deep sombreness. "The trouble, sir, is that the dawn won't come for many decades afterwards. Perhaps not for centuries. The plan was laid a long time ago."

Allan was so excited that he moved to the edge of his chair and his voice rose: "I know! My God, it's some comfort to realise that others know, too! Shouting, never getting an answer except grins and mockery, until now." He added abruptly, "I think a war is coming."

In spite of what Richard had said, Allan watched him closely for the faintest smile of incredulity. But Richard did not smile. He nodded slowly, over and over. "Of course," he said. "That is part of the plot. Induced wars to destroy a capitalistic world. And how can such wars be induced? By giving governments unlimited revenues. Our enemies are all for those revenues. I don't know if you know how Parliament operates. Each year, the tax rates, as we call them, come up for repeal or extension. We have no such thing as you have—Amendments of the Constitution. I always vote against extensions. I voted against the Finance Act of 1907, which is a nefarious plot against England, well executed, well thought out. The graduated tax, as expounded and recommended by Karl Marx. ' From each according to his ability . . .'"

He drew his slight hands slowly and with a dragging motion over his tired face. "It began so many years ago. That day is accursed when we gave asylum to Karl Marx. But sometimes I'm a fatalist. When, in history, did the people of any nation ever listen when a few men ' cried havoc.' The working class in England was very pleased by the Finance Act of 1907. It would help ' put the nobs in their places,' they said, to be heavily taxed. What they did not realise was that the universal plot was directed against them, too. They will know it when it is too late." Again he rubbed his face. " Even when the wars come—and there won't be just one war—I'm afraid they won't realise, not until the day they are enslaved by worse masters than we, and masters so inhuman that they'll be without mercy."

He hesitated. " When the first blow against mankind will come I don't know. I think it will be soon. There is such a stir in all the capitals of Europe. Who will be the ' enemy,' who will fire the first gun? It is my guess that it will be Germany. I think that was decided upon even as long ago as 1906. There is another thing: when war comes, I will be called up, you know. I will have to join my regiment. And there is Dolores, and our child."

"My God, no!" exclaimed Allan.

"I'm afraid so, sir." He lifted his head, and his smile was extremely sad. "Listen to the birds. They would ' wake the dead,' as our cook says. But they won't be able to ' wake the dead ' in the evil days which are almost upon us. The millions of dead, everywhere, in their untimely graves. The millions of dead in a universal gaol. And perhaps, in the future, there won't be a single human ear to hear or a single human soul to love the songs of the birds. Not in the prison house."

Allan beat his fist on the arm of his chair. "What can we do, before it is too late?"

Richard stood up and shook his head. "It's already too late, sir. But there is just one thing we can do: shout, warn, cry havoc. Protest if we die for it. Perhaps someone will hear us, eventually. Perhaps a few. We can only pray."

The first beams of gauzy sunlight suddenly struck into the room. Richard stood in the light, and spare as he was, he seemed to acquire stature and a quiet dignity which could never be overthrown. "The sun will always come up," he said. "There will always be the mornings. Who knows but that, generations in the future, there will be a new morning for our grand-children, if not for us? After all, there is always God."

Allan was so moved that he could not speak. But he got up and put his hands on Richard's shoulders and bent his head to kiss him on the cheek, as he had kissed his son Tony.

CHAPTER FORTY-FIVE

"So STUPID of your father," said Cornelia to her son, the Reverend Rufus Anthony Marshall. "The Germans would never dare to sink any British ships carrying Americans, and really, hundreds of Americans are still going to Paris and the Riviera. Exciting, in a way. Knowing that not too far off there are trenches and things, and fighting. But no, your father obstinately refused to leave America even for a moment after war was declared last summer. It isn't that he's afraid, either. He's just enraged."

"Everyone of sense," she continued, annoyed, fanning herself in the unseasonable May heat, "knows that Wilson's ' New Freedom,' as he calls it, is just politics, and no one takes the man seriously. But your father, God help us! He yammers day and night about this being ' the first open blow against liberty.' He's been talking about ' blows ' for years, and now he feels his prophecy is coming true. Norman just doesn't dare visit us any more, and though it's all your father's fault and Estelle is hysterical about it, I feel it is a blessing. I can't stand the man, even if he is my half-brother. Please don't laugh, Tony, but do you know what your father has recently done? Sold his millions of investments in armament stocks, just when they're booming! Said he couldn't have it on his conscience, for God's sake! What if we are supplying England and France and Germany with a fine neutral hand? But he thinks it's immoral, or something. He's gone out into the garden, and for that, I suppose, I should offer praise, for he becomes intolerable when he drinks, and I'm tired of him infuriating guests. By the way, how do you like Mr. Regan? You haven't seen him since you were a child."

Tony, in the black habit of the priesthood, stood straight and tall in the cool drawing-room of the Portersville house. Guests surged through the rooms and out into the gardens with glasses in their hands. The house and the land tinkled and clamoured with their talk and laughter. Tony sipped at his sherry and glanced anxiously about for his sister Dolores. But she was nowhere in sight. Probably, he thought, upstairs with the child. How pale and cold and distant she is, thought Tony. Is it possible she is worrying about her husband, the colonel, who was with his regiment "somewhere in France?"

"Tony, you aren't listening," said Cornelia, more annoyed than ever. Her white linen dress was draped tightly about her splendid figure, and there was a slit in it almost to the knee. Her red hair was dressed in the latest fashion, bunched thickly about her head and over her ears. Delicate white lace cascaded over her full breast, sprinkled with glittering diamonds.

"I'm sorry, Mamma," said Tony. "I was listening, though. Mr. Regan? The son of the man Grandpa used to talk about? He looks like a deceptively friendly monster in ambush. Isn't he one of those who are helping finance the armaments trade?"

"How unrealistic you are!" said Cornelia impatiently. "Just like your father. By the way, our guests will be leaving soon, and you will oblige me by going to look for him? I can't see him from the terraces, and it wouldn't surprise me if he's hidden himself far down in that grotto with a private bottle. By the way, when are you going to be a monsignor or a bishop or something?"

Tony smiled sadly. "I don't want to be anything but a parish priest, and now that Father Dugan is dead, and I have taken his place, I'm quite content with the Church of the Holy Family and hope I'll be allowed to remain there. Yes, I'll go and look for my father."

He regarded his mother gravely. He loved her, and knew that he knew nothing at all about her. She's like a conflagration, he thought, growing stronger as it devours. There was an insatiable hunger in her eyes, and her coarse face was seamed, here and there, about the painted lips and the lavender eyelids, with the deep lines of avarice. How hard and sure she is, thought Tony with sorrow.

"It's a nice party, isn't it?" she said, as her son began to move off.

"But my father hasn't been around very much," he answered, with more anxiety.

Cornelia laughed boisterously. "That's what made it a nice party!" she exclaimed. Her fan fluttered before her face, and now he saw that her eyes were full of contemptuous malice. "Oh, I love your father, but there are many times, and they come more often now, when I can't stand him and am glad when he's out of my sight." She waved him away and returned to her guests and to have her glass refilled.

Tony, smiling uncertainly and vaguely as he encountered the curious eyes of the swarming guests, moved towards the tall french windows which led into the gardens. He had almost reached them when he heard the gentle voice of his aunt, Ruth Peale, calling him. She was with her husband Miles, and she limped towards Tony eagerly, with her delicate face flushed with the heat, her golden head like a flake of sunlight in the shadowed room. At thirty-seven, she appeared much younger, for there was such a look of innocence on her shy face, such an unspotted tenderness. She gave Tony her almost boneless hand and smiled up at him. "I didn't have an opportunity to talk to you before, dear," she said. She sighed, and the thin blue silk which covered her meagre breast fluttered with her embarrassed breath. "How are you, Tony? I haven't seen you for a long time."

"No one ever sees Tony much; we're heretics or something," said Miles. His mahogany curls came just to his wife's eyebrows, but in spite of his stature there was in Miles what Tony had seen in his own mother: indomitable strength, surety, and command. There was no coarseness about him, however, but only elegance and poise. He gave Tony the benefit of an absolutely blue stare. "How's the priest business these days?"

"Oh," said Ruth, distressed and flushing, "I'm sure Tony doesn't think we are heretics or heathens, do you, Tony?"

"I'm certain you are one of God's angels, Aunt Ruth," said Tony affectionately.

Ruth was fumbling with the pearls at her thin white throat. She stammered, "I—I went to—your church—last Sunday, dear. High Mass. It was very beautiful. I didn't understand—but so holy—so full of grandeur. And what a wonderful sermon! The ministers all talk about the war in Europe, or ' social conditions ' in America, these days. But you talked of God, and God's mercy and love. I was very comforted."

Do you need mercy and comfort? wondered Tony with compassion. But then, who does not? He hoped that Ruth was happy. He believed she was, and was relieved when he saw her glance at her husband timidly, but with a whole shining of her pretty eyes. Miles did not return the glance. He was studying Tony, and his amusement was brighter on his face. Someone came sauntering up loosely, his tall "tan coloured" brother Fielding, his assistant. "Hallo, Tony," said Fielding negligently, his light brown hair falling in a straight lock over his yellowish forehead. "Still a holy Joe, I see. Not tired of it yet, eh?"

"Fielding!" protested Ruth, and touched her husband's arm as if urging him to rebuke his gangling brother, who was grinning in quite a loathsome fashion at Tony.

Tony tried to hold back his temper; he said coldly, "How can I tire of it? I am doing the work God created me to do."

Fielding shrugged his broad and bony shoulders. He raised his glass and studied the amber champagne. "So am I," he said, and turned his grin on Miles. "We all are. That's predestination, isn't it? Heard about it in Sunday School. Pa's always talking about it. Predestination. It doesn't matter what you do—God makes you do it. No choice."

Tony felt his ridicule. He knew he should bow and move off, but he was still young, and his temper was rising. "You never heard of free will, did you, Field?"

"Oh, you holy Joes," said Fielding. "I'm no match for your dogma. I just help to run the road—which brings you in a nice penny, too."

541

Charity or not, Tony decided that he hated that long, spade-chinned, ochre-coloured face with its malignant, pale brown eyes. Miles was looking at his brother forbiddingly now, and Fielding, under the weight of his eyes, shrugged again and said, "Hell, I didn't mean to offend you, Tony. Excuse me; someone's waving. My wife, of course." He moved on gawkily towards the former Cynthia Brownell, the banker's granddaughter, a little sallow girl with a petulant face. Tony watched him go, and then a curious sensation came to him. Danger. There was danger in this house, danger in Miles and Fielding. Miles was watching, half-smiling. "What's the matter, Tony?" he asked. "Don't mind old Field. He must always have his joke. Where are you going?"

"I'm going home," said Tony.

He suddenly remembered that he must say good-bye to his brother DeWitt. He had not seen DeWitt for a considerable time until to-day. He found the younger man in a chair near the french windows, his cane beside him, his neat black skull outlined against the red satin, his small dark face wearing its usual cryptic smile. Mary was beside him in rosy linen, looking like a graceful young cat, with a cat's agelessness. Her dusky curls had been bobbed, and she kept tossing them so that they danced about her cheeks and over her forehead. Her black eyes gleamed and glittered as she saw Tony approaching. It was a pointed feline face which she turned up to him, with a mischievous mouth. She had almost recovered from the disappointment of bearing a daughter less than two years ago, for there was another child three months on the way. With dainty teeth, she was eating a tiny sandwich.

"Well, Tony, are you going?" she asked, and there was a purr in her laughing voice, a purr of derision.

But DeWitt turned to his brother alertly. "We never have time to talk together," he said. Tony put his hand lovingly on that narrow and twisted shoulder, and DeWitt became very still. "No, but I always pray for you, youngster," he said, and pressed the shoulder. "I wanted to thank you, in person, for that french rose window, instead of writing."

"It came from France," said DeWitt unnecessarily. "Some old church they were tearing down. I thought you'd like it, in your church."

Tony laughed. "The church is in one of the ' worst ' sections of Portersville, but it's one of the sights of the city. Thanks to —everybody. Why don't you come in sometime and see the window in place?"

"How do you know," said DeWitt in his flat tones, "that I don't come?" Tony, startled, looked down into those slanted eyes. "Do you?" he asked in astonishment.

Mary giggled. "Not too often," she said. "He wanted to see that Italian altar Father Marshall gave you a year ago. He was afraid it would be too grand in your church. Too overpowering. And it was, really."

"I don't think so," said Tony shortly. "And the Sisters made a beautiful lace cloth for it. They're very proud of the altar. And the marble statue of Our Lady is one of the finest I have seen anywhere in the world. Some experts think it is an authentic Michelangelo."

"Well, it cost nearly fifty thousand dollars," said Mary jeeringly. "It ought to be *something*."

"Shut up," said her husband, without raising his voice. But Mary went on: "Anyway, it's too good for a church in the slums. DeWitt told me you could hear the trains all the time, roaring away in the back. Almost drowned out the bells Dolores sent you from Spain."

DeWitt did not move. It was as if he were afraid Tony would remove his hand. "You shouldn't have become a priest," he said. "We need you . . . in the business."

DeWitt was looking at his cane, and there was a crease between his eyes. He said, "Dad's become a sot. I suppose you know that." He added, "Oh, he keeps up, in the offices. But he drinks himself blind when he isn't there. It's bound to affect him adversely, one of these days, and I'm not yet even twenty-five. Too young for president, I suppose they'd say."

Tony's heart became constricted. "I am looking for him now, for I must go. It'll soon be time for Benediction."

Where was Dolores? There was no sign of his sister in the surging of the guests. He must leave without seeing her. He smiled at DeWitt and went through the windows and into the gardens. A trio of musicians were playing somewhere, and the jangling discord of the ragtime music offended Tony's ears. But worse than anything else was his formless fear. What did DeWitt mean? He had spoken with concern for his father. There had been something else in his voice, expressionless though it

543

had been. Tony had been so detached from the family business for so many years that he had given up thinking of it seriously. Now he stood uncertainly under a great oak and frowned with concentration. Miles and Fielding. Miles's power had been growing on the road, and he had assisted his brother to advancing power, also. Miles was married to the daughter of Jim Purcell; she must have considerable stock, and she was slavishly devoted to her young husband. Fielding had married the only grandchild of the banker Brownell, one of the directors of the road. Patrick Peale, father of Miles and Fielding, was also a director. Laura Peale, mother of the two young men, owned considerable stock—Tony was uncertain how much. On the other hand, DeWitt was not only executive vice-president now, he was married to Mary Peale, who had inherited stocks and bonds from Jim Purcell. Fifty-one per cent of the stock was held by his, Tony's parents. He supposed, vaguely, that the advantage lay with his own family—the Marshalls.

Tony moved slowly down the green terraces. May had come in a tide of flowers, a sea of bursting green, spilling the overflow of rose and yellow and white and blue over the stones of the walls and the terraces and the rock gardens. The sun flung blue shadows away from the clustering trees and spread them on the young grass. It was as if the earth was rioting in joy and colour, dancing in an exuberance of praise and innocence. The green mountains lifted themselves in the background, almost sparkling in the sunlight. But what of the torn fields and the broken walls of Belgium and France? What of the trampled new grain and the smashed vineyards and the ruined churches? Was there any joy in Europe now, any flowering to give gladness to the eye? Tony sighed. He did not believe that Europe was engaged in any "fight for freedom," as was proclaimed in the British, French, Austrian, Belgian, German, and Russian press. His father had often despairingly asserted that ancient evil was again breaking out in Europe among a silent congress of men, and with it had exploded a war for the world's markets. Yes, thought Tony, still descending the terraces to the lower gardens, all that is true, but it is something else besides. The old murderous instinct of man, atavistic, buried in him like a red seed which would not die, was leafing once more in a resurgence of unbounded death. The evil plotters could not flourish, there would be no wars for world markets, without that instinct in man which impelled him to hate his brother and desire his annihilation.

"Lord have mercy upon us—Christ have mercy upon us," murmured Tony, thinking of the boys in the trenches of Europe, thinking of the thousands of graves, thinking of the weeping of women and children, and the sound of Cain's guns in the meadows and the forests. "Holy Mary, Mother of God, pray for us sinners now and at the hour of our death," he prayed. Sinners, he said to himself. We are all responsible for the riot of murder in Europe, which will never end, never end.

He shivered as though he had heard a tremendous and warning whisper. But what can I do?" he asked himself. There were some who were already scolding in the American press that "religion had failed the world." No. Man had failed religion; he had failed God. Tony remembered the grandeur of the churches and the cathedrals of Europe and America. How empty they were during holy services! How few knelt at the altars or filled the pews! The priests and the ministers were always there, anxiously waiting for millions who never came. They waited to speak of God and mercy and love and justice—but the millions never came.

But what if the churches suddenly spoke up with a single and sonorous cry: "Thou shalt not kill!" What if the men of God stood in the trenches and commanded that all men lay down their arms? What if all priests and ministers descended in a body on The Hague and called the statesmen and the generals what they were: murderers? They could not kill us all, thought Tony with a sad smile. The women would stand beside us, and perhaps the lusting world, lifting its bloodstained guns, would be startled into hearing, and be ashamed, and the primordial instinct would wither away.

Tony found himself standing beside the glittering poplar he had planted as a child. He looked up into its high branches in which birds were nesting. The pointed tree seemed to turn on its trunk like a gigantic green candle in the soft wind and under the sun. How many millions of Europeans—young men like himself—had planted trees about their own peaceful little homes! And now the trees were blackened stumps and the birds had gone. For what? For what? "Defence of country?" "Liberty?" Lies, lies. There was only Cain, at the beginning, and at the last.

The grotto, green-walled, stood before the young priest, and he pushed aside the thick shrubbery and entered. There, as he had feared, sat his father on an old marble bench, drinking. A bottle stood beside him; there was a glass in his hand. His whitened head was bent, and he slumped on the bench like a motionless and emaciated statue of despair. He did not look up as Tony approached him; his stained eyelids had closed over his sunken eyes; his mouth sagged with agony. Tony sat down near his father and said very softly, "Tell me about it, Dad."

Allan stirred. Slowly, he lifted his head, and as he looked at his son, Tony knew that he did not see him. He was away in some terrible dream of his own, and was only barely conscious that someone was with him, and listening. He said thickly, "It was that Christmas—they broke the windows." He raised his hand and clenched it and brought it down on his knee with heavy and measured strokes like the beat of a heart. "The stone fell on the crèche. The Christ Child was smashed in His cradle." He peered at Tony as if trying to see him. "I had known all the time what men are like, from the time I was a lad. But, sure, and that stone brought it home to me. I nailed up the window with the hammer, and I was striking at the rascals. . . ." He dragged his hands over his haggard face and stared off into the distance with bloodshot eyes. "And I've been striking at them all my life, I'm thinking, and hating them. . . ."

Tony said very gently, and with love and pity, "No, you've been hating the evil in them, but not the men themselves. Didn't you know?"

Allan was shaking his head. It was apparent that a few of his son's words had penetrated into the black storminess of his drugged mind. "The evil is man, and man is the evil. The sin is man, and man is the sin. If there was a God, man would never have been created."

His livid face was covered with cold moisture. Tony took out his handkerchief and wiped it away. What could assuage this anguish and this grief? Tony put his hand on the top of that bowed head, and prayed. Again he wiped away his father's sweat, which seemed to stream from his soul like blood. Tony thought of his mother, and he thought with bitterness. She had only careless scorn for her husband now; her eyes, when they stared at him, were calculating and thoughtful. She could do so much for him! thought Tony sorrowfully. She could comfort him. Did she still love her husband? Now, for the first time, Tony began to doubt. Once, perhaps, she had loved him. Had his drinking revolted her? No, it was something else. Cornelia wanted something.

I'm imagining things, Tony thought. Such cruelty isn't possible. But he knew it was possible, for Cornelia. He recalled a letter she had written him before Christmas, a ruthless and derisive letter: "Your father grows more violent and incompetent every day. I don't know what is to become of us. He is quite a fool, as you know, my dear."

She had added brutally: "I had often heard that the Irish are a gay and lively people. I don't believe it. They're belligerent and sombre. . . . I saw them, when we were last in Ireland, gloomily drinking their grog in their pubs, not speaking for a long time, and then beginning to shout, and sometimes fight, wildly. Politics—' wrongs '—the landlords—anything as long as they could indulge their moroseness. And your father is just like them."

What had the strong, realistic and buoyant Cornelia to do with the sepulchral Celts, who had one foot precariously on earth and the other deep in mysticism? To her, they were ridiculous. The one to whom she was married, was the most ridiculous of them all. She was pretending, less and less, to be concerned about him.

If only I could take him away! thought Tony. If he could only go into retreat somewhere, where he could be healed. But there was no retreat for a man who had lost his faith.

"The farm," Tony said urgently to Allan. "Dad, can you hear me? The farm."

But his father was muttering in his slurred voice, "Dolores, my baby, my love, my little colleen. It's leaving the child with us she is. But she must return to England. Duty, says she. Responsibilities. Her husband gone—a good lad, that Dick, and it's hoping, I am, that he won't be killed. But he will! My soul is telling me. It was last night I heard the banshees, but Cornelia laughed and said it was the hoot owls. Why did my colleen leave me?"

Tony turned to his father. He had believed what his mother had told him, that his father had desired this marriage, had urged it on his daughter. Lies! Lies! His mother must always have her way; nothing could turn her from it. Tony's breath came fast. Dolores had been deceived; she had tried to please her father, to do what he wished. But he had never wished it. No wonder, now, that Dolores was so cold and withdrawn, and why she would not speak with her father and her brother.

"Dolores loves you, Dad," said Tony, full of despairing pity. "She will come back. She trusts you. She is leaving little Alex with you. You must take him to the farm."

Allan cried, "God, God, God!" Someone was shaking him, but he was in darkness again. Someone was calling him, and he struggled to answer. It was becoming light; the sun was everywhere, and the sound of the spring wind in the trees was the sound of surf. He came to himself with lightning sobriety, his heart shaking, and a long shiver passing over his flesh. His son Tony was beside him, his anxious face turned to him, his hands on his father's shoulders. "What is it, Dad?" he asked. "Why did you shout? Can you hear me?"

"Yes, yes, I hear," said Allan faintly. His face was dripping. Tony dried it tenderly. "You must have fallen asleep for a few minutes, Dad," he said. His father had called to God in a voice of the utmost extremity, in his nightmare. Tony put his arm about his father's shoulders and thought: He has come almost to the end. "I was talking about Dolores," he said. "She is leaving little Alex with you."

Allan threw off his son's arm violently and half-rose. "No!" he cried. "She can't go back! The whole damn sea's infested with submarines! The German Embassy has been warning the idiot Americans to stay off British ships, but still they go, thinking it all wonderful fun, and exciting. Tony! Dolores must stay with us."

Tony frowned anxiously. "But Dad, she came on the *Lusitania*, and she's returning on it to-morrow. It'll be convoyed, just as all the other British ships are convoyed. She'll be perfectly safe. Why, scores of Americans will be on it . . . the Germans wouldn't dare——"

"The Germans!" exclaimed Allan, more and more excited, and almost violent now, in his passion of fear. "Who said anything about the Germans? We need an 'incident.' Can't you understand? The American people don't want war, but something must be done to make them want it. I tell you, I had a dream!" He stood up, and staggered, and Tony stood up also, and caught his father's arm. "The *Lusitania* won't be convoyed, not this time! Not this time!"

Tony said imploringly, "Dad, Dad, listen to me. Do you think the Germans would sink the *Lusitania*—Almighty God forbid it!—just to get us into the war against them? It doesn't make sense. Think a moment. They'd be more anxious not to sink it."

Allan was wringing his hands, and he was breathing like a man just rescued from death. He regarded his son with the wildest eyes. "I've tried to tell you, but it does no good. You only listen with your ears, Tony. If a great ship like the *Lusitania* is sunk, with many Americans, yes, it will be a German torpedo. But who will give the order to loose that torpedo? The German government alone? No, I tell you! It will be many others, here in America, in England . . . men you can't see, won't ever see, safe men who've been plotting all this for many years, fanatical men——" His arms fell to his sides, and he shook his head over and over. "It's no use. You'll never understand, in spite of all I've told you all these years."

"I believe what you've told me; you had the proof," said Tony. frightened for his father. "What shall we do? Ask Dolores not to sail? Mamma told me that Dolores must return to England. We can only pray."

Allan slowly looked about him, at the earth and then at the sky. Then he said in a strange voice of the utmost bitterness, "To whom? To what?" Tony was silent, and Allan studied him with narrowed eyes. "No, I shouldn't have asked you, boy. You have the stock answers, don't you? Or you think I would turn away from you. Tony, I can't talk to Dolores. You must; she is your twin. Tell her she can't go, in the name of God."

Tony found his sister Dolores in her sitting-room with her three-year-old boy in her arms. A nurse stood nearby while Dolores rocked and murmured to the child, and kissed him and begged him to be "very good while Mamma is away for a little while." The little fellow listened to her obediently, his light brown eyes, so serious and glistening, fixed on his mother. No one noticed Tony for a few minutes. He thought he had never seen so beautiful a picture in that early twilight. Dolores, in a long and flowing gown of blue, had let down her masses of pale hair and had tied them back from her face with a blue ribbon. She seemed, to Tony, to be the very embodiment of the Madonna, all the youth and grace and loveliness, bending over her child tenderly, her mouth gentle yet stern with anxiety for him, her eyes shining with love.

"You will be so happy with Grandma and Grandpa," she was saying. "And Alex must be away from the awful zeppelins, and then he shall come home to Mamma and Papa." Her voice had already acquired an English inflection, and Tony reflected that his sister had gone far from him. She was, to everyone but her child, cold and distant and indifferent, as if nothing held interest for her anywhere in the world.

He spoke up now: "A very nice little boy, Dolores. I've only seen him once or twice."

Dolores glanced up and he saw the sweetness of her eyes harden. Tony sat down on his heels and held out his arms to Alexander. "I'm your uncle, child," he said. "Won't you come to me?"

The boy hesitated, staring at the strange young man in his priestly black. He peeped up at his mother. She did not move, though she had relaxed her arms. She neither urged him nor detained him, and her face was fixed and expressionless. "Come, dear," said Tony urgently. Again the child hesitated, then he suddenly smiled and his small and slender face became radiant. He slipped from his mother's lap and ran to Tony and shyly put his arms about his uncle's neck. Tony rose with him, holding him tightly, and looked at Dolores above his head. He was too moved to speak. But Dolores said to the nurse, "You may take Alexander in a few moments." Her voice was as cold as her eyes. She folded her hands on her knees and gazed at the windows, which were turning a deep turquoise.

Tony fondled his nephew and kissed him. He ruffled the feathery brown hair on the child's head. "Such a nice boy," he said helplessly. "Alex. I'll come to see you often."

Alexander nestled against his uncle, then stirred with childish restlessness, eager to return to his mother. Tony reluctantly set him down and the child ran to Dolores, who gave him to his nurse. She waited until the woman and the boy had left the room and then said, still gazing at the windows, "I suppose you came to say good-bye, Tony." Her profile was as lifeless and impervious as marble in the evening light.

He sat down near her and fumbled for his pipe. He took considerable time filling it and lighting it. He puffed at it for a minute of two. He said at last, "No. I came to ask you not to go back to England until the war is over."

She slowly turned to him and smiled faintly. "That is out of the question. Dick has only an old senile uncle and a distant cousin. Neither could manage his affairs in England. I'm needed there. I can't run away like a coward. There are the people, our tenants, our dependants. It is impossible to desert them. Dick relies on me." She smoothed a fold of her gown in her white fingers. "I am sailing to-morrow, as you know, on the *Lusitania*." Her smile was a little mocking now. "Why should any of you be afraid? The *Lusitania* was convoyed by British destroyers coming over; it will be convoyed on the way back."

Tony said, out of his hopelessness, "Dad told me this afternoon that he thinks that this time it won't be."

Dolores laughed stiffly. "How ridiculous. How could he know? I understand that many Americans will be on board. Who would dare kill them? Germany? Tony, that sounds very foolish."

Tony lifted his hands and let them drop on his knees. "I've had a lot of talks with Dad. He has convinced me that something is brewing in the world, something deathly. And that to bring it about they will stop at nothing."

"Who are ' they '?" asked Dolores with a light note of derision in her voice. "Dad has changed for the worst in the past years. He's haunted by unreal fears. Possibly because of his constant drinking; he must be having hallucinations. If you were about your business, Tony, you'd be helping him overcome his alcoholism, and getting him to overcome his unhealthy delusions." She lightly threw the fold of her dress from her. "I'm really very vexed; Dad even convinced Dick with his fantasies."

"Your husband probably had his own reasons to suspect something," said Tony, alerted. "After all, he is a member of the House of Lords."

But Dolores had withdrawn into cool indifference again. "Really, I don't know. I'm not concerned with those things."

Tony said with involuntary passion, "Dolores, are you concerned about anything at all?" He stood up and approached her. "What is wrong with you? Why have you gone away like this? You are living a kind of death life. . . ."

She was affronted. She drew her gown closely about her, rejecting him.

"Don't be dramatic, Tony. It seems to me that I've been very docile and obliging—to everybody. What more do any of you want?"

He was so distressed that in spite of her attitude he put his hand on her shoulder tightly. "Dolores, you'll deny anything I accuse you of. So, I can only ask you a question: do you love your husband?"

She did not move under his hand, but all her flesh repudiated him. She looked up at him, and he thought that not even a dead face could be so aloof as this. "Of course not," she said. "I never did. I like him considerably, but I don't love him. However, what does that matter to anyone? I think your question is insolent."

But something was stirring in her eyes, and Tony knew it for bottomless pain. "Did you ever love anyone else, Dolores?"

She replied in a very matter-of-fact voice, "Yes, I did. Miles Peale."

He drew his hand away from her rapidly. "Miles Peale! Miles Peale!" He shook his head dazedly. "I can't believe it. I thought you detested him." He felt sick and weak.

Dolores smiled bitterly. "I thought so, too. But all the time I loved him. I planned on marrying him. Then Grandpa died, and Dad was in a mess and couldn't be talked to, Mamma said. He had burdens enough of his own. She remarked that if I should tell Dad about Miles and me, it would be the last thing he could bear. She convinced me that Dad wanted me to marry Dick. I didn't need much convincing, for only a few weeks after Grandpa died Dad complained that it was evident I would be an old maid. I admit he seemed confused. I"—she halted for an instant, and Tony could see her swallowing painfully—"loved Dad very much. I couldn't add more to his worries. I married Dick so that I could get away from Miles, whom Dad disliked; he would never have given his consent. And he really wanted me to marry Dick. There was a night when he had been drinking, and I went to him in the library, to help him, and he shouted out to me that I could marry Dick if I wanted to, and be damned to me. That is what he said, Tony."

Tony sat down again, for his knees were trembling. He looked at his sister, who would be gone to-morrow. He could not help himself, and he said, "Dolores, you can't go away believing a lie. But the truth might be too terrible for you. Shall I tell you, I wonder?"

Curiosity changed the hard outline of her face. "Tell me what, Tony?"

He prayed that he was doing what was right. "You can't go away believing cruel things about our father. Dolores, Dad never wanted you to marry Dick. Remember the months after Grandpa died. Dad was almost beside himself with worry. You see, he never really had much confidence in his own power; he was always afraid, all his life. He hardly knew what was going on in his own home." He paused, completely shaken. "I'm afraid our mother used those months to her advantage. Dolores, what did she tell you about Miles Peale?"

Dolores was very white. "I told her I loved him and wanted to marry him. And she said, ' Well, if it'll give you any pleasure, your father will drop dead if you ever mention that boy's name to him. He hates him as much as he hates his father.'"

Tony got up and began to wander about the room. "It is true that Dad disliked Miles. But he did not hate him. That was proved when he gave him a position on the road, and by the responsibilities he has turned over to him. Dad loves you, Dolores. If you had wanted to marry a savage he would have given his consent, if you had been convinced it would have made you happy. How could you doubt him, knowing him as you did, knowing that you were his favourite child?"

Dolores could only whisper, as she stared at her brother distractedly, "I thought he wanted me to marry Dick. I thought, from what Mamma said, that it would make him happy when he was so miserable and distraught over everything. I did it for Dad."

She suddenly put her hand over her mouth and sobbed dryly. "Now I know what he meant, two years ago, when he asked me why I did it! I didn't understand. I was offended." Tears rushed into her eyes. She started to her feet and caught her brother's arm. "I must go to him immediately and tell him about Mamma, about everything."

"No," said Tony inflexibly. "That is one thing, now, that you dare not do. For his sake. I honestly think it would kill him. You can't even tell Mamma about it. You must keep it to yourself, and it will help you bear your own wretchedness."

But Dolores was weeping uncontrollably and wringing her hands. "No, I can't tell him. You are right. I stayed away from the party to-day—I couldn't bear to see Miles. We love each other. I don't know what to do!"

"You can go to Dad to-night and tell him that you love him, and you can remain here until the war is over."

She went up and down the room as her brother had done, shaking her head until her hair fell over her face in a cascade of agony and despair. Tony watched her until he could endure the sight no longer. He went to his sister and put his arms about her and drew her head to his shoulder. "Dolores, Dolores," he murmured. "Dear sister, dear child."

She clung to him, crying mournfully, her hair streaming about her in a tangled mass. "Oh, God," she stammered. "What can I do, what can I do!"

"You told me just now that you like poor Dick. He is a good fellow, Dolores, and the best of husbands and fathers. You can remember that. You can do your duty. I know, I feel that you would have been wretched in the end with Miles. Perhaps you have been granted a great mercy."

But she rolled her head on his shoulder. "No. We'd have been happy. And I could have stopped—anything he has in mind."

Tony lifted her face. "What do you mean?"

Her cheeks ran with tears. "Don't you know, Tony? It isn't something for which I have proof. But Miles—he wants what DeWitt has. Dad, the road, are in danger. I know it with all my heart."

Danger. Tony put aside his sister and turned his back to her. But there is nothing we can do, he thought. There is, though, always my mother, and DeWitt, and the fifty-one per cent of the stock in the family's hands. He returned to Dolores and tried to console her with these facts. However, she shook her head silently.

"When someone wants something, as Miles does, he always gets it, Tony," she said after a moment or two.

She pushed her hair back from her face resolutely. "I'll take your advice, of course, and assure Dad that I've always loved him. But, Tony, I must go back to England. Nothing can persuade me to the contrary. Watch out for little Alex. You can do so much for him, and he needs you—in this family. Mamma mustn't be allowed to—to corrupt him."

On May 7, 1915, the *Lusitania*, mysteriously not convoyed this time, was struck by a German torpedo off the green and smiling coast of Ireland, and went down with the loss of over a thousand lives, including one hundred and twenty-four American citizens.

Among those who perished was Lady Dolores Gibson-Hamilton. A letter from the British War Office was awaiting her at home, informing her, with regret, that her husband, Richard Gibson-Hamilton, had died of wounds "somewhere in France" several days before. She went down into the waters remembering only that she had been reconciled to her father and thinking of her son.

CHAPTER FORTY-SIX

PATRICK PEALE returned from the Johns Hopkins Hospital on a very hot day in June. He had told his wife one of the very few lies he had ever uttered, not to spare her any anxiety, but because he did not want to express to anyone his own fears for himself. He came back to Portersville, ghastly and wizened, and though the day was extremely warm he had frequent rigours during which he pressed his arms convulsively to his sides.

He was only sixty-one, but he had become an old man during the past two months. Laura had seen it, and had urged a medical examination upon him, which he had refused petulantly, and with the usual contempt he now invariably expressed for her. But fear had come to him eight months previously. He had had a bad cold late in October, which he had seemed unable to shake off; a heavy cough remained with him, which did not slacken even when warm weather had come. When, one day in late March, he coughed up a slight portion of blood, he had been seized with extreme terror. Tuberculosis? He was afraid of consulting any physicians. Now he became obsessed with his private fear. Heretofore his one unremitting obsession had been Allan Marshall. He added this other to the original one, and in his characteristically confused and narrow thinking, he blamed Allan for this mysterious invader in his life.

He had done much reading about a new science: psychosomatic medicine. Always meticulously careful of his health, with the concentrated absorption of one in love with himself and who believed himself to be of the utmost value and importance, he had followed every medical advance submitted to the public. He was convinced that the desperate resentment and chronic rage in which he lived—all provoked by Allan Marshall—had "psychosomatically" brought on the unnamed illness which afflicted him. But still, in March, he was afraid to have an examination. He bought tomes on the subject of phthisis. He looked for sputum, for night sweats, for loss of weight, for early evening fever. He took his temperature. He was relieved to find that though he was losing weight he had none of the other symptoms. Just a cough, he told himself with prayerful thanksgiving. Coughs had a way of remaining, especially in a man of his age. His chest was very painful. Neuritis, probably.

There was no more blood until the latter part of May, and then there was a considerable amount of it. He was terribly frightened. He waited a few more days, his cough becoming alarmingly more harsh and hacking. It was then that he called Johns Hopkins, told his wife gloomily that he had some business in New York, and went to Baltimore.

The verdict was swift and sure: cancer of the lungs, a very extensive cancer for which nothing could be done. His doctors gave him a box of tiny grey pills, and they looked at him with pity. They also gave him an unlimited prescription for morphine and informed him that he must not be hesitant about using it. Patrick, stunned, would not believe at first. It was impossible. He neither drank nor smoked; he had always lived a blameless life. He had given up his pipe many years ago. "Impossible," he said to his doctors, looking at them with terror. "I have always been a good man, according to my lights." They thought him piteous, but a little stupid. One said, "If disease attacked only the unrighteous, then we'd have such a religious revival that there wouldn't be churches enough to accommodate the people." But Patrick thought only of Allan Marshall. He said to his doctors, "I have been killed, murdered, as surely as if I had had a bullet shot into me."

He arrived home in great pain and weakness, and went at once to bed. He called for Laura, who came to him immediately. There he lay on his pillows, shrunken and still, his large brown eyes, once so serious in his youth, bulging with the agony and dread of those mortally stricken. When Laura entered the room, he glared at her with accusation mingled with hatred and fury and fear. He said, before she could speak in her anxiety for him, "I am going to die. I'll live, with luck, about two months." The accusation flamed in his eyes, as she sank into a chair near him. She was unable to speak, for her throat had tightened and she was trembling violently, uncontrollably.

"Allan Marshall killed me," added Patrick, and closed his eyes against her. The tall lean house was very chill, for even the June heat could not penetrate those gaunt walls or invade this narrow bedroom with the sombre furniture. Patrick was seized with a spasm of coughing. Now blood foamed to his lips, but he was too distraught and too numbed to wipe it away. He knew it was there; he derived some satisfaction, some malicious contentment, that Laura could see the signs of his coming dissolution.

She cried out, so he knew that she had seen. He felt her standing over him. She was using a handkerchief on his mouth. He turned aside his head and groaned. "Let me alone." Sharp pain knifed through his chest and he put one withered hand to it.

"Patrick, Patrick!" she was weeping. "What is wrong? What do you mean? Oh, God, why are you bleeding? I must call the doctor. . . ." A scent of lilacs floated from her, and he sickened at the perfume and drew in his nostrils.

"I said," he repeated feebly, "that Allan Marshall has finally succeeded in killing me."

He's ill, and mad, thought Laura distractedly. "I must call the doctor," she said again. But he held up his hand.

"Too late," he answered. "Too late for anything. I have cancer of the lungs. They told me yesterday, at Johns Hopkins. That is where I went, and not to New York, as I told you." He pointed to the table at his side. "Morphine. For my pain."

There was no dignity in him, no compassion for his wife, no desire to spare anyone pain. There was only terror, outrage, hatred, that this thing had come to him. The Pharisee—confronted with reality, stripped of precise theories and dogmas and pride, face to face with majestic Death, who could not be placated with self-righteous cries and the spurious importance of men like Patrick Peale—could only whimper to himself and long for vengeance.

Laura, undone by pity, suffering her own terror, fell into her chair again. "Oh, Patrick," she murmured frantically. "I know you haven't looked well for some time—I wanted you to have an examination. Oh, Patrick. Oh, my dear. Are—are they certain?"

As if he were determinedly and deliberately throwing stones at her, he gave her the facts. His voice was stronger. He watched her shocked face and tear-filled eyes, pleased. Let her suffer, too. She had made his life wretched enough. A dim-witted, colourless, silly woman, hysterical and mindless! How often she had opposed him in the past; how often she had begged him, long ago, not to "poison" their children's minds against that foul wretch, Marshall. How she had pleaded with him to persuade Miles not to marry Ruth Purcell, and Mary not to marry DeWitt Marshall. She had stood in his way wherever he had turned. She had refused to entertain Norman deWitt, and when Patrick had insisted, she had treated the visitor coldly and with evident distaste. He, Patrick, could remember nothing of her now but womanish petulance and foolishness. She had resisted, for years, turning over to him her sixteen per cent of the Interstate stock.

"They are absolutely certain," he said to her now. "There is nothing that can be done, except temporary easing of pain. I believe they said I might live two months."

Laura put her hands over her face and wept aloud. Patrick, poor Patrick; cold, silent, hating, gloomy Patrick. Her sobs were deep and broken. Patrick moved restlessly. "Now, Laura," he said in his old tone of disdain and repudiation, "let's not be hysterical, as usual. Hysterical people never feel strongly, I've heard. Spare me superficiality, at least."

She dropped her hands from her wet face and looked at him speechlessly. Her pity was a fire in her. She could not go to him and console him; she dared not take him in her arms. His bitter eyes were mocking her, enjoying her grief, taking satisfaction in her pain. She closed her eyes, for she could not endure that light in his.

"My children will remember," he was saying. "My sons will avenge me."

He's mad; he's boundlessly vindictive, she thought, in spite of her compassion. But she could not let him die with that evil obsession in his soul. She could not let him use his sons, as he had long plotted, to strike at Allan Marshall, Allan away in the sanatorium where he had been sent after his collapse over the death of his daughter.

"Have pity," she stammered imploringly. "Have pity on

yourself, Patrick. Allan may have hurt you, once; we all hurt each other. Some out of cruelty, some out of necessity, some out of greed or expediency. Think of Allan now. It is feared he is dying; he is out of his mind with sorrow. Dolores, poor Dolores. The little boy—without parents. Patrick, you can't—you can't —go on, hating like that, carrying it with you. . . . You can't do that to yourself, you can't continue to hate yourself like this."

He regarded her with sombre outrage and disgust. "Are you insane?" he asked. "But then, you never had any intelligence. ' Hate ' myself! That comes of your having very limited comprehension, and a sheltered existence, and poor heredity. I was told your mother was a fool. It is a good thing she didn't live to have other children, to burden the world with more feeble-mindedness."

Her grey eyes became enormous as she looked at him, and her slender body stiffened. For a moment she forgot to pity him, and she felt the hot thrust of loathing in herself. How could he, even in this extremity, be so cruel, so contemptible, so self-righteous? The dying were supposed to gain some comprehension, some mercy for others, some tenderness, some wisdom. But there her husband lay, and he was as he had always been, and all his twisted egotism was burning more vividly than ever.

But then, Laura thought with a resurgence of pity, he is so frightfully afraid. He always speaks of God; he attends church with fanatical regularity. But he never believed in God, never once in his life. He is the complete atheist.

He was dismissing her with a wave of his hand. "Send for Miles and Fielding," he said in the voice of one scornfully speaking to the meanest of servants. "And leave me alone for a little while. I think I want to sleep."

But he did not sleep. Left alone, while Laura telephoned his sons and quietly called the family physician, who promised to arrange for nurses and to visit Patrick the next day, the slowly dying man suddenly thrust his knuckles against his teeth and a sick whining sound began to rise in his throat. He choked it down; it rose again and again. His nightshirt became damp and clammy against his quivering flesh. The curtains had been drawn far back from the slits of windows, and he could see the scarlet sunset flaring over the dark mountains. He began to stare at it, and he thought: I am all alone. I was always alone. No one ever cared for me at any time in my life. He muttered prayers like an incantation, a plea not for mercy but for explanation. Why should this awful terror have come to him instead of to his enemies? He contemplated himself on his pillows, a good and virtuous man, completely abandoned to silence and death and lovelessness, and he was moved to overwhelming commiseration for himself.

His sons entered the house and Laura met them, examining their faces for any sign of the real grief she prayed they felt for their father. But she saw at once that the excessively solemn Fielding was inwardly excited. She turned from him with a brief closing spasm of her eyes, and looked at Miles. He was actually looking at her with solicitude, and this startled and warmed her; she did not know that this solicitude was for herself, nor did she know that of all her children only Miles did not consider her a fool or a nonentity. Miles, the debonair, the exquisite, was thinking: Hard on you, old girl, but better for you in the long run. You won't be losing anything. Like Fielding, he kissed his mother's cheek, but his kiss had genuineness in it. He said, "It's certain, then?" She nodded, and sat down weakly on the narrow crimson bench before the meagre fireplace of the hall. Then she gazed earnestly and imploringly at her sons.

"Be kind to him," she whispered. Be merciful, she wanted to add. "Comfort him."

"It's frightful, frightful," said Fielding, leaning against the wall, all the long and gangling length of him. He pulled at his yellowish nose and glanced sideways at his brother. "At the most, two months, I think you said, Mother?"

"Sometimes there are mistakes, even among the best of doctors," said Miles, putting his hand on his mother's shoulder and frowning at his brother. His eyes were a cold blue flash in the duskiness of the hall. "We'll do what we can. We've always humoured him, you remember."

"He never found out we thought him a——" Fielding began, then was stopped by another flash from Miles.

Laura wrung her hands tightly together. "I wish you had known your father as I knew him, when I was a very young girl. So serious, so thoughtful, so idealistic. And so very, very upright. I think it was his uprightness which really—really caused him trouble later, and distorted his original character.

You see, he could never compromise; he could never accept people for what they were." She swallowed, and stopped.

"If anyone opposed him, he thought of the man as a personal enemy, who ought to be destroyed. The enemy became not only Pa's enemy, but the enemy of God and the angels," said Miles. He put his hand over his mother's twisting fingers, and pressed them. "A common, and dangerous, disease of the idealists. History is full of the cities they burned, the people they hanged, the children they orphaned, the fields they laid waste." Miles's voice was thoughtful, but hard. "Uncle Allan opposed him, I suppose. Therefore Uncle Allan must be destroyed, as an enemy of the people. I know. I'm sure that's what he wants to talk to us about—Uncle Allan, the poor devil."

Laura gazed at her older son with intense amazement. "Why, Miles, I didn't know you . . . !" She stopped, and cried without restraint. Fielding looked bored and impatient, and yawned. But Miles watched his mother with fresh solicitude. He knew what he wanted; he was determined to have it, no matter what he had to do. Nevertheless, he was sorry for Allan Marshall, as a man who was suffering, as a man who found the fierce world at last too much for him. It'll never be too much for me, thought Miles, for I'll never permit myself to be caught up in its emotions. I loved Dolores; I suppose Uncle Allan and Tony and myself were the only ones who really mourned her. But I have my life to live. I have no time to waste.

His mother, in spite of everything, loved her children, and so he was sorry for her. Perhaps if she had not had children, she would have left her intolerant and bigoted husband a long time ago and might have found some happiness. He said, "What about Mary? Does she know?"

"No, there was the baby to think of," replied Laura. "Later, I'll tell her her father is just very ill, and perhaps I can persuade him to keep her in ignorance."

Miles commented wryly to himself that it was doubtful if Mary would feel any shock or sorrow. Laura was pushing back her soft dark hair, and her face gleamed in the shadows, purely carved and white. She touched Miles's sleeve timidly. "I think, in a way, that I am beginning to understand you, my dear." But she did not look at the bored and squinting younger son. Fielding thought: It's all right for Miles to "play-act"; he is the perfect diplomat, but why waste it on a fluttering and totally insignificant woman? Fielding tugged at his nose again, and said, "Well, shall we get it over? I've got a dinner engagement with Cynthia."

Laura, as if she had committed some offence, immediately stood up. All at once, as she stood there, tall and slim and strangely young and silent, there was a faint resemblance in her to Dolores and Miles was struck with a violent pang. Now, control yourself, he thought, with cool anger at his folly. But he went upstairs with his brother, walking surely. Only a fool quarrels with his own bargains.

Miles threw away his cigarette before entering his father's rooms with his brother. A sedative had finally calmed Patrick; fear was less overpowering; he could use his mind, and he knew he must use it now. He watched his sons enter, and his eyes became intent in his quietly desperate face. Despite what Laura had flung at him wildly, years ago, he steadfastly believed that his sons loved and respected him and waited upon his word at all times. Had he not been a just and devoted father? Had his sons ever quarrelled with him or taken issue with him? No, at all times they had gravely agreed with his convictions. Fine young men, my sons, thought Patrick Peale, men of principle, seriousness, and ideals. He held out his hand first to Miles, who pressed it briefly, and then to Fielding, who, with a pretence of youthful emotion and awkwardness, suddenly bent down and kissed his father's forehead.

"Your mother has told you?" Patrick asked faintly. Miles said, "Yes. And there is nothing I can say, I suppose, except that I'm terribly sorry." Fielding said in a loud voice, "Perhaps it isn't true! We've got to believe it isn't." Miles pursed his lips again and sat down, while Patrick looked with mournful fondness at his younger son. "It is true, I'm afraid," he said. "But I didn't call for you to discuss me. . . . I wanted to talk things over with you. I have so little time now."

He clasped his hands over his chest, and now his eyes were even more intent on his sons. "It hurts me to talk. I'll try to be brief. You know the history of the DeWitt and the Peale families. You know that your grandfather, Stephen deWitt, was robbed of his position, his house, and his money, by his brother Rufus. The law may not agree—man's law—that the grandsons of Stephen deWitt have been robbed of their rightful heritage. But there is a moral law, which, at the end, inexorably comes into effect."

Miles and Fielding listened with the proper and solemn attention, but Miles was annoyed at the pompous and old-fashioned phrasing of his father's words. Why didn't the poor old devil just come out and say: "I want you to have what those I hate have, and I don't care how you get it so long as I have my revenge?" But that would be too honest for Patrick Peale.

Patrick lifted his hands and began to mark off what he was about to say: "I have sixteen per cent of Interstate stock, which I acquired through your mother. You, Miles, through your wife Ruth, have control of four per cent. I have another five per cent, in addition to the original sixteen per cent. That makes twenty-five per cent in our hands. Against—their—fifty-one per cent." He paused. "DeWitt will be president one of these days, perhaps soon, with that fifty-one per cent. Of course, he is married to my daughter Mary."

Miles said, "Of course, we can't count on Mary. After all, she'd stand with her husband, and the other Marshalls."

Patrick winced. He would have preferred that his son not be so blunt. He replied, "That is so. I'm afraid that Mary has become very selfish and expedient; that comes of her association with those people. We can expect nothing but opposition from Mary, so let us not discuss her." He hesitated, then coughed. "Let us continue. Twenty-five per cent in the hands of this family. We also have a great deal of money. Your mother inherited a good deal of cash and investments from her aunt, Lydia Purcell, and also from her uncle, Rufus deWitt, who was apparently, and belatedly, trying to make some amends. My own private holdings are not to be despised, and I have control of your mother's. Your mother has no head for finances, as you know, and turned all over to me."

At your insistence, after your endless nagging and recriminations and accusations, and because she wanted peace for her children's sake, thought Miles. And you had made her feel guilty.

Patrick was now speaking in a louder, faster voice: "The Interstate really belongs to us! And my sons must have it! The details I shall leave to you. Who stands in your way? A miserable cripple, DeWitt Marshall, who is also quite young. A conscience-less alcoholic and very sick man, Allan Marshall, who will probably never be very potent in the concerns of the company again. Money is power! You will have it. Miles, you also have the money Jon deWitt left you, and you have invested it wisely, on the advice of Mr. Regan. You are general superintendent, now, of the Interstate Railroad Company, and Fielding is your assistant. Why, you are in the camp of the enemy, and you can do what you wish!"

Miles, always so discreet, could not prevent himself from saying, "But who gave me my opportunity there? Allan Marshall, of course. He could have kept us out. If we are in the ' camp of the enemy ' we were invited in."

His father rose on his pillows at this stupid enormity, and glared at his son. "Why? Why? I know! First of all, he needed your ability. Second, it was his bribe to you not to pursue his daughter any longer. He held your position in the company over your head: attempt to marry his daughter and he would throw you out! I know all the workings of his mind. He forced her to marry that Englishman in order to remove her from you, And how did a just God visit punishment upon him?" Patrick's eyes gloated. "By her death, on the *Lusitania*."

"Of course, of course," murmured Fielding, in a sepulchral tone.

Miles slowly and carefully crossed his legs. Self-righteous liar, he thought. There is no mercy or honour in you. He folded his arms on his chest and regarded his father enigmatically. Patrick had begun to beat a pillow with a clenched fist. "There is always God's justice, at the end. And the day of justice for my sons is almost here. And you have a friend in the very camp of the enemy: Norman deWitt. When I last saw Norman, in New York, he told me that he is so unwelcome in the family that he rarely sees his poor old mother, who is prematurely senile with her grief. . . ."

"She is seventy-five or so," said Miles. "And not a very bright woman at any time, if I remember correctly." He paused, and was amused at himself for this almost unique impulse towards integrity.

Fielding turned his pale brown eyes in bewilderment on his brother. The diplomatic, careful Miles! But there he sat now, staring at his father with that complete blueness of eye, that reserved expression which indicated some hidden disgust. Even Patrick was caught by his son's look, and silenced momentarily by his words. Then he sank back on his pillows, and began to pluck vaguely at his sheet. "I thought you were very congenial with Norman," he said. "After all, you were in Norman's Harvard Socialist Club—one of the charter members, I believe."

"He had a student chapter there, among many other chapters in other universities," said Miles coldly. "I was just eighteen when I joined."

Now, what in hell is wrong with Miles? thought Fielding. He could see the delicate skin of his brother's forehead flushing. Is he trying to antagonise the old boy, just now when everything depends on his keeping his mouth shut?

Patrick became excited. "Miles! But you believed what Norman and his friends taught you. You believe in the theories——"

"Such as government control of the means of production?" asked Miles casually. "Under such a system, what would become, for instance, of the Interstate Railroad Company? *Our* Company, as you have just said."

Patrick stared at him in silence. He began to rub his right index finger slowly over his lips. He blinked. Then he said reflectively, "You know what Norman has told you. The friends of the government will not have their property socialised. When you and Fielding are in control of the Interstate, all will be well with you. But if you are not, then eventually, and the day is not far off, the company will be seized by the government, for the benefit of all the people, including the exploited workers."

Why is it impossible for him to think without confusion? Miles asked himself. Why does he insist upon self-deception? There are so many wealthy fools like him in America. If the day he prophesies ever comes, they are going to cry out in protest: "But you don't mean me! You mean my brother!" Miles reflected that it might almost be worth while to be present on such an occasion, for the joy of Olympian laughter.

But men like Norman deWitt were neither confused nor the victims of self-deception. They knew what they wanted. And they used men like Patrick Peale to help them. However, this was no time to attempt to clear Patrick's mind. So Miles said soothingly, "Of course, you are right." Fielding relaxed, and stretched out his long legs.

Now Miles's voice became brisk and hard. "Yes, I know that Norman will help us. You've reviewed the whole situation pretty thoroughly, Pa. I have something to add. DeWitt is executive president of the company; he will be, one of these days, president. But he's not capable of holding such a position, though I don't underestimate his intelligence and ability. He's not the man his father was, or his grandfather. He wants power, not as they wanted power, for the sake of power itself, but for his own self-aggrandisement. He was always the ' little one,' even before he was crippled. His crippling only accentuated his intrinsic littleness. He's ruthless and egotistic and small-minded and crafty."

Patrick nodded eagerly. "Go on, Miles." Fielding sat up.

Miles considered, and glanced about the dusky room. The last shreds of the scarlet sunset lingered over the black mountains. Miles stood up and turned on a few lamps. He studied the last, as if it held all his thoughts. He began to speak again, musingly.

"This is another day. Some blame it on Wilson. But no one is to blame. The day of the absolute, autocratic industrial baron has ended. It is a natural development, and theorists, with their shouts of the brotherhood of man and their outcries against the profit system and free enterprise, have had nothing to do with it. The source of a more equitable and decent industrial society was the middle class. As that class invaded industry and business they decentralised the power of the great barons and tycoons. All the anti-trust acts and other laws against monopolies would have forever remained impotent if the middle-class businessmen and smaller industrialists hadn't breeched the narrow fortresses held by the Rockefellers, the Belmonts, the Vanderbilts, the Gunthers, to name only a few."

"Well, well?" demanded Patrick impatiently. He had not followed his son in the least. "What are you getting at?"

Miles lifted his eyebrows briefly, but did not turn to his father. "More and more, thoughtful people in industry are beginning to realise that the success of any business depends upon the people in it. And the public it serves well. Personal power is no longer feasible, among intelligent men, and no longer very desirable. The barons will struggle against this a little longer, and then they will learn. Some of them have already learned; they've created benevolent foundations in behalf of all the people of America. They've distributed millions of their profits."

"Yes, yes," muttered Patrick restlessly. Miles glanced at Fielding, and smiled a little. He continued: "DeWitt Marshall is an anachronism. He thinks of himself as one of the tycoons, one of the barons. With that attitude, he will ruin the company. And that is why he must be got out, some way."

Patrick exclaimed, still without the slightest understanding, "That is what I mean! Exactly!"

Miles came to his father's bedside and looked down at him ironically. What a fool this was, to be sure. He said, "But there is some great and hidden evil in the world. I think I know what it is. Men like DeWitt unknowingly sustain that evil. He must be got rid of, if America is to remain free. And we must get rid of that evil, too; it's an ancient one, and was born in Europe centuries ago. We can't work fast enough."

Fielding wrinkled his sallow forehead, and Patrick put on an expression of solemnity. Miles was highly amused. He found it sardonically satisfying to hold these spoken soliloquies with himself in the presence of those who could not understand and believed that they understood.

"There is a trusteeship in public service," said Miles. He reached into his pocket for a cigarette, then withdrew his hand, empty. He said, "I think you can trust us, Pa. We'll get what you want for us." He turned to his brother. "We've learned a lot these past years, haven't we, Field?"

"We sure have," replied Fielding. He was puzzled. He looked at this exquisite, his brother, at the bland, almost beautiful face of the older man; he felt Miles's indomitable and silent power, his assurance, his puissant masculinity. Fielding was no fool; he knew that he had very little of his brother's intellect, but there had been a time when Miles had talked with him gaily, lightly and informingly. Now he merely gave Fielding orders, without bothering to explain them or enlarge upon them. Fielding felt a thrust of envy and resentment, but he admired his brother so thoroughly, and respected him so abjectly, that the thrust was almost immediately blunted. There was no use trying to follow old Miles all the time, Fielding thought. It was better just to obey.

Patrick lay limply in his bed. "I can die in peace now," he murmured. Then he stiffened and sat up again, aghast. "We have forgotten one thing: Cornelia deWitt Marshall! She's not only a director of the company, she's DeWitt's mother! How will you eliminate *her*?"

Miles patted his father's shoulder. "When the time comes, we'll eliminate Aunt Cornelia. She's more formidable than

DeWitt—but we'll eliminate her. Have you forgotten? Since your retirement from the board I've been a director, too."

Miles went alone that night down to the yards. He often went there, at least twice a week, and usually at night, driving his own great black automobile to his own reserved spot. The men were accustomed to see that Dresden figure moving about over the rails, looking around thoughtfully, smoking his special cigarettes, one after another, wandering in and out of the round-houses, rarely speaking, seeing everything. Sometimes he would just stand for a long time, in all weather, seeing the glittering of tracks in the moonlight, studying the switchmen thawing out switches in zero cold, seemingly fascinated by unburdened engines roaring up out of the darkness on the various lines, spewing out a wake of fire and sparks. The crash of engines automatically coupling with freight cars and passenger coaches sometimes made his face take on a sharpened look, as if he had heard an awakening sound out of an unremembered past. Often he stood by men impatiently attending to a hot-box. He stood by other men waving lanterns at huge and sprawling crossings; when monster trains clangoured and pounded into the great station—where freight and passenger cars were sometimes switched to other engines for other destinations—he would stand and look and watch like some yokel come down to the depot for the daily local. Cool, remote, uncommunicative, he was every-where, stepping like a cat over high rails, appearing suddenly out of nowhere, endlessly smoking, his hat on the back of his mahogany curls, his gloved hands holding his " dandy" cane. The brassy hosanna of bells, the shuddering of rails, the piercing hiss of steam, the lights against the night sky, the thunder of coming and departing trains, the hubbub of men and their shouts and curses, the glimmer of lanterns far down the tracks, the shunting of engines—all these seemed of interest to him.

"Coming down to spy on us, the little dancin' feller." So a group of three engineers, two conductors, and a few switchmen and other workers in one of the roundhouses to-night, muttered among themselves. The June evening was very hot; there was much traffic lately, and an inexplicable prosperity, and the men were pleased. But in the immemorial way of railroaders they grumbled. "Comin' down to see if we're doin' all right, with all the work, and not scroungin' on the job."

568

Never Victorious, Never Defeated

"You ain't right," said a very old man, a sweeper in the station. His eyes were bleared; he was like some ancient bird, leaning on his broom. He shook his head. But no one listened to him. Old Billie was daffy; everybody knew that, and usually the men were kind to him. He had been a railroader since very early youth, and he was always mixing up "Mister Aaron, Mister Rufus, Mister Stephen" with the mighty men now the owners of the Interstate Railroad Company.

"He's only general superintendent; you'd think he owned the damn road," said one engineer churlishly, and spat into the cold black stove in the room.

"'Course he'll own it," said Old Billie, nodding so vigorously that he staggered. "Why shouldn't he? He owned it in the first place, didn't he? I could tell you what he did way back. . . ."

One of the engineers, an older man, took a moment's kindly notice of him. "How old are you, Pop? You must'a' been born on the road!"

"Pretty near," chortled Old Billie, delighted by this crumb of recognition, and pecking at it eagerly. "You fellers don't know what railroadin' is. Sometimes you'd go out with a train in the winter and the snow high as mountains and you'd never know if you'd get to Philly or anywheres. But we sang like all hell in the cabs, and the firemen'd throw on more coal, and there you'd go a-pantin' up the grade with all the bells shoutin' and the passengers scared to death and freezin' but laughin', too, for you wouldn't know if you'd be spendin' the night in the hills, brewin' coffee with coals from the engine, right out by the side of the road, and settin' up fires, and the people comin' out of the coaches to warm theirselves, and the engineers and the firemen and the conductors a-minglin' with 'em, and soon everybody laughin', and passin' bottles and no talk about germs, and sharin' sandwiches, and a big white moon comin' over the white mountains, and waitin' for the snow to melt or the ploughs come, screamin' with bells like angels roarin' up——"

He shook his head sorrowfully. "You fellers never knew what railroadin' was, in the old days. Excitin'. Everybody knowin' everybody else on the road, and workin' together, and bein' proud of the road. . . . Old Aaron, now, he was a son of a bitch, but he was a railroader. Many's the time he'd ride in the cab with us; no fancy private cars; and he'd have a bottle of whisky, and he could cuss better than any damn engineer I ever

569

knowed. Screw the last penny out of you and the road, but he was a railroader. What you got now? Men in the big offices in Philly and New York and in town, here, and never comin' down, and just sittin' over their ledgers and talkin' with the big feenanciers on Wall Street, and goin' out with their yachts and spendin' their time in Europe raisin' hell with the whores I heerd all about—and not knowin' a single damn thing about the road, 'cept their private cars and their stocks and bonds." The old man sighed. "There's Mr. Marshall. He hated the road. It was just money to him. And it's just money to DeWitt, and Miss Cornelia, and the rest of 'em." The old man's eyes began to shine brilliantly as he stared at the men smiling at him indulgently. "But it ain't just money to Mr. Aaron! No, sir! And when I see him out there, steppin' over the rails careful like he used to, and smokin' and watchin' everything, I tell you, it's just like old times and I'm a fireman again, and I go up to speak to him, touchin' my forehead, and I says, ' Mr. Aaron, I'm glad you come back, and it's good to see you,' and he says, ' Thanks, Billie, I'm glad to be back, too.'"

"You're daffy; old Aaron deWitt's been dead a thousand years," said one of the younger men good-humouredly. "That's Mr. Miles Peale, general superintendent, out there to-night, checkin' up on everythin' and watchin' to see if a damn piece of coal gets wasted. He ain't Mr. Aaron."

"That's all you know, Jim!" shrilled Old Billie, and he shook his broom at the speaker. "It's Mr. Aaron, and I've knowed him for seventy years or more. And I know his voice. . . . !"

One of the men crossed himself furtively, and then was embarrassed. The men went to the window. There was Miles now, seriously walking along, studying a long freight train which had just come in, sometimes tapping on the high and secret sides with his cane. "What's he doing that for?" asked a conductor. He snickered. "Looking for gold or something? Just a regular freight."

"No, it isn't," said another, with interest. "It's a special; it's being shunted on to New York. Dozens of those special freights coming in now, almost every day. Ever notice the guards on 'em? They ain't our own fellers."

But the men were not interested. They looked at watches, caught up lunch pails, and went off sullenly to their work. Their wages were high these days; the union leaders were talking

570

of still higher wages, and "benefits." But the men were sullen. Just a job.

Old Billie wistfully watched "Mr. Aaron" through the smoky window, then suddenly threw down his broom and crept out on creaking legs. He followed Miles far down the tracks, and finally caught up with him, gasping a little. "Mr. Aaron!" he screamed against the uproar. Miles turned at once, saw him, smiled. "Good evening, Billie," he said. The old man sighed happily. It was wonderful, Mr. Aaron being so young again, and his hair just the way it always was, and his cane in his hand as usual, and the way he walked—small, sure steps. "Great big freight, ain't it, Mr. Aaron?" he asked. "Three, four, five times bigger than the old days. Still call it old Forty-two, but it ain't the same train. What you think they got in there, and what're those fellers doin' with guns on the platforms and glarin' as if you don't own the whole business?"

Miles folded his gloved hands on the top of his cane, an old-remembered gesture which thrilled the ancient Billie, and stared at the freight. "Well," said Miles, "it's munitions, Billie." He lifted his cane, pointed briefly at the name of a mighty munitions maker on the side of a car. "For the war. Explosives, guns, bombs, everything else. Going to England, France, and Germany with a wonderful, fine, impartial indifference. That's what is known as neutrality, Billie. That is known as ' being fair.' Of course, booming profits have nothing to do with it. We're very virtuous in this country, you see; all of us, everywhere, are very virtuous. It would be very unkind for anyone to insist that we say: ' We don't care who dies, or what becomes after, or what governments are destroyed. There's a profit to be made. We'll deal with any tyrants later; we'll buy them, if necessary.'" Miles leaned on his cane again. "Perhaps we won't be able to buy them this time, Billie. Perhaps they want more than money. Perhaps they want the whole damned world."

The old man listened, fascinated. He had listened decades before to the soliloquies of Mr. Aaron. He had never understood; but he had always been happy at the sound of that wry and vigorous voice, and the odd implications in it. There, now Mr. Aaron was shrugging; always well-dressed and beautifully turned out—Mr. Aaron. He could shrug and there'd never be so much as a slipped cravat or shoulder.

"You see, Billie," said Miles, "I don't ' love ' humanity so much that I believe I know what's 'best' for it, and so try to impose my will on it. And I don't hate it enough to want to subjugate and rule it absolutely. I don't think there is a great deal of difference, after all, between the 'love' of the Socialist idealists and the hate of the murderers. I think any honesty in the whole business lies with the murderers; the naked steel and lash are open and immediate, and you can see the faces behind them and know what they are. It's the 'lovers of humanity' who do their work behind a fog of fine and noble words, and keep the steel and the lash hidden until they dare come out with them."

"You're certainly right, Mr. Aaron," said the old man emphatically. He peered vaguely at the monster cars, which were now rolling smoothly down the tracks. "What war, sir?" He was bewildered.

"It's always the same war," said Miles kindly. "The name doesn't matter."

Red lights changed to green far down the rails; the freight moved faster and faster. Faster and faster, thought Miles. But perhaps, at the end, there'll be a few of us left to derail you forever. We'll kill you because you're wolves and boars and insane monsters out of some primeval jungle, nightmares still roaming around in the light of the day.

He turned to the old man standing so devotedly at his side; he saw the blinking, unknowing, and curiously innocent eyes. He smiled at the old man. "You see, Billie, men like me will have to fight for men like you. Some of us won't like to fight; too much trouble. But we shall; you'll see. It'll be a case of survival, for all of us."

"Sure, Mr. Aaron, you was always a fighter," said Old Billie with pride. He began to walk down towards the station with Miles.

"I wonder," Miles mused, swinging his cane in the little circles Old Billie remembered so well, "what perverted men are coming to maturity behind the guns and the shattered cities and the trenches of Europe? What are their names? Sure as the devil they are there, waiting, as they've always been waiting. English names, French names, German names, Russian names? And who are the Americans who are watching and waiting, too, until the European nightmares emerge from the smoke and the ruins and show themselves? Yes, we'll have to fight them, just to live, we millionaires and plumbers, we physicians and bricklayers, we railroaders and industrialists and businessmen and factory hands and farmers."

He touched Old Billie, stumbling along beside him, with the gold head of his fine cane. "I've got a feeling, Billie, that it'll be your kind, at the end, who will kill off the tyrants. Because, you see, you won't be able to compromise. You haven't the money."

"You can always count on me, Mr. Aaron," said Old Billie with passionate vigour.

Miles smiled a little. "Yes, I think we can. Not something to be proud of, perhaps—but I think we can."

He gave the old man ten dollars. Billie protested a little. Miles said, "You've given me a lot to-night, old fellow."

Billie watched him go, swelling with joy in himself at the small straight back of "Mr. Aaron." He'd been gone a long time, Mr. Aaron. But now he was here again, and the road was safe. Some fellers said he was a hard man. They didn't know what a fighter was, the young boys.

When Miles reached home he was met by his tearful wife, Ruth, who informed him that his father had died an hour before, very suddenly.

CHAPTER FORTY-SEVEN

ARCHBISHOP RUFUS ANTHONY MARSHALL of St. Louis alighted from his long black limousine in the golden haze of the early November afternoon. He had not been in Pennsylvania for over four years; he told himself that he had almost forgotten how lovely the countryside was here, how scarlet the mountains in the autumn, how cobalt the autumnal skies, how bronze the reaped fields, how turquoise the river reflecting all this pure colour in sheets and shafts, how sweet and cool the air, and in what lofty silence the land lay. The lightest wind sent crumpled russet leaves scuttling over the empty road; they scrambled like the feet of little mice. The white farmhouse stood in a nest of red maples; the unclouded sun poured down on the red barns and the red roofs of the silos. How had he forgotten? He smiled at his chauffeur, standing respectfully near him. "I think you'd better go back to Portersville and call for me about seven," he said. The man touched his cap, entered the car, and drove off in a spume of yellow dust. The archbishop, tall and stately in his black garments, watched him go. He gently touched the cross on his breast, and wished, for a nostalgic moment, that he had remained a parish priest. But God had chosen for him.

He stood on the gravelled path leading to the long white farmhouse for some moments. At forty-two, he had not lost his youthful expression of wise, grave innocence, though his fair skin was lined and his face had taken on the austere and spare boniness of a dedicated man. His pale blue eyes were still crystal-line, but very tired, and there was a slight amount of grey in his very blond hair. He permitted the profound peace of the countryside to flow over him like refreshing water. He saw the cattle in the distant field, he heard a horse neigh. Far up in the abyss of the deep blue sky he saw the last of the migrant birds flying southward; they cast a broken shadow over the earth, like the shadow of leaves. The gravelled path was bordered with marigolds and zinnias in one last blaze of bloom. Two rabbits bounced timidly past him, on lawns still green and thick. A blue jay screamed, flashing like a piece of the sky itself into the burning maples.

No one was about. Tony slowly walked towards the farmhouse. And then, on that still and perfumed air, he, unbelievingly, heard the fairy-like singing of a harp. He stopped, bewildered. The music, fey and wild and unbearably poignant, seemed part of the earth itself.

Where had he heard that song before? And who was playing it? Faint memories returned to him. He began to hum, still incredulous: "By Killarney's lakes and fells . . ." A voice joined the harp, as strong and sure as the instrument was tender, a hearty baritone. My father, thought Tony, and he was not ashamed of the tears in his eyes. My father, singing again, as he sang to us when we were children.

The song of the harp and the song of the man died away on the golden air. Tony went quickly to the farmhouse. He stopped in the cool blue shade of the deep veranda and peered through the screen door. He was a boy again, coming to visit his grand-parents, dead all these years. He could see the long hall, and the screened door at the end of it, leading to the gardens. He could see the soft dusk of the rooms on either side. He heard his father talking: "I'll make an Irishman of you yet, Alex. Now, if you'll go into the kitchen, you'll be finding some cold beer in the ice box; take it out while Bessie isn't looking; she thinks I shouldn't drink it, the Baptist!"

A young man of about seventeen emerged from the parlour, laughing. A light-skinned, slender, tall young man, moving with the grace of youth, his smooth brown head resting delicately on a thin neck, his brown eyes smiling. Tony pulled the bell, and the young man stopped, startled, and looked at the door. The archbishop could see his narrow face and elegant features. "Alex?" said Tony through the screen. "Alex!" He had not seen his nephew Alexander, Lord Gibson-Hamilton, for over twelve years. His voice was uncertain and eager. Was it possible that this young man, in his rough British tweeds, was actually the child he remembered? Alex, smiling courteously, came to the door, trying to see against the brighter light in which Tony stood. "Yes?" he murmured. Then he saw Tony clearly, the shining cross on his breast. "Uncle Tony?" he exclaimed. "Uncle Tony!" He stood there on the other side of the screen door, and his gentle face beamed with disbelief and pleasure.

"Now, who in hell are you talking to?" asked Allan, and came into the hall. Then he stood there, petrified, a thin, dark-faced man with rough white hair, a cigarette in his lean fingers. Suddenly he shouted incoherently. He ran to the door, thrust aside his grandson with the strong gestures of a young man, opened the door, and threw his arms about his son. "Tony!" he cried brokenly, "Tony, you spalpeen, you rascal! Sure, and you've dropped from heaven. . . . Tony!"

The brogue was thick on his tongue, but Tony could not detect any odour of whisky. He hugged his father close to him and laughed. "Well, aren't you going to ask me in? I've come all the way from St. Louis, on my way to New York, and Rome." He held out his hand to his nephew, who grasped it strongly. Allan, his arm still about his son's shoulders, said severely, "Where're your manners, boy? You kiss the archbishop's ring. You bend the knee. Don't they teach you that in England? That's the way to do it." He released Tony, hesitated, then dropped to his knee and kissed the ring, himself. All his movements were quick and supple, Tony noticed. "I never thought," said Allan in a grumbling voice, "that I'd be kissing the hand, or ring, of my own son." But he was full of pride. "Come in, come in." He took Tony's arm and pulled him into the cool shade of the parlour, where all was as Tony remembered, from the wax flowers under a glass bell on the old marble table before the fireplace to the stiffly starched lace curtains at the wide windows, from the old red carpet on the floor to the horsehair furniture which had pricked his bare calves as a child. A small crimson fire burned on the brick hearth, and a scent of apple wood rose from it. The wooden walls and ceiling glimmered with the light reflected from outside.

"So, it's the archbishop you are now," said Allan, when the three men had seated themselves on the stiff furniture. "I—I couldn't go to your installation, Tony." He dropped his head a moment. "I know," said Tony. His father had been very ill again, at that time. He had been told that Allan had not recognised any member of his family for nearly six months. It was hard to believe that this man, so brown, so youthful, so strong and alert, was the sick and broken man he remembered. Tony sighed contentedly. He had been afraid on receiving the news of his father's last, and almost fatal, "breakdown" of a year ago. His father, since Dolores's death in 1915, had lived in a nightmare agony of unreality. There had been a vague rumour that he had attempted suicide late in 1916, and again in 1917, when America had entered the European war. And each time I could never go to him, thought Tony. I could never have let him know; I had to stay away for his own sake. The newspapers had been kind. Newspapermen were usually very discreet about rich and powerful men.

The beer was so cold that moisture gathered on the outside of the big glasses. A stout, middle-aged woman had disapprovingly brought in a tray of fine old cheeses. She had stared with umbrage at Tony, and had waddled out, flouncing a little. "Bessie's a good woman," said Allan, smiling. His small black eyes twinkled at his son. "And her husband's my right arm on the farm. We have two families living in their own houses here; we need all the hands we can get. Had a hard time for a while, with the high wages in the cities. But during the past year help has been more plentiful; and now that the stock market has crashed, I suppose it'll be still more easy to come by." He spoke as if the disastrous debacle of a few weeks ago had occurred on the moon and had nothing to do with him.

Never Victorious, Never Defeated

"Four years since I've seen you, Tony," said Allan. "How many times have I seen you in the last twelve years or so? I could count them on the fingers of my hand. First you went to Philadephia, then to Chicago, then to Seattle, then to San Francisco——" He shook his head. Tony said, "I know. I was all over the country, it seems." His father had forgotten his son's visits, apparently. There had been only one reality in his life, the tragic death of his daughter, and his mountainous hatred. After the war, Tony had spent much time in Rome; he had gone to the Riviera in 1926, only to find that the family had left hastily for America, because of another breakdown of his father's. He had arrived once in Newport; Allan was again immured in a sanatorium. Tony had visited him there, had talked with him, had prayed for him, kneeling beside his father's bed. Allan had not remembered.

Yet, here he was now, bronzed and restlessly vital as in his youth, seeing everything, knowing everything. "You look so well, Dad," said Tony. Allan laughed, and lit a cigarette for his son, and then for himself. "Why not, Tony? It was the damned railroad—my retiring four months ago was the best thing I ever did for myself. And I'm not missed. Your mother, and DeWitt, send me reports occasionally, or papers for me to sign, and that's all I want of it. I've come back to the land, and this is where I intend to live and die." He looked about the ugly, pleasant room and settled deeper in the old rocking chair. "Yes, they'll be leaving the cities, I hope, and the factories, for the land. Perhaps the Crash will be salutary for the whole nation."

Tony was not so sure. He swirled the last of the beer in his glass.

"It was bound to come," said Allan. "I sold out my holdings, a great part of them, in August. They laughed at me in New York. But all the signs were there. The country was mad; it was stupid and trivial, excitable and greedy. I talked with Regan and the rest of them, and warned them. And they exchanged looks, and I knew they were thinking I was out of my mind." He laughed with a ringing sound. "Now they write me and ask 'how in God's name' I knew."

But Tony was very grave. "What you say about the American people having been stupid and trivial, excitable and greedy, since the war, is very true, Dad. It has caused us considerable concern. There is an excuse that they wished to 'forget' the war.

That is nonsense. We suffered almost nothing in comparison with other nations. Yet we dare to talk of ourselves as being ' disillusioned! ' With the exception of our boys who died on the useless battlefields, and their relatives, the whole nation actually enjoyed the war, delighted in it. The antics of our prominent people and our politicians, and the nation as a whole, following them, has proved it. Criminal childishness. A new style in women's clothing, the visit of a foreign prince, the junket of some obscure queen of some obscure nation, a new brand of automobile, and other trivialities, have been enough to throw the whole nation into a convulsion of ecstasy and excitement and delirium. Because," said Tony. "I am afraid we have become a trumpery people, completely demoralised with our own trumpery."

Allan looked at Alex's golden harp near the window and smiled. "All this no longer concerns me," he said.

He believes that, thought Tony with amusement, and dismay.

"I visited Europe several times since 1919," said the archbishop. "And the Near East, too. The Holy Father is very concerned these days, and alarmed." He paused. "But before I tell you about that, I want to tell you that Europe is not joyous, idiotically excited, and in a state of euphoria, as is America. It is enormously, and honestly, and fearfully disillusioned. I remember what you once said to me: ' Who are the men who are waiting behind the smoke of guns and the shattered cities, for their turn to come?' Well, Dad, we have their names now. Mussolini, Stalin. That is why the Holy Father is so alarmed these days. For we know something else; we know these names are only symptoms."

Allan smiled, and it was his old dark and cynical smile. "Isn't Mussolini the boy who is making the Italian trains run on time, and who dislikes Italian gaiety and the civilisation and maturity? Isn't Stalin the expression of the medieval emotions of the Russian people? What have they to do with America?" He stood up and began to prowl restlessly up and down the room, shaking his head. "I told you I don't care any longer. Let the whole world go to hell, as long as I am safe here on the land." He pushed aside a lace curtain and stared fiercely out on to the cool November lawns and shade.

"But you are *not* safe; none of us is safe, anywhere," said Tony. He turned to look at his nephew. Young Alex had not spoken; he just sat in his old chair near his uncle. There was a silent quality about him which reminded Tony of his sister Dolores.

Alex smiled shyly, and suddenly it was Dolores's smile, sweet and comprehending. His mother lives in him, thought the archbishop with gratitude and an old pang of sorrow.

Allan swung from the window, frowning. "You priests! You are always seeing the ' abomination of desolation ' in everything. The hell with Europe. We'll have nothing to do with the League of Nations. Why should we be embroiled in the ancient quarrels of Europe, anyway?"

Tony sighed. He put his hand to his large cross. "Dad, I wouldn't be talking like this to you now, in view of your past, and real fears, which upset you for years and made you ill, if I didn't believe you have the stamina and the courage to know, and to act.

"Look at us, a strumpet nation which until a few weeks ago lived in a delirium of easy money and immorality and silly excitements, saved temporarily from the monstrous depression of a post-war period by the earnest efforts of a few men in Washington. They can no longer save us from that depression. It has begun. It will get immeasurably worse. And that will give the hordes of shadowy men the opportunity they have been waiting for for over two hundred years."

"Go get us some more beer, Alex," said Allan to his grandson. He sat down and watched the young man leave the room. He had planted his sun-browned hands on his knees, and sat rigid, now staring at the floor. He shook his head. "I'll have my peace if it is the last thing I'll ever have." He lifted his head and looked at Tony suddenly, and now his black eyes narrowed and sharpened. "What ' shadowy men ? '"

"Over two hundred years ago," said Tony, with relief, "there was organised, both in Germany and France, and in England and Russia, too, a society called The Silent Masters. There were not too many of them, perhaps a few thousands. But they saw that liberty for all men was a growing concept in the world, and they were outraged. So, the plot was created that they should some day take over the world, as the élite, to subdue mankind to slavery once more, to destroy the dignity of man, to subserviate mankind to ruthless masters, for the invincible power of these masters. They were content to wait, these men, for hatred has no birth and no death."

Again, Tony touched his cross. "The age they dreamed of has arrived. And millions of men like them have been born; there

579

are so many of them now, waiting to serve, to murder, to instigate wars which will overthrow liberty and create depressions, which will eradicate democratic governments. Wars, crushing taxations, depressions: these are the three deaths which will eliminate Judeo-Christian civilisation and deliver the whole world to the new, indoctrinated Silent Masters.

"No, please let me finish," said Tony, lifting his hand. His fair face had darkened, become full of stern prophecy. "The secret movement, everywhere, goes under the names of fascism, socialism, communism. They did not 'create' Mussolini and Stalin. These creatures are just their weapons, as their philosophies are just their weapons. The Silent Masters know each other very well; they recognise each other. And we have them in America, too, in such well-organised platoons of hatred and treachery that it is almost incredible. Have you forgotten my uncle, Norman deWitt, so soon? Have you forgotten the Socialist Clubs which were organised as long ago as 1905, or even earlier? Have you forgotten that Norman owns four newspapers, five magazines, and an organisation which constantly litters the country with sly propaganda?"

Alex returned with more beer and some sandwiches. He put them down before his uncle on a small table. He moved dreamily, but his large and intelligent eyes fixed themselves with intense seriousness on the archbishop. "I know," he said in his gentle English voice. "I know all about it. One hears it at Oxford all the time, among the young men."

But Allan clenched his fists on his knees. "Norman deWitt," he said. "I've tried to put the whole family out of my mind. I had almost forgotten him."

He looked at Tony, and he became grim. "Is that why you came to see me to-day?"

Tony hesitated. "I came to see you because you are my father, whom I love, and I was anxious about you. No one would give me any news at all, of any importance, except Ruth and Aunt Laura. Not even DeWitt would tell me much." He regarded his father straightly. "Yes, I came to see you to-day because there is no time to be lost. You are a tremendously rich man. You knew, long ago, that what is happening now would happen. The world of free men needs powerful and rich men like yourself, for, you see, the evil men have all the money they need in Europe. And in America. Even through these prosperous American years, the evil men have been working, calling themselves Communists and Socialists, in secret and constant communication with their European counterparts."

Allan's brown forehead was glistening with sweat. He had turned quite grey under his tan. "But what in hell can I do?" he shouted. Alex glanced at him apprehensively. "What can I do? Who will listen?"

"You can buy a few newspapers, yourself," said Tony. "You can staff them with men who are as much afraid as you used to be afraid. Through these newspapers you can tell the American people the truth. You can cry ' havoc ' without stopping. Your editors can denounce war, destroying taxation, hatred, communism, socialism, fascism. Your papers can support politicians and statesmen of intelligence and integrity, who are already suspecting the ancient plot. You can, with your money, set up a foundation or something, to keep the people informed with pamphlets and publications and books. You can use the same means of public communication as the enemy is already using.

"It is late, very late. Perhaps it is already too late," said Tony. "But perhaps, with the grace of God, we still might win, we free men everywhere in the world, we men who love freedom and dignity and God more than we love our very lives."

"If the people of the world succumb to these terrible things, it will be their own fault," said Allan.

"They will succumb, if they do, out of ignorance," said Tony. "It is your duty to lift their ignorance. You could speak with your friends in all the industries. If ignorant, inform them. If not ignorant, but part of the plot, themselves, you will soon detect them. And you can expose them."

Allan said in a stifled voice, "I am seventy-one years old, almost seventy-two."

Tony stretched out his hand and laid it on his nephew's shoulder, "And Alex is only seventeen." There was suddenly a desperate silence in the room.

Allan said dully. "He should be back in England, at Oxford. But he wanted to stay with me this year. I'm one of his guardians, and I had to fight the English ones. . . ." He looked at the young man, and his greying eyebrows drew together. "You mean, I should use these last few years of mine to fight again, for Alex?"

"Yes," said Tony. "And for all the endless millions of Alexes all over the world, the young men in their schools, tens of thousands of them already being poisoned by their enemies—all the Alexes who will die in the plotted wars of the future, who will be enslaved, if we do not work fast and surely, by the men who hate them."

He put his hand on his father's knee. "Dad. You are very tired. You became ill because what you had was not what you wanted. You became ill because you suspected the truth, and knew the first battle against man opened with the war. You did not know where to start the fight; your energies were being drained away in channels which no longer interested you. Now you know where to begin the struggle for which you were really born."

Again, Allan looked about the room which his parents had furnished, and loved. "Is it too much to ask that a man of my age have a little peace?"

"But such peace is alien to you," said Tony, smiling. His blue eyes were very tired now, but they also sparkled. "How much longer would you have been able to stand this withdrawal from life? Oh, you can talk to me until doomsday of your passionate addiction to crops, your absorption in the land! And I'd know you were lying to yourself. You were not born to the land. You are a fighter."

Allan glared at him, then slowly began to smile. He rubbed his sunburned cheek. "Well, I suppose I must confess that I was getting a little bored. . . . A man can't read all the time. I have good men on this farm. It's always a retreat, waiting for me. I can always grow food. . . ." He looked at Tony and exclaimed, "All right, then, you devil in holy clothing!" He stood up, and rested his arms on Tony's shoulders. "You'll be the death of me, you understand. You'll be saying the Mass for me one of these days, and there'll be the guilt on your soul."

Tony turned his stately head, and as simply as a child, he kissed the back of his father's hand. "You've come a long way, Dad," he said, and smiled up into Allan's moved face. "A long way around, back to the day when you decided you wanted to be a priest."

No, Tony said, he could not stay for supper. Cornelia was giving a dinner for him. No, he had not seen her yet; he had telephoned her, and had given his promise.

Allan said, "Your mother is indestructible. At sixty-four she still has her old flair for living, and verve and robustness. When DeWitt became president, after my retirement, there she was, right behind him, like an eager girl blazing with ambition. She manipulates him, as she wanted to manipulate me. She probably did, quite a number of times, I suppose, without my being aware of it, especially when I was—ill. She didn't like Miles Peale becoming executive vice-president, but there was nothing she could do about it. After all, Miles's wife is Cornelia's half-sister. And there was all that stock in Miles's hands. Perhaps there's some truth in her suspicions that Miles wants to be president; I don't know. But the family has its fifty-one per cent of the stock, and I suppose we're safe, even from such a one as Miles—whom I don't dislike, incidentally."

Tony was alarmed. "I never liked Miles, I'm afraid; and I don't trust him. And there's Fielding, who's general superintendent now."

Allan laughed. "I thought you weren't supposed to be interested in worldly things. Have some of this fine Camembert."

Tony waved away the proffered dish. "How can you be so uninterested, Dad?"

Allan, who seemed to have acquired fresh life, said, "Why should I be interested, particularly? I was not merely babbling when I said I was finished with the road. And DeWitt hardly seems my son. We have nothing to say to each other. But you've forgotten your mother; she's always there."

Twilight was drifting down in blue and purple shadows over the mountains and the valley. "Yes," said Allan thoughtfully, "your mother is always there. She writes me; we see each other very seldom, perhaps not more than two or three times a year. It's best that way. She despises me, and I don't like being openly despised, having my normal share of vanity. I'm not the man she married. In fact, I don't think I ever was. I served my purpose; I'm no more use to her. Once we loved each other; that wasn't an illusion. But I finally bored her, and Cornelia can stand anything but boredom. She never felt intensely about anything except the road."

They talked of many things, as the twilight deepened. Allan showed disinterest in his grandson, son of DeWitt, young Rufus deWitt Marshall. "Fourteen years old, and with old Rufus's eyes and hair and general appearance," said Allan. "He's Cornelia's pet aversion, strange to say." Allan was not concerned

583

with his granddaughter Shelley, daughter of DeWitt. "A nice girl, almost sixteen," he said. "A little colourless, however. Cornelia is fond of her. When Cornelia last drove down here, with a sheaf of papers for me to sign, relinquishing my last hold on the road, she mentioned she thought it would be 'nice' if Alex, here, married Shelley later."

He smiled at his son. "My main visitors are poor Ruth, who comes for consolation, she being Miles's wife and he having quite a way with the ladies; and Laura. Are you going to be outraged, Tony? After all, I'm in my seventies, and Laura is sixty-three. We comfort each other. Cornelia thinks it is 'amusing.'"

Alex said, "I am fond of Grandmother, though sometimes she is a little—overpowering. I ought not to say that, for she is very kind to me, and I think she has some affection for me. I often go to dinner at her home. Grandfather, here, pretends to be entirely indifferent about what is happening in the house on the mountain, but if I don't give him a full accounting he is put out."

"I loved that house once," said Allan, after his son had stopped chuckling. "I never cared for the other damned mausoleums in France and England and Newport and New York. But now it's full of strangers. It's full of people I never knew, and who never knew me: my son DeWitt, my wife, my brother-in-law Norman (who goes there regularly these days), and Mary, my daughter-in-law, and her children. Mary! That was my mother's name, and it's the dearest name in all the world, I'm thinking, for a woman. But my son's wife is no Mary, for all her name."

They talked of the time when the government had taken over the operation of the railroads. "Your mother," said Allan, "almost went out of her mind with rage. But even then I was becoming detached."

"That was an indication of the future," said Tony sombrely. But Allan would have no more serious conversation. He was beginning to show his age; the lamps which had been lighted—old oil lamps—revealed the seams about his mouth and eyes, the weariness like a shadow over his whole face. He began to speak of his daughter Dolores, and it was as though he were thinking aloud. Grief rose in water to his eyelids. It was then that young Alex went out and returned with a bottle of medicine and a spoon. Allan took it with surprising docility. He looked at Alex and said, "Here is all I have left—my grandson and my son." He paused, and added softly, "And Laura. We sit on the veranda, two old people, and talk of nothing, and everything, with Alex as chaperon somewhere about."

Allan and Tony walked in the twilight to the road where the limousine was waiting. They paused, and regarded each other gravely. "I often remember what Woodrow Wilson said in 1912," said Tony. "The history of liberty is a history of the limitations of governmental power, not the increase of it. When we resist concentration of power, we are resisting the powers of death, because concentration of power is what always precedes the destruction of human liberties."

"I shall use that on the masthead of my newspapers, which I don't yet own, and shall order my editors to emphasise it, editors I haven't yet hired," replied Allan. He paused. "Tony, my little spalpeen, will you give me your blessing?"

He watched the limousine disappear into the purple distance towards town. A glittering orange sunset shone through high black pines. Allan contemplated it for a long time, then went back to the farmhouse. Alex was waiting for him. He said, with his shy smile, "Grandfather, you look like a man of resolution again, and not a man of peace."

But Allan sat down in a chair, leaned back his head, and closed his eyes. He said softly, "I know it in my heart, that I'll never see my Tony again. But this time it is I who'll be going. After my last battle."

Cornelia said to Tony, "There's anything you want to drink, my dear. But, of course, seeing we have that dreadful Prohibition, and you a churchman, you won't drink anything." She smiled at him slyly, and touched his black sleeve. "Shouldn't you be a cardinal, or something? By the way, you look very handsome and majestic, and such. How was your father?"

"Very well, I'm happy to say," replied Tony.

"I asked Alex to come to dinner to-night, too," said Cornelia. "But it is always ' Grandfather needs me.' There's something maternal about that boy. He reminds me of poor Dicky. Always seriously wanting to be of help. Tiresome people. They can never be gay or light or amusing. Your father's like that, too. For years I tolerated it, and then it got too much. I hate morose people, not that Alex is morose, yet."

"I never thought of Dad as being ' maternal,'" said Tony, smiling.

"No, nor particularly helpful, I suppose. He was quite a man, in his young days."

"He is quite a man still," said Tony in a cold voice.

It was evident that Cornelia still loved this house on the mountain. The old furniture was always carefully kept in repair. It was almost as it had been when old Aaron had bought it from the artist. However, electricity had replaced oil lamps, and the great chandelier in the hall had been artfully fitted with electric candles. The effect was not so soft, and there were no gentle shadows in the corners of the hall, as Tony had remembered.

"I've invited everyone of consequence in Portersville to see you to-night," said Cornelia. "And some from New York. You see, I'm quite proud of you." At sixty-four she was still erect and had still retained her magnificent figure, though it was deplorably dressed to-night in a glittering, very short sequin sheath, so that she looked like a tall statue clad in blue lightning. A belt of diamonds hugged her hips; her short red hair, shingled, was moulded to her large head. Expert care had kept her face from becoming that of an old woman's, but the rouge and the powder and the blazing lipstick gave her a raddled and raffish look, coarse, if vibrant. Her big hands betrayed her age; they were dark, veined, and mottled, and afire with gems. Diamond bracelets, in distracting quantity, raced up and down her arms; a long string of mingled pearls and diamonds dangled from her seamed neck. She moved like a strong young woman, quickly and surely, and her laugh boomed out as in her youth. Her eyes were bits of polished amber, and they glowed with a wicked light. Tony reminded himself that he loved his mother, and he kissed her again. She smelled of expensive French scent, and the best whisky. Tony said, "Dad just drinks beer, he tells me."

"Well," said Cornelia, shrugging, "that's something to be encouraged about, anyway. He never really could drink hard liquor. It did something frightful to him." She laughed loudly. "Did he tell you how old Laura visits him? I think it's ridiculous. They always had a thing about each other; I knew it for years. I offered him a divorce two years ago, so he could marry her if he wanted to. He was quite outraged; so silly. But come into the living-room. Everybody's there."

There was a time when she loved my father more than anything in the world, probably more than the road, thought Tony. But he reverted to what he really was, and so was no longer the man she had married.

Cornelia had linked her arm into that of her son's, and she led him into the living-room, already crowded with members of the family and a number of strangers. "My son, the archbishop, who is going to be a cardinal soon," Cornelia introduced him. "Now, Tony, stop protesting. Why else are you going to Rome?" She turned to a short, rather stout, dark man with brilliant black eyes. "Tony, this is George Richberg, of New York, who owns all those newspapers. We call him Izzy. Don't glare, Izzy. That was your name before you changed it to George, wasn't it? George writes all those editorials about the ' rising enemy in America '; you must have read some. He thinks there're Communists and such, right here in this country, plotting in little dark holes somewhere, and especially in Washington. Of course, that's just newspaper stuff; makes for good circulation."

Tony, startled, took the little man's strong fat palm, and looked into the quick and intelligent eyes. Mr. Richberg said, "It isn't just newspaper stuff. It's the truth. I wonder if you know anything about it—sir?"

Tony nodded. He was filled with excitement. "I understand running newspapers is a strenuous business," he suggested tentatively.

Mr. Richberg shrugged eloquently. "Terrible, I'm nearly sixty, and I had a heart attack six months ago. I wish I could sell out a couple of my papers to a younger man, who would understand our policy."

"I know a ' younger man,' said Tony, as the guests moved about them. "My father. Let me give you his address. He wants to buy a newspaper or two, perhaps more."

"I was supposed to return to New York to-night," said Mr. Richberg, carefully tucking away Tony's card, on which he had scribbled Allan's address. His eyes quickened. "Your father? Allan Marshall? He's retired, hasn't he? He wants to buy some newspapers? How about some magazines, too? I tell you— sir——"

But Cornelia had returned from a brief sortie into the crowd of her guests, and had seized Tony's arm again. Mr. Richberg lifted his hand. "I'll stay over. I'll go to see your father to-morrow."

Bemused, Tony permitted himself to be introduced to other curious strangers. He came here so rarely now that he wanted to steep himself in the atmosphere of the old house where his mother and he had been born. He wanted to wander out on to the terraces and smell the wood smoke. He wanted to see the fine and glimmering rooms, alone. He wanted to see how tall the poplar he had planted had grown. And, as always, he missed his sister; he kept finding himself looking for her in some remote corner, beautiful as a classic statue, faintly smiling and remote.

He eventually found DeWitt sitting in a chair with his cane beside him, DeWitt who was almost forty, and "the youngest railroad president in the United States." DeWitt was a silent gnome now, sallow-skinned, ageless, watching, his shrivelled lips fixed in a cynical smile. Then Tony appeared before him he said nothing, but he held out his hand. "Hallo," said Tony gently, and pressed that small hand with its fine bones. Allan called his younger son an anachronism, and Tony unwillingly had to admit that there was some truth in the remark. DeWitt, though still under forty, looked old and static and oddly out of date, too precise, too fastidious, too set. His eyes were never still, but they were cold.

"When did I see you last?" he asked of Tony. "Never mind; don't tell me. You aren't interested in the family any longer." Now his eyes changed, became accusing and strange. "I thought you'd never forget me, but you did."

"No," began Tony, bending over him. But Mary Marshall, his sister-in-law, had appeared, chic and shining and perfumed, her pointed face as mischievous as ever. "Well, Tony!" she exclaimed, and her voice was derisively shrill. "You've come a long way, haven't you? Don't scowl; the clergy shouldn't scowl. Have you seen Rufus and Shelley, our kids? They always try to slip away from us elderly folk so they can go to some nice bootleg place where they can kick their legs and drink moonshine. They tell me Rufus looks just like old Rufus deWitt, who died such ages ago; I remember him. But he certainly doesn't have old Rufus's personality." She patted DeWitt carelessly on the shoulder and wandered off with a glass in her hand. DeWitt watched her go, and said nothing. His small face was inscrutable.

He said in a very low voice, "I think I hate practically everything. But perhaps I always did. Eh, Tony?"

"Yes, I think so," said Tony with sadness.

DeWitt lifted his eyes to his brother's face, and they were the eyes of a basilisk. "Except you," he said. "And that's something

I don't understand. You were always such a damned prig." He raised his cane and touched Tony's black coat. "Miles is here, and Field. We call Miles ' the dancer.' I don't know why; he never dances. I'm keeping my eye on him." He saw Cornelia approaching in a welter of fresh guests. "Here's the old girl again. Do you know something? I think she always tried to keep us apart when we were children. Why, I wonder?"

But she always kept everyone apart, thought Tony. She never trusted anyone. He found himself at the long glimmering table in the dining-room. He looked about him with satisfaction. Nothing had changed here. There was the same ponderous silver, the same chairs, and now again there was candlelight. A fire burned on the old hearth, and dark blue and gold draperies had been drawn against the autumn chill. Across from Tony sat Norman deWitt, queerly youthful and disarmingly smiling like a boy, though he was about fifty years old. There was no grey in his fine brown hair, no wrinkles about his wide brown eyes. No one could have looked more innocent, more gentle, more interested, than this strange man who was so dangerous. The ladies on each side of him listened to his soft voice eagerly. He spoke so winningly to them, and he spoke of nothing. But when he glanced at Tony, the corners of his eyes tightened and the pupils were as still and lifeless as stone. They had, as yet, not spoken to each other, this uncle and his nephew. Tony felt that between them lay a treacherous glacier, like a battlefield.

Tony listened to the frivolous chatter all about him. He remembered that as a very young boy he had heard serious discussions during dinner parties in this very room. There had been good talk, intelligent and mature. But now the whole conversation revolved about the latest illegal deliveries of whisky, the newest and most flamboyant gangster (whom the ladies, young and old, declared they "adored"), the latest national or international scandal, passionate eulogies about the Prince of Wales, the newest and most notorious murder case, golf and other sports, the latest attempt of some man or woman to swim the English Channel, and similar trivialities. There was little or no mention, even among the men, about the stock market crash, and the rising tide of panic and the ominous hints of widespread depression in America. The men had their secure fortunes; they had not suffered measurably, though here and there there was an exaggerated and amusing groan about "paper profits."

Never Victorious, Never Defeated

They do not know, thought Tony, that America stands at the door of doom. If some know, they do not care. They have fortunes tucked away in invincible places; their businesses will not collapse. But what of the millions of the foolish, who invested earnings as clerks and mechanics, as bookkeepers and cashiers, in the monstrous bubble of the market? One can pity them even while censuring these poor creatures, who had not had the intelligence to know that Santa Claus does not exist. And what of the slowly closing factories, the scent of disaster in the air, the dawning of the age of the evil men? Who knew, or knowing, cared?

Tony, with another part of his mind, noticed that, as usual, his mother's incredible magnetism drew involuntary glances even amidst the feverish chatter about the table. Her flair made other women appear colourless, and two-dimensional. Her voice caught the ear in fascination, for all its husky ribaldry. Vulgar as she was, and shouting frivolously, there was yet a pungency and meaning in her remarks absent in the conversation of other women. Sometimes she caught Tony looking at her; she winked at him humorously. It is possible, then, to despise people and yet inspire their devotion, thought Tony. He then reflected on Mussolini and Stalin. They, too, had this diabolical gift. Who, in the America of the near future, would appear with the same endowment?

Cornelia suddenly shouted down the table to her son: "Tony! I thought archbishops travelled with entourages. Where's yours?"

He answered uncomfortably: "Monsignor Burke and my two secretaries are waiting for me at the Philadelphia House, Mother." He added, "We leave at midnight for New York."

Cornelia winked at her guests. "That remark means he is bored," she said.

They all looked at him with their blank or curious faces. I ought not to have come, thought Tony. But my mother invited me—and I love her, in spite of everything. He began to flush. He saw Miles smiling at him cryptically, as if in sympathy, and all at once Tony lost his dislike of his kinsman. He knew all the stories about Miles, about his debonair and very calm unfaithfulness to his fifty-one-year-old wife Ruth, who sat in such silence far down the table, her golden hair heavily streaked with grey, her head bent timidly, her features wretchedly sharpened

590

with the years and with grief. He knew with all surety that Miles would never relent until he had what he wanted, and suddenly Tony knew that he would get it. There was such strong and masculine youth about Miles, such poised ruthlessness, such quiet, such intelligence.

Tony saw DeWitt watching Miles, with still, dark hatred. DeWitt will lose, inevitably, thought Tony, and he was sorrowful for his brother. He glanced at Fielding Peale, so lanky, so yellow, so ugly. Fielding was enjoying his dinner and ignoring everyone else. Yet there emanated from him a primordial strength.

Norman deWitt spoke to his nephew for the first time: "Tony, I hear that the influence of religion is steadily disappearing in these happy and prosperous times. Can it flourish only during misery?" His eyes were as shining and as interested as a very young man's, and his expression was friendly. Tony regarded him without answering for a moment, and all the ascetic planes of his face sprang out clearly.

He remembered what an old priest had once told him: "Only an inspired saint can dispute with an evil man effectively. Such men argue from materialistic premises, with which all are familiar, and which appear valid. But you would have to argue from spiritual premises, which are strange to most men, invalid to many more, and ridiculous to the so-called intellectual."

Tony said, "Norman, in the first place, I dispute your premises. The times are neither happy nor prosperous. They never were, except for a few. If religion is not "flourishing," as you say, it is because men have ignored or rejected the moral law of God. These occasions, or crises, occur throughout history, and men pay for them in blood and despair."

"What a gloomy prophecy!" cried Cornelia. She lifted her wine glass and screamed with laughter. "To doomsday!" she shouted. "To doomsday!" the others responded, and lifted their glasses, and laughed with jeering politeness. But Tony and Norman stared at each other across the table and neither laughed nor drank. "The moral law of God," Norman repeated softly, and smiled. "What is it?"

Tony said, under cover of the unlistening mirth of the others, "You know, don't you? And the law will always prevail; it always has. Remember that."

Norman did not answer. His smile remained, musing and secret. He moved his glass a little, back and forth. Then suddenly he looked at Tony again, and Tony saw all his powerful detestation and contempt for him as a priest, as an antagonist, as an enemy. He almost whispered, "No. This time you shall not prevail."

Now Norman lifted his glass, bent his head courteously to his nephew, and said, "To doomsday." Only Tony heard him.

Tony went alone to the library after dinner. He closed the door behind him. He stood there with closed eyes, remembering. Here his father, on hot summer days, worked on his papers while the family was briefly in Portersville. Tony could smell the heat, and the immemorial odour of sealing wax, the mowed grass outside, the fragrance of the wind blowing from the gardens. He went to the desk his father had once used and opened it. A box of red wax, mostly used, remained, and Allan's seal. Tony lit the wax, and his youth returned to him.

He did not hear the door open and close, and he started when a man's voice said, "Sir—well, I don't know what I should call you. But I think I'm getting an idea."

Tony swung round and saw the fattish little figure of George Richberg near him. The newspaper magnate was smiling subtly. He held out his hand and Tony took it. "I think," said Mr. Richberg, "that I know all about it. That uncle of yours, Norman deWitt. And your father wanting to buy some newspapers and other publications. We've got a terrible fight coming up—sir. But you know that. What can I say? Good luck, good luck."

"We'll win, Mr. Richberg," said Tony. "You know, we always have."

CHAPTER FORTY-EIGHT

"WE'VE GONE over this, and over this, until I could puke," said Miles Peale rudely both to the president, DeWitt Marshall, and to the assembled board of directors. "I'm not going to apologise to you, Aunt Cornelia, for the verb. I see I don't need to," he added.

"It's one of my favourites," said Cornelia. "But I don't agree with anything you say, Miles, and neither does DeWitt. As for the other gentlemen present, I'm not sure they agree either."

Never Victorious, Never Defeated

The board of directors looked down at the papers on the long table and said nothing. Cornelia, usually so sharp, did not see them exchange glances. But Miles saw. The cloven lines about his lips relaxed a trifle. He ran his delicate hand through his mahogany curls, which were threaded with grey. He examined the papers before him again. Then he looked at DeWitt. My God, he thought, he's only forty-four, two years younger than I am, and he's as out of date as a victoria. What had he just said in that precise and flattened voice of his: "It may be 1934, but I believe that it is always possible to bend men and events to one's will." He had added this *non sequitur*: "I have the promise of Standard Oil to lend us tens of millions if necessary, for the expansion of the freight business."

Miles said, "I don't believe they'll lend any money at all to the Interstate Railroad Company. They're more interested in the New York Central and the Pennsylvania and the Union Pacific."

DeWitt smiled his cold and superior smile and said nothing. He should be wearing a wide black silk cravat and a pearl pin and a Prince Albert coat and striped trousers, thought Miles. He still thinks of the railroad industry as old kings thought of their kingdoms: a thing over which to reign absolutely and to drain absolutely, for the profit of the royal family. And no end to the possibilities of draining. "We owe the public nothing," said DeWitt.

"That attitude, these days, usually ends by the public saying they owe us nothing, either, and taking their business elsewhere," said Miles. He looked sidelong at the board of directors, and all, except Cornelia, nodded almost imperceptibly.

DeWitt shrugged his small shoulders. His hand played with the head of his cane. "We are doing excellently with the freight business," he said, "in spite of—everything. We've modernised the whole thing to the ultimate; we have ten class-one line-hauls operating electrically, in addition, more than any other railroad. Our equipment is perfect."

He looked at Miles with icy hatred. "As for the passenger service, I must remind you that we've even introduced air conditioning on some of our trains."

Miles said, "It still remains that our passenger service, as is the case with other roads too, is terrible. Old, obsolete Pullmans, rattling along like freight cars. Oh, some of them are not bad, but they're in the minority. In the majority, the passengers are still subjected to smoke and cinders in the Pullmans. As for the day-coaches, they belong to the nineties or even the eighties. Speed? Oh, yes, we've done wonders on speed. You keep reminding me of that. Ten per cent of our passenger runs average more than seventy miles an hour; and shake hell out of the people in the process. Speed, you said. Haven't you heard? The airlines. They're already beginning to prophesy great things in the very immediate future: speed without dirt; cheapness; air-freight, too."

"Do you seriously believe that the airlines will ever be a serious competitor?" asked DeWitt, and he laughed his contemptuous little laugh. "Passenger *or* freight?"

"Trucking is already a serious threat to us," said Miles. "So much for the freight business. How many times do I have to go over this with you? We've got to concentrate on passenger service, if we are to survive. We've got to put on light, fast, aluminium or stainless-steel cars as quickly as we can, to compete with the airlines. Other railroaders know this; only we don't."

DeWitt looked at his mother, who was smiling sardonically. He said, "And where, Miles, are we going to get the money? Let us go over these figures again? Before the Crash, in 1929, our stock was selling for $110, and now it is 28⅛. Dividends? What dividends?"

"Look," said Miles wryly, "I have stock in this company, too. I know all about dividends. But we have our own private fortunes, aside from the company. We should use a large part of them to modernise passenger service."

"That's nice," said Cornelia. "As for myself, I wouldn't put a cent of my private cash into the thing. Call me unprogressive, if you will, Miles, but there I stand. DeWitt?"

"That goes without saying," replied her son.

The directors said nothing. Miles sighed. "I tell you, within a very few short years, the airlines will be our serious competitor for passenger service. Our freight is doing well now, in spite of the Depression; but the motor-trucking industry is steadily eating away at it, and the airlines will take their share, too. We not only need to begin to modernise our passenger service; we should begin, at once, to launch a vast programme of public education about the advantages of travelling by rail." He continued, when no one commented: "The days of the autocrats have gone, and with their going there will be real progress.

594

You can't treat the public any longer as just a source of immediate revenue. There is the long-range programme to consider. The people are reading more; they understand more things. They demand service, and they have a right to it, and we can survive only if we cater to this right."

"You talk like one of Roosevelt's brains-trusters," said Cornelia, with a loud burst of laughter in which, curiously, only DeWitt joined. She stuck a cigarette in her mouth and her neighbour lit it. She puffed a cloud of smoke at Miles. "Have you become a New Dealer, child?"

Miles kept his temper. "No," he said evenly. "But I do know that if we go on as we are now going, we'll be run into the ground. Not by the New Dealers; not by anyone but ourselves. We modernise, prepare to meet the threat of the airlines, or we're finished, freight or not." He pointed at DeWitt. "In spite of the freight, we're in frightful difficulties, you know that. Do you think anybody, including Standard Oil, will lend us money on equipment which is growing more and more obsolete all the time? Do you think anyone will be interested in just increasing our private fortunes, so that at the end we'll be stuffed with cash and the road will be a pile of junk? Organisations which lend money look to the future, not to the past."

He put those almost-dainty hands of his on the table and they were the hands of power; most of the directors stared at them, fascinated. "We've got to do as other railroads are already beginning to do: plan, at least. And carry out the plans. Once we have a programme we can borrow, even if we don't use our own money. There it stands. We go on, or we go back."

"You still talk like a New Dealer," said Cornelia. "When we throw out Roosevelt in 1936, business will go on as usual."

"It never has," said Miles.

DeWitt stood up. "I am opposed to all this, and so is my mother. Gentlemen, please excuse us." Cornelia rose, superb in her white silk suit and her "Eugénie" hat sweeping with plumes. She turned the full force of her magnetism on the silent directors, ignoring Miles. "I still think we have a lot of common sense around here. I'm relying on you boys." They stood about her, admiring her: only Miles saw the stiff fixity of their eyes, in spite of the admiration. She swept out with DeWitt, towering over her son like a female colossus. The door banged behind her.

The directors, with the exception of old Mr. Hill, who

was almost eighty, were all vigorous men in their fifties and early sixties. Mr. Hill sat and blinked his rheumy eyes, and said, "Cornelia's a railroader; always was. She was her father's right-hand man; she never made a mistake. I think I'm coming around to her way of thinking; sorry, Miles."

"All right," said Miles courteously. "I wouldn't quarrel with you for all the world, Mr. Hill." The old man blinked at him with fondness. "You're just a boy still, Miles, only forty-six, forty-seven? I'm afraid you'll have to continue to learn from us old-timers for a while longer. Airlines? Fantastic. But there is such a jumpiness in the air these days; no stability, no reason, no planning, no sound caution."

"All right, sir," repeated Miles. He lit a cigarette, and behind the smoke his intensely blue eyes gleamed. Mr. Hill coughed, glanced about, and rose. "I've got to get back to Philadelphia. My train leaves in less than forty-five minutes." He croaked affectionately. "My good train, with all those fine 'obsolete' Pullmans. We've come a long way."

When he had gone, a whole quickening came over the remaining directors. Fielding Peale said, "Well, Miles, what now?"

Miles said. "Very simple. DeWitt will have to go. And the sooner the better. I'm working on the last details now."

The directors sighed with relief. "Old Cornelia might once have had some excellent ideas; at least, that is the history of the company. But now she thinks only of her own money; it's become a fetish to her. That, and her hatred for Roosevelt—in spite of her brother Norman. She mentioned at a dinner recently that the State Department and the Commerce Department can 'handle' Roosevelt all right. I have a feeling that is true, to Roosevelt's undoing, and ours, unless the people wake up in time." The director added: "Too bad, about Cornelia. She was always a symbol to us, of the road. But DeWitt ought to be embalmed along with his ancestors."

"Give me a little time longer," said Miles. He stared at each man in turn, slowly and carefully. "With your help, the embalming can proceed."

Cornelia and DeWitt drove from Philadelphia to Portersville. Cornelia said, "I think we've spiked little Miles's guns for a while. Permanently, I should say. When it comes down to a serious vote, we'll win."

"Of course," said DeWitt. He firmly believed it. "But I'd give several years of my life to get him out."

"We can't," said his practical mother. "So let's not dream. But we can make him impotent. Impotent. A nice old-fashioned word." She laughed raucously. "More ways than one, DeWitt. Even though Ruth was in her middle thirties when they married, she could have given him a child or two."

DeWitt said indifferently, "I understand two other women did. One in New York, one in Paris." His mother was incredulous. DeWitt went on: "We could use that against him, if necessary."

Cornelia laughed again. "DeWitt, you're precious! You sound like an old melodrama. Do you actually think the revelation of Miles's ' inconstancy,' as the dear old word is, would be dangerous to him? Do you think our directors would give a damn? DeWitt, you aren't serious!"

The heat of the summer day was not so evident in Portersville. A cool wind blew from the mountains and river. Another car met the large black limousine in which Cornelia and DeWitt had travelled. "Are you sure you want to go to see the old man?" asked DeWitt as the chauffeur assisted him to the other car. "And what for?"

"Some trifles," said Cornelia airily. "Run on home; I'll be back for dinner. Remember, we leave for Newport to-morrow." She added, leaning from the window of her car: "Tell Rufus not to go out to-night. I want to see him. He's almost twenty, and he'd better begin thinking about the road."

She was driven rapidly along the countryside. She smoked and hummed to herself, but there was a crease in the rough skin between her eyes. Progress, the fool of a Miles had said. Who knew more about progress than herself? "Cornelia is always in the day after to-morrow," her father had declared fondly. She thought of young Rufus now, her grandson, who looked so much like his great-grandfather. He might be a sullen rascal, but he was no fool. He might not have his great-grandfather's charm and power, but he was dogged and intelligent. One day he would be president of the Interstate Railroad Company. He would be graduated from Harvard soon. Then he would enter the company and the whole satisfying cycle would begin again. She, Cornelia, was only sixty-eight. She sat up in the car, not stiffly, but as easily and buoyantly as a very young woman. She had a long way to go.

597

Never Victorious, Never Defeated

Allan was surprised to see her car draw up before his farm-house. He had not seen his wife for nearly two years, for he did much travelling, and they had lost what little touch had remained between them long ago. He went to the door, and then began to walk down the path to greet her. Sixty-eight, Cornelia, with the face of a vital harridan; painted, rude, and full of quenchless strength. Her white plumes blew in the breeze; her stride was not the stride of an old woman. It was graceful and powerful. When she walked towards Allan, lifting a gloved hand in greeting, the hot sun struck into her eyes and they were the wicked and hungry eyes of a young lioness.

She gave Allan her hand, grinned at him, and said, "Surprised? I'm only staying a few minutes. Well, how fine you look! And you seventy-six. You could be taken for sixty at the most, Allan. Your work must agree with you." She tilted her head and her eyes crinkled mockingly. "Lochinvar. Whoever would have thought it, in the old days?"

She linked her arm confidingly in his, as she had done so many decades ago, and they walked together into the ancient house. "Cool in here, thank God," said Cornelia. "It was a furnace in Philadelphia. What? Oh, we just had one of those tiresome board meetings. Nothing important. Not that you are interested any more. Damn these horsehair chairs! This has given me a run in my stocking."

Her ankles were neat and still beautifully turned. She crossed her legs, relaxing, and they were the legs of some glamorous actress. She took a gold cigarette case from her white bag, and before Allan could move she had lit her cigarette briskly with a gold lighter. "How you can live in such a damned old ruin I don't know," she said. "You who loved our house almost more than anything else. Do you remember the first day we met? We talked; I don't remember about what. But all at once you looked up at the house, and there was something in your eyes, and I knew you felt about it as I did, and it was then that I fell in love with you. Ah, me," she said, and smiled at him. "You don't think about the house now, do you?"

"No," said Allan. "I never lived there, I think."

"For God's sake, let's not get cryptic," said Cornelia, waving her cigarette and frowning. "I always hated subtleties. Have you anything to drink in that den you call a kitchen?"

Allan brought her a highball, which she regarded with

satisfaction. He himself had a bottle of beer. Cornelia sipped. "Good Scotch," she commented. She looked about her. "How do you stand this monstrous old place, with only one servant?"

"I'm not here much of the time, Cornelia." His voice was as vibrant as in his youth. "I go everywhere. At a moment's notice. But I'm giving myself a holiday in August. I'm going to visit Alex in England, and meet the nice girl he is to marry. Lady Elizabeth Scott-Hardley."

"I know," said Cornelia. "We met her family last spring. 'Nice girl' is right. A frump. Like most English girls. But her Catholic family has money, and that's a rarity in England since the war. Now, don't begin to tell me that Alex isn't marrying her for her money; he's a sensible boy, and so of course he is. His father married Dolores for hers, didn't he?"

Allan did not reply. He drank his beer slowly. He was in his shirt sleeves and his fingers were stained with ink. His thick white hair glimmered in the cool dusk of the parlour. He was wondering why Cornelia had come to see him. She never did anything without shrewd thought. She was grinning at him again. "How's Laura?" she asked.

"I haven't seen her this time," he answered unsmilingly.

Cornelia drank deeply. "You know," she said after a moment or two, "you would never have married Laura. You didn't really love her at all. She was just the 'cool marble unattainability,' to you. You liked to have her for a point of reference in that poor hot mind of yours, something holy, like a saint. Some little shrine where you could retire when I got too much for you at times. Isn't that so?"

Cornelia nodded. "But Laura really loved you, poor old wreck. She must have given Pat some bad moments. I've heard that she was a lot like her father, my Uncle Steve. I remember him a little. I liked him, though one could never remember just what he looked like ten minutes after seeing him. No character. Laura's just like him. Yes, she really loved you. That's why you find her comforting now. No doubt she thinks you never loved me. But you did."

Allan was silent with shock. He suddenly realised that Cornelia had spoken the truth. Laura had been his 'comforter,' his 'shrine.' But Cornelia had been his love, in spite of all she had been and all she was.

"What romantics men are, no matter how old they get!" said

Cornelia. "I'm sorry if I've just kicked over another one of your delusions, my dear. You look very shaken."

"Let me get you another drink," said Allan. Cornelia watched him leave the room and she laughed to herself, and lit another cigarette. When Allan returned she saw that he had put on a tie and a coat. We're to be formal, now, she thought with amusement. Why was it that men who wished to remove themselves from personalities always put on ties and coats? Did that make them feel less vulnerable? DeWitt was vulnerable. One never saw him other than impeccably and formally dressed. Once Cornelia had asked him, during a dinner, if, like aristocratic Mohammedans, he went to bed with his wife fully clothed and with gloves on his hands.

Cornelia gave him news of the family; Allan listened politely. He had acquired only one gesture of the old; he twiddled his fingers against his thumb, as if rolling pills. "But of course, you aren't much interested in any of your grandchildren, except Alex," said Cornelia. "And that puzzles me; you disliked Dicky so, and could never stand him."

"You are wrong," said Allan. He thought of that morning so long ago when he and Richard, Lord Gibson-Hamilton, had talked in the English dawn. He remembered the young Englishman so often these days; he remembered the morning light on his kind and diffident face and the ringing assurance of his voice at the last, when he had reaffirmed his faith in God and man. "You are wrong," repeated Allan, while Cornelia stared at him in surprise. "I loved him; I still do."

A strange expression ran over Cornelia's face, almost like relief. "A nice young fellow," she commented carelessly, looking at her cigarette. For a few moments they sat in silence, both thinking of Dolores and her husband. "I wish," said Allan, almost inaudibly, "that my brother Mike could have met him. They would have had a lot in common."

"Oh, yes, your brother," said Cornelia, and she smiled almost gently. "He told me so much of you, when DeWitt was ill. Too bad that he remained only a monk. He died some years ago in India, didn't he? What makes men become missionaries, anyway? Some psychiatrist told me that they do that to compensate for some guilt in their youth, or something equally nasty."

A gust of anger began to blow in Allan. He remembered, just in time, that his friend George Richberg had warned him to husband his anger for necessary occasions. He also remembered what his doctor had told him only a month ago. So he swallowed his rage and answered with quietness: "That's stupid. I can't recall a single vice in Mike. But you wouldn't understand. There are men who prefer, above all other things, to serve God. Their love for God is so tremendous that it is the only thing in their lives."

Cornelia laughed. "You know, I never get over your speaking of God so easily and naturally. You've certainly become a different man. . . . God? What God? A remnant of primitive superstition."

Allan did not answer. Cornelia was goading him, as she had always goaded him. He detached himself from her. But he had loved her. Did he still love her? He studied her earnestly, the haggish but fascinating face, the verve, the magnetism, the charm. I suppose I still love Cornelia, he thought. All at once he was compassionate for this robust and hearty and ribald woman who had never had compassion for anyone in her life—except perhaps me, thought Allan. He would forever be grateful to her for this tenderness, which now had left her forever. He would forever pity her because some part of her had been truncated, or had not been included in her personality.

"I've seen Tony three times the past year," said Cornelia. She was becoming restive, and she glanced at the diamond watch on her wrist. "He complains he never seems to catch up with you; when he is in Rome, thinking to meet you, you are in London. When he is in New York, you're off in Los Angeles. And so it goes."

"He calls me at least twice a week," said Allan. "And I write him regularly."

But Cornelia's restless mind was off again. "I can't get over how young you look," she said musingly. "By the way, I understand Miles has become fond of you and that he sometimes visits you out here."

"That's true," said Allan, and his face closed. Cornelia sipped at her drink and her hazel eyes widened and stared fixedly over the edge of her glass. "We're having a little trouble with Miles. He has the most extravagant ideas these days. He takes entirely too much authority on himself, even though he is only executive vice-president. But I—I mean DeWitt—is quite able to control him."

"Are you trying to find out what Miles and I talk about?" asked Allan, smiling a little sadly. "You aren't in the least subtle, Cornelia. I don't intend to tell you, however. You know, I'm not very interested any longer in the road. We discuss it only briefly. We talk of other things."

"I thought so," said Cornelia, and put down her glass. Now her expression was very unpleasant. "And that brings me to why I am here. I am going to divorce you, Allan, for desertion, mental cruelty, and all the other things my lawyers can think of. In fact, I'm leaving for Reno very soon."

"Divorce me?" asked Allan with disbelief. "Are you out of your mind, Cornelia? You are looking towards seventy now, and I'm in my late seventies. What in hell for? A divorce?" He stared at her. "You aren't thinking of marrying again, at your age, are you?"

"Well, that's complimentary, I must say. My doctors tell me my biological age is about forty." But Cornelia laughed. "I can live practically forever, and I intend to. No, I'm divorcing you for quite another reason. You're an embarrassment to me these days. Your association with that New York newspaper Jew, Izzy Richberg—you with your newspapers, and he with his, screaming ' havoc ' all the time. You writing a monthly editorial for his yelling sheets. Really, ' at your age,' to quote your own words, it's ridiculous. A crusader. I never liked Izzy; frankly, I think he's a sensation-monger, and it's dangerous to be a sensation-monger against the present Administration these days."

Allan had flushed a deep crimson. "Very interesting," he said, keeping his voice down. "So it seems that, for the first time in the history of this country it is ' dangerous ' to disagree with the party in power. I don't believe it. I don't think Roosevelt is that kind of man. I don't agree with many of his ideas—but after all he respects the Constitution."

"It *is* dangerous to disagree," said Cornelia. "A sensible person acknowledges the facts. Roosevelt? Who cares about him? There are powerful people behind him who manipulate him."

"I know more about that than you do," said Allan. "I know all about those people. Mr. Roosevelt doesn't. If he ever learns—it might kill him. It is our duty to inform him. To alert the country. I can't talk about this with you, Cornelia, for you'd either sneer at me incredulously, or you'd know exactly what I mean, and still sneer to try to divert me." He paused. He looked

602

at her grimly. "There's your brother Norman. An assistant to the Secretary of Commerce, European Department. He is in charge, as you know, of assigning commercial attachés to European embassies.

"He was appointed to that post on the ground that he is a 'liberal.' But you and I know exactly what he is. There are hundreds of his kind now in government posts in Washington. How did they get there? How did they manage to infiltrate into very important positions, which will have tremendous weight on our domestic and foreign policies? Who are the villains who sought them out, and appointed them? Who are the many unseen men who hate America so much that they want to destroy her? We intend to expose them all."

Cornelia's eyes narrowed on him until they were gleaming yellow slits. She sat in thoughtful silence for a few moments. Then she said, "You don't know what you are doing, or perhaps you do. Everything you say in your papers, everything Izzy says, is laughed at by the American people. But the men you attack aren't laughing; they are out for you. They have ways of destroying men like you and Izzy, and they're prepared to use them."

"Did Norman tell you that?"

Cornelia only smiled. She shrugged, and drank. "Don't talk to me of ' freedom of speech, and the press,' she said. "One of the most powerful newspapers in New York hates you and Izzy; they rarely have an issue without an attack on you and your ideas. Inspired attacks, I suppose you'd call them. I'm a realist. I don't want to be part of your ruination. I don't want to be associated with you, even by our marriage. The road is in danger, by your being my husband, even though you're retired. Remember the last Sunday issue? They had a violent article by Gregory Sanders about you. ' Malefactor of great wealth, who opposes all progressive and liberal reforms. . . . Millionaire reactionary.' And such. That is dangerous for the road. Yes, Norman has warned me. I repeat, I'm a realist. Realists don't try to change history; they accept it."

Allan turned to his wife. "Norman? He warned you, eh? And what does Norman promise you about the road? For he did promise you something."

Cornelia turned her cigarette over and over in her fingers. "Let me make this clear to you, Allan. I don't like the situation any more than you do. I suppose what you've told me is the truth. But once again, I'm a realist, and the road is more to me than anything else in the world, as it always was. If I divorce you—and I admit I don't mind the idea at all—the road won't be mentioned in connection with your activities again. Norman has promised me that. How I hate him! How I always did!" Her face became violent for a moment, and Allan moved towards her almost involuntarily, his hand extended. But she did not take it; she shook her head, rejecting. "I'm sorry I was emotional for a moment or two. We have to accept the fact that hundreds of Normans are now in power in Washington. We dare not antagonise them, whether we are railroad magnates or shop-keepers. They are determined to silence all their enemies. I don't want to be pilloried as one of them, by being married to you."

"And this is America," said Allan softly.

"This is a new America," said Cornelia. "It's the America you prophesied was coming, centuries ago, it seems. You were right. So, being a realist, I want to adjust to it. If I adjust to it, and the others like me, we'll be spared in the 'coming New Order,' as Norman calls it."

Allan sat down and just looked at her, and again he was compassionate. "America means nothing to you, then?"

"Not particularly, my dear. But my money does."

Allan sighed. "I won't oppose your divorce, Cornelia."

"That's good. I knew you wouldn't. You couldn't have, anyway. You deserted me. But I thought I owed it to you, considering the wonderful young years we had together, to tell you first."

Now Cornelia's face gentled. She put out her hand and laid it on his knee. "My dear, my dear," she said, and was silent a little. "Allan, it isn't too late to stop your work. There is your Foundation for the Preservation of the Constitution. You're pouring tens of thousands of dollars into it regularly, and you've got a number of powerful men like yourself to contribute to it. You cover the country with pamphlets and 'libertarian' books. You issue leaflets and even a newspaper in its name. Norman hates that Foundation more than anything else you do."

"I'm glad," said Allan, and he lifted his head triumphantly. "I couldn't have had better news. One of these days Norman will face the Senate, and his accusers will be there, and with him will be hundreds of men like him. One of these days the people will know all about him and his kind—through the work of men like me and George Richberg; through the work of our Foundation. Through the scores of fine speakers we send out all over the country. The Normans can't silence us. And one of these days they'll stand before the nation they betrayed, and answer to it."

He smiled at Cornelia. "In a way, I'm glad you are getting a divorce. I won't have to leave you anything then. I have already made a will leaving the greater part of my money to the Foundation, and my newspapers. The family is well provided for, with its own fortunes."

"And we intend to keep them." The dark scarlet thread of Cornelia's lips twisted. "With Norman's undercover help."

She stood up, and Allan rose with her. She contemplated him quietly, and her hazel eyes were very still. Then she put her arms about his neck and kissed him on the lips, very simply. He held her to him. He was not sure, but he thought that a little moisture touched his cheek. "Good-bye, my dear," said Cornelia. "Good-bye—Allan."

Allan worked far into the night on a pamphlet he was writing, on an editorial he was doing for one of George Richberg's most influential newspapers and on an editorial he was finishing for one of his own. The yellow oil-lamps glimmered; the face of the round white moon poured through the windows; great yellow moths and myriads of other insects crawled and flew against the screens. Night birds cried to the sky; trees murmured endlessly in an ancient language. Allan wrote on. Occasionally he reached with an absentminded gesture to a bottle of pills and swallowed a tablet, especially when the familiar cramping pain in his chest heightened with his growing weariness. Once or twice he thought: This damned old body of mine! I'm a young man in spirit, and I could work forever. But this shrivelling flesh gets in my way.

At ten o'clock George Richberg called him from New York. It was good to Allan to hear that rich and determined voice, which had such fortitude, such courage, behind it. "When do we get that editorial?" he demanded in his affectionately dictatorial way. "Well, I didn't call you about that. I was just anxious about you. Why don't you join me for a short vacation at my home in Maine? You haven't the time? What damned nonsense. Here I am, with a bad heart, and I work like three dogs, but I take a holiday at times. And I'm younger than you are." There was an undertone of anxiety in his voice. "Look, we can't have you dying on us, or something, Allan. I promised Tony. . . ."

Allan frowned. "You promised Tony? He's an old woman. I feel in perfect health, George." He told his friend of his whole conversation with Cornelia that day. George listened without interrupting. Then he said, "Poor old girl. And think, too, of the poor old boys like her, in just the same position. They don't know that they're the first on the lists of liquidation—if the devils once really control the country. Hope you aren't worrying too much about the divorce. Take things easy, won't you?"

When Allan hung up he had a satisfied feeling. His loneliness had gone. The night was filled with the presences of his friends, everywhere, men who were working as he was working. Courage, courage, he said to them. Don't despair. Hell never prevails. But let us never relax, not even for a moment. The enemy does not relax; his mind is always cool and clear and focused on the deadly plans he has for the world. He does not drink, for he wishes to be conscious at every moment of all that is said about him, and he wishes to see all that can be seen. If you must drink for pleasure and for social gaiety, be certain of your company, for your enemy has a thousand ears and a thousand eyes; he is ubiquitous. He is a distinct personality, stern, rigid, cruel, and coldly intellectual and hating; he was born as he is; he can never change himself. He is as old as death, as old as the world, but each generation sees him born anew. Watch for him, but have courage. You are stronger than he, for God is with you.

Allan picked up his pen again and resumed his rapid writing. In his editorial for George Richberg's largest newspaper he wrote: "I voted for Franklin Delano Roosevelt because he declared that any political power which is entrenched too long becomes a danger to free institutions. I agree with him. A law should be passed which prohibits any one man serving more than two terms as president. It is not likely that the tradition laid down by George Washington will ever be violated, but I fear such an attempt will be made. A third term is unthinkable to the American people at this time; they might not find it unthinkable in the future. Therein lies the danger. A president under such conditions is no longer the leader of his party; he is its slave.

Never Victorious, Never Defeated

An opportunity is also presented to certain elements in his party to press its more sinister designs—and there are sinister designs among sinister men in any political party. Long power assists them in carrying these designs to their ultimate conclusion. . . ."

The moon flooded the room, but somewhere in the distance there was a sound of faint thunder, as if a giant had turned over on the earth.

Allan picked up a small pamphlet written by Norman deWitt six months before, in which Norman expressed his cold aversion for the President. " While it is uncivilised for one to deride a man for any physical handicap, it is the opinion of many that Franklin Delano Roosevelt is a symbol, in his person, of the distorted and unhealthy deformity of capitalism."

Yet, thought Allan, he is there, in a high and powerful position in the government. Who is so strong in this government to keep him where he is? He thought of the evil men sleeplessly working behind the façade of constitutional government, men whose names were not yet known, except to a few like himself. He thought of their minions who were already teaching corruption in the secular colleges in every corner of the nation, who were already seizing control of the public means of communication through radio, books, newspaper columns, and moving pictures, who were moving silently into the public schools of America, armed with their monstrous philosophy of hatred, envy, and murder.

Their creatures had written of the first Roosevelt cabinet: "The new Wall Street hunger and war cabinet. . . . Yes, the New Deal may prove to be fascism. The smiling India-rubber liberal in the White House is destined to destroy all remaining American liberals."

But a change in propaganda was subtly taking place now. It had begun with the recognition of Russia by the United States; it had gathered force with the rise of Hitler. The hidden and evil men—so smilingly and disastrously belittled by the President, in all sincerity—were preparing to use him and his party for their own awful ends. Why can't he see? thought Allan desperately. How can he believe they are so small a group, so impotent a one? Their name is legion. There is no spot in all the world which does not bear the lesions of their disease.

There was a sudden crimson flare at the windows and a roar from the sky. The trees, which had been whispering together, now threshed wildly, like a sea struck by a cyclone, and from the alarmed earth rose a strong and pungent breath like an exhalation of fear. Allan went to the windows; the mountains started at him out of blackness in a new flare of lightning, then disappeared in a crash of thunder. Rain, mingled with hail, flew down on the land, and Allan could hear the deep groaning of the trees.

The telephone rang. Another voice came to him, that of the young and energetic Milton Richberg, one of George Richberg's three nephews, who worked with him on his newspapers. "I knew you'd still be up," said Milton accusingly. Then he chuckled affectionately. "I've been trying to reach you since six, but all the circuits were busy."

"How's it in Washington, Milton?" asked Allan. "There's a storm here."

"Oh, I suppose you shouldn't be using the phone, then. But I wanted to tell you something. I talked with Martin Dies to-day." He paused. "I think it's worse than we know. It's appalling. They're moving in more every day; no one's challenging them. They're taking over. That's what Martin told me. Got a pencil? Here are some of the names."

Allan incredulously wrote them down, one by one, and stared at them. Impossible. "Doesn't he—the President—have the slightest idea?"

"Martin's not exactly a silent man, Mr. Marshall."

There was a silence. Then Milton went on: "Incidentally, the President is a very sick man. I have a feeling, myself, that when he does know all about it, it will strike him down as if he'd been shot. In the meantime—they'll have moved in completely. It'll be too late."

"No," said Allan, swallowing a sudden burning sickness in himself. "History is full of epidemics which killed a half or two-thirds of a whole continent. But man survived, and the epidemics were conquered, finally. This is a disease of the mind. . . ."

"And millions might die because of it," said the younger man quietly.

"No doubt. But it is their fault because they took no measures in time to preserve themselves from infection."

Milton sighed. "Martin's suffering from prematurity. The American people aren't yet ready to believe what his committee is trying to tell them. After all, their enemies talk so nobly about ' human rights ' and ' social justice.' Aren't they the clever ones ? They use the terminology of virtue to destroy virtue."

"They always did, from the first page of recorded history. What shall I do with these names?"

"They're just for your information. We have three writers now, who are doing books on them. God knows if any publisher will publish the books; if not now, then later, perhaps." He sighed again. "Martin's going to be martyred. But someone else will come up, in the future, in Washington. He's bound to; and he won't be martyred, for the people will be ready for the truth."

"After Armageddon," said Allan.

"After Armageddon," repeated Milton Richberg. He added: "The only thing which worries me is that when the people do know, and go after the murderers, thousands of innocent people will suffer, too. Peoples never do things by halves, or with any temperance, after they're enraged."

Allan was alone again. The storm was all about him now in a welter of fire and noise. It seemed symbolic to him. The room was stuffy, though the windows were still open. Allan found it hard to breathe. All at once he was overwhelmed with a profound physical weakness and inertia. He lay back in his chair and closed his eyes. He began, without volition, to think of his wife Cornelia.

He had loved Cornelia. There was no reason in it, for he knew what she was. Strange thoughts came to him. Perhaps if it had not been for Cornelia, Dolores, his daughter, would be alive. Some way, that marriage had happened; he had had nothing to do with it. If it had not been for Cornelia . . . . His mind began to wander, but he did not sleep. He could feel pain somewhere, devastating pain such as one feels under a partial anaesthetic. My pills, he thought. The storm had retreated from him and he no longer heard it. A light was pulling at his eyes, and it took all his strength to open them. The storm rushed in on him again; the lamplight stung his eyeballs. He tried to reach for his pills, but there was no power in his arm. Slowly, very slowly, he was able to pull the telephone to him. He called his son Tony in St. Louis, and then sat there, bent over his desk, overcome with agony.

While he waited, he could hear a rough and rapid sound in the room; he did not know it was his own breath. He listened to it with a vague curiosity. Then Tony's voice, sharp and disturbed, came to him, and Allan smiled. He must not alarm his son. He gathered what force he had left and tried to make his own voice cheerful and assured. "Tony? I know this is an ungodly hour to call you, but I wanted to hear you. No, nothing in particular. Tony."

"Yes, Dad?" The voice in the receiver was urgent and full of fear.

"Nothing, Tony. I only wanted to hear you."

"I can hear you breathing. Dad, are you ill?"

Allan was silent. All at once the pain was gone and there was a lightness in him, almost a gaiety. "No, no! There's nothing wrong with me, Tony, I just wanted to talk with you a moment. It's good to know you're there. That noise? There's a storm, but it's subsiding now. Tony, you rascal, my boy, Tony. . . ."

Tony controlled himself and spoke evenly. "Old Betsy's there, isn't she? Call her, Dad. Take your medicine. Go to bed. Don't be alone. Promise me."

Allan looked about the room, and all at once it was filled with joy and comfort. "I'm not alone," he said. "There's something, someone—I can't tell you. Good night, Tony. God bless you, my boy."

He hung up very gently. The sense of lightness and gaiety filled him so completely that he almost cried with the delight of it. He leaned back in his chair and fell asleep. But Archbishop Rufus Anthony Marshall did not sleep. He was calling long distance. "Give me the Reverend Joseph Hogan of the Church of the Holy Family, in Portersville, Pennsylvania. At once, at once; this is an emergency." While he waited, the archbishop was no longer an ascetic and quiet man. Tears began to run down his cheeks. His lips moved; he prayed. Even after he had completed his call, and summoned his secretary out of bed to prepare him for a journey, he did not think of his mother. The secretary was at the telephone, making reservations on the next train.

Allan dreamed. He was a young man again, and a hoe was in his hand and beside him stood a young girl with fierce golden eyes and hair like a fire. They were looking up at a house far above them on terraces. Flowers clustered all about them. The girl said, "I live there." She turned to him, and smiled, and it was a sad smile. "You think you'll live there. But you never will. Never."

"No," said Allan thoughtfully, "I never will. At one time I

thought it was what I wanted; all I could ever want. But now I know it isn't what I wanted at all." He moved his hoe along the ranks of the flowers. They were so large and fragrant. "It took me a long time to see them," he said. "It took me almost a lifetime." He turned to the girl, but she had gone. He was sorrowful at this, and shook his head.

The hillside darkened, and all at once the house far up its flank burst into flame. The sky blackened behind it. The whole world was full of thunder and red flashes. Near at hand someone moaned, over and over, but Allan could not see him. "There's a storm," said Allan in his dream, "A frightful storm. Millions will die in it. I have done all I could. Perhaps it wasn't enough. But it was all I could do." He tried to see in the red-lighted darkness of utter chaos. Then he was shouting, "Don't give up! Fight, fight! We'll win. We always have!"

Allan opened his eyes. The sound of the storm was still in his ears, but it was not over the living land. He heard trees dripping; pale lightning occasionally lighted up windows turning grey with dawn. The room was swept with sweet cool winds. Birds were calling and leaves rustling. Allan shook his head dazedly. He could reach for his pills now, but it was very hard to swallow. Something like an iron collar was about his throat. He pushed himself to his feet, and it took much of his strength. I worked and slept the night through, he thought. He did not remember calling his son. I'm getting too old, he thought angrily. A man reaches wisdom when it's too late to give it to others. He had a sudden urge to go into his garden in this dawn light and sweetness. But he found that he had to lean on furniture as he left the room and went into the dusky hallway. "I must go out," he said aloud. Now some strength returned to him; he could feel his heart beating weakly but steadily. He pushed open the outer back door and let himself carefully over the sill; he could not remember that it was so high. It was like stepping down over a wall. Then he was in the garden.

He looked to the east. Black storm clouds were flying westward, tinged with purple. They boiled over him like smoke from giant cauldrons. Below them streamed a reddish-purple river of light, swelling into brightness, and below this river was a pool of gold, seeming to palpitate on the top of a mountain. It became more radiant each moment. The mountains stepped nearer, black and silent, but sharper. All the trees about Allan rippled with fragrant moisture, like fountains. The willows swung their long green tresses in the morning wind; birds ran about over the grass, they whistled on brown branches. But all the flowers were still white, their colour not yet restored. A long blue shadow flew over the earth, melting into a heliotrope mist under the trees.

"The morning," said Allan, "is always new. It is the first day of earth's creation." He walked with infinite slowness along the banks of flowers. He reached the rose bed; from it rose a cloud of perfume; here and there a rose was turning yellow or pink. Tenderly, he touched a few buds. Birds hopped near him, watching him. Men so seldom see the morning, he thought. The air rang with gentle crystal; the grass sent up its incense. A rabbit scuttled along a gravel path and stopped to twitch its nose and stare at the old man. Allan turned his head to smile at him, and then stopped. He was not alone.

Two men and two women were standing at a little distance from him, and he strained to see them, for the mist was rising about them in brightening clouds. He felt no wonder; the joy he had experienced earlier returned to him. It was his father, there, and his mother, and his brother Michael, and Dolores. The dawn became concentrated in them. "But of course, you never died," said Allan. "None of you ever died, my dears, my darlings. It was just a terrible dream."

"Just a terrible dream," said Michael, and he smiled. Now they were all smiling. Allan moved towards them. "Wait," said his brother. "Someone is coming down the path."

The weight of clay was on Allan's body, but he turned obediently. An old priest was hurrying towards him, and Allan saw how he was dressed and what he carried in his hand reverently. With incredible effort he began to walk towards the priest. But his strength dropped from him. He fell to his knees and lifted up his hands. "Bless me, Father," he whispered. The old priest knelt beside him, there on the gravelled path.

CHAPTER FORTY-NINE

Tony saw that his mother, in spite of her jauntiness, looked pale and sunken. Her voice might be practical and rousing, but sometimes she paused to stare emptily into the distance.

"We kept it out of the papers, that he died right here on a garden path, like some tramp," she said. "The old priest who mysteriously had appeared, and his old servant, Betsy, didn't have the strength to carry him into the house, after he died. So they had to wait for help. Imagine, Allan Marshall, former railroad magnate, dying like that!"

"Does it matter where a man dies?" asked Tony absently. His mother glanced at him with rare solicitude.

"Well, after all, he was an old man," she said. "It was to be expected, I suppose. But I'd just seen him; he looked in the best of health." She turned her eyes from her son, and he noticed they were furtive. However, he was not interested in that final conversation between his parents. His own grief was too great.

"Don't look as if the end of the world's come," said Cornelia. "It's strange in a way. You—officiated, is that the word?—at his funeral, and everyone came. You were magnificent, and the choir sounded like a host of angels. Touching—comforting...."

Tony gave all his attention to his mother. "Yes, dear," he said gently. "All the services of the Church are so. I have been praying you would come to the conclusion——"

Cornelia gave an echo of her usual robust laughter. "Tony! You know me better than that. Don't be ridiculous. I never believed in anything but myself all my life, though once I believed in your father. That was when he was young. He had such power, such force." She drew in a quick breath, then grinned at her son. "I was proud of you. Why aren't you a cardinal yet?"

Tony said, "Alex has asked me to come to England in August to perform his marriage. I hope I can do it." He added, "Did Dad leave no written word, or anything?"

"No. Only some letters to that Izzy Richberg; editorials, or something. We mailed them, and then his desk and his house were all cleaned out, before you arrived. Did you ever hear of such an outrageous will, leaving almost all his money to his newspapers and Foundation, and practically nothing to me and his sons? If—if I didn't have some regard left for your father, I think I should contest that will." But Tony knew that she had never had any such intention. Her eyes had a dim film over them, and her conversation was disjointed. Was it possible that she still loved his father?

"Have you seen old Laura?" she asked, and now her face hardened into viciousness.

"Mother," said Tony earnestly, "you've always hated Aunt Laura. You had no reason to hate her. There was never—anything—such as you may have suspected, between them."

"Oh, I know your father never really cared about her," said Cornelia, holding out her cigarette for her son to light. They were sitting in her sitting-room in the house in Portersville. "But she thought so. She'd look at him with sheep's eyes; she made poor old Pat wretched. Well, how is she? I thought she looked very complacent in church, as if she'd won something."

"She won peace, a long time ago," said Tony. "She isn't lonely, though she doesn't see her children and grandchildren often. There are some people who never know peace among others; Aunt Laura is one of them. She showed me her garden, the day after the funeral, and she talked a little of Dad and said he had won a great victory."

Cornelia laughed now in open raucousness. "What victory? He gave up everything. If he hadn't worked so hard over his damned Foundation and newspapers, he might be alive now." She stared suddenly at her son. "How did you know he was dying? You arrived late last night. I've been wondering."

"He called me; it was about three in the morning. I knew there was something wrong, though he sounded cheerful. It was as if he had called to say good-bye. I seemed to know."

Cornelia studied him shrewdly. "I see. And that is how the old priest got there. You must have asked him. Such a doddering old man. Did you actually think it was of such importance to your father to have a priest before he died? Don't look so stern. I suppose it was a comfort to him. Dear me, how I hate funerals."

And then she was crying, covering her face with her ringed and mottled hands. "I can't remember him as he was, lying in his casket in the church. I can't remember him as he was these last forty years." She was stammering almost piteously. "He was a stranger to me. I can remember him only as I knew him before we were married, and a few years after that. He was such a man! My father adored him. And then something happened to him; he began to drink and get morose and made our lives wretched. I sometimes think something happened to his mind. I've talked with psychiatrists. They agree with me. His childhood, perhaps."

"Yes," said Tony. "His childhood."

He went to his brother DeWitt, who was sitting alone on an upper terrace. DeWitt watched him come, in silence, his black eyes like bits of jet. Tony sat down near him in a chair. Then DeWitt said, "We could have used the money he spent on that damned trash of his. I can't forgive him."

Tony said, "You never forgave him from the time you were a very little boy, DeWitt. You never forgave him because you could never be like him."

DeWitt shrugged. "That's true, though I'd never admit it to anyone else. I was a ' real railroader,' he once told me. That was a lie. I never was, in the sense he meant, the old sense. The road is something to run for profits. Never mind; you're a clergyman, and you wouldn't understand. You wouldn't even know the market quotations on our stock."

"How many millions have you, DeWitt?" asked Tony quietly. "Twenty? Isn't that enough?"

DeWitt smoked nervously. "Not for me. I once had over forty. It's dwindled."

"No doubt you now think of yourself as a very poor man." Tony could not help smiling a little. "However, there's Mother's money, which will come to you."

"She'll live forever," said DeWitt gloomily. "But she'll leave some to you, and Alex. I don't mind you, but I do mind him. His father got plenty from the family."

"His mother was our sister," Tony reminded him. But DeWitt merely shrugged again. "I've left you a quarter of my own money," he said grudgingly. "I suppose you'll build churches or schools or hospitals, with it, or something equally valueless." He eyed his brother, and the wizened face changed and the black eyes became coldly violent. "Why did you have to go into this thing? Don't you know I'm all alone, that I have nobody? I never had anyone but you. Looking back, I think I never cared

615

about anybody but you, in spite of your priggishness and all that religion. I'm all alone, I tell you! There's nothing——"

"I pray for you constantly," said Tony, and braced himself for ridicule or contempt. But De Witt was staring at him strangely. "Do you?" he asked, without any intonation. "Do you know I need it? Oh, hell. What is there to pray to? Anyway, it's some comfort to know that you haven't forgotten me."

He twisted his dark little hands together, as if wringing them. "Why did you have to go away? I wouldn't have wanted you in the road; I hoped all the time you'd never come in. But at least I knew that you—that you . . ."

"What?" asked Tony, and he reached out to the wringing hands and quieted them.

DeWitt looked down at the strong white fingers over his own. "That someone cared a damn for me. I don't know why you ever did, frankly. Never mind; don't get sentimental and talk of brotherly love. I was a pig of a kid. I suppose I'm a pig of a man. But when you are here, it's like a peace to me. And that's very funny, for you were not, and are not, a peaceable kind of fellow. Did you know that Miles is after the road? He won't get it, of course, for we have our fifty-one per cent. But I feel exposed. I think I always did. Did you know he often went out to see the old man? We never found out what their discussions were. Miles has gone ' modern.' He wants to bankrupt the road. Ma laughs, but I have a feeling the directors are with him, all except herself. I, too, have my intuitions. What can he do? Nothing. Did you see him at the funeral? Such a damnable hypocrite. He looked at the old man as if Dad were his own father, and we all know what the Peales thought of us. Do you think the old man gave him hints as to what to do to ruin us?"

"No," said Tony. The fingers under his hand were tense. "I think it was something else. It might have been about Dad's Foundation and newspapers. Some of the editorials had a certain ring which was not Dad's style at all. Measured. Reasonable. The duty of big business to the public. The duty of big business to fight socialism in America in order to preserve not only big business but competition among big business; the survival of small businesses, and the liberty of all the people. I've heard Miles talk many times on these subjects. I'm sure he writes those editorials."

"I don't know what he's after, if he does write those things," said DeWitt. "Washington would like to see the Foundation smashed, and those newspapers and magazines. We can't afford to be at loggerheads with Washington these days."

"You can't afford not to," said Tony. He stood up. DeWitt, like a child, caught at his arm. "Are you going?" His thin voice was suddenly desolate. "My God, my God, I tell you I can't stand this loneliness! Never mind. If you have to leave, I suppose you have to."

He watched his brother mounting the stone steps to the house again, and his face contorted like the face of a suffering gnome.

CHAPTER FIFTY

THIS IS the day, thought Miles Peale, as he stood at his window and looked out at the black river with its banks heaped with snow. The sky was white and still; the voice of the river filled Miles's bedroom as it struggled with the floes of ice upon it. It would soon be spring. Even though it was February, there was a feeling in the air, a sense of powerful thrust and stir. The old house about Miles creaked a little in all its timbers and walls. He liked Jim Purcell's house, in spite of the draughty halls and big sombre rooms. Some of the family joked with him about it; he was so "modern" yet he did not mind living in a house "built in the dark ages." He never bothered to explain to them that there was no real cleavage between the past and the present.

He lived sparely. He did not have a valet for himself. But his great old room was comfortable, and he was very neat and fastidious. The three servants in the house were enough. He heard some crackling movement in the corridor outside; one of his wife's nurses going briskly about her business. He frowned. He liked old Ruth, for she had never troubled him, and he had found her adoration pleasant. He wished she would die; she had been bedridden for years with arthritis, and he knew how she suffered in spite of her constant gentle smiles and absence of complaints. It hurt something in him to see her on her pillows, so wasted, the once-golden hair white and thin, the deep lines of torment on the sweet face. Perhaps that new drug they were prophesying for the future would help her. If not, it would be better for her to die. She was very tired. Miles carefully adjusted his tie. He supposed he had caused her some pain, himself. Everyone thought her without intelligence, a frail shadow who could experience no real emotion, and who never suspected anything. They were wrong. Thinking about her now, he came to the conclusion that not only did he like her but that he had considerable fondness for her. She loved him; he did not believe that anyone else ever had, even his mother, dead these past three months.

A photograph of his mother stood on his dresser and he looked at it closely, the serene and quiet old face, the cloud of white hair, the deep and thoughtful eyes. Poor old girl, he thought. What a life she had. She had slipped away from the living earth like a shadow, and no one remembered her now except himself. He had no photograph or painting of his father, Patrick. He had never wanted one. He smiled at his mother's image, and said aloud, "This isn't what you'd want, is it? But you see, in a way it is justice."

He went in to see Ruth. Her room was rosy with firelight, and she was supported by pillows. A newspaper lay on her twisted knees, and her distorted hands rested on the sheets. She had always tried to read books and periodicals in order to interest her husband and talk brightly to him. Now, as he entered, her face became radiant, though he guessed that she had spent a sleepless night of agony. When she smiled, as now, she seemed less than her fifty-seven years, in spite of her disease. It was almost the face of a young girl, shy and adoring. Miles bent and kissed her forehead, and the crippled hands raised themselves painfully to touch him.

"How are you, dear?" he asked.

"Quite well. Hardly any pain now, Miles." She beamed at her nurse. "I slept quite well, didn't I, Sally?"

"That's what the report says," replied the nurse cheerily, with a meaning look for Miles. He was such a handsome man, Mr. Peale, with all those auburn-grey curls and his very blue eyes and his courteous ways. He moved so surely and with such youth, though the nurse guessed that he must be almost forty-eight. He had no paunch like other men his age; his figure might be that of a man of thirty, and his clothing was exquisite. Hardly a line on his face, either, and such a charming smile. Pity, thought the nurse, that he's so short.

Miles rested his hand on the blue brocade of the bed's headboard. "I might not be back until late, Ruth," he said. "I'm going to Philadelphia this morning. Business of the board, you know."

"Always business," she replied. She was so proud of him. What did it matter if he had had his women in the past, and even now? It was nothing to her. He was her husband, and she loved him. Humbly, she considered all those faceless women in all those strange beds. What did it matter? She was still grateful to God that Miles had married her; if she had had to pay some price, it was only just. Once she had felt anguish, but when she had finally come to know that he would never leave her for any of the others, she had regained some contentment. It was still a miracle to her that she was Miles's wife.

"I've been reading so many serious things," she said, feeling his restlessness and wanting to hold him a few moments longer. "This is one of poor Allan's newspapers. Such sinister matters. Hitler—and something they call a purge because some people tried to kill him last year—1934. This editorial says that Hitler will declare war against the whole world in a few years. But in another part of the paper, Mr. Roosevelt is just amused. He says Hitler wouldn't dare."

"Don't worry yourself," said Miles. "America has outlived both her domestic and foreign enemies before. Perhaps Roosevelt is just trying to reassure the American people. Presidents do that, you know."

"They shouldn't," said Ruth with gentle vehemence. "We aren't children. We should know the truth at all times." She touched the paper again. "Allan's papers always tell us the truth, though some politicians call them sensation-mongers."

"That's what they called Jeremiah, too," smiled Miles. "And I believe there was also something to that effect about Christ."

She touched his sleeve again longingly, wistfully, and he kissed her with that old gratitude for her affection. "Ruth, dear," he said, "you are perhaps going to read, or hear, something about me soon, and it may cause you some anxiety. But you must trust me."

Now the soft blue eyes widened and became strangely wise. "I always trusted you, Miles," she said quietly. She smiled. "Even when I had no reason to."

No, she is no fool, he thought. He waved his hand to her

gallantly at the door and went down to his car, which he always drove himself. He drove to Fielding's house, which had once belonged to Cynthia's grandfather, Old Brownell. A very handsome Georgian house, of which Miles approved. Fielding was waiting at the door and got into his brother's car with a dexterous fold of his legs. He let out a gusty breath. "Well," he said, "this is our day, isn't it? Think we can manage it?"

"No doubt," said Miles. Fielding peered at him with his tan-coloured eyes and began to hum. "By the way," said Fielding, with one of his loud laughs, "I've just heard a legend about you. It seems there was an old fellow who worked on the road for centuries and who died a long time ago. Old Billie, they called him. The men say that Old Billie insisted that you were 'Mr. Aaron,' our great-grandfather, in person. He used to call you that, they said. So I looked it up in that book, *The History of American Roads*, which was written about us by John Butzer."

"A foolish, lyrical piece of junk," said Miles with a rare irritability. "He made our road out to be the benefactor of the human race, or something. Either big business is an all-wise and noble benefactor, operating in behalf of humanity and with no eye for honest profits, or it is ' a devourer of the labour of honest men and an exploiter of the public.' I don't like either version. Why is it right for a working man to make as much money as he can, and wrong for a big industrial organisation to do the same thing? Socrates mentioned something like that. ' It has become dangerous for a man to let it be known that he is rich.' People don't change. Some might find it comforting; I find it pretty terrible. It's about time we got out of the trees, in our thinking."

His small and competent hands smoothly guided the big car over the icy streets. Other cars might slide and churn, but not Miles's. Fielding studied his china-clear profile with his usual mingling of envy and admiration. "Well, anyway, I sat a long time over our great-grandpappy's photograph, and damned if I don't admit that you do look like him, in spite of the goat's beard he had. Same forehead, hair, nose, and general appearance. You may call that book a ' piece of junk,' but did you know that old Aaron had his trouble with organisations very peculiarly like the socialists these days? That was just after thousands of Germans came here to escape Bismarck's socialism, and spies mingled with them, bringing the idea in with them. Just a flurry, though; the free Germans handled them, themselves, with a few clubs and things."

"It always ends that way," said Miles. "It always comes back to the people in the end; governments that don't please the people, no matter how powerfully entrenched they are, usually get kicked out."

The Pullman they boarded for Philadelphia was, as usual, creaking, obsolete, full of cinders, and chilly. Miles prowled about the car, the trainmen watching him apprehensively. Damned old arks, thought Miles. He talked with some of his fellow-travellers, who were strange to him, travellers who had transferred to this train from other points. "What do you think of these rattling boxcars?" he would ask. They were eager to answer him. They spoke of the very few aluminium or stainless-steel trains in which they had journeyed before, belonging to other lines. Warm, fullwindows, modern, comfortable. Miles nodded. "But this line thinks only of money," a man grumbled. "I wouldn't travel on it if there was any other way. One of these days the airlines will have what we want."

Miles trusted no one, with the possible exception of his wife, to whom he told nothing of importance. He did not trust even Fielding; avarice made men untrustworthy, even when they were allies, and especially if they were brothers. Fielding had the Brownell money, and he was willing to throw its powerful weight on the side of Miles, as he was about to do to-day. But still, no one was ever hanged for simply holding his tongue. Let not even your heart be fully aware of what your brain is doing, thought Miles, as he sat beside his brother. He began to smile. Fielding saw that smile and knew that Miles had "something up his sleeve." It sometimes irked him that Miles never told him "everything," but he admired Miles too much to be overly annoyed. What a mind he had! And what had he been doing in Washington a week ago? No one but Fielding knew of that visit.

Miles was thinking of it. He was thinking of his long years of pretence with the dangerous Norman deWitt, the smiling, shining-eyed, scholarly Norman, the mad, cool-nerved, and ruthless Norman. The man who hated and bowed and talked of nothing in company, but who had his secret places, and his secret comrades in the hidden places of Washington. Jon would have been easier to handle, had he lived, thought Miles, for Jon was not really a madman. But then, one can handle madmen, if one is willing to learn. It was irksome and sometimes boring, and often nauseating, and I frequently wanted to slam his face in, but I was willing to be patient, to lie, to agree, to smile significantly. For something very important; for a part of the world, perhaps. Frankly, if a nation wants slavery, I suppose it is its own business. But I don't want to be enslaved along with it, in its idiot's ecstasy of prostration before murderers. So, finally, I must fight for America in the years ahead.

Miles crossed his elegant legs and concentrated on his last visit to Norman deWitt, who held such a powerful position in the Department of Commerce. Norman liked him; there was no unhealthiness in his liking, as there had been in the case of his brother Jon. Miles was "progressive." He was thoughtful, serious, intellectual; he was charming, and he discussed rather than argued. He had also expressed his amused disdain of Allan Marshall, and had even permitted himself to become slightly heated on the subject, to Norman's satisfaction.

An egotist, thought Miles, is always under the impression that he is much cleverer than anyone else. The way to manipulate a powerful egotist is to let him believe that. He remembered how, when he had been still only a youth, he had felt the evil current beginning to flow in America. He had set himself out to discover those who had unfurled their sails upon it. Some enormous intuition in himself, even in those days, had informed him that some day it would be very valuable to know about these men. He had not been wrong.

It had not been too hard to gain Norman's trust. A show of open admiration and serious listening, at first, had been enough. Later had come Miles's pretended reluctant conviction that Norman was right. He had sought Norman's advice; if it all came to nothing, as Miles intended, Miles expressed his anger and it was Norman who had consoled him with mysterious promises for the future. It was Norman who spoke to the powerful, secret men about him, and convinced them of Miles's true convictions. "He's been my apt pupil for more years than I like to remember," Norman had said. "We can't have too many like him in big business—when the time comes." They were pleased that they had so many allies in the mighty industries, especially women who had inherited position and fortunes from their more intelligent husbands, idle women who could never get enough publicity in the newspapers for all their wealth.

Miles had gone, a week ago, to Norman's very modest apartment in Washington. Norman might be a multimillionaire of fantastic assets, but he lived modestly. That was the way with those people, Miles often thought. Until they can strike, they live in a Spartan manner. It is a part of their stage property. Norman did not even have a servant; he ate in obscure restaurants with obscure men who would not be exposed until twenty years later for what they were. His furnishings were old and ramshackle and out of date. Miles said to him, as he always did when entering that apartment on the back street, "If nothing else would ever convince me of your absolute integrity and sincerity, this damned old hole would."

Norman had whisky in quantity for those whose tongues he wished to loosen. But Miles, all these years, had been careful never to drink whisky in Norman's company. He pretended to like "a light sherry," of which Norman approved, or a martini which tasted like witch hazel, which Norman preferred even more. Neither of these, taken sparingly, confused Miles in the slightest.

Norman gave Miles sherry to-night. It was a cheap sherry, of course, but Miles sipped it with the air of a connoisseur. Norman, who knew nothing of good wines, was pleased. He poured a glass for himself. He had become thinner with the years, more wiry, but more intent, more aware, more focused. At fifty-five, he seemed almost as young as Miles, his kinsman, for there was no grey in his fine brown hair, which had thinned to partial baldness on the top of his narrow skull. His large brown eyes shone with life and quiet eagerness; his smile was almost as charming as the younger man's. He had a gracious way with him, a confiding and gentle mannerism, calculated to disarm. "Well, what is on your mind, fella?" he asked of Miles. "You sounded urgent on the phone to-day."

Miles became very sober. He twisted the cheap glass in his fingers. He pretended to hesitate. He peeped at Norman apologetically. "Sometimes I wonder if I'm right in telling you so much, Norman, about the road. Oh, I know you should know, of course. But at times I have twinges. . . ."

Norman's face became stern and his eyes flashed fanatically. "Miles, I think we've gone over this so much in the past. If you have ' twinges,' it should be in behalf of the proletariat, not a lot

623

of stupid damned plutocrats in Portersville, Philadelphia, and New York."

Miles regarded him sombrely. He thought: You dog, you dog who believe your own lies. Plutocrat! And who the hell has more money than you, you swine? But it isn't just money you want. You want the almighty power to judge who shall live and who shall die; who shall starve in concentration camps and who shall crawl around your knees. You, you Torquemada, want what all of you have always wanted, since first Cain raised his club against his brother.

Norman softened at Miles's expression. "All right, boy. I won't say that again. You've come to tell me you are about to move against that old hag Cornelia, and that slug, DeWitt. Good. The time has come. How can I help you, now?" To show that he had regretted his denunciation, he refilled Miles's glass. He sat down again on the worn and billowy chair which had been fashionable twenty years ago.

Miles began to speak, and he let a pleading note come into his voice as if attempting to persuade Norman deWitt: "I've gone over this with you before. I know"—he hesitated—"that you hate Roosevelt. . . ."

Norman nodded; his eyes hardened. "Of course; we all do. But we know we can use him and the Northern element of his party. We can be expedient, too, you know." He smiled contemptuously.

"Well," said Miles, with an answering smile, "the President is anxious to create and increase prosperity. You and I know that the National Industrial Recovery Act will be declared unconstitutional by the Supreme Court very shortly, in spite of the President. You told me that the last time. Too bad. But it's only a temporary delay, after all. The country will recover in spite of what the Supreme Court can do."

Norman nodded again, and a strangely mysterious smile hovered on his mouth. "Yes, when we have a war. It is my opinion of course, but it may be sooner than we think. Perhaps in four or five years. The public must be educated to it. But, go on."

"In the meantime," said Miles, "the working people will suffer. As you know, I have a plan to modernise our entire railroad, in which you hold quite a block of shares picked up by you during the depression. If I can accomplish that, our closed repair shops will be reopened; we can place large orders with car builders, thus stimulating employment and prosperity everywhere. Our example might goad other roads into doing the same thing." He stopped and bit his tongue. He had almost used the "accursed word, competition." "But we can't move, can't accomplish anything, until your half-sister Cornelia, and your nephew DeWitt, are made powerless—and I become president of the road. You know what damned conservatives they are, hoarding their private fortunes and refusing to disgorge any part of them for the benefit of the road and the workers."

"I've agreed with you before that DeWitt will have to go," said Norman reprovingly. "Cornelia, I suppose, will have to remain a director. What can we do about DeWitt?"

Miles laughed. "We can ' elevate ' him to the safe and powerless post of chairman."

Norman moved in his chair, and laughed also. "All right, Miles, what do you want me to do?"

The game was dangerous, but the odds were with Miles. He told Norman what he wished him to do.

"We're coming into the station," said Fielding to his reflective brother. "What've you been dreaming about the past fifteen minutes?"

"I," said Miles indifferently, "was thinking about a murderer."

When they reached the Philadelphia offices of the Interstate Railroad Company, they found the board of directors already waiting for them. It was a matter of astonishment to Fielding that the directors, who were so much older than Miles, stood up when Miles entered, with expressions of deference. But Miles accepted the gesture as perfectly normal. He sat down in his seat near the head of the long table, and glanced at the empty chairs usually used by DeWitt and Cornelia. He said, "Aunt Cornelia told me last night that she ' understood,' and that she would not tell DeWitt of our invitation to her to-day, until this session has been completed. However, I asked her, for the sake of DeWitt, who is not any too well lately, not to tell him until the day after to-morrow, because of the dinner we are having here in Philadelphia to-morrow night to honour her and the one hundredth birthday of the road. She's a wily old girl; she doesn't require reams of paper to explain things to her. She gets on to things immediately. We," added Miles, glancing around the table, "are going to have a hard time with her. She may be old, but there's no fuzziness in her mind.".

The white glare of the snow outside shone starkly on his face, and his eyes were a brilliant stare of blueness. The directors nodded soberly; they were fascinated, as always, by this small man's aura of absolute power and compact authority. He communicated complete confidence to them.

"But Aunt Cornelia will have no weight if you are with me," Miles went on. "A few days ago I went to Washington and talked with Norman deWitt."

The intent faces around the board darkened and tightened. Miles smiled. "Criminals always believe, and fanatics with them, that they are so much more intelligent than others. We must never forget that we are just as bright or brighter. It is the one weapon we have against then. But we must never let them know we know the truth.

"Norman is willing to intercede in behalf of our road with the Interstate Commerce Commission, if, gentlemen, I am elected president of our company. This intercession will take the form of rate adjustments and other privileges, such as financing new issues for passenger modernisation of the road. Well, gentlemen?"

The only other director not present was old Mr. Hill. One of the others said, "Hill, Miles? You know how devoted he is to Cornelia."

"We'll manage Hill, shortly. After all, he may be old and very rich, but he wants even more money. He has what is called the 'dynasty complex,' and he has scores of great-grandchildren. When it comes brutally down to just dollars and cents, old Hill will weep with Cornelia, and throw in his vote with ours."

"We'll take the preliminary vote to-day," said another director. "In Cornelia's presence. She's a very wise woman, and later she'll begin to think how much money she'll also make, herself, when we modernise the road."

"Good," said Miles. He opened his gold cigarette case and a director, his senior by at least fifteen years, sprang to his feet and lit the cigarette. Fielding grinned. What a boy was Miles! Miles was nodding in acknowledgment of the courtesy. Then he studied the papers on his desk, smiled, leaned back in his chair. He began to talk of casual and personal matters, and to inquire about the families of the directors. It was one of his rules that when a matter was precariously settled, it did nothing but unsettle it again if the thing were constantly discussed. He conveyed to the directors the idea that they had no alternative but to do what he wished, and that what he wished was to their advantage. He did this without any words, but only with the strong tone of his voice, his interest in their personal lives, the state of the weather, and plans they all had for the coming summer.

Cornelia arrived in about fifteen minutes, wrapped in the finest Russian sables, perfumed, swift-moving, and smilingly composed. Her small blue hat sat closely on her dyed red hair, and its veil was studded with diamonds. The men rose as one; she nodded to them gaily, sat down in her chair, and took off her gloves. While she did this, her alert eyes scrutinised each face. She continued to smile but a few of her facial muscles twitched.

"Well, here I am, boys, and I'm all intrigued about this mystery. Did I ever tell you I love mysteries? Miles can be very mysterious in such a calm way, and so I feel quite excited. Did someone inquire about DeWitt? Well, his cold is getting better, but he broods. I don't know why. It can't be the road, I don't think. I do hope he won't turn out to be like his father." For an instant her smile was gone, and then it returned, more robust than ever, her fine white. teeth flashed between her painted lips. She sighed, laughed. "You all look like undertakers, my dears. Except Miles." She studied Miles. "The executioner, I think, would never look like a mortician. He usually takes such relish in his work."

Miles rested his hands on the table. "Aunt Cornelia," he said, "I am no executioner." He was relieved that Cornelia had caught some inkling of what this session might portend. "Perhaps you could call me a surgeon."

"Odd that a surgeon is present but not the—shall we say— victim?" She drew a deep breath and stared at Miles with all her formidable power. "You're quite a dog, Miles, my little one. But I never underestimated you. However, I want to tell you now that you'll find me a very good antagonist." She continued to stare at him. "Little Miles, little Mr. Aaron. Yes, I've heard about that ancient sentimentality. But I'm going to give you some credit, Miles; you're not sentimental. I doubt whether you ever considered yourself the adequate successor of my grandfather, your great-grandfather."

The directors were becoming uneasy; they played with their papers and pretended to study them. Miles smiled gently. "No, I'm not sentimental, Aunt Cornelia. I'm a businessman, and I control twenty-nine per cent of the stock of the road. Naturally, I'm interested in its welfare, and continued success. And," he added more slowly, "I'm also interested in eliminating those who stand in the way of our common property."

Cornelia let out a boom of genuine laughter. "Miles, I'm almost coming to believe in the story of ' little Mr. Aaron!' You do resemble him, if my father's reports, and the reports of others are true. ' Eliminating.' Do you know, I prefer that word to the one Hitler uses: ' liquidation.' But it amounts to the same thing, doesn't it?"

One of the directors murmured, "Cornelia, that——" But she shook her head at him archly, and her hazel eyes glittered through the blue web of her veil. "Oh, hell, Bertie, let's not get into semantics. I knew from the very moment Miles called me the other night that you were all plotting something. Why else the secrecy? I've known, too, that he's met you all very often, right here. But here I am, Cornelia deWitt Marshall, and here I sit, and I shall listen. What do you want?"

Miles waited, but the shamefaced directors suddenly became silent. Miles did not waste his time in trying to force them to look at his contemptuous eyes. He addressed himself softly to Cornelia: "You are one of the directors of the road, Aunt Cornelia, and we intend to let you remain a director. What else can we do? But, after endless sessions, we've all come to the conclusion that DeWitt cannot remain as president. For reasons we've discussed with you before. It is now life or death for the road. DeWitt stands for its death. We stand for its life, and I expect that you will, too, eventually. The directors have agreed that I must be president; DeWitt will be chairman." He lifted his hands, smiled at Cornelia, let his hands drop. "That is all there is to the whole thing."

"So simple," said Cornelia. She opened her case and took out a cigarette. Miles himself lit it for her, and she inclined her head in acknowledgment. "Thank you, dear. You were always such a courteous and quick little boy. You still are. Yes, so simple. Why are the other lads so quiet, Miles? Are they remembering that we control fifty-one per cent of the stock?"

"They are remembering," said Miles, "that they have the power to vote me in as president, with your consent."

Cornelia let her eyes wander acutely from one face to another. The men looked up, smiled miserably or sheepishly or grimly, according to their present emotions. But she had her answer. Her red eyebrows drew together thoughtfully; she dropped an ash from her cigarette, put the white cylinder into her mouth again. Her eyes narrowed to slits, shifted to a window. Then she spoke abstractedly; "And that is what they intend to do. I'm thinking of dear old Mr. Hill. But you'll get around to him. Miles, you never do anything until you are sure, do you? Don't bother to answer. You wouldn't have called me in to-day if you hadn't been sure."

All at once the directors were speaking together in a babble of voices. Cornelia listened politely. They were terribly sorry, they wouldn't have done this for worlds if there had been any other way—the road—concessions were necessary from the government, which would not grant concessions if DeWitt's ideas prevailed—the road—modernise—surely she could see that for herself—future profits, unlimited expansion—she knew how devoted they all were to her, how much they admired her wisdom and understanding, and respected her opinions—the road—it was all for the best—she was still a director—DeWitt would be chairman—the road——

Cornelia nodded gravely as the men stood about her, gesticulating, pleading, arguing. But her eyes were beginning to dance. She said at last, "All right, boys, sit down. You've got it all settled. Let's have no post-mortems. But aren't you a little cowardly to leave it to me to tell DeWitt?"

Miles said, "I think the idea was cowardly—yes. I'm sorry. We'll have a session next Monday, and we'll tell him, ourselves. We should not even have considered leaving it all to you, Aunt Cornelia. But, in a way, it's a compliment."

She contemplated him seriously. "As you are not sentimental, I won't remind you that you are my sister's husband, and that your sister is married to my son."

Miles said, as seriously, "It isn't necessary to remind me. I've thought about it very often. But nothing is as important as the road. For all of us."

Fielding interjected, "Yes, Aunt Cornelia, the road." But she ignored him.

"Miles, have you Norman with you, Norman, my brother?"

Miles replied without hesitation. "Yes. We have. Norman and I are great friends."

Cornelia emitted such a roar of laughter that the directors were startled. She laughed until the tears ran down her raddled cheeks; she even slapped one of her silken thighs. "I thought so; I knew it! God, but this is wonderful! You and Norman! Such ' great friends!' And how he hates me. Miles, you are a genius, a genius!" She paused to wipe her wet eyes, and shook her head over and over with unaffected mirth. "I'm going to live to be a hundred or more! I just couldn't bear to miss the final episode between you and Norman, the swine that he is. For there will be that final episode. There's no use in my telling him all about you, my dear child. He wouldn't listen; I'm just the dyed old plutocrat, sitting on her bags of gold. Miles, I repeat, you are a genius." She touched his coat sleeve lightly with her painted fingernails. "The future is going to be so interesting. I can't wait."

"Very interesting, and very profitable for all of us," said Miles. But Cornelia was laughing again in that silent room, without hysterics, and only with a kind of Homeric ecstasy. The men listened, and to them Cornelia had never appeared so gallant, so powerful, as she was now in her capitulation. They smiled at each other, and there was something sad in their smiles. Her laughter was dying away, gustily, and in enjoyment. She was looking at Miles again. "Yes, dear, I've no doubt that under you, as president, the road will prosper. I've no doubt that I'll become a whole lot richer. But, do you know, I hate you like death."

She turned away from him, and she was very quiet. "There is an old saying—' man is never victorious, never defeated.' DeWitt has a son. I'm remembering so many things. Your grandfather was defeated by my father, and your grandfather's son has defeated the offspring of my father in return. Yes, DeWitt has a son."

Now she looked at Miles and she was young and zestful again, glowing with purpose and exhilaration. "You are a railroader, Miles," she said, and her coarse voice vibrated. "I can see it all, now. You know everything about the intricacies of the road, all about its management. You went to a good school—the Interstate. To you, as it has always been to me, the railroad is the first thing in your life, the dominant thing. You are more than clever; you are wise and subtle and shrewd. You've managed to get the promise of the present Administration to give its approval to your plans—if DeWitt is removed. If by some trick I could get the Administration to withhold its approval of you, I wouldn't do it. No, Miles, I wouldn't do it. For then the road would suffer. There would be the meanest of pressures and harassments, for nothing can be more vicious than a bureaucrat. Not even DeWitt and all his money, and Mary's money, and mine, could stop the vindictive persecution. The road would go down."

She put up her hand when Miles tried to speak. "Wait, my little man. I'm not finished yet. Rufus DeWitt's son, is my grandson. This past year or more he has begun to show authentic interest in the road. I've been watching him. I'm going to coach him, and tell him all I know. You have no son. But there will be Rufus in the future."

Fielding squinted his pale brown eyes at her. "Aunt Cornelia, you're forgotting I have two boys, myself, younger than Rufus, of course. But my boys."

For the first time she gave him her attention. "Your sons, Fielding?" she asked in contemptuous astonishment. "I've seen the little fellows. No, Fielding, not your sons." She shook her head emphatically.

"If Rufus ever becomes the better man, then I won't hold on to the presidency," said Miles, and he was very grave. "If he ever becomes that better man, twenty years from now, I'll be glad to withdraw. In fact, I'll help him. As you have said, the road is first with me. When Rufus is ready to come into the road next year, I'll teach him, too. As if he were my own son."

She regarded him fixedly. It was as if she had never seen him before, and was struck with amazement. The directors turned in a body to look at Miles with profound respect. He stood there near Cornelia, short, forceful, but very quiet and sincere, and he saw no one but her. Fielding blinked his eyes; ran a long and lanky hand over his lips. For the first time in his life he hated his brother. But wait, he thought to himself. You've all forgotten me, but I'm here, and I'm not the clown you think I am. He put a white knuckle against his teeth and pressed it, hard.

"Miles," said Cornelia. She put another cigarette into her mouth and Miles lit it for her. "Well, Miles," she murmured. "Damned if I don't believe you."

She stood up quickly and she appeared to tower over them all.

She put her hand on Miles's shoulder and shook it indulgently. "You're going to need me, Miles. I'm a director. No one knows more about the road than I do. I hate you, but I'll help you." She laughed down at him and shook his shoulder again, then turned and offered her big strong hand to each of the directors in turn. She had all the exuberance and resilience of youth about her, all its animal magnetism and fire. The men shook her hand with deep and honest feeling. A trouper, one said to himself. There's no one like old Cornelia. But as Fielding shook her hand she could feel his malignance. She stopped to look at him intently, and said to Miles, "Your brother, my dear. I don't think he likes any of us to-day."

Fielding grinned easily. "You were never so wrong, Aunt Cornelia."

But Miles looked contemplatively at his brother and fine wrinkles appeared on his forehead. "However," said Cornelia, "I think we can manage." She studied Fielding slowly, thoroughly. "There are two genuine railroaders here, Fielding, but you are not one of them." She dismissed him, returned her attention to Miles. "Do you know, I think, with you and me, it will be almost like the old days. When Allan was young."

Miles escorted her down to her car and assisted her inside. He stood on the bleak and icy sidewalk in silence. But she blew a kiss to him and laughed, and was driven away. Her last words were: "I'm going to enjoy to-morrow night's party, in a way. And the next day, I'll tell DeWitt."

When Miles returned to the board room, one of the directors said, "I knew we could always rely on old Cornelia, in a pinch. I can't remember her ever looking so brisk and young. It was as if she'd been given new life."

"Yes," said Miles. "For a few years she had forgotten what it was to be a real railroader. Now she has remembered."

CHAPTER FIFTY-ONE

ARCHBISHOP RUFUS ANTHONY MARSHALL supported his brother DeWitt along some of the gentle garden paths below the Portersville house. Full summer burned in the marigolds, the zinnias, the canna lilies and the salvias. The trees, however, were not so bright green and lush as they had been in July; the grass had a dusty smell. Fountains leaped and glittered in the hot air, and there was a scent of stone near them. Here and there, in open places, the lawns were burned. The sunlight flamed on the windows of the old mansion above, and its red roof glowed as if on fire. Far down in the valley the city smouldered under a grey fog of heat and smoke, and the river between the mountains had dwindled.

"There'll be an early fall," said Tony, as he gently helped his brother to sit down on a marble bench beneath a tree. He smiled up at the poplar, which he had planted. It was so large now, so pointed, like a spire, every leaf turning in the soft wind, and sparkling. But DeWitt saw nothing; he did not hear the shrilling of the cicadas or the tinkle of the fountains. He sat sunken on the bench, his hands fallen between his thin knees, his head on his breast. His face was livid and shrivelled, like an old leaf, and his eyes were dull as muddy stones.

He said, "I hate this house. I always hated it. As soon as my new house is finished in November, Mary and Shelley and Rufus and I are leaving. Leaving it to—her."

His voice was very quiet, but loaded with sick rage and hatred. Tony sat beside him, and the sunlight struck on the large cross on his breast. His brother was just recovering from an illness suffered last March, but the doctors reported that he was "doing very well." But his soul is "not doing very well," thought Tony with a momentary pang of despair, for which he immediately prayed forgiveness. He had been with his brother for three days now; all his consolations, his sympathy, his love, had not stirred the mighty rock of loathing and anger in the younger man. Tony's pale and ascetic face was like that of a statue's under the light of the hot sky.

"I think it will be best for you to have your own home," he said. He hesitated. "But you mustn't leave without becoming at least slightly reconciled to Mother."

DeWitt laughed, a thin and acrid laugh. "I haven't spoken to her since the day she informed me that she would vote with the directors against me, and put in—him."

Tony sighed. "It was expedient business, for her. I've heard all the arguments. I suppose they had to do it, considering everything. But, DeWitt, you are such a wealthy man. You will be wealthier. What more can you want?"

DeWitt's dark little hands tightened to fists on his knees. He lifted his head and stared emptily before him. "You wouldn't understand. It was the power, not the money. And now, this degradation, this public humiliation. . . ."

"No one," said Tony with some wry bitterness, "regards it as degradation or public humiliation to be a multimillionaire."

But DeWitt was speaking as if Tony had not spoken. "A man wants power because he despises other men. He wants to force them to admire and humble themselves before him. Money alone doesn't accomplish that. Power does." He turned a sick but almost baleful smile on Tony. "Surely you understand that. People kneel to you and kiss your ring, don't they?"

Tony said, "It isn't I who am honoured; it is God."

DeWitt nodded, and parroted him: "It isn't I who was honoured; it was my power."

"DeWitt, you are ill, more than your body has been ill. There are other things in the world besides power."

"I know; you've named them. What is the use of my talking to you? We don't even use the same connotations. What is desirable to you is incomprehensible to me, what is desirable to me is incomprehensible to you. We can never meet on the same semantic grounds. You're wasting your time, Tony. It's just enough for you to be here with me. I don't want your arguments."

"But you'll have my prayers."

"Good," said DeWitt, and smiled again, as one smiles at a beloved imbecile. "Will God be very kind and restore to me the presidency of the company? This is all I want. Just a small matter."

"Perhaps God has a merciful reason in permitting this thing to happen to you."

DeWitt laughed, and the sound was acid and ugly. "I think

' God's mercy ' is just a little more than I can stand now. Could you ask Him to withdraw it, for my sake?" He hit his leg with his cane, and though the gesture was slight it expressed an inner violence. "You've said, Tony, that God permits painful things to happen to men in order that they may draw nearer to Him. I think I prefer not to draw nearer to Him. It's too costly."

He laughed again. "What nonsense we are talking! And I only upset you. Just be still and let me know you're here."

Someone was coming along the path, a tall, red-haired young man with high colouring and hazel eyes and a sullen expression. He saw DeWitt and Tony, and stopped. The sullen expression disappeared and dark anger and resolution replaced it.

"Rufus," called Tony, and the young man approached unwillingly. DeWitt glanced with brief indifference at his son and looked away. He closed his eyes as if the very sight of this big young fellow was a weariness to him, as all other things were these days, except his brother. Rufus stood in silence before his father and his uncle, and Tony tried to remember whether DeWitt loved this strapping boy or was proud of him. He could not remember whether DeWitt had ever mentioned him in his letters, or had ever spoken of him except with the faint derision he used in speaking of everyone. To DeWitt, Rufus was just the son who might have controlled the Interstate Railroad Company.

"Sit down, Rufus," said Tony in his grave and quiet voice. Rufus folded himself up on the grass. Tony recalled having very few conversations with his nephew; he feared that he bored the boy by his very existence. But now, as Rufus sat there on the grass, it seemed to Tony that his own sight sharpened, and he saw that Rufus, who resembled his grandmother and his great-grandfather so closely, in all their colouring, stature, and primitive splendour, was not in more imponderable ways like them at all. What Tony had taken for sullenness was sombre concentration; what he had taken for boorish conduct was a hard young sincerity, what he had taken for insistent selfishness was a desperate if silent desire for tenderness and attention, all of which had been consistently denied him.

Tony continued his dazed study as if with preternatural sight. This was no hulking boy, preoccupied by facile things. He was intelligent, determined, and a trifle morose, full of great reserve and strength. Tony saw that Rufus had forgotten his presence;

he was gazing at his father, and there was the strangest intensity in his tawny eyes.

Then Tony saw that the young man loved his little, dark, and crippled father who almost invariably ignored him.

Before this blinding revelation, this miracle revealed to him, Tony shut his own eyes, and there was a moisture behind his lids. Who could explain the marvel of love given to one who could neither return it nor had desired it? But then, thought Tony, God gives His love unasked to mankind, and unknown to it. It is just there, like the sun itself. What Rufus feels for his father is a tiny reflection of what God feels for man, and that in itself is a miracle.

"Rufus," said Tony very softly. Rufus started, frowned, then turned with brusqueness to his uncle, and waited. The sun changed his eyes to the colour of hard gold. "Your father has been very ill," Tony went on, holding the boy's attention with his willpower.

"Good God, he knows that," said DeWitt in a spent voice. "Wasn't he called from school?"

But Rufus was staring fixedly at his uncle. Tony repeated, "Your father has been very ill."

Rufus nodded very slightly. He fumbled for a cigarette and lit it, and his big hands, so like Cornelia's, trembled ever so little. Tony prayed inwardly for help, then began to speak slowly.

"I am reminded of what St. Augustine wrote in his Confessions."

DeWitt stirred impatiently, but when he looked into his brother's eyes he saw a strange and radiant light in them, which had the effect of impaling him.

"'But I, being miserable, sought for things over which I could grieve, and over which I could shed tears. But that was no marvel, as I was a straying sheep from Thy flock, and so was infected with the sad disease of my soul. In the weariness of my heart I became inflamed with my own sorrow, which increased my own original suffering. My life being such, was it life, O my God?'"

His voice seemed to dominate the hot silence of the gardens, to ring back from the clustered trees, the stone walls, the hillside, the very sky. The little crippled man on the marble bench could not move his body, but his head sank to his chest and his face was hidden. The cigarette burned unheeded in Rufus's hand, and his eyes fastened themselves on his father.

Then DeWitt said with bitter mockery, "' My life being such, was it life, O my God?'"

Tony put his hands on his brother's shoulders and said in command, "Look up. But don't look at me. Look at your son, for the first time in your life."

DeWitt obeyed. Slowly he lifted his head and looked at Rufus. Across the little space of sunburned grass the father and the son regarded each other. Rufus did not move; he gazed at his father, and all his love—open now, offering, unashamed—stood on that broad young face, simple, not pleading, not demanding, but held out as a gift. And DeWitt stared at that gift, unbelieving, half-rejecting, incredulous. He put up his hand and touched his son's cheek, his mouth, his lips, like a man in a dream.

"Yes," said Tony, and his voice broke, "your son loves you. But you never looked at him before, and you never knew his love, for in your heart you have always believed that you were not worthy of love."

Rufus got to his feet and came to his father and took one of the diminutive hands in his own. He said nothing.

"But we are all worthy of love, otherwise God would not love us," said Tony. "Why did you cling to me all these years? Because you knew, deep in your soul, that I loved you. And now, there are two of us who love you, though you thought I was the only one."

DeWitt said in a harsh voice like a cricket, "And now I know, too, that I have nothing to give my son, but money. What I had was taken from me."

Then Rufus spoke, quick and sure and loud, "You never had it, Father. You never had the power you thought you had. It was Grandmother's all the time. I don't want any power such as you think you wanted for yourself and me. If it comes anyway, through my own efforts, well and good. If I don't have the capacity for it, I don't particularly care." He hesitated. "I suppose it's because I never hated anyone very much."

DeWitt's face twisted, but Tony saw that his small fingers were clinging to his son's hand.

"Listen to me, Father," pleaded Rufus. "No one has ever bothered to tell you the truth. When you had your nervous collapse, after being voted out as president, you spent four weeks in bed. Do you know that if you hadn't been forced by accident into that bed you would not be alive now?"

DeWitt looked at him in disbelieving astonishment. Rufus nodded at him, and smiled. He knelt down near his father, and his face was on a level with DeWitt's.

"You see, it seems that you've had a heart condition for years, probably since your childhood, and it was building up for a long time to what would probably have been a fatal heart attack. The enforced rest saved your life." The young man averted his head. "Think what it would have meant to me if you had died. I—well, I'm not the religious type, but when your doctors told me, I went to a church, and I thanked . . ."

DeWitt had turned very pale. He looked at his son for a long time; then, with an almost imperceptible movement, he lifted his hand and placed it on Rufus's red head. Rufus knelt there, very still, and to Tony it seemed that something powerful and unbearably moving flowed between the two.

"Rufus," said Tony, "I didn't know, myself. Tell me, what is your father's condition now?"

Rufus looked up at his uncle, and the golden eyes were wet. "I suppose Grandmother never thought it necessary to tell Father, for the resignation from the presidency had already been proffered by him. But if he had continued to attend board meetings, and to carry on the affairs as president, he would have died. Now he can live, possibly a full lifetime, if he lives quietly."

So, Mother really has some compassion hidden away in her, thought Tony. But she was wrong; she should have told him that he could not have remained president under any circumstances. What does she know of real bitterness and grief? Is it possible that not experiencing them in herself she believes others do not experience them? Then Tony's heart involuntarily hardened against Cornelia. She was still a powerful director; she attended every meeting of the board. Her voice was still loud and assured, still listened to with respect. While DeWitt, thought Tony, wanders in loneliness about this house and has no comfort from his mother, and no tenderness from his wife, whose one desire is pleasure and romping about the world and getting her parties prominently publicised in the newspapers, and trying to marry off her daughter advantageously.

"But what shall I do with my life?" asked DeWitt feebly. "With all the years I can live?"

"You are still chairman, and you can attend an occasional meeting," said Rufus. He smiled at his father. "And you and I

638

can be together. I have just another year at Harvard. And then I'll be home, and you can teach me about the road, and we can travel comfortably, and we can find out everything about each other."

"And you can read, and you can learn, and you can think a little about God," said Tony. "Just a little, each day. That you must promise me."

DeWitt began to laugh, at first faintly, and then with a stronger sound.

"You two!" he exclaimed. "What shall I do for amusement when you are both away?" He turned his eyes from his son to his brother, and they were like fragments of shining jet, glinting with new-born energy. "You'll be the death of me."

"No," said Tony, "we'll be the life."

He helped his brother to his feet, and Rufus took his father's arm. Side by side, with DeWitt in the middle, the three men—the priest, the red-haired young giant, the dry twig which was DeWitt—moved up the long garden path together. No one spoke; DeWitt appeared engrossed in bottomless thought. All at once he stopped, and turned to look up and down at the gardens, at the walls, at the trees and sky. A peculiar dark kindling ran over his face; his meagre chest rose and fell quickly.

"It's very funny," he said, "but I never noticed that summer had come. In fact, I think I never noticed it ever came. Until now."

Tony watched him, and it was as if some little shrivelled bough on a tree had suddenly pointed with buds, as if the bough would open into flower, not swiftly, not all in one day, but through cool and quiet weeks, through frosts and through nights.

DeWitt linked his arm through his son's, and tightened his fingers on the young flesh. But he looked at Tony. "There's something, perhaps, I can do about your charities. Put me on a board, or something." He looked about him again, and he seemed bewildered. Then he began to laugh soundlessly. They watched him, deeply moved. He nodded at Tony. "There's our Pa's infernal Foundation. While I've been lounging around since March, I've been reading some of the literature, and the newspapers. I have an idea or two, myself."

He pointed to the mighty poplar blowing in the sun. "You thought I didn't know, but I knew you planted that. They've wanted to cut it down; shading the flowers, or something. But I prevented it. I've an idea, now, what it really means."

He looked up at his son. "Rufe, we've a long way to go, the two of us. I think we'll start to-morrow. You and I."

Tony fell behind a pace or two and watched the big young man and his father go slowly up the path together. If man is never victorious, he is also never defeated, thought Tony.

The sun suddenly blazed on the cross on his breast.

THE END